Text Mining: Challenges, Algorithms, Tools and Applications

Text Mining: Challenges, Algorithms, Tools and Applications

Guest Editor

Fei Liu

MDPI

Basel • Beijing • Wuhan • Barcelona • Belgrade • Novi Sad • Cluj • Manchester

Guest Editor
Fei Liu
Department of Computer
Science & Information
Technology
La Trobe University
Melbourne
Australia

Editorial Office
MDPI AG
Grosspeteranlage 5
4052 Basel, Switzerland

This is a reprint of the Special Issue, published open access by the journal *Information* (ISSN 2078-2489), freely accessible at: https://www.mdpi.com/journal/information/special_issues/S5XR368PW3.

For citation purposes, cite each article independently as indicated on the article page online and as indicated below:

Lastname, A.A.; Lastname, B.B. Article Title. *Journal Name* **Year**, *Volume Number*, Page Range.

ISBN 978-3-7258-6139-2 (Hbk)
ISBN 978-3-7258-6140-8 (PDF)
https://doi.org/10.3390/books978-3-7258-6140-8

Contents

About the Editor . . . . **vii**

Saeede Anbaee Farimani, Majid Vafaei Jahan and Amin Milani Fard
From Text Representation to Financial Market Prediction: A Literature Review
Reprinted from: *Information* **2022**, *13*, 466, https://doi.org/10.3390/info13100466 . . . . **1**

Yousef H. Alfaifi
Recommender Systems Applications: Data Sources, Features, and Challenges
Reprinted from: *Information* **2024**, *15*, 660, https://doi.org/10.3390/info15100660 . . . . **26**

Tingyao Jiang, Zilong Wang, Ming Yang and Cheng Li
Aspect-Based Sentiment Analysis with Dependency Relation Weighted Graph Attention
Reprinted from: *Information* **2023**, *14*, 185, https://doi.org/10.3390/info14030185 . . . . **51**

Jai Prakash Verma, Shir Bhargav, Madhuri Bhavsar, Pronaya Bhattacharya, Ali Bostani, Subrata Chowdhury, et al.
Graph-Based Extractive Text Summarization Sentence Scoring Scheme for Big Data Applications
Reprinted from: *Information* **2023**, *14*, 472, https://doi.org/10.3390/info14090472 . . . . **66**

Veronika Belcheva, Tatiana Ermakova and Benjamin Fabian
Understanding Website Privacy Policies—A Longitudinal Analysis Using Natural Language Processing
Reprinted from: *Information* **2023**, *14*, 622, https://doi.org/10.3390/info14110622 . . . . **94**

Liu Yang, Gang Wang and Hongjun Wang
Reimagining Literary Analysis: Utilizing Artificial Intelligence to Classify Modernist French Poetry
Reprinted from: *Information* **2024**, *15*, 70, https://doi.org/10.3390/info15020070 . . . . **121**

Paolo Fantozzi, Valentina Rotondi, Matteo Rizzolli, Paola Dalla Torre and Maurizio Naldi
Detecting Moral Features in TV Series with a Transformer Architecture through Dictionary-Based Word Embedding
Reprinted from: *Information* **2024**, *15*, 128, https://doi.org/10.3390/info15030128 . . . . **144**

Md Saiful Islam and Fei Liu
Domain-Specific Dictionary between Human and Machine Languages
Reprinted from: *Information* **2024**, *15*, 144, https://doi.org/10.3390/info15030144 . . . . **171**

Natalia Vanetik, Margarita Tiamanova, Genady Kogan and Marina Litvak
Genre Classification of Books in Russian with Stylometric Features: A Case Study
Reprinted from: *Information* **2024**, *15*, 340, https://doi.org/10.3390/info15060340 . . . . **188**

Keyi Liu and Yunpeng Cui
Automated Knowledge Extraction in the Field of Wheat Sharp Eyespot Control
Reprinted from: *Information* **2024**, *15*, 367, https://doi.org/10.3390/info15070367 . . . . **218**

Paolo Fantozzi, Guglielmo Maccario and Maurizio Naldi
Uncovering Tourist Visit Intentions on Social Media through Sentence Transformers
Reprinted from: *Information* **2024**, *15*, 603, https://doi.org/10.3390/info15100603 . . . . **235**

Ricardo Hernández-Pérez, Pablo Lara-Martínez, Bibiana Obregón-Quintana, Larry S. Liebovitch and Lev Guzmán-Vargas
Correlations and Fractality in Sentence-Level Sentiment Analysis Based on VADER for Literary Texts
Reprinted from: *Information* **2024**, *15*, 698, https://doi.org/10.3390/info15110698 . . . . **254**

Daniel S. Soper
Quickly Finding the Semantically Optimal Presentation Order for a Set of Text Artifacts
Reprinted from: *Information* **2025**, *16*, 59, https://doi.org/10.3390/info16010059 . . . . **268**

Khaled Abdalgader, Atheer A. Matroud and Ghaleb Al-Doboni
Temporal Dynamics in Short Text Classification: Enhancing Semantic Understanding Through Time-Aware Model
Reprinted from: *Information* **2025**, *16*, 214, https://doi.org/10.3390/info16030214 . . . . **282**

Chih-Yuan Li, Soon Ae Chun and James Geller
Perspective-Based Microblog Summarization
Reprinted from: *Information* **2025**, *16*, 285, https://doi.org/10.3390/ info16040285 . . . . **311**

Peng Ye, Yujin Jiang and Yadi Wang
CHTopo: A Multi-Source Large-Scale Chinese Toponym Annotation Corpus
Reprinted from: *Information* **2025**, *16*, 610, https://doi.org/10.3390/info16070610 . . . . **344**

Daniyar Rakhimzhanov, Saule Belginova and Didar Yedilkhan
Automated Classification of Public Transport Complaints via Text Mining Using LLMs and Embeddings
Reprinted from: *Information* **2025**, *16*, 644, https://doi.org/10.3390/info16080644 . . . . **362**

Xiaoying Fu, Wenyi Zhang and Zhi Li
Internet Governance in the Context of Global Digital Contracts: Integrating SAR Data Processing and AI Techniques for Standards, Rules, and Practical Paths
Reprinted from: *Information* **2025**, *16*, 697, https://doi.org/10.3390/info16080697 . . . . **387**

About the Editor

Fei Liu

Fei Liu received her PhD degree in Computer Science from La Trobe University, Melbourne, Australia. Her research area is Artificial Intelligence including text mining, automated reasoning and semantic web. In her over 30 years' academic career, she worked as a lecturer/senior lecturer in the Department of Computer Science & Information Technology, La Trobe University; School of Computing Technologies, RMIT University and School of Computer & Information Sciences, University of South Australia. She has authored/co-authored over 80 conference and journal articles.

information

MDPI

Article

From Text Representation to Financial Market Prediction: A Literature Review

Saeede Anbaee Farimani [1], Majid Vafaei Jahan [1,*] and Amin Milani Fard [2]

[1] Department of Computer Engineering, Mashhad Branch, Islamic Azad University, Mashhad 91871-47578, Iran
[2] Department of Computer Science, New York Institute of Technology, Vancouver, BC V5M 4X3, Canada
* Correspondence: vafaeijahan@mshdiau.ac.ir

Abstract: News dissemination in social media causes fluctuations in financial markets. (Scope) Recent advanced methods in deep learning-based natural language processing have shown promising results in financial market analysis. However, understanding how to leverage large amounts of textual data alongside financial market information is important for the investors' behavior analysis. In this study, we review over 150 publications in the field of behavioral finance that jointly investigated natural language processing (NLP) approaches and a market data analysis for financial decision support. This work differs from other reviews by focusing on applied publications in computer science and artificial intelligence that contributed to a heterogeneous information fusion for the investors' behavior analysis. (Goal) We study various text representation methods, sentiment analysis, and information retrieval methods from heterogeneous data sources. (Findings) We present current and future research directions in text mining and deep learning for correlation analysis, forecasting, and recommendation systems in financial markets, such as stocks, cryptocurrencies, and Forex (Foreign Exchange Market).

Keywords: text mining; sentiment analysis; financial market prediction; big data analytics; news; social media

1. Introduction

The efficient market hypothesis [1], introduced by Fama in 1965, showed that financial time series are influenced by the information available to investors. This motivated behavioral economics [1,2], which studies the psychological behavior of investors and the role of social, cultural, and emotional factors in their decision making to justify market anomalies [3]. Most investors are influenced by news of political, economic, social, or emotional events that are posted on social media. Thus, information on web newsgroups, social networks, and stock chat boards are examples of important sources of information that can be used toward better business decision making. In the past decades, the field of behavioral economics was motivated by technical analysis, and a great deal of research was conducted recently through the fundamental analysis of unstructured textual data using embedding techniques [4–6].

In a technical analysis, indices such as World Bank reports on the GDP, analyzed by human experts, and also the technical analysis of market indicators are used [7–9], while in a fundamental analysis, text mining methods are applied to identify important events that influence investors and cause market fluctuations. To understand fundamental subjects that affect the market, one needs to represent text according to the contextual information in a document as well as the proximity of the information in news streams that report various aspects of events; however, most works that were published before 2006 only analyzed the market response to simple parameters, such as news counts. In this survey, we study methods for identifying the contextual information published in social media related to financial markets. Text mining techniques, such as a sentiment analysis [10–13], part of speech tagging (POS) [14,15], text representation, such as transformer-based word embedding [16–22], and machine learning techniques [23–31], have been used in this area after 2006. Recently, researchers have focused on using deep learning-based natural language processing (NLP), such as Bidirectional Encoder Representations from Transformer (BERT) [18,21,32–34] or seq2seq architecture with an attention mechanism [20,35–38], to structure textual web data. BERT-contextualized word embedding, announced by Google in 2018, is used as a word sense disambiguation technique for summarizing and selecting important news for investors' behavior analysis [21,25]. Recent works have investigated the use of an attention mechanism in a deep encoder–decoder network that applies transfer learning from pre-trained models or calculating the impact of each news feed as well as assigning heavy weights for important time intervals in a time series [19,39,40]. Other recent research is on the implementation of graph embedding and knowledge graph mining with deep learning-based predictive models [20,24,41–43].

We study the literature that was published in the intersection of behavioral economics and the NLP field and analyzed various data, such as market indicators and textual sources. We review the ways of structuring text and the retrieval of attractive patterns that are extracted from unstructured text or market time-series data using deep feature fusion strategies and machine learning approaches. Figure 1 depicts our survey organization. We review the usage of the text-structuring approach from Bag of Words (BoW) as a traditional text representation method to contextualize transformer-based text representation in a deep neural network. We then study the sentiment analysis, graph mining, and deep feature fusion methods for information retrieval. Finally, we explore studies that present new ways in one of the three areas of forecasting models, investor behavior analysis techniques, or trading strategy recommendation systems that jointly use financial data and media information.

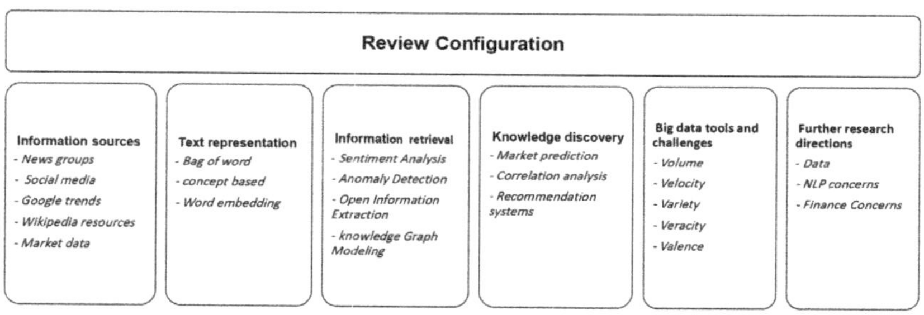

Figure 1. Organization of our review process.

Most of the reviewed works survey fundamental or technical analysis methods [44–48]. We review the literature that processed various heterogeneous data sources for financial decision support by exploring prestigious journals and top-rank conferences to find representative works during the past 13 years that cover the intersection of fundamental and technical analysis approaches. A distinctive aspect of our review is covering the literature from three mainstream viewpoints, including predictive models, correlation analysis methods, and recommendations for trading strategies. Another aspect of our work is studying big data challenges, such as the veracity of textual information and the impact of fake news on the stock market or the valence of groups of investor's behavior, and introducing tools for the huge amount of real-time data storage and processing.

Previous review papers, such as [44,47], present some hypotheses and earlier efforts in the domain. Compared to Li et al. [45], published in 2017, we include other aspects, such as covering the recent deep learning-based NLP approaches. Unlike [46,49], we not only cover a sentiment analysis but also other information retrieval approaches from the text. Compared to [48,50–52], we only focus on interactions between web media and the stock market. The authors in [53,54] review the literature from an information science perspective, while we review the technical characteristics of predictive models or trading strategy recommendations methods.

Our main contributions in this survey are as follows:

- We provide state-of-the-art use cases of fundamental analysis studies in financial market prediction, trading strategy recommendation, and correlation analysis, which distinguishes this study from the existing surveys.
- We systematically review the structuring heterogeneous data sources, such as knowledge graph mining or tensor decomposition techniques, and discuss the lag analysis or significance indication methods, which are often neglected in other surveys.
- We organize our review into four main categories of heterogeneous data sources, text structuring, analysis of information, and knowledge discovery methods.
- We present the future research directions in all of these categories.
- We discuss various big data aspects, such as variety, veracity, volume, valence, and velocity, as well as the tools and challenges in this field.

Outline: In Section 2, we discuss the background concepts and overview of the research methodology. Section 3 describes the review organization. Section 4 presents the big data, tools, and challenges. Section 5 presents the future directions of the research, and the conclusion is presented in Section 6.

2. Background and Methodology

In this section, we first explain our review methodology for selecting the studied resources and then present the motivation from the three viewpoints of information sources, textual representation, and financial predictive models.

2.1. Methodology

Figure 2 depicts the distribution of published papers in terms of years and text representation approaches that they investigated. The growing number of papers in recent years shows the importance of applied studies in the intersection of behavioral finance and artificial intelligence. This figure clearly shows the investigation of text mining methods after 2006 in the reviewed literature and the increasing number of embedding techniques used in the literature over the past two years. We explore papers published in prestigious journals and conferences by searching for keywords such as "financial market prediction", "financial sentiment analysis", "news text mining". We select papers that contribute to the intersection of behavioral finance and financial newsgroups and social media analysis. Table 1 depicts the most cited related works published in journals and conferences. The citation statistics were extracted from Google Scholar as of 10 September 2022. Most journals do not have commercial or advertiser relationships, while some conferences are sponsored by financial companies and stakeholders. The *Expert Systems and Applications*, with 14 publications, has the greatest number of related publications among other sources, and the *Association for Computational Linguistics (ACL)* conference with 4 publications has the most papers among other conferences. Bollen et al. [55], who proposed stock market mood estimation, from Twitter, have the most cited work since 2010.

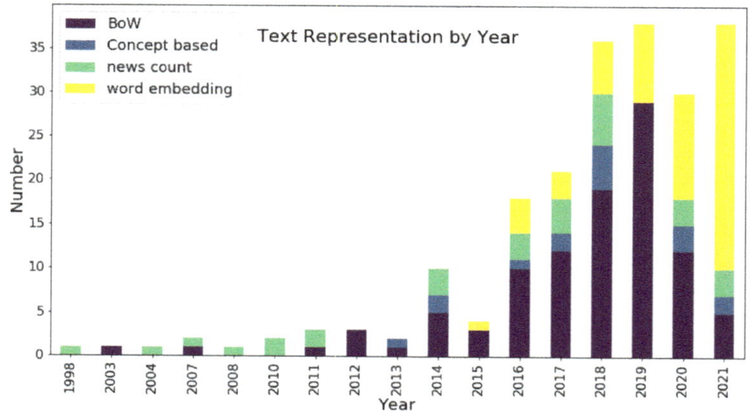

Figure 2. Distribution of reviewed works based on the text representation methods.

Table 1. Information sources in terms of citations.

Source	Papers	No. of Papers	Citation
Journal of Finance	[56–58]	3	6137
Journal of Computational Science	[55]	1	2801
Expert Systems with Applications	[9,22,47,48,52,59–66]	14	1229
Decision Support Systems	[24,67–74]	9	785
Information Processing & Management	[28,75–78]	5	406
Knowledge-Based Systems	[12,23,79–82]	7	162
Neurocomputing	[17,83–85]	4	158
The Journal of Finance and Data Science	[86,87]	2	111
International Review of Financial Analysis	[3,88]	2	100
International Journal of Data Science and Analytic	[50,51,89,90]	4	28
Neural Computing and Applications	[13,91,92]	3	99
Applied Soft Computing	[20,93,94]	2	77
Physica A: Statistical Mechanics and its Applications	[95,96]	3	50
IEEE Transactions	[45,97,98]	3	45
AAAI Conference on Artificial Intelligence	[99,100]	2	1080
Empirical Methods in Natural Language Processing (EMNLP)	[101,102]	2	320
Association for Computational Linguistics (ACL)	[21,25,103,104]	4	232

2.2. Information Sources

Applied studies that we reviewed in this work mainly used various information sources, including market- and media-based sources. Figure 3 depicts the distribution of market based on corresponding countries. Refs. [10,88,91,105] examined the predictability of US stock market, including Dow Jones, NYSE, and S&P 500 stocks. Refs. [15,21,60,95,96,106] have studied the predictability of the Foreign Stock Exchange (Forex) and cryptocurrencies market, where a currency is traded based on the ratio of two currency pairs, such as the EUR/USD, UDS/JPY, or BTC/USD. News [13,86,89,107]; social network data, such as Twitter [55,108,109], Stocktweet [88,108,110], or Sina Weibo [111]; as well as trends in search engines [95,112]; referring to Wikipedia page statistics [59]; and online reviews of customers about firm's products [113] are the types of media-based sources available to investors.

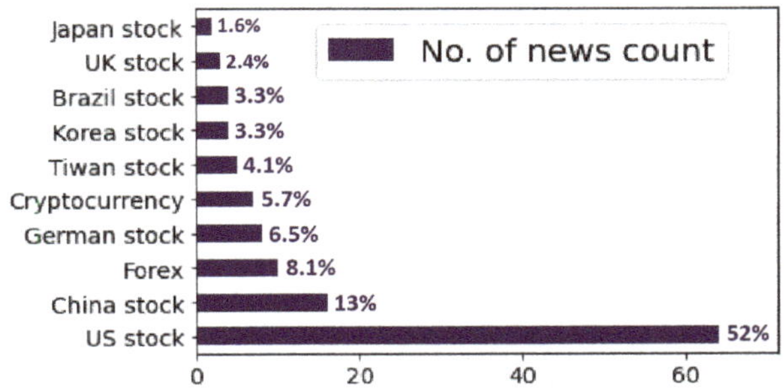

Figure 3. Distribution of reviewed works with respect to the analyzed market. Stock markets are mentioned with country names.

Thomson Reuters and Bloomberg newsgroup are the mainstream news resources in this category; however, it is a basic challenge to utilize relevant texts to the target market because of redundancy and noise in the associated texts. Most of the review papers have manually selected the target market-related news based on manually predefined rules [15,60,114]; however, there are some researchers that proposed a method for selecting the stock-related news, including summarizing the news, measuring the news information gain analysis, and knowledge graph techniques [21,39,67,115]. Farimani et al. [12,16] explored 12 specialized newsgroups that specifically publish for Forex, cryptocurrencies, and commodities and select relevant news to the target market based on judgments of specialized authors. They made public RESTFul APIs (https://robonews.robofa.cscloud.ir/Robonews/v1/, accessed on 2 December 2021) and *MarketNews* (https://figshare.com/articles/dataset/MarketData_for_MarketPredict_RESTFul_API_including_News_and_Market_Data/14754966, accessed on 21 September 2018) datasets so that the research community can access these news sources. For example, Figure 4 presents the number of news indicated for Bitcoin via 25 specialized authors among 592 authors in Cryptocurrency category of *MarketNews* dataset.

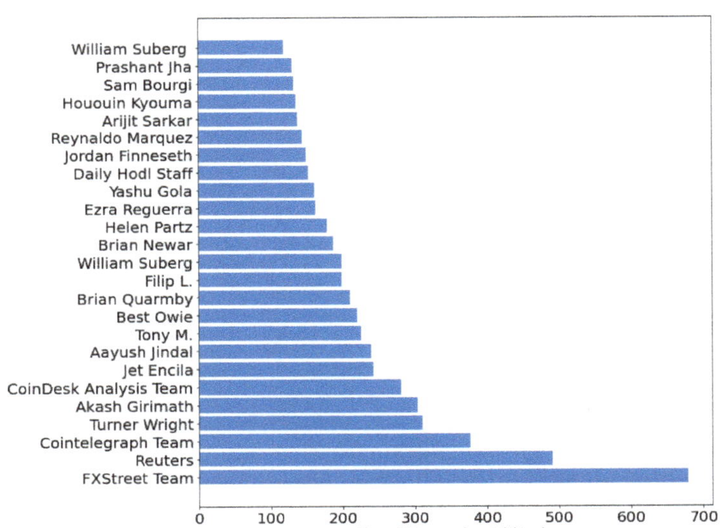

Figure 4. Number of news related to Bitcoin in *MarketNews* dataset in terms of authors.

2.3. Text Representation

The distributional semantic hypothesis [116] states that words that occur in similar contexts tend to have similar meanings, and words with similar distributional properties often have similar meanings. Salton presented a vector space model (VSM) for representing text documents in vector space called Bag of Words based on word occurrences in a text corpus [117]. This method suffers from the curse of dimensionality and sparse representation of TFIDF matrix with the growth of the vocabulary size. Latent Semantic Analysis (LSA) [118] decomposes the singular values of the TFIDF matrix for constructing some latent concepts and reducing the dimension size of word vector representation in a linear space. Feuerriegel and Gordon used LSA for stochastic concept modeling in the process of forecasting macroeconomic indices [119]. Another dimension reduction approach is Latent Dirichlet Allocation (LDA) which factorizes the TFIDF matrix with 3 levels Bayesian approximation [120,121]. Atkin et al. used LDA to extract some topics and each news document is vectorized through these topics for sentiment analysis in financial news [86]. However, with the growth of vocabulary size, it is relatively computationally time expensive.

Recently, neural network-based word embedding techniques have emerged. The word2vec method proposes a word vector representation that reflects both syntactic and semantics roles of words [5]. The main idea of word2vec is to predict a word vector based on its surrounding words instead of directly capturing co-occurrence counts [107]. Predictive methods, such as [18,36,122], consider the semantic relationships between words and use the word embedding technique [5] with long short-term memory predictive model to forecast S&P500 stock market. Lutz et al. [123] used Doc2vec embedding technique [4] for predicting the sentence-level sentiment for developing their financial decision support system. Devlin and his colleagues at Google fine-tuned Bidirectional Encoder Representations from Transformers (BERT) [32] with bidirectional pre-training model for language representations. Ref. [21] proposed a news summarization method for Forex market prediction based on the BERT [32]. They summarized news with SOTA extractive summarization method proposed in [115] and selected news based on the attention score of news headlines to some embedded financial indices. By using BERT, their method captures the deep semantic information effectively. Authors in [124] used BERT for calculating sentiment index of the market using news published in Chinese social media.

2.4. Predictive Models

A broad variety of predictive models have analyzed diverse portfolios [125–128] with an average of 5 years duration. Figure 5 depicts the duration of analysis in reviewed articles in the year. For example, bar '0–3' shows the number of methods with less than three years of duration of the analysis stacked based on the trading timeframe that the scholars focused on. There are two mainstream predictive methods. One predicts the real value of price based on regression models and the other uses a classifier for predicting the trend direction. Researchers have studied the change in the close price and have examined the different duration of time for analyzing the impact of news on the market for short term (minutes to a day) or long term (weekly to monthly). The latter are those [18,36,79,122] that focused on trend (up/down) prediction and formulated the problem as the binary or multiclass classification that was determined based on the change in close price due to two consequent time frames. In terms of news labeling, a few methods labeled news by considering asymmetric time intervals before and after news publishing. For example, Chen et al. [21] analyzed the influence of input time and prediction time on Forex trading in an asymmetric manner. They labeled news based on the change in close price within t1 minutes before news input timestamp and t2 minutes after news announcement.

Different methods have adopted different data types. Some works on predicting stock markets only use text information from daily news [19,39,61,99,101], while others [18,25,34,124] consider a combination of textual and market-based features. Traditional models split data into train and test in chronological order for model training, while in the recursive model, training in rolling window strategy is used. In the rolling window training strategy, dynamic updating of the model parameters is investigated with respect to structural change in market, whereas in traditional train and test split, the training process is static. In some cases [23,28,61,91,129], cross-validation is used for evaluating the accuracy of prediction. Figure 6 shows the distribution of predictive models in the reviewed methods by publication year categorized into 4 groups of deep learning, machine learning, price regression, and statistical analysis of inter-dependencies between media and price fluctuations.

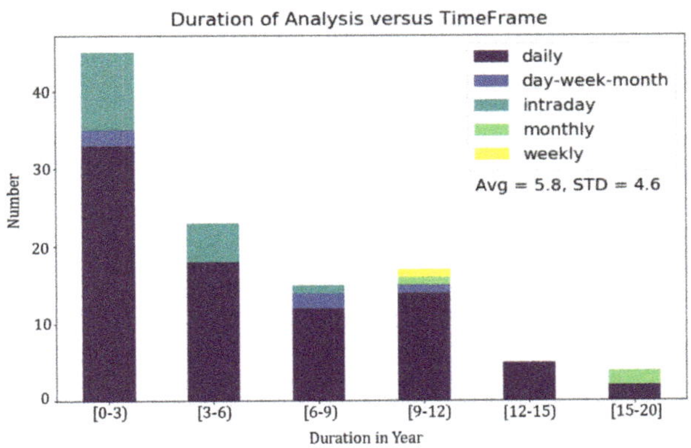

Figure 5. Histogram plot of duration of analysis in the surveyed papers versus time frames.

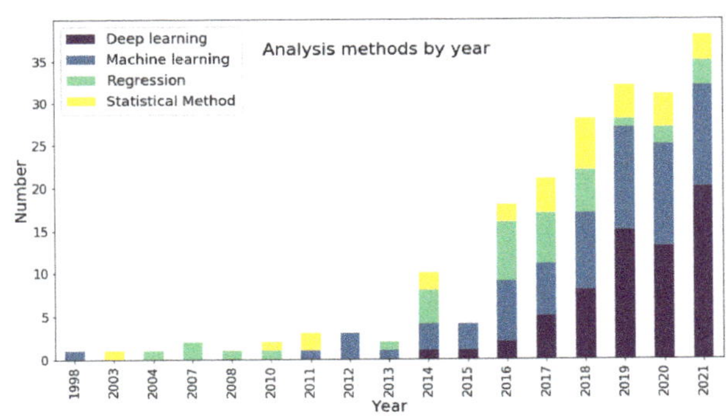

Figure 6. Distribution of predictive models used in the reviewed methods by publication year.

3. Review Configuration

We explore the prominent methods that evaluate some hypotheses related to behavioral economies via a sentiment analysis or text-based features. In Section 3.1, we study text representation methods, including Bag of Words, concepts-based approaches, and word embedding-based techniques. Then, in Section 3.2, we discuss in detail the sentiment analysis, the popular lexicons in the finance domain, the application of the sentiment analysis in the reviewed methods, and finally, focus on OpenIE and knowledge graph-based methods for real-world event detection. In Section 3.3, we address the popular taxonomy of the traits of market analysis models and some graceful issues for evaluating the hypothesis, predictive models, and trading strategies proposed in the literature.

3.1. Textual Representation

In this section, we investigate the main methods in the literature that contributed to the text representation step of the financial analysis, from earlier efforts by Wuthrich et al. [9] in *1998* to the GPT3 [130] presentation in *2020* as a powerful text-structuring method.

3.1.1. Bag of Words

The first leading studies, such as [56,57,131,132], provide regression models based on parameters, such as the amount of news, to examine the rate of the stock return. With the development of text mining techniques and the increasing volume of textual data on the Internet, various methods have been employed to organize documents based on term frequencies by the Bag-of-Words (BoW) matrix. The BoW approach suffers from the existence of noisy and rare terms as issues of scalability, especially in the case of growing words in a dictionary, and challenges such as high dimensionality or the sparse matrix problem that reduce the accuracy of the sentiment analysis. The scholars in [60,68–70] used feature selection methods or proposed term weighting approaches to increase the importance of the word which is unevenly distributed between the up and down classes. In all of the methods mentioned, the feature selection process will be effective as long as we do not face the big data challenge. However, as the use of the Internet grows, investors are facing a huge amount of data.

3.1.2. Concepts-Based Approaches

The Latent Dirichlet Allocation (LDA) and Latent Semantic Analysis (LSA) are two matrix factorization techniques that can also be used for dimensionality reduction. These methods produce some interpretable latent variables in low dimensions. The main purpose of these methods is to reduce the dimensions of the problem features to overcome the sparse matrix problem in the vocabulary integration model. The proposed methods in [86,91,105,125] extracted some topics from textual news with LDA to validate the hypothesis that news is a powerful proxy for market prediction. Ref. [119] proposed a latent variable extraction method, which develops a semantic path model, together with an estimation technique based on regularization in order to yield the full interpretability of the forecasts. Although the concepts in an LSA generally capture a better representation compared to the BoW, they fail to incorporate the nonlinear semantics between the words due to linear space matrix decomposition [83]. Moreover, the LDA distribution estimation has a limitation of time complexity.

3.1.3. Word Embedding

The word embedding technique [5] used a neural network to produce a dense vector for each word based on its occurrences within a contextual window of words. Recently, scholars [18,22,79,122,129,133] have used the word2vec [5] or Doc2vec [4] representation of news headlines and content in their financial decision support systems; however, transformer-based language models [6,130] have shown better results in reflecting deep semantic and syntactic news information compared to traditional word embedding in the financial domain. Liu, in [35], used long-term and short-term event embedding methods which contain the stack ELMO embedding of the t-days set of news headlines for the prediction of the S&P500 index. The authors of [21,25,35] used BERT-contextualized word embedding representation for market prediction. Farimani et al. [16] proposed context-aware conceptual document representation to model the relevance between the news based on all the information in financial news titles and bodies via the clustering of contextualized BERT word embedding. The BERT-BoEC method in [16] leveraged the conceptual relationship in the news that outperforms other concept-based approaches as well as other embedding techniques, such as BERT-based [cls] embedding.

3.1.4. Discussion

Introducing word embedding in 2013 by Mikolov [5] has led to a significant progress in NLP, especially for generating new language models, such as ELMO, BERT, GPT2, and GPT3. The main challenging task for representing a word in a vector space is the ability to reflect the proximity information of the semantic and syntactic roles, in which the transformer-based models can effectively capture the deep semantic and syntactic roles of words by presenting the contextualized word embedding technique. Applying transfer learning from pre-train models, such as ELMO or BERT, in the financial domain is still a challenging problem. The need for semantic similarity modeling between the news documents that report various aspects of an important event remains debatable in the financial domain. Table 2 shows a comparison of methods based on text representation techniques and describes the data and analysis modes.

Table 2. Comparison of methods based on text representation manner.

		Data Attributes					Analysis	
	Literature	Data	Market	Media Source	Duration	Feature Selection	Time Frame	Machine Learning
BOW	[69]	news	S&P500	Yahoo Finance	October 2005–November 2005	POS	20 min	SVR
	[70]	news	DGAP	DGAP and EuroAdhoc	1997–2011	two-word combination	Intraday	SVM
	[60]	news	Forex	MarketWatch.com	2008–2011	Ontology	2 h	SVM
	[15]	news	Forex	MarketWatch.com	2008–2011	POS	Intraday	SVM
	[91]	news	NSYE and NASDAQ	MarketWatch.com	2013	BOW	Daily	NN
Concept Based	[125]	social media	2008 America bank crisis	Yahoo! Finance	January 2008–December 2008	LDA	20 min	Regression
	[134]	News	CSI100	Hexun	January 2015–December 2015	LDA	Daily	Naive Bayes
	[86]	News	NASDAQ	Reuters	September 2011–September 2012	LDA	Minutes	Naive Bayes
	[105]	News	Forex	Reuters	2012–2016	LDA	Daily	MLP
	[119]	News	CDAX	Website of the EQS Group	July 1996–April 2006	Latent Variable	monthly	Lasso Regression
Word Embedding	[122]	News	S&P500	Thomson Reuters, Bloomberg	2006–2014	word2vec	Day–week	LSTM
	[18]	News	S&P500	Reuter	2006–2013	word2vec	Daily	HCAN
	[79]	news, social media	HK and CSI100	Xueqiu and Guba and Sina and Hexun	January 2015–December 2015	word2vec	Daily	MFC
	[133]	News	TWSE	TWSE Official Website	2007–2017	word2vec	Daily	CNN-LSTM
	[22]	News	CDAX	DGAP	January 2001–September 2017	Doc2vec	Daily	LSTM
	[129]	News	Indian stock market	Indian news wires	January 2013–December 2016	pharagraph 2vec	Daily	LSTM
	[35]	News	S&P 500	Reuters and Bloomberg	October 2006–October 2013	Word embedding	Daily	LSTM
	[21]	News	Forex	Reuters	2013–2017	BERT Word embedding	Daily	LSTM
	[25]	News	S&P500	Google Trends	January 2004–December 2015	BERT Word embedding	Weekly	NN

3.2. *Information Retrieval*

We study the representative methods in the two categories of sentiment analysis and open information extraction for organizing information. For the sentiment analysis, we focus on the adopted methods for in-domain or cross-domain sentiment analysis processes for the finance-specific domain, and for the open information extraction, we investigate the challenge of finding structural dependencies between textual resources that report different aspects of real-world events with knowledge graph mining.

Sentiment Analysis. There have been two lines of work predicting stock markets using a sentiment analysis. In the first one, researchers extract the sentiment (positive, negative, or neutral) from documents as features [23,79], and in the other line of work, the public mood time series is calculated by aggregating a sentiment score for each time interval [25,71,108]. From the market perspective, there are two categories, coarse grained and fine grained, in the domain-specific usage of the financial sentiment analysis (FSA). The fine-grain sentiment analysis embraces tasks on a sub-sentence level related to a specific firm, while the coarse-grained SA often analyzes the whole document or a sentence-level analysis. From an NLP viewpoint, the types of approaches applied for the sentiment analysis can be divided into two categories, lexicon-based and machine learning-based approaches. The lexicon-based methods analyze the text sentiment based on the high quality of the emotion dictionary and word polarity, while machine learning approaches rely on supervised learning and word features. In lexicon-based approaches, a domain-specific or domain adaptation lexicon is constructed based on pre-defined manual rules. Lexicons such as Sentiwordnet [135] and Loughran–McDonald [136] are common domain adaptation and finance-specific lexicons in the financial sentiment analysis, respectively. However, studies such as [11,72] presented a method for constructing a financial domain-specific lexicon with machine learning-based techniques. In machine learning approaches, the supervised methods are investigated for a sentiment analysis, and then, based on the document-, sentence-, or aspect-level sentiment, the in-domain classifier is trained to be used in the sentiment analysis phase. However, with some pre-trained models, more embedding methods, and significant improvements in attention mechanisms, deep learning methods are growing in the FSA [75,80–82,137,138].

Lexicon-based methods. Most of the lexicon-based methods in the FSA [28,60,69,139,140] focus on statistically evaluating the correlation between different moods extracted from lexicon-based SA and the fluctuations in target market indices. Most domain-specific lexicons, such as Loughran–McDonald [136] and RavenPack [140], are usually provided by human expert intervention, while the process of manually labeling words' sense is a time-consuming process. Challenges, such as defining the context-aware polarity of a certain word, especially in the financial domain, still exist for an accurate lexicon-based sentiment analysis. Issues such as existing Out-of-Vocabulary Words (OOV), especially in social media texts, cause more frequent updates in lexicons and a poor performance in financial prediction.

Machine Learning-based Methods. In this line of work, a classifier, such as naive Bayes, SVM, or Random Forest, are used to determine the sentiment of features extracted from a textual document [141,142]. There are two strategies for training-set labeling. The first one is training classifiers based on a seed of manually labeled features and the other that usually labels based on the alignment of the lag correlation between headlines' release time and the rate of the stock return. For example, if the stock returns at time t are lower than the time $t - \Delta$, then the news released at time t will be labeled negative. These methods [60,90] often suffer from the problem of market endogeneity [143]. In [11,26], a piece of news is considered good/bad if the market volatility before and after the news publishing is positive/negative, while [128] shows investors overreact to bad news in a short time even in a bullish market and under-react to good news in bad times; thus, the classification is endogenous to the market volatility.

Deep learning-based methods. The main difference between deep learning-based methods and the traditional machine learning models is the better performance of such methods using more data. General domain transformer models, such as BERT, have been used for a sentiment analysis in the literature [16,34,35,90]. In [124], the authors fine-tuned an uncased version of the BERT model for an FSA based on manually labeled firm-specific data from Weibo and then measured the time series of emotions from BERT. This work tried to use a cross-domain sentiment analysis based on a pre-trained BERT model and applied transfer learning for the sentiment analysis through financial news documents. The result indicated that the BERT-based SA outperforms other embedding techniques, such as FastText, Bidirectional Long Short-Term Memory, and Multichannel CNN. The cross-domain sentiment analysis refers to investigating a general domain pre-trained model for finance sentiment analysis problems. Araci et al. fine-tuned BERT for an FSA based on the human expert-labeled TRC2 dataset [144]. The scholars in [12,145] showed the superiority of the FinBERT model [144] as a fine-tuned version of BERT for an FSA.

3.2.1. Discussion about Sentiment Analysis

The empirical findings in the literature show that news and social media messages exhibit a persistent predictive power on financial market movement [18,55,85]. Twitter posts are very short messages less than 140 characters, averaging 11 words per message, and most of the tweets have simple meaning and complicated sentiment structure due to one or more aspects, while news stories contain both a news headline and article body which are longer than tweets. In addition to the linguistic differences between them, there are also differences in the timing behavior of their impact. Tweets are faster than news in exhibiting new market information, whereas news is broadly considered a more trustworthy source of information than tweets. The rumor-essence word-of-mouth statements that investors post on social media may cause earlier fluctuations in the market, while the news has a persistent effect. The ability of a transformer-based sentiment analysis, especially in the recently proposed finer-grained sentiment analysis approaches [63,76,78,146,147], can help scholars to analyze the different aspects of news and social media posts on investors' trading behaviors. Table 3 demonstrates a comparison between news and social media sentiment analysis methods.

Table 3. Comparison of news and social media sentiment analysis methods.

Category		Data Attributes				Analysis		
		Literature	**Media Source**	**Market**	**Duration**	**Feature Selection**	**Time Frame**	**Machine Learning**
News	Lexicon Based	[62]	Belgian financial newspaper *De Tijd*	Dutch Company	May 2012	BoW	Daily	SVM
		[72]	Twitter		December 2012–October 2015	LSA	Daily	Regression
		[58]	*Wall Street Journal*	DJIA	1935–1961	News count	Daily	Regression
	Machine Learning	[23]	Sina Weibo	Shanghai Stock SSEC	December 2014–April 2016	BoW	Intra- day	Logistic regression
		[148]	Reuters and Moneycontrol	NIFTY	Five month	POS	Daily	SVM
		[14]	LexisNexis	NIFTY		BoW	Monthly	ARM
	Deep Learning	[142]	Yahoo Finance	NASDAQ-100	2008–2018	BoW	Daily	MLP
		[22]	Deutsche Gesellschaft (DGAP)	CDAX	January 2001–September 2017	Doc2vec	Daily	LSTM
		[12]	Fxstreet, NewsBTC, Cointelegraph	Forex, Cryptocurrency	October 2018–July 2021	FinBERT	Hourly	LSTM
Social Media	Lexicon Based	[149]	Indian Financial	NIFTY	January 2009–December 2009	BoW	hourly	SVM
		[90]	Yahoo Finance, Reuters	Tokyo Stock Exchange	September 2015 and January 2007–December 2016	Word embedding	Daily	MLP
		[79]	Sina, Hexuan websites	HK, CSI100	January 2015–December 2015	Word embedding	Daily	Tensor decomposition
		[139]	twitter	NYSE	October 2011–March 2012	BoW	Daily	ARM
	Machine Learning	[55]	Twitter	Dow Jones	February 2008–December 2008	News count	Daily	Fuzzy neural network
		[110]	Reuters and Forbes	Amazon, Google	2017	BoW	Daily	Lasso regression, SVR
		[141]	Baidu news	Shanghai 50ETF	2008–2015	BoW	Daily	Naive Bayes, LSTM
	Deep Learning	[124]	Tencent, Ping An, CCB, Weibo	Hong Kong Market	January 2016–December2018	Word embedding	Daily	LSTM, VAR

3.2.2. Event Detection

The mainstream works [10,150] identify important events based on sudden changes in factors, such as the volume of the tweet, the sentiment score, word frequency, or distinct pattern in the occurrence of the words being reported, using the likelihood and point-wise mutual information. The other category of works apply knowledge graph mining approaches [24,39,42,61] and open information extraction (OpenIE) [19,40,99].

Knowledge Graph Modeling. Various knowledge graph-based techniques have been used in the literature to determine the structural relations between news items for a fundamental market analysis. Ref. [102] proposed a Semantic Stock Network (SSN) based on the stock-related cash-tag on Twitter and use it to predict stock based on the summarization of the latent semantics of stocks from social discussions. In their semantic stock graph, stocks are nodes and the frequency of multiple occurrences of two stocks in tweets is the weight of edges. Ref. [61] proposed a graph construction method to leverage both the bi-gram features from news content words and the information structures hiding in the relations between them for predicting the market direction. However, this method leverages a similar subjective relation between news items, and it suffers from the sparsity problem with respect to extracted bi-gram features. The GRU-based attention mechanism in [39] modeled a weighted knowledge graph based on the attention score between similar word embedding representations of news disclosures and corresponding movements in the target market. Ren et al. [24] presented a news recommendation system based on a target company and interested users using a knowledge graph that includes users, news, companies, concepts, and industry categories. The node2vec representation of this knowledge graph is used for predicting the relations between interested users, companies, and related news. Ref. [42] proposed a multimodality graph neural network (MAGNN) to learn from these multimodal inputs for financial time-series prediction, which facilitate the way of handling heterogeneity.

Open Information Extraction. OpenIE aims at extracting structural triples in the form of (subject, relation, object) from textual resources. In [101], entity-relation extraction in the form (Actor, Action, Object) was applied over web-scale data for an event based S&P 500 prediction. Ding [99] employed the event embedding as input features of a deep learning network. They proposed tensor embedding techniques and then applied a deep convolution neural network that processes an event embedding sequence in chronological order for combining the long-term event and short-term event on stock price movements. Following [99], Ding, in [19], used the YAGO knowledge base for incorporating a knowledge graph in the learning process of event embedding. The result indicated the incorporation of knowledge graph-based information, and OpenIE-based structured events to encode background knowledge help with a better prediction of stock movement. Deng [40], after the extraction of events in the form of tuples, constructed a knowledge graph based on Freebase and Wikipedia, and then used graph embedding for the event representation and estimation of the power of an event to move the market. In this article, the author proposed an equation for measuring the impact of events in their predictive models.

Discussion. Table 4 depicts the comparison of the above-mentioned methods. While there has been substantial progress in OpenIE for NLP tasks [151,152] and deep learning-based knowledge graph modeling [100], event detection from financial text remains challenging. Important events with long-term effects and minor effects with short-term effects can influence the market differently. The growth of relation extraction methods based on transformer models and knowledge graph embedding [97,103] can help to facilitate the way for extracting important information from heterogeneous sources in the finance domain.

3.3. Knowledge Extraction

In this section, we investigate a text-based market analysis and discuss issues from three viewpoints: predictive models, the statistical analysis of stakeholders' behavior, and recommendations for portfolio selection. Figure 7 depicts the taxonomy of traits researchers considered while designing their market analysis models. Some aspects in Figure 7 were explained in the background section and here we discuss the other characteristics.

Table 4. Comparison of event detection methods.

	Literature	Media	Data Attributes Market	Duration	Feature Selection	Analysis Time Frame	Machine Learning
Anomalous changes	[10]	Twitter	Dow Jones, S&P500	September 2013–September 2015	Hashtag	Daily	SVR
	[150]	Twitter	Tesco, Booker	January 2017	Hashtag	Minutes	Naive bayes
	[153]	*Irish Farmers Journal*	Irish Beef Market	2005–2015	BOW	Day–week–month	SVM, log-likelihood
OpenIE	[101]	Reuters, Bloomberg	S&P 500	October 2006–November 2013	OpenIE-based tuples	Day–week–month	MLP
	[99]	Reuters, Bloomberg	S&P500	October 2006–November 2013	OpenIE-based tuples	Day–week–month	MLP
	[19]	Reuters, Bloomberg	S&P500	October 2006–November 2013	Event embedding	Daily	SVM
Knowledge Graph	[24]	GF Securities	Airbnb Market	May 2017–May 2018	word2vec	News release time	Bi-LSTM
	[39]	Reuters, Bloomberg	S&P 500	October 2006–November 2013	Word embedding	Daily	Bi-LSTM
	[61]	ifeng.com (Financial China)	SZ002424	September 2012–March 2017	2-gram	Daily	Kernel SVM
	[40]	Reddit WorldNews Channel	DJIA	July 2008–January 2016	Price vector and event embedding	Daily	Temporal CNN
	[102]	Twitter	S&P500	January 2013	BoW	Hourly	Vector auto-regression model

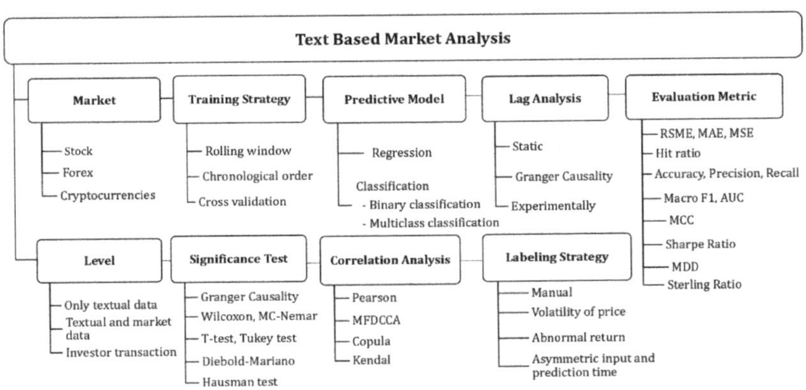

Figure 7. Taxonomy of trait for text-based market analysis models.

Lag analysis. One of the essential characteristics in a time-series analysis is the lag determination. Lag refers to a duration of time between the announcement of new information and the time the stock market adapted itself to a new equilibrium. Some research methods [15,23,92,154] have used a fixed lag size based on related works, while others [21,61,85,104,119] experimentally determine the lag size or use a Granger analysis test [129,142,155]. The Granger causality test [156] is a statistical hypothesis test for determining whether a time series X is useful in forecasting another time series Y. Time series X is considered as impacting Y, if it can be shown that X values provide significant information about future values of Y.

Evaluation Metrics. Accuracy, precision, and recall are three common metrics for evaluating the classifier for *trend prediction* (up/down classes). In the case of an unbalanced dataset due to an up or down trend in the market volatility regime, the weighted Macro F1, Area Under Curve (AUC), Receiver Operating Characteristic (ROC), and Matthews Correlation Coefficient (MCC) are more reliable metrics. The RMSE, MSE, MAE, and hit ratio are traditional metrics for the residual evaluation of *regression-based* predictive models. Some predictive models proposed a trading strategy and evaluated the effectiveness of such models based on profitability and investment metrics, such as the cumulative profit, Sharpe ratio, and Maximum Drawdown (MDD). In Section 3.3.3, we discuss these metrics and methods. Figure 8 depicts the distribution of the evaluation metrics used in publications, which shows about 60 papers focused on the trend prediction evaluation with an accuracy metric. Moreover, most predictive methods consider the trend (up/down) prediction and are less focused on price regression.

Significance test. Various statistical tests have been used in the literature. Most of the research indicated the effect of news information based on the regression-based Granger causality test and used the unit root test or Dickey–Fuller test for satisfying the stationary behavior of the market during the analysis period [55,129,141,157].

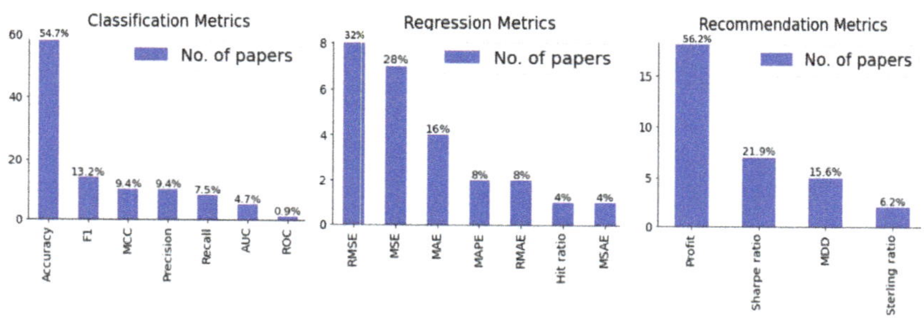

Figure 8. Distribution of evaluation metrics.

3.3.1. Predictive Models Based on Heterogeneous Data Fusion

In this section, we focus on studies about the insider influence of heterogeneous information on investors. Tensor decomposition has been used for handling the heterogeneity of information sources [23,59,79,154]. Tensor-based approaches have shown good results in handling heterogeneous data sources, while the iterative estimation of parameters for each mode of data is a time-consuming process and makes it difficult for models to learn the lead–lag effect of the news on market movements. The concatenation of extracted features from a deep neural network was also used to handle various information sources in market decision support [12,16,21]. Ref. [104] presented a novel deep generative model that jointly exploits text and price signals for assessing continuous latent variables for the superior treatment of stochasticity. Their deep model includes three components, the Market Information Encoder, Variational Movement Decoder, and Attentive Temporal Auxiliary, for the prediction of 80 stocks listed in S&P500. Ref. [17] proposed a hierarchical attention network for handling information fusion from news titles, bodies, and sentiment as well as market based information for stock prediction. Table 5 shows the trait of these reviewed predictive models.

Table 5. Detailed trait of predictive models based on chaotic data.

Literature	Data Attributes Media	Market	Duration	Analysis Feature Selection	Time Frame	Machine Learning
[92]	Caihua	HIS	2001	BoW	Daily	MLP
[154]	Sina, eastmoney	CSI100	2011	BoW	Minute	High-order tensor regression
[23]	Sina Weibo	Shanghai Stock SSEC	September 2014–April 2016	Tensor decomposition	Intraday	Logistic regression
[21]	Thomson Reuters	Forex	2013–2017	BERT word embedding, MLP-based feature extraction	Intraday	LSTM
[104]	Twitter	NASDAQ	2014–2016	Word embedding, latent variable extraction	Daily	Bi-GRU
[20]	CITIC Securities, GF Securities, China Pingan	Chinese stock	March 2012–July 2018	Graph embedding	Daily	Bi-LSTM

3.3.2. Statistical Analysis of Investors' Behavior

Various cross-correlation analyses have been used for revealing the correlation between investor sentiment and market returns on the non-stationary behavior of the market. Traditional correlation analysis methods, such as Pearson, cannot capture nonlinear relations. Ref. [158] adopted the Kendall correlation for the analysis of the news effect on FBOVESPA, because unlike the Pearson, instead of measuring linear relationships, it measures the monotonic relationship between two variables. Ref. [159] presented a nonlinear dynamic model to study the fractal influence of good and bad news and the actions of various market participants (fundamentalists, chartists, and insiders) on the change in market prices. Nonlinear long-term correlation analysis methods, such as the Multifractal Detrended Cross-Correlation Analysis (MF-DCCA) [160], in [95,161], were used in a rolling window-based strategy and revealed that there is a decreasing trend for the cross-correlations between the change in Google Trends and Bitcoin returns over time. The conditional Copula test was used in [128] to evaluate the nonlinear and asymmetric market effects of economic news that may vary with news intensity. Adopting the Granger causality test for the analysis of a linear causal relationship between the sentiment index and the market is a common task, while [67] used transfer entropy for the analysis of the nonlinear causal relationship between the news and the Korean stock market. Moreover, researchers, such as [162–164], have studied the simultaneous co-movements of the financial markets due to the disclosure of relevant news, macroeconomic announcements, and trending market-related words in Google searches for the short-term analysis. Table 6 depicts the finding that indicates the statistical analysis of the research hypothesis.

Table 6. Findings in behavior analysis methods.

Literature	Sentiment Analysis	Market	Analysis Method	Time Frame	Parameter	Finding
[96]	Yes	Forex	Mathem-atical model	5 min	volatility	Their findings show that the model with multiplicative noise can reproduce the dynamics observed in the real financial market affected by the arrival of high-impact news.
[158]	No	FBOVE- SPA	Kendall cross correlation	15 min	average price, trading volume	Besides demonstrating that sector is indeed influenced contrastingly by news, they also show that the machine learning models utilized performed better than random and other less complex baselines for all sectors in FBOVESPA, in this manner giving proof that news information conveys in reality a significant signal for comprehension of BM and FBOVESPA dynamics.

Table 6. *Cont.*

Literature	Sentiment Analysis	Market	Analysis Method	Time Frame	Parameter	Finding
[126]	Yes	NYSE	Regression	Daily	trading volume, volatility	Their results suggest that significant price discovery related to news stories occurs through institutional trading before the news announcement date.
[128]	No	US	Copulas Statics	Daily	equity returns	The finding shows the market reacts strongly and negatively to the most unfavorable macroeconomic news but appears to largely discount the good news.
[165]	Yes	S&P 500	Correlation	Week	volatility	Their findings show a statistically and economically significant relationship between stale news stories on unemployment and next week's S&P 500 returns. This effect is then completely reversed during the following week.
[95]	No	Bitcoin market	MF-DCCA	Daily	trading volume	By employing the Multifractal Detrended Cross-Correlation Analysis method, they find that the change in Google Trends (CGT) and the Bitcoin market, i.e., returns and changes of volume, is an overall higher degree of multifractal in the long term and weak multifractal in the short term.
[166]	Yes	S&P 500	DCCA-MIDAS	Daily	return	The results show that the composite index of investor sentiment has a significantly positive influence on the long-term stock–bond correlation, and the shock of crises significantly decreases the average correlation, but the effect of sentiment does not change significantly.
[87]	Yes	FTSE 100	Correlation	Daily	close price	Their findings show there is evidence of causation between public sentiment and the stock market movements, in terms of the relationship between MOOD and the daily closing price, and the time-lag findings of MOOD and PRICE.
[163]	No	DAX	Impulse response analysis	5 min	volatility	Show that 50 percent of the total accumulated impact of US macroeconomic news on the DAX 30 and CAC 40 volatilities is attained after 90 min.
[164]	No	Forex	Impulse response analysis	Intra-day	volatility	News surprise moderates extreme pure news effects that have nearly all positive (negative) coefficients in both regimes for volatility and depth (spread). In addition, volatility and depth respond positively to good and bad unscheduled news in both states (with more intensity during the expansion), while spread decreases in both states.

3.3.3. Recommendation Trading Strategies

Automated portfolio selection and designing trading strategies are challenging tasks due to differences between short-term and long-term investment risks. Short-term investments carry a heavy risk. The Sharpe ratio, Maximum Drawdown (MDD), and Sterling ratio are three measures for evaluating the utility of trading strategies based on risk adjustment. The authors of [85] proposed an optimal trading strategy using investors' sentiment feedback strength through news and tweets with the objective to maximize a risk-adjusted return measured by the Sterling ratio. Ref. [84] designed a business strategy recommendation system based on the public mood index and trend indicators and then according to rankings produced by a neural network-based learning-to-rank algorithm. Ref. [133] exploited the word embedding representation of news items and the local feature extraction capacity of CNN, and the temporal and long conditions of prices and news are taken care of by long short-term memory (LSTM) networks. Scholars have used a deep Q-network for training trading agents, in [27,64–66,94,167], based on financial market data. It seems the application of leveraging news information in the deep Q-learning approaches is not well explored. Table 7 depicts the detailed characteristics of the reviewed methods in strategy recommendation.

Table 7. Comparison of trading strategies models.

Literature	Media	Data Attributes Market	Duration	Feature Selection	Analysis Machine Learning	Evaluation Metrics
[84]	Thomson Reuters	S&P500	2006–2014	BoW	ListNet, RankNet	Sharpe ratio, MDD
[133]	TWSE Official Website	TWSE	2007–2017	word2vec	CNN, LSTM	RSME, profit
[85]	Twitter	NASDAQ, S&P 500	1 August 2012–30 January 2015	BoW	Genetic programming	Sterling ratio, Sharpe ratio, profit
[73]	Reuters	S&P500	September 2006–August 2007	BOW	NN, DT, SLR	Profit
[74]	DGAP	CDAX	2004–2011	BOW	Reinforcement learning	Profit

4. Big Data, Tools, and Challenges

In this section, we review some big data issues in the literature on financial market prediction based on textual data.

Volume: To meet the challenge of the huge volume of data, organizations need to look at distributed platforms, such as distributed Hadoop Eco-Systems, as big data management distributed systems and also use the No-SQL MongoDB database. For example, in SMeDA-SA [139], a Hadoop 1.1.2 cluster was utilized that comprised four nodes distributed through a WAN for each group in order to create separate processes for the classification tasks. Farimani et al. [16] proposed a restful microservice architecture for market prediction based on news and market data, where news data came from MongoDB-Flask-based APIs. MongoDB was also used in [168] to store around 31 million collected messages from Twitter, holding hashtags of all the traded stocks.

Velocity: The authors in [110] leveraged Apache Spark to deal with user-generated big data and to have a scalable system for stream processing. Most deep learning-based methods are implemented with TensorFlow [12,18,122,129,133] or PyTorch [21].

Variety: In terms of a market analysis, the methods are in three levels of data variety. The first category only uses text-based features for the stock prediction problem, in which the market information is often explicitly used for labeling the training set [19,39,61,99,101]. The other group presents mood criteria based on the firm, category, or market-related information via a sentiment analysis of text-based resources, especially stock board discussions [12,18,55,143]. Finally, the third group is methods that extract features based on the combination of market data, mood analysis, and feature selection from unstructured news documents [16,154]. Our analysis shows more than 30% of the works explored in this work use Python programming languages and Tensorflow APIs for implementing their decision support systems.

Veracity:The first step in big data analytics is to assure the originality of the data and production source [169]. One of the important areas of behavioral economics research is considering the impact of fake news and rumors on the market and investors. Kiymaz [170] examined the impact of rumors published in Turkish newspapers on the Istanbul Stock Exchange. Rumor identification in this research has been carried out by a human expert, while in recent years, research has been conducted on identifying rumors and fake news on social networks [77], and of course, the automatic identification of fake rumors and news in the behavioral economics domain is an open field of research.

Valence: Yang [85] used the big data valence concern among users with similar interests in the financial domain, extracting from the community of Twitter users and the messages diffused between members. Moreover, the authors in [171] proposed community detection for extracting relevant tweets for the target firms.

Value: The consideration of the different levels of these six V features depends on the type of business that faces the big data, and the organization determines the level of variety according to its cost and needs.

5. Open Research and Future Directions

Based on our quantitative analysis, some possible research questions for the future are:

- What is the effect of famous authors and influential persons working for financial newsgroups on market fluctuations?
- Do investors respond to the news, social media posts, or other information resources in the same way?
- Does the representation of contextual information in news documents and the proximity between a sequence of news help with improving financial decision supports?
- How do rumor and fake news diffusion patterns in financial social media correlate with market fluctuation?

We present possible research directions from three perspectives: data, NLP applications, and finance-related concerns.

5.1. Data

The methods presented over the past two years have been focusing on the use of multiple sources of information, as discussed in Section 3.3.1, and hence the integration of such data from multiple sources as well as data variety need to be investigated more. While our study (Figure 3) shows that the US and China stock markets have been well studied, the Forex market issues, such as pair selection based on news influence, are not well explored to the best of our knowledge. Cryptocurrency fluctuations under the news effect are also disregarded, which might be due to a lack of relevant news datasets. Recently, Farimani et al. gathered the Forex and Cryptocurrency news datasets in [12] which can facilitate the research in this domain. The early detection of rumors and fake news is of a great importance in behavioral economics. Very little research is currently conducted on identifying rumors and fake news in the behavioral economics domain which can be due to the complexity of this issue and the lack of appropriate datasets in this domain.

5.2. NLP Applications

Our survey shows that the use of word embedding methods for text structuring in behavioral economics has been growing over recent years. Future research could be incorporating other recent language models, such as RoBERTA, GPT3, and PEGASUS, presented in [172,173] and [174], respectively, for applying pre-training on a large corpus of text followed by the fine-tuning of a financial domain or for summarizing news. An accurate financial sentiment analysis can lead to better market mood identification, even in making soft real-time trading decisions. Usually, financial news is reported with ambivalence terms, hence focusing on a finer-grained sentiment analysis, such as recent deep learning-based methods [63,76,78,146,147], can be investigated. In terms of OpenIE, higher-level event detection methods, such as multiple event extraction [37], can extract more accurate features for market prediction. Deep feature extraction from various data sources, such as candle chart images, news text, news authors' roles, the trading transaction of investors, and social media comments, is recommended for research in financial market prediction.

5.3. Finance Applications

Deep learning approaches have been proposed in stock data and news releases over the past few years. Another interesting domain of study is investigating the impact of the information stream from news and social networks on investment transfers from one financial market to another. Investors move their investments from one market to another, influenced by news of some events for greater security. Modeling the impact of news events on markets that have co-movement is therefore a possible research direction. For instance, techniques based on information theory can be used to estimate the impact of news on financial markets. Portfolio selection based on textual information also requires more attention from the research community.

6. Conclusions

In this study, we reviewed the research on information retrieval from data sources, such as news and social networks, and the impact of such information on financial markets from the computer science perspective. During the review process, qualitative and quantitative analyses of behavioral economics knowledge extraction were performed in the four domains of heterogeneous data, contextual text representation and sentiment analysis, predictive models, and the correlation analysis of media behavior and investors' trading behavior. The purpose of this review is to cover different aspects of text mining interaction and behavioral economics and to identify research pathways in this domain. We studied the latest text mining techniques used in predicting financial markets, analyzing investor behavior, and reporting the trading strategy recommendation systems. This review can serve as a source of study for computer science researchers from the applied perspective in adopting long-term strategies and utilizing contextual text mining and behavior analysis. It is also desirable for market investors to reduce investment risk by leveraging decision support systems. From the financial perspective, the application of financial news recommendations and automatic trading agents leveraging media information in real-time decision support systems is another line of future work.

Author Contributions: S.A.F.: conception and design of study, acquisition of data, software, interpretation of data, and writing—original draft. M.V.J.: conception and design of study, supervision, review, and editing. A.M.F.: conception and design of study, supervision, and writing—review and editing. All authors have read and agreed to the published version of the manuscript.

Funding: This research received no external funding.

Data Availability Statement: Not applicable.

Conflicts of Interest: We declare that the authors have no competing interests as defined by MDPI or other interests that might be perceived to influence the results and/or discussion reported in this paper.

References

1. Fama, E.F. The behavior of stock-market prices. *J. Bus.* **1965**, *38*, 34–105. [CrossRef]
2. Shiller, R.J. From efficient markets theory to behavioral finance. *J. Econ. Perspect.* **2003**, *17*, 83–104. [CrossRef]
3. Ramiah, V.; Xu, X.; Moosa, I.A. Neoclassical finance, behavioral finance and noise traders: A review and assessment of the literature. *Int. Rev. Financ. Anal.* **2015**, *41*, 89–100. [CrossRef]
4. Le, Q.; Mikolov, T. Distributed representations of sentences and documents. In Proceedings of the International Conference on Machine Learning, Beijing, China, 21–26 June 2014; pp. 1188–1196.
5. Mikolov, T.; Chen, K.; Corrado, G.; Dean, J. Efficient estimation of word representations in vector space. *arXiv* **2013**, arXiv:1301.3781.
6. Devlin, J.; Chang, M.W.; Lee, K.; Toutanova, K. BERT: Pre-training of Deep Bidirectional Transformers for Language Understanding. In *Proceedings of the 2019 Conference of the North American Chapter of the Association for Computational Linguistics: Human Language Technologies, Volume 1 (Long and Short Papers)*; Association for Computational Linguistics: Minneapolis, Minnesota, 2019; pp. 4171–4186. [CrossRef]
7. Cutler, D.M.; Poterba, J.M.; Summers, L.H. What moves stock prices? Technical report; National Bureau of Economic Research: Cambridge, MA, USA, 1988.
8. Barber, B.M.; Loeffler, D. The "Dartboard" Column: Second-Hand Information and Price Pressure. *J. Financ. Quant. Anal.* **1993**, *28*, 273–284. [CrossRef]
9. Wuthrich, B.; Cho, V.; Leung, S.; Permunetilleke, D.; Sankaran, K.; Zhang, J. Daily stock market forecast from textual web data. In *SMC'98 Conference Proceedings, Proceedings of the 1998 IEEE International Conference on Systems, Man, and Cybernetics (Cat. No. 98CH36218), San Diego, CA, USA, 14 October 1998*; IEEE: Piscataway, NJ, USA, 1998; Volume 3, pp. 2720–2725. [CrossRef]
10. Daniel, M.; Neves, R.F.; Horta, N. Company event popularity for financial markets using Twitter and sentiment analysis. *Expert Syst. Appl.* **2017**, *71*, 111–124. [CrossRef]
11. Sun, Y.; Fang, M.; Wang, X. A novel stock recommendation system using Guba sentiment analysis. *Pers. Ubiquitous Comput.* **2018**, *22*, 575–587. [CrossRef]
12. Anbaee Farimani, S.; Vafaei Jahan, M.; Milani Fard, A.; Tabbakh, S.R.K. Investigating the informativeness of technical indicators and news sentiment in financial market price prediction. *Knowl.-Based Syst.* **2022**, *247*, 108742. [CrossRef]
13. Passalis, N.; Avramelou, L.; Seficha, S.; Tsantekidis, A.; Doropoulos, S.; Makris, G.; Tefas, A. Multisource financial sentiment analysis for detecting Bitcoin price change indications using deep learning. *Neural Comput. Appl.* **2022**, 1–12. [CrossRef]

14. Krishnamoorthy, S. Sentiment analysis of financial news articles using performance indicators. *Knowl. Inf. Syst.* **2018**, *56*, 373–394. [CrossRef]
15. Seifollahi, S.; Shajari, M. Word sense disambiguation application in sentiment analysis of news headlines: An applied approach to FOREX market prediction. *J. Intell. Inf. Syst.* **2019**, *52*, 57–83. [CrossRef]
16. Anbaee Farimani, S.; Vafaei Jahan, M.; Milani Fard, A.; Haffari, G. Leveraging Latent Economic Concepts and Sentiments in the News for Market Prediction. In Proceedings of the 8th IEEE International Conference on Data Science and Advanced Analytics (DSAA), Porto, Portugal, 6–9 October 2021.
17. Chen, X.; Ma, X.; Wang, H.; Li, X.; Zhang, C. A hierarchical attention network for stock prediction based on attentive multi-view news learning. *Neurocomputing* **2022**, *504*, 1–15. [CrossRef]
18. Vargas, M.R.; dos Anjos, C.E.; Bichara, G.L.; Evsukoff, A.G. Deep leaming for stock market prediction using technical indicators and financial news articles. In Proceedings of the 2018 International Joint Conference on Neural Networks (IJCNN), Rio de Janeiro, Brazil, 8–13 July 2018; IEEE:Piscataway, NJ, USA, 2018; pp. 1–8. [CrossRef]
19. Ding, X.; Zhang, Y.; Liu, T.; Duan, J. Knowledge-Driven Event Embedding for Stock Prediction. In Proceedings of COLING 2016, the 26th International Conference on Computational Linguistics, Osaka, Japan, 11–16 December 2016; Technical Papers; The COLING 2016 Organizing Committee: Osaka, Japan, 2016; pp. 2133–2142.
20. Long, J.; Chen, Z.; He, W.; Wu, T.; Ren, J. An integrated framework of deep learning and knowledge graph for prediction of stock price trend: An application in Chinese stock exchange market. *Appl. Soft Comput.* **2020**, 91, 106205. [CrossRef]
21. Chen, D.; Ma, S.; Harimoto, K.; Bao, R.; Su, Q.; Sun, X. Group, Extract and Aggregate: Summarizing a Large Amount of Finance News for Forex Movement Prediction. In *Proceedings of the Second Workshop on Economics and Natural Language Processing*; Association for Computational Linguistics: Hong Kong, 2019; pp. 41–50. [CrossRef]
22. Lutz, B.; Pröllochs, N.; Neumann, D. Predicting sentence-level polarity labels of financial news using abnormal stock returns. *Expert Syst. Appl.* **2020**, *148*, 113223. [CrossRef]
23. Wang, H.; Lu, S.; Zhao, J. Aggregating multiple types of complex data in stock market prediction: A model-independent framework. *Knowl.-Based Syst.* **2019**, *164*, 193–204. [CrossRef]
24. Ren, J.; Long, J.; Xu, Z. Financial news recommendation based on graph embeddings. *Decis. Support Syst.* **2019**, *125*, 113115. [CrossRef]
25. Yang, L.; Xu, Y.; Ng, J.; Dong, R. Leveraging BERT to improve the FEARS index for stock forecasting. In Proceedings of the First Workshop on Financial Technology and Natural Language Processing, Macao, China, 12 August 2019; ACL: Stroudsburg, PA, USA, 2019.
26. Zhang, Z.; Zohren, S.; Roberts, S. Deep reinforcement learning for trading. *J. Financ. Data Sci.* **2020**, *2*, 25–40. [CrossRef]
27. Gao, Z.; Gao, Y.; Hu, Y.; Jiang, Z.; Su, J. Application of Deep Q-Network in Portfolio Management. In Proceedings of the 2020 5th IEEE International Conference on Big Data Analytics (ICBDA), Xiamen, China, 8–11 May 2020; pp. 268–275. [CrossRef]
28. Li, X.; Wu, P.; Wang, W. Incorporating stock prices and news sentiments for stock market prediction: A case of Hong Kong. *Inf. Process. Manag.* **2020**, *57*, 102212. [CrossRef]
29. Moews, B.; Ibikunle, G. Predictive intraday correlations in stable and volatile market environments: Evidence from deep learning. *Phys. A Stat. Mech. Appl.* **2020**, 124392. [CrossRef]
30. Teng, X.; Wang, T.; Zhang, X.; Lan, L.; Luo, Z. Enhancing Stock Price Trend Prediction via a Time-Sensitive Data Augmentation Method. *Complexity* **2020**, *2020, 6737951.* [CrossRef]
31. Wong, S.Y.K.; Chan, J.S.K.; Azizi, L.; Xu, R.Y.D. Time-varying Neural Network for Stock Return Prediction. *Int. J. Intell. Syst. Account. Financ. Manag.* **2022**, *29*, 3–18. [CrossRef]
32. Devlin, J.; Chang, M.W.; Lee, K.; Toutanova, K. Bert: Pre-training of deep bidirectional transformers for language understanding. *arXiv* **2018**, arXiv:1810.04805
33. Lu, Z.; Du, P.; Nie, J.Y. VGCN-BERT: Augmenting BERT with Graph Embedding for Text Classification. In Proceedings of the European Conference on Information Retrieval, Lisbon, Portugal, 14–17 April 2020; Springer: Berlin, Germany, 2020; pp. 369–382. [CrossRef]
34. Wang, T.; Yuan, C.; Wang, C. Does Applying Deep Learning in Financial Sentiment Analysis Lead to Better Classification Performance? *Econ. Bull.* **2020**, *40*, 1091–1105.
35. Liu, X.; Huang, H.; Zhang, Y.; Yuan, C. News-Driven Stock Prediction With Attention-Based Noisy Recurrent State Transition. *arXiv* **2020**, arXiv:2004.01878.
36. Liu, Q.; Cheng, X.; Su, S.; Zhu, S. Hierarchical complementary attention network for predicting stock price movements with news. In Proceedings of the 27th ACM International Conference on Information and Knowledge Management, Torino, Italy, 22–26 October 2018; pp. 1603–1606. [CrossRef]
37. Liu, X.; Luo, Z.; Huang, H. Jointly multiple events extraction via attention-based graph information aggregation. *arXiv* **2018**, arXiv:1809.09078.
38. Zhao, R.; Deng, Y.; Dredze, M.; Verma, A.; Rosenberg, D.; Stent, A. Visual attention model for cross-sectional stock return prediction and end-to-end multimodal market representation learning. *arXiv* **2018**, arXiv:1809.03684.
39. Yang, L.; Zhang, Z.; Xiong, S.; Wei, L.; Ng, J.; Xu, L.; Dong, R. Explainable text-driven neural network for stock prediction. In Proceedings of the 2018 5th IEEE International Conference on Cloud Computing and Intelligence Systems (CCIS), Nanjing, China, 23–25 November 2018; IEEE: Piscataway, NJ, USA, 2018; pp. 441–445. [CrossRef]

40. Deng, S.; Zhang, N.; Zhang, W.; Chen, J.; Pan, J.Z.; Chen, H. Knowledge-Driven Stock Trend Prediction and Explanation via Temporal Convolutional Network. In Proceedings of the Companion Proceedings of The 2019 World Wide Web Conference, San Francisco, CA, USA, 13–17 May 2019; Association for Computing Machinery: New York, NY, USA, 2019; WWW '19 ; pp. 678–685. [CrossRef]
41. Prokhorov, V.; Pilehvar, M.T.; Collier, N. Generating Knowledge Graph Paths from Textual Definitions using Sequence-to-Sequence Models. *arXiv* **2019**, arXiv:1904.02996.
42. Cheng, D.; Yang, F.; Xiang, S.; Liu, J. Financial time series forecasting with multi-modality graph neural network. *Pattern Recognit.* **2022**, *121*, 108218. [CrossRef]
43. Kim, R.; So, C.H.; Jeong, M.; Lee, S.; Kim, J.; Kang, J. HATS: A Hierarchical Graph Attention Network for Stock Movement Prediction. *arXiv* **2019**, arXiv:1908.07999.
44. Kumar, B.S.; Ravi, V. A survey of the applications of text mining in financial domain. *Knowl.-Based Syst.* **2016**, *114*, 128–147. [CrossRef]
45. Li, Q.; Chen, Y.; Wang, J.; Chen, Y.; Chen, H. Web media and stock markets: A survey and future directions from a big data perspective. *IEEE Trans. Knowl. Data Eng.* **2017**, *30*, 381–399. [CrossRef]
46. Man, X.; Luo, T.; Lin, J. Financial sentiment analysis (fsa): A survey. In Proceedings of the 2019 IEEE International Conference on Industrial Cyber Physical Systems (ICPS), Taipei, 6–9 May 2019; IEEE: Piscataway, NJ, USA, 2019; pp. 617–622. [CrossRef]
47. Nassirtoussi, A.K.; Aghabozorgi, S.; Wah, T.Y.; Ngo, D.C.L. Text mining for market prediction: A systematic review. *Expert Syst. Appl.* **2014**, *41*, 7653–7670. [CrossRef]
48. Jiang, W. Applications of deep learning in stock market prediction: Recent progress. *Expert Syst. Appl.* **2021**, *184*, 115537. [CrossRef]
49. Rajendiran, P.; Priyadarsini, P. Survival study on stock market prediction techniques using sentimental analysis. *Mater. Today Proc.* **2021.** [CrossRef]
50. Saha, S.; Gao, J.; Gerlach, R. A survey of the application of graph-based approaches in stock market analysis and prediction. *Int. J. Data Sci. Anal.* **2022**, 14, 1–15. [CrossRef]
51. Cao, L.; Yang, Q.; Yu, P.S. Data science and AI in FinTech: An overview. *Int. J. Data Sci. Anal.* **2021**, *12*, 81–99. [CrossRef]
52. Kumbure, M.M.; Lohrmann, C.; Luukka, P.; Porras, J. Machine learning techniques and data for stock market forecasting: A literature review. *Expert Syst. Appl.* **2022**, *197*, 116659. [CrossRef]
53. Agarwal, S.; Kumar, S.; Goel, U. Stock market response to information diffusion through internet sources: A literature review. *Int. J. Inf. Manag.* **2019**, *45*, 118–131. [CrossRef]
54. Xing, F.Z.; Cambria, E.; Welsch, R.E. Natural language based financial forecasting: A survey. *Artif. Intell. Rev.* **2018**, *50*, 49–73. [CrossRef]
55. Bollen, J.; Mao, H.; Zeng, X. Twitter mood predicts the stock market. *J. Comput. Sci.* **2011**, *2*, 1–8. [CrossRef]
56. Tetlock, P.C. Giving content to investor sentiment: The role of media in the stock market. *J. Financ.* **2007**, *62*, 1139–1168. [CrossRef]
57. Tetlock, P.C.; Saar-Tsechansky, M.; Macskassy, S. More than words: Quantifying language to measure firms' fundamentals. *J. Financ.* **2008**, *63*, 1437–1467. [CrossRef]
58. Baker, M.; Wurgler, J. Investor sentiment and the cross-section of stock returns. *J. Financ.* **2006**, *61*, 1645–1680. [CrossRef]
59. Weng, B.; Ahmed, M.A.; Megahed, F.M. Stock market one-day ahead movement prediction using disparate data sources. *Expert Syst. Appl.* **2017**, *79*, 153–163. [CrossRef]
60. Nassirtoussi, A.K.; Aghabozorgi, S.; Wah, T.Y.; Ngo, D.C.L. Text mining of news-headlines for FOREX market prediction: A Multi-layer Dimension Reduction Algorithm with semantics and sentiment. *Expert Syst. Appl.* **2015**, *42*, 306–324. [CrossRef]
61. Long, W.; Song, L.; Tian, Y. A new graphic kernel method of stock price trend prediction based on financial news semantic and structural similarity. *Expert Syst. Appl.* **2019**, *118*, 411–424. [CrossRef]
62. Van de Kauter, M.; Breesch, D.; Hoste, V. Fine-grained analysis of explicit and implicit sentiment in financial news articles. *Expert Syst. Appl.* **2015**, *42*, 4999–5010. [CrossRef]
63. Do, H.H.; Prasad, P.; Maag, A.; Alsadoon, A. Deep Learning for Aspect-Based Sentiment Analysis: A Comparative Review. *Expert Syst. Appl.* **2019**, *118*, 272–299. [CrossRef]
64. Shavandi, A.; Khedmati, M. A multi-agent deep reinforcement learning framework for algorithmic trading in financial markets. *Expert Syst. Appl.* **2022**, *208*, 118124. [CrossRef]
65. Chen, J.; Luo, C.; Pan, L.; Jia, Y. Trading strategy of structured mutual fund based on deep learning network. *Expert Syst. Appl.* **2021**, *183*, 115390. [CrossRef]
66. Carta, S.; Ferreira, A.; Podda, A.S.; Reforgiato Recupero, D.; Sanna, A. Multi-DQN: An ensemble of Deep Q-learning agents for stock market forecasting. *Expert Syst. Appl.* **2021**, *164*, 113820. [CrossRef]
67. Nam, K.; Seong, N. Financial news-based stock movement prediction using causality analysis of influence in the Korean stock market. *Decis. Support Syst.* **2019**, *117*, 100–112. [CrossRef]
68. Shynkevich, Y.; McGinnity, T.M.; Coleman, S.A.; Belatreche, A. Forecasting movements of health-care stock prices based on different categories of news articles using multiple kernel learning. *Decis. Support Syst.* **2016**, *85*, 74–83. [CrossRef]
69. Schumaker, R.P.; Zhang, Y.; Huang, C.N.; Chen, H. Evaluating sentiment in financial news articles. *Decis. Support Syst.* **2012**, *53*, 458–464. [CrossRef]

70. Hagenau, M.; Liebmann, M.; Neumann, D. Automated news reading: Stock price prediction based on financial news using context-capturing features. *Decis. Support Syst.* **2013**, *55*, 685–697. [CrossRef]
71. Ho, C.S.; Damien, P.; Gu, B.; Konana, P. The time-varying nature of social media sentiments in modeling stock returns. *Decis. Support Syst.* **2017**, *101*, 69–81. [CrossRef]
72. Oliveira, N.; Cortez, P.; Areal, N. Stock market sentiment lexicon acquisition using microblogging data and statistical measures. *Decis. Support Syst.* **2016**, *85*, 62–73. [CrossRef]
73. Geva, T.; Zahavi, J. Empirical evaluation of an automated intraday stock recommendation system incorporating both market data and textual news. *Decis. Support Syst.* **2014**, *57*, 212–223. [CrossRef]
74. Feuerriegel, S.; Prendinger, H. News-based trading strategies. *Decis. Support Syst.* **2016**, *90*, 65–74. [CrossRef]
75. Xiang, C.; Zhang, J.; Li, F.; Fei, H.; Ji, D. A semantic and syntactic enhanced neural model for financial sentiment analysis. *Inf. Process. Manag.* **2022**, *59*, 102943. [CrossRef]
76. Yang, C.; Zhang, H.; Jiang, B.; Li, K. Aspect-based sentiment analysis with alternating coattention networks. *Inf. Process. Manag.* **2019**, *56*, 463–478. [CrossRef]
77. Zhang, X.; Ghorbani, A.A. An overview of online fake news: Characterization, detection, and discussion. *Inf. Process. Manag.* **2020**, *57*, 102025. [CrossRef]
78. Ghorbanali, A.; Sohrabi, M.K.; Yaghmaee, F. Ensemble transfer learning-based multimodal sentiment analysis using weighted convolutional neural networks. *Inf. Process. Manag.* **2022**, *59*, 102929. [CrossRef]
79. Zhang, X.; Zhang, Y.; Wang, S.; Yao, Y.; Fang, B.; Philip, S.Y. Improving stock market prediction via heterogeneous information fusion. *Knowl.-Based Syst.* **2018**, *143*, 236–247. [CrossRef]
80. Liang, B.; Su, H.; Gui, L.; Cambria, E.; Xu, R. Aspect-based sentiment analysis via affective knowledge enhanced graph convolutional networks. *Knowl.-Based Syst.* **2022**, *235*, 107643. [CrossRef]
81. Consoli, S.; Barbaglia, L.; Manzan, S. Fine-grained, aspect-based sentiment analysis on economic and financial lexicon. *Knowl.-Based Syst.* **2022**, *247*, 108781. [CrossRef]
82. Wu, H.; Zhang, Z.; Shi, S.; Wu, Q.; Song, H. Phrase dependency relational graph attention network for Aspect-based Sentiment Analysis. *Knowl.-Based Syst.* **2022**, *236*, 107736. [CrossRef]
83. Kim, H.K.; Kim, H.; Cho, S. Bag-of-concepts: Comprehending document representation through clustering words in distributed representation. *Neurocomputing* **2017**, *266*, 336–352. [CrossRef]
84. Song, Q.; Liu, A.; Yang, S.Y. Stock portfolio selection using learning-to-rank algorithms with news sentiment. *Neurocomputing* **2017**, *264*, 20–28. [CrossRef]
85. Yang, S.Y.; Mo, S.Y.K.; Liu, A.; Kirilenko, A.A. Genetic programming optimization for a sentiment feedback strength based trading strategy. *Neurocomputing* **2017**, *264*, 29–41. [CrossRef]
86. Atkins, A.; Niranjan, M.; Gerding, E. Financial news predicts stock market volatility better than close price. *J. Financ. Data Sci.* **2018**, *4*, 120–137. [CrossRef]
87. Nisar, T.M.; Yeung, M. Twitter as a tool for forecasting stock market movements: A short-window event study. *J. Financ. Data Sci.* **2018**, *4*, 101–119. [CrossRef]
88. Sun, A.; Lachanski, M.; Fabozzi, F.J. Trade the tweet: Social media text mining and sparse matrix factorization for stock market prediction. *Int. Rev. Financ. Anal.* **2016**, *48*, 272–281. [CrossRef]
89. Li, Y.; Pan, Y. A novel ensemble deep learning model for stock prediction based on stock prices and news. *Int. J. Data Sci. Anal.* **2022**, *13*, 139–149. [CrossRef] [PubMed]
90. Ito, T.; Sakaji, H.; Izumi, K.; Tsubouchi, K.; Yamashita, T. Ginn: Gradient interpretable neural networks for visualizing financial texts. *Int. J. Data Sci. Anal.* **2020**, *9*, 431–445. [CrossRef]
91. Hájek, P. Combining bag-of-words and sentiment features of annual reports to predict abnormal stock returns. *Neural Comput. Appl.* **2018**, *29*, 343–358. [CrossRef]
92. Li, X.; Xie, H.; Wang, R.; Cai, Y.; Cao, J.; Wang, F.; Min, H.; Deng, X. Empirical analysis: Stock market prediction via extreme learning machine. *Neural Comput. Appl.* **2016**, *27*, 67–78. [CrossRef]
93. Jahan, M.V.; Akbarzadeh-T, M.R. Extremal optimization vs. learning automata: Strategies for spin selection in portfolio selection problems. *Appl. Soft Comput.* **2012**, *12*, 3276–3284. [CrossRef]
94. Shi, Y.; Li, W.; Zhu, L.; Guo, K.; Cambria, E. Stock trading rule discovery with double deep Q-network. *Appl. Soft Comput.* **2021**, *107*, 107320. [CrossRef]
95. Zhang, W.; Wang, P.; Li, X.; Shen, D. Quantifying the cross-correlations between online searches and Bitcoin market. *Phys. A Stat. Mech. Appl.* **2018**, *509*, 657–672. [CrossRef]
96. Ochiai, T.; Nacher, J. A model for the dynamic behavior of financial assets affected by news: The case of Tohoku–Kanto earthquake. *Phys. Lett. A* **2011**, *375*, 3552–3556. [CrossRef]
97. Rodrigues, F.B.; Giozza, W.F.; de Oliveira Albuquerque, R.; García Villalba, L.J. Natural Language Processing Applied to Forensics Information Extraction With Transformers and Graph Visualization. *IEEE Trans. Comput. Soc. Syst.* **2022**, 1–17. [CrossRef]
98. Jahan, M.V.; Akbarzadeh-T, M.R. From local search to global conclusions: Migrating spin glass-based distributed portfolio selection. *IEEE Trans. Evol. Comput.* **2010**, *14*, 591–601. [CrossRef]
99. Ding, X.; Zhang, Y.; Liu, T.; Duan, J. Deep learning for event-driven stock prediction. In Proceedings of the Twenty-fourth international joint conference on artificial intelligence, Buenos Aires, Argentina, 25–31 July 2015.

100. Liu, W.; Zhou, P.; Zhao, Z.; Wang, Z.; Ju, Q.; Deng, H.; Wang, P. K-BERT: Enabling Language Representation with Knowledge Graph. In Proceedings of the AAAI, New York, NY, USA, 7–12 February 2020; pp. 2901–2908. [CrossRef]
101. Ding, X.; Zhang, Y.; Liu, T.; Duan, J. Using Structured Events to Predict Stock Price Movement: An Empirical Investigation. In Proceedings of the 2014 Conference on Empirical Methods in Natural Language Processing (EMNLP), Doha, Qatar, 25–29 October 2014; Association for Computational Linguistics: Doha, Qatar, 2014; pp. 1415–1425. [CrossRef]
102. Si, J.; Mukherjee, A.; Liu, B.; Pan, S.J.; Li, Q.; Li, H. Exploiting social relations and sentiment for stock prediction. In Proceedings of the 2014 Conference on Empirical Methods in Natural Language Processing (EMNLP), Doha, Qatar, 25–29 October 2014; pp. 1139–1145.
103. Papaluca, A.; Krefl, D.; Suominen, H.; Lenskiy, A. Pretrained Knowledge Base Embeddings for improved Sentential Relation Extraction. In Proceedings of the 60th Annual Meeting of the Association for Computational Linguistics: Student Research Workshop, Dublin, Ireland, 22–27 May 2022; Association for Computational Linguistics: Dublin, Ireland, 2022; pp. 373–382. [CrossRef]
104. Xu, Y.; Cohen, S.B. Stock movement prediction from tweets and historical prices. In Proceedings of the 56th Annual Meeting of the Association for Computational Linguistics (Volume 1: Long Papers); Association for Computational Linguistics: Melbourne, Australia, 2018; pp. 1970–1979. [CrossRef]
105. Hajek, P.; Barushka, A. Integrating Sentiment Analysis and Topic Detection in Financial News for Stock Movement Prediction. In Proceedings of the 2nd International Conference on Business and Information Management, ICBIM '18, Barcelona, Spain, 20–22 September 2018; Association for Computing Machinery: New York, NY, USA, 2018; pp. 158–162. [CrossRef]
106. Jin, F.; Self, N.; Saraf, P.; Butler, P.; Wang, W.; Ramakrishnan, N. Forex-foreteller: Currency trend modeling using news articles. In Proceedings of the 19th ACM SIGKDD International Conference on Knowledge Discovery and Data Mining, Chicago, IL, USA, 11–14 August 2013; pp. 1470–1473. [CrossRef]
107. Sontag, D.; Roy, D. Complexity of inference in latent dirichlet allocation. In Proceedings of the Advances in neural information processing systems, Granada, Spain, 12–15 December 2011; pp. 1008–1016.
108. Zhang, X.; Fuehres, H.; Gloor, P.A. Predicting stock market indicators through twitter I hope it is not as bad as I fear. *Procedia-Soc. Behav. Sci.* **2011**, *26*, 55–62. [CrossRef]
109. Wang, Q. Cryptocurrencies asset pricing via machine learning. *Int. J. Data Sci. Anal.* **2021**, *12*, 175–183. [CrossRef]
110. Atzeni, M.; Dridi, A.; Recupero, D.R. Using frame-based resources for sentiment analysis within the financial domain. *Prog. Artif. Intell.* **2018**, *7*, 273–294. [CrossRef]
111. Zhang, K.; Zi, J.; Wu, L.G. New event detection based on indexing-tree and named entity. In Proceedings of the 30th annual international ACM SIGIR conference on Research and development in information retrieval, Amsterdam, The Netherlands, 23–27 July 2007; pp. 215–222. [CrossRef]
112. Da, Z.; Engelberg, J.; Gao, P. The sum of all FEARS investor sentiment and asset prices. *Rev. Financ. Stud.* **2015**, *28*, 1–32. [CrossRef]
113. Wu, J.; Xu, K.; Zhao, J. Online reviews can predict long-term returns of individual stocks. *arXiv* **2019**, arXiv:1905.03189.
114. Wu, G.G.R.; Hou, T.C.T.; Lin, J.L. Can economic news predict Taiwan stock market returns? *Asia Pac. Manag. Rev.* **2019**, *24*, 54–59. [CrossRef]
115. Liu, Y. Fine-tune BERT for extractive summarization. *arXiv* **2019**, arXiv:1903.10318.
116. Harris, Z.S. Distributional Structure. *WORD* **1954**, *10*, 146–162. [CrossRef]
117. Salton, G. *Automatic Text Processing: The Transformation, Analysis, and Retrieval of Information by Computer*; Addison-Wesley: Boston, MA, USA, 1989; Volume 169.
118. Dumais, S.T. Latent semantic analysis. *Annu. Rev. Inf. Sci. Technol.* **2004**, *38*, 188–230. [CrossRef]
119. Feuerriegel, S.; Gordon, J. News-based forecasts of macroeconomic indicators: A semantic path model for interpretable predictions. *Eur. J. Oper. Res.* **2019**, *272*, 162–175. [CrossRef]
120. Blei, D.M.; Ng, A.Y.; Jordan, M.I. Latent dirichlet allocation. *J. Mach. Learn. Res.* **2003**, *3*, 993–1022.
121. Anbaee Farimani, S.; Tabatabaee, H.; Kaffashan, M. An Investigation into the Process of Organizing and Retrieving Web Texts Based on the Integration of Semantic Concepts In order to organize knowledge. *Iran. J. Inf. Process. Manag.* **2019**, *34*, 1879–1904.
122. Huynh, H.D.; Dang, L.M.; Duong, D. A new model for stock price movements prediction using deep neural network. In Proceedings of the Eighth International Symposium on Information and Communication Technology, Nha Trang City, Viet Nam, 7–8 December 2017; pp. 57–62. [CrossRef]
123. Lutz, B.; Pröllochs, N.; Neumann, D. Sentence-Level Sentiment Analysis of Financial News Using Distributed Text Representations and Multi-Instance Learning. *arXiv* **2018**, arXiv:1901.00400.
124. Hiew, J.Z.G.; Huang, X.; Mou, H.; Li, D.; Wu, Q.; Xu, Y. BERT-based Financial Sentiment Index and LSTM-based Stock Return Predictability. *arXiv* **2019**, arXiv:1906.09024.
125. Jiang, C.; Liang, K.; Chen, H.; Ding, Y. Analyzing market performance via social media: A case study of a banking industry crisis. *Sci. China Inf. Sci.* **2014**, *57*, 1–18. [CrossRef]
126. Hendershott, T.; Livdan, D.; Schürhoff, N. Are institutions informed about news? *J. Financ. Econ.* **2015**, *117*, 249–287. [CrossRef]
127. Gupta, K.; Banerjee, R. Does OPEC news sentiment influence stock returns of energy firms in the United States? *Energy Econ.* **2019**, *77*, 34–45. [CrossRef]

128. Medovikov, I. When does the stock market listen to economic news? New evidence from copulas and news wires. *J. Bank. Financ.* **2016**, *65*, 27–40. [CrossRef]
129. Verma, I.; Dey, L.; Meisheri, H. Detecting, quantifying and accessing impact of news events on Indian stock indices. In Proceedings of the International Conference on Web Intelligence, Sogndal, Norway, 25–27 May 2011; pp. 550–557. [CrossRef]
130. Dale, R. GPT-3: What's it good for? *Nat. Lang. Eng.* **2021**, *27*, 113–118. [CrossRef]
131. Tetlock, P.C. Does public financial news resolve asymmetric information? *Rev. Financ. Stud.* **2010**, *23*, 3520–3557. [CrossRef]
132. Tausch, F.; Zumbuehl, M. Stability of risk attitudes and media coverage of economic news. *J. Econ. Behav. Organ.* **2018**, *150*, 295–310. [CrossRef]
133. Lee, C.Y.; Soo, V.W. Predict Stock Price with Financial News Based on Recurrent Convolutional Neural Networks. In Proceedings of the 2017 Conference on Technologies and Applications of Artificial Intelligence (TAAI), Taipei, 1–3 December 2017; pp. 160–165. [CrossRef]
134. Rao, Y.; Zhong, X.; Lu, S. Research on News Topic-Driven Market Flucatuation and Predication. In Proceedings of the 2016 International Conference on Identification, Information and Knowledge in the Internet of Things (IIKI), Beijing, China, 20–21 October 2016; pp. 559–562. [CrossRef]
135. Baccianella, S.; Esuli, A.; Sebastiani, F. SentiWordNet 3.0: An Enhanced Lexical Resource for Sentiment Analysis and Opinion Mining. In Proceedings of the Seventh International Conference on Language Resources and Evaluation (LREC'10), Paris, France, 17–23 May 2010; European Language Resources Association (ELRA): Valletta, Malta, 2010.
136. LOUGHRAN, T.; MCDONALD, B. When Is a Liability Not a Liability? Textual Analysis, Dictionaries, and 10-Ks. *J. Financ.* **2011**, *66*, 35–65. [CrossRef]
137. Zhang, H.; Li, Z.; Xie, H.; Lau, R.Y.; Cheng, G.; Li, Q.; Zhang, D. Leveraging statistical information in fine-grained financial sentiment analysis. *World Wide Web* **2022**, *25*, 513–531. [CrossRef]
138. Zhao, M.; Yang, J.; Zhang, J.; Wang, S. Aggregated graph convolutional networks for aspect-based sentiment classification. *Inf. Sci.* **2022**, *600*, 73–93. [CrossRef]
139. Li, B.; Chan, K.C.; Ou, C.; Ruifeng, S. Discovering public sentiment in social media for predicting stock movement of publicly listed companies. *Inf. Syst.* **2017**, *69*, 81–92. [CrossRef]
140. Shi, Y.; Liu, W.M.; Ho, K.Y. Public news arrival and the idiosyncratic volatility puzzle. *J. Empir. Financ.* **2016**, *37*, 159–172. [CrossRef]
141. Zhang, G.; Xu, L.; Xue, Y. Model and forecast stock market behavior integrating investor sentiment analysis and transaction data. *Clust. Comput.* **2017**, *20*, 789–803. [CrossRef]
142. Bouktif, S.; Fiaz, A.; Awad, M. Augmented Textual Features-Based Stock Market Prediction. *IEEE Access* **2020**, *8*, 40269–40282. [CrossRef]
143. Shi, Y.; Ho, K.Y.; Liu, W.M. Public information arrival and stock return volatility: Evidence from news sentiment and Markov Regime-Switching Approach. *Int. Rev. Econ. Financ.* **2016**, *42*, 291–312. [CrossRef]
144. Araci, D. Finbert: Financial sentiment analysis with pre-trained language models. *arXiv* **2019**, arXiv:1908.10063.
145. Vora, V.; Shah, M.; Chouhan, A.; Tawde, P. Stock Market Prices and Returns Forecasting Using Deep Learning Based on Technical and Fundamental Analysis. In *Proceedings of the Information and Communication Technology for Competitive Strategies (ICTCS 2021)*; Kaiser, M.S., Xie, J., Rathore, V.S., Eds.; Springer Nature Singapore: Singapore, 2022; pp. 717–728. [CrossRef]
146. Sun, C.; Huang, L.; Qiu, X. Utilizing BERT for aspect-based sentiment analysis via constructing auxiliary sentence. *arXiv* **2019**, arXiv:1903.09588.
147. Huang, J.; Xing, R.; Li, Q. Asset pricing via deep graph learning to incorporate heterogeneous predictors. *Int. J. Intell. Syst.* **2022.** *37*, 8462–8489. [CrossRef]
148. Yadav, A.; Jha, C.; Sharan, A.; Vaish, V. Sentiment analysis of financial news using unsupervised approach. *Procedia Comput. Sci.* **2020**, *167*, 589–598. [CrossRef]
149. Yadav, R.; Kumar, A.V.; Kumar, A. News-based supervised sentiment analysis for prediction of futures buying behaviour. *IIMB Manag. Rev.* **2019**, *31*, 157–166. [CrossRef]
150. Vilas, A.F.; Redondo, R.P.D.; Crockett, K.; Owda, M.; Evans, L. Twitter permeability to financial events: An experiment towards a model for sensing irregularities. *Multimed. Tools Appl.* **2019**, *78*, 9217–9245. [CrossRef]
151. Kruiper, R.; Vincent, J.F.; Chen-Burger, J.; Desmulliez, M.P.; Konstas, I. In Layman's Terms: Semi-Open Relation Extraction from Scientific Texts. In Proceedings of the 58th Annual Meeting of the Association for Computational Linguistics, Online, 5–10 July 2020.
152. Zhou, S.; Yu, B.; Sun, A.; Long, C.; Li, J.; Yu, H.; Sun, J.; Li, Y. A Survey on Neural Open Information Extraction: Current Status and Future Directions. *arXiv* **2022**, arXiv:2205.117252022.
153. Gurin, Y.; Szymanski, T.; Keane, M.T. Discovering news events that move markets. In Proceedings of the 2017 Intelligent Systems Conference (IntelliSys), London, UK, 21–22 September 2016; IEEE: Piscataway, NJ, USA, 2017; pp. 452–461.
154. Li, Q.; Chen, Y.; Jiang, L.L.; Li, P.; Chen, H. A tensor-based information framework for predicting the stock market. *ACM Trans. Inf. Syst. (TOIS)* **2016**, *34*, 1–30. [CrossRef]
155. Checkley, M.; Higón, D.A.; Alles, H. The hasty wisdom of the mob: How market sentiment predicts stock market behavior. *Expert Syst. Appl.* **2017**, *77*, 256–263. [CrossRef]
156. Granger, C. Testing for causality: A personal viewpoint. *J. Econ. Dyn. Control* **1980**, *2*, 329–352. [CrossRef]

157. Wei, Y.C.; Lu, Y.C.; Chen, J.N.; Hsu, Y.J. Informativeness of the market news sentiment in the Taiwan stock market. *North Am. J. Econ. Financ.* **2017**, *39*, 158–181. [CrossRef]
158. de Araújo, J.G.; Marinho, L.B. Using Online Economic News to Predict Trends in Brazilian Stock Market Sectors. In Proceedings of the 24th Brazilian Symposium on Multimedia and the Web, Salvador, Brazil, 16–19 October 2018; WebMedia '18; Association for Computing Machinery: New York, NY, USA, 2018; pp. 37–44. [CrossRef]
159. Romanov, V.; Naletova, O.; Panteleeva, E.; Federyakov, A. Fractal model of estimating news and insider influence on market volatility. *Autom. Doc. Math. Linguist.* **2007**, *41*, 141–149. [CrossRef]
160. Zhou, W.X. Multifractal detrended cross-correlation analysis for two nonstationary signals. *Phys. Rev. E* **2008**, *77*, 066211. [CrossRef]
161. Alamatian, Z.; Vafaei Jahan, M.; Milani Fard, A. Using Market Indicators to Eliminate Local Trends for Financial Time Series Cross-Correlation Analysis. In Proceedings of the 34th Canadian Conference on Artificial Intelligence (Canadian AI), Vancouver, BC, Canada, 25–28 May 2021. [CrossRef]
162. Chen, K.; Luo, P.; Liu, L.; Zhang, W. News, search and stock co-movement: Investigating information diffusion in the financial market. *Electron. Commer. Res. Appl.* **2018**, *28*, 159–171. [CrossRef]
163. Omrane, W.B.; Hussain, S.M. Foreign news and the structure of co-movement in European equity markets: An intraday analysis. *Res. Int. Bus. Financ.* **2016**, *37*, 572–582. [CrossRef]
164. Omrane, W.B.; Tao, Y.; Welch, R. Scheduled macro-news effects on a Euro/US dollar limit order book around the 2008 financial crisis. *Res. Int. Bus. Financ.* **2017**, *42*, 9–30. [CrossRef]
165. Birz, G. Stale economic news, media and the stock market. *J. Econ. Psychol.* **2017**, *61*, 87–102. [CrossRef]
166. Fang, L.; Yu, H.; Huang, Y. The role of investor sentiment in the long-term correlation between US stock and bond markets. *Int. Rev. Econ. Financ.* **2018**, *58*, 127–139. [CrossRef]
167. El Akraoui, B.; Daoui, C. Deep Reinforcement Learning for Bitcoin Trading. In *Proceedings of the Business Intelligence*; Fakir, M., Baslam, M., El Ayachi, R., Eds.; Springer International Publishing: Cham, Switzerland, 2022; pp. 82–93. [CrossRef]
168. Oliveira, N.; Cortez, P.; Areal, N. The impact of microblogging data for stock market prediction: Using Twitter to predict returns, volatility, trading volume and survey sentiment indices. *Expert Syst. Appl.* **2017**, *73*, 125–144. [CrossRef]
169. Ghasemaghaei, M. The role of positive and negative valence factors on the impact of bigness of data on big data analytics usage. *Int. J. Inf. Manag.* **2020**, *50*, 395–404. [CrossRef]
170. Kiymaz, H. The effects of stock market rumors on stock prices: Evidence from an emerging market. *J. Multinatl. Financ. Manag.* **2001**, *11*, 105–115. [CrossRef]
171. Ranjan, S.; Sood, S. Investor community sentiment analysis for predicting stock price trends. *Int. J. Manag. Technol. Eng.* **2019**, *9, 6012–6020.*
172. Liu, Y.; Ott, M.; Goyal, N.; Du, J.; Joshi, M.; Chen, D.; Levy, O.; Lewis, M.; Zettlemoyer, L.; Stoyanov, V. Roberta: A robustly optimized bert pretraining approach. *arXiv* **2019**, arXiv:1907.11692.
173. Brown, T.B.; Mann, B.; Ryder, N.; Subbiah, M.; Kaplan, J.; Dhariwal, P.; Neelakantan, A.; Shyam, P.; Sastry, G.; Askell, A.; et al. Language models are few-shot learners. *arXiv* **2020**, arXiv:2005.14165.
174. Zhang, J.; Zhao, Y.; Saleh, M.; Liu, P.J. Pegasus: Pre-training with extracted gap-sentences for abstractive summarization. *arXiv* **2019**, arXiv:1912.08777.

information

MDPI

Systematic Review

Recommender Systems Applications: Data Sources, Features, and Challenges

Yousef H. Alfaifi

Faculty of Computers and Information Technology, University of Tabuk, Tabuk 71491, Saudi Arabia; y_alfaifi@ut.edu.sa

Abstract: In recent years, there has been growing interest in recommendation systems, which is matched by their widespread adoption across various sectors. This can be attributed to their effectiveness in reducing an avalanche of data into individualized information that is meaningful, relevant, and can easily be absorbed by a single person. Several studies have recently navigated the landscape of recommendation systems, attending to their approaches, challenges, and applications, as well as the evaluation metrics necessary for effective implementation. This systematic review investigates the understudied aspects of recommendation systems, including the data input into the systems and their features or outputs. The data in (input) and data out (features) are both diverse and vary significantly from not just one application domain to another, but also from one application use case to another, which is a distinction that has not been thoroughly addressed in the past. In addition, this study explores several application domains, providing a comprehensive breakdown of the categorical data consumed by these systems and the features, or outputs, of these systems. Without focusing on any particular journals or their rankings, this study collects and reviews articles on recommendation systems published from 2018 to April 2024, in four top-tier research repositories, including IEEE Xplore Digital Library, Springer Link, ACM Digital Library, and Google Scholar.

Keywords: recommender system; recommendation system; applications; data sources; features; challenges

1. Introduction

There is a plethora of definitions and interpretations of recommendation or recommender systems (RSs) in information science literature. According to [1], RSs are web applications capable of predicting the future opinion of a user about a set of items. Similarly, in [2], RSs are defined as systems that help users to decide on appropriate items and find preferred items within a collection. Additionally, in [3], they are defined as web-based tools that tailor vendor's offerings to consumers according to their preferences [4]. However, one widely accepted definition of RSs is that they are systems that suggest items to users based on their preferences, interests, or behaviors. Based on this definition, the main components of RSs include the user (either individuals or businesses), the item (products or services), and the user's preferences or interests.

The term "recommendation system" initially appeared as a branch of data or knowledge retrieval [5] and filtering before becoming an independent science about four decades ago [6,7]. In recent years, research on RSs has significantly increased. Several factors are responsible for this increased interest, including the rapid and exponential growth of data (particularly big data); the ubiquitous nature of information on the internet or web, which has inevitably caused information overload; and, last but not least, global demand for digital devices including computers and mobile phones. While each of these factors has played a huge role in the unprecedented excitement around RSs, the most compelling factor for researchers to study and investigate RSs has undoubtedly been the internet environment itself. Because the internet is crowded with information accessible through multiple applications, filtering out what is relevant for an everyday user is a challenging task. Thus, researchers have proposed RSs as viable solutions to information overload. Furthermore, the internet provides a platform for collecting data from users, which is subsequently utilized by RSs to suggest relevant items, making RSs particularly adept for this task.

RSs aim to not only retrieve the most relevant information for the user from a vast amount of data but also to predict the most appropriate elements for the user based on the characteristics depicted in their preferences and behavior. Besides recommending previously seen items, RSs also suggest new and unexpected items to users. This diversity and randomness have been deemed useful and effective in RSs as of late, as they ensure that the user does not get bored of repetitive recommendations [8].

A multitude of real-world applications benefit from RSs. From e-commerce, social media, and messaging, to audio and video content streaming, RSs are widely adopted to enhance the customer experience. Amazon (https://www.amazon.com, accessed on 4 March 2024), eBay (https://www.ebay.com, accessed on 4 March 2024), and Alibaba (https://www.alibaba.com, accessed on 4 March 2024) are some of the most popular business-to-consumer (B2C) sites with powerful RSs engines. They have adopted the collaborative filtering (CF) technique, which recommends products to a customer based on the correlation between the customer and other consumers who have purchased similar products [9]. CF aggregates user-provided ratings, typically assessed on a scale of 1 to 5 (with increasing level indicating a preference or likeability), in order to generate new recommendations for customers.

Motivated by the breadth of underexplored aspects in RSs, this study conducts a comprehensive survey of existing literature on RSs to uncover details on the input and outputs of RSs. Upon a preliminary review of the recent literature from 2018 to April 2024, this study identifies, and focuses on, six carefully chosen application domains, studying three fundamental aspects pertaining to the input and outputs of RSs. These three fundamental aspects of rapidly evolving RSs are: (1) the data (the input into RSs) that is provisioned to RSs to enable them to function, (2) the features or functions (the output from RSs), and (3) the challenges faced in the research, development, and implementation of the aforementioned systems. This study organizes recent and current knowledge pertaining to these aspects into the different application domains or fields.

Based on the above, the main contributions of this work include the following: (1) classifying RSs into several domains according to their applications in business and (2) studying the features, challenges, and data sources for each application of RSs.

The remainder of this paper is organized as follows. First, Section 2 reviews critical studies and articles. This is followed by Section 3, which describes the data collection methods used in this study. This paper utilized four stages (Identification, Scanning, Eligibility, and Inclusion) adopted from the Preferred Reporting Items for Systematic Reviews and Meta-Analyses (PRISMA) statement (see Supplementary Materials). The next section (Section 4) breaks down the various RSs application domains, providing an independent and distinct review for each, concentrating on the data (inputs), features (outputs), and challenges faced by RSs applications in their respective domains. Finally, the paper summarizes the literature review's findings in the discussion Section 5 followed by the conclusion in Section 6.

2. Related Work

The number of literature reviews or surveys focused on RSs has increased significantly over the past few years. Many of these surveys explore one or more of the following topics: (1) Approaches or techniques of RSs; (2) Challenges or problems facing RSs; (3) Applications of RSs; and (4) Methods for evaluating RSs [10–17].

Several approaches [10,13,15,18], models [11], or techniques [17,19], as they are sometimes called, play an essential role in building RSs. The aforementioned approaches, as they are referred to in this study, are critically examined in almost every literature review of RSs [10–14,16,18–20]. The approaches are usually divided into three main categories: content-based filtering (CBF), collaborative filtering (CF), and hybrid filtering (HF) [10,11,13,14,16–20]. CBF is further divided into two approaches, which are model-based and memory-based [10–12,14,17], whereas HF comprises several classifications such as weighted, switching, and mixed hybrid [11,16,18]. In addition, these literature reviews also cover other approaches, such as knowledge-based filtering [13–15,17].

Within the most important topics examined in the literature review of RSs, the problems [10,11] encountered—commonly termed as "challenges" [14,15,17–20]—are considered to be the second most important subject, after the approaches of RSs. Cold start, data sparsity, and scalability [10,11,13,15,17–19] are the most common challenges presented in these studies. Challenges such as gray sheep [11,17], running time [10], and privacy issues [19] are also addressed in these reviews, albeit to a lesser extent. These challenges have been studied in order to reduce their impact on recommendation systems; for example, the cold start challenge has been managed by proposing a combined collaborative filtering technique that integrates a rating-oriented approach with a pairwise ranking-oriented approach [21]. Data sparsity has been addressed by providing a customized recommendation with hybrid feedback to improve implicit data [22]. It is important to know that, although there are general challenges to RSs as a field, some RS applications face challenges that others do not [23]. This study focuses on the challenges specific to each RS application type without attempting to address the proposed solutions for them, as that is beyond the scope of this work.

As mentioned earlier in Section 1, this study focuses on three aspects of RSs applications: the inputs, outputs, and challenges faced by these systems. To better understand them, RS applications were studied and analyzed. These applications are examined extensively in five literature reviews [11,13,15,17,20]. One study [11] classified the applications of RSs into seven service categories as follows: streaming, social network, tourism, e-commerce, healthcare, education, and academic information services. The second [13] classified RSs applications into a myriad of categories, including tourism, movies, consumer electronic products, education, research papers, medical treatments, music, electronic books, and job opportunities. A third study [15] created five classifications, which were e-commerce, transportation, agriculture, healthcare, and media. A fourth study [20] sorted RSs applications into four main groups, mobile, social, cloud, and traditional (such as e-commerce, e-shopping, e-learning, and e-library). Finally, in [17], RSs applications were defined as one of four types: e-commerce/e-shopping, entertainment, content, and service oriented. Table 1 categorizes this literature on RSs applications. Of note is that the above five studies [11,13,15,17,20] examined multiple applications of RSs without reviewing their data sources, features, and challenges. In other words, the data sources, features, and challenges of RSs have not been reviewed before, leaving a critical gap in the literature.

Table 2 summarizes the literature reviews or surveys on RSs, indicating the particular subject on which they focused their investigations. Figure 1 further shows the percentage of topics treated in these studies. As seen in these visuals, approaches are the most widely studied RSs subject, followed by challenges, then evaluation, and finally applications.

Table 1. Various works with a classification list of their respective RSs application domains. 'NA' indicates that the number of categories for RSs is not available or mentioned explicitly.

Existing Studies	No. of Categories	Categories
[11]	Seven	Streaming, social network, tourism, e-commerce, healthcare, education, and academic information services
[13]	NA	Tourists, movies, consumer electronics products, education, research papers, medical treatments, music, electronic books, and job opportunities
[15]	Five	E-commerce, transportation, agriculture, healthcare, and media

Table 1. *Cont.*

Existing Studies	No. of Categories	Categories
[20]	Four	Mobile, social, cloud, and traditional (e.g., e-commerce, e-shopping, e-learning)
[17]	Four	E-commerce/E-shopping, entertainment, content, and service oriented

Table 2. A summary of previous literature reviews on RSs and the subjects they cover. The symbol '✓' indicates that the subjects are covered in the study, while 'NA' means the subjects were not covered in the study.

Existing Studies (References)	Approaches	Challenges	Evaluation Metrics	Applications
[10]	✓	✓	✓	NA
[11]	✓	✓	✓	✓
[12]	✓	NA	NA	NA
[13]	✓	✓	✓	✓
[14]	✓	✓	NA	NA
[15]	✓	✓	✓	✓
[18]	✓	✓	NA	NA
[20]	✓	✓	NA	✓
[16]	✓	✓	NA	NA
[17]	✓	✓	✓	✓
[19]	✓	✓	✓	NA

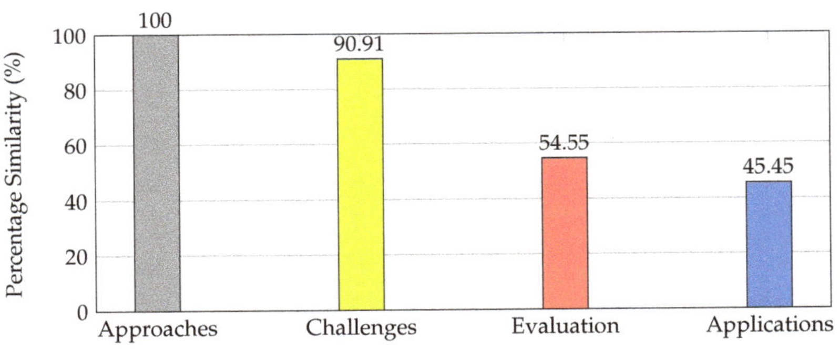

Figure 1. Percentage of topics included in literature reviews of the RSs.

After an extended review of the literature, this study discovered that most of the focus has been on the methods and techniques of RSs, while only a small amount of attention has been paid to the inputs and outputs of RSs. This leaves a gap, which this study investigates.

3. Methodology

The field of RSs is evolving rapidly and has garnered much attention in recent years. As result, the number of recommendation systems has increased due to the exponential growth of data, especially on the Internet, and the need for systems to manage this vast amount of information. Previous relevant studies discussed recommendation systems over different periods. For example, study in [11] examined recommendation systems from 2003 to 2018, while study in [13] covered recommendation systems from 2010 to 2021. This study focuses on recommendation systems in the last approximately six years, specifically from 2018 to April 2024.

3.1. Search Criteria

This study limits its investigation to four popular digital libraries that serve as repositories for top-tier journals and conference papers in information science. These libraries include IEEE Xplore Digital Library (https://ieeexplore.ieee.org/Xplore/home.jsp, accessed on 2 April 2024), Springer Link (https://link.springer.com/, accessed on 7 April 2024), ACM (https://dl.acm.org/, accessed on 11 April 2024), and Google Scholar (https://scholar.google.com/, accessed on 15 April 2024) (up to the first 20 pages of search results). Despite the rich history of RSs dating back over four decades [24], this paper only considers studies from 2018 to April 2024. This was done with the intention of capturing recent trends and benefitting from the recent uptick in RS adoption. Key search phrases were used to search and retrieve articles. These included "recommendation systems", "recommender system", "recent trends of recommendation systems", "recommendation system applications", and "data mining technology/technique". These key phrases are predominantly used in RS articles, and including them thereby ensures the retrieval of recent and relevant studies.

3.2. Article Selection and Exclusion

This paper adopted a structured selection process, only choosing articles that fulfilled at least one the following conditions: (1) The article's title included the phrase "recommendation system", "recommender system", or "data mining"; (2) The article's title or abstract indicated the proposal or development of am RS for a specific domain; (3) The article's title or abstract depicted the proposal or development of an RS framework for a specific domain; or (4) The article's title or abstract addressed one of the following: challenges, data sources, and/or features for a specific type of RS application.

Subsequently, this study excluded the following articles: (1) non-English articles; (2) pre-prints (in any language) awaiting publication and other unpublished articles that were not associated with any mainstream journal or conference; (3) partial studies; and (4) publications dated before 2018.

Data Analysis and Findings

Following the Preferred Reporting Items for Systematic Reviews and Meta-Analyses (PRISMA) statement [25], this study used four stages to select articles for inclusion. In the first stage (identification), 1878 papers were identified based on the keywords mentioned in preceding section. In the second stage (scanning), 1620 papers were retained after duplicate articles were removed. Additionally, at this stage, a preliminary review of titles and abstracts was conducted based on the inclusion and exclusion criteria noted above, which resulted in 622 articles requiring full-text reading. During the third stage (eligibility), 345 articles were identified as irrelevant, citing the following reasons: they did not discuss the applications of recommendation systems (for example). In the final stage (inclusion), 139 studies were retained for the full analysis conducted in this research. Figure 2 illustrates this search strategy.

The 139 studies included in this research were meticulously reviewed, with particular attention given to discussions on RS applications, their inputs (or data sources), features (or functions), and challenges. Additionally, these articles were categorized into their respective application domains (Section 5).

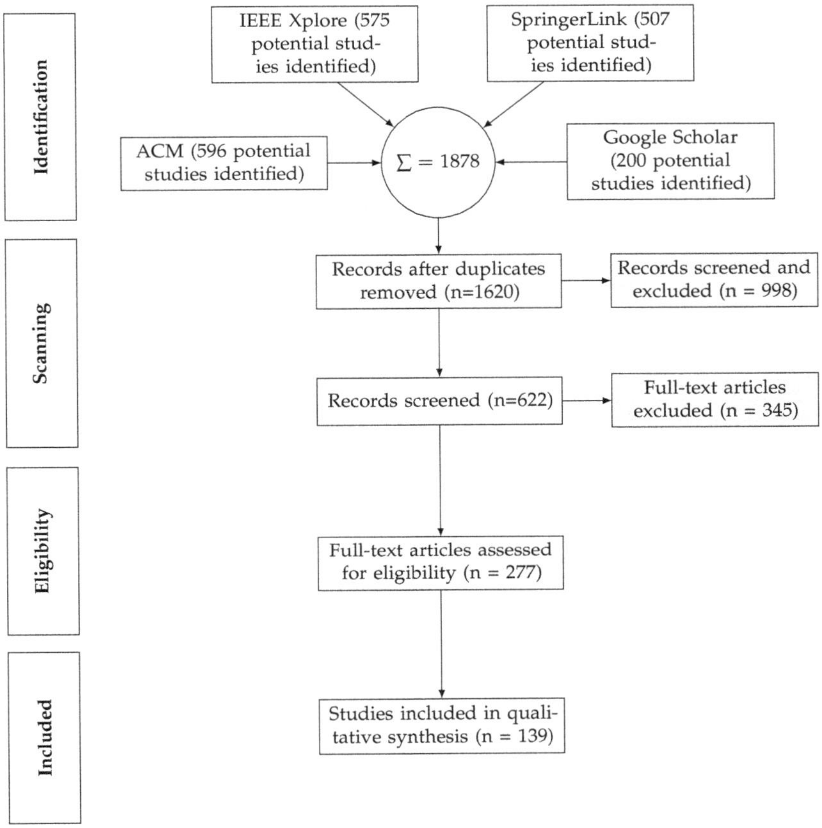

Figure 2. The structured and systematic process of collecting and then filtering out studies for the survey on RSs.

4. Recommendation System Applications

The popularity of RSs has transcended e-commerce sites that aim to sell various items to consumers. RSs have been adopted in a wide range of established business-to-business (B2B) and B2C websites and applications [26]. Current research trends reveal that RSs are being explored for several additional scenarios, some of which include drug recommendations [27–29], as well as disease and diagnosis predictions in healthcare [30,31]. Likewise, education stakeholders have begun using them for recommending personalized learning pathways and courses [32,33], to students using ontology [34,35]; for example, farmers are also using them to recommend agricultural items that would lead to optimal production in different seasons [36].

This section conducts a comprehensive survey of RS applications from 2018 to April 2024. It extensively discusses various RS-oriented aspects in the application domain. These include data sources available in the domain, its features, and the challenges faced in the application domain.

Key terms in the following subsections include the following:

Data sources: A recommendation or suggestion provided to an RS end-user premised on existing data, which may be user-generated. Examples of such include reviews, feedback, preferences, and social media data [37]; content-based data such as product attributes [38]; and context and demographic data such as gender, income, age, location, and time [39].

Features: This denotes the functionalities and/or services of RSs, which vary from one application domain to another. Each of these RS can have practical applications in, and a great impact on, human life [17].

Challenges: These are the unique obstacles faced by RS applications. These challenges could be generic or domain specific.

This investigation focuses on six application domains, because there is a plethora of prior work on them within the literature on RSs. These domains include e-learning, e-commerce, e-health, tourism, entertainment, and jobs.

4.1. E-Learning

E-learning RSs provide personalized suggestions in the form of learning material such as courses, learning pathways, and solutions to tasks for online learners [40–42].

Data: E-learning RSs leverage user data categorized under the following:

- Learner personal data: This includes personal demographic data (name, date of birth, and addresses) [43,44].
- Learner profile data: This includes a user's background qualifications, preferred learning style (e.g., course work or group learning) and level of progress (beginner, intermediate or experienced) [45].
- Learning objectives: This indicates the user's preferred learning outcomes [45,46].
- Log files: This includes a history of the user's queries [40].

Features: Features in e-learning are learning objects, which, conceptually, are items or services that an e-learner expects to be recommended by the RS. Formally, a learning object has been defined as an entity, digital or non-digital, that may be used for learning, education, or training [47], or any digital resource that can be reused to support learning [48]. A feature of an e-learning system may entail one or more learning objects. Below is a classification of the main features discussed in prior literature:

- Learning paths or pathways: This feature aims to retrieve personalized learning paths for e-learners based on their current profile. A learning path is an optimized sequence of modules and tasks that a learner can follow to achieve a learning objective or outcome [49–51].
- Course or modules: This feature suggests relevant courses or learning programs to users (e.g., learners) based on their profile (e.g., preferences and requirements) [43,44]. In addition, this feature aims to analyze a learner's skills and knowledge gaps based on their performance and assessments and then subsequently recommend specific modules, courses, or learning resources to address those gaps and facilitate skill development [45,52].
- Material: This feature recommends content such as topics, articles, books, and lessons to an e-learner [53].
- Activity: This feature suggests learning tasks such as a class, group discussion, or conference to a learner [42,54].

Challenges: Despite the similarities between this and other RS application domains, recommendations in e-learning are quite ambiguous and complex [55]. Often, an e-learner may have inadequate knowledge on what kind of item they need despite knowing what qualification they want. Thus, they are left unsatisfied with the recommendations presented. For instance, Figure 3 shows a scenario where an e-learner interested in a data analyst qualification is recommended a list of courses that are related to his preferred qualification; however, they are not necessarily relevant or suitable in actually obtaining the qualification, as depicted by the Venn diagram on the right. In contrast, all seven courses recommended are related to the data analyst qualification, they are not necessarily relevant for the e-learner to attain the qualification, i.e., only three of them are prerequisite courses (C1, C5, and C7). According to [55], this conundrum of narrowing down a large pool of related learning objects to a finite set of objects that are suitable and relevant is a challenge for tutors or teachers preparing learning material.

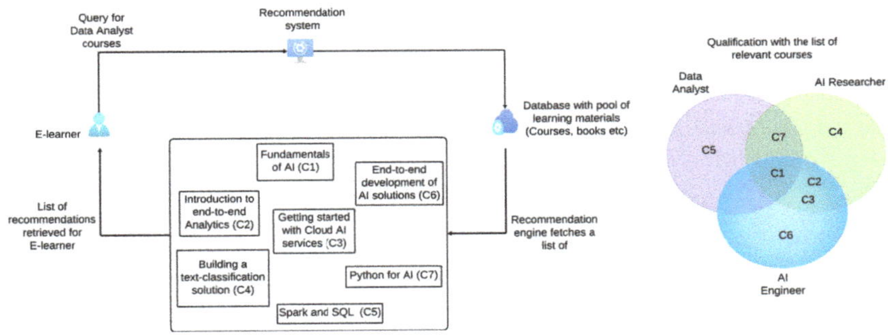

Figure 3. An example of an RS retrieving a list of courses for an e-learner interested in a data analyst qualification.

4.2. E-Commerce Recommendation System

Retailers, wholesalers, traders, and businesses that target the e-market have been the biggest beneficiaries of RSs since their inception [56,57]. They leverage RSs to achieve two main goals: to firstly suggest products to their customers and, secondly, to provide information to help their customers in making decisions on which product to purchase [57,58]. To achieve this, these RSs analyze customer data such as browsing behavior, purchase history, demographic information, and user preferences [26,39].

Data: Unlike RSs in other application domains such as e-learning, where the customer's initial profile can effectively inform the RS of his or her preferences [49,51], as well as the most relevant entity required to generate recommendations in e-commerce is the customer's behavior, which is hinged on the customer's interaction with the e-commerce site [59]. Customer behavior is obtained after customers perform tasks on the site such as liking, rating, viewing, or/and purchasing a product.The authors in [26,59] discussed how likes, ratings, views, and purchases can subsequently be used to create a customer preference matrix and a product feature matrix, both of which are significant inputs for the e-commerce RSs. Table 3 includes examples of a product feature matrix and a preference matrix. Whether a user has an existing profile (expecting a personalized recommendation) or not (expecting a non-personalized recommendation) [26,59], the product feature matrix would suffice in generating a recommendation solely based on the feature statistics drawn from the product matrix. From Table 4, *Dell* (Dell Inc., Round Rock, TX, USA) computers will be recommended, because they have the highest scores across most features, achieving 3 out of 5. Conversely, *Acer* (Acer Inc., Taipei, Taiwan) products would not be recommended, because it has no best scores at all.

Table 3. Customer preference matrix.

Computer	Likes	Dislikes	Ratings (0–10)	Purchases
Dan	Macbook, Dell	Acer	Macbook, Dell, HP	Macbook
Alec	Dell, Acer, HP	-	Macbook, Dell, HP, Acer	Dell, HP
Ed	Macbook	Acer, HP	Macbook	Macbook
Greg	Dell, Acer, HP	-	Macbook, Dell, HP, Acer	HP

In addition to customer behavior, product characteristics are another commonly discussed variable that influences customers in e-commerce. The study conducted by [60] categorized attributes into two categories: hedonic and utilitarian. The latter refers to cognitively driven, instrumental, and goal-oriented attributes that demonstrate what a product accomplishes. Hedonic products, on the other hand, are effective and sensory, being more concerned with aesthetics or sensual pleasure, fantasy, and fun. Broadly, the hedonic–utilitarian attribute [61] has been shown to influence consumer product search behavior, purchase decisions, and even consumers' value of products [62].

Table 4. A product feature matrix used in generating recommendations. Numbers in bold indicate the best score for that particular feature.

Computer	Likes	Dislikes	Ratings (0–10)	Views	Purchases
MacBook	**4**	1	8	100	5
Dell	**4**	2	**9**	98	**6**
HP	3	1	6	**110**	**6**
Acer	1	3	3	20	2

Features: Traditionally, e-commerce RSs only output products as their recommendations to the user; however, this has recently changed, with RSs recommending lists of products ranked in order to relevance [57,63]. The most common RSs in this domain are Amazon (https://www.amazon.com, accessed on 4 March 2024), Netflix (https://www.netflix.com/sa-en/, accessed on 6 March 2024), and eBay (https://www.ebay.com, accessed on 4 March 2024).

Challenges: The burden of RSs in the e-commerce application domain is incomparable because of its huge client-base, which is rapidly expanding every day. This vast, exponential demand inevitably creates a need to constantly scale the RSs, as well as their resources, such as the data stores available in order to keep clients satisfied. Because of this, scalability is a largely documented challenge for e-commerce RSs [17,64–66]. For instance, Amazon has to provide recommendations to over 20 million clients from their pool of over 18 million products [64]. In addition to scalability, another very pertinent challenge in e-commerce is data sparsity, which results from some items or products lacking a rating, score, or any metric value that is informative of the product's likeability. Data sparsity is largely connected to the cold start challenge, which implies that there is insufficient information about an item or a user for a RS to make a recommendation.

4.3. E-Health Recommendation Systems

E-health RSs are designed to provide personalized recommendations to users, which can include patients, healthcare providers, or medical researchers. The primary goal of e-health RSs is to improve various aspects of healthcare delivery and decision-making processes through the generation of personalized suggestions tailored to the specific needs and preferences of the users [67].

Data: E-health RSs consume and analyze data from various sources to provide personalized medical and health recommendations. Some of the most commonly used sources are outlined below:

- Electronic Health Records (EHRs): EHRs are a primary source of patient data recorded at various patient care levels by different healthcare workers, including physicians, nurses, consultants, clinical researchers, etc. Data in EHRs includes medical history or progress notes, diagnostic information, treatment outcomes, and more [68,69].
- Commercial and free health apps and systems: Patient-generated inputs through apps or health portals include subjective data regarding well-being, treatment outcomes, and health status [70].
- Wearable devices: These include smartwatches, fitness trackers, and other health-monitoring devices that offer up-to-the-minute information on a person's physical activity [71], heart rate, sleep patterns, and other relevant data [72–74].
- Clinical research repositories: These are databanks that store publicly accessible biomedical literature published after clinical tasks and activities such as clinical trials, genomics, etc. For example, see PubMed (https://pubmed.ncbi.nlm.nih.gov/, accessed on 8 March 2024) [67].

- Social media: Social media platforms generate vast amounts of user-generated content, including posts, comments, likes, shares, and connections. In recent years, adopting social media data for healthcare research has become common practice [75].
- Internet of Things (IoT) devices: Beyond wearables, other connected devices in home or healthcare settings can provide continuous data streams about patient behavior and their environment [68,76,77].
- Pharmacy data: These are records of pharmaceutical purchases and dispensations, which help in monitoring drug adherence and interactions [31].

Features: The recommendation items provided by e-health recommendation systems are categorized into five main categories below:

1. Treatment-based recommendations: These focus on suggesting information that relieves, alleviates, or controls unwanted escalations of symptoms and other health related challenges, e.g., drug recommendation systems [27,28,78].
2. Healthcare management-based recommendations: These focus on providing strategies or methods to manage, handle, respond, and live with or without certain conditions. These may range from personalized diet and nutrition recommendations [79–82] to physical activity and exercise recommendations [71,83,84], health hazard alerts, and tips [85].
3. Lifestyle and behavioral management-based recommendations: These focus on providing recommendations for daily habits, behaviors [86], and lifestyle as a whole [87].
4. Condition-specific recommendations: These are tailored to meet distinctive needs for specific conditions. For example, mental health [88,89], emotional health (e.g., depression) [90], and well-being [91,92] RSs provide therapy to mental health patients and those suffering from chronic diseases [93] such as diabetes [94] and heart disease [95].
5. Specialist care recommendations: These focus on suggesting the most suitable clinicians or trained personnel to provide medical care to patients [96–98].

Challenges: Several challenges have hampered research on e-health RSs. This is due, in part, to the fact that there are ethical issues revolving around the dissemination and use of health–related data, especially data from EHR systems [99–101]. EHR data are not readily available, and even when they are made available, researchers have to comply to a multitude of data protection and impact assessment policies. Besides the challenge of ensuring the privacy and security of sensitive health data, researchers are confronted by the absence of standardized specifications or classifications that are universally recognized and used. The study conducted by [102] refers to this as the proliferation of healthcare standards, essentially implying that different entities or organizations will use different specifications and classifications for healthcare attributes such as drugs, diseases, and examinations.

Accuracy is another pertinent challenge for e-health RSs because of the tragic consequences that can result from inaccurate recommendations. This is applicable not only to recommendation systems, but to healthcare information technology as a whole [99]. As a result, establishing trust and providing transparent explanations for the recommendations generated by e-health systems becomes crucial for user acceptance and adoption. Furthermore, handling large-scale health data, real-time recommendations, and ensuring efficient and scalable algorithms all present essential challenges in e-health recommendation systems. Needed too is the need to develop appropriate evaluation metrics and methodologies to assess the effectiveness and impact of e-health recommendation systems, which is considered to be a significant challenge for researchers and practitioners [103].

4.4. Tourism Recommendation Systems

E-tourism RSs aim to provide personalized and relevant recommendations to users in the tourism domain [104]. They seek to assist users in making informed decisions about their travel plans [105], destinations or locations [106,107], attractions [108,109], accommodations, hotels [110], restaurants, and activities [104,111].

E-tourism recommendations are is built on the concept of personalization. On several occasions, this personalization has been credited for significantly contributing to the success of the tourism industry [112,113]. The European IST project CRUMPET (Creation of User-friendly Mobile Services Personalized for Tourism) [114] describes the following as features of personalization:

- Adaptation to user's tourism-related interests and other preferences [115].
- Adaptivity, i.e., the automatic update of the user model based on the user's interaction history.
- Location-awareness, i.e., the awareness of a user's current spatial context.

The technologically oriented upheaval in the tourism industry has allowed for the collection of vast amounts of data through internet devices (such as mobile phones) from websites, social media applications, and other web portals [109].

Stakeholders—including researchers, hospitality and catering providers, and tourism service providers—are leveraging this rich source of data to discover more about the interests and preferences of tourists [109]. Subsequently, in consuming this data, researchers have explored RSs and proposed a variety of RS techniques aimed at enhancing tourism services for destinations worldwide [116–118].

Data sources: RSs acquire data from various sources, which can be summarized as follows:

- User preferences: These consist of the specific or implied choices users have in relation to their travel selections, encompassing favored destinations, types of attractions, and accommodations. These preferences can be gathered through surveys, and questionnaires, or by studying user interactions and behavior within the recommendation system [109,119].
- Tourist reviews and ratings: User-generated content such as reviews and ratings provided by users are pivotal in tourism recommendation systems. They offer valuable insights into the viewpoints and experiences of past travelers, aiding in the assessment and recommendation of destinations, accommodations, attractions, and activities. Review data can be obtained from various platforms like online travel agencies, review websites, and social media [109].
- Geographical information: This type of data plays a vital role in tourism recommendation systems by furnishing details about the geographical locations of destinations, attractions, and accommodations [120].
- Social media: This is a valuable resource for tourism recommendation systems as social platforms contain copious amounts of user-generated content related to travel experiences. This data can be utilized to grasp user preferences, interests, and connections in order to derive insights into trending destinations, attractions, and influencer-based suggestions [119,120].
- Contextual and environmental data: This type of acquired data comprises details such as weather conditions, seasonal variations, local events, transportation choices, and other environmental aspects that might influence travel decisions. Integrating this data enables the system to offer contextually aware and pertinent recommendations [104,119].

The primary features of tourism RSs can be broadly classified into three main categories:

- Restaurant recommendation systems: These are designed to provide personalized suggestions for restaurants based on user preferences, location, and other relevant factors [115].
- Tourism destination recommender systems: These provide personalized recommendations for travel destinations based on user preferences, interests, and other relevant factors [121].
- Tourist activities recommendation systems: The system provides personalized suggestions for leisure activities, experiences, or events based on user preferences, interests, and other relevant factors [119].

Challenges: Tourism recommendation systems face several challenges. Firstly, data sparsity is a hurdle due to the difficulty of obtaining comprehensive and diverse data on user preferences, reviews, and geographical information. Sparse data can impact the quality of recommendations. Secondly, scalability becomes a challenge as the number of users and tourism-related entities both increase. Efficiently processing recommendations for a large userbase while maintaining real-time performance is demanding. Similarly, ensuring diversity and serendipity in recommendations is another challenge. While personalization is important, introducing novelty and unexpected suggestions to enhance user experiences is necessary. Additionally, subjectivity and trust pose challenges as recommendations are subjective and dependent on individual preferences. Building trust in the system is challenging due to differing expectations and perceptions of relevance and quality. Incorporating contextual information, such as weather and local events, adds further complexity to recommendations. Thus, these dynamic factors require sophisticated modeling techniques and up-to-date data sources. Lastly, privacy and data protection are concerns, as these systems rely on user data. Safeguarding user information while delivering personalized recommendations requires robust data protection mechanisms and compliance with privacy regulations [104,111].

4.5. Entertainment Recommendation Systems

This type of RS suggests a variety of entertainment content to users based on factors like interests, preferences, user ratings, and viewing history [122]. Recommended items may include music, movies [122,123], games, books [124], and other items used for entertainment purposes, typically including genres like romances, mysteries, or novels. However, this type of RS excludes scientific books, publications, and scientific journals, which are often classified under e-learning.

This kind of system aims to help users find content that is suitable and compatible with their preferences and interests, including discovering the right music or movie. User behavior analysis, user ratings, and other factors are employed to offer suitable recommendations [125,126].

Data sources: Entertainment RSs acquire data from various sources, which can be summarized as follows:

- User preferences and behavior: When users interact with the recommendation system, their views, ratings, reviews, and likes are logged in their profile. These data assist the system in anticipating the user's interests and preferences. Some entertainment recommendation systems can anticipate user behavior, enhancing the user profile and delivering recommendations based on behavior [127,128].
- Content metadata: Here, information about movies, music, and books is gathered. This data source involves collecting source information such as details about movies (e.g., director and actors), music (e.g., singers and keywords), and books (e.g., author(s) and titles) [123].
- Third-party application programming interfaces (APIs): Entertainment recommendation systems are distinguished by their capacity to acquire data from external sources, including social media data, which are commonly known as third-party APIs. Third-party APIs function as a unique supplement to the algorithms of entertainment RSs, improving the precision of their recommendations.

The primary features of entertainment RSs can be broadly classified into the four main categories below:

- Movie RS: This type of recommendation system suggests TV shows, movies, and documentaries to users [129]. These systems not only provide support and assistance to users, but they also benefit content creators by boosting and expanding movie viewership. A prominent example of a movie recommendation system is the Netflix RS, which offers personalized movie suggestions tailored to viewers' preferences [122,130,131].

- Music RS: Music recommendation systems suggest music objects such as songs that align with user preferences, listening history, and ratings [132]. These systems help listeners by recommending music that resonates with their preferences, benefiting content creators by boosting the listenership of their content [133,134]. Some of the websites that perform music recommendations include Soundcloud (https://soundcloud.com/, accessed on 2 May 2024), lastfm.com (https://www.last.fm/, accessed on 2 May 2024), and AllMusic (https://www.allmusic.com/, accessed on 2 May 2024).
- Game or video game RS: A game recommendation system suggests games that are tailored for the user based on factors like preferences, interests, and gaming history. These systems help users discover games that match their preferences while also supporting game developers by boosting game usage or downloads [135–137].
- Book RS: A book recommendation system suggests books to readers based on factors like their preferences and reading history [126]. One notable book recommendation system is Goodreads (www.goodreads.com, accessed on 3 May 2024), a subsidiary of Amazon. The Goodreads website recommends books using various factors, including reader ratings [124].

Challenges: Entertainment RSs comprise such an enormous collection of items available for recommendation [138]. However, a significant portion of this collection is less known or unpopular [139]. These unpopular or new items belong to the long tail of item distribution [140]. Recommending these less-popular items presents a challenge for entertainment RSs, given that there is virtually no prior knowledge of user preference or interest in the items. Striking a balance between suggesting less popular and more popular items is essential to offer users a set of diverse recommendations.

Unless an RS is domain-specific, such as a movie RS, a generic entertainment RS will often have a pool of diverse items to recommend to users. This poses the challenge of accurately recommending a collection of distinct items. Thus, accuracy is crucial for delivering relevant advice, but the lack of diversity restricts the exploration of new user preferences that could be utilized as future recommendations [141].

Obtaining an adequate number of ratings and comments from users is particularly challenging, especially in video game or book RSs. This is particularly evident when compared to other domains within entertainment RSs (such as music). This scarcity of data leads to incomplete insights, resulting in a lack of understanding of user preferences and choices, thereby leading to inaccurate recommendations [141].

4.6. *Job Recommendation Systems*

Internet-based online recruiting platforms [142], e-recruitment platforms [143], or job RSs are designed to provide guidance not only to job seekers based on their academic qualifications, job experience, preferences, and interests, but they also aid employers based on their hiring needs. These systems analyze job applicants' profiles, including CVs, and compare them with job requirements to offer relevant advice for job seekers. Similarly, job RSs can provide guidance to employers based on their conditions and compare them with job applicant profiles to suggest suitable candidates for their job requirements [143]. Online recruitment using RS is considered to be one of the most successful business platforms, because it has brought about a change not only in the recruitment of candidates by employers but also in matching job seekers with jobs that suit their abilities and qualifications [142].

Job RSs are required to align or match two different types of stakeholders: job seekers and employers. This approach is referred to, in some studies, as Two-Sided Engagement (TSE). This is in stark contrast to other RSs, whose success is often measured by unilateral user actions (such as recommending a movie to a viewer on the Netflix platform based on their previous preferences or viewings) [142]. This type of RS therefore faces challenges that generally differ from those of other recommendation systems.

Data sources: Job RSs acquire data from various sources, which can be summarized as follows:

- Job seeker applications: This includes qualifications, skills, experience, previous jobs, location, and working hours. This information is typically available in the job applicant's CV [144,145].
- Employer requirements: This encompasses the specifications of the job offered or available by the employer, detailing the job nature, required skills, qualifications, experience, and additional information [146] such as workplace, working hours, and salary.
- Job postings: Job recommendation systems utilize job postings or advertisements published or submitted by employers as a data source to inform job recommendations. These advertisements outline the requirements and qualifications needed for the job [147]. Platforms like LinkedIn can be used to capture and identify available job postings.
- Feedback and ratings: The advice provided by the system is rated by either the job seeker regarding their satisfaction with the recommended job, or by the employer regarding their satisfaction with the candidate. This, in turn, leads to improved advice in the future [148].

The primary features of job RSs can be broadly classified into two main categories:

- Job seeker RS: This type focuses on providing advice to job seekers. It compares professional skills, qualifications, and experiences with job requirements to suggest suitable job opportunities for the job seeker [144,145,149].
- Job employer RS: This type functions conversely, as it provides advice to the employer rather than the job seeker. It compares job requirements, including qualifications, experience, skills, and required salary, with job applicants to offer appropriate recommendations to the employer [144,146].

Challenges: One of the challenges facing job RSs is finding relevant information [143,150]. As a result, inaccurate or unhelpful advice or recommendations may be provided to the stakeholder, whether it be the job seeker or the employer. This is attributed to numerous factors, with the most significant being the need to align job seekers' preferences with the job requirements, as previously mentioned. One more challenge that job recommendation systems deal with sensitive data, especially for job seekers. These data are linked to the job seeker's CV (such as their date of birth, gender, age, and address). Thus, ensuring data privacy and the non-violation of data is one of the challenges facing job RSs [148]. Additionally, recommender systems, in general, and job RSs, in particular, suffer from well-known biases. Providing a fair and transparent recommendation in job RSs is more important than in other types of RSs because it is a high-risk area, as job seeking has a long-term impact on people's careers and lives. In addition, work plays an important role in shaping and formatting the competitive advantage of institutions and companies in the market. E-recruitment has been classified as a high-risk area according to the EU's Artificial Intelligence Act (proposal) [143]. Considering fairness, merit, and racial bias are among the most prevalent challenges faced by job RSs compared to other domains of RSs [150].

By the end of this section, the main goal of this paper has been achieved, which is to study the data sources, features, and challenges of different applications of recommendation systems (RSs). A full list of the references reviewed for all six categories of the RSs applications studied above can be found in Table 5.

Table 5. RS Application Studies by Use and Category.

Category	Application	Reference
E-learning	Activities (e.g., tests) recommendations	[42]
	Courses or/and modules recommendations	[43,44,46]
	Material content suggestions	[53]
	Path recommendations for learners	[49–51,54]
E-commerce	Fashion (e.g., retail) recommendation	[57,63,151–154]
	Product recommendations	[62,155–157]
	Taxi recommendations	[158–160]
E-health	Drug recommendations	[27,28,78]
	Diet, nutrition, or food recommendations	[79–81,161–163]
	Physical activities or exercises recommendations	[71,83,84]
	Behavior recommendations	[86,164]
	Lifestyle recommendations	[87]
	Behavior recommendations	[86]
	Mental health recommendations	[88,89]
	Emotion (e.g., depression) recommendations	[90]
	Chronic diseases recommendations (e.g., diabetes and heart disease)	[93,95,165]
E-tourism	Hotels recommendation	[110,166–168]
	Restaurant recommendations	[169,170]
	Destination, location, attraction or travel recommendations	[105–109]
E-Entertainment	Movie recommendations	[123,130,171–176]
	Music recommendations	[133,177–182]
	Game recommendations	[135,137,183]
	Book recommendations	[184,185]
E-Job	Job seeker recommendations	[144–146,149,186]
	Job employer recommendations	[144,146]

5. Discussion

RSs are central to how organizations and business operate and deliver services to their clients. Previously, organizations relied on traditional data gathering techniques such as questionnaires, surveys, interviews, and focus groups to gain intel on user preferences. However, all of that can be digitally accomplished today using RSs. Many businesses boast large customer bases as a result of leveraging RSs, including Amazon, Netflix, Google, LinkedIn, etc.

RSs have attracted a lot of attention in computer science research in recent years. Discussions on improving the quality of recommendations provided by RSs have been further intensified by prediction-based algorithms based on machine learning and artificial intelligence. The breadth of application use-cases for RSs has been widening in recent years.

This study systematically selected research articles on RSs that were published from 2018 to April 2024, and it surveyed them with a keen focus on three fundamental aspects of RSs: data sources, features, and challenges. While investigating several application domains, this study observed that although user-generated data obtained through end-users (such as personalized and demographic data, reviews, ratings, and preferences) are the main source of information for RSs, other sources have been adopted for the same purpose. Public social media networks were identified data sources for RSs such as tourism and entertainment, particularly because the nature of recommendations can benefit from discourse on public forums. To present a simple example, if there are many people praising a tourist destination on Facebook, it benefits an RS to recommend that destination to users.

In terms of features, it was noted that, as expected, features or functionalities of RSs are domain-specific. In other words, the type of recommendation varies from one domain to another. E-commerce recommends retail or wholesale products, e-learning recommends learning objects or learning materials, and e-health recommends therapies that could be informed about of drugs, behaviors, etc. Moreover, this study found that the products, items, and/or services recommended can be categorized into different groups for their respective RSs. Example of such include e-health sharing treatment-based recommendations and lifestyle and behavioral managed-based recommendations, etc. Similarly, e-learning has learning-pathways-based recommendations, skills-based recommendations, courses, module-based recommendations, etc.

This study also analyzed the challenges faced in the development and implementation of RSs. Unsurprisingly, data sparsity or the cold-start problem, where there is little to no information available for a RS to make a recommendation, is the most widely documented challenge among RSs. Other significant issues included the multiplicity of demands from RSs and their inaccuracies, which can be damaging depending on the nature of recommendation. It was also revealed that there is a consensus among researchers on the necessity of more robust systems. These enhanced systems are needed not only to meet the escalating demand of users but also to provide high-quality and reliable recommendations.

As displayed in Table 5, it is evident that e-health and e-entertainment RS applications are deemed to be the most prevalent, ranking first and second, respectively. They are followed by e-tourism and e-economic RS applications. In contrast, e-learning and e-job RS applications are the least common. Figure 4 illustrates the relative proportions of these applications, thus providing a visual representation of their distribution.

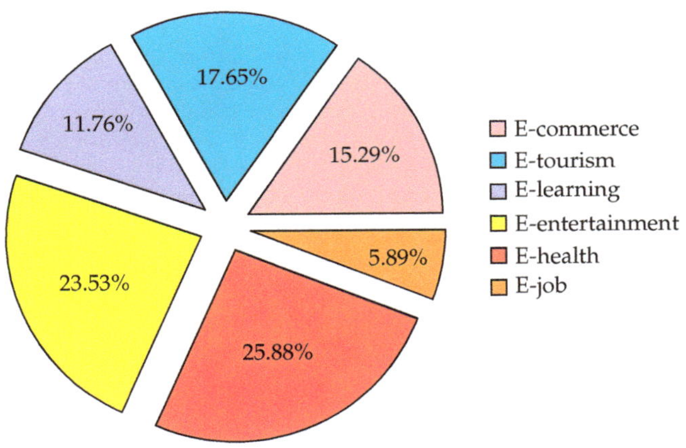

Figure 4. The percentage of studies addressing different RS domains.

The limitations of this study can be summarized as follows. One of the most important is the lack of studies related to all three aspects of this study (data sources, features, and challenges), especially since, in some cases, there was no explicit and clear statement of these aspects in applications' studies of recommendation systems; as such, this study had to infer/assume these three aspects from context. In addition, there is an overlap in RS system applications, such as e-commerce RSs with e-tourism (e.g., restaurant RSs) and e-commerce and e-entertainment (e.g., game RSs). It can be difficult to distinguish between categories when there is extensive overlap. Moreover, some features of RS applications are complex, which makes it further difficult to distinguish between them; take, for example, behavior and lifestyle applications in e-health RSs. These limitations are managed and addressed by referring to many studies in the field to obtain a breadth of information that provides a full picture of the knowledge of that field.

6. Conclusions and Future Work

This review explored three understudied aspects of RSs applications: data sources, features, and challenges. To fulfill the primary objective of this study, RS applications were reviewed and classified into six distinct categories: e-learning, e-commerce, e-health, e-tourism, e-entertainment, and e-job recommendation systems. The Preferred Reporting Items for Systematic Reviews and Meta-Analyses (PRISMA) statement was used to select relevant papers by implementing four different stages (identification, filtering, eligibility, and inclusion). This resulted in the review of 139 papers included in this study from four (top-tier) research repositories: the IEEE Xplore Digital Library, Springer Link, ACM Digital Library, and Google Scholar (first 20 pages of search results). Additionally, this study included a review of the RS literature (Section 2), which in turn helped identify weaknesses in the field of RSs and thus define the research parameters. To this extent, the analysis in Section 4 revealed that researchers and RSs developers are adopting other data sources such as social media platforms to supplement the existing array of user-generated data sources for RSs. The various functionalities or features for RSs were deemed domain-specific, since they varied from one application domain to another. This study further reported that data sparsity or the cold-start problem as the most widely documented challenge of RSs. In light of the prevailing challenges encountered in research and development of RSs, the need for more robust RSs is indisputable.

In future work, other RS applications, such as social media platforms (e.g., Facebook and Instagram), should be studied as well, instead of focusing only on the six most common applications of RSs. Such an expansion would be beneficial to a broader audience, as it would address the critical aspects investigated in this study: data sources, features, and functionalities, as well as the challenges of RSs. Additionally, the research could be expanded to include other digital libraries, such as Elsevier and SpringerLink platforms. In addition, possible solutions to these challenges of RSs applications should be analyzed and studied. Furthermore, future work should provide accurate explanations to the user about why a particular item of advice was provided, which is an area that still requires research. This is especially true for recommendations derived from the user's behavior and feelings, which undoubtedly represents a major challenge for those interested and researchers in the RSs. Providing these explanations, which requires deep learning algorithms, enhances user trust and satisfaction in RSs and increases the chance of users using and relying on them.

Supplementary Materials: The following supporting information can be downloaded at: https://www.mdpi.com/article/10.3390/info15100660/s1, PRISMA Checklist [187].

Funding: This research received no external funding.

Conflicts of Interest: The author declares no conflicts of interest.

References

1. Bhattacharya, S.; Sarkar, D.; Kole, D.K.; Jana, P. Recent trends in recommendation systems and sentiment analysis. In *Advanced Data Mining Tools and Methods for Social Computing*; Elsevier: Amsterdam, The Netherlands, 2022; pp. 163–175.
2. Gunawardana, A.; Shani, G.; Yogev, S. Evaluating recommender systems. In *Recommender Systems Handbook*; Springer: Berlin/Heidelberg, Germany, 2012; pp. 547–601.
3. Jawaheer, G.; Weller, P.; Kostkova, P. Modeling user preferences in recommender systems: A classification framework for explicit and implicit user feedback. *Acm Trans. Interact. Intell. Syst. (TiiS)* **2014**, *4*, 8. [CrossRef]
4. Li, S.S.; Karahanna, E. Online recommendation systems in a B2C E-commerce context: A review and future directions. *J. Assoc. Inf. Syst.* **2015**, *16*, 2. [CrossRef]
5. Abaho, M.; Alfaifi, Y.H. Select and Augment: Enhanced Dense Retrieval Knowledge Graph Augmentation. *J. Artif. Intell. Res.* **2023**, *78*, 269–285. [CrossRef]
6. Goldberg, D.; Nichols, D.; Oki, B.M.; Terry, D. Using collaborative filtering to weave an information tapestry. *Commun. ACM* **1992**, *35*, 61–70. [CrossRef]

7. Lu, J.; Wu, D.; Mao, M.; Wang, W.; Zhang, G. Recommender system application developments: A survey. *Decis. Support Syst.* **2015**, *74*, 12–32. [CrossRef]
8. Castells, P.; Hurley, N.; Vargas, S. Novelty and diversity in recommender systems. In *Recommender Systems Handbook*; Springer: Berlin/Heidelberg, Germany, 2021; pp. 603–646.
9. Wei, K.; Huang, J.; Fu, S. A survey of e-commerce recommender systems. In Proceedings of the 2007 International Conference on Service Systems and Service Management, Chengdu, China, 9–11 June 2007; pp. 1–5.
10. Saifudin, I.; Widiyaningtyas, T. Systematic Literature Review on Recommender System: Approach, Problem, Evaluation Techniques, Datasets. *IEEE Access* **2024**, *12*, 19827–19847. [CrossRef]
11. Ko, H.; Lee, S.; Park, Y.; Choi, A. A survey of recommendation systems: Recommendation models, techniques, and application fields. *Electronics* **2022**, *11*, 141. [CrossRef]
12. Raikwar, V. Review on Recommendation System and its Classification. *Int. J. Tech. Sci. Explor.* **2022**, *3*, 16–18.
13. Monti, D.; Rizzo, G.; Morisio, M. A systematic literature review of multicriteria recommender systems. *Artif. Intell. Rev.* **2021**, *54*, 427–468. [CrossRef]
14. Sharma, M.; Mittal, R.; Bharati, A.; Saxena, D.; Singh, A.K. A survey and classification on recommendation systems. In Proceedings of the International Conference on Big Data, Machine Learning, and Applications, Taiyuan, China, 3–5 December 2021; Springer: Berlin/Heidelberg, Germany, 2021; pp. 569–585.
15. Fayyaz, Z.; Ebrahimian, M.; Nawara, D.; Ibrahim, A.; Kashef, R. Recommendation systems: Algorithms, challenges, metrics, and business opportunities. *Appl. Sci.* **2020**, *10*, 7748. [CrossRef]
16. Gupta, S. A literature review on recommendation systems. *Int. Res. J. Eng. Technol.* **2020**, *7*, 3600–3605.
17. Raghuwanshi, S.K.; Pateriya, R.K. Recommendation systems: Techniques, challenges, application, and evaluation. In Proceedings of the Soft Computing for Problem Solving: SocProS, Bhubaneswar, India, 23–24 December 2017, Springer: Berlin/Heidelberg, Germany, 2019; Volume 2, pp. 151–164.
18. Narke, L.; Nasreen, A. A comprehensive review of approaches and challenges of a recommendation system. *Int. J. Res. Eng. Sci. Manag.* **2020**, *3*, 381–384.
19. Kumar, P.; Thakur, R.S. Recommendation system techniques and related issues: A survey. *Int. J. Inf. Technol.* **2018**, *10*, 495–501. [CrossRef]
20. Alhijawi, B.; Kilani, Y. The recommender system: A survey. *Int. J. Adv. Intell. Paradig.* **2020**, *15*, 229–251. [CrossRef]
21. Feng, J.; Xia, Z.; Feng, X.; Peng, J. RBPR: A hybrid model for the new user cold start problem in recommender systems. *Knowl.-Based Syst.* **2021**, *214*, 106732. [CrossRef]
22. Feng, J.; Wang, K.; Miao, Q.; Xi, Y.; Xia, Z. Personalized recommendation with hybrid feedback by refining implicit data. *Expert Syst. Appl.* **2023**, *232*, 120855. [CrossRef]
23. Ricci, F.; Rokach, L.; Shapira, B. Recommender systems: Techniques, applications, and challenges. In *Recommender Systems Handbook*; Springer: Berlin/Heidelberg, Germany, 2021; pp. 1–35.
24. Dong, Z.; Wang, Z.; Xu, J.; Tang, R.; Wen, J. A brief history of recommender systems. *arXiv* **2022**, arXiv:2209.01860.
25. Moher, D.; Liberati, A.; Tetzlaff, J.; Altman, D.G.; PRISMA Group. Preferred reporting items for systematic reviews and meta-analyses: The PRISMA statement. *Ann. Intern. Med.* **2009**, *151*, 264–269. [CrossRef]
26. Hussien, F.T.A.; Rahma, A.M.S.; Wahab, H.B.A. Recommendation systems for e-commerce systems an overview. *J. Phys. Conf. Ser.* **2021**, *1897*, 12024.
27. Garg, S. Drug recommendation system based on sentiment analysis of drug reviews using machine learning. In Proceedings of the 2021 11th International Conference on Cloud Computing, Data Science & Engineering (Confluence), Noida, India, 28–29 January 2021; pp. 175–181.
28. Suryadevara, C.K. Towards Personalized Healthcare—An Intelligent Medication Recommendation System. *IEJRD-Int. Multidiscip. J.* **2020**, *5*, 16.
29. Bhimavarapu, U.; Chintalapudi, N.; Battineni, G. A fair and safe usage drug recommendation system in medical emergencies by a stacked ANN. *Algorithms* **2022**, *15*, 186. [CrossRef]
30. Chen, J.; Li, K.; Rong, H.; Bilal, K.; Yang, N.; Li, K. A disease diagnosis and treatment recommendation system based on big data mining and cloud computing. *Inf. Sci.* **2018**, *435*, 124–149. [CrossRef]
31. Pincay, J.; Terán, L.; Portmann, E. Health recommender systems: A state-of-the-art review. In Proceedings of the 2019 Sixth International Conference on eDemocracy & eGovernment (ICEDEG), Quito, Ecuador, 24–26 April 2019; pp. 47–55.
32. Dhananjaya, G.; Goudar, R.; Kulkarni, A.; Rathod, V.N.; Hukkeri, G.S. A Digital Recommendation System for Personalized Learning to Enhance Online Education: A Review. *IEEE Access* **2024**, *12*, 34019–34041.
33. Alfaifi, Y.H. Towards an Ontology-Based E-Learning Recommendation System. In Proceedings of the 2023 3rd International Conference on Computing and Information Technology (ICCIT), Sanya, China, 10–12 February 2023; pp. 652–656.
34. Alfaifi, Y. Ontology development methodology: A systematic review and case study. In Proceedings of the 2022 2nd International Conference on Computing and Information Technology (ICCIT), Tabuk, Saudi Arabia, 25–27 January 2022; pp. 446–450.
35. Elfaki, A.O.; Alfaifi, Y.H. Ontology Driven for Mapping a Relational Database to a Knowledge-based System. *Int. J. Adv. Comput. Sci. Appl.* **2024**, *15*. [CrossRef]

36. Vaishnavi, S.; Shobana, M.; Sabitha, R.; Karthik, S. Agricultural crop recommendations based on productivity and season. In Proceedings of the 2021 7th International Conference on Advanced Computing and Communication Systems (ICACCS), Coimbatore, India, 19–20 March 2021; Volume 1, pp. 883–886.
37. Bank, M.; Franke, J. Social networks as data source for recommendation systems. In Proceedings of the E-Commerce and Web Technologies: 11th International Conference, EC-Web 2010, Bilbao, Spain, 1–3 September 2010; Proceedings 11; Springer: Berlin/Heidelberg, Germany, 2010; pp. 49–60.
38. Javed, U.; Shaukat, K.; Hameed, I.A.; Iqbal, F.; Alam, T.M.; Luo, S. A review of content-based and context-based recommendation systems. *Int. J. Emerg. Technol. Learn. (iJET)* **2021**, *16*, 274–306. [CrossRef]
39. Keerthika, K.; Saravanan, T. Enhanced product recommendations based on seasonality and demography in ecommerce. In Proceedings of the 2020 2nd International Conference on Advances in Computing, Communication Control and Networking (ICACCCN), Noida, India, 18–19 December 2020; pp. 721–723.
40. Khanal, S.S.; Prasad, P.; Alsadoon, A.; Maag, A. A systematic review: Machine learning based recommendation systems for e-learning. *Educ. Inf. Technol.* **2020**, *25*, 2635–2664. [CrossRef]
41. Liu, T.; Wu, Q.; Chang, L.; Gu, T. A review of deep learning-based recommender system in e-learning environments. *Artif. Intell. Rev.* **2022**, *55*, 5953–5980. [CrossRef]
42. Bhaskaran, S.; Marappan, R.; Santhi, B. Design and analysis of a cluster-based intelligent hybrid recommendation system for e-learning applications. *Mathematics* **2021**, *9*, 197. [CrossRef]
43. Ali, S.; Hafeez, Y.; Humayun, M.; Jamail, N.S.M.; Aqib, M.; Nawaz, A. Enabling recommendation system architecture in virtualized environment for e-learning. *Egypt. Inform. J.* **2022**, *23*, 33–45. [CrossRef]
44. Jena, K.K.; Bhoi, S.K.; Malik, T.K.; Sahoo, K.S.; Jhanjhi, N.; Bhatia, S.; Amsaad, F. E-learning course recommender system using collaborative filtering models. *Electronics* **2022**, *12*, 157. [CrossRef]
45. Rahayu, N.W.; Ferdiana, R.; Kusumawardani, S.S. A systematic review of ontology use in E-Learning recommender system. *Comput. Educ. Artif. Intell.* **2022**, *3*, 100047. [CrossRef]
46. Rahhali, M.; Oughdir, L.; Jedidi, Y.; Lahmadi, Y.; El Khattabi, M.Z. E-learning recommendation system based on cloud computing. In Proceedings of the WITS 2020: The 6th International Conference on Wireless Technologies, Embedded, and Intelligent Systems, Fez, Morocco, 14–16 October 2020; Springer: Berlin/Heidelberg, Germany, 2022; pp. 89–99.
47. Sinclair, J.; Joy, M.; Yau, J.Y.K.; Hagan, S. A practice-oriented review of learning objects. *IEEE Trans. Learn. Technol.* **2013**, *6*, 177–192. [CrossRef]
48. Wiley, D.A. Connecting learning objects to instructional design theory: A definition, a metaphor, and a taxonomy. *Instr. Use Learn. Objects* **2000**, *2830*, 1–35.
49. Shi, D.; Wang, T.; Xing, H.; Xu, H. A learning path recommendation model based on a multidimensional knowledge graph framework for e-learning. *Knowl.-Based Syst.* **2020**, *195*, 105618. [CrossRef]
50. Saito, T.; Watanobe, Y. Learning path recommendation system for programming education based on neural networks. *Int. J. Distance Educ. Technol. (IJDET)* **2020**, *18*, 36–64. [CrossRef]
51. Saito, T.; Watanobe, Y. Learning path recommender system based on recurrent neural network. In Proceedings of the 2018 9th International Conference on Awareness Science and Technology (iCAST), Fukuoka, Japan, 19–21 September 2018; pp. 324–329.
52. Tarus, J.K.; Niu, Z.; Mustafa, G. Knowledge-based recommendation: A review of ontology-based recommender systems for e-learning. *Artif. Intell. Rev.* **2018**, *50*, 21–48. [CrossRef]
53. Qomariyah, N.N.; Fajar, A.N. Recommender system for e-learning based on personal learning style. In Proceedings of the 2019 International Seminar on Research of Information Technology and Intelligent Systems (ISRITI), Yogyakarta, Indonesia, 5–6 December 2019; pp. 563–567.
54. Troussas, C.; Krouska, A. Path-based recommender system for learning activities using knowledge graphs. *Information* **2022**, *14*, 9. [CrossRef]
55. De Medio, C.; Limongelli, C.; Sciarrone, F.; Temperini, M. MoodleREC: A recommendation system for creating courses using the moodle e-learning platform. *Comput. Hum. Behav.* **2020**, *104*, 106168. [CrossRef]
56. Alamdari, P.M.; Navimipour, N.J.; Hosseinzadeh, M.; Safaei, A.A.; Darwesh, A. A systematic study on the recommender systems in the E-commerce. *IEEE Access* **2020**, *8*, 115694–115716. [CrossRef]
57. Hwangbo, H.; Kim, Y.S.; Cha, K.J. Recommendation system development for fashion retail e-commerce. *Electron. Commer. Res. Appl.* **2018**, *28*, 94–101. [CrossRef]
58. Jiang, L.; Cheng, Y.; Yang, L.; Li, J.; Yan, H.; Wang, X. A trust-based collaborative filtering algorithm for E-commerce recommendation system. *J. Ambient. Intell. Humaniz. Comput.* **2019**, *10*, 3023–3034. [CrossRef]
59. Wakil, K.; Alyari, F.; Ghasvari, M.; Lesani, Z.; Rajabion, L. A new model for assessing the role of customer behavior history, product classification, and prices on the success of the recommender systems in e-commerce. *Kybernetes* **2020**, *49*, 1325–1346. [CrossRef]
60. Zhou, L. Product advertising recommendation in e-commerce based on deep learning and distributed expression. *Electron. Commer. Res.* **2020**, *20*, 321–342. [CrossRef]
61. Colombo-Mendoza, L.O.; Valencia-García, R.; Rodríguez-González, A.; Colomo-Palacios, R.; Alor-Hernández, G. Towards a knowledge-based probabilistic and context-aware social recommender system. *J. Inf. Sci.* **2018**, *44*, 464–490. [CrossRef]

62. Khatter, H.; Arif, S.; Singh, U.; Mathur, S.; Jain, S. Product recommendation system for E-commerce using collaborative filtering and textual clustering. In Proceedings of the 2021 Third International Conference on Inventive Research in Computing Applications (ICIRCA), Coimbatore, India, 2–4 September 2021; pp. 612–618.
63. Chakraborty, S.; Hoque, M.S.; Rahman Jeem, N.; Biswas, M.C.; Bardhan, D.; Lobaton, E. Fashion recommendation systems, models and methods: A review. *Informatics* **2021**, *8*, 49. [CrossRef]
64. Almahmood, R.J.K.; Tekerek, A. Issues and solutions in deep learning-enabled recommendation systems within the e-commerce field. *Appl. Sci.* **2022**, *12*, 11256. [CrossRef]
65. Huang, Z.; Zeng, D.; Chen, H. A comparative study of recommendation algorithms in e-commerce applications. *IEEE Intell. Syst.* **2007**, *22*, 68–78. [CrossRef]
66. Abdul Hussien, F.T.; Rahma, A.M.S.; Abdulwahab, H.B. An e-commerce recommendation system based on dynamic analysis of customer behavior. *Sustainability* **2021**, *13*, 10786. [CrossRef]
67. De Croon, R.; Van Houdt, L.; Htun, N.N.; Štiglic, G.; Abeele, V.V.; Verbert, K. Health recommender systems: Systematic review. *J. Med. Internet Res.* **2021**, *23*, e18035. [CrossRef]
68. Sahoo, A.K.; Mallik, S.; Pradhan, C.; Mishra, B.S.P.; Barik, R.K.; Das, H. Intelligence-based health recommendation system using big data analytics. In *Big Data Analytics for Intelligent Healthcare Management*; Elsevier: Amsterdam, The Netherlands, 2019; pp. 227–246.
69. Mantey, E.A.; Zhou, C.; Mani, V.; Arthur, J.K.; Ibeke, E. Maintaining privacy for a recommender system diagnosis using blockchain and deep learning. *Hum.-Centric Comput. Inf. Sci.* **2023**, *13*. [CrossRef]
70. Gräßer, F.; Tesch, F.; Schmitt, J.; Abraham, S.; Malberg, H.; Zaunseder, S. A pharmaceutical therapy recommender system enabling shared decision-making. In *User Modeling and User-Adapted Interaction*; Springer: Berlin/Heidelberg, Germany, 2022; pp. 1–44.
71. Ferretto, L.R.; Bellei, E.A.; Biduski, D.; Bin, L.C.P.; Moro, M.M.; Cervi, C.R.; De Marchi, A.C.B. A physical activity recommender system for patients with arterial hypertension. *IEEE Access* **2020**, *8*, 61656–61664. [CrossRef]
72. Çelik Ertuğrul, D.; Elçi, A. A survey on semanticized and personalized health recommender systems. *Expert Syst.* **2020**, *37*, e12519. [CrossRef]
73. Roy, S.N.; Srivastava, S.K.; Gururajan, R. Integrating wearable devices and recommendation system: Towards a next generation healthcare service delivery. *J. Inf. Technol. Theory Appl. (JITTA)* **2018**, *19*, 2.
74. Kaneriya, S.; Chudasama, M.; Tanwar, S.; Tyagi, S.; Kumar, N.; Rodrigues, J.J. Markov decision-based recommender system for sleep apnea patients. In Proceedings of the ICC 2019—2019 IEEE International Conference on Communications (ICC), Shanghai, China, 20–24 May 2019; pp. 1–6.
75. Anandhan, A.; Shuib, L.; Ismail, M.A.; Mujtaba, G. Social media recommender systems: Review and open research issues. *IEEE Access* **2018**, *6*, 15608–15628. [CrossRef]
76. Erdeniz, S.P.; Menychtas, A.; Maglogiannis, I.; Felfernig, A.; Tran, T.N.T. Recommender systems for IoT enabled quantified-self applications. *Evol. Syst.* **2020**, *11*, 291–304. [CrossRef]
77. Erdeniz, S.P.; Maglogiannis, I.; Menychtas, A.; Felfernig, A.; Tran, T.N.T. Recommender systems for IoT enabled m-health applications. In Proceedings of the Artificial Intelligence Applications and Innovations: AIAI 2018 IFIP WG 12.5 International Workshops, SEDSEAL, 5G-PINE, MHDW, and HEALTHIOT, Rhodes, Greece, 25–27 May 2018; Proceedings 14; Springer: Berlin/Heidelberg, Germany, 2018; pp. 227–237.
78. Promkot, A.N.; Arch-int, S.; Arch-int, N. The personalized traditional medicine recommendation system using ontology and rule inference approach. In Proceedings of the 2019 IEEE 4th International Conference on Computer and Communication Systems (ICCCS), Singapore, 23–25 February 2019; pp. 96–104.
79. Sookrah, R.; Dhowtal, J.D.; Nagowah, S.D. A DASH diet recommendation system for hypertensive patients using machine learning. In Proceedings of the 2019 7th International Conference on Information and Communication Technology (ICoICT), Kuala Lumpur, Malaysia, 24–26 July 2019; pp. 1–6.
80. Abhari, S.; Safdari, R.; Azadbakht, L.; Lankarani, K.B.; Kalhori, S.R.N.; Honarvar, B.; Abhari, K.; Ayyoubzadeh, S.; Karbasi, Z.; Zakerabasali, S.; et al. A systematic review of nutrition recommendation systems: With focus on technical aspects. *J. Biomed. Phys. Eng.* **2019**, *9*, 591. [CrossRef]
81. Agapito, G.; Simeoni, M.; Calabrese, B.; Caré, I.; Lamprinoudi, T.; Guzzi, P.H.; Pujia, A.; Fuiano, G.; Cannataro, M. DIETOS: A dietary recommender system for chronic diseases monitoring and management. *Comput. Methods Programs Biomed.* **2018**, *153*, 93–104. [CrossRef]
82. Mahajan, P.; Kaur, P.D. A Systematic Literature Review of Food Recommender Systems. *SN Comput. Sci.* **2024**, *5*, 174. [CrossRef]
83. Chiang, P.H.; Wong, M.; Dey, S. Using wearables and machine learning to enable personalized lifestyle recommendations to improve blood pressure. *IEEE J. Transl. Eng. Health Med.* **2021**, *9*, 2700513. [CrossRef]
84. Xie, J.; Wang, Q. A personalized diet and exercise recommender system for type 1 diabetes self-management: An in silico study. *Smart Health* **2019**, *13*, 100069. [CrossRef]
85. Nagaraj, P.; Deepalakshmi, P. A framework for e-healthcare management service using recommender system. *Electron. Gov. Int. J.* **2020**, *16*, 84–100. [CrossRef]
86. Chaudhuri, A.; Samanta, D.; Sarma, M. Modeling user behaviour in research paper recommendation system. *arXiv* **2021**, arXiv:2107.07831.

87. Chatterjee, A.; Prinz, A.; Gerdes, M.; Martinez, S.; Pahari, N.; Meena, Y.K. ProHealth eCoach: User-centered design and development of an eCoach app to promote healthy lifestyle with personalized activity recommendations. *BMC Health Serv. Res.* **2022**, *22*, 1120. [CrossRef] [PubMed]
88. Cheng, V.W.S. Recommendations for implementing gamification for mental health and wellbeing. *Front. Psychol.* **2020**, *11*, 586379. [CrossRef]
89. Lewis, R.; Ferguson, C.; Wilks, C.; Jones, N.; Picard, R.W. Can a Recommender System Support Treatment Personalisation in Digital Mental Health Therapy? A Quantitative Feasibility Assessment Using Data from a Behavioural Activation Therapy App. In Proceedings of the CHI Conference on Human Factors in Computing Systems Extended Abstracts, New Orleans, LA, USA, 29 April–5 May 2022; pp. 1–8.
90. Yang, S.; Zhou, P.; Duan, K.; Hossain, M.S.; Alhamid, M.F. emHealth: Towards emotion health through depression prediction and intelligent health recommender system. *Mob. Netw. Appl.* **2018**, *23*, 216–226. [CrossRef]
91. Gyrard, A.; Sheth, A. IAMHAPPY: Towards an IoT knowledge-based cross-domain well-being recommendation system for everyday happiness. *Smart Health* **2020**, *15*, 100083. [CrossRef]
92. Mojarad, R.; Attal, F.; Chibani, A.; Amirat, Y. Context-aware adaptive recommendation system for personal well-being services. In Proceedings of the 2020 IEEE 32nd International Conference on Tools with Artificial Intelligence (ICTAI), Baltimore, MD, USA, 9–11 November 2020; pp. 192–199.
93. Afolabi, A.O.; Toivanen, P. Integration of recommendation systems into connected health for effective management of chronic diseases. *IEEE Access* **2019**, *7*, 49201–49211. [CrossRef]
94. Ihnaini, B.; Khan, M.A.; Khan, T.A.; Abbas, S.; Daoud, M.S.; Ahmad, M.; Khan, M.A. A smart healthcare recommendation system for multidisciplinary diabetes patients with data fusion based on deep ensemble learning. *Comput. Intell. Neurosci.* **2021**, *2021*, 4243700. [CrossRef]
95. Jabeen, F.; Maqsood, M.; Ghazanfar, M.A.; Aadil, F.; Khan, S.; Khan, M.F.; Mehmood, I. An IoT based efficient hybrid recommender system for cardiovascular disease. *Peer-Peer Netw. Appl.* **2019**, *12*, 1263–1276. [CrossRef]
96. Waqar, M.; Majeed, N.; Dawood, H.; Daud, A.; Aljohani, N.R. An adaptive doctor-recommender system. *Behav. Inf. Technol.* **2019**, *38*, 959–973. [CrossRef]
97. Han, Q.; Ji, M.; De Troya, I.M.D.R.; Gaur, M.; Zejnilovic, L. A hybrid recommender system for patient-doctor matchmaking in primary care. In Proceedings of the 2018 IEEE 5th International Conference on Data Science and Advanced Analytics (DSAA), Turin, Italy, 1–3 October 2018; pp. 481–490.
98. Tran, T.N.T.; Felfernig, A.; Trattner, C.; Holzinger, A. Recommender systems in the healthcare domain: State-of-the-art and research issues. *J. Intell. Inf. Syst.* **2021**, *57*, 171–201. [CrossRef]
99. Meingast, M.; Roosta, T.; Sastry, S. Security and privacy issues with health care information technology. In Proceedings of the 2006 International Conference of the IEEE Engineering in Medicine and Biology Society, New York, NY, USA, 30 August–3 September 2006; pp. 5453–5458.
100. Ambulkar, H.D.; Pathan, A. Recommender system challenges and methodologies in social network: Survey. *Int. J. Sci. Res. (IJSR)* **2015**, *4*, 286–289.
101. Sahoo, A.K.; Pradhan, C.; Barik, R.K.; Dubey, H. DeepReco: Deep learning based health recommender system using collaborative filtering. *Computation* **2019**, *7*, 25. [CrossRef]
102. Iroju, O.; Soriyan, A.; Gambo, I.; Olaleke, J. Interoperability in healthcare: Benefits, challenges and resolutions. *Int. J. Innov. Appl. Stud.* **2013**, *3*, 262–270.
103. Etemadi, M.; Abkenar, S.B.; Ahmadzadeh, A.; Kashani, M.H.; Asghari, P.; Akbari, M.; Mahdipour, E. A systematic review of healthcare recommender systems: Open issues, challenges, and techniques. *Expert Syst. Appl.* **2023**, *213*, 118823. [CrossRef]
104. Hamid, R.A.; Albahri, A.S.; Alwan, J.K.; Al-Qaysi, Z.; Albahri, O.S.; Zaidan, A.; Alnoor, A.; Alamoodi, A.H.; Zaidan, B. How smart is e-tourism? A systematic review of smart tourism recommendation system applying data management. *Comput. Sci. Rev.* **2021**, *39*, 100337. [CrossRef]
105. Herzog, D.; Laß, C.; Wörndl, W. Tourrec: A tourist trip recommender system for individuals and groups. In Proceedings of the 12th ACM Conference on Recommender Systems, Vancouver, BC, Canada, 2–7 October 2018; pp. 496–497.
106. Figueredo, M.; Ribeiro, J.; Cacho, N.; Thome, A.; Cacho, A.; Lopes, F.; Araujo, V. From photos to travel itinerary: A tourism recommender system for smart tourism destination. In Proceedings of the 2018 IEEE Fourth International Conference on Big Data Computing Service and Applications (BigDataService), Bamberg, Germany, 26–29 March 2018; pp. 85–92.
107. Baizal, Z.A.; Tarwidi, D.; Wijaya, B. Tourism destination recommendation using ontology-based conversational recommender system. *Int. J. Comput. Digit. Syst.* **2021**, *10*. [CrossRef]
108. Cepeda-Pacheco, J.C.; Domingo, M.C. Deep learning and Internet of Things for tourist attraction recommendations in smart cities. *Neural Comput. Appl.* **2022**, *34*, 7691–7709. [CrossRef]
109. Abbasi-Moud, Z.; Vahdat-Nejad, H.; Sadri, J. Tourism recommendation system based on semantic clustering and sentiment analysis. *Expert Syst. Appl.* **2021**, *167*, 114324. [CrossRef]
110. Ray, B.; Garain, A.; Sarkar, R. An ensemble-based hotel recommender system using sentiment analysis and aspect categorization of hotel reviews. *Appl. Soft Comput.* **2021**, *98*, 106935. [CrossRef]
111. Sarkar, J.L.; Majumder, A.; Panigrahi, C.R.; Roy, S.; Pati, B. Tourism recommendation system: A survey and future research directions. *Multimed. Tools Appl.* **2023**, *82*, 8983–9027. [CrossRef]

112. Ricci, F. Travel recommender systems. *IEEE Intell. Syst.* **2002**, *17*, 55–57.
113. Schmidt-Belz, B.; Nick, A.; Poslad, S.; Zipf, A. Personalized and location-based mobile tourism services. In Proceedings of the "Mobile Tourism Support Systems" in Conjunction with Mobile HCI, Pisa, Italy, 17 September 2002.
114. Poslad, S.; Laamanen, H.; Malaka, R.; Nick, A.; Buckle, P.; Zipl, A. Crumpet: Creation of user-friendly mobile services personalised for tourism. In Proceedings of the 3G Mobile Communication Technologies, London, UK, 26–28 March 2001.
115. Gomathi, R.; Ajitha, P.; Krishna, G.H.S.; Pranay, I.H. Restaurant recommendation system for user preference and services based on rating and amenities. In Proceedings of the 2019 International Conference on Computational Intelligence in Data Science (ICCIDS), Gurugram, India, 6–7 September 2019; pp. 1–6.
116. Buhalis, D.; Amaranggana, A. Smart tourism destinations enhancing tourism experience through personalisation of services. In *Information and Communication Technologies in Tourism 2015, Proceedings of the International Conference in Lugano, Switzerland, 3–6 February 2015*; Springer: Berlin/Heidelberg, Germany, 2015; pp. 377–389.
117. Kontogianni, A.; Alepis, E.; Patsakis, C. Promoting smart tourism personalised services via a combination of deep learning techniques. *Expert Syst. Appl.* **2022**, *187*, 115964. [CrossRef]
118. Volchek, K.; Law, R.; Buhalis, D.; Song, H. Exploring ways to improve personalisation: The influence of tourist context on service perception. *E-Rev. Tour. Res.* **2020**, *17*, 737–752.
119. Rehman Khan, H.U.; Lim, C.K.; Ahmed, M.F.; Tan, K.L.; Bin Mokhtar, M. Systematic review of contextual suggestion and recommendation systems for sustainable e-tourism. *Sustainability* **2021**, *13*, 8141. [CrossRef]
120. Yochum, P.; Chang, L.; Gu, T.; Zhu, M. Linked open data in location-based recommendation system on tourism domain: A survey. *IEEE Access* **2020**, *8*, 16409–16439. [CrossRef]
121. Zheng, X.; Luo, Y.; Sun, L.; Zhang, J.; Chen, F. A tourism destination recommender system using users' sentiment and temporal dynamics. *J. Intell. Inf. Syst.* **2018**, *51*, 557–578. [CrossRef]
122. Goyani, M.; Chaurasiya, N. A review of movie recommendation system: Limitations, Survey and Challenges. *ELCVIA Electron. Lett. Comput. Vis. Image Anal.* **2020**, *19*, 0018-37.
123. Kumar, S.; De, K.; Roy, P.P. Movie recommendation system using sentiment analysis from microblogging data. *IEEE Trans. Comput. Soc. Syst.* **2020**, *7*, 915–923. [CrossRef]
124. Anwar, K.; Siddiqui, J.; Sohail, S.S. Machine learning-based book recommender system: A survey and new perspectives. *Int. J. Intell. Inf. Database Syst.* **2020**, *13*, 231–248. [CrossRef]
125. Aggarwal, S.; Goswami, D.; Hooda, M.; Chakravarty, A.; Kar, A.; Vasudha. Recommendation systems for interactive multimedia entertainment. In *Data Visualization and Knowledge Engineering: Spotting Data Points with Artificial Intelligence*; Springer: Berlin/Heidelberg, Germany, 2020; pp. 23–48.
126. Nawar, A.; Toma, N.T.; Al Mamun, S.; Kaiser, M.S.; Mahmud, M.; Rahman, M.A. Cross-content recommendation between movie and book using machine learning. In Proceedings of the 2021 IEEE 15th International Conference on Application of Information and Communication Technologies (AICT), Virtual Event, 13–15 October 2021; pp. 1–6.
127. Dhelim, S.; Aung, N.; Bouras, M.A.; Ning, H.; Cambria, E. A survey on personality-aware recommendation systems. In *Artificial Intelligence Review*; Springer: Berlin/Heidelberg, Germany, 2022; pp. 1–46.
128. Moscato, V.; Picariello, A.; Sperli, G. An emotional recommender system for music. *IEEE Intell. Syst.* **2020**, *36*, 57–68. [CrossRef]
129. Gomez-Uribe, C.A.; Hunt, N. The netflix recommender system: Algorithms, business value, and innovation. *ACM Trans. Manag. Inf. Syst. (TMIS)* **2015**, *6*, 13. [CrossRef]
130. Reddy, S.; Nalluri, S.; Kunisetti, S.; Ashok, S.; Venkatesh, B. Content-based movie recommendation system using genre correlation. In *Smart Intelligent Computing and Applications, Proceedings of the Second International Conference on SCI, Xi'an, China, 16–17 August 2018*; Springer: Berlin/Heidelberg, Germany, 2019; Volume 2, pp. 391–397.
131. Zhang, J.; Wang, Y.; Yuan, Z.; Jin, Q. Personalized real-time movie recommendation system: Practical prototype and evaluation. *Tsinghua Sci. Technol.* **2019**, *25*, 180–191. [CrossRef]
132. Song, Y.; Dixon, S.; Pearce, M. A survey of music recommendation systems and future perspectives. In Proceedings of the 9th International Symposium on Computer Music Modeling and Retrieval, London, UK, 19–22 June 2021; Volume 4, pp. 395–410.
133. Ayata, D.; Yaslan, Y.; Kamasak, M.E. Emotion based music recommendation system using wearable physiological sensors. *IEEE Trans. Consum. Electron.* **2018**, *64*, 196–203. [CrossRef]
134. Paul, D.; Kundu, S. A survey of music recommendation systems with a proposed music recommendation system. In *Emerging Technology in Modelling and Graphics: Proceedings of IEM Graph, Kolkata, India, 6–7 September 2018*; Springer: Berlin/Heidelberg, Germany, 2020; pp. 279–285.
135. Yang, L.; Liu, Z.; Wang, Y.; Wang, C.; Fan, Z.; Yu, P.S. Large-scale personalized video game recommendation via social-aware contextualized graph neural network. In Proceedings of the ACM Web Conference 2022, Lyon, France, 25–29 April 2022; pp. 3376–3386.
136. Cheuque, G.; Guzmán, J.; Parra, D. Recommender systems for online video game platforms: The case of steam. In Proceedings of the Companion: The 2019 World Wide Web Conference, San Francisco, CA, USA, 13–17 May 2019; pp. 763–771.

137. Pérez-Marcos, J.; Martín-Gómez, L.; Jiménez-Bravo, D.M.; López, V.F.; Moreno-García, M.N. Hybrid system for video game recommendation based on implicit ratings and social networks. *J. Ambient. Intell. Humaniz. Comput.* **2020**, *11*, 4525–4535. [CrossRef]
138. Christensen, I.A.; Schiaffino, S. Entertainment recommender systems for group of users. *Expert Syst. Appl.* **2011**, *38*, 14127–14135. [CrossRef]
139. Schedl, M.; Knees, P.; McFee, B.; Bogdanov, D. Music recommendation systems: Techniques, use cases, and challenges. In *Recommender Systems Handbook*; Springer: Berlin/Heidelberg, Germany, 2021; pp. 927–971.
140. Park, Y.J.; Tuzhilin, A. The long tail of recommender systems and how to leverage it. In Proceedings of the 2008 ACM Conference on Recommender Systems, Lausanne, Switzerland, 23–25 October 2008; pp. 11–18.
141. Deldjoo, Y.; Schedl, M.; Cremonesi, P.; Pasi, G. Recommender systems leveraging multimedia content. *ACM Comput. Surv. (CSUR)* **2020**, *53*, 106. [CrossRef]
142. Al-Otaibi, S.T.; Ykhlef, M. A survey of job recommender systems. *Int. J. Phys. Sci.* **2012**, *7*, 5127–5142. [CrossRef]
143. Mashayekhi, Y.; Li, N.; Kang, B.; Lijffijt, J.; De Bie, T. A challenge-based survey of e-recruitment recommendation systems. *ACM Comput. Surv.* **2024**, *56*, 252. [CrossRef]
144. Hu, X.; Cheng, Y.; Zheng, Z.; Wang, Y.; Chi, X.; Zhu, H. Boss: A bilateral occupational-suitability-aware recommender system for online recruitment. In Proceedings of the 29th ACM SIGKDD Conference on Knowledge Discovery and Data Mining, Long Beach, CA, USA, 6–10 August 2023; pp. 4146–4155.
145. González-Briones, A.; Rivas, A.; Chamoso, P.; Casado-Vara, R.; Corchado, J.M. Case-based reasoning and agent based job offer recommender system. In Proceedings of the International Joint Conference SOCO'18-CISIS'18-ICEUTE'18, San Sebastián, Spain, 6–8 June 2018; Proceedings 13; Springer: Berlin/Heidelberg, Germany, 2019; pp. 21–33.
146. Tondji, L.N. Web Recommender System for Job Seeking and Recruiting. Partial Fulfillment of a Masters II at AIMS 2018. Available online: https://www.researchgate.net/profile/Lionel-Tondji/publication/323726564_Web_Recommender_System_for_Job_Seeking_and_Recruiting/links/5aa799a20f7e9bbbff8cfc0d/Web-Recommender-System-for-Job-Seeking-and-Recruiting.pdf (accessed on 6 May 2024).
147. Elsafty, A.; Riedl, M.; Biemann, C. Document-based recommender system for job postings using dense representations. In Proceedings of the 2018 Conference of the North American Chapter of the Association for Computational Linguistics: Human Language Technologies, New Orleans, LA, USA, 1–6 June 2018; Volume 3, pp. 216–224.
148. Mishra, R.; Rathi, S. Efficient and scalable job recommender system using collaborative filtering. In Proceedings of the ICDSMLA 2019: The 1st International Conference on Data Science, Machine Learning and Applications, Pune, India, 21 May 2020; Springer: Singapore, 2020; pp. 842–856.
149. Appadoo, K.; Soonnoo, M.B.; Mungloo-Dilmohamud, Z. Job recommendation system, machine learning, regression, classification, natural language processing. In Proceedings of the 2020 IEEE Asia-Pacific Conference on Computer Science and Data Engineering (CSDE), Gold Coast, Australia, 16–18 December 2020; pp. 1–6.
150. De Ruijt, C.; Bhulai, S. Job recommender systems: A review. *arXiv* **2021**, arXiv:2111.13576.
151. Bellini, P.; Palesi, L.A.I.; Nesi, P.; Pantaleo, G. Multi clustering recommendation system for fashion retail. *Multimed. Tools Appl.* **2023**, *82*, 9989–10016. [CrossRef] [PubMed]
152. Shin, Y.G.; Yeo, Y.J.; Sagong, M.C.; Ji, S.W.; Ko, S.J. Deep fashion recommendation system with style feature decomposition. In Proceedings of the 2019 IEEE 9th International Conference on Consumer Electronics (ICCE-Berlin), Berlin, Germany, 8–11 September 2019; pp. 301–305.
153. Stefani, M.A.; Stefanis, V.; Garofalakis, J. CFRS: A trends-driven collaborative fashion recommendation system. In Proceedings of the 2019 10th International Conference on Information, Intelligence, Systems and Applications (IISA), Patras, Greece, 15–17 July 2019; pp. 1–4.
154. Ye, T.; Hu, L.; Zhang, Q.; Lai, Z.Y.; Naseem, U.; Liu, D.D. Show me the best outfit for a certain scene: A scene-aware fashion recommender system. In Proceedings of the ACM Web Conference 2023, Austin, TX, USA, 30 April–4 May 2023; pp. 1172–1180.
155. Shahbazi, Z.; Hazra, D.; Park, S.; Byun, Y.C. Toward improving the prediction accuracy of product recommendation system using extreme gradient boosting and encoding approaches. *Symmetry* **2020**, *12*, 1566. [CrossRef]
156. Mandalapu, S.R.; Narayanan, B.; Putheti, S. A hybrid collaborative filtering mechanism for product recommendation system. *Multimed. Tools Appl.* **2024**, *83*, 12775–12798. [CrossRef]
157. Sharma, A.K.; Bajpai, B.; Adhvaryu, R.; Pankajkumar, S.D.; Gordhanbhai, P.P.; Kumar, A. An efficient approach of product recommendation system using NLP technique. *Mater. Today Proc.* **2023**, *80*, 3730–3743. [CrossRef]
158. Hwang, R.H.; Hsueh, Y.L.; Chen, Y.T. An effective taxi recommender system based on a spatio-temporal factor analysis model. *Inf. Sci.* **2015**, *314*, 28–40. [CrossRef]
159. Wang, X.; Zhang, H.; Wang, L.; Ning, Z. A demand-supply oriented taxi recommendation system for vehicular social networks. *IEEE Access* **2018**, *6*, 41529–41538. [CrossRef]
160. Wan, X.; Ghazzai, H.; Massoud, Y. A generic data-driven recommendation system for large-scale regular and ride-hailing taxi services. *Electronics* **2020**, *9*, 648. [CrossRef]

161. Subramaniyaswamy, V.; Manogaran, G.; Logesh, R.; Vijayakumar, V.; Chilamkurti, N.; Malathi, D.; Senthilselvan, N. An ontology-driven personalized food recommendation in IoT-based healthcare system. *J. Supercomput.* **2019**, *75*, 3184–3216. [CrossRef]
162. Toledo, R.Y.; Alzahrani, A.A.; Martinez, L. A food recommender system considering nutritional information and user preferences. *IEEE Access* **2019**, *7*, 96695–96711. [CrossRef]
163. Iwendi, C.; Khan, S.; Anajemba, J.H.; Bashir, A.K.; Noor, F. Realizing an efficient IoMT-assisted patient diet recommendation system through machine learning model. *IEEE Access* **2020**, *8*, 28462–28474. [CrossRef]
164. Zhao, Y.; Wang, S.; Wang, Y.; Liu, H. MbSRS: A multi-behavior streaming recommender system. *Inf. Sci.* **2023**, *631*, 145–163. [CrossRef]
165. Torrent-Fontbona, F.; López, B. Personalized adaptive CBR bolus recommender system for type 1 diabetes. *IEEE J. Biomed. Health Inform.* **2018**, *23*, 387–394. [CrossRef] [PubMed]
166. Kaya, B. A hotel recommendation system based on customer location: A link prediction approach. *Multimed. Tools Appl.* **2020**, *79*, 1745–1758. [CrossRef]
167. Forhad, M.S.A.; Arefin, M.S.; Kayes, A.; Ahmed, K.; Chowdhury, M.J.M.; Kumara, I. An effective hotel recommendation system through processing heterogeneous data. *Electronics* **2021**, *10*, 1920. [CrossRef]
168. Chen, T. A fuzzy ubiquitous traveler clustering and hotel recommendation system by differentiating travelers' decision-making behaviors. *Appl. Soft Comput.* **2020**, *96*, 106585. [CrossRef]
169. Fakhri, A.A.; Baizal, Z.; Setiawan, E.B. Restaurant recommender system using user-based collaborative filtering approach: A case study at Bandung Raya Region. *J. Phys. Conf. Ser.* **2019**, *1192*, 012023. [CrossRef]
170. Asani, E.; Vahdat-Nejad, H.; Sadri, J. Restaurant recommender system based on sentiment analysis. *Mach. Learn. Appl.* **2021**, *6*, 100114. [CrossRef]
171. Darban, Z.Z.; Valipour, M.H. GHRS: Graph-based hybrid recommendation system with application to movie recommendation. *Expert Syst. Appl.* **2022**, *200*, 116850.
172. Singh, R.H.; Maurya, S.; Tripathi, T.; Narula, T.; Srivastav, G. Movie recommendation system using cosine similarity and KNN. *Int. J. Eng. Adv. Technol.* **2020**, *9*, 556–559. [CrossRef]
173. Wang, Y.; Wang, M.; Xu, W. A sentiment-enhanced hybrid recommender system for movie recommendation: A big data analytics framework. *Wirel. Commun. Mob. Comput.* **2018**, *2018*, 8263704. [CrossRef]
174. Wu, C.S.M.; Garg, D.; Bhandary, U. Movie recommendation system using collaborative filtering. In Proceedings of the 2018 IEEE 9th International Conference on Software Engineering and Service Science (ICSESS), Beijing, China, 23–25 November 2018; pp. 11–15.
175. Aljunid, M.F.; Manjaiah, D. Movie recommender system based on collaborative filtering using apache spark. In Proceedings of the Data Management, Analytics and Innovation: ICDMAI 2018, Pune, India, 19–21 January 2018; Springer: Berlin/Heidelberg, Germany, 2019; Volume 2, pp. 283–295.
176. Ahuja, R.; Solanki, A.; Nayyar, A. Movie recommender system using k-means clustering and k-nearest neighbor. In Proceedings of the 2019 9th International Conference on Cloud Computing, Data Science & Engineering (Confluence), Noida, India, 10–11 January 2019; pp. 263–268.
177. Wen, X. Using deep learning approach and IoT architecture to build the intelligent music recommendation system. *Soft Comput.* **2021**, *25*, 3087–3096. [CrossRef]
178. Sheikh Fathollahi, M.; Razzazi, F. Music similarity measurement and recommendation system using convolutional neural networks. *Int. J. Multimed. Inf. Retr.* **2021**, *10*, 43–53. [CrossRef]
179. Yousefian Jazi, S.; Kaedi, M.; Fatemi, A. An emotion-aware music recommender system: Bridging the user's interaction and music recommendation. *Multimed. Tools Appl.* **2021**, *80*, 13559–13574. [CrossRef]
180. Fessahaye, F.; Perez, L.; Zhan, T.; Zhang, R.; Fossier, C.; Markarian, R.; Chiu, C.; Zhan, J.; Gewali, L.; Oh, P. T-recsys: A novel music recommendation system using deep learning. In Proceedings of the 2019 IEEE International Conference on Consumer Electronics (ICCE), Berlin, Germany, 8–11 September 2019; pp. 1–6.
181. Katarya, R.; Verma, O.P. Efficient music recommender system using context graph and particle swarm. *Multimed. Tools Appl.* **2018**, *77*, 2673–2687. [CrossRef]
182. Abdul, A.; Chen, J.; Liao, H.Y.; Chang, S.H. An emotion-aware personalized music recommendation system using a convolutional neural networks approach. *Appl. Sci.* **2018**, *8*, 1103. [CrossRef]
183. Bertens, P.; Guitart, A.; Chen, P.P.; Perianez, A. A machine-learning item recommendation system for video games. In Proceedings of the 2018 IEEE Conference on Computational Intelligence and Games (CIG), Maastricht, The Netherlands, 14–17 August 2018; pp. 1–4.
184. Jomsri, P. FUCL mining technique for book recommender system in library service. *Procedia Manuf.* **2018**, *22*, 550–557. [CrossRef]
185. Kommineni, M.; Alekhya, P.; Vyshnavi, T.M.; Aparna, V.; Swetha, K.; Mounika, V. Machine learning based efficient recommendation system for book selection using user based collaborative filtering algorithm. In Proceedings of the 2020 Fourth International Conference on Inventive Systems and Control (ICISC), Coimbatore, India, 8–10 January 2020; pp. 66–71.

186. Mughaid, A.; Obeidat, I.; Hawashin, B.; AlZu'bi, S.; Aqel, D. A smart geo-location job recommender system based on social media posts. In Proceedings of the 2019 Sixth International Conference on Social Networks Analysis, Management and Security (SNAMS), Granada, Spain, 2–25 October 2019; pp. 505–510.
187. Page, M.J.; McKenzie, J.E.; Bossuyt, P.M.; Boutron, I.; Hoffmann, T.C.; Mulrow, C.D.; Shamseer, L.; Tetzlaff, J.M.; Akl, E.A.; Brennan, S.E.; et al. The PRISMA 2020 statement: An updated guideline for reporting systematic reviews. *BMJ* **2021**, *372*, n71.

information

MDPI

Article

Aspect-Based Sentiment Analysis with Dependency Relation Weighted Graph Attention

Tingyao Jiang, Zilong Wang *, Ming Yang and Cheng Li

College of Computer and Information, China Three Gorges University, Yichang 443002, China; jiangty@ctgu.edu.cn (T.J.)
* Correspondence: wzl@ctgu.edu.cn

Abstract: Aspect-based sentiment analysis is a fine-grained sentiment analysis that focuses on the sentiment polarity of different aspects of text, and most current research methods use a combination of dependent syntactic analysis and graphical neural networks. In this paper, a graph attention network aspect-based sentiment analysis model based on the weighting of dependencies (WGAT) is designed to address the problem in that traditional models do not sufficiently analyse the types of syntactic dependencies; in the proposed model, graph attention networks can be weighted and averaged according to the importance of different nodes when aggregating information. The model first transforms the input text into a low-dimensional word vector through pretraining, while generating a dependency syntax graph by analysing the dependency syntax of the input text and constructing a dependency weighted adjacency matrix according to the importance of different dependencies in the graph. The word vector and the dependency weighted adjacency matrix are then fed into a graph attention network for feature extraction, and sentiment polarity is predicted through the classification layer. The model can focus on syntactic dependencies that are more important for sentiment classification during training, and the results of the comparison experiments on the Semeval-2014 laptop and restaurant datasets and the ACL-14 Twitter social comment dataset show that the WGAT model has significantly improved accuracy and F1 values compared to other baseline models, validating its effectiveness in aspect-level sentiment analysis tasks.

Keywords: aspect-based sentiment analysis; dependent syntactic analysis; dependency weighting; graph attention network; pretrained model

1. Introduction

Sentiment analysis is one of the current research hotspots in natural language processing [1]. With the development of information technology, increasingly more text with emotional tendencies is appearing on the internet [2], and the analysis of this information to understand people's views is crucial for solving practical problems, as well as for informative decision making.

The main types of text sentiment analysis are chapter-level sentiment analysis, sentence-level sentiment analysis, and aspect-level sentiment analysis [3]. Both chapter-level and sentence-level sentiment analyses are coarse-grained sentiment analyses that analyse an entire document or an entire sentence as a basic unit, respectively, and can only analyse a single sentiment of the text, not multiple aspects. Aspect-level sentiment analysis is a more fine-grained sentiment analysis that addresses specific aspects of a sentence [3]. For example, the emotional polarity of "The food at this restaurant is good, but the service is terrible" is positive and negative. In this case, it is not possible to accurately analyse the sentiment of the whole sentence, and specific aspects need to be analysed. With increasingly complex semantic environments and increased analysis requirements, coarse-grained sentiment analysis techniques can no longer meet today's needs, and more fine-grained sentiment analysis has become a key research problem in natural language processing [4].

Early approaches for aspect-based sentiment analysis used machine learning to manually engineer features, such as building sentiment dictionaries and then classifying sentiments through machine learning classifiers such as decision trees and support vector machines [5]. Particularly complex feature engineering is often needed, which is costly and poorly generalised.

With the development of neural network technology, deep learning methods have become the main approach for current aspect-based sentiment analysis research [6]. Deep learning overcomes the traditional machine learning problem of relying on manual extraction of text features, and it is able to automatically learn the emotional information embedded in text through neural networks and map words in text to low-latitude word embedding vectors. Some researchers further combined attentional mechanisms with deep learning [7–9], obtaining desirable results. To be specific, the attention mechanism enables the model to concentrate more on words with high similarity during sentiment classification by calculating the semantic similarity of the aspect word embedding vector to other word embedding vectors in the text. However, merely taking into account semantic similarity without considering the syntactic structure between words may cause the model to focus excessively on sentiment words that are not syntactically correlated with aspectual words and, thus, make incorrect judgments [10,11]. Nonetheless, traditional neural networks can only process data in Euclidean space and cannot make effective use of syntactic information.

To cope well with these problems, some researchers have conducted systematic and comprehensive dependency syntactic analysis on texts, generated dependency syntactic graphs to express the syntactic dependencies between words, and extracted the syntactic information from them through graph neural networks, which has materialised a considerably noticeable improvement in the model effect [11]. Nevertheless, the majority of current studies simply take into consideration the syntactic dependencies between words, ignoring the important feature of the type of dependency. Aside from that, in the process of classifying aspectual words for sentiment, the model needs to fix attention on the dependencies that are more important for the sentiment judgement of aspectual words. As a consequence, we incorporated dependency types into the graph neural network. Under such circumstances, the model can focus more on the dependencies that are important for sentiment classification. To achieve this, we set the weights of the dependencies in accordance with their importance and weight them as trainable parameters in the graph neural network for feature extraction, so that the model can fix its attention on the important dependencies. In the word embedding layer, we also use a sentiment pretraining model for word embedding. This enables the word embedding weights to be better adapted to the sentiment analysis task.

This paper presents the following main work:

1. We use a BERT-pretrained sentiment corpus for word embedding of input text. In such case, BERT can better capture the sentiment information in the text during pretraining, and demonstrate the superiority of the sentiment pretraining model compared to the normal pretraining model in sentiment analysis tasks through experimental results.
2. We probe deep into the text for dependency syntax, set initial weights for dissimilar dependencies in line with their relative importance for sentiment classification, and further optimise them through model training.
3. We come up with a relation-weighted graph attention network model (WGAT). This model ameliorates the existing attention mechanism and weights the attention score. In this way, the model can assign weights according to the importance of different types of dependencies, so as to concentrate more on important dependencies and heighten classification accuracy.
4. Experiments on different datasets prove the effectiveness of our proposed method, whereby the effect of our model is better than other baseline models.

2. Related Work

The main aim of aspect-based sentiment analysis is to examine the sentiment categories of the different aspects of a sentence. One of the main approaches used for aspect-based sentiment analysis based on machine learning involves using supervised classification algorithms such as plain Bayes algorithm [12] and support vector machines [13]. Although such an approach has achieved good performance, it relies heavily on manual feature engineering, which is costly. The performance of the model is also directly affected by how well the features are manually extracted; the manually extracted features are only valid in the corresponding domain and have poor generalisation capabilities.

In recent years, the rise of neural networks has led to the widespread use of deep learning methods in natural language processing tasks. Compared to traditional machine learning methods, deep learning can automatically extract text features without the need for particularly complex feature engineering and has greater expressive power. However, the large number of parameters used in various neural network models and the often small corpus for downstream tasks in natural language processing (sentiment analysis, machine translation, etc.) prevent the neural network parameters from being better trained. For this reason, pretraining on a large-scale corpus and then applying the resulting word embeddings to downstream natural language processing tasks is currently a proven approach [14].

Early word embedding techniques represented each word as a vector, where words that were closer in semantics were represented as vectors that were also closer in space. The word2vec model proposed by Mikolov et al. [15] uses a CBOW (predicting central words with surrounding words) and skip-gram (predicting surrounding words with central words). The Glove model proposed by Pennington et al. [16] constructs a co-occurrence matrix of words based on the corpus and then vectorises the word list on the basis of the co-occurrence matrix and the Glove model. The above two are static word vectors, which have been widely used in sentiment analysis tasks.

Recurrent neural networks (RNNs), with their temporal nature, exhibit great advantages in natural language processing tasks, but RNNs experience gradient disappearance for longer text. The long short-term memory (LSTM) network can solve this problem; hence, various aspect-based sentiment analysis models based on LSTM networks have been proposed. Tang et al. [7] proposed a target-dependent LSTM (TD-LSTM) model to address the inadequate attention given to target words in LSTM networks by using two LSTM networks, modelled separately on the left and right of the target words. They further proposed a target-connected LSTM (TC-LSTM) model, which further strengthens the relationship between target words and context by splicing target word vectors with contextual word vectors in the input part of the LSTM model based on TD-LSTM. The attention mechanism can focus on important parts of the text and has been successfully applied to a variety of natural language processing tasks. Wang et al. [8] proposed an attention-based LSTM (ATAE-LSTM) model using target embeddings, where the context and aspectual word splicing is fed into the LSTM for encoding, and the encoded vector is spliced with the aspectual word vector to obtain the sentiment category by computing through the attention mechanism. Tang et al. [17] applied the idea of memory networks to the aspect-based sentiment analysis task by storing the contextual information of a given aspect into a memory network and capturing the degree of aspect word–context association through an attention mechanism, which has a higher computational speed than LSTM. However, all these models use static word vectors and cannot dynamically adjust the meaning of words according to the context during model training to address the multiple meanings of words.

BERT is pretrained by working on a large corpus and fine-tuned in downstream tasks. It has better word embedding representation and stronger feature extraction than traditional word vectors. Song et al. [18] proposed the BERT_AEN model to address the excessive training data required for LSTM by using a multiheaded attentional encoder network for modelling between contextual words and aspect words and learning the interaction information between them. Zeng et al. [19] suggested that the sentiment polarity of aspectual words is related to nearby contextual words, and that distant words can interfere with words that may interfere with the final classification; hence, they proposed an aspect-based sentiment classification mechanism that focuses on local context. However, the emotional polarity of aspectual words is not always related to words that are close' for example, in the sentence "So delicious were the noodles but terrible were the vegetables", the aspectual word "noodles" is closer to "terrible", but its affective polarity is negative. In addition, calculating weights between words through a self-attentive mechanism fails to consider syntactic knowledge and may assign greater weights to words unrelated to aspectual word sentiment classification, leading to misclassification [10,11].

In recent years, some scholars have applied knowledge of dependent syntactic analysis to aspect-based sentiment analysis. Dependent syntactic analysis focuses on analysing the dependencies between words in a sentence [20], explaining the dependencies between word nodes through a kind of graph structure. For example, in the above example, the adjective "delicious" directly modifies the aspectual word "noodles" through a dependency relation, and they are at a distance of 1 in the syntactic map, while the aspectual word "noodles" has no path to reach the adjective "terrible". Syntactic distance is, therefore, preferable over spatial distance. Graph convolutional networks (GCNs) [21] can better handle graph structured data by aggregating and messaging neighbouring nodes. Because traditional neural networks cannot address the syntactic constraints and long-term dependencies of text, Zhang et al. [11] built graph convolutional networks in syntactic dependency trees to facilitate the use of syntactic information and dependencies of text. Huang et al. [22] proposed a graph attention network based on target dependency [23], which represents sentences as dependency graphs and directly connects aspect words to related words to extract information through graph attention networks. Wang [24] et al. proposed the relational graph attention (R-GAT) network model to reconstruct syntactic graphs using dependencies with aspectual words as root nodes and to encode dependencies for feature extraction through relational graph attention networks. Current research has enabled models to learn rich syntactic knowledge by combining syntactic graphs with graph neural networks, but less consideration has been given to the types of dependencies. Although R-GAT encodes dependencies, it does not consider that different types of dependencies have different importance and may assign larger weights to unimportant nodes when calculating the attention weights of two nodes.

3. Methodology

3.1. Task Definition

The data for an aspect-based sentiment analysis task can usually be defined as a binary group (W, A) consisting of a sentence and the aspect words therein, where $W = \{w_1, w_2, \ldots w_n\}$ is an emotionally charged sentence consisting of m words and $A = \{w_i, w_{i+1}, \ldots w_{i+n-1}\}$ represents the n aspect words in the sentence. Its affective polarity includes positive, negative, and neutral. For example the text "The staff should be more friendly.", W is a sequence of words within the text, i.e., W = {"the", "staff", "should", "be ", "more", "friendly", "."}, and A is the sequence of aspectual words in it, i.e., A = {"staff"}. The goal of the task is to input W and A into Model M to predict the sentiment polarity of aspectual word A, as shown in Equation (1). y_pred is the model prediction result.

$$y\_pred = M(W, A). \tag{1}$$

This paper proposes a graph attention network aspect-based sentiment analysis (WGAT) model based on sentiment pretraining and the weighting of dependencies. The model mainly consists of a word embedding layer, a dependency syntactic analysis layer, a graph attention network layer, and a classification layer. The original text is encoded at the word embedding layer as an input feature to the graph attention network. Dependency syntax analysis is performed on the text at the syntactic analysis layer to generate a dependency syntax graph and construct a dependency-weighted adjacency matrix based on the dependency relationships between nodes. Lastly, the weighted adjacency matrix and input features are fed into the graph attention network for feature extraction and sentiment prediction through the classification layer. The specific model structure is shown in Figure 1.

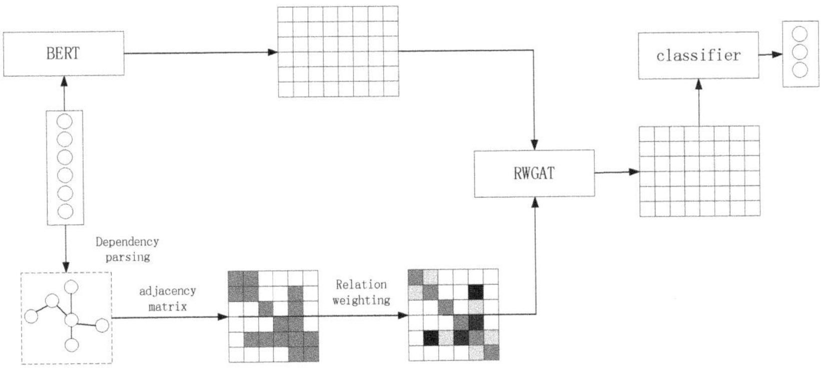

Figure 1. Model structural diagram.

3.2. Word Embedding Layer

The BERT model uses a bidirectional transformer [25] encoder structure, which, at its core, uses a self-attentive mechanism to encode text. The self-attention mechanism allows the model to focus on the important parts of the text during training by calculating the attention weight of each word in the text in relation to all other words. Although the pretrained model has performed well in a variety of NLP tasks, it is pretrained on a generic corpus based on its inability to better capture sentiment relations in text [26], limiting its performance in sentiment analysis tasks. This paper, therefore, uses a BERT model pretrained on a large-scale sentiment corpus for word embedding, making its pretrained weights better suited for sentiment analysis.

In this paper, the input text sequence is $W = \{w_1, w_2, \ldots w_m\}$, which is mapped into a low-dimensional semantic vector $H^{m \times bert\_dim}$ by the BERT model, where m is the input text length and bert_dim is the BERT word embedding dimension. The features that are graph nodes are then fed into the graph neural network for training. This is shown in Equation (2).

$$H = \{h_1, h_2, \ldots h_m\} = BERT(W). \tag{2}$$

3.3. Syntactic Analysis Layer

Dependency syntactic analysis focuses on the dependency relationships between words in a sentence [24]. Although the attention mechanism can focus on important parts of text, it cannot adequately capture the syntactic dependencies in sentences [21], which affects the classification effect. This paper, therefore, requires syntactic analysis of the input text. The StanfordNLP syntactic parser was used to convert the sentences into a syntactic dependency graph. Taking "Great food but the service was dreadful!" as an example, the syntactic dependency graph is shown in Figure 2.

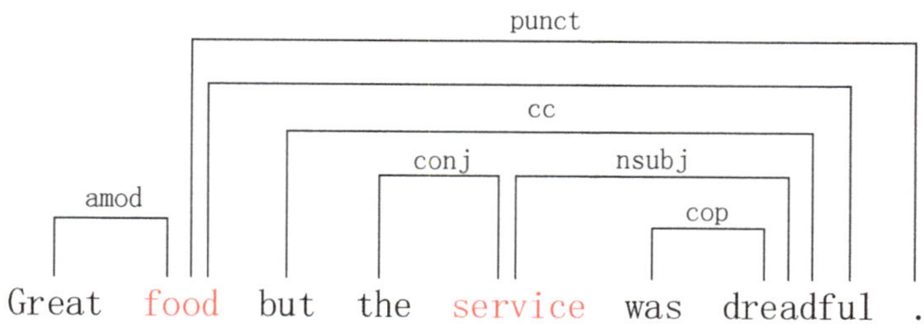

Figure 2. Dependency syntax example 1.

In Figure 2, the results of the syntactic analysis of dependencies include both the syntactic dependencies that exist between words and the types of dependencies. Different dependencies contribute differently to the affective classification of aspectual words, e.g., the aspectual word 'food' is related to the words "great", "dreadful", and "," in a modifying way. Different dependencies contribute differently to the affective classification of aspectual words; for example, the aspectual word "food" has a modifying relationship with the words "great", "dreadful", and ",", whose dependencies are "amod", "conj", and "punct", respectively. "Great" is an emotion word for the aspect word "food", indicating that its emotional overtone is positive and that it plays a positive role in the classification of emotions. "Punct" is usually connected with punctuation and can potentially interfere with the final classification. "Food" is linked to the word "dreadful" via "conj" with negative emotional overtones, which can lead to misclassification. For the aspectual word "service", the dependency "nsubj" can be directly connected to its affective word "dreadful", but "det" has no effect on affective classification. Different types of dependencies have different effects on the affective prediction of aspectual words. Therefore, this paper sets different weights for different types of dependencies, with larger weights used for dependencies that have an affective effect on aspectual words and smaller weights for the rest of the dependencies so that the model can focus on the important parts in the process of extracting the syntactic dependency graph. In addition to aspectual words, adverbial relations modifying adjectives or verbs play a crucial role in classification, as shown in Figure 3.

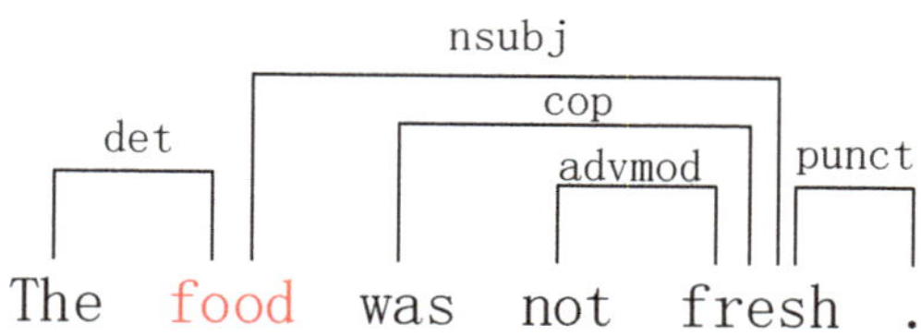

Figure 3. Dependency syntax example 2.

In Figure 3, the aspectual word "food" is modified by the emotion word "fresh". The emotion polarity could be positive; however, since "fresh" is not modified by the adverb "not", the emotion polarity of food should be negative.

The StanfordNLP syntactic parser used in this paper has more than 50 dependencies [27]. On the basis of a priori knowledge, we set larger weights for dependencies that are more important for aspectual word sentiment classification, such as amod, nsubj, and advmod, and smaller weights for other dependencies, such as det, punct, and cop. Here, the initialisation weight of important dependencies is set to 3, the weight of other dependencies is set to 0.5, and they are stored in the dependency dictionary wei.

After setting the dependency weights, we construct the dependency weighted adjacency matrix on the basis of the dependency weights. The construction method is shown in Equation (3).

$$A_{ij}^{weight} = \begin{cases} wei(r(i,j)) & i \neq j \; and \; \mathrm{j} \in \mathrm{N}(i) \\ 1 & i = j \\ 0 & other \end{cases}, \tag{3}$$

where $r(i,j)$ denotes the type of dependency relationship corresponding to node i and node j. The $wei(r(i,j))$ function denotes the weight of the relationship between node i and node j, and $N(i)$ denotes all the neighbouring nodes of node i. If node j is a neighbour node of node i (i.e., node i and node j are at a distance of 1), then the value of A_{ij}^{weight} is the weight of the relationship between node i and node j; otherwise, the value of A_{ij}^{weight} is 0. In addition to preserving the information of the node itself, we also add self-connected edges for the node, i.e., the value of node i with respect to itself is 1.

3.4. Graph Attention Network Layer

Ordinary GCNs are aggregated by averaging the characteristics of each of the node's neighbours. However, neighbouring nodes with different dependencies are of different importance to the aspect word nodes, and some may even lead to incorrect classification results. Therefore, this paper uses the GAT model for feature extraction of syntactic graphs.

The GAT network is essentially a variant of the upper GCN, where the attention weights of the current node and each neighbouring node are calculated according to the different importance of the neighbouring information and the weighted average when aggregating the neighbouring information. However, the use of the attention mechanism alone to calculate the neighbour node weights may cause the aspect nodes to focus too much on error messages. In this paper, we propose a graph attention network based on dependency weighting based on the GAT model. By adding dependency weights to the calculation of attention weights between neighbouring nodes, the model is trained to focus more on the important parts of the sentence by giving greater weights to important dependencies, as shown in Equation (4).

$$\partial = W^r A^{weight} + b. \tag{4}$$

Equation (4) shows the dependency weight matrix, where W^r and b are the weight and bias, respectively. The dependency weight matrix is set as a trainable parameter by setting the weights and biases, and the model dynamically adjusts the relationship weights during training according to the initial values we set.

The attention weights of different nodes are then calculated by weighting the dependencies, as shown in Figure 4. The calculation is shown in Equations (5) and (6).

$$e_{ij} = \partial_{ij}[Wh_i||Wh_j]. \tag{5}$$

$$a_{ij} = \frac{exp(LeakyRelu(\partial_{ij}[Wh_i||Wh_j]))}{\sum\limits_{u \in N(i)} exp(LeakyRelu(\partial_{iu}[Wh_i||Wh_u]))}. \tag{6}$$

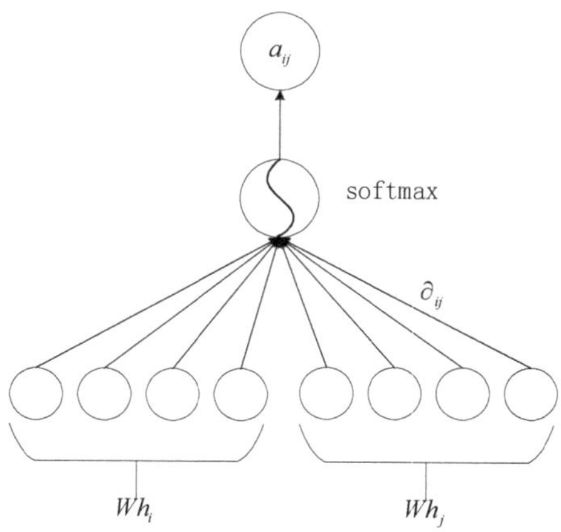

Figure 4. Attention calculation diagram.

Equation (5) calculates the attention weights of two nodes. The two nodes are stitched together by a linear transformation and multiplied by the corresponding relationship weights of the two nodes. ∂ is the weight of trainable dependencies in Equation (4), and $||$ is the splicing operation. Equation (6) performs a softmax operation on the computed attention mechanism so that it maps to a probability between 0 and 1, where $N(i)$ denotes the neighbouring nodes of node i, and $LeakyRelu()$ is the activation function.

Lastly, all neighbouring nodes of node i are multiplied by their corresponding attention weights for weighted summation, and the final attention characteristics of node i are obtained through the nonlinear layer, as shown in Equation (7).

$$h'_i = \sigma\left(\sum_{j\in N(i)} a_{ij}Wh_j\right). \tag{7}$$

To improve the model fitting ability, this paper adopts a multiheaded attention mechanism for information extraction. The calculation method is shown in Equation (8).

$$h'_i = \mathop{||}_{k=1}^{K} \sigma\left(\frac{1}{K}\sum_{k=1}^{K}\sum_{j\in N(i)} a_{ij}^{k}W^{k}h_j\right). \tag{8}$$

In Equation (8), σ is the activation function, where K denotes the number of attention heads. We obtain the feature h'_i of node i after aggregating information about its neighbours by multiplying the weights calculated from the K attention heads by the weighted average of the corresponding nodes. Lastly, we obtain the output vector $H' = \{h'_1, h'_2, \ldots h'_m\}$ of the dependency weighted graph attention network.

3.5. Emotional Classification Layer

As this paper implements a multiclassification task, a softmax function is used for the final sentiment classification. In this paper, the features extracted from the graph attention network layer are passed through a fully connected layer and a softmax layer to obtain the probability values of various sentiments of the corresponding aspect words. The feature with the highest probability is the final prediction result, as in Equation (9), where W and b are the weight and bias, respectively.

$$y\_pred = softmax(WH' + b). \tag{9}$$

The loss function of the model uses a cross-entropy loss function, as shown in Equation (10), where y is the true label. To prevent overfitting of the model, L2 regularisation is used in this paper to train parameters and weights, and λ is the regularisation parameter.

$$L(\theta) = -\sum ylog(y\_pred) + \lambda||\theta||_2. \quad (10)$$

4. Experiment

4.1. Dataset

This paper conducts experiments on publicly available aspect-based sentiment analysis datasets, namely, the Semeval2014 Task4 dataset [28] and the ACL-14 [29] dataset. Among them, Semeval2014 includes two review datasets, laptop and restaurant, and ACL-14 is a Twitter social review dataset. Each dataset is divided into a training set and a test set and has three types of labels: positive, negative, and neutral. The specific information of the three datasets is shown in Table 1.

Table 1. Experimental data statistics.

Dataset	Positive		Negative		Neutral	
	Train	Test	Train	Test	Train	Test
Laptop	994	341	870	128	464	169
Restaurant	2164	728	807	196	637	196
Twitter	1561	173	1560	173	3127	346

4.2. Hyperparameter Setting

In this paper, experiments are conducted on 12 models for each of the three datasets. Seven of the models are based on the Glove word vector, and five are based on the BERT pretrained model. The word embedding dimension is 300 for Glove and 768 for the BERT-pretrained model. As the BERT-pretrained model requires a relatively low learning rate while fine-tuning the shared layer [10], the learning rate is set to 2×10^{-5} for the BERT-based model and 1×10^{-3} for the Glove-based model. The BERT model used above is bert-base-uncased, and the sentiment pretrained model used in this paper is bert-base-uncased-emotion. Other hyperparameters are shown in Table 2.

Table 2. Training parameters.

Parameter	Value
Batch size	16
Dropout rate	0.1
Epoch	6
L2 regularisation coefficient	0.000001
Optimiser	Adam
Maximum sentence length	80

4.3. Evaluation Metrics

The main model evaluation metrics commonly used for sentiment analysis are accuracy, precision, recall, and F1 value. Accuracy indicates the proportion of correctly predicted samples with respect to all samples, as shown in Equation (11). Precision is the proportion of positive predictions in the sample that are actually positive, as shown in Equation (12). Recall is the proportion of positive cases in the original sample that are correctly predicted, as shown in Equation (13). The F1 value combines precision and recall and is the summed average of the two, as shown in Equation (14). Some of the datasets in this experiment have a large difference in the numbers of categories, while macro-F1 (macro-F1) can consider the number of each category and is more suitable for unevenly distributed samples, as shown in Equation (15). To evaluate the model results, accuracy and macro-F1 are used as evaluation metrics, and the model is tested five times on each of the three datasets. The best result is taken as the final result.

$$Accuracy = \frac{TP + TN}{TP + TN + FP + FN}, \tag{11}$$

$$Precision = \frac{TP}{TP + FP}, \tag{12}$$

$$Recall = \frac{TP}{TP + FN}, \tag{13}$$

$$F1 = \frac{2 \times TP}{N + TP \times TN}, \tag{14}$$

$$Macro - F1 = \frac{1}{n}\sum_{i=1}^{n} F1_i, \tag{15}$$

where N is the total number of samples, TP is the number of samples with positive labels predicted by the model to be positive, TN is the number of samples with negative labels predicted to be negative, FP is the number of samples with negative labels predicted to be positive, and FN is the number of samples with positive labels predicted to be negative.

4.4. Comparison Models

To verify the validity and reasonableness of the model proposed in this paper, 11 baseline models used in aspect-based sentiment analysis were selected for comparative analysis.

TD-LSTM [7]: LSTM is extended by using two LSTM networks to model a left context with a target and a right context with a target. The left and right target-dependent representations are connected and used to predict the affective polarity of the target.

ATAE-LSTM [8]: ATAE-LSTM is an improved AE-LSTM model. The aspect word vector is spliced with the context vector in the input part of the model and fed into the LSTM network, enabling the context hidden states to carry information from the aspects.

MEMNET [17]: MEMNET stores the context of a particular aspectual word into a memory network and captures the importance of the aspectual word in relation to the contextual word through an attention mechanism.

IAN [9]: This model proposes an interactive attention network that extracts contextual and aspectual features through two LSTM models and interactively learns the representation of context and aspectual words through an attention mechanism.

Bi-GCN [30]: Bi-GCN uses global lexical graphs to encode word co-occurrence information and designs interactive graph convolutional networks to learn syntactic and lexical graphs.

ASGCN [11]: A multilayer GCN is constructed to extract syntactic information based on the ability of LSTM to capture word order information, and a masking mechanism is used to remove non-aspect word information and retain only aspectual high-level features.

TD-GAT [22]: Syntactic graphs using aspectual targets directly linked to related targets are applied to GAT networks instead of word sequences, and node features are updated by LSTM.

BERT-SPC [18]: This model uses a pretrained BERT classification model to generate word vectors and extracts the vectors corresponding to the sign bit [CLS] for final classification based on each vector output from the BERT model containing full text information.

AEN-BERT [18]: This model uses BERT for pretraining to generate context and target word vectors and an attention encoder to model the context and target.

LCF-BERT [19]: This model uses a local context-focusing mechanism that uses a dynamic masking layer for contextual features and a dynamic weighting layer for contextual features to focus on local contextual words.

Mem + BERT [31]: The syntactic structure information is extracted using GCN, and the attention mechanism is used to fuse syntactic structure information, semantic information, lexical information, location information, and aspects.

SEDC-GCN [32]: A two-channel graph convolutional network model based on GCN structural enhancement is proposed.

R-GAT-BERT [24]: R-GAT-BERT involves the pruning of dependent syntactic graphs, reconstruction of syntactic graphs with aspectual words as root nodes, and feature extraction via relational graph attention networks.

SenticGCN [33]: This model incorporates affective common-sense knowledge into graph networks to facilitate model extraction of affective dependencies between contextual words and specific aspects.

4.5. Experiment Results

Table 3 shows the results of the different models on the three datasets, where data marked with "*" refer to the model results in the published paper, while "-" refers to the results not given in the original paper, and the bolded parts are the models in this paper. The model results show that, among the word vector-based models, the ATAE_LSTM, IAN, and AOA models based on the attention mechanism have better results than the TD_LSTM model based on LSTM alone on both the notebook and the restaurant datasets due to the inclusion of the attention mechanism. However, the static word vector limits the performance of the model, with accuracy rates on the Twitter, restaurant, and laptop datasets topping out at approximately 70%, 77%, and 72%, respectively. Moreover, as the attention mechanism cannot use the syntactic information of the text, it is possible to assign larger attention weights to irrelevant or even wrong word nodes, leading to classification errors and limiting the performance of the model. ASGCN and Bi-GCN use GCNs for text syntactic feature extraction and show a large improvement over the attention-based mechanism model on all three datasets. The GAT model improves the effect of the TD-GAT model compared to the above two GCN models due to the consideration of the different importance between different nodes. The BERT_SPC model combines aspect words with context as input only by constructing auxiliary sentence pairs, and then uses the first output vector of BERT for classification. The model is relatively simple but also achieves better results, with accuracy improvements of 1.77%, 1.91%, and 2.6% compared to the best static word vector-based model. The R-GAT model discards all dependencies between non-aspect words by pruning the dependency tree, which reduces redundant information but may also ignore information that is important for sentiment classification. The model in this paper sets the corresponding weights for the dependencies of different importance and optimises them through model training. The best results are improved by 1.39%, 0.89%, and 1.36% compared to those of the best model above, proving the effectiveness of the model.

Table 3. Experimental results contrasting.

Dataset	Twitter		Restaurant		Laptop	
	Acc	F1	Acc	F1	Acc	F1
TD-LSTM	-	-	75.63 *	-	68.13 *	-
ATAE-LSTM	-	-	77.20 *	-	68.70 *	-
MEMNET	68.50	67.48	77.36	67.36	71.56	65.34
IAN	67.92	65.61	76.47	67.49	71.88	66.16
ASGCN	70.95	69.46	77.92	69.98	73.41	69.05
Bi-GCN	70.12	68.94	78.25	70.21	74.15	69.12
TD-GAT	71.35	69.17	79.11	71.64	75.21	72.09
BERT-SPC	73.12	71.32	81.02	72.81	77.81	73.41
BERT-AEN	73.70	72.10	81.69	73.64	77.19	72.57
BERT-LCF	73.84	72.87	82.13	74.52	78.12	73.43
Mem-BERT	73.13	71.94	84.76	78.46	78.70	74.06
SEDC-GCN	73.56	71.34	84.33	79.12	77.74	74.68
R-GAT-BERT	74.86	72.52	84.55	78.34	78.73	75.12
SenticGCN	74.69	72.28	84.82	79.37	79.13	76.06
WGAT-SBERT	**76.25**	**74.56**	**85.71**	**80.23**	**80.49**	**77.21**

* in the table refers to the model results in the published paper.

4.6. Ablation Studies

To further verify the effect of the different modules of the model on the final experimental results, several sets of ablation experiments were performed on the three datasets above, as described below.

GAT-Glove: GAT-Glove performs word embedding using the Glove word vector and LSTM for feature extraction, trained by a general graph attention network.

WGAT-Glove: WGAT-Glove performs word embeddings using Glove word vectors and LSTM for feature extraction, trained with a relational weighted graph attention network.

GAT-SBERT: To verify the effect of dependency weighting on the experimental effect, the dependency weights are removed, and only the weights between two nodes are calculated by the attention mechanism.

WGAT-BERT: To verify the effect of sentiment pretrained models on experimental effects, word embeddings are performed on text using a pretrained model on a large-scale general corpus.

As shown in Table 4, changing either part of the model resulted in a lower final classification. First, the use of different word embedding methods had a large impact on the model effects. Both Glove word embedding-based models showed a significant decrease in effectiveness compared to the BERT word embedding-based models, demonstrating the powerful feature extraction capability of the BERT model. The BERT model pretrained on the sentiment corpus was better than the BERT model pretrained on the general corpus, which shows the positive effect of domain data on model training. The dependency weights also had a greater impact on the models for the same word embedding cases. The accuracy of the models increased by 2.13%, 3.2%, and 3.6% with the addition of dependency weights in the Glove word embedding case and 2.27%, 2.12%, and 2.37% with the addition of dependency weights in the SBERT word embedding case. This is because graph attention networks may assign larger attention weights to unimportant nodes in the process of calculating the importance between two nodes. With the addition of dependency weights, the model can assign greater attention weights to nodes that have a strong influence on the classification, reducing the interference of non-disjoint points, with a significant improvement in accuracy.

Table 4. Ablation experiment.

Dataset	Twitter		Restaurant		Laptop	
	Acc	F1	Acc	F1	Acc	F1
GAT-Glove	69.92	67.68	76.64	67.91	72.35	67.37
WGAT-Glove	72.05	69.23	79.84	70.11	75.95	72.24
GAT-SBERT	73.12	71.39	83.16	76.69	77.12	73.50
WGAT-BERT	75.13	72.76	84.75	78.53	79.32	76.03
WGAT-SBERT	**76.25**	**74.56**	**85.71**	**80.23**	**80.49**	**77.21**

4.7. Effect of Initial Values of Weights

To study the effect of the initialisation weights of the dependencies on the effectiveness of the model, we set different initialisation weights for the dependencies and conducted comparative experiments to observe the results and explore the best initialisation weights. Here, we denote the important dependency weights mentioned in Section 3.2 (a) and denote the other dependency weights (b). The range of a values is [1,5], and the range of b values is [0.1, 1]. The control variable method was used to find the optimal solution, and the experimental results are shown in Figure 5.

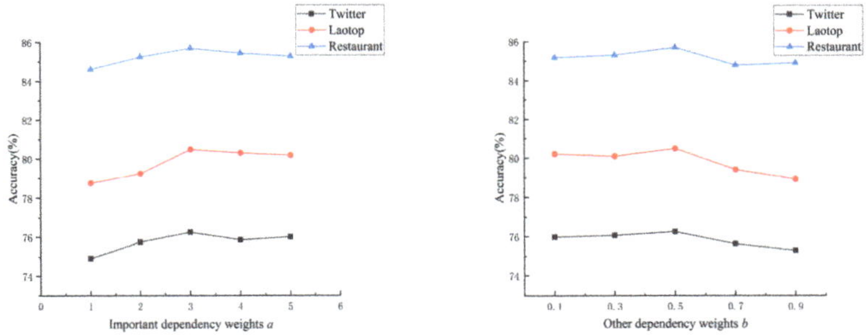

(**a**) Important dependency weights a (**b**) Other dependency weights b

Figure 5. Performance of WGAT model on each dataset under different a and b.

In Figure 5a, $b = 3$, and different values of a are set. The accuracy of the model increases as the value of a decreases, and the model performance is optimal when $a = 0.5$, after which the model performance stabilises and decreases as the value of a decreases. In Figure 5b, $a = 0.5$, and different values of b are set. As the value of b increases, the accuracy of the model gradually increases and reaches an optimum performance at $b = 3$. Figure 5a,b show that setting larger a values and smaller b values allows the model to assign greater weight to important dependencies when calculating attention scores, which helps to improve classification accuracy. However, too large a values or too small b values may also lead to a degradation in model performance. This is due to the model focusing too much on important dependencies, which may lead to classification errors in some specific sentence types. For example, in the sentence "The staff should be more friendly.", the adjective "friendly" modifies the aspect word "staff" through the dependency nsubj, and the adverb "more" modifies the emotive word "friendly" through the dependency advmod. When $a < 0.5$ and $b > 3$, the aspectual word "staff" is predicted to be positive. However, since this sentence is a dummy, the aspectual word is negative.

4.8. Visualisation of Attention Mechanisms

WGAT makes the model focus more on the words that contribute more to the aspect words in the calculation of attention through dependencies. Here, we visualise the attention weights for the sentence "Great food but the service is dreadful!". The attention weights for this sentence are shown in Figure 6.

(**a**) Unweighted attention weight matrix (**b**) Weighted attention weight matrix

Figure 6. Attention visualisation.

As shown in the figure, it is possible for GAT to assign larger weights to unimportant words when calculating the attention of two nodes. For example, the attention weights calculated without relational weights in Figure 6a, where the aspect word "food" is assigned a larger weight for "dreadful", may cause the model to predict "food" as being negative, affecting model accuracy. The addition of dependency weights in Figure 6b allows the aspectual word "food" to focus more on "great" and the aspectual word "service" to focus more on "dreadful", reducing the interference of irrelevant words in the sentiment classification of aspectual words. The example in the figure above shows that the weights we set are better able to help the model find sentiment words corresponding to aspect words during the training process.

5. Conclusions

In this paper, we proposed a graph attention network aspect-level sentiment analysis model (WGAT) based on the weighting of dependencies. On the one hand, the influence of different dependencies on sentiment classification is analysed, corresponding weights are set for them, and the optimal weights are found through experiments. On the other hand, the incorporation of relational weights into the graph attention network allows the model to pay more attention to words that are more important to the aspectual sentiment and to ignore words that have a negative impact on the outcome during the training process. In addition, this paper achieved better results by using a BERT model pretrained on a sentiment corpus for word embedding of text. According to comparative experiments on three datasets, the WGAT model achieved the best results in terms of accuracy and F1 values compared to other baseline models, demonstrating the effectiveness of our approach. We also analysed specific cases of this to show more visually how relational weighting contributes to our task.

Although our model achieves better results, it is significantly less accurate than the normal text when faced with abnormal text (e.g., Twitter dataset). In addition, the model sometimes fails to correctly identify the sentiment in complex sentences such as virtual speech, leading to errors in judgment. In the future, more in-depth syntactic analysis will be conducted on more complex sentences to improve the prediction accuracy.

Author Contributions: Conceptualisation, T.J., Z.W., M.Y. and C.L.; data curation, T.J., Z.W., M.Y. and C.L.; methodology, T.J. and Z.W.; writing—original draft, T.J. and Z.W. All authors have read and agreed to the published version of the manuscript.

Funding: This research was funded by the National Natural Science Foundation of China, grant number 61871258.

Data Availability Statement: https://alt.qcri.org/semeval2014/task4/ (accessed on 7 March 2023).

Conflicts of Interest: The authors declare no conflict of interest.

References

1. Zhang, L.; Wang, S.; Liu, B. Deep Learning for Sentiment Analysis: A Survey. *Wiley Interdiscip. Rev. Data Min. Knowl. Discov.* **2018**, *8*, e1253. [CrossRef]
2. Wang, T.; Yang, W. Review of Text Sentiment Analysis Methods. *Comput. Eng. Appl.* **2021**, *57*, 11–24.
3. Zhang, Y.; Li, T. Review of Comment-oriented Aspect-based Sentiment Analysis. *Comput. Sci.* **2020**, *47*, 7. [CrossRef]
4. Tang, X.; Liu, G. Research Review on Fine-grained Sentiment Analysis. *Libr. Inf. Serv.* **2017**, *61*, 132–140.
5. Wang, S.Y.; Yuan, K. Sentiment analysis model of college student forum based on RoBERTa-WWM. *Comput. Eng.* **2022**, *48*, 292–298, 305.
6. Shen, Y.; Zhao, X. A Review of Research on Aspect-based Sentiment Analysis based on Deep Learing. *Inf. Techol. Stand.* **2020**, *1*, 50–53.
7. Tang, D.; Qin, B.; Feng, X.; Liu, T. Effective LSTMs for target-dependent sentiment classification. In Proceedings of the 26th International Conference on Computational Linguistics, Osaka, Japan, 11–16 December 2016; pp. 3298–3307.
8. Wang, Y.; Huang, M.; Zhu, X.; Zhao, L. Attention-based LSTM for aspect-based sentiment classification. In Proceedings of the 2016 Conference on Empirical Methods in Natural Language Processing, Austin, TX, USA, 1–5 November 2016; pp. 606–615.
9. Ma, D.; Li, S.; Zhang, X.; Wang, H. Interactive attention networks for aspect-based sentiment classification. In Proceedings of the 26th International Joint Conference on Artificial Intelligence, Melbourne, Australia, 19–25 August 2017; pp. 4068–4074.

10. Meng, F.; Feng, J.; Yin, D.; Chen, S.; Hu, M. Sentiment Analysis with Weighted Graph Convolutional Networks. In *EMNLP (Findings)*; Association for Computational Linguistics: Stroudsburg, PA, USA, 2020; pp. 586–595.
11. Zhang, C.; Li, Q.; Song, D. Aspect-based Sentiment Classification with Aspect-specific Graph Convolutional Networks. In Proceedings of the 2019 Conference on Empirical Methods in Natural Language Processing and the 9th International Joint Conference on Natural Language Processing, Hong Kong, China, 3–7 November 2019; ACL: Stroudsburg, PA, USA, 2019; pp. 4560–4570.
12. Mubarok, M.S.; Adiwijaya; Aldhi, M.D. Aspect-based sentiment analysis to review products using Naïve Bayes. *AIP Conf. Proc.* **2017**, *1867*, 020060.
13. Kiritchenko, S.; Zhu, X.; Cherry, C.; Mohammad, S. NRC-Canada-2014: Detecting Aspects and Sentiment in Customer Reviews. In Proceedings of the 8th International Workshop on Semantic Evaluation, Dublin, Ireland, 23–24 August 2014; pp. 437–442.
14. Devlin, J.; Chang, M.W.; Lee, K.; Toutanova, K. Bert: Pre-training of deep bidirectional Transformer for language understanding. In Proceedings of the 2019 Conference of the North American Chapter of the Association for Computational Linguistics: Human Language Technologies, Minneapolis, MN, USA, 2–7 June 2019; Association for Computational Linguistics: Stroudsburg, PA, USA, 2019; pp. 4171–4186.
15. Mikolov, T.; Sutskever, I.; Chen, K.; Corrado, G.; Dean, J. Distributed representations of words and phrases and their compositionality. In Proceedings of the 27th Annual Conference on Neural Information Processing Systems 2013, Lake Tahoe, NV, USA, 5–10 December 2013; pp. 3111–3119.
16. Pennington, J.; Socher, R.; Manning, C.D. Glove: Global Vectors for Word Representation. In Proceedings of the 2014 Conference on Empirical Methods in Natural Language Processing (EMNLP), Doha, Qatar, 25–29 October 2014; pp. 1532–1543.
17. Tang, D.; Qin, B.; Liu, T. Aspect level sentiment classification with deep memory network. In Proceedings of the 2016 Conference on Empirical Methods in Natural Language Processing, Austin, TX, USA, 1–5 November 2016; pp. 214–224.
18. Song, Y.; Wang, J.; Jiang, T.; Liu, Z.; Rao, Y. Targeted sentiment classification with attentional encoder network. In *International Conference on Artificial Neural Networks*; Springer: Cham, Switzerland, 2019; pp. 93–103.
19. Zeng, B.; Yang, H.; Xu, R.; Zhou, W.; Han, X. LCF: A Local Context Focus Mechanism for Aspect-Based Sentiment Classification. *Appl. Sci.* **2019**, *9*, 3389. [CrossRef]
20. Tang, X.; Xiao, L. Research on Micro-Blog Topics Mining Model on Dependency Parsing. *Inf. Sci.* **2021**, *57*, 11–24.
21. Kipf, T.N.; Welling, M. Semi-supervised classification with graph convolutional networks. *arXiv* **2016**, arXiv:1609.02907.
22. Huang, X.; Carley, K. Syntax-aware aspect level sentiment classification with graph attention networks. In Proceedings of the Conference on Empirical Methods in Natural Language Processing and the 9th International Joint Conference on Natural Language Processing(EMNLP-IJCNLP), Hong Kong, China, 3–7 November 2019; pp. 5469–5477.
23. Veličković, P.; Cucurull, G.; Casanova, A.; Romero, A.; Liò, P.; Bengio, Y. Graph attention networks. *arXiv* **2017**, arXiv:1710.10903.
24. Wang, K.; Shen, W.; Yang, Y.; Quan, X.; Wang, R. Relational Graph Attention Network for Aspect-based Sentiment Analysis. In Proceedings of the 58th Annual Meeting of the Association for Computational Linguistics, Online, 6–8 July 2020; pp. 3229–3238.
25. Vaswani, A.; Shazeer, N.; Parmar, N.; Uszkoreit, J.; Jones, L.; Gomez, A.N.; Kaiser, Ł.; Polosukhin, I. Attention is all you need. In Proceedings of the 31st Conference on Neural Information Processing Systems (NIPS 2017), Long Beach, CA, USA, 4–9 December 2017; p. 30.
26. Zhang, D.; Huang, L.; Zhang, R.; Xue, H.; Lin, J.; Yao, L. Fake Review Detection Based on Joint Topic and Sentiment Pre-Training Model. *J. Compt. Res. Dev.* **2021**, *58*, 1385–1394.
27. de Marneffe, M.C.; Manning, C.D. *Stanford Typed Dependencies Manual*; Technical report; Stanford University: Stanford, CA, USA, 2008.
28. Pontiki, M.; Galanis, D.; Pavlopoulos, J.; Papageorgiou, H.; Androutsopoulos, I.; Manandhar, S. SemEval-2014 task 4: Aspect based sentiment analysis. In Proceedings of the 8th International Workshop on Semantic Evaluation, Dublin, Ireland, 23–24 August 2014; 24 August 2014; pp. 27–35.
29. Dong, L.; Wei, F.; Tan, C.; Tang, D.; Zhou, M.; Xu, K. Adaptive recursive neural network for target-dependent twitter sentiment classification. In Proceedings of the 52nd Annual Meeting of the Association for Computational Linguistics, Baltimore, Maryland, 22–27 June 2014; Volume 2, pp. 49–54, Short papers.
30. Zhang, M.; Qian, T. Convolution over Hierarchical Syntactic and Lexical Graphs for Aspect Level Sentiment Analysis. In *Empirical Methods in Natural Language Processing*; Association for Computational Linguistics: Stroudsburg, PA, USA, 2020; pp. 3540–3549.
31. Wang, G.; Li, H.; Qiu, Y.; Yu, B.; Liu, T. Aspect-based Sentiment Classification via Memory Graph Convolutional Network. *J. Chin. Inf. Process.* **2021**, *35*, 98–106.
32. Zhu, L.; Zhu, X.; Guo, J.; Dietze, S. Exploring rich structure information for aspect-based sentiment classification. *J. Intell. Inf. Syst.* **2022**, *60*, 97–117. [CrossRef]
33. Liang, B.; Su, H.; Gui, L.; Cambria, E.; Xu, R. Aspect-based sentiment analysis via affective knowledge enhanced graph convolutional networks. *Knowl.-Based Syst.* **2022**, *235*, 107643. [CrossRef]

information

MDPI

Article

Graph-Based Extractive Text Summarization Sentence Scoring Scheme for Big Data Applications

Jai Prakash Verma [1], Shir Bhargav [1], Madhuri Bhavsar [1], Pronaya Bhattacharya [2,3], Ali Bostani [4], Subrata Chowdhury [5,*], Julian Webber [6] and Abolfazl Mehbodniya [6,*]

1 Department of Computer Science and Engineering, Institute of Technology, Nirma University, Ahmedabad 382481, Gujarat, India; shirbhargav18@gmail.com (S.B.)
2 Department of Computer Science and Engineering, Amity School of Engineering and Technology, Amity University, Kolkata 700135, West Bengal, India; pbhattacharya@kol.amity.edu
3 Research and Innovation Cell, Amity University, Kolkata 700135, West Bengal, India
4 College of Engineering and Applied Sciences, American University of Kuwait, Salmiya 20002, Kuwait
5 Department of Computer Science and Engineering, Sreenivasa Institute of Technology and Management Studies, Chittoor 517127, Andra Pradesh, India
6 Department of Electronics and Communication Engineering, Kuwait College of Science and Technology (KCST), 7th Ring Road, Kuwait City 13133, Kuwait; jwebber@ieee.org
* Correspondence: subrata895@gmail.com (S.C.); a.niya@kcst.edu.kw (A.M.)

Abstract: The recent advancements in big data and natural language processing (NLP) have necessitated proficient text mining (TM) schemes that can interpret and analyze voluminous textual data. Text summarization (TS) acts as an essential pillar within recommendation engines. Despite the prevalent use of abstractive techniques in TS, an anticipated shift towards a graph-based extractive TS (ETS) scheme is becoming apparent. The models, although simpler and less resource-intensive, are key in assessing reviews and feedback on products or services. Nonetheless, current methodologies have not fully resolved concerns surrounding complexity, adaptability, and computational demands. Thus, we propose our scheme, *GETS*, utilizing a graph-based model to forge connections among words and sentences through statistical procedures. The structure encompasses a post-processing stage that includes graph-based sentence clustering. Employing the Apache Spark framework, the scheme is designed for parallel execution, making it adaptable to real-world applications. For evaluation, we selected 500 documents from the WikiHow and Opinosis datasets, categorized them into five classes, and applied the recall-oriented understudying gisting evaluation (ROUGE) parameters for comparison with measures ROUGE-1, 2, and L. The results include recall scores of 0.3942, 0.0952, and 0.3436 for ROUGE-1, 2, and L, respectively (when using the clustered approach). Through a juxtaposition with existing models such as BERTEXT (with 3-gram, 4-gram) and MATCHSUM, our scheme has demonstrated notable improvements, substantiating its applicability and effectiveness in real-world scenarios.

Keywords: text mining; extractive text summarization; sentence scoring scheme; graph analytics; graph-based clustering; opinion mining

1. Introduction

Modern Internet communication has shifted towards microblogging, community formation (on Twitter, Facebook, and other sites), and opinion-based polling. Most of the generated information falls under the wider umbrella of text mining (TM) schemes, where the data or information are gathered from devices and distributed to different users for consumption [1]. Another field is crowdsourcing [2], which includes the involvement of public opinions, work distribution, and community shares from a large group of persons. Mostly, the information is generated by mobile devices and the content is user-generated, with a significant amount of textual information. In social communities, many people post raw data, which need to be analyzed for opinions in real time to make informed decisions. The problem is considered challenging in TM applications as a micro-blog post is usually very short and colloquial, and traditional opinion mining algorithms in the TM scope do not cater to a one-fit-all scheme in such scenarios.

Thus, effective text analytics schemes have been widely studied over the last decade [3,5**?** ,6], which has improved interactions in human life. Social media, blogs, and e-shopping are those domains that have benefited from this study. A rich environment for expressing ideas about a variety of topics, including service providers, logistics, and e-commerce platforms, has been created within the social community landscape thanks to the growth in feedback channels, customer reviews, and polling systems [7]. The tremendous amount of data that have been produced by this ecosystem makes it difficult to sort through. Specialized mining approaches are needed to analyze these data to find patterns, preferences, and behavior. Deploying artificial intelligence (AI) models is also essential in light of the emergence of open application programming interfaces (APIs), which enable the seamless exchange of information across social media and e-commerce platforms. These models assist in trend forecasting and allow for a more complex comprehension of consumer behavior in the digital market. The concern, however, remains that the data are shared over open public channels (Internet), and, thus, at the security front, crypto-primitives and privacy preservation techniques are important [8]. Once data are collected, different statistical and machine learning (ML) models are built for text summarization (TS), from which effective predictions can be made, which facilitates business decisions in smart communities [9,10].

Considering the scenario of e-commerce portals, the text document generally includes reviews, comments, and feedback provided by users on the purchased product [11]. In such cases, document summarization becomes an effective tool for analysis [12] as it filters out important and necessary information from multiple text documents. However, on the downside, as the number (frequency) of documents generated increases, the prediction analytics models become bulkier and costlier, which limits organizations to implement them due to budgetary constraints [13]. This limitation presents the requirement of robust algorithms for abstractive text summarization (ATS) [14] systems, which generate summaries of the documents based on the provided ML algorithm [15]. Figure 1 shows the classification taxonomy of ATS, where a three-tier classification is presented, namely based on the file size, the summarization approach, and the summarization algorithm approach [14].

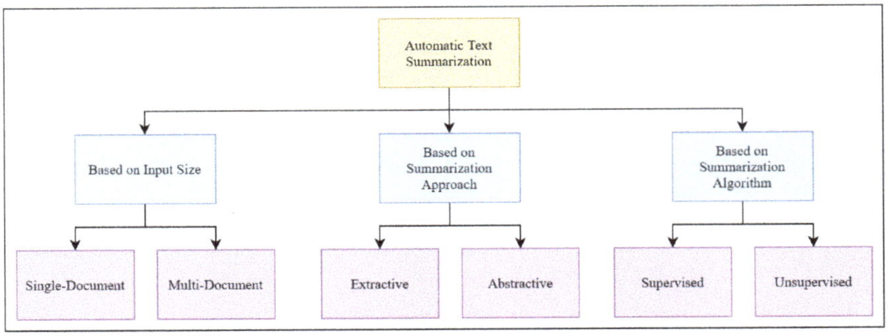

Figure 1. A classification taxonomy of ATS ecosystem [14].

Input-based ATS systems are further classified into two types, single-document and multi-document classification [16]. Single-document ATS, as the name suggests, summarizes the content of one document, whereas multiple-document ATS takes many documents in parallel and provides the summarization output [13]. Based on the document retrieval and semantic value obtained from the summary, an ATS is classified as an extractive or abstractive ATS, respectively [14]. An experimental review comparing abstractive and extractive summarization methods is presented in Refs. [17,18]. The review likely examines their effectiveness and performance in generating summaries. Computationally, Extractive ATSs are less computationally expensive but suffer from semantic misinterpretation. An ATS involves semantic nets and grammar rules, which renders it ineffective for real-time applications. It is useful in cases where the quality of information is more important and thus accurate summary generation is highly required. Further, the classifications can be both supervised and unsupervised for the extraction of relationships from the main text document [19–21]. The primary goal of this study is to implement extractive text summarization (ETS) in a big data analytics environment. Based on a comprehensive literature survey, we have considered a substantial volume of text for summarization while simultaneously reducing computational expenses. As a result, this paper advocates for a statistical analysis approach to text summarization in contrast to abstractive text summarization. The discussion on this subject is also prominently highlighted in the paper.

Mostly in big data applications, owing to the text content bulk, an extractive ATS is a preferred choice. Figure 2 presents a generic overview of the extractive ATS, which can be further classified into three phases.

1. *Pre-processing:* Most text mining big data are unstructured and in raw form, and, thus, pre-processing steps are required to handle the text documents, along with natural language processing (NLP) schemes [22]. With NLP, the pre-processing steps include noise removal from text [23]. The noise removal comprises steps like case removal, tokenization, stemming, stop-word removal, parts of speech tagging, and many others. Once data are pre-processed, two types of feature extraction mechanisms are presented based on sentence level and word level. Sentence-level features include sentence length, sentence position, and frequency of word type in a sentence. Word-level features include word-related statics like word type, term frequency inverse document frequency (TF-IDF), and other related schemes.
2. *Sentence Scoring*: In this phase, rank is calculated from the given sentences based on which sentence selection. Different methods of sentence scoring are employed, namely TF-IDF, TextRank, word2vec, and others based on the similarity of the occurrence of nouns and numerical values [24]. However, the method of rank calculation is not universal and differs based on end application requirements. Recently, graph-based schemes have used the ranking algorithm PageRank based on graph traversal. ML models pose summarization as a classification problem [25].
3. *Summary Generation*: This phase generates the initial summary based on the rank calculated in the previous phase. For a graph-based model, it just selects the top required number of sentences based on rank. An ML model then just selects the sentences and classifies them as a true label and generates the summary.
4. *Post-processing*: The initial summary often contains different sentences having the same information, which increases redundancy and decreases the overall quality of a generated summary. So, various redundancy elimination techniques are implemented in this phase. Grouping techniques like clustering and itemset mining are preferred in this phase to group similar types of sentences. Miscellaneous processes like rearranging the sentences in summary based on their occurrence in the original document or inclusion of additional information like tables, figures, equations, and others are conducted.

In the ETS scheme, the task is to generate a mined document that contains the important information, without any hindrance to the semantical construct. In such cases, graph-based schemes are proven to be highly effective [26]. Graph-based ETS methods are powerful enough to capture the underlying structure of the text and form a graph $G = \{V, E\}$, where the vertices V (nodes) are the sentences in the text and edges E denote the relationship. The edges are formed based on similarity and coherence criteria. Thus, they are better than feature-based ETSs as they tackle the complex relationships between sentences and can be extensible as new sentences (nodes) can be added as required. Thus, graph-based ETSs are adaptable and highly flexible. The popular graph-based ETS methods include PageRank, LexRank, TextRank, Sumbasic, and the ensemble methods [27,28].

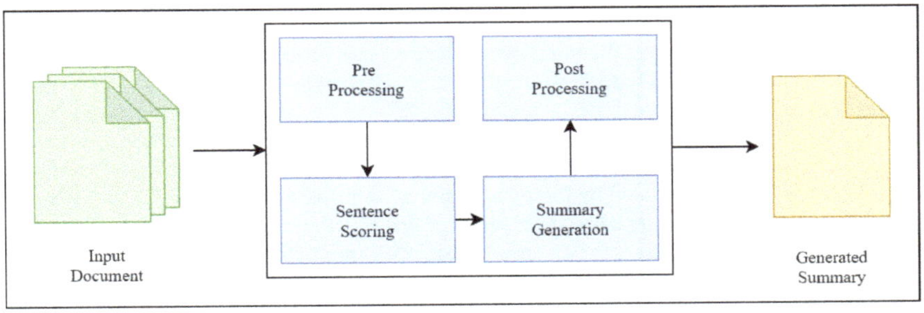

Figure 2. A generic model for extractive ATS [14].

1.1. An Illustration of Graph-Based ETS with Sentence Scoring Mechanism

In this subsection, we present the basics of graph algorithms to represent and process documents and illustrate the sentence scoring mechanism with details of ETS. Formally, we view a document as a graph $G = (V, E)$, where V represents a set of nodes and E presents a set of edges. Any node $v_i \in V$ corresponds to a sentence in the document, and an edge $(v_i, v_j) \in E$ indicates a semantic relationship between sentences v_i and v_j.

To indicate the strength of the semantic relationships between nodes and edges, we introduce weight w_{ij} of the edge connecting v_i and v_j. The weight computation is based on different similarity measures, like cosine similarity [29], Jaccard similarity [30], and semantic similarity [31]. Formally, the similarity measure Sim can be connected to w_{ij} as follows.

$$w_{ij} = Sim(v_i, v_j) \tag{1}$$

To score sentences, we consider the centrality measure, which quantifies the significance of the document (node) in the graph. A common choice is the degree of centrality, which is presented as follows.

$$C_D(v_i) = \sum_{j \in V} w_{ij} \tag{2}$$

The degree centrality $C_D(v_i)$ of a sentence v_i is thus the sum of the weights of the edges connected to it. Sentences with a higher degree of centrality are more likely to be selected for the summary as they are deemed more important.

As an example, let us consider four sentences as follows.

1. "The cat is on the roof."
2. "The dog is in the garden."
3. "The cat, from the roof, watches the dog."
4. "The dog is unaware of the cat."

The corresponding graph G would have four nodes, v_1, v_2, v_3, v_4, each representing a sentence. An edge is established between nodes that share semantic relationships, like, for example, between v_1 and v_3, and v_2, v_3, and v_4. Edge weights w_{ij} are assigned based on the strength of the semantic relationship. Applying the degree centrality measure, v_3 has the most connections (highest degree), and, thus, it would be deemed as an important sentence.

1.2. Novelty

In contemporary research, recent graph-based ETS schemes have instigated a migration towards optimized ranking algorithms. These algorithms are based to facilitate opinions, provide recommendation services, and work in a multitude of NLP applications. For ETS, in most of the existing approaches, simple heuristics (similarity matrix) are mainly used to rank the importance of nodes, which might not be the global picture of the entire text [32]. However, it is essential to recognize that these methods might not always capture the full contextual nuances and coherence necessary to represent the global picture of the entire text [33]. As research in ETS advances, there is a growing emphasis on exploring more sophisticated algorithms and techniques that can address the limitations of these heuristics and yield more comprehensive and cohesive extractive summaries. By delving into more context-aware and holistic models, ETS systems are striving to produce summaries that better reflect the overarching narrative and essence of the original text, thereby enhancing their utility and value for various applications. Motivated by these discussions, we present our scheme, *GETS*, which is tailored to extract use opinions based on sentence scoring algorithms. It enhances linguistic and contextual attributes, such as sentence length, relevance to the subject, and grammatical construction. Consequently, this fosters a superior level of semantic comprehension of the text, facilitating the creation of more refined and comprehensive summarizations. The scheme harbors the capacity to substantially augment the accuracy of the summaries generated, by integrating more sophisticated and exhaustive attributes into the scoring framework.

1.3. Research Contributions

The section provides the research objectives presented in the paper as follows.

1. Develop a graph-based sentence selection model to generate summaries for selected datasets. The text conversion to the graph model is conceptualized, and the relationships are presented.
2. Analyze the impact of sentence clustering as post-processing with the proposed scheme. Clustering applied at the post-processing level for the selection of the final summary can enhance the attainability of the summary of large documents.
3. Evaluate the proposed scheme by comparing it with the bidirectional encoder representations from Transformer (BERT)-based ETS.
4. The comparative analysis is presented in terms of ROUGE-1, ROUGE-2, and ROUGE-L for clustered and non-clustered work on the WikiHow dataset. The presented results indicate the scheme viability in real practical application setups.

1.4. Paper Organization

The rest of the paper is structured as follows. Section 2 presents a literature review and discusses the basic schemes and scoring algorithms that have been proposed by various researchers in the graph text summarization domain. Section 3 describes the proposed scheme with system architecture and execution of the proposed scheme and its components. Section 4 presents the methodology and concept applied to achieve defined objectives with a comparative analysis of various ranking algorithms. Sections 5 and 6 present the experimentation analysis, results, and discussion, respectively. Section 7 presents the conclusion and future scope for this paper. Table 1 shows the abbreviations and intended meanings used in the paper.

Table 1. Abbreviations and their meanings.

Abbreviations	Meanings	Abbreviations	Meanings
AI	Artificial Intelligence	LSTM	Long Short-Term Memory
ALBERT	A Lite BERT	ML	Machine Learning
API	Application Programming Interface	NLP	Natural Language Processing
ATS	Abstractive Text Summarization	NNW	Non-Noun Words
BERT	Bidirectional Encoder Representations from Transformers	POS	Parts of Speech
BLEU	Bilingual Evaluation Understudy	PPF	Positional Power Function
DBSCAN	Density-Based Spatial Clustering of Applications with Noise	RAKE	Rapid Automatic Keyword Extraction
ETS	Extractive Text Summarization	RDD	Resilient Distributed Datasets

Table 1. *Cont.*

Abbreviations	Meanings	Abbreviations	Meanings
GAN	Generative Adversarial Networks	ROBERTa	A Robustly Optimized BERT Pretraining Approach
GloVe	Global Vectors for Word Representation	ROUGE	Recall-Oriented Understudying Gisting Evaluation
GPT	Generative Pretrained Transformers	SCU	Summary Content Unit
GRU	Gated Recurrent Unit	SVD	Singular Value Decomposition
HITS	Hyperlink Induced Topic Search	TF-IDF	Term Frequency Inverse Document Frequency
IDF	Inverse Document Frequency	TM	Text Mining
LCS	Longest Common Subsequence	TS	Text Summarization
LSA	Latent Semantic Analysis	UMLS	Unified Medical Language Systems

2. Background Schemes

As discussed in the introduction section, researchers have demonstrated the capability of the graph in the ATS system. It ranges from the simple implementation, for example, PageRank, to various combinations to improve the specific task of an ETS system, like domain coverage or the semantic value of summary, and others. The details are presented as follows.

2.1. Graph Analytics Frameworks

With the surge in graph applications, many graph-related frameworks have been established [34,35]. Neo4j is one of them, which is ACID-compliant, open-source, and supports the REST for device-to-device communications. Meanwhile, the GraphX framework provides support for multiple data sources, like CSV, MySQL, AWS storage, and others. It also provides faster execution of graph operations by using a distributed computing environment with Spark's Resilient Distributed Datasets (RDDs) to persist the data in RAM for in-memory execution. Apart from these, various high-scale graph frames are also defined [34], like Pregel, a vertex-centric graph processing framework, Blogel, the block-level type of graph processing framework, and PEGASUS, which focuses on the matrix representation of a graph and improves the processing power for the matrix-related operations by implementing functionality on map-reduce architecture.

2.2. Graph Model Generation

Based on the vertex type used in the graph, the graph model can be further divided into two approaches: 1. sentence-centric approach [36] and 2. word-centric approach [37], discussed as follows. In the later sections, different ranking algorithms and similarities are discussed, which are mainly used in the sentence-centric approach.

Sentence-centric approach: This model uses a sentence as a node, and various similarity measures like cosine, Jaccard, and others are used as a weight of an edge between two nodes (sentences). After that, a node-ranking algorithm is used to calculate the rank of a node. Based on the rank, sentences are selected either for the summary directly or by using the post-processing steps. The sentence-based model is preferable over the word-based model because it is less complex, requires small numbers of computation steps, and is visually more understandable. However, it also has a drawback as these types of graphs are generally fully connected. So, for the document with a higher count of sentences, it loses its simplicity and becomes a computer-intensive model. Figure 3 shows the graph model proposed by [37], which is the fully connected graph. Figure 4 demonstrates a basic process to generate the graph-based model.

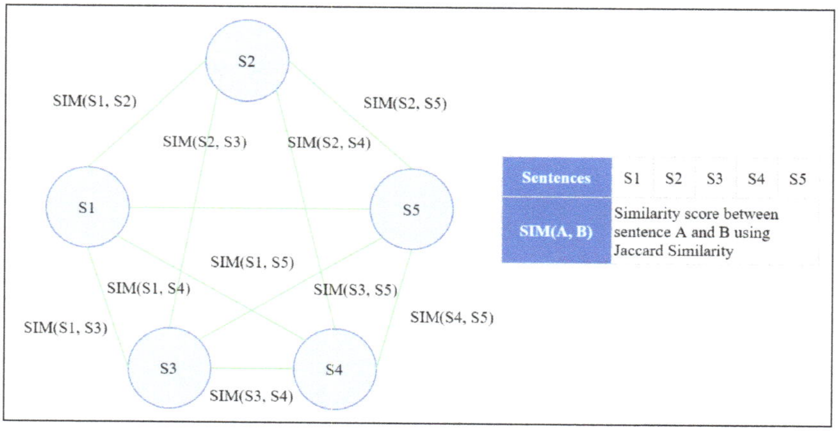

Figure 3. Sentence-based model proposed by [37].

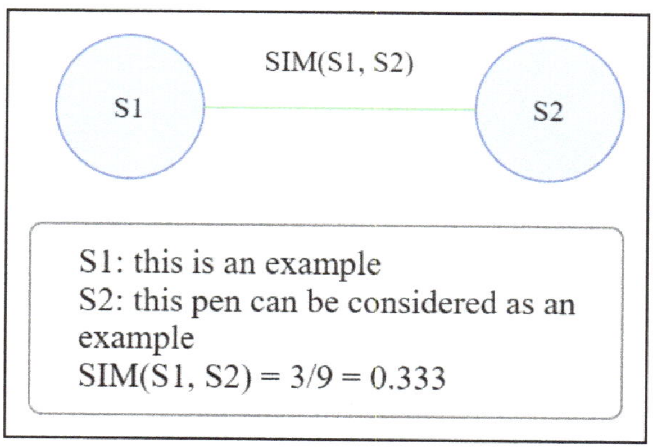

Figure 4. An example to generate sentence-centric model.

Word-centric approach: Opposite to the sentence-based model, the word is assigned as a node in a given scheme. The main challenge in this type of approach is to assign weights to the edges. Many parameters are considered, like N-gram pairs of words, adjacency words with position, POS tags, and others, but very few models have been implemented based on the given approach for the ATS system. There are several parameters behind this situation; first is the identification of a set of words for calculating the weight of the edge, as mentioned earlier, and the most impactful parameter is the number of words. With the comparison of the number of sentences, the count of words in each document is much higher, which leads to the high count of the nodes to represent in a graph as well as compute the high numbers of weights for each edge. So, in other words, this type of approach demands a more computation-intensive process. Some researchers have proposed a word-based model. We have used the model proposed by [38] to explain the basic idea behind this approach. Figure 5 shows the directed graph model proposed by them.

We first applied POS tagging to identify the grammar label of each word. Then, based on the grammar label, a graph is generated. As shown in Figure 5 above, they have assigned proper nouns as a node and words between two nouns as a directed edge. Each noun word has assigned some weight based on the position, count, occurrence in sections, and relation to the domain of the document. After the graph has been generated, each sentence is ranked by traversing words in the graph with respect to the given sentence. Averaged weight is assigned to sentences, based on which the sentence selection process takes place. To demonstrate the graph, we used a single sentence to generate its word graph, which is shown in Figure 6.

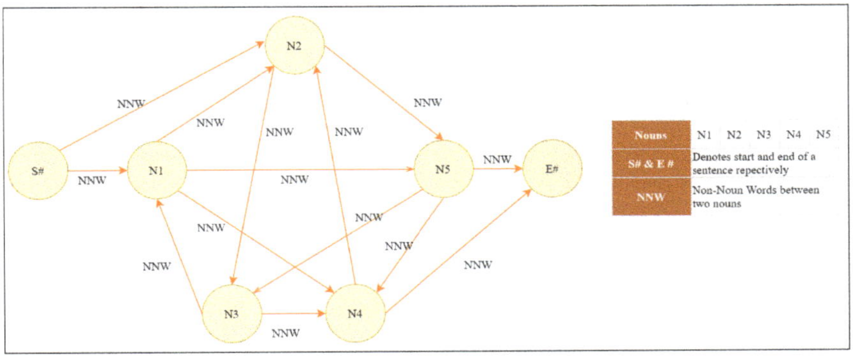

Figure 5. Word-based model proposed by [38].

In the sentence "In a word-based graph, a noun is represented as a node and other words between two nouns represented as a directed edge", "word", "graph", "noun", and "edge" are identified nouns in a test sentence, so these words will act as a node. Non-noun words (NNWs) are shown as an edge value. For example, in a sentence, NNW between ("Noun", "Edge") is "represented as a directed", which also reflects in a graph.

The similarity between sentences was measured using Jaccard similarity. As shown in Figure 6, it is a ratio between the common words and total words from both sentences. After this, a sentence-scoring algorithm has been applied to measure the node score. Then, with some post-processing steps, top-n sentences are selected for the summary.

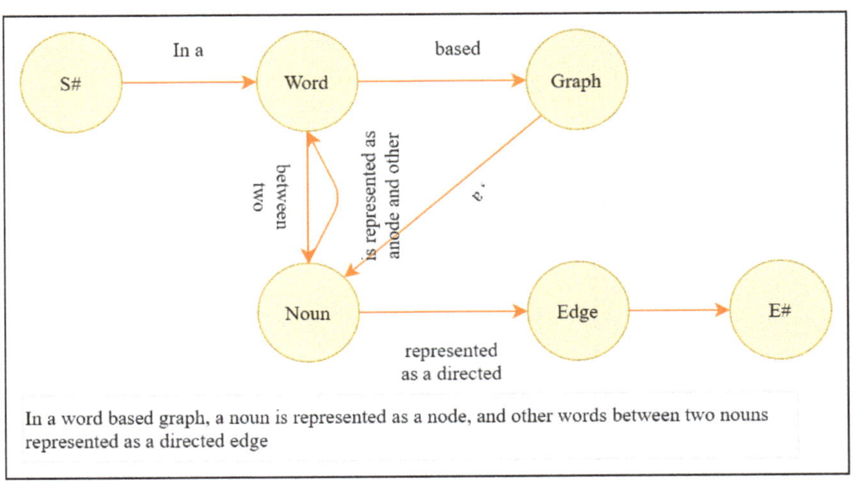

Figure 6. Example of word graph of a sentence.

2.3. *Sentence Scoring Algorithms with Graph-Based Analytics*

This section shows the sentence-scoring algorithms that can be applied with graph-based analysis models.

2.3.1. Hyperlinked Induced Topic Search (HITS)

As the name suggests, HITS is a link-ranking algorithm to identify important pages that contain information related to the search query. It was introduced by Jon Kleinberg in

1998 [39]. Even though it is targeted for webpage ranking in a WWW, it is used in many graph analytics processes. It calculates scores of the webpages based on pages that are linked with it as well as information stored in those pages. It generally maintains two parameters, 1. *Authorities:* It is a set webpage that contains highly related information related to the search query. 2. *HUBs:* It is a set of webpages with a link to the pages in authorities. So, HUB pages do not need to contain information regarding the search query.

2.3.2. PageRank

PageRank is another webpage ranking algorithm to estimate the importance of the webpage based on the number of pages that it links to and the quality of the pages. It was first presented by Sergey Brin and Lawrence Page [40]. PageRank mainly focuses on the outgoing links from webpages. Equation (3) provides the simplified version of PageRank.

$$PR(u) = \sum_{v \in B_u} \frac{PR(v)}{L(v)} \tag{3}$$

where u = Current webpage, B_u = Set of webpages linked to u, $L(v)$ = Number of outgoing links from webpage v, $PR(x)$ = PageRank of webpage x.

2.3.3. TextRank

TextRank is a widely used sentence-ranking method in the field of text summarization, originally proposed by [41]. It finds application in two essential areas of NLP: sentence ranking and keyword extraction. In both cases, the algorithm leverages the PageRank approach to analyze a generated graph. For keyword extraction, TextRank applies the PageRank algorithm to a directed word-based graph. This graph is constructed based on the occurrence of words in the sentences (see Figure 5 for reference). By utilizing this graph, TextRank effectively identifies and ranks keywords within the text. On the other hand, for sentence ranking, TextRank adopts a sentence-centric graph-based model and applies the PageRank model to rank the sentences [17,42,43]. This method allows TextRank to determine the importance of each sentence in the text, leading to an effective text summarization process. It combines outgoing links from sentences and nodes with the similarity between two sentences, as mentioned in Equation (4).

$$TR(u) = \sum_{v \in B_u} \frac{sim(u,v) * TR(v)}{L(v)} \tag{4}$$

where u = Current sentence node, B_u = Set of sentence node linked to u, $sim(u,v)$ = Similarity score between sentence node u and v, $L(v)$ = Number of outgoing links from sentence node v, $TR(x)$ = TextRank of sentence node x.

2.3.4. LexRank

All the above-mentioned ranking algorithms use similarity measures that either work with the frequency of words or use common words between sentences. They do not capture the weight of words based on their, e.g., keywords. LexRank tackles this problem by including an extra measurement called inverse document frequency (IDF). LexRank combines IDF with cosine similarity (IDF-modified cosine) and uses it along with the PageRank algorithm, which can be derived in Equation (5).

$$LR(u) = \sum_{v \in B_u} \frac{IDF\_modified\_sim(u,v) * LR(v)}{\sum_{z \in B_v} IDF\_modified\_sim(z,v)} \tag{5}$$

where u = Current sentence node, B_x = Set of sentence node linked to x (adjacent nodes of x), $IDF\_modified\_sim(u,v)$ = IDF based similarity score of sentence node u and v, $L(v)$ = Number of outgoing links from sentence node v, $LR(x)$ = LexRank of sentence node x.

Table 2 provides the abstract view of the usage of different ranking algorithms in the research area. From the table, it is clear that PageRank is a much more trusted and used sentence-scoring method by researchers in the summarization domain.

Table 2. Ranking algorithms in research area.

Ref.	Objective	Pros	Cons	Node	1	2	3	4	5
Moradi et al. [44]	Comparison of effects of different input encoders in graph-based models.	Inclusion of domain-specific word embedding improves the generated summary	Cannot be used for general-purpose summarization as it more relies on the domain of the document.	S	✓	X	X	✓	X
Alzuhair et al. [45]	Implementation the combinations of two similarity measures and two ranking algorithms to find the optimal one.	Can be used for both single and multiple document summarization.	Results comparison can be improved by including more similarity and ranking algorithms.	S	✓	X	X	✓	X
Yang et al. [46]	Use combined weightage of words, bigrams, and trigrams to generate better sentence scores.	An integrated graph can learn and use semantic relatedness from three different dimensions.	It may require a high amount of resources in case of a big number of documents.	S	X	✓	X	X	X
Bhargava et al. [47]	Improve semantic values in summary by considering word position and overlapping of words.	A simple POS tag can be used to improve semantic value in summary.	A model can be complex for an extractive ATS system.	W	X	X	X	X	✓
Mao et al. [48]	Optimal balance between machine learning and graph-based sentence selection method.	ML model and graph model combined provide a better summary.	Author has not implemented any redundancy handling technique.	S	X	X	✓	X	X
Fang et al. [37]	Inclusion of importance of words during sentence score calculation to improve the sentence selection process.	Less complex and easy to implement	The assumption has taken that, initially, all words have the same weightage.	S	✓	X	X	X	X
El-Kassas et al. [38]	Induce word's weightage based on its type and position to improve the sentence selection process.	Model can generate great results for domain-specific documents or scientific papers.	Complex to implement; may require a high amount of resources.	W	X	X	X	X	✓

1: PageRank; 2: TextRank; 3: LexRank; 4: Hyperlinked Induced Topic Search (HITS); 5: Word-based; S: Sentence; W: Word; X: None.

3. Literature Review

Text summarization with basic features has been demonstrated in earlier research works. In our literature review, the oldest research work in text summarization was performed on scientific documents. In 1958, Ref. [49] proposed the method for summarization using basic features like word frequency, phrase frequency, and position in the sentence. In 1969, Ref. [50] performed the same task but used key phrases as an extra feature. After that, a better probabilistic model and features were introduced. Research work published by [51] in 1999 used the naïve Bayes classifier with the TF-IDF feature for improvement in the summarization model. After this, new methods like graph ranking algorithms and machine learning/deep learning models have been introduced. Recent research work has mainly focused on these methods.

Table 3 shows a comparative analysis of methodologies used by researchers in different models for text summarization processes. It shows that researchers mainly used schemes like extractive or abstractive text summarization on single or multiple documents [52]. The methodologies like deep learning, machine learning, data mining, and graph-based text summarization are compared along with the findings. The methodologies presented in these papers are mainly emphasizing preprocessing steps. It has emerged that improvised text summarization can be achieved by applying post-processing with a text summarizing model. Sentence selection algorithms are generally used to display sentences with the most information. They have various applications in different domains [53]. Nowadays, many users buy from e-stores and review the products. Most purchases are completed based on these reviews given by the users, but reading all reviews can be time-consuming. The solution to this problem is to select a certain amount of top sentences from all reviews and display them as a summarized review.

Table 3. Comparativeanalysis of state-of-the-art schemes.

Author	Methodology	Type	1	2	3	4	5	I/p Type
Patel et al. [54]	Combination of word-level and sentence-level features to obtain best results for multiple documents. Word Features: Given fixed weightage to a word based on its specific position (title, keyword), type (noun, numerical), and domain. Sentence Features: Sentence position, length, and cosine similarity.	E	X	X	X	✓	X	M
Mao et al. [48]	Use of LexRank for calculating scoring of node. Three models: (1) Linear combination. (2) Use graph score as a feature. (3) Use the decision of supervised result in graph scoring.	E	✓	X	✓	X	X	S
Van Lierde et al. [55]	Use DBSCAN for semantic clustering of words to generate a topic-based model with the constructed hypergraph	E	X	X	✓	X	✓	S
Chaves et al. [15]	Calculate cosine similarity between sentence words and keywords as well as with words of other sentences. Obtain averaged similarity of all words in a sentence and assign it as a sentence score.	E	X	✓	X	X	X	S
Jindal et al. [56]	Apply TF-TDF and rapid automatic keyword extraction (RAKE) for word-level features. Find optimal no. of clusters and apply fuzzy c clustering for sentence-level features.	E	X	X	X	✓	✓	S
Du et al. [57]	Apply genetic algorithm for optimal weights of above features. Uses a fuzzy logic system to calculate sentence scores.	E	X	X	X	✓	✓	S
Moradi et al. [58]	Find topic-wise using itemset mining. Apply hierarchical clustering on support values to group similar types of sentences.	E	X	X	X	✓	✓	Both
Bhargava et al. [59]	Label generation by mapping document and its pre-summary made by human. Convert sentence to vector using embedded layer. Then, pass it through the convolution layer for feature extraction.	E	X	✓	X	X	X	S
Anand et al. [60]	Generate labeled data by using various similarity measures between legal documents and head notes. Generate embedded vector combined with cosine similarity.	E	X	✓	X	X	X	M
Alami et al. [61]	Generation of word2vec model. Used three variations of autoencoders: a. auto encoder b. variation AR c. extreme learning machine AE 3. Use the voting method to obtain cumulative ranks of sentences.	E	X	✓	X	X	X	S
Azadani et al. [62]	Map document to concept using MetaMap developed for Unified Medical Language System (UMLS). Use the itemset mining method to obtain frequent itemsets from documents. Jaccard similarity to obtain similarity measure between two itemsets.	E	X	X	✓	X	✓	S
Liang et al. [63]	Combination of cross-entropy and reinforcement learning to improve performance of seq2seq attention model	A	X	X	X	X	X	S
Adelia et al. [64]	Vectorize sentence with word2vec model.	A	X	✓	X	X	X	S
Moirangthem et al. [65]	Seq2seq attention model and pointer generator network. Improve performance of model and sentiment value of summary for large documents.	A	X	✓	X	X	X	S
Ghodratnama et al. [13]	Posed as a classification problem. First cluster the sentences and then send information to the classifier for weight updating of features. Linguistic feature: each sentence is a subgraph of three forms: subject, predicate, and object.	E	X	X	X	X	✓	M
Guo et al. [66]	Improvement in the grammar of summary. Used pointer network for out-of-vocabulary problems. Multi-head self-attention model is used to generate a semantic summary.	A	X	✓	X	X	X	S
Mackey et al. [12]	Generate an inverted index of training dataset in Hadoop. Use the TF-IDF score to rank sentences.	E	X	X	X	X	X	S
Cagliero et al. [67]	Generate word to sentence frequent itemset matrix. Apply Singular Value Decomposition (SVD) on the resulting matrix to identify concepts covered by sentences. Select the sentence with the most covered concepts.	E	X	X	X	X	✓	S
Fang et al. [37]	Calculate word's rank using sentence rank. Calculate new sentence rank by using the weight of every word. Use a linear combination of each sentence rank as sentence selection rank	E	X	X	✓	X	X	S
Giarelis et al. [17]	Presented an in-depth analysis on the TS process, datasets, and outlined the evaluation methods and metric selection principles	Both A and E	✓	✓	N	N	✓	M
El-Kassas et al. [38]	Calculate node weightage using parameters like word type, the domain of the word, and the position of the word in the document (e.g., title, subject, keyword, etc.). Generate candidate summary by calculating the average weight nodes of the selected path. Apply K-means clustering in the candidate summary to remove redundancy.	E	X	X	✓	X	✓	M
Alomari et al. [18]	A comprehensive review of the application of deep reinforcement learning and transfer learning techniques in the context of abstractive text summarization. The study delves into the current state-of-the-art works and explores how these methods can be utilized to generate concise and coherent summaries from large textual content.	A	X	✓	X	X	✓	M

E: Extractive; A: Abstractive; 1: Machine Learning; 2: Deep Learning; 3: Graph; 4: Fuzzy-logic-based; 5: Data Mining Techniques (Itemset mining and clustering); S: Single Document; M: Multiple Documents.

With the recent research advancements in machine learning methods, researchers proposed many models for extractive text summarization with machine learning models. Oussam Rouane et al. [68] proposed a model with K-means clustering for concept recognition, which prevents the repetition of a particular type of sentence and covers the major concepts in a generated summary. Chih-Fong Tsai et al. [69] utilized multiple reviews of a hotel by classifying it into a helpful review or not and used this feature to improve the sentence-scoring method. Mudasir Mohd et al. [70] derived a novel method for sentence ranking, which is applied to clusters generated with the use of K-means clustering on word2vec vectors. B. Cao et al. [71] present an unsupervised learning-based text summarization approach for short text extracted for patients about their disease with consideration of privacy issues.

Deep learning models have also promised a significant amount of advancement in document summarization [46]. Recurrent neural network (RNN) and its different variants are one of the most preferred models by researchers because of their capability to model complex underlying relationships in sequential data. Mohamed Seghir Hadj Ameur et al. [72] used a bi-directional gated recurrent unit (GRU) to learn dependencies between words for extractive text summarization. Qingyu Zhou et al. [73] applied a two-layer normalized RNN model on vectors encoded (BERT) to extract summary sentences, which are also discussed in [74]. Rupal Bhargava et al. [36] proposed a paraphrase detection algorithm to reduce redundancy in the text by removing similar paraphrases along with generative adversarial network (GAN).

Milad Moradi et al. [44] proposed an undirected graph model with sentence vectors as nodes and cosine similarity as the weight of an edge. They used bidirectional encoder representations from Transformers (BERT) encoding for sentence2vec conversion. Three different ranking algorithms, PageRank, HITS, and positional power function (PPF), are used to calculate sentence rank. Abeer Alzuhair et al. [45] compared different similarity measures and ranking methods in an undirected weighted graph model. Cosine similarity, Jaccard similarity, and identity similarity are used for similarity measures comparison and PageRank and HITS for a ranking method comparison. Kang Yang et al. [46] implemented three different graph models by including three different sets of extra information with the sentence as a node and cosine similarity as a weighted edge. They used words along with their POS tags, Bigrams, and Trigrams as extra information for each graph, respectively. The TextRank method has been used to rank a sentence on a single graph made by combining all three different graphs using a naïve Bayesian fashion. Rupal Bhargava et al. [47] used a directed graph model for ATS with the use of the word, its POS-Tag, and its relative position in sentences.

4. *GETS*: The Proposed Scheme

In this paper, the graph-based sentence-centric scheme for the selection of representative sentences to generate a summary for the given input text approach is proposed, in which sentence is used as a node and Jaccard similarity as a weight of the edge between nodes (sentences). We used the ROUGE metric to evaluate the model. It demonstrates the influence of words in the sentence-scoring process. To generate an improved version of the summary, one of the important parameters can be word weightage. So, we have identified and implemented one extra process that can be employed to extend the capabilities of the proposed scheme, which is implemented in the data pre-processing phase and post-processing phase. Figure 7 shows the complete process flow and execution flow with different components of the proposed scheme.

4.1. System Architecture and Flowchart

As shown in Figure 7, the given model can be divided into three parts: 1. pre-processing—containing text pre-processing and feature extraction; 2. processing; and 3. post-processing, described as follows and also shown in Figure 8. The process starts with sentence segmentation, which extracts sentences from the raw CSV. Consequently, a sentence-level CSV is generated and saved in a Spark-based database. PySpark APIs will then be used to perform all actions on the Spark tables. Pre-processing includes fundamental operations like lowercasing, white noise removal, etc. The flow continues with additional activities, including POS tagging and Jaccard similarity calculation, which aid in rank generation during the processing stage. The feature extraction flow involves word frequency computation and keyword generation, both of which contribute to word weighting. Graphs are generated using the Jaccard similarity score in the process flow, and a combined rank is determined using the random walk algorithm and word weighting. Subsequently, the flow splits into two branches. The first branch generates summaries based on the combined rank, while the second branch utilizes GraphFrames to perform graph clustering on the sentence graphs, producing a cluster-based rank. A summary is then generated based on this rank. As the summary of the flow, both of these summaries are evaluated during the evolution stage using the ROUGE score across various document lengths.

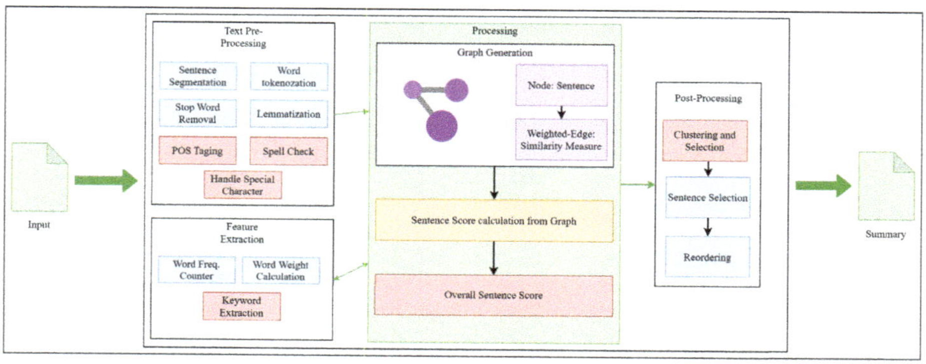

Figure 7. Graph-based extractive text summarization architecture.

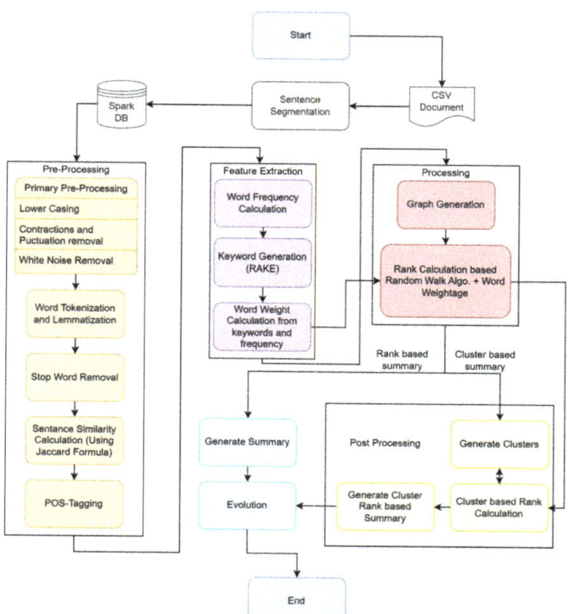

Figure 8. Flowchart for execution flow of proposed scheme.

4.1.1. Phase I—Data Pre-Processing Steps

The most used pre-processing steps are identified and implemented; these processes are as follows: spell check, case removal, tokenization, stopword removal, handle special characters, stemming/lemmatization, POS tagging, TF-IDF, word frequency calculation, and keyword extraction. Following equations are used to calculate the rank of each sentence.

Random Walk: Equation (6) is used to calculate a graph-based random walk score for each sentence node.

$$R_i = (1-d) + d\sum_{i,j=0}^{N} \frac{SM_{i,j}}{SM_j} R_j \quad (6)$$

where R = Rank list of sentences, R_i = Rank of ith sentence, d = damping factor to handle node with zero degree; $\in [0,1]$, N = Number of sentences, SM = Similarity score matrix $(N \times N)$ calculated using Jaccard Similarity, $SM_{i,j}$ = Element at ith row and jth column of SM.

Frequency-based word score: Equation (7) calculates a score of each word based on sentence scores obtained through the random walk.

$$WSf_j = \frac{\sum_{i=1}^{N} C_{ij} R_i}{\sum_{i=1}^{N} C_{ij}} \quad (7)$$

where WSf = Frequency-based Word score, WSf_j = Score of jth word, M = Total numbers of words, C = Count matrix $(N \times M)$, contains count of each word in sentence, C_{ij} = Frequency of jth word in ith sentence.

Type-based word score: Equations (8) and (9) calculate normalized score if the word is noun, keyword, or both. Meanwhile, Equation (10) combined both mentioned scores, so, for words that are not nouns and keywords, the WSt score will be 0.

$$Word_{noun} = \frac{freq(word)}{\sum_i freq(Noun_i)} \quad (8)$$

$$Word_{keyword} = \frac{freq(keyword)}{\sum_i freq(KeyWord_i)} \quad (9)$$

$$WSt = Word_{noun} + Word_{keyword} \quad (10)$$

where $Word_{noun}$ = Normalized score if the word is a noun, $Word_{keyword}$ = Normalized score if word is keyword, WSt = Type based Word score, $freq(word)$ = Frequency of word in a document, $Noun$ = List of nouns present in a document, $KeyWord$ = List of keywords present in a document.

Word Score: Equation (11) simply combines both different types of word scores to assign a final score.

$$WS = WSt + WSf \quad (11)$$

where WS = Final word score.

Word influenced rank: Include word weightage into sentence score using Equation (12).

$$R_i^* = \frac{\sum_{j=1}^{M} SC_{ij} WS_j}{\sum_{j=1}^{M} C_{ij}} \quad (12)$$

where R^* = Word influenced rank list of sentences, R_i^* = Word influenced rank of ith sentence, SC_{ij} = Similarity between ith sentence and jth sentence.

Hybrid Rank: The linear combination has been used to include the influence of random walk score and word-influenced score as shown in Equation (13).

$$R_i = \alpha R_i + (1-\alpha) R_i^* \quad (13)$$

where $\alpha \in [0,1]$; to balance the overall score.

Smoothing Counts: The word count for every sentence has been normalized using Equation (14) to improve processing time.

$$SC_{ij} = \frac{C_{ij}}{\sum C_i} \quad (14)$$

where SC = Normalized count matrix $(N \times M)$ of C, C_{ij} = Frequency of jth word in ith sentence.

Cluster Rank: Calculates the rank of the cluster based on the similarity scores of sentences for a given cluster.

$$CR_i = \sum_{j \in Ne} SM_{ij} \quad (15)$$

where CR_i = Cluster Rank of ith cluster, SM_{ij} = Similarity score between ith and jth sentence, i and $j \in C_i$ cluster.

4.1.2. Phase II—Processing with Graph

Three processes come under graph processing, namely graph generation, graph-based score calculation, and overall score calculation. In graph generation, the sentences are modeled as nodes and Jaccard similarity scores between those nodes are modeled as the weight of edges between them. This scenario is represented as a similarity matrix mentioned in data pre-processing. In graph-based score calculation, the score is computed based on the random walk Equation (6). In overall score calculation, it combines both the graph-based score and word-influence score to finalize the rank of given sentences. Algorithm 1 describes step-by-step execution of the processing phase.

Algorithm 1 *GETS*: Sentence Scoring Algorithm

```
Input: S_i: Sentence list
        SM: Sentence Similarity Matrix/Graph
        SC: Sentence–word Smoothen Count Matrix calculated using Equation (14)
        d, α, ϵ: Parameters
        NOS: Number of sentences to be selected
Output: S_o: a set of sentences
Initialize i ← 0
Initialize R^i
while ||R^i − R^{i−1}||^2 ≥ ϵ
        Calculate R^{i−1} using Equation (6)
        Calculate WS using Equation (11)
        Calculate R* using Equation (12)
        Calculate R^i using Equation (13)
        i ← i + 1
S_i ← sort-in-score-descending-order (S_i)
Selection: S_o ← S_o ∪ top_S_i(NOS)
```

4.1.3. Phase III—Post Processing

This stage includes the miscellaneous processes like sentence sorting based on rank, sentence selection, and sentence rearrangement, as mentioned in Algorithm 1. We have included graph clustering as an additional process to understand the effect of graph clustering in the sentence selection process. Algorithm 2 represents the detailed steps of post-process stage:

1. *Graph Clustering:* Connected components algorithm has been used to identify the clusters within the graph. Initially, the sentence graph generated in the previous stage will be fully connected. To remove the edges, first are edges between sentences that do not have any similarity; secondly, a new threshold β is used. So, if the weight of an edge is less than the threshold, β is removed.

2. *Cluster Rank sort:* This stage sorts the sentences within the cluster based on the sentence ranks. Given rank is calculated using Equations (13) and (15).
3. *Sentence Selection and Reordering:* As the sentence is sorted, top sentences are selected from each cluster based on the number of required sentences, then reordered based on their occurrence in the original document.

Algorithm 2 Sentence selection process using Graph Clustering

```
Input: G: Sentence graph
        β: Parameters
        NOS: Number of sentences to be selected
Output: S_o: a set of sentences
For each edge(E) in G:
        if weight(E) < β:
          remove(E)
clusters = get_clusters(G)
For each cluster(C) in clusters:
        For each node(N) in cluster(C):
          Calculate cluster_rank using Equation (15)
          Calculate final_rank using cluster_rank and Equation (13)
        S_i ← sort − in − score − descending − order(C, final_rank)
Selection: S_o ← S_o ∪ top_S_i(NOS)
```

5. *GETS*: Performance Analysis

5.1. Dataset Selection

We have used large-scale dataset "WikiHow" as well as "Opinosis" for the training and testing of the proposed scheme. WikiHow dataset contains instruction articles on different topics, hosted on wikihow.com. It includes more than 230,000 articles [75]. Diversity is the main advantage of this dataset. Most of the preferred datasets are composed of news articles. These articles are written by journalists, which often use the same type of writing methods, like inverted pyramid writing style [75]. Meanwhile, topics on WikiHow were written by different individuals. We have used a small subset of this dataset, which is available with the sentence along with its labels for inclusion. As the given dataset comes with the extractive type of reference summaries, the WikiHow dataset is used to evaluate the quality of generated extractive summaries by the proposed scheme with the mentioned base model.

We have also used a small-scale dataset named "Opinosis" to further test the proposed scheme for justification of the post-processing step included in the proposed scheme. It comprises 51 topics with reviews from multiple users for each topic. It contains an average of 100 sentences for each topic [76]. The dataset also comes with the reference summary known as the gold summary made by humans. The main advantage of the mentioned dataset is that it contains the repetitive type of sentences in the documents; because of that, this dataset is used to evaluate our post-processing method, which is focused on reducing the similar type of sentences in summary.

5.2. Evaluation Measures

In this subsection, we present the details of different metrics that are used to evaluate extractive text summaries generated by the photograph-based text summarization model [77–81]. Evaluation of the summary can be completed on multiple bases. For example, consider the evaluation based on the application of the ATS system. In some scenarios, ATS systems have been employed to extract useful information. In this case, summaries are evaluated based on information covered in the input document, and, opposite to the given case, some researchers have developed ATS systems to generate human-like summaries. So, in this situation, evaluation is completed based on the presence of grammatical errors in the summaries. To cover most types of measures, we have followed categories defined by

Ref. [82] for the evaluation of summaries. In this paper, we applied content-based measures for evaluation of the extractive summary generated by the proposed scheme [79,83,84].

1. **Cosine Similarity [85]:** It is a vector-space-based similarity measure. Sentences are first converted into vectors and then their similarity score is calculated using Equation (16).

$$Cosine\,Similarity(X,Y) = \frac{\sum_i x_i y_i}{\sqrt{\sum_i (x_i)^2}\sqrt{\sum_i (y_i)^2}} \tag{16}$$

where X and Y are a vector representation of generated summary and referenced summary, respectively.

2. **Unit Overlap [86]:** It measures similarity based on the common words or lemmas between generated summary and referenced summary, which can be formulated using Equation (17).

$$Overlap(X,Y) = \frac{\|X \cap Y\|}{\|X\| + \|Y\| - \|X \cap Y\|} \tag{17}$$

where X and Y are the set of words or lemmas of generated summary and referenced summary, respectively.

3. **Longest Common Subsequence (LCS) [87]:** It is the simplest similarity measure, which calculates similarity based on the longest common subsequence between generated summary and referenced summary. Equation (18) provides the basic formula of LCS measure.

$$LCS(X,Y) = \frac{length(X) + length(Y) - edit(X,Y)}{2} \tag{18}$$

where X and Y are a sequence of words or lemma form of generated summary and referenced summary, respectively. The $edit(X,Y)$ is the edit distance between X and Y. Edit distance is the number of operations required to convert X into Y.

4. **Bilingual Evaluation Understudy (BLEU) [79]:** BLEU is frequently used in the field of machine translation. BLEU is defined by Equation (19).

$$BLEU = BP \cdot \exp(\sum_{n=1}^{N} w_n \log p_n) \tag{19}$$

where BP is the brevity penalty, w_n are the weights for each N-gram (usually equal when N = 4), and p_n is the precision for each N-gram.

5. **ROUGE [78]:** Recall-oriented understudying for gisting evaluation (ROUGE) is a powerful evaluation measure to assess the generated summary [88]. It evaluates the generated summary by comparing it with various human-generated reference summaries. Based on its comparison method, it has various variants, for example, the ROUGE-N comparison of N-gram, the ROUGE-L comparison of the longest subsequence, and ROUGE-S, which uses the skip-gram model. The basic formula of ROUGE-N is presented in Equation (20).

$$ROUGE-N = \frac{\sum_{S \in \{ReferenceSummaries\}} \sum_{gram_n \in S} Count_{match}(gram_n)}{\sum_{S \in \{ReferenceSummaries\}} \sum_{gram_n \in S} Count(gram_n)} \tag{20}$$

where $gram_N$ is an N-gram, $Count_{match}(gram_N)$ is the maximum number of N-grams co-occurring in a candidate summary and a set of reference summaries, and $Count(gram_N)$ is the number of N-grams in the reference summaries.

6. **Latent Semantic Analysis (LSA) [80].** LSA is a method mainly used to reduce dimensionality within a given text corpus and transforms a document to the term–document

matrix, which we denote by A. On the document, we apply the SVD, which is presented in Equation (21).

$$A = U\Sigma V^T \tag{21}$$

where U and V are orthogonal matrices, and Σ is a diagonal matrix containing singular values. The dimensionality reduction in LSA is mainly attributed to matching the top k largest singular values in Σ and corresponding columns/rows in U and V^T. The resultant matrix is denoted as $\hat{A} = \hat{U}\hat{\Sigma}\hat{V}^T$, where $\hat{(.)}$ function represents the lower dimensional semantic space. LSA is not a metric in itself; rather, it employs cosine similarity in between document vectors to measure the semantic similarity.

7. **Pyramid [81]:** This method defines a new unit called summary content unit (SCU) to compare information covered in generated summary with the reference summary. SCU is defined by human judges, which is semantically motivated, variable length, and can be of one or more words/lemmas. The best try is that SCU covers most of the information stored in the sentences. So, sentences are given a rank based on the SCUs covered by them. The pyramid is generated based on these SCUs. At the top of the pyramid are those SCUs that appeared in most of the summaries.

Table 4 presents a comparative overview of evaluation metrics. The metrics are summarized in terms of objective, relative metrics, and the applications in which they are used. From the table, it can be inferred that the metric selection for a given application depends on the nature of the application, its associated tasks, and the associated performance measures. For example, cosine similarity is suitable for vector space models and should be used when semantic similarity is paramount. Unit overlap and LCS are effective in tasks where sequence preservation is important, like machine translation and text-to-speech analysis. Complex metrics like BLEU, ROUGE, and Pyramid are more suitable for the TS domain. While BLEU and Pyramid are widely used in summarization and understanding of the context, ROUGE is more suitable and adjustable for ETS, where recall is a critical component.

Table 4. Summary of TS evaluation metrics.

Metric	Objective	Merits	Applications
Cosine Similarity	Measures the cosine of the angle between two vectors.	Captures semantic similarity, efficient for high-dimensional vectors.	Information retrieval, text mining.
Unit Overlap	Computes the overlap of words in two texts.	Simple to calculate, highly interpretable.	Text similarity, text classification.
LCS	Finds the longest subsequence common to two sequences.	Robust to paraphrasing.	Plagiarism detection, genetic sequences analysis.
ROUGE	Measures the overlap of N-grams, word sequences, and word pairs.	Captures recall-based metrics with variants (ROUGE-N, ROUGE-L, and others).	Text summarization, machine translation.
Pyramid	Evaluates content units in summaries.	Comprehensive assessment of summaries.	Text summarization, particularly multi-document.
BLEU	Compares N-grams of machine output with that of a human reference.	Precision-oriented, good for aggregate data.	Machine translation, text summarization.
LSA	Unearths the latent semantic relationships within a corpus.	Can capture contextual and conceptual similarity.	Information retrieval, text summarization, topic modeling.

5.3. Selection Choice

The aforementioned metrics offer a unique perspective to the summarization problem. In particular, we have selected the ROUGE-N metric (including ROUGE-1 and ROUGE-2) as the principal metric [78]. The selection choice is based on the robustness and wide acceptance of this metric in ETS. In ETS, it is more important to capture details about the information source, and, thus, recall is a critical measure. However, the BLEU metric is more oriented towards precision than recall value, which makes it a weak candidate for extractive summarization tasks. Similarly, the LSA metric operates under the assumption that words used in similar contexts share semantic meaning. Due to this, LSA might overlook nuances in sentence construction and semantic orientation. Further, LSA requires a high semantic space for computation, which slows down the processing of real-time big data frameworks. The Pyramid scoring metric evaluates the weight of summary content but is labor-intensive and not suitable for large-scale dataset evaluations. The considered framework on the dataset focuses to maximize the semantic context, and, as these metrics do not directly measure the impact of the recall on the information, a high score on precision would not correlate directly with the summary effectiveness. Applying these metrics to our dataset, thus, the application of metrics BLEU, LSA, and Pyramid would fetch high precision scores owing to the semantic overlap but reduce the model's ability to capture key information, which is the most crucial aspect of ETS.

In our evaluation, we have considered the WikiHow [75] and Opinosis datasets [76]. The WikiHow dataset is normally sequential and structured, and the Opinosis dataset is known for user reviews. In these datasets, the evaluation of cosine similarity, overlap coefficient, and LCS would fundamentally revolve around the semantic and textual overlap. For WikiHow, the semantic relationships would be captured by these metrics; thus, they would yield high scores. In contrast, the Opinosis dataset, being user-generated, is prone to contain repetitive phrases and sentiments. Thus, the model's capability to render the overlaps into succinct summaries would be limited. The metrics might fall short in assessing whether the summary captures the key ideas and information of the original text, which is a crucial aspect of ETS.

In this context, the ROUGE metric measures the overlap of the N-grams between system and reference summaries and thus is contextually meaningful to our framework. Unlike other metrics, the ROUGE metric is not primarily dependent on the structural and semantic overlap but focuses on the salient information of the source text. Given the diversity of the datasets, using ROUGE as the primary evaluation measure allows the framework to assess summaries more effectively in terms of relevance. Thus, a balanced assessment of semantic equivalence and information makes it an effective fit for the problem.

6. Evaluation Setup

To evaluate the proposed scheme, the "WikiHow" and "Opinosis" datasets have been used. In the WikiHow dataset, 500 documents have been selected and classified into the five different classes as shown in Table 5. Each class was assigned 100 documents, which is useful to learn the ability to model over the different lengths of the documents. In this study, two different models have been used. Model M1 follows Algorithm 1, while model M2 is an extension to M1, which employs graph clustering as the post-processing phase that uses Algorithm 2. The parameters are set as defined in Table 6 for the execution of respective operations described in the third column. We have used the recall-based ROUGE parameter to evaluate our model. The length of the generated summary is the same as the reference summary. The project's source code, dataset, and all relevant supporting documents have been deployed on GitHub, utilizing a public shared repository. This allows for easy access and collaboration with the broader community (Source Code Link: https://github.com/shirbhargav/Graph-based-Extractive-Text-Summarization-Sentence-Scoring-Scheme-for-Big-Data-Applications (accessed on 14 August 2023)).

Table 5. Classes of documents based on the length.

Class	Length of Documents
C1	Between 0–50
C2	Between 50–100
C3	Between 100–150
C4	Between 150–200
C5	Greater Than 200

Table 6. Parameters.

Parameter	Values	Description
d	0.8	Damping factor to handle node with zero degrees (refer Equation (6))
α	0.6	Where $\alpha \in [0,1]$; to balance the word-infused rank and random walk rank (refer Equation (13))
ϵ	10^{-5}	A convergence factor for word-based rank calculation (refer Algorithm 1)
β	Q3 percentile of all similarity values	To remove the edge with very low similarity relations between sentences in the graph (refer Algorithm 2)

6.1. Discussion and Limitations

As per the discussion, the recall-oriented understudying for gisting evaluation (ROUGE) evaluation measure is selected. Table 7 shows the average ROUGE-1, 2, and L values obtained for each class using models M1 and M2. If we focus on the individual performance of each model, then it is clear that both models provide the better result for class C3 in all three ROUGE score areas. Another visible trend that can be observed is that the ROUGE-2 value is very low compared to the other two ROUGE scores. The reason behind this trend is that ROUGE-2 compares the pairs of consecutive words between the generated and reference summary for each sentence and the probability of having the same pair of consecutive words in a generated summary becomes very low.

Table 7. Recall-based ROUGE score with/without clustering for WikiHow dataset.

	Without Clustering			With Clustering		
	ROUGE-1	**ROUGE-2**	**ROUGE-L**	**ROUGE-1**	**ROUGE-2**	**ROUGE-L**
C1	0.4121	0.1116	0.3523	0.3942	0.0952	0.3436
C2	0.4492	0.1194	0.3742	0.4219	0.0946	0.3572
C3	0.4850	0.1304	0.3780	0.4397	0.0915	0.3505
C4	0.4761	0.1171	0.3654	0.4296	0.0828	0.3333
C5	0.4487	0.1004	0.3536	0.4007	0.0714	0.3137

Figures 9–11 show the performance comparison between model M1 and M2 in terms of ROUGE-1, ROUGE-2, and ROUGE-L, respectively. If we compare these results with the selected base model (BERT-based state of art extractive text summarization model presented by Ming Zhong et al. [89]), it is clear from Figure 12 and Table 8 that both of the proposed schemes M1 and M2 outperform the base model. The proposed schemes have generated better results on ROUGE-1 and ROUGE-L scores compared to the base model. According to the result presented in Table 8 and the referenced paper [89], the authors propose a

model called "MATCHSUM", and they claim that it outperforms other competing models, including "BERTEXT" and "BERTEXT + 3gram-Blocking", "BERTEXT + 4gram-Blocking", and even the baseline model with "BERT-large" as the pre-trained encoder. The comparison is completed using the ROUGE-1 score, which is a common metric used to evaluate the quality of text summarization.

From Figures 9–11, it is visible that M2 does not perform as well as model M1. Figure 12 discusses the ROUGE score comparison against models without clusters and with clusters for different parameters.. Further, we evaluate the proposed post-processing model (M2) on the Opinosis dataset, which contains the repetitive sentences in the documents. As shown in Table 9 and Figure 13, it is clear that the proposed post-processing model (M2) provides better results compared to model M1 (without post-processing). All three ROUGE scores improve for model M1 over model (M1). The reason that M2 does not perform as well as model M1 with the "WikiHow" dataset is the characteristics of the dataset. Documents in the WikiHow dataset comprise the instruction-type sentences related to the topic and the instructions have a low probability to be repeated in the later part of a document. So, during the clustering process, for a sufficient number of documents, sentences either fall under the same clusters or just become dangling nodes, which leads to the poor quality of the summary. From the graphs, it is clear that, as the length of the document increases, the imbalance in clustering also increases, which can be reflected by the differences between the results of the two models for classes C4 and C5.

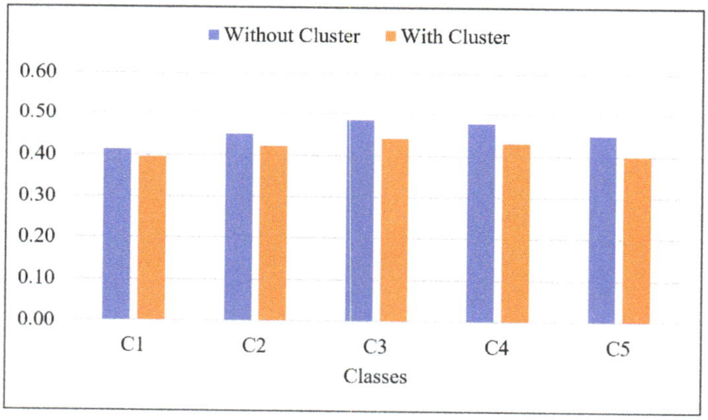

Figure 9. ROUGE-1 score comparison between models M1 and M2 for WikiHow dataset.

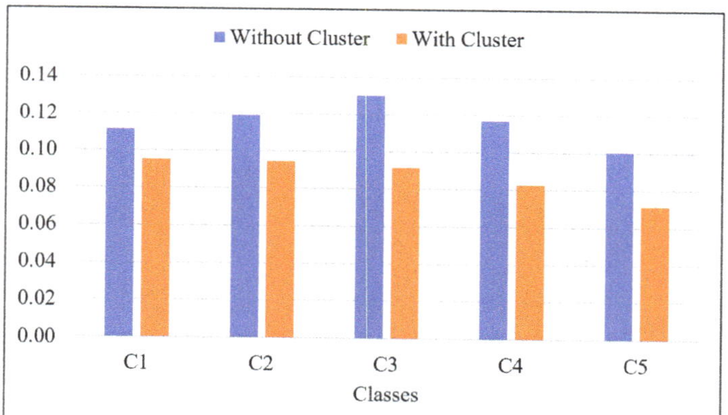

Figure 10. ROUGE-2 score comparison between models M1 and M2 for WikiHow dataset.

Table 8. Recall-based ROUGE score with/without clustering and BERT model [89] for WikiHow dataset.

	ROUGE-1	ROUGE-2	ROUGE-L
Without Clustering (M1)	0.4542	0.1158	0.3647
With Clustering (M2)	0.4172	0.0871	0.3396
BERTEXT [89]	0.3031	0.0871	0.2824
BERTEXT + 3gram-Blocking [89]	0.3037	0.0845	0. 2828
BERTEXT + 4gram-Blocking [89]	0.3040	0.0867	0.2832
MATCHSUM (BERT-base) [89]	0.3185	0.0898	0.2958

Table 9. Recall-based ROUGE score with/without clustering for Opinosis dataset.

	Without Clustering	With Clustering	Improvement %
ROUGE-1	0.2225	0.2622	4%
ROUGE-2	0.0429	0.0376	−1%
ROUGE-L	0.1954	0.2216	3%

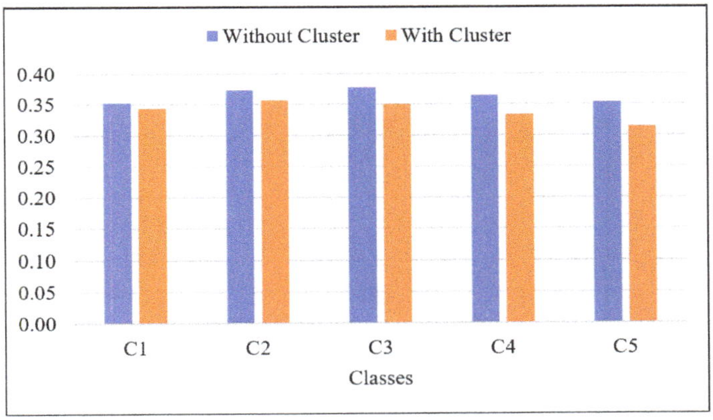

Figure 11. ROUGE-L score comparison between models M1 and M2 for wikiHow dataset.

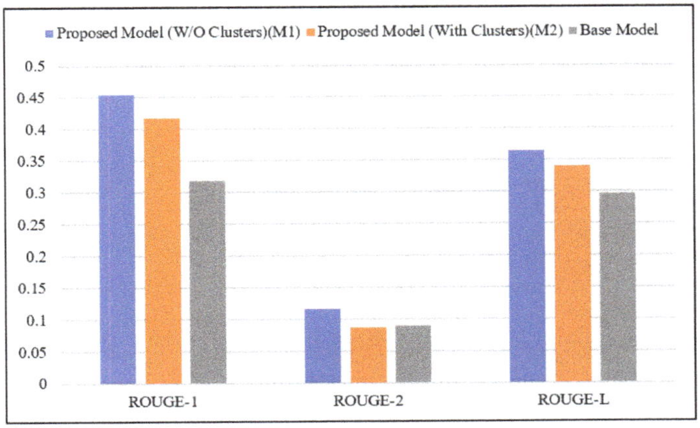

Figure 12. ROUGE score comparison between model proposed scheme (average of all five clusters) and base model [89].

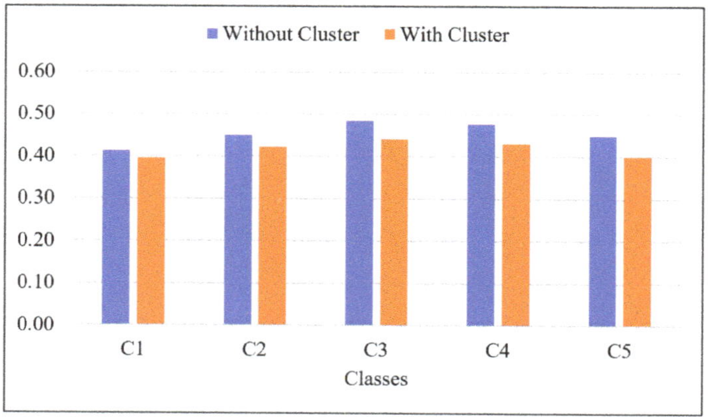

Figure 13. ROUGE score comparison between models M1 and M2 for Opinosis dataset.

Text summarization and sentiment analysis are highly correlated processes. The reason behind the high correlation is that one model can be used to improve or optimize another model. The outcome of the experimental analysis presented may be used to improvise businesses on e-commerce portals analyzing target customer reviews and feedback. The same model can be applied to opinion and sentiment analysis for large-scale crowdsourcing for launching a new product, service, or policy by the government or an enterprise. It can be applied to recommendation systems (RSs) for e-commerce businesses because the RS for many e-commerce and social media sites mainly considers the statistical datasets for predictive and descriptive models. The proposed scheme provides a new direction where text data can be used more effectively for these systems.

6.2. The Way Forward

The proposed framework paves the way toward the design of a hybrid framework, where both abstractive and extractive summarization can be unified. The motivation for the integration of both schemes is to address the dual issue of context richness provided by ETS and concise, human-like summaries generated by ATS. To achieve this, the framework should map out the semantic network information in a coherent manner. To address this, deep neural architectures, such as BERT and generative pretrained Transformers (GPT) [90], could be instrumental. These architectures are integrated with the self-attention mechanism [91], which allows the model to learn about contextual relationships between words in the text and the semantics of the document. In addition, the encoder–decoder models, like Seq2Seq [92], can be integrated with attention models to aid in the translation of extracted semantics (from ETS) to ATS.

BERT variants such as Robustly optimized BERT approach (RoBERTa) [93], A Lite BERT (ALBERT) [94], and DistilBERT [95] employ a bidirectional Transformer to understand the deep understanding of the context. RoBERTa improves the BERT model by inclusion of mode training data and optimization of the BERT process. ALBERT reduces the parametric performance loss of BERT, which makes it an effective fit for large-scale big data applications. DistilBERT is designed for minimized model sizes, with comparable performance to BERT, suitable for low-powered and constrained applications such as IoT.

GPT, on the other hand (successors GPT-2 [96], GPT-3 [97], and GPT-4 [98]), is based on Transformer architecture and is useful in the abstractive part of the framework. The architecture includes the unidirectional or casual self-attention mechanism. It can generate highly fluent and coherent text. GPT-2 is trained with 1.5 billion parameters and uses a 48-layer Transformer architecture. GPT-3 has 175 billion parameters, with 137 Transformer layers, and GPT-4 has 100 trillion parameters, with 175 layers. The increase in parameters allows the Transformer model to learn long-range dependencies better, which generates more realistic and coherent text. The optimization algorithm of GPT models has improved, which makes it more real-time and effective, with more layers.

The hybrid framework could significantly benefit the realm of big data, specifically in the context of social media analytics. The vast amount of user-generated content on social media requires extractive as well as realistic summarization, and thus the hybrid framework could serve as a potent tool in this direction. It can leverage contextual sentiment analysis, information extraction, and trend summarization in a scalable manner. A notable example of the hybrid framework is the application of big data e-commerce platforms for product recommendation engines, where the framework could identify key features and descriptions of a product, which should resonate with customers based on demographics and relevant information like gender, age, previous selection choices of buyer, and popular opinion choices extracted from social communities.

7. Conclusions and Future Work

In recent years, e-commerce web portals have exponentially increased the amount of textual data over the internet in the form of reviews and comments about a product or service. This paper proposes a graph-based sentence scoring scheme for sentence selection to represent the summary of a given text. As an extension of the proposed scheme, graph-based clustering is applied as a post-processing step for the selection of representative sentences as a required summary of a given dataset. It shows that the proposed schemes provide better results than a BERT-based extractive text summarization model. The results show that the graph clustering process is not an ideal selection as a post-processing step for all types of datasets. The datasets with repetitive sentences benefit more from the proposed post-processing model. It can apply to applications where the impact of user reviews and comments may be analyzed.

As an extension of the work, the authors intend to propose a hybrid scheme of extractive and abstractive text summarization, where the designed model would be capable to handle multi-modal data summarization, where the hybrid framework would be designed as a staged framework. Initially, the extractive model would be trained on salient features of the input, and then the abstractive model would generate concise summaries. The architecture would be Transformer-based with a self-attention supervised training process over a large corpus of text documents. For visual and sequential data, convolutional neural networks and long short-term memory would be combined. This extension would have significant implications in digital content generation and social analytics, where the end-to-end framework would address a wide range of challenges with intelligent solutions.

Author Contributions: Conceptualization: J.P.V., S.B. and M.B.; writing—original draft preparation: J.P.V., S.B. and M.B.; methodology: P.B., A.B. and S.C.; writing—review and editing: P.B., A.B. and S.C.; Software: J.P.V., S.B., P.B., A.B., J.W. and A.M.; Visualization: J.W. and A.M.; Investigation: A.B., S.C., J.W. and A.M. All authors have read and agreed to the published version of the manuscript.

Funding: This research received no external funding.

Data Availability Statement: No data are associated with this research work.

Acknowledgments: Authors would like to thank Kuwait College of Science and Technology (KCST) for supporting this work.

Conflicts of Interest: The authors declare no conflict of interest.

References

1. Essameldin, R.; Ismail, A.A.; Darwish, S.M. An Opinion Mining Approach to Handle Perspectivism and Ambiguity: Moving Toward Neutrosophic Logic. *IEEE Access* **2022**, *10*, 63314–63328. [CrossRef]
2. Elahi, S.; Nika, A.; Tekin, C. Online Context-Aware Task Assignment in Mobile Crowdsourcing via Adaptive Discretization. *IEEE Trans. Netw. Sci. Eng.* **2023**, *10*, 305–320. [CrossRef]
3. Hassani, H.; Beneki, C.; Unger, S.; Mazinani, M.T.; Yeganegi, M.R. Text Mining in Big Data Analytics. *Big Data Cogn. Comput.* **2020**, *4*, 1. [CrossRef]

4. Miah, S.J.; Vu, H.Q.; Alahakoon, D. A social media analytics perspective for human-oriented smart city planning and management. *J. Assoc. Inf. Sci. Technol.* **2022**, *73*, 119–135. [CrossRef]
5. Bhattacharya, P.; Patel, S.B.; Gupta, R.; Tanwar, S.; Rodrigues, J.J.P.C. SaTYa: Trusted Bi-LSTM-Based Fake News Classification Scheme for Smart Community. *IEEE Trans. Comput. Soc. Syst.* **2022**, *9*, 1758–1767. [CrossRef]
6. Devlin, J.; Chang, M.W.; Lee, K.; Toutanova, K. Bert: Pre-training of deep bidirectional transformers for language understanding. *arXiv* **2018**, arXiv:1810.04805.
7. Schouten, K.; Frasincar, F. Survey on Aspect-Level Sentiment Analysis. *IEEE Trans. Knowl. Data Eng.* **2015**, *28*, 813–830. [CrossRef]
8. Bhattacharya, P.; Trivedi, C.; Obaidat, M.S.; Patel, K.; Tanwar, S.; Hsiao, K.F. BeHAutH: A KNN-Based Classification Scheme for Behavior-Based Authentication in Web 3.0. In Proceedings of the 2022 International Conference on Communications, Computing, Cybersecurity, and Informatics (CCCI), Dalian, China, 17–19 October 2022; pp. 1–5. [CrossRef]
9. Mansour, S. Social Media Analysis of User's Responses to Terrorism Using Sentiment Analysis and Text Mining. *Procedia Comput. Sci.* **2018**, *140*, 95–103. [CrossRef]
10. AL-Khassawneh, Y.A.; Hanandeh, E.S. Extractive Arabic Text Summarization-Graph-Based Approach. *Electronics* **2023**, *12*, 437. [CrossRef]
11. Novgorodov, S.; Guy, I.; Elad, G.; Radinsky, K. Descriptions from the Customers: Comparative Analysis of Review-Based Product Description Generation Methods. *ACM Trans. Internet Technol.* **2020**, *20*, 44. [CrossRef]
12. Mackey, A.; Cuevas, I. Automatic text summarization within big data frameworks. *J. Comput. Sci. Coll.* **2018**, *33*, 26–32.
13. Ghodratnama, S.; Beheshti, A.; Zakershahrak, M.; Sobhanmanesh, F. Extractive Document Summarization Based on Dynamic Feature Space Mapping. *IEEE Access* **2020**, *8*, 139084–139095. [CrossRef]
14. El-Kassas, W.S.; Salama, C.R.; Rafea, A.A.; Mohamed, H.K. Automatic text summarization: A comprehensive survey. *Expert Syst. Appl.* **2020**, *165*, 113679. [CrossRef]
15. Chaves, A.; Kesiku, C.; Garcia-Zapirain, B. Automatic Text Summarization of Biomedical Text Data: A Systematic Review. *Information* **2022**, *13*, 393. [CrossRef]
16. Deng, Z.; Ma, F.; Lan, R.; Huang, W.; Lu, X. A Two-stage Chinese text summarization algorithm usingkeyword information and adversarial learning. *Neurocomputing* **2020**, *425*, 117–126. [CrossRef]
17. Giarelis, N.; Mastrokostas, C.; Karacapilidis, N. Abstractive vs. Extractive Summarization: An Experimental Review. *Appl. Sci.* **2023**, *13*, 7620. [CrossRef]
18. Alomari, A.; Idris, N.; Sabri, A.Q.M.; Alsmadi, I. Deep reinforcement and transfer learning for abstractive text summarization: A review. *Comput. Speech Lang.* **2022**, *71*, 101276. [CrossRef]
19. Dave, N.; Mistry, H.; Verma, J.P. Text data analysis: Computer aided automated assessment system. In Proceedings of the 2017 3rd International Conference on Computational Intelligence Communication Technology (CICT), Ghaziabad, India, 9–10 February 2017; pp. 1–4. [CrossRef]
20. Jigneshkumar Patel, H.; Prakash Verma, J.; Patel, A. Unsupervised Learning-Based Sentiment Analysis with Reviewer's Emotion. In Proceedings of the Evolving Technologies for Computing, Communication and Smart World, Singapore, 26 November 2020; pp. 69–81.
21. Zaeem, R.N.; German, R.L.; Barber, K.S. PrivacyCheck: Automatic Summarization of Privacy Policies Using Data Mining. *ACM Trans. Internet Technol.* **2018**, *18*, 1–18. [CrossRef]
22. Cai, M. Natural language processing for urban research: A systematic review. *Heliyon* **2021**, *7*, e06322. [CrossRef]
23. Verma, J.P.; Patel, B.; Patel, A. Web Mining: Opinion and Feedback Analysis for Educational Institutions. *Int. J. Comput. Appl.* **2013**, *84*, 17–22.
24. Priyadarshana, Y.H.P.P.; Ranathunga, L. Verb Sentiment Scoring: A Novel Approach for Sentiment Analysis Based on Adjective-Verb-Adverb Combinations. In Proceedings of the 2017 IEEE/ACM International Conference on Advances in Social Networks Analysis and Mining (ASONAM), Sydney, Australia, 31 July–3 August 2017; pp. 533–540.
25. Arya, C.; Diwakar, M.; Singh, P.; Singh, V.; Kadry, S.; Kim, J. Multi-Document News Web Page Summarization Using Content Extraction and Lexical Chain Based Key Phrase Extraction. *Mathematics* **2023**, *11*, 1762. [CrossRef]
26. Bichi, A.A.; Keikhosrokiani, P.; Hassan, R.; Almekhlafi, K. Graph-based extractive text summarization models: A systematic review. *J. Inf. Technol. Manag.* **2022**, *14*, 184–202.
27. Srivastava, R.; Singh, P.; Rana, K.; Kumar, V. A topic modeled unsupervised approach to single document extractive text summarization. *Knowl.-Based Syst.* **2022**, *246*, 108636. [CrossRef]
28. Huang, J.; Wu, W.; Li, J.; Wang, S. Text Summarization Method Based on Gated Attention Graph Neural Network. *Sensors* **2023**, *23*, 1654. [CrossRef]
29. Hernandez-Castaneda, A.; García-Hernández, R.A.; Ledeneva, Y.; Millan-Hernández, C.E. Extractive Automatic Text Summarization Based on Lexical-Semantic Keywords. *IEEE Access* **2020**, *8*, 49896–49907. [CrossRef]
30. Jayashree, R.; Vinay, S. A Jaccards Similarity Score Based Methodology for Kannada Text Document Summarization. In Proceedings of the 2020 International Conference on Advances in Computing, Communication & Materials (ICACCM), Dehradun, India, 21–22 August 2020; pp. 8–11. [CrossRef]
31. Bidoki, M.; Moosavi, M.R.; Fakhrahmad, M. A semantic approach to extractive multi-document summarization: Applying sentence expansion for tuning of conceptual densities. *Inf. Process. Manag.* **2020**, *57*, 102341. [CrossRef]

32. Tkachuk, A. Robustness of rank minimization heuristics for form-finding of tensegrity structures. *Comput. Struct.* **2022**, *266*, 106786. [CrossRef]
33. Fatima, Z.; Zardari, S.; Fahim, M.; Andleeb Siddiqui, M.; Ibrahim, A.A.A.; Nisar, K.; Naz, L.F. A novel approach for semantic extractive text summarization. *Appl. Sci.* **2022**, *12*, 4479. [CrossRef]
34. Yan, D.; Huang, Y.; Liu, M.; Chen, H.; Cheng, J.; Wu, H.; Zhang, C. Graphd: Distributed vertex-centric graph processing beyond the memory limit. *IEEE Trans. Parallel Distrib. Syst.* **2017**, *29*, 99–114. [CrossRef]
35. Stewart, E. (Blog) Facebook's Fake Accounts Problem Seems Bad. Available online: Vox.com (accessed on 3 December 2020).
36. Bhargava, R.; Sharma, G.; Sharma, Y. Deep Text Summarization using Generative Adversarial Networks in Indian Languages. *Procedia Comput. Sci.* **2020**, *167*, 147–153. [CrossRef]
37. Fang, C.; Mu, D.; Deng, Z.; Wu, Z. Word-sentence co-ranking for automatic extractive text summarization. *Expert Syst. Appl.* **2017**, *72*, 189–195. [CrossRef]
38. El-Kassas, W.S.; Salama, C.R.; Rafea, A.A.; Mohamed, H.K. EdgeSumm: Graph-based framework for automatic text summarization. *Inf. Process. Manag.* **2020**, *57*, 102264. [CrossRef]
39. Kleinberg, J.M. Authoritative Sources in a Hyperlinked Environment. *J. ACM* **1999**, *46*, 604–632. [CrossRef]
40. Brin, S.; Page, L. The Anatomy of a Large-Scale Hypertextual Web Search Engine. *Comput. Netw. ISDN Syst.* **1998**, *30*, 107–117. [CrossRef]
41. Mihalcea, R.; Tarau, P. TextRank: Bringing Order into Texts. In Proceedings of the 2004 Conference on Empirical Methods in Natural Language Processing, Barcelona, Spain, 16–25 July 2004; pp. 404–411.
42. Talpur, B.A.; O'Sullivan, D. Multi-class imbalance in text classification: A feature engineering approach to detect cyberbullying in twitter. *Informatics* **2020**, *7*, 52. [CrossRef]
43. Margaris, D.; Vassilakis, C. Exploiting rating abstention intervals for addressing concept drift in social network recommender systems. *Informatics* **2018**, *5*, 21. [CrossRef]
44. Moradi, M.; Dashti, M.; Samwald, M. Summarization of biomedical articles using domain-specific word embeddings and graph ranking. *J. Biomed. Inform.* **2020**, *107*, 103452. [CrossRef]
45. Alzuhair, A.; Al-Dhelaan, M. An Approach for Combining Multiple Weighting Schemes and Ranking Methods in Graph-Based Multi-Document Summarization. *IEEE Access* **2019**, *7*, 120375–120386. [CrossRef]
46. Yang, K.; Al-Sabahi, K.; Xiang, Y.; Zhang, Z. An Integrated Graph Model for Document Summarization. *Information* **2018**, *9*, 232. [CrossRef]
47. Bhargava, R.; Sharma, Y.; Sharma, G. ATSSI: Abstractive Text Summarization using Sentiment Infusion. *Procedia Comput. Sci.* **2016**, *89*, 404–411. [CrossRef]
48. Mao, X.; Yang, H.; Huang, S.; Liu, Y.; Li, R. Extractive summarization using supervised and unsupervised learning. *Expert Syst. Appl.* **2019**, *133*, 173–181. [CrossRef]
49. Luhn, H.P. The automatic creation of literature abstracts. *IBM J. Res. Dev.* **1958**, *2*, 159–165. [CrossRef]
50. Edmundson, H.P. New methods in automatic extracting. *J. ACM* **1969**, *16*, 264–285. [CrossRef]
51. Aone, C.; Okurowski, M.E.; Gorlinsky, J. Trainable, scalable summarization using robust NLP and machine learning. In Proceedings of the 36th Annual Meeting of the Association for Computational Linguistics and 17th International Conference on Computational Linguistics, Montreal, QC, Canada, 10–14 August 1998; Volume 1, pp. 62–66. [CrossRef]
52. Etaiwi, W.; Awajan, A. SemG-TS: Abstractive Arabic Text Summarization Using Semantic Graph Embedding. *Mathematics* **2022**, *10*, 3225. [CrossRef]
53. Huang, Y.; Sun, L.; Han, C.; Guo, J. A High-Precision Two-Stage Legal Judgment Summarization. *Mathematics* **2023**, *11*, 1320. [CrossRef]
54. Patel, D.; Shah, S.; Chhinkaniwala, H. Fuzzy logic based multi document summarization with improved sentence scoring and redundancy removal technique. *Expert Syst. Appl.* **2019**, *134*, 167–177. [CrossRef]
55. Van Lierde, H.; Chow, T.W. Query-oriented text summarization based on hypergraph transversals. *Inf. Process. Manag.* **2019**, *56*, 1317–1338. [CrossRef]
56. Jindal, S.G.; Kaur, A. Automatic Keyword and Sentence-Based Text Summarization for Software Bug Reports. *IEEE Access* **2020**, *8*, 65352–65370. [CrossRef]
57. Du, Y.; Huo, H. News Text Summarization Based on Multi-Feature and Fuzzy Logic. *IEEE Access* **2020**, *8*, 140261–140272. [CrossRef]
58. Moradi, M. CIBS: A biomedical text summarizer using topic-based sentence clustering. *J. Biomed. Inform.* **2018**, *88*, 53–61. [CrossRef]
59. Bhargava, R.; Sharma, Y. Deep Extractive Text Summarization. *Procedia Comput. Sci.* **2020**, *167*, 138–146. [CrossRef]
60. Anand, D.; Wagh, R. Effective Deep Learning Approaches for Summarization of Legal Texts. *J. King Saud Univ. Comput. Inf. Sci.* **2019**, *34*, 2141–2150. [CrossRef]
61. Alami, N.; Meknassi, M.; En-nahnahi, N. Enhancing unsupervised neural networks-based text summarization with word embedding and ensemble learning. *Expert Syst. Appl.* **2019**, *123*, 195–211. [CrossRef]
62. Azadani, M.N.; Ghadiri, N.; Davoodijam, E. Graph-based biomedical text summarization: An itemset mining and sentence clustering approach. *J. Biomed. Inform.* **2018**, *84*, 42–58. [CrossRef]

63. Liang, Z.; Du, J.; Li, C. Abstractive Social Media Text Summarization using Selective Reinforced Seq2Seq Attention Model. *Neurocomputing* **2020**, *410*, 432–440. [CrossRef]
64. Adelia, R.; Suyanto, S.; Wisesty, U.N. Indonesian Abstractive Text Summarization Using Bidirectional Gated Recurrent Unit. *Procedia Comput. Sci.* **2019**, *157*, 581–588. [CrossRef]
65. Moirangthem, D.S.; Lee, M. Abstractive summarization of long texts by representing multiple compositionalities with temporal hierarchical pointer generator network. *Neural Netw.* **2020**, *124*, 1–11. [CrossRef]
66. Guo, Q.; Huang, J.; Xiong, N.; Wang, P. MS-Pointer Network: Abstractive Text Summary Based on Multi-Head Self-Attention. *IEEE Access* **2019**, *7*, 138603–138613. [CrossRef]
67. Cagliero, L.; Garza, P.; Baralis, E. ELSA: A Multilingual Document Summarization Algorithm Based on Frequent Item-sets and Latent Semantic Analysis. *ACM Trans. Inf. Syst.* **2019**, *37*, 1–33. [CrossRef]
68. Rouane, O.; Belhadef, H.; Bouakkaz, M. Combine clustering and frequent itemset mining to enhance biomedical text summarization. *Expert Syst. Appl.* **2019**, *135*, 362–373. [CrossRef]
69. Tsai, C.F.; Chen, K.; Hu, Y.H.; Chen, W.K. Improving text summarization of online hotel reviews with review helpfulness and sentiment. *Tour. Manag.* **2020**, *80*, 104122. [CrossRef]
70. Mohd, M.; Jan, R.; Shah, M. Text Document Summarization using Word Embedding. *Expert Syst. Appl.* **2020**, *143*, 112958. [CrossRef]
71. Cao, B.; Wu, J.; Wang, S.; Gao, H.; Fan, J.; Deng, S.; Yin, J.; Liu, X. Unsupervised Derivation of Keyword Summary for Short Texts. *ACM Trans. Internet Technol.* **2021**, *21*, 1–23. [CrossRef]
72. Ameur, M.S.H.; Belkebir, R.; Guessoum, A.A. Robust Arabic Text Categorization by Combining Convolutional and Recurrent Neural Networks. *ACM Trans. Asian Low-Resour. Lang. Inf. Process.* **2020**, *19*, 1–16. [CrossRef]
73. Zhou, Q.; Yang, N.; Wei, F.; Huang, S.; Zhou, M.; Zhao, T. A Joint Sentence Scoring and Selection Framework for Neural Extractive Document Summarization. *IEEE/ACM Trans. Audio Speech Lang. Process.* **2020**, *28*, 671–681. [CrossRef]
74. Abdel-Salam, S.; Rafea, A. Performance study on extractive text summarization using BERT models. *Information* **2022**, *13*, 67. [CrossRef]
75. Koupaee, M.; Wang, W.Y. WikiHow: A Large Scale Text Summarization Dataset. *arXiv* **2018**, arXiv:1810.09305.
76. Ganesan, K.; Zhai, C.; Han, J. Opinosis: A graph-based approach to abstractive summarization of highly redundant opinions. In Proceedings of the 23rd International Conference on Computational Linguistics, Beijing, China, 23–27 August 2010; pp. 340–348.
77. Jalil, Z.; Nasir, M.; Alazab, M.; Nasir, J.; Amjad, T.; Alqammaz, A. Grapharizer: A Graph-Based Technique for Extractive Multi-Document Summarization. *Electronics* **2023**, *12*, 1895. [CrossRef]
78. Lin, C.Y. Rouge: A package for automatic evaluation of summaries. In Proceedings of the Workshop on Text Summarization Branches Out, Barcelona, Spain, 25–26 July 2004; pp. 74–81.
79. Papineni, K.; Roukos, S.; Ward, T.; Zhu, W.J. Bleu: A method for automatic evaluation of machine translation. In Proceedings of the 40th Annual Meeting of the Association for Computational Linguistics, Philadelphia, PA, USA, 7–12 July 2002; pp. 311–318.
80. Landauer, T.K.; Foltz, P.W.; Laham, D. An introduction to latent semantic analysis. *Discourse Process.* **1998**, *25*, 259–284. [CrossRef]
81. Nenkova, A.; Passonneau, R.J. Evaluating content selection in summarization: The pyramid method. In Proceedings of the Human Language Technology Conference of the North American Chapter of the Association for Computational Linguistics: Hlt-Naacl 2004, Boston, MA, USA, 2–7 May 2004; pp. 145–152.
82. Steinberger, J.; Jezek, K. Evaluation measures for text summarization. *Comput. Inform.* **2009**, *28*, 251–275.
83. Zhang, T.; Kishore, V.; Wu, F.; Weinberger, K.Q.; Artzi, Y. Bertscore: Evaluating text generation with bert. *arXiv* **2019**, arXiv:1904.09675.
84. Sellam, T.; Das, D.; Parikh, A.P. BLEURT: Learning robust metrics for text generation. *arXiv* **2020**, arXiv:2004.04696.
85. Takano, Y.; Iijima, Y.; Kobayashi, K.; Sakuta, H.; Sakaji, H.; Kohana, M.; Kobayashi, A. Improving Document Similarity Calculation Using Cosine-Similarity Graphs. In *Advanced Information Networking and Applications*; Barolli, L., Takizawa, M., Xhafa, F., Enokido, T., Eds.; Springer: Cham, Switzerland, 2020; pp. 512–522.
86. Kryściński, W.; Keskar, N.S.; McCann, B.; Xiong, C.; Socher, R. Neural text summarization: A critical evaluation. *arXiv* **2019**, arXiv:1908.08960.
87. Yavuz, S.; Chiu, C.C.; Nguyen, P.; Wu, Y. CaLcs: Continuously Approximating Longest Common Subsequence for Sequence Level Optimization. In Proceedings of the 2018 Conference on Empirical Methods in Natural Language Processing, Brussels, Belgium, 31 October–4 November 2018; pp. 3708–3718. [CrossRef]
88. Plaza, L.; Daaz, A.; Gervas, P. A semantic graph-based approach to biomedical summarisation. *Artif. Intell. Med.* **2011**, *53*, 1–14. [CrossRef]
89. Zhong, M.; Liu, P.; Chen, Y.; Wang, D.; Xuanjing Huang, X.Q. Extractive Summarization as Text Matching. In Proceedings of the 58th Annual Meeting of the Association for Computational Linguistics, online, July 2020; pp. 6197–6208.
90. Zhu, Q.; Luo, J. Generative Pre-Trained Transformer for Design Concept Generation: An Exploration. *Proc. Des. Soc.* **2022**, *2*, 1825–1834. [CrossRef]
91. Vaswani, A.; Shazeer, N.; Parmar, N.; Uszkoreit, J.; Jones, L.; Gomez, A.N.; Kaiser, Ł.; Polosukhin, I. Attention is All you Need. In *Advances in Neural Information Processing Systems*; Guyon, I., Luxburg, U.V., Bengio, S., Wallach, H., Fergus, R., Vishwanathan, S., Garnett, R., Eds.; Curran Associates, Inc.: Red Hook, NY, USA, 2017; Volume 30.
92. Zhang, Y.; Xiao, W. Keyphrase Generation Based on Deep Seq2seq Model. *IEEE Access* **2018**, *6*, 46047–46057. [CrossRef]

93. Liu, Y.; Ott, M.; Goyal, N.; Du, J.; Joshi, M.; Chen, D.; Levy, O.; Lewis, M.; Zettlemoyer, L.; Stoyanov, V. RoBERTa: A Robustly Optimized BERT Pretraining Approach. *arXiv* **2019**, arXiv:1907.11692.
94. Lan, Z.; Chen, M.; Goodman, S.; Gimpel, K.; Sharma, P.; Soricut, R. ALBERT: A Lite BERT for Self-supervised Learning of Language Representations. *arXiv* **2019**, arXiv:1909.11942.
95. Sanh, V.; Debut, L.; Chaumond, J.; Wolf, T. DistilBERT, a distilled version of BERT: Smaller, faster, cheaper and lighter. *arXiv* **2020**, arXiv:1910.01108.
96. Radford, A.; Wu, J.; Child, R.; Luan, D.; Amodei, D.; Sutskever, I. Language models are unsupervised multitask learners. *OpenAI Blog* **2019**, *1*, 9.
97. Brown, T.B.; Mann, B.; Ryder, N.; Subbiah, M.; Kaplan, J.; Dhariwal, P.; Neelakantan, A.; Shyam, P.; Sastry, G.; Askell, A.; et al. Language Models are Few-Shot Learners. *arXiv* **2020**, arXiv:2005.14165.
98. Bubeck, S.; Chandrasekaran, V.; Eldan, R.; Gehrke, J.; Horvitz, E.; Kamar, E.; Lee, P.; Lee, Y.T.; Li, Y.; Lundberg, S.; et al. Sparks of Artificial General Intelligence: Early experiments with GPT-4. *arXiv* **2023**, arXiv:2303.12712.

information

MDPI

Article

Understanding Website Privacy Policies—A Longitudinal Analysis Using Natural Language Processing

Veronika Belcheva [1], Tatiana Ermakova [2] and Benjamin Fabian [1,3,*]

1 Information Systems, Humboldt-Universität zu Berlin, 10178 Berlin, Germany; veronika.belcheva@gmail.com
2 School of Computing, Communication and Business, Hochschule für Technik und Wirtschaft, University of Applied Sciences for Engineering and Economics, 10318 Berlin, Germany; tatiana.ermakova@htw-berlin.de
3 EDIH pro_digital, Technical University of Applied Sciences Wildau, 15745 Wildau, Germany
* Correspondence: benjamin.fabian@th-wildau.de or bfabian@wiwi.hu-berlin.de

Abstract: Privacy policies are the main method for informing Internet users of how their data are collected and shared. This study aims to analyze the deficiencies of privacy policies in terms of readability, vague statements, and the use of pacifying phrases concerning privacy. This represents the undertaking of a step forward in the literature on this topic through a comprehensive analysis encompassing both time and website coverage. It characterizes trends across website categories, top-level domains, and popularity ranks. Furthermore, studying the development in the context of the General Data Protection Regulation (GDPR) offers insights into the impact of regulations on policy comprehensibility. The findings reveal a concerning trend: privacy policies have grown longer and more ambiguous, making it challenging for users to comprehend them. Notably, there is an increased proportion of vague statements, while clear statements have seen a decrease. Despite this, the study highlights a steady rise in the inclusion of reassuring statements aimed at alleviating readers' privacy concerns.

Keywords: privacy policy; longitudinal analysis; text analysis; NLP; readability; vagueness

1. Introduction

Natural language privacy policies serve as the primary means of disclosing data practices to consumers, providing them with crucial information about what data are collected, analyzed, and how they will be kept private and secure. By reading these policies, users can enhance their awareness of data privacy and better manage the risks associated with extensive data collection. However, for privacy policies to be genuinely useful, they must be easily comprehensible to the majority of users. Lengthy and vague policies fail to effectively inform the average user, rendering them ineffective in ensuring data privacy awareness.

Research by Meier et al. [1] revealed that users presented with shorter privacy policies tend to spend more time understanding the text, indicating their willingness to engage with more concise information. Another study suggested that missing comprehension is a major burden for reading privacy policies. In the study, 18% of participants reported experiencing difficulty in understanding policies from popular websites, and over 50% did not actually understand the content [2]. Moreover, readability is essential for users' trust, as other studies have emphasized [3].

Privacy policies are often excessive in length, requiring a substantial amount of time to read through. Estimates show that the average Internet user would spend around 400 h per year reading all encountered privacy terms [4]. This time investment may deter users from thoroughly reviewing policies, leading them to hurriedly click the "I agree" button without fully understanding the implications.

Addressing the significance of readability and privacy regulations, such as General Data Protection Regulation (GDPR), mandate that privacy policies should be concise, easy to understand, and written in plain language. Additionally, the California Consumer Privacy Act (CCPA) emphasizes the need to present policies in a clear and straightforward manner, avoiding technical or legal jargon.

To enhance clarity and conciseness, the GDPR guidelines recommend the use of active voice instead of passive voice in writing [5]. The active voice directs the reader's attention to the performer of the action, reducing ambiguity and making the text more straightforward.

Additionally, policies become less comprehensible due to ambiguity, which occurs when a statement lacks clarity and can be interpreted in multiple ways. The use of imprecise language in a privacy policy hinders the clear communication of the website's actual data practices. For example, when websites summarize their data practices without specifying the exact conditions under which actions apply, vague policies emerge. Ambiguous policies allow websites to maintain flexibility in future changes to data practices without requiring policy updates [6].

The presence of language qualifiers like "may", "might", "some", and "often" contributes to ambiguity, as noted by the European Commission's GDPR guidelines [5]. Recent research suggests an increasing use of terms such as "may include" and "may collect" in privacy policies, which may result in policies becoming more ambiguous over time [7]. Vague language not only renders policies inaccurate but may also mislead readers, limiting their ability to interpret policy contents accurately. Consequently, ambiguity can erode users' trust and raise privacy concerns, leading to reduced willingness to share personal information [8].

In addition to vague language, policies also contain expressions such as "we value your privacy" or "we take your privacy and security seriously". Despite their intention to alleviate privacy concerns, these phrases do not convey crucial policy information. Positive language, at its best, redirects user focus away from privacy implications and, at its worst, can lead to misinformation.

This study examines the comprehensibility of English-language privacy policies between the years 2009 and 2019, utilizing natural language processing (NLP), machine learning and text-mining methods to analyze a large longitudinal corpus. The research focuses on the following indicators of clarity:

- Reading difficulty in terms of readability test and text statistics;
- Privacy policy ambiguity measured by the usage of vague language and statements;
- The use of positive phrasing concerning privacy.

The analysis encompassed several key factors: policy length, quantified through sentence count; passive voice index, indicating passive voice usage degree; and reading complexity, assessed via the new Dale–Chall readability formula, which considers semantic word difficulty and sentence length. Evaluating policy ambiguity involved identifying and counting vague terms from a defined taxonomy. Additionally, a pre-trained BERT model was utilized for multi-class sentence classification, predicting sentence vagueness levels within each policy. The study also explored the presence of positive phrasing related to privacy, examining the prevalence of phrases like "we value your privacy" or "we take your privacy and security seriously" across policies.

Some scholars have previously evaluated policy comprehensibility, focusing on shorter periods or single time points [4,7,9–12]. In contrast, this study advances the literature on consumer comprehension by conducting a large-scale analysis covering an extended period and a wide range of websites. It explores trends across website categories, top-level domains, and popularity ranks. Additionally, examining policy development in the context of the GDPR provides insights into the impact of regulations on policy writing practices. By shedding light on the lack of transparency in the privacy policy landscape, this research advocates for the design of more comprehensible and valuable privacy policy statements.

Wagner [4] examined length (words and sentences), passive voice, various readability formulas (Flesch Reading Ease (FRE), Coleman–Liau score (CL), and Simple Measure Of

Gobbledygook (SMOG)). Srinath et al. [12] reported on the length of the privacy policy and the use of vague words in their private policy corpus. Compared to Srinath et al. [12], Libert et al. [13] and Wagner [4], the present work is based on the dataset of Amos et al. [7], which extends substantially over several years. Furthermore, herein the length and indeterminacy are analyzed in function of the GDPR, website category, popularity level, and domain.

The analysis of policy length reported by Amos et al. [7] in the form of a word-based analysis is complemented by a sentence-based analysis in this paper. Instead of the Flesch–Kincaid Grade Level (FKGL) readability metric used by Amos et al. [7], Dale–Chall's readability formula is used, which takes into account the semantic difficulty of words. In addition to analyzing the length based on the popularity of the website, our work considers additional aspects such as website category, GDPR and non-GDPR policies, and top-level domain. Although Amos et al. [7] found an increase in terms such as "may contain" and "may collect" in privacy policies in a general trend analysis and assumed that privacy policies become more ambiguous over time, this has not been systematically studied. This prompted us to investigate this specifically, based on the taxonomy of vague words by Reidenberg et al. [6] and a corpus of 4.5K sentences by Lebanoff and Liu [14] with a human-commented vagueness value to train a BERT classification model.

2. Regulatory Background

This section provides legal context to understand the foundation of privacy policies in the European Union and the United States. In the European Union, the Data Protection Directive (DPD) and its successor, the General Data Protection Regulation (GDPR), have shaped the landscape of data privacy. In the United States, data privacy regulations have historically taken a sectoral approach, meaning that privacy laws and regulations have been developed for specific sectors or industries.

2.1. Data Protection in the European Union

The Data Protection Directive (DPD) of 24 October 1995 aimed to regulate the processing of personal data in the European Union, harmonizing data protection legislation across member states [15,16]. The law builds upon the concept of *personal data*, which is defined as "any information relating to an identified or identifiable natural person ("data subject"); an identifiable person is one who can be identified, directly or indirectly, particularly with reference to an identification number or to one or more factors specific to their physical, physiological, mental, economic, cultural, or social identity" (Article 2). Such data include names, phone numbers, addresses and personal identification numbers.

The directive established supervisory authorities, data subject rights, and principles for data quality and processing. Special rules were introduced for sensitive data, prohibiting the processing of certain categories of information. Data controllers were required to provide transparent information to data subjects, often performed through privacy policies.

With the rise of the Internet and networked society, the need for enhanced data protection regulations became evident. The General Data Protection Regulation (GDPR), adopted in 2016 and effective from 25 May 2018, replaced the Data Protection Directive. Unlike its predecessor, the GDPR was a regulation directly applicable in Member States without the need for national legislation.

Under the regulation, the definition of personal data should be interpreted as broadly as possible to reflect the ways that organizations collect data about individuals [17]. Personal data are defined as any information that can be used alone or together with other data to identify an individual. In the current technological context, this includes location data, IP addresses, device identifiers, biometric data, audio and visual formats and profiling based on browsing and purchasing behavior. Personal data do not need to be objective; it can also be data about opinions, preferences and posts on social media. The GDPR aims to give EU citizens more control over their data by requiring explicit consent ("opt-in") and giving individuals the right to withdraw their consent and request the deletion of their data.

The GDPR also expanded its territorial scope, applying to all companies processing the personal data of EU residents, regardless of location. Privacy policies, a fundamental aspect of the GDPR's transparency principle, must be easily accessible and written in clear and plain language. They should provide concise information about:

- The data retention period;
- The data subject's rights;
- Information about the automated decision-making system, if used;
- The data controller's identity and contact details;
- The data protection officer's contact details, where applicable;
- All the purposes of and the legal basis for data processing;
- Recipients of the personal data;
- If the organization intends to transfer to a third country or international organization.

The GDPR emphasizes making privacy policies accessible and easy to understand. The information provided in them must be "in a concise, transparent, intelligible, and easily accessible form, using clear and plain language". Furthermore, "the information shall be provided in writing, or by other means, including, where appropriate, by electronic means" (Article 12).

2.2. *"Notice and Choice" in the United States*

In the US, there is no single national law regulating the collection and use of personal information. The government has approached privacy and security by only regulating certain sectors: the so-called "sectoral" or "patchwork" approach. One of the first federal laws was the Children's Online Privacy Protection Act (COPPA) from 1998, which regulated online data collection of data from children under 13 years old.

The leading framework for Internet privacy in the US is guided by the fair information practice principles of the Federal Trade Commission, a set of guidelines for privacy-friendly data practices in the online marketplace [18]. They take the form of recommendations and are not legally enforceable. At the heart of these recommendations are the principles of "notice and choice", also known as "notice and consent". Companies are required to inform individuals about data collection and use through privacy notices, and individuals must consent to data processing before it takes place.

While no generally applicable law exists in the United States, some states have implemented legislation governing privacy policies. The California Online Privacy Protection Act (CalOPPA) of 2003, for instance, required commercial websites that collect personally identifiable information about California residents to include a privacy policy on their homepage.

A more recent and comprehensive law was the California Consumer Privacy Act (CCPA), which came into force in 2020. This law requires companies to explain their privacy practices in a notice and gives consumers more control over their personal information. The CCPA established privacy rights, including the right to know what personal information a business collects and how it is shared, the right to delete collected personal information upon request, and the right to opt-out of the sale of personal information. Similar laws will come into force in Colorado, Connecticut, Virginia and Utah from 2023.

3. Automated Privacy Policy Research

Automated privacy policy analysis, including machine learning methods, has grown in popularity during the last decade. The main goal was to grant users a better understanding of how their data are used and help them make informed decisions regarding their privacy. This section provides an overview of the recent research efforts with a focus on English language website policies.

3.1. Privacy Policy Datasets

Various privacy policy datasets have been made accessible to researchers (see Table 1), with the Usable Privacy Policy Project [19] playing a significant role in this regard. Their OPP-115 corpus [20] contains annotated segments from 115 website privacy policies, enabling advanced machine learning research and automated analysis. Another dataset from the same project is the OptOutChoice-2020 corpus [21], which includes privacy policy sentences with labeled opt-out choices types. PolicyIE [22] offers a more recent dataset with annotated data practices, including intent classification and slot filling, based on 31 web and mobile app privacy policies. Nokhbeh Zaeem and Barber [23] created a corpus of over 100,000 privacy policies, categorized into 15 website categories, utilizing the DMOZ directory. PrivaSeer [12] is a privacy policy dataset and search engine containing approximately 1.4 million website privacy policies. It was built using web crawls from 2019 and 2020, utilizing URLs from "Common Crawl" and the "Free Company Dataset". Finally, Amos et al. [7] released the Princeton-Leuven Longitudinal Corpus of Privacy Policies, a large-scale longitudinal corpus spanning two decades, consisting of one million privacy policy snapshots from around 130,000 websites, enabling the study of trends and changes over time.

Table 1. Publicly available privacy policy datasets.

Dataset	# Policies	# Websites	Timeframe	Labeling
OPP-115	115	115	2015	Yes
OptOutChoice-2020	236	236	-	Yes
PolicyIE	400	400 (websites + apps)	2019	Yes
DMOZ-based Corpus	117,502	-	2020	No
PrivaSeer	1,005,380	995,475	2019	No
Princeton-Leuven Corpus	910,546	108,499	1997–2019	No

3.2. Classification and Information Extraction

Classification and information extraction from privacy policies have been widely explored using machine learning techniques. Kaur et al. [11] employed unsupervised methods such as Latent Dirichlet Allocation (LDA) and term frequency to analyze keywords and content in 2000 privacy policies. Supervised learning approaches have also been utilized, including classifiers trained on the OPP-115 dataset. Audich et al. [24] compared the performance of supervised and unsupervised algorithms to label policy segments, while Kumar et al. [25] trained privacy-specific word embeddings for improved results. Deep learning models like CNN, BERT, and XLNET have further enhanced their classification performance [26–28]. Bui et al. [29] tackled the extraction of personal data objects and actions using a BLSTM model with contextual word embeddings. Alabduljabbar et al. [30,31] proposed a pipeline called TLDR for the automatic categorization and highlighting of policy segments, enhancing user comprehension. Extracting opt-out choices from privacy policies has also been studied [21,32,33]. In the field of summarization, Keymanesh et al. [34] introduced a domain-guided approach for privacy policy summarization, focusing on labeling privacy topics and extracting the riskiest content. Several studies have worked on developing automated privacy policy question-answering assistants [35–37].

Furthermore, the PrivacyGLUE [38] benchmark was proposed to address the lack of comprehensive benchmarks specifically designed for privacy policies. The benchmark includes the performance evaluations of transformer language models and emphasizes the importance of in-domain pre-training for privacy policies.

3.3. Privacy Policy Applications for Enhancing Users' Comprehension

Applications enhancing the comprehension of privacy policies have been developed to provide users with useful and visually appealing presentations of policy information. PrivacyGuide [39] employs a two-step multi-class approach, identifying relevant privacy aspects and predicting risk levels using a trained model on a labeled dataset. The user interface utilizes colored icons to indicate risk levels. Polisis [40,41] combines a summarizing tool, policy comparison tool, and chatbot. The query system employs neural network classifiers trained on the OPP-115 dataset and privacy-specific language models. PrivacyCheck is a browser extension that extracts 10 privacy factors and displays their risk levels through icons and text snippets [42–45]. Opt-Out Easy is another browser extension that utilizes the OptOutChoice-2020 dataset to identify and present opt-out choices to users during web browsing [21,46].

3.4. Regulatory Impact

User research has also focused on evaluating privacy policies for regulatory compliance, particularly in response to the implementation of General Data Protection Regulation (GDPR) in Europe. The tool Claudette detects unfair clauses and evaluates privacy policy compliance with GDPR [47,48]. KnIGHT ("Know your rIGHTs") utilizes semantic text matching to map policy sentences to GDPR paragraphs [49]. Cejas et al. [50] and Qamar et al. [51] leveraged NLP and supervised machine learning to identify GDPR-relevant information in policies and assess their compliance. Similarly, Sánchez et al. [52] used manual annotations and machine learning to tag policies based on GDPR goals, offering both aggregated scores and fine-grained ratings for better understanding. Degeling et al. [53] and Linden et al. [54] examined the effects of GDPR on privacy policies through longitudinal analysis, observing updates and changes in policy length and disclosures. Zaeem and Barber [55] compared pre- and post-GDPR policies using PrivacyCheck, highlighting deficiencies in transparency and explicit data processing disclosures. Libert [56] developed an automated approach to audit third-party data sharing in privacy policies.

3.5. Comprehensibility of Privacy Policies

Studies on privacy policy comprehensibility have examined deficiencies in readability, revealing that privacy policies are difficult to read and demonstrating correlations between readability measures [9,10]. Furthermore, researchers have examined the changes in length and readability of privacy policies over time [4,7].

Other scholars have studied ambiguous content in privacy policies. Kaur et al. [11] and Srinath et al. [12] analyzed the use of ambiguous words in a corpus of 2000 policies. Furthermore, Kotal et al. [57] studied the ambiguity in the OPP-115 dataset and showed that ambiguity negatively affects the ability to automatically evaluate privacy policies. Srinath et al. [12] reported on privacy policy length and the use of vague words in their PrivaSeer corpus of policies. Lebanoff and Liu [14] investigated the detection of vague words and sentences using deep neural networks. The present work improved the prediction performance regarding sentence classification using a BERT architecture. This paper also contributed to the literature by providing a longitudinal analysis of trends related to ambiguity.

3.6. Mobile Applications

While the focus of the present overview is on website policies, the research community has also examined privacy policies in the context of mobile applications, establishing several corpora of mobile app privacy policies [58,59]. Those policies are well-suited for compliance analysis, because they are studied along with the app code and the traffic generated by the app [59,60].

4. Data and Methods

4.1. The Princeton-Leuven Longitudinal Corpus of Privacy Policies

This analysis of the privacy policy landscape is based on the Princeton-Leuven Corpus, a historical dataset of English-language privacy policies spanning over two decades [7]. It contains 910,546 policy snapshots of 108,499 distinct websites, which have been selected based on the Alexa's top 100,000 lists between 2009 and 2019. The original dataset consisted of 1,071,488 policy snapshots of over 130,000 sites. In the course of additional quality control, Amos et al. [7] removed real policies that might lead to a biased analysis (e.g., the policies of domain-parking services). The remaining dataset they refer to as the "analysis subcorpus", which is the one used in this study. The websites are distributed over 575 different top-level domains, with ".com" being the most frequent (76% of the websites). Figure 1 shows the distribution across the remaining domains.

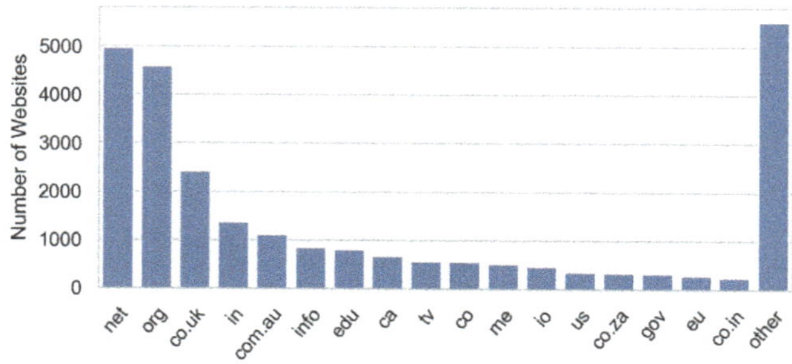

Figure 1. Distribution of top-level domains in the dataset (.com excluded).

For each website, two snapshots per year were retrieved, creating a crawler that discovered, downloaded, and extracted archived privacy policies from the Internet Archive's Wayback Machine [61]. Available snapshots were included for the years before 2009 and up to the first year for which Internet Archive has crawls. One snapshot was retrieved from the first half of the year (January–June) and another from the second half (July–December). These six-month spans were referred to as intervals and they were the basic time units in the data analysis. After the crawling, there was a series of validation and quality control steps, including language checks to remove non-English policies. For detailed information about the data collection methodology, consult the original paper by Amos et al. [7]. Figure 2 presents the distribution of the policy snapshots over time and across the most frequent website categories.

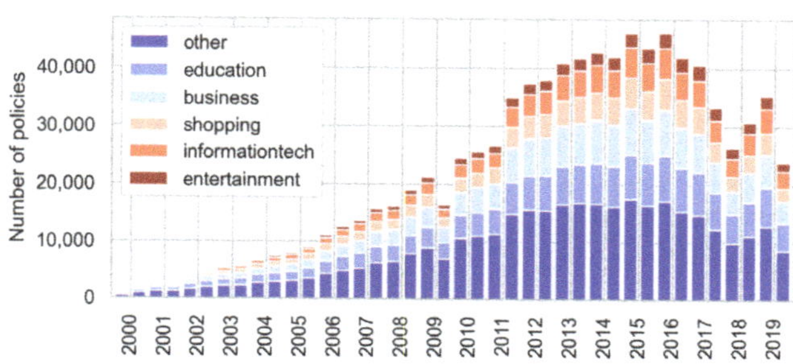

Figure 2. Distribution of policy snapshots per interval and category. Each bar represents an interval (two intervals per year).

The analysis in this paper focuses on the period after 2009, as the majority of policies are from these years. Additionally, Alexa rank data are only available for this timeframe. Since the provided dataset only covers up to 2019, we do not consider the period beyond that. Our data preparation phase involved extracting only the sentence text from privacy policies. This step was necessary because the analysis relied on sentence counts and sentence classification. Non-sentence content such as headers, short lists, tables, and links was removed. After applying various data cleaning steps, each policy text was segmented into sentences using the sentence tokenizer from the NLTK library [62]. A manual check revealed that short sentences were mostly noisy, so those containing fewer than three words were removed. Data extraction and preparation stages are illustrated in Figure 3.

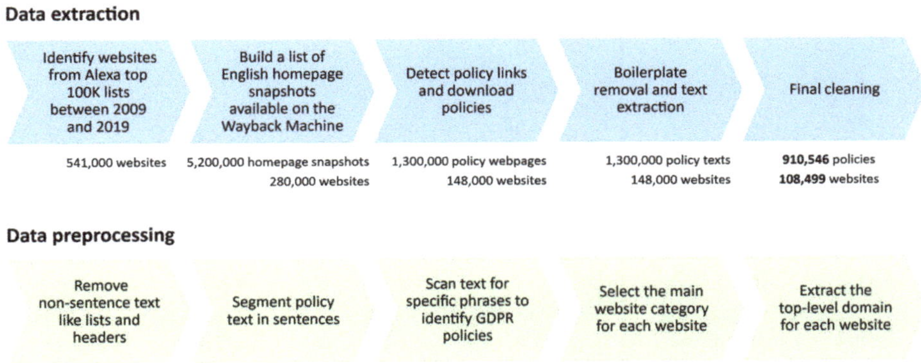

Figure 3. Data extraction (by Amos et al. [7]) and further preprocessing (this study).

The dataset included information on website categories from the domain categorization API Webshrinker [63]. The websites were distributed over 481 unique combinations of 27 top-level categories like business, shopping, and education, but a small number of categories dominated the dataset.

To identify GDPR policies, the text was scanned for "GDPR", "General Data Protection Regulation" or one of the GDPR-related phrases provided by Amos et al. [7]. Refer to Appendix A for comprehensive information on category distribution and the measure of GDPR content.

4.2. Measuring Readability of Privacy Policies

The analysis of privacy policy readability focused on three key factors: policy length, passive voice usage, and reading difficulty, as measured by the Dale–Chall readability formula. To assess the policy length, the mean and median sentence counts were reported for each interval. Passive voice usage was quantified using a passive voice index. This index was derived by dividing the number of passive voice structures by the total number of sentences in a given policy. In essence, the passive voice index represents the average number of passive voice structures per sentence. The identification of passive voice structures in the policy text followed a methodology similar to that presented by Linden et al. [54].

Many readability metrics, such as the Flesch Readability Ease Score (FRES), the Flesh-Kincaid Grade Level (FKG), the Simple Measure of Gobbledygook (SMOG), rely on word complexity measured by the number of characters or syllables and sentence length. A drawback of most of these formulas is their failure to account for the semantic difficulty of the words used [7].

To analyze the development of policies' reading complexity, we used the new Dale–Chall readability formula (see Equation (1)). Unlike other formulas, the Dale–Chall uses a count of semantically difficult words, classified as such because they do not appear on a list of common words familiar to most fourth-grade students. The new Dale–Chall formula expanded the list of the initial 763 familiar words to 3000 words [64]. The expanded list of words is available here: https://readabilityformulas.com/word-lists/the-dale-chall-word-list-for-readability-formulas (accessed on 15 November 2023). An adjusted version of the Dale–Chall score was converted to US grade level based on a correction table (see Table 2).

$$DC = 0.1579 \times \left(\frac{\text{difficult words}}{\text{words}} \times 100\right) + 0.0496 \times \left(\frac{\text{words}}{\text{sentences}}\right) \quad (1)$$

Table 2. Readability grades according to the new Dale–Chall formula.

Adj. Score	Grade Level
5.0–5.9	Grades 5–6
6.0–6.9	Grades 7–8
7.0–7.9	Grades 9–10
8.0–8.9	Grades 11–12
9.0–9.9	College
10–above	College graduate

Please consult Appendix B for the outlier analyses of the calculated measures presented in this and the following section.

4.3. Measuring Ambiguity in Privacy Policies

4.3.1. Taxonomy of Vague Terms

Qualifiers like "may", "can", "could", and "possibly" introduce uncertainty, creating imprecision and ambiguity. This study refers to these words as "vague terms". Similarly, phrases such as "depending", "as needed", and "as applicable" indicate conditional validity, complicating readers' ability to discern specific circumstances for described processes. For instance, "We may disclose your personal information if necessary to enforce our User Agreement".

Additionally, phrases like "including" and "such as" within lists imply incomprehensive specification (refer to example in Table 3). Generalizing terms like "generally" or "usually" lead to abstraction, hampering precise information identification, as seen in "Generally we will store and process your information within the UK".

In their research on "Ambiguity in Privacy Policies and the Impact of Regulation", Reidenberg et al. [6] developed a comprehensive vague term taxonomy. Analyzing 15 policies across different sectors, they categorized 40 vague terms into four types, as illustrated in Table 3. This taxonomy served as a foundation for ambiguity measurement in privacy policies. For each policy, the number of sentences containing at least one, two, or three vague terms was divided by the overall number of sentences. To show the progression of ambiguity over time, we used the median number of all policies for each time interval.

4.3.2. Language Model for Vagueness Prediction

A further evaluation of the ambiguity was conducted using the corpus on vagueness in privacy policies made available by Lebanoff and Liu [14]. The corpus consisted of human-annotated sentences extracted from 100 privacy policies. A group of five annotators were instructed to rate the sentences on a scale from 1 to 5, where 1 meant "clear" and 5 meant "extremely vague". The authors only selected potentially vague sentences to help balance the dataset using the taxonomy of vague words introduced in this section. Sentences containing at least 1 of the 40 cue words were considered to have a higher chance of being labeled as vague by the annotators. The overall size of the corpus amounted to 4500 sentences.

To predict the vagueness of the sentences, a language model was trained on these data. The annotations were aggregated according to the majority voting rule: if three or more annotators agreed on a given score, it was considered the final score. In the case of disagreement between the annotators, the average of the five scores was taken. Following the methodology of Lebanoff and Liu [14], the aggregate score s was grouped into four categories:

$1 \leq s < 2 \rightarrow$ clear
$2 \leq s < 3 \rightarrow$ somewhat clear
$3 \leq s < 4 \rightarrow$ vague
$4 \leq s \leq 5 \rightarrow$ extremely vague

Figure 4 shows the distribution of the categories. An "ambiguity score" for each policy snapshot in the longitudinal dataset illustrates the development of ambiguity over time. This score represents the number of sentences classified either as vague or extremely vague and normalized by the total number of sentences in the policy (i.e., the percentage of vague sentences). Another metric we reported was the percentage of sentences, labeled as clear.

Table 3. Taxonomy of vague terms. Adapted from Reidenberg et al. [6].

Category	Key Words and Phrases	Example Sentence
Condition Action performed is dependent on a variable or unclear trigger	depending, necessary, appropriate, inappropriate, as needed, as applicable, otherwise reasonably, sometimes, from time to time	"As a result, Pokemon will not collect more personal information than is reasonably **necessary**".
Generalization Action/information type is vaguely abstracted with unclear conditions	generally, mostly, widely, general, commonly, usually, normally, typically, largely, often, primarily, among other things	"**Generally** we will store and process your information within the UK."
Modality Vague likelihood of action or ambiguous possibility of action or event	may, might, can, could, would, likely, possible, possibly, probably, optionally	"If you are logged in to the site, we **could** associate information about your site usage that is collected by cookies, web beacons and web logs with your user account."
Numeric quantifier Vague quantifier of action/information type	anyone, certain, everyone, numerous, some, most, few, much, many, various, including but not limited to, such as	"You hereby consent to the collection, use, disclosure and retention by edX of your personal information as described under this privacy policy, **including but not limited** to the transfer of your personal data between edX and the third parties, affiliates and subsidiaries described in this privacy policy."

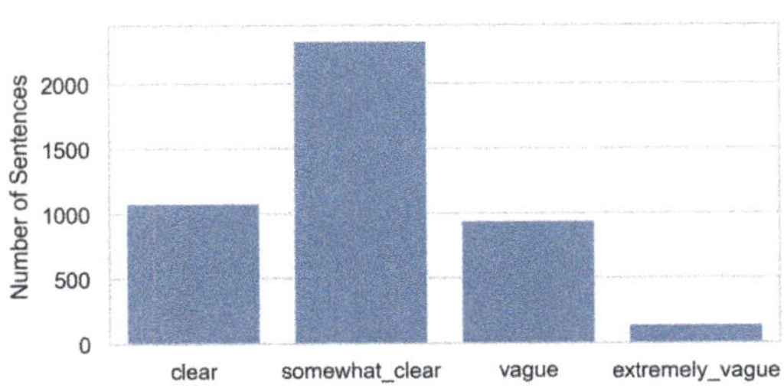

Figure 4. Distribution of vagueness categories.

Predicting the vagueness level of a sentence is a multi-class sentence classification task that we approached using transfer learning with a pre-trained BERT model.

The model was fine-tuned using Fast-BERT, a deep learning Python library for training BERT-based models for text classification. The library repository is located at https://github.com/utterworks/fast-bert (accessed on 15 November 2023). Fast-BERT is built on the foundations of the Hugging Face BERT PyTorch interface [65]. For this study, we used the "BertForSequenceClassification" model, a BERT model with an added linear layer for classification, as a sentence classifier. The small "BERT base" version was used in particular; it consists of twelve layers, each including 768 hidden units and 12 attention heads resulting in a total of 110 million parameters.

Devlin et al. [66] suggested fine-tuning only on few parameters: the epochs, learning rate, and batch size. They recommended training for just two to three epochs with the Adam optimizer and a batch size of 16 or 32. Table 4 shows the training parameter chosen after manual evaluation. The tokenized input sequence was limited to 256-word piece tokens. Taking into account the length of the sentence, this was sufficient to capture almost all the information it contained.

Table 4. BERT fine-tuning parameters.

Model	BERT Base Uncased
Batch size	16
Epochs	2
Learning rate	4×10^{-4}
Max length	256
Optimizer type	Adam

For the fine-tuning, the dataset was divided into the train, test, and validation sets, each the size of, respectively, 3499, 500, and 500 sentences. As Figure 4 shows, the sentences were very unevenly distributed across the four categories. For an imbalanced classification problem, accuracy is not the most suitable measure, because high accuracy is achievable through even a simple model only predicting the majority class. For this kind of problem, the F1 score, composed of precision and recall, is more appropriate. We report those metrics in Table 5.

Table 5. BERT for sentence classification: model evaluation.

	Baseline		BERT		ACGAN
		Train	Validation	Test	
Accuracy	0.5172	0.6499	0.6120	0.5960	
F1-Score					
Macro average	0.1705	0.4658	0.4477	0.4098	
Micro average	0.3526	0.6327	0.5955	0.5783	0.5234
Precision					
Macro average	0.1293	0.4747	0.4540	0.4157	
Micro average	0.2675	0.6240	0.5878	0.5669	0.5290
Recall					
Macro average	0.2500	0.4635	0.4482	0.4085	
Micro average	0.5172	0.6499	0.6120	0.5960	0.5464

The BERT model was compared to a baseline model and the Auxiliary Classifier Generative Adversarial Networks (AC-GAN) used in the original paper by Lebanoff and Liu [14]. The baseline model is a simple rule-based model that always predicts the majority class. In this case, for every sentence in the validation and test datasets, the "somewhat clear" class is assigned, because this is the most common category in the training dataset. The prediction power of BERT was by far greater than a baseline model and also showed an improvement over the AC-GAN model. However, the results are not directly comparable, because they use a slightly different annotations aggregation scheme. Lebanoff and Liu [14] did not use majority voting and simply took the average of all the annotators. More details about the performance of the model are presented in Appendix C.

4.4. Unveiling Positive Framing in Privacy Policies

Many Internet users have likely encountered phrases like "we value your privacy" or "we take your privacy and security seriously" while using online services. These phrases, aimed at alleviating privacy concerns, are not essential policy information. Positive language, at best, diverts user attention from privacy implications, and at worst, can mislead.

Libert et al. [13] investigated the prevalence of such potentially insincere statements and found that they occur more frequently in privacy policies than in documents such as terms of use. Our study built on this by manually identifying additional phrases beyond those examined by Libert et al. [13]. These phrases were then matched within policy texts using regular expression patterns. The aim was to identify trends in the use of positive phrases, but not to create an exhaustive list. Table 6 provides the illustrative examples of those phrases, while the complete list can be found in Appendix D.

Table 6. Examples of pacifying statements concerning privacy and security.

Website	Category	Example Sentence
cheapflights.com	travel, business	Cheapflights Media (USA) Inc., which publishes Cheapflights.com, has created this privacy statement in order to demonstrate our **firm commitment to user privacy.**
direct-golf.co.uk	business, shopping	The personal information which we hold will be **held securely** in accordance with our internal security policy and governing UK law.
tumblr.com	blogs and personal, social networking	Tumblr, Inc. takes the private nature of your information **very seriously**.
learningstrategies.com	business, education	We are **committed to safeguarding** the privacy of our website visitors, subscribers, and clients.
imdb.com	entertainment	IMDb knows that you care how information about you is used and shared, and we appreciate your trust that we will do so **carefully and sensibly**.
alibaba.com	shopping	We at Alibaba.com **recognize the importance** of privacy and confidentiality of personal information.

5. Results

5.1. Readability

Figure 5 shows the mean and median sentence counts for every interval since 2001. Over 19 years, the average policy length has doubled, with around 30 sentences in 2001 rising up to 60 by 2019. Policy lengths increased more steeply after the first interval of 2018, when the GDPR came into force. Indeed, the length of policies mentioning the GDPR or related phrases was on average double that of those classified as "non-GDPR" (Figure 6-right).

The trend of increasing length remains true across different rank tiers, website top-level domains, and categories. However, the results confirm previous findings that sites ranked higher by Alexa tend to have longer policies [56] and this trend has remained stable over time (Figure 6-left). In 2019, the median length of the top 1000 ranked policies in the dataset was 114.5 sentences, nearly twice the length of website policies with rankings between 100,000 and 1,000,000 (59 sentences).

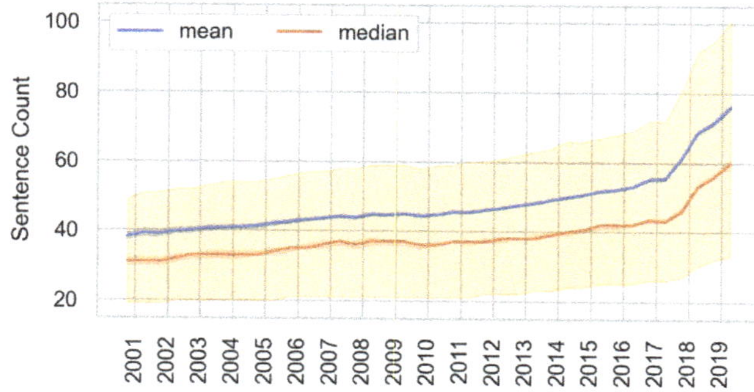

Figure 5. Sentence count of privacy policies over time. The shaded area indicates the data between the 25th and 75 percentiles.

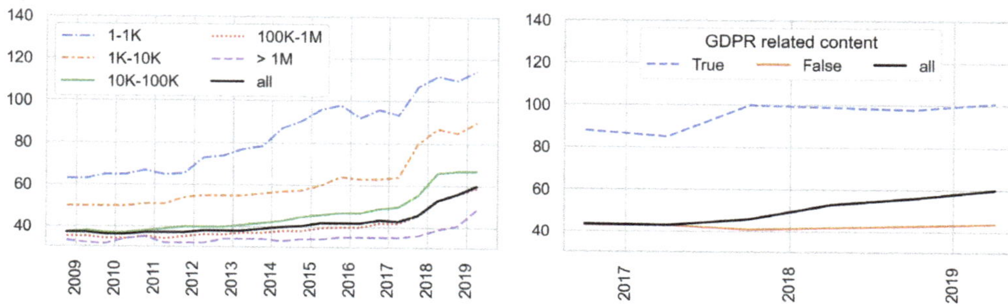

Figure 6. Median sentence count of privacy policies by Alexa ranking (**left**) and by GDPR content (**right**).

Regarding the top-level domain, the holders of the co.uk and com.au domains provide policies of above-median lengths. These domains are typically used for UK and Australian commercial websites. In contrast, .edu and .net websites have the shortest policies, averaging around 40 sentences in 2019 (Figure 7-left). We also analyzed the policy length of the most frequent categories of websites present in the dataset. Shopping and business websites have longer policies, whereas information tech sites' policies are shorter on average. However, the results showed that the differences between categories remain small in size (Figure 7-right).

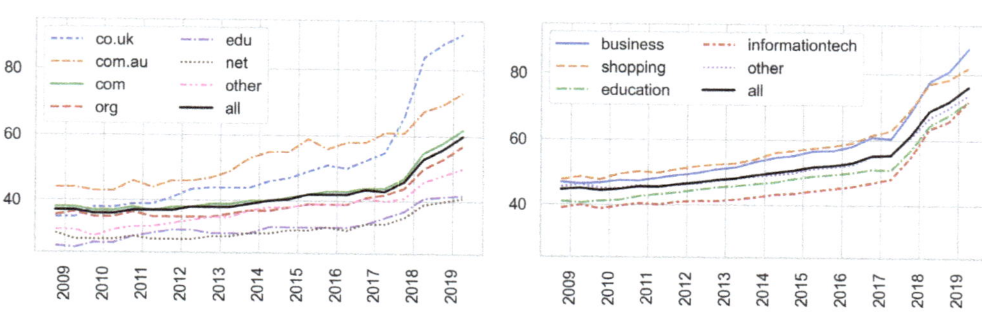

Figure 7. Median sentence count of privacy policies by top-level domain (**left**) and by website category (**right**).

Concerning passive voice structures, the results showed that their usage remained stable over time, with values of 0.15–0.16 (Figure 8). These index values signified the use of one passive voice structure every six sentences on average. The index did not vary considerably across different domains.

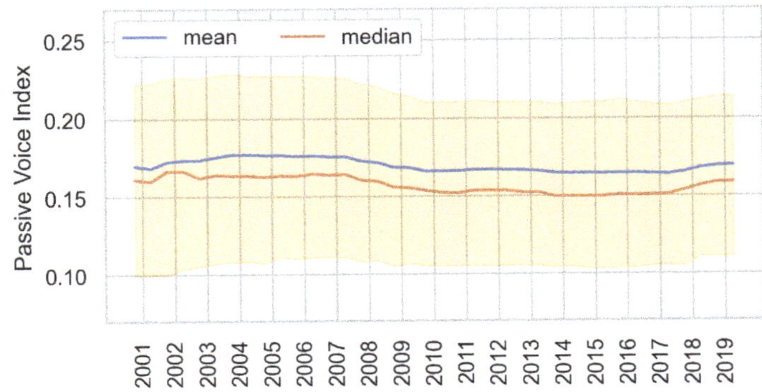

Figure 8. Average passive voice index of privacy policies. The shaded area indicates the interquartile range.

Figure 9 shows the distribution of polices across reading grades over time. The analysis only included polices with more than 100 words, as this metric is not suitable for shorter policies. Furthermore, the 61 policy snapshots requiring 7th or 8th high-school grade are excluded from the visualization (they comprise less than 0.00001% of all snapshots).

More than 90% of the policies in the dataset were at the reading level of a college student or college graduate. Indeed, 2019 was the first year in which the proportion of polices requiring a college degree was higher than all other groups. These results confirmed the previous findings that privacy policies are difficult to comprehend. This has been shown to be true across all popularity ranks, website categories, and domains. The median DC score increased slightly over time, from 9.8 to 10 over a 10 year span. The GDPR's policies were shown to be less readable with a DC score of about 0.2 higher than the median. Policies in the .edu domain were also less readable (scoring about 0.6 higher than the median). See Figure 10.

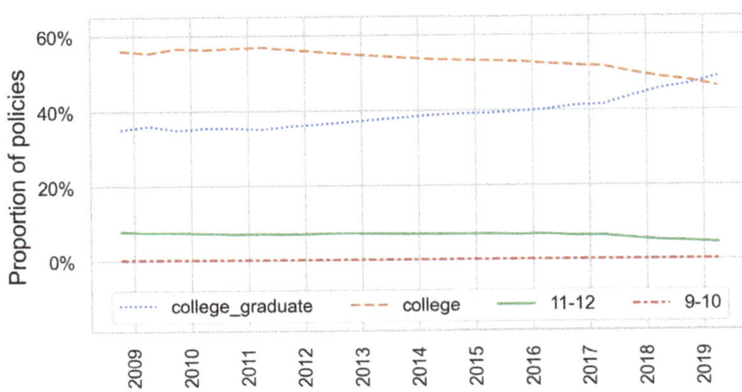

Figure 9. Distribution of the Dale–Chall reading grade levels of privacy policies.

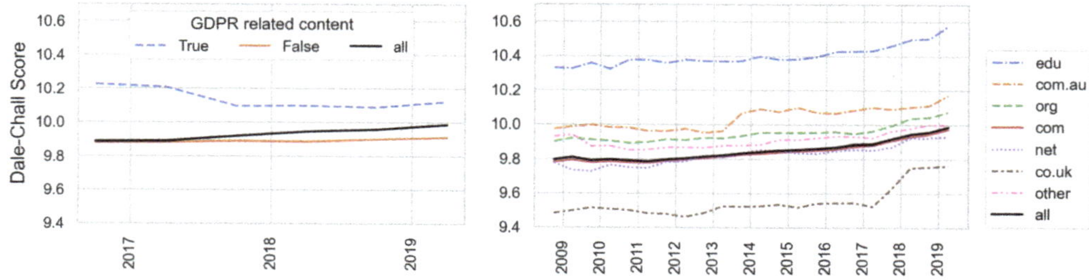

Figure 10. Median Dale–Chall readability score of privacy policies by GDPR content (**left**) and by top-level domain (**right**).

5.2. Ambiguity

The results showed that the proportion of sentences containing vague terms increased (Figures 11 and 12). The fraction of sentences containing at least one vague term rose constantly over time, from 38% in 2001 to 47% in 2019. On average, nearly every second sentence in a policy contained at least one vague term. The percentage of the sentences the model classified as vague also increased, while clear sentences decreased. Those findings paint a similar picture of the results of Srinath et al. [12] between the years 2019 and 2020.

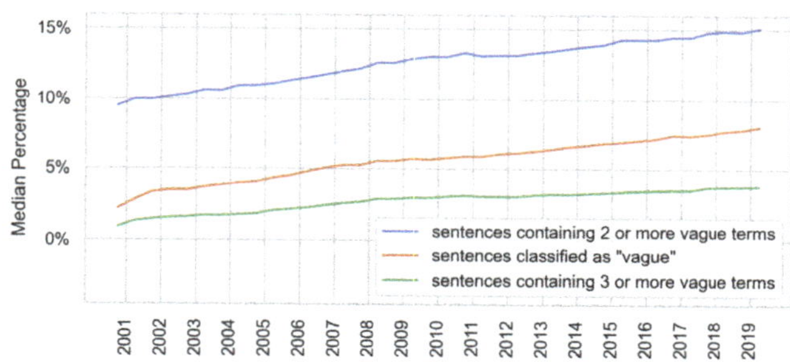

Figure 11. Median percentage of "vague" sentences in privacy policies.

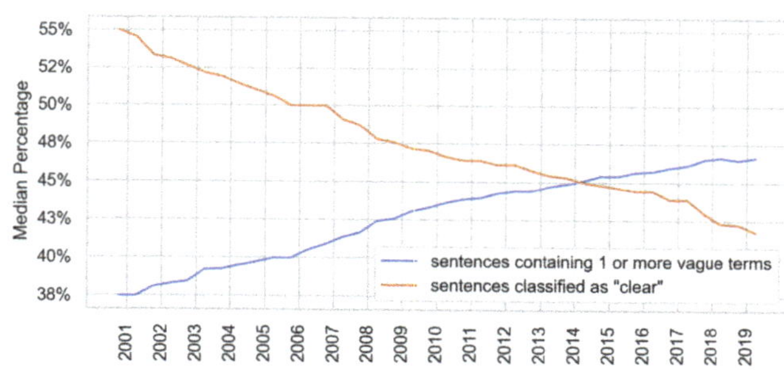

Figure 12. Median percentage of "vague" and "clear" sentences in privacy policies.

The results also confirm the assumption that privacy policies are becoming more ambiguous over time [7]. This trend holds for different website categories, top-level domain, and popularity ranks. Figure 13 illustrates that popular websites tend to have a higher number of vague and less clear sentences. The different categories of websites followed the overall trend of increasing policy ambiguity. However, for education and information technology websites, it was generally higher, while for business websites, it was lower. Nevertheless, those differences were not particularly large (Figure 14). It is noteworthy that the holders of Australian commercial websites (com.au domain) provided more ambiguous polices. The fraction of clear sentences in those policies was consistently around 8% lower than the median fraction for all websites (35% versus 42% in 2019). The opposite trend was visible the vague sentences, as can be seen in Figure 15.

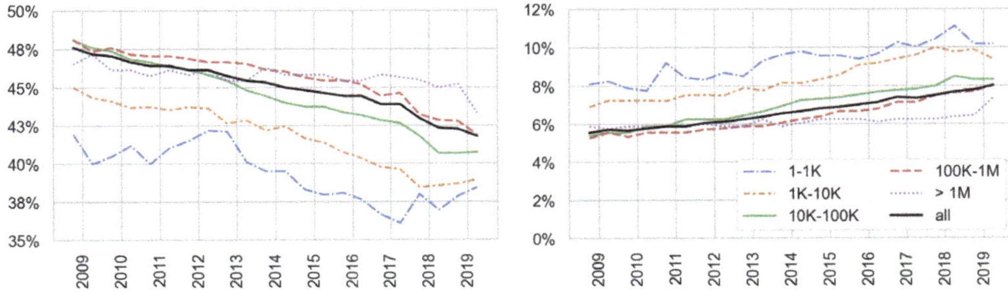

Figure 13. Median proportion of sentences classified as "clear" (**left**) and as "vague" (**right**) by Alexa rank.

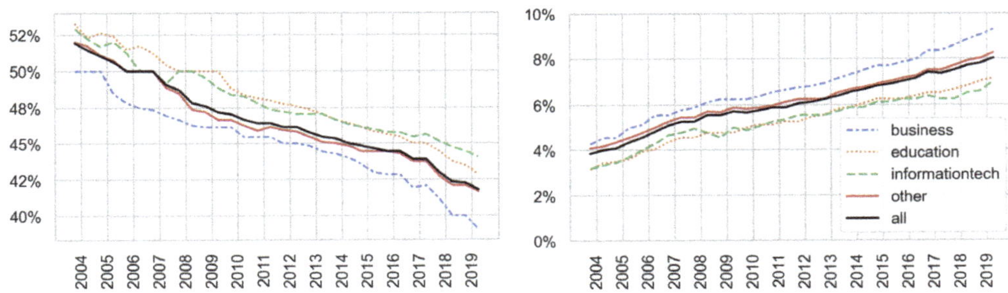

Figure 14. Median proportion of sentences classified as "clear" (**left**) and as "vague" (**right**) by website category.

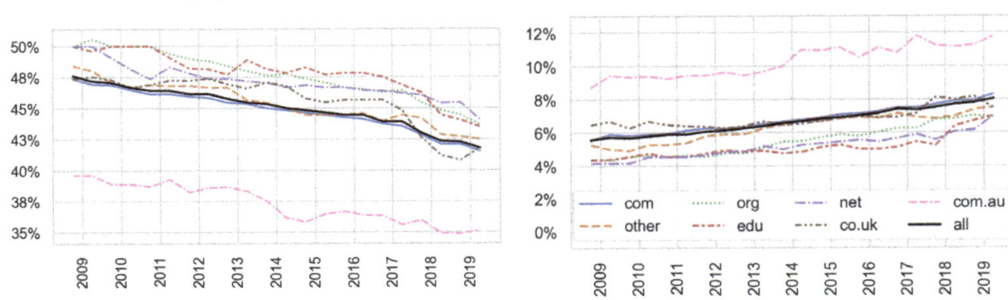

Figure 15. Median proportion of sentences classified as "clear" (**left**) and as "vague" (**right**) by top-level domain.

To analyze whether GDPR policies are ambiguous, Figure 16 shows the fraction of clear and vague sentences grouped by whether the policy contains some GDPR key terms or not. The results indicate that the GDPR policies have a lower fraction of clear sentences of about 2%. In contrast, the fraction of vague ones is higher.

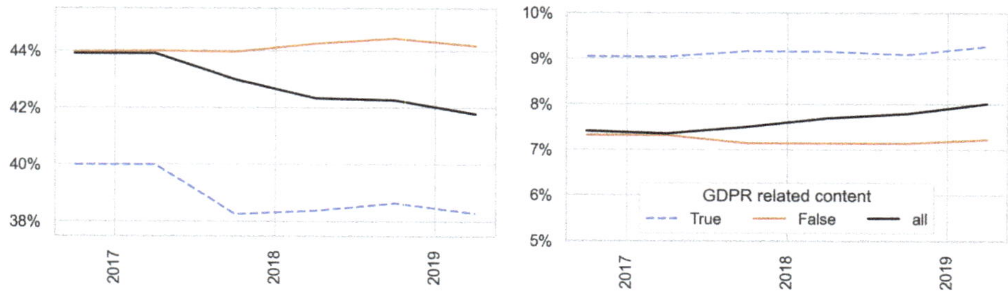

Figure 16. Median proportion of sentences classified as "clear" (**left**) and as "vague" (**right**) by GDPR content.

5.3. Positive Phrases

Figure 17 displays a large increase in policies using positive language. In 2019, two-thirds of privacy policies contained at least one of the listed phrases. This is more than double the result reported by Libert et al. [13] for the year 2021, which may be due to the fact that we added more words to the list of pacifying phrases. The findings indicated that the policies of the top 1000 websites more often contained such phrases than less popular websites (Figure 18-left). Furthermore, Figure 18-right shows that, in 2019, 78% percent of GDPR policies contained positive framing, whereas for the "non-GDPR" polices, this fraction was only 65%. Considering the top-level domain and website categories, this illustrated the fact that educational websites use those positive statements less often in their policies (Figure 19).

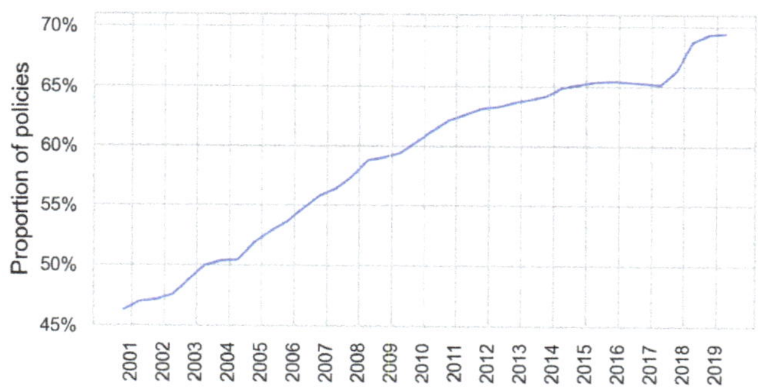

Figure 17. The proportion of policies containing one or more pacifying phrases.

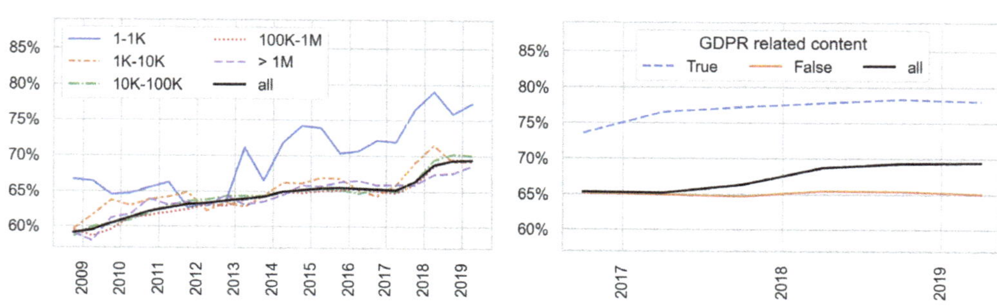

Figure 18. Proportion of policies containing one or more pacifying phrases by Alexa ranking (**left**) and by GDPR content (**right**).

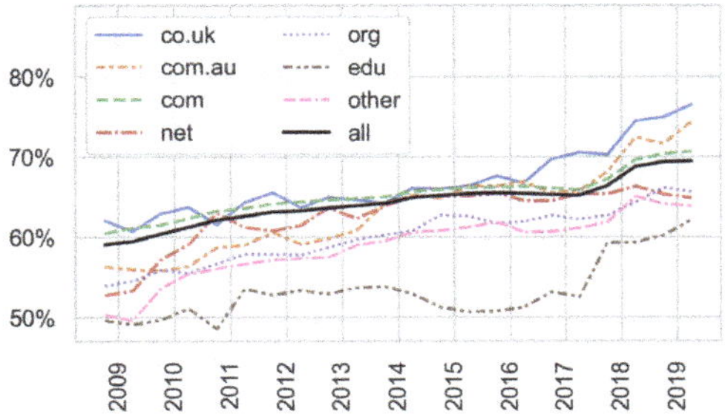

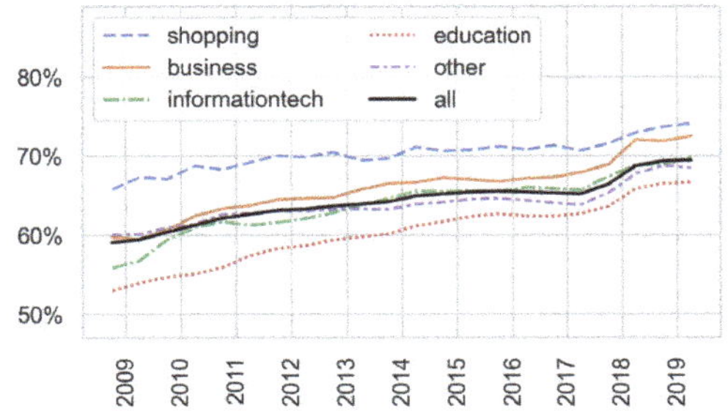

Figure 19. Proportion of policies containing one or more pacifying phrases by top-level domain (**left**) and by website category (**right**).

6. Discussion

The longitudinal analysis of more than 900,000 policy snapshots showed a concerning picture of the privacy policy landscape. To begin with, these policies were shown to be long and difficult to read. Since 2001, the average policy length has doubled, and nearly half the policies in the dataset required a college degree. In the age of information overload, the increasing complexity of privacy policies forces Internet users into a "transparency paradox" [67]. Transparency requires the detailed explanations of all data practices and user rights, which might result in terms that are lengthy and difficult to understand. Alternatively, summarizations lead to more ambiguous notices. The policies an average user encounters on a daily basis are simply too extensive and too long. When faced with yet another one, users most simply click "accept" and hope for the best.

Moreover, policies mentioning the GDPR or related wording were double the length of "non-GDPR" ones. This result confirmed findings from previous studies, indicating that the rise in policy length in recent years is likely connected to the regulation. A possible explanation is that policies were required to add information on data sharing practices, users rights, contact information, and other areas. Furthermore, to ensure compliance with the new regulations, lawyers might have used more detailed and lengthy legal language. This contradicts the GDPR's transparency guidelines, which require that websites avoid the need for users to scroll through large amounts of text, causing information fatigue. Furthermore, "the quality, accessibility, and comprehensibility of the information is as important as the actual content".

The key finding of this study was that privacy policies have become more ambiguous over time. They are increasingly using vague terms; in 2019, on average, nearly every second sentence in a policy contained at least one vague term. The results of the language model showed that the fraction of vague statements in policies has increased over time, while clear statements have decreased. This is troubling because it indicates that the policies fail to clearly communicate websites' actual practices. This in turn limits not only the ability of human readers to precisely interpret their contents, but also machines' ability to "understand" them. Kotal et al. [57] found that NLP-based text segment classifiers are less accurate for policies that are more ambiguous.

The greatest lack of overall clarity, however, was found in the policies of popular websites—in other words, in those that accounted for a larger portion of web traffic. However, the bigger part of these policies contained pacifying statements. One possible explanation is that those websites are using user data in a greater variety of ways and require more exhaustive policies. It could also be that the popular sites are the only ones with the resources to afford teams of lawyers to write complex policy texts. There appears to be a lack of incentives to make privacy policies not only beneficial for their writers, but also useful for their readers. While companies "take your privacy very seriously", they have failed to take the effective communication of data practices seriously enough.

The presented readability analysis focused on specific aspects such as sentence count for length, passive voice usage, and the Dale–Chall readability score. However, it has limitations as it does not encompass other factors that can influence the overall comprehension difficulty of the text. Policy features such as highlighting relevant information, the organization of the text, and formatting are equally important. One possible direction for research is the examination of the overall user-friendliness, including the question of whether policies are easily accessible and if they contain additional media such as videos or images. Furthermore, the use of specific legal jargon should be explored as it may make the text less understandable.

Concerning ambiguity, the frequency of vague terms in a text may indicate ambiguous content. Nevertheless, to achieve accurate results, it is important to study the context in which those words are used. The presented key terms can be used in a way that is not vague or in a context that is not relevant for the analysis, for example, in descriptions. One possibility for the future research is to identify sentences in which vague terms are used in tandem with relevant content, for example, data sharing practices (e.g., the co-occurrences of "may" and "share").

As part of an additional measurement of ambiguity, a BERT model was trained. However, there are several limitations regarding the training data. First, the corpus is based on privacy policies from the year 2014. There is no evidence for whether the model trained with these data can be applied on policies from 2009 to 2019. The policy content or phrasing might change in the course of the time and this could distort the predictions. Second, with only 4500 sentences, the corpus is relatively small and very unbalanced. This makes it difficult to train accurate classifiers, especially regarding the "vague" category. A larger and more balanced annotated dataset is necessary to further improve the overall performance of the model. Third, annotations are made on a sentence basis. However, the context beyond the scope of the single sentence may be important for annotators to judge the clarity of the statements. Lastly, the concept of vagueness is a very subjective one and even human annotators often disagree. The underlying pattern may be too complex for a language model to accurately reproduce.

Furthermore, the relationship between GDPR policies and ambiguity should be investigated in future work to obtain more decisive results. Another open question is why the policies of Australian commercial websites (com.au) are on average longer and more ambiguous. This might be due the local legal framework or specific language characteristics of Australian English.

With respect to pacifying language, the heuristic approach of matching pacifying statements in privacy policies has revealed that their use is increasing. User studies and more complex NLP techniques such as sentiment analysis are needed to gain a deeper understanding of how policy authors influence the user's perception of privacy risks.

Furthermore, recent advancements in NLP methodologies underscore the potential of large language models (LLMs) for the future analysis of privacy policies. Recent papers by Chanenson et al. [68] and Tang et al. [69] exemplify this potential.

7. Conclusions

The key finding of this study was that privacy policies have become more ambiguous over time. They are increasingly using vague terms; in 2019, on average, nearly every second sentence in a policy contained at least one vague term. The results of the language model showed that the fraction of vague statements in policies has increased over time, while clear statements have decreased. This is troubling because it indicates that the policies fail to clearly communicate the websites' actual practices. This, in turn, limits not only the ability of human readers to precisely interpret their contents but also machines' ability to "understand" them.

Author Contributions: Conceptualization, V.B., T.E. and B.F.; methodology, V.B., T.E. and B.F.; software, V.B.; validation, V.B., T.E. and B.F.; formal analysis, V.B.; investigation, V.B.; resources, V.B.; data curation, V.B.; writing—original draft preparation, V.B.; writing—review and editing, V.B., T.E. and B.F.; visualization, V.B.; supervision, T.E. and B.F.; project administration, B.F.; All authors have read and agreed to the published version of the manuscript.

Funding: This research received no external funding.

Data Availability Statement: The corpus of policies is available at https://github.com/citp/privacy-policy-historical (accessed on 15 November 2023). To get access to the data in the form of an SQL-database, send an email to privacy-policy-data@lists.cs.princeton.edu stating your name and affiliation. The dataset containing vague statements used for training the sentence classificator is available here: https://loganlebanoff.github.io/mydata (accessed on 15 November 2023).

Conflicts of Interest: The authors declare no conflict of interest.

Appendix A. Website Categories and GDPR Content

Figure A1 illustrates the distribution of categories among websites. During the analysis phase, if a website was linked to multiple categories, including "business", the last one was removed, leaving only the more descriptive categories. This enabled the better visualization of trends across categories.

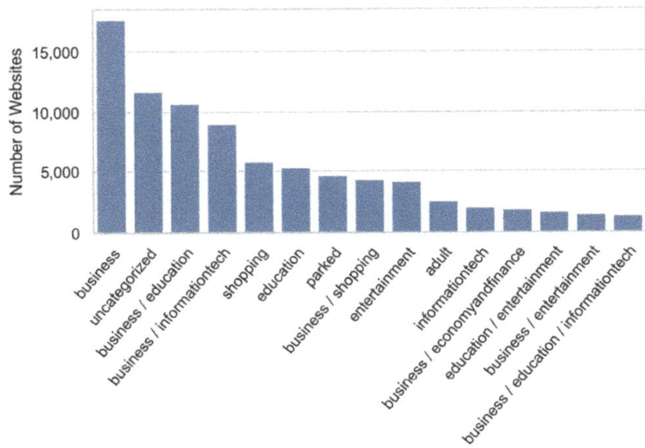

Figure A1. Website count per category. If no category information is available, the "uncategorized" bin applies.

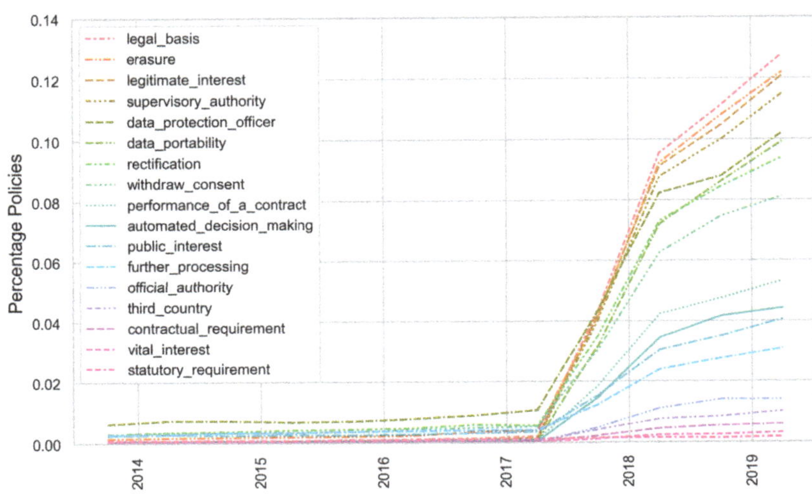

Figure A2. Usage of phrases specific to the GDPR (selection based on Amos et al. [7]).

The data repository by Amos et al. [7] contains a list of potential keywords that are frequently used with GDPR policies, a subset of which is shown in Figure A2. Also inspired by a similar approach, namely that of Degeling et al. [53], and further testing, the final set of phrases we selected are: legal basis, erasure, legitimate interest, supervisory authority, data portability, performance of a contract, automated decision making, public interest, further processing, and withdraw consent.

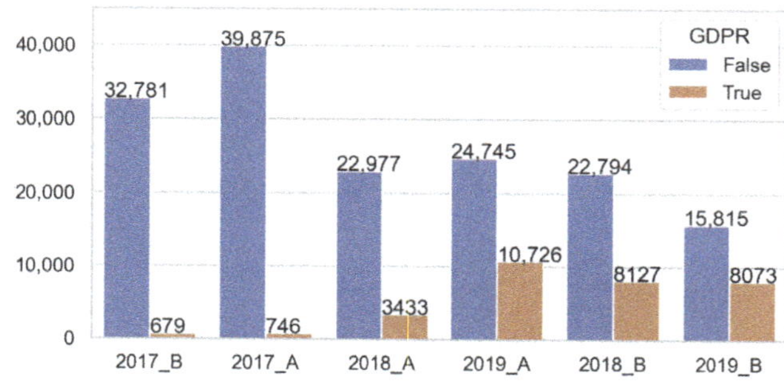

Figure A3. Distribution of GDPR and non-GDPR policies per interval.

Appendix B. Outlier Analysis

Appendix B.1. Policy Length

The outlier analysis pointed out one unusually long policy. This policy contained 25 times the same text and it was manually adjusted to its regular length.

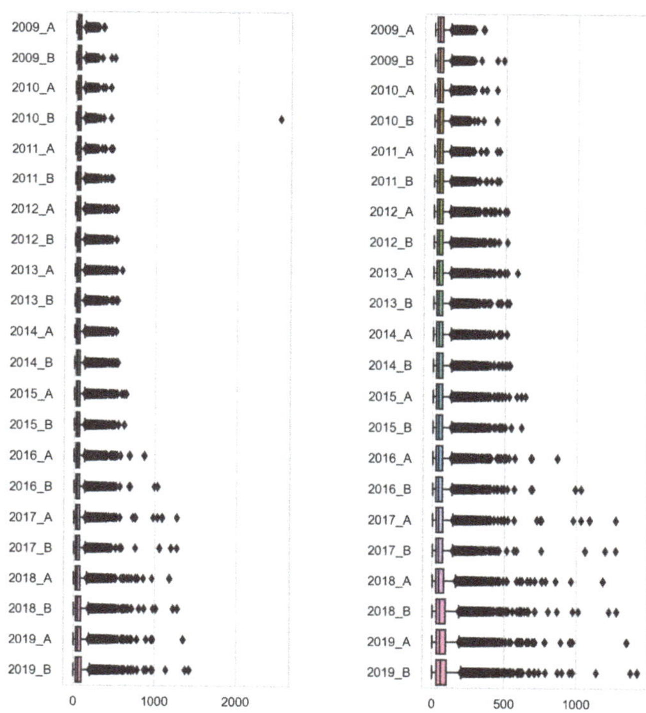

Figure A4. Sentence count distribution: original (**left**) and after cleaning (**right**).

Appendix B.2. Readability Score

A manual check showed that the content of three policies that scored unusually high on the Dale–Chall test is not valid and those policies had to be removed.

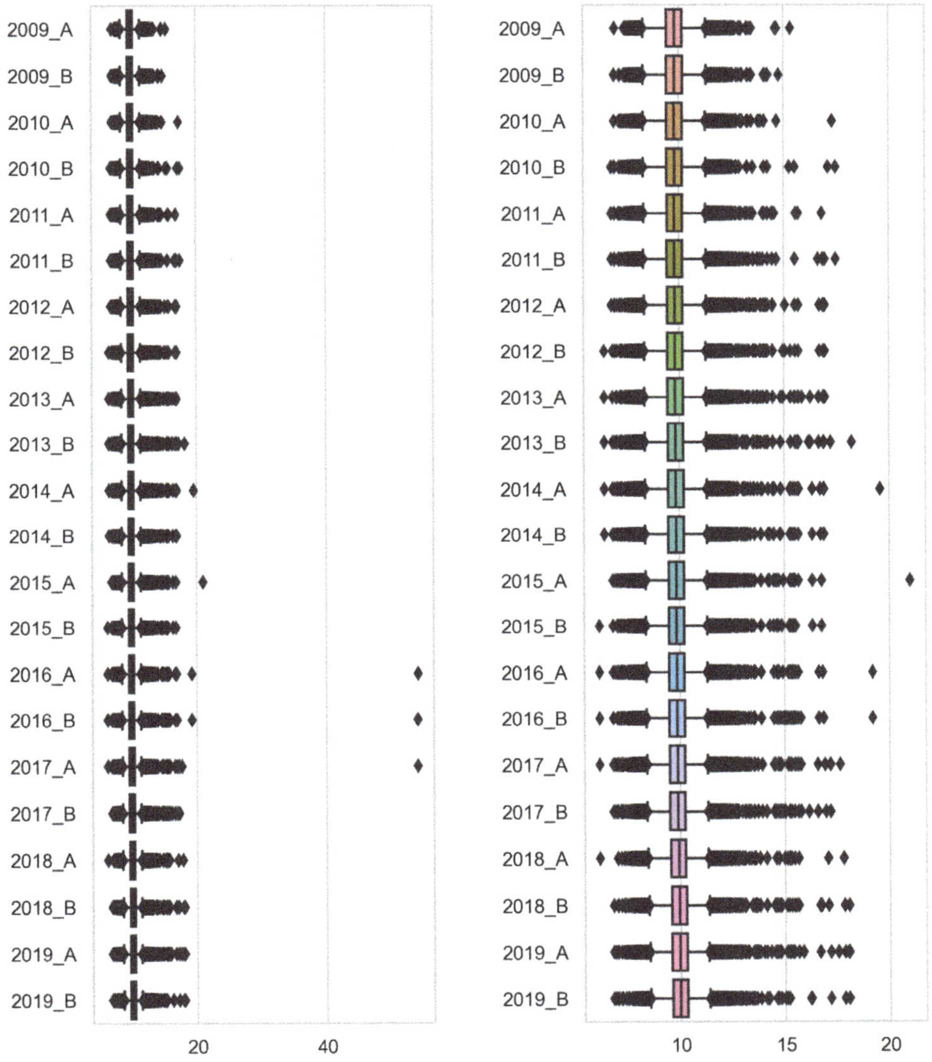

Figure A5. Dale–Chall score distribution: (**left**) and after cleaning (**right**).

Appendix B.3. Vague Sentences

Some policies contain almost no vague sentences and some only contain vague sentences. The manual evaluation of the policies in the two extremes of the distribution showed that most of them are very short, but they are valid and remained in the corpus.

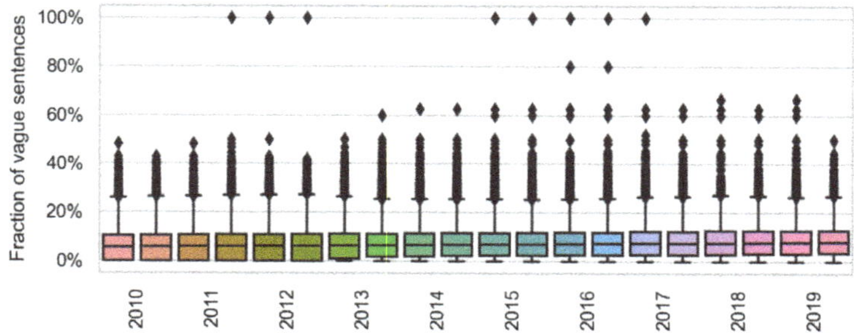

Figure A6. Vagueness score distribution.

Appendix C. Model Performance

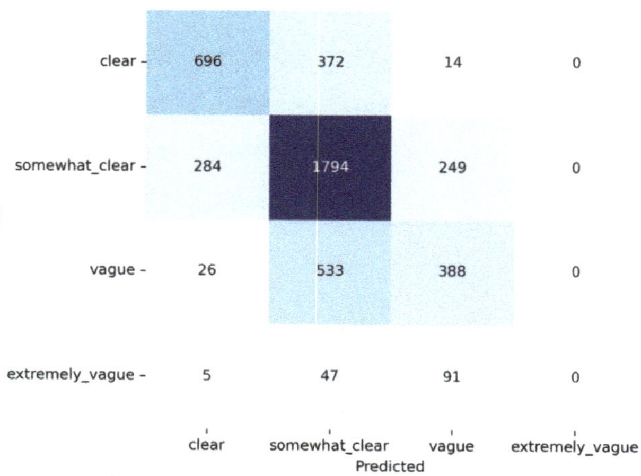

Figure A7. BERT performance evaluation: confusion matrix (stronger color indicates higher numbers).

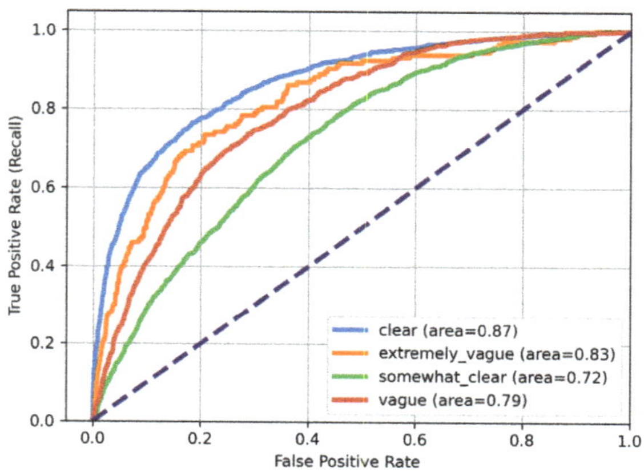

Figure A8. BERT performance evaluation: ROC curves.

Appendix D. Positive Phrasing

Table A1. Positive phrases identified in privacy policies.

we value	transparency	protect your (personal) information
we respect	trust us	protect your (personal) data
we promise	safe and secure	protect your privacy
care about	committed to protecting	provides protection
with care	committed to safeguarding	serious about your privacy
responsibly	committed to respecting	takes your security (very) seriously
important to us	respect your privacy	takes your privacy (very) seriously

References

1. Meier, Y.; Schäwel, J.; Krämer, N. The Shorter the Better? Effects of Privacy Policy Length on Online Privacy Decision-Making. *Media Commun.* **2020**, *8*, 291. [CrossRef]
2. Ibdah, D.; Lachtar, N.; Raparthi, S.M.; Bacha, A. "Why Should I Read the Privacy Policy, I Just Need the Service": A Study on Attitudes and Perceptions Toward Privacy Policies. *IEEE Access* **2021**, *9*, 166465–166487. [CrossRef]
3. Ermakova, T.; Krasnova, H.; Fabian, B. Exploring the Impact of Readability of Privacy Policies on Users' Trust. In Proceedings of the 24th European Conference on Information Systems (ECIS 2016), Istanbul, Turkey, 12–15 June 2016.
4. Wagner, I. Privacy Policies Across the Ages: Content and Readability of Privacy Policies 1996–2021. Technical Report. *arXiv* **2022**, arXiv:2201.08739.
5. Article 29 Working Party: Guidelines on Transparency under Regulation 2016/679. Available online: https://ec.europa.eu/newsroom/article29/items/622227/en (accessed on 15 November 2023).
6. Reidenberg, J.R.; Bhatia, J.; Breaux, T.; Norton, T. *Ambiguity in Privacy Policies and the Impact of Regulation*; SSRN Scholarly; Social Science Research Network: Rochester, NY, USA, 2016. [CrossRef]
7. Amos, R.; Acar, G.; Lucherini, E.; Kshirsagar, M.; Narayanan, A.; Mayer, J. Privacy Policies over Time: Curation and Analysis of a Million-Document Dataset. In Proceedings of the Web Conference 2021, Ljubljana, Slovenia, 19–23 April 2021; pp. 2165–2176. [CrossRef]
8. Bhatia, J.; Breaux, T.D.; Reidenberg, J.R.; Norton, T.B. A Theory of Vagueness and Privacy Risk Perception. In Proceedings of the 2016 IEEE 24th International Requirements Engineering Conference (RE), Beijing, China, 12–16 September 2016; pp. 26–35, ISSN 2332-6441. [CrossRef]
9. Fabian, B.; Ermakova, T.; Lentz, T. Large-scale readability analysis of privacy policies. In Proceedings of the International Conference on Web Intelligence (WI '17), Leipzig, Germany, 23–26 August 2017; Association for Computing Machinery: New York, NY, USA, 2017; pp. 18–25. [CrossRef]
10. Ermakova, T.; Fabian, B.; Babina, E. Readability of Privacy Policies of Healthcare Websites. In Proceedings of the 12th International Conference on Wirtschaftsinformatik, Osnabrück, Germany, 4–6 March 2015.
11. Kaur, J.; Dara, R.A.; Obimbo, C.; Song, F.; Menard, K. A comprehensive keyword analysis of online privacy policies. *Inf. Secur. J. Glob. Perspect.* **2018**, *27*, 260–275. [CrossRef]
12. Srinath, M.; Sundareswara, S.N.; Giles, C.L.; Wilson, S. PrivaSeer: A Privacy Policy Search Engine. In *Proceedings of the Web Engineering*; Brambilla, M., Chbeir, R., Frasincar, F., Manolescu, I., Eds.; Lecture Notes in Computer Science; Springer International Publishing: Cham, Switzerland, 2021; pp. 286–301. [CrossRef]
13. Libert, T.; Desai, A.; Patel, D. Preserving Needles in the Haystack: A Search Engine and Multi-Jurisdictional Forensic Documentation System for Privacy Violations on the Web. 2021. Available online: https://timlibert.me/pdf/Libert_et_al-2021-Forensic_Privacy_on_Web.pdf (accessed on 15 November 2023).
14. Lebanoff, L.; Liu, F. Automatic Detection of Vague Words and Sentences in Privacy Policies. In Proceedings of the 2018 Conference on Empirical Methods in Natural Language Processing, Association for Computational Linguistics, Brussels, Belgium, 31 October–4 November 2018; pp. 3508–3517. [CrossRef]
15. Data, Movement of Such. Directive 95/46/EC of the European Parliament and of the Council of 24 October 1995 on the Protection of Individuals with Regard to the Processing of Personal Data and on the Free Movement of Such Data. *Off. J. L* **1995**, *281*, 0031–0050.
16. Robinson, N.; Graux, H.; Botterman, M.; Valeri, L. *Review of the European Data Protection Directive*; Technical report; RAND Corporation: Cambridge, UK, 2009.
17. GDPR-Personal Data. Available online: https://gdpr-info.eu/issues/personal-data/ (accessed on 5 August 2023).
18. Federal Trade Comission, Privacy Online: A Report to Congress. Federal Trade Commission, 1998. Available online: https://www.ftc.gov/sites/default/files/documents/reports/privacy-online-report-congress/priv-23a.pdf (accessed on 5 August 2023).
19. Usable Privacy Policy Project. Available online: https://usableprivacy.org/ (accessed on 18 June 2023).

20. Wilson, S.; Schaub, F.; Dara, A.A.; Liu, F.; Cherivirala, S.; Giovanni Leon, P.; Schaarup Andersen, M.; Zimmeck, S.; Sathyendra, K.M.; Russell, N.C.; et al. The Creation and Analysis of a Website Privacy Policy Corpus. In Proceedings of the 54th Annual Meeting of the Association for Computational Linguistics (Volume 1: Long Papers), Berlin, Germany, 7–12 August 2016; Association for Computational Linguistics: Berlin, Germany, 2016; pp. 1330–1340. [CrossRef]
21. Bannihatti Kumar, V.; Iyengar, R.; Nisal, N.; Feng, Y.; Habib, H.; Story, P.; Cherivirala, S.; Hagan, M.; Cranor, L.; Wilson, S.; et al. Finding a Choice in a Haystack: Automatic Extraction of Opt-Out Statements from Privacy Policy Text. In Proceedings of the Web Conference 2020, Virtural, 20–24 April 2020; ACM: Taipei, Taiwan, 2020; pp. 1943–1954. [CrossRef]
22. Ahmad, W.U.; Chi, J.; Le, T.; Norton, T.; Tian, Y.; Chang, K.W. Intent Classification and Slot Filling for Privacy Policies. *arXiv* **2021**, arXiv:2101.00123.
23. Nokhbeh Zaeem, R.; Barber, K.S. A Large Publicly Available Corpus of Website Privacy Policies Based on DMOZ. In Proceedings of the Eleventh ACM Conference on Data and Application Security and Privacy, Virtual, 26–28 April 2021; ACM: New York, NY, USA, 2021; pp. 143–148. [CrossRef]
24. Audich, D.; Dara, R.; Nonnecke, B. Privacy Policy Annotation for Semi-Automated Analysis: A Cost-Effective Approach. In *Trust Management XII. IFIPTM 2018. IFIP Advances in Information and Communication Technology*; Springer: Cham, Switzerland; Toronto, ON, Canada, 2018; pp. 29–44. [CrossRef]
25. Kumar, V.B.; Ravichander, A.; Story, P.; Sadeh, N. Quantifying the Effect of In-Domain Distributed Word Representations: A Study of Privacy Policies. In AAAI Spring Symposium on Privacy-Enhancing Artificial Intelligence and Language Technologies. 2019. Available online: https://usableprivacy.org/static/files/kumar_pal_2019.pdf (accessed on 18 June 2023).
26. Liu, F.; Wilson, S.; Story, P.; Zimmeck, S.; Sadeh, N. Towards Automatic Classification of Privacy Policy Text. Technical Report, CMU-ISR-17-118R, Institute for Software Research and Language Technologies Institute, School of Computer Science, Carnegie Mellon University, 2018. Available online: http://reports-archive.adm.cs.cmu.edu/anon/isr2017/CMU-ISR-17-118R.pdf (accessed on 18 June 2023).
27. Mousavi, N.; Jabat, P.; Nedelchev, R.; Scerri, S.; Graux, D. Establishing a Strong Baseline for Privacy Policy Classification. In Proceedings of the IFIP International Conference on ICT Systems Security and Privacy Protection, Maribor, Slovenia, 21–23 September 2020.
28. Mustapha, M.; Krasnashchok, K.; Al Bassit, A.; Skhiri, S. Privacy Policy Classification with XLNet (Short Paper). In *Data Privacy Management, Cryptocurrencies and Blockchain Technology*; Garcia-Alfaro, J., Navarro-Arribas, G., Herrera-Joancomarti, J., Eds.; Springer International Publishing: Cham, Switzerland, 2020; Volume 12484, pp. 250–257. [CrossRef]
29. Bui, D.; Shin, K.G.; Choi, J.M.; Shin, J. Automated Extraction and Presentation of Data Practices in Privacy Policies. *Proc. Priv. Enhancing Technol.* **2021**, *2021*, 88–110. [CrossRef]
30. Alabduljabbar, A.; Abusnaina, A.; Meteriz-Yildiran, U.; Mohaisen, D. Automated Privacy Policy Annotation with Information Highlighting Made Practical Using Deep Representations. In Proceedings of the 2021 ACM SIGSAC Conference on Computer and Communications Security, Virtual, 15–19 November 2021; CCS '21; Association for Computing Machinery: New York, NY, USA, 2021; pp. 2378–2380. [CrossRef]
31. Alabduljabbar, A.; Abusnaina, A.; Meteriz-Yildiran, U.; Mohaisen, D. TLDR: Deep Learning-Based Automated Privacy Policy Annotation with Key Policy Highlights. In Proceedings of the 20th Workshop on Workshop on Privacy in the Electronic Society, Virtual, 15 November 2021; ACM: New York, NY, USA, 2021; pp. 103–118. [CrossRef]
32. Sathyendra, K.M.; Schaub, F.; Wilson, S.; Sadeh, N.M. Automatic Extraction of Opt-Out Choices from Privacy Policies. In AAAI Fall Symposia, 2016, Association for the Advancement of Artificial Intelligence. 2016. Available online: https://api.semanticscholar.org/CorpusID:32896562 (accessed on 18 June 2023).
33. Sathyendra, K.M.; Wilson, S.; Schaub, F.; Zimmeck, S.; Sadeh, N. Identifying the Provision of Choices in Privacy Policy Text. In Proceedings of the 2017 Conference on Empirical Methods in Natural Language Processing, Copenhagen, Denmark, 7–11 September 2017; Association for Computational Linguistics: Copenhagen, Denmark, 2017; pp. 2774–2779. [CrossRef]
34. Keymanesh, M.; Elsner, M.; Parthasarathy, S. Toward Domain-Guided Controllable Summarization of Privacy Policies. In Proceedings of the 2020 Natural Legal Language Processing (NLLP) Workshop, Virtual Event/San Diego, CA, USA, 24 August 2020; ACM: New York, NY, USA, 2020; pp. 18–24.
35. Ravichander, A.; Black, A.W.; Wilson, S.; Norton, T.; Sadeh, N. Question Answering for Privacy Policies: Combining Computational and Legal Perspectives. *arXiv* **2019**, arXiv:1911.00841.
36. Ahmad, W.U.; Chi, J.; Tian, Y.; Chang, K.W. PolicyQA: A Reading Comprehension Dataset for Privacy Policies. *arXiv* **2020**, arXiv:2010.02557.
37. Keymanesh, M.; Elsner, M.; Parthasarathy, S. Privacy Policy Question Answering Assistant: A Query-Guided Extractive Summarization Approach. *arXiv* **2021**, arXiv:2109.14638.
38. Shankar, A.; Waldis, A.; Bless, C.; Andueza Rodriguez, M.; Mazzola, L. PrivacyGLUE: A Benchmark Dataset for General Language Understanding in Privacy Policies. *Appl. Sci.* **2023**, *13*, 3701. [CrossRef]
39. Tesfay, W.B.; Hofmann, P.; Nakamura, T.; Kiyomoto, S.; Serna, J. PrivacyGuide: Towards an Implementation of the EU GDPR on Internet Privacy Policy Evaluation. In Proceedings of the Fourth ACM International Workshop on Security and Privacy Analytics, Tempe, AZ, USA, 19–21 March 2018; IWSPA '18; Association for Computing Machinery: New York, NY, USA, 2018; pp. 15–21. [CrossRef]

40. Harkous, H.; Fawaz, K.; Lebret, R.; Schaub, F.; Shin, K.G.; Aberer, K. Polisis: Automated Analysis and Presentation of Privacy Policies Using Deep Learning. In Proceedings of the 27th USENIX Security Symposium, Baltimore, MD, USA, 15–17 August 2018; USENIX Association: Berkeley, CA, USA, 2018; pp. 531–548.
41. PriBOT. Available online: https://pribot.org/ (accessed on 24 June 2023).
42. Zaeem, R.N.; German, R.L.; Barber, K.S. PrivacyCheck: Automatic Summarization of Privacy Policies Using Data Mining. *ACM Trans. Internet Technol.* **2018**, *18*, 53:1–53:18. [CrossRef]
43. Nokhbeh Zaeem, R.; Anya, S.; Issa, A.; Nimergood, J.; Rogers, I.; Shah, V.; Srivastava, A.; Barber, K.S. PrivacyCheck v2: A Tool that Recaps Privacy Policies for You. In Proceedings of the 29th ACM International Conference on Information & Knowledge Management, Virtual, 19–23 October 2020; Association for Computing Machinery: New York, NY, USA, 2020; CIKM '20, pp. 3441–3444. [CrossRef]
44. Nokhbeh Zaeem, R.; Ahbab, A.; Bestor, J.; Djadi, H.H.; Kharel, S.; Lai, V.; Wang, N.; Barber, K.S. PrivacyCheck v3: Empowering Users with Higher-Level Understanding of Privacy Policies. In Proceedings of the Fifteenth ACM International Conference on Web Search and Data Mining, Virtual, 21–25 February 2022; WSDM '22; Association for Computing Machinery: New York, NY, USA, 2022; pp. 1593–1596. [CrossRef]
45. Privacy Lab | Center for Identity. Available online: https://identity.utexas.edu/privacy-lab (accessed on 24 June 2023).
46. Opt-Out Easy. Available online: https://optouteasy.isr.cmu.edu/ (accessed on 24 June 2023).
47. Contissa, G.; Docter, K.; Lagioia, F.; Lippi, M.; Micklitz, H.W.; Pałka, P.; Sartor, G.; Torroni, P. *Claudette Meets GDPR: Automating the Evaluation of Privacy Policies Using Artificial Intelligence*; SSRN Scholarly; Social Science Research Network: Rochester, NY, USA, 2018. [CrossRef]
48. Liepina, R.; Contissa, G.; Drazewski, K.; Lagioia, F.; Lippi, M.; Micklitz, H.; Palka, P.; Sartor, G.; Torroni, P. GDPR Privacy Policies in CLAUDETTE: Challenges of Omission, Context and Multilingualism. In Proceedings of the Third Workshop on Automated Semantic Analysis of Information in Legal Text (ASAIL 2019), Montreal, QC, Canada, 21 June 2019.
49. Mousavi, N.; Scerri, S.; Lehmann, J. KnIGHT: Mapping Privacy Policies to GDPR. In *Knowledge Engineering and Knowledge Management*; Faron Zucker, C., Ghidini, C., Napoli, A., Toussaint, Y., Eds.; Springer International Publishing: Cham, Switzerland, 2018; Volume 11313, pp. 258–272.
50. Cejas, O.A.; Abualhaija, S.; Torre, D.; Sabetzadeh, M.; Briand, L. AI-enabled Automation for Completeness Checking of Privacy Policies. *IEEE Trans. Softw. Eng.* **2021**, *48*, 4647–4674. [CrossRef]
51. Qamar, A.; Javed, T.; Beg, M.O. Detecting Compliance of Privacy Policies with Data Protection Laws. *arXiv* **2021**, arXiv:2102.12362.
52. Sánchez, D.; Viejo, A.; Batet, M. Automatic Assessment of Privacy Policies under the GDPR. *Appl. Sci.* **2021**, *11*, 1762. [CrossRef]
53. Degeling, M.; Utz, C.; Lentzsch, C.; Hosseini, H.; Schaub, F.; Holz, T. We Value Your Privacy ... Now Take Some Cookies: Measuring the GDPR's Impact on Web Privacy. In Proceedings of the 2019 Network and Distributed System Security Symposium, San Diego, CA, USA, 24–27 February 2019. [CrossRef]
54. Linden, T.; Khandelwal, R.; Harkous, H.; Fawaz, K. The Privacy Policy Landscape After the GDPR. *arXiv* **2019**, arXiv:1809.08396.
55. Zaeem, R.N.; Barber, K.S. The Effect of the GDPR on Privacy Policies: Recent Progress and Future Promise. *ACM Trans. Manag. Inf. Syst.* **2020**, *12*, 2:1–2:20. [CrossRef]
56. Libert, T. An Automated Approach to Auditing Disclosure of Third-Party Data Collection in Website Privacy Policies. In Proceedings of the 2018 World Wide Web Conference on World Wide Web-WWW '18, Lyon, France, 23–27 April 2018; pp. 207–216. [CrossRef]
57. Kotal, A.; Joshi, A.; Pande Joshi, K. The Effect of Text Ambiguity on creating Policy Knowledge Graphs. In Proceedings of the 2021 IEEE Intl Conf on Parallel & Distributed Processing with Applications, Big Data & Cloud Computing, Sustainable Computing & Communications, Social Computing & Networking (ISPA/BDCloud/SocialCom/SustainCom), New York City, NY, USA, 30 September–3 October 2021; IEEE: New York City, NY, USA, 2021; pp. 1491–1500. [CrossRef]
58. Zimmeck, S.; Story, P.; Smullen, D.; Ravichander, A.; Wang, Z.; Reidenberg, J.; Cameron Russell, N.; Sadeh, N. MAPS: Scaling Privacy Compliance Analysis to a Million Apps. *Proc. Priv. Enhancing Technol.* **2019**, *2019*, 66–86. [CrossRef]
59. Story, P.; Zimmeck, S.; Ravichander, A.; Smullen, D.; Wang, Z.; Reidenberg, J.; Russell, N.; Sadeh, N. Natural Language Processing for Mobile App Privacy Compliance. In Proceedings of the PAL: Privacy-Enhancing Artificial Intelligence and Language Technologies AAAI Spring Symposium, Palo Alto, CA, USA, 25–27 March 2019.
60. Hashmi, S.S.; Waheed, N.; Tangari, G.; Ikram, M.; Smith, S. Longitudinal Compliance Analysis of Android Applications with Privacy Policies. *arXiv* **2021**, arXiv:2106.10035.
61. Internet Archive: Wayback Machine. Available online: https://archive.org/web/ (accessed on 5 August 2023).
62. NLTK: nltk.tokenize Package. Available online: https://www.nltk.org/api/nltk.tokenize.html (accessed on 5 August 2023).
63. Webshrinker. Available online: https://webshrinker.com/ (accessed on 5 August 2023).
64. Chall, J.S.; Dale, E. *Readability Revisited: The New Dale-Chall Readability Formula*; Brookline Books: Brookline, MA, USA, 1995; Google-Books-ID: 2nbuAAAAMAAJ.
65. Wolf, T.; Debut, L.; Sanh, V.; Chaumond, J.; Delangue, C.; Moi, A.; Cistac, P.; Rault, T.; Louf, R.; Funtowicz, M.; et al. HuggingFace's Transformers: State-of-the-art Natural Language Processing. *arXiv* **2020**, arXiv:1910.03771.
66. Devlin, J.; Chang, M.W.; Lee, K.; Toutanova, K. BERT: Pre-training of Deep Bidirectional Transformers for Language Understanding. *arXiv* **2019**, arXiv:1810.04805.

67. Nissenbaum, H. A Contextual Approach to Privacy Online. *Daedalus* **2011**, *140*, 32–48. [CrossRef]
68. Chanenson, J.; Pickering, M.; Apthorpe, N. Automating Governing Knowledge Commons and Contextual Integrity (GKC-CI) Privacy Policy Annotations with Large Language Models. *arXiv* **2023**, arXiv:cs.CY/2311.02192.
69. Tang, C.; Liu, Z.; Ma, C.; Wu, Z.; Li, Y.; Liu, W.; Zhu, D.; Li, Q.; Li, X.; Liu, T.; et al. PolicyGPT: Automated Analysis of Privacy Policies with Large Language Models. *arXiv* **2023**, arXiv:cs.CL/2309.10238.

information

MDPI

Article

Reimagining Literary Analysis: Utilizing Artificial Intelligence to Classify Modernist French Poetry

Liu Yang [1,*], Gang Wang [2] and Hongjun Wang [2]

[1] School of Foreign Studies, Zhongnan University of Economics and Law, Wuhan 430073, China
[2] School of Computing and Artificial Intelligence, Southwest Jiaotong University, Chengdu 611756, China; 2022wg@my.swjtu.edu.cn (G.W.); wanghongjun@swjtu.edu.cn (H.W.)
* Correspondence: yarres@zuel.edu.cn

Abstract: Aligned with global Sustainable Development Goals (SDGs) and multidisciplinary approaches integrating AI with sustainability, this research introduces an innovative AI framework for analyzing Modern French Poetry. It applies feature extraction techniques (TF-IDF and Doc2Vec) and machine learning algorithms (especially SVM) to create a model that objectively classifies poems by their stylistic and thematic attributes, transcending traditional subjective analyses. This work demonstrates AI's potential in literary analysis and cultural exchange, highlighting the model's capacity to facilitate cross-cultural understanding and enhance poetry education. The efficiency of the AI model, compared to traditional methods, shows promise in optimizing resources and reducing the environmental impact of education. Future research will refine the model's technical aspects, ensuring effectiveness, equity, and personalization in education. Expanding the model's scope to various poetic styles and genres will enhance its accuracy and generalizability. Additionally, efforts will focus on an equitable AI tool implementation for quality education access. This research offers insights into AI's role in advancing poetry education and contributing to sustainability goals. By overcoming the outlined limitations and integrating the model into educational platforms, it sets a path for impactful developments in computational poetry and educational technology.

Keywords: AI in literary analysis; machine learning; modern french poetry classification; feature extraction techniques; SVM in poetry analysis

1. Introduction

In digital humanities, AI's role is transformative, especially in analyzing complex literary genres like Modernist French poetry [1]. This study uses AI to classify Modernist French poetry, aligning with the United Nations Sustainable Development Goals, particularly in education and reducing inequalities [2]. We aim to bridge cultural and linguistic divides through AI-driven analysis, opening new pathways for appreciating diverse literary traditions [3].

Modernist French poetry, with its audacious departure from traditional forms, offers a unique challenge for AI with its symbolism, unconventional syntax, and thematic depth [4]. Its distinct characteristics make it well-suited for AI analysis, providing a rich dataset for machine learning algorithms [5]. Despite its richness, the AI analysis of this genre is still emerging, with a focus on traditional forms, leaving a gap in Modernist French poetry exploration [4].

This study develops an AI framework for classifying Modernist French poetry, enhancing digital humanities and understanding this literary movement. We apply AI to delve into linguistic patterns, stylistic innovations, and thematic elements of the genre [6]. The defining features of Modernist French poetry—fragmentation, symbolism, subconscious exploration, and reflections of urbanization—present a compelling AI analysis subject [7].

An AI-driven analysis can preserve and disseminate Modernist French poetry, making it accessible and fostering global appreciation [8]. It also promises educational applications, enhancing critical thinking and diverse perspectives in literary studies [9]. AI serves as a complementary tool in literary criticism, enriching traditional methods with new insights [10].

Our research, focusing on modern French poetry, blends AI with poetic expression and establishes new benchmarks in literary research. We prioritize a narrative style over complex mathematics, aiming for accessibility in an interdisciplinary context. This approach highlights AI's role in augmenting literary analysis and comprehension [11].

This research marks an interdisciplinary breakthrough by applying AI to analyze and classify modern French poetry, integrating AI with a literary analysis. We highlight three major contributions:

- **Innovative AI in Literary Research:** This study introduces AI, particularly SVM and advanced feature extraction like TF-IDF and Doc2Vec, into modern French poetry analysis. This approach not only brings new analytical tools to literary research but also enriches education and cross-cultural understanding.
- **Enhancing Literary Comprehension:** Our work advances literary understanding through AI, dissecting stylistic elements of modern French poetry. This enriches educational methodologies and opens new avenues for cross-cultural studies, deepening the appreciation of literary diversity.
- **Technical Enrichment:** We focus on efficient SVM deployment and diverse feature extraction methods, ensuring data integrity for machine learning classification. Our research employs various classifiers, enhancing the accuracy and applicability of AI in a literary analysis.

In summary, our study extends existing AI methodologies to literary analysis, particularly focusing on modern French poetry. We blend AI analysis with a deep understanding of poetic expression, setting new benchmarks for literary AI application. The study avoids complex mathematics for accessibility and clarity, emphasizing AI's role in augmenting literary comprehension and analysis.

2. Related Works

Research in computer-generated poetry and literature analysis is extensive [12]. Key advancements include the Quality-Aware Masked Language Model for high-quality quatrain generation and cross-cultural poetry generation research [13]. Educational applications in poetry writing and computational tools for analysis have also been explored [14,15]. Notably, AI's role in Arabic poetry classification and analysis is emerging [16].

2.1. *Challenges of Text Classification in Poetry*

Text classification in poetry faces challenges like ambiguity, subjectivity, and varied styles [17–19]. Additional issues include feature reduction, sentiment analysis, dataset domain and sources [20], bilingual text recognition challenges [21], and benchmarking difficulties [22,23]. Other limitations are semantic label information neglect, modeling restrictions in image-text concatenation [24], and cross-domain text classification issues [25]. Challenges in short text classification [26], incremental few-shot learning [27], human-designed feature biases [28], and the inadequacy of "bag of words" models [29] are also significant.

In summary, text classification in poetry requires a multifaceted approach integrating machine learning, NLP, and domain-specific knowledge to address its diverse challenges.

2.2. *Categorizing Existing Works Based on Approaches and Contributions*

Poetry classification research divides into rule-based and data-driven methodologies. Rule-based methods, utilizing predefined rules often grounded in linguistic analysis, are praised for their interpretability and domain expertise integration. Abel and Lantow's 2019 framework [30] and Wang and Hong's study on rule-based feature selection [31] illustrate these methods' structured approach. Additionally, associative the rule-based classification [32] and association rule mining [33] demonstrate rule-based methods' diversity and applicability.

Conversely, data-driven approaches employ machine learning algorithms to autonomously learn from text data that are adaptable for handling large datasets. Liu et al.'s 2020 work [34] and Fragoso's 2019 evaluation [35] showcase these methods' flexibility. The use of hierarchical models for offensive content classification [36] and genetic programming [34] exemplifies advancements in data-driven techniques. Additionally, privacy concerns in data-driven classification [37] highlight the multifaceted nature of these approaches.

These references collectively provide an overview of poetry classification research, outlining the varied methodologies and contributions of both rule-based and data-driven approaches to the field.

2.3. Critically Evaluating Strengths and Weaknesses of Each Work

The evaluation of text classification methods, particularly in poetry, reveals distinct strengths and weaknesses. Rule-based methods, as shown in Abel and Lantow's study [30], offer interpretability and expert knowledge integration but may lack flexibility and struggle with poetic ambiguity. Data-driven approaches excel in adaptability and handling large datasets, but their reliance on extensive training and sometimes opaque processes can be limitations. Their ability to capture complex patterns, as discussed in recent studies [38,39], is countered by concerns over interpretability and overfitting risks. Hybrid models, combining rule-based and data-driven methods, enhance effectiveness but add complexity, as highlighted by Wang et al. [40]. Emerging techniques, such as graph neural networks and weakly supervised learning [41,42], offer innovative solutions but face challenges like data requirements and computational demands. In summary, this section critically assesses various methodologies in text classifications within poetry, underscoring the balance between strengths and limitations and the need for innovative approaches to address the unique complexities of poetic texts.

2.4. Beyond Boundaries: Recent AI Advancements Illuminate Modernist French Poetry Analysis

This comprehensive review of text classification literature, especially in poetry, synthesizes key advancements and future directions. Recent studies [43] emphasize advancements in data processing, showcasing the evolution of text classification methods. The integration of NLP techniques [44] highlights the effectiveness of combined methodologies in enhancing model accuracy and applicability. The applications of text classification across various domains, including news and job market analysis [45,46], demonstrate its versatility. Challenges such as decision jumps, data imbalance, and algorithm complexity are outlined in recent research [47], underscoring the importance of feature selection and model establishment in developing accurate classification models. Our review extends beyond traditional boundaries, incorporating AI advancements to enrich the Modernist French poetry analysis. For example, the PF-BiGRU-TSAM method [48] adeptly handles complex data, an approach adaptable to poetic language analysis. Challenges in poetry classification, like ambiguity and complex structures, are informed by studies on feature reduction and sentiment analysis [20–22]. Recent developments, such as contrastive learning and adversarial training [40], offer novel methods to tackle classification challenges relevant to Modernist French poetry. By integrating these advanced AI techniques, we aim to develop a more nuanced model for the poetry analysis.

In conclusion, the text classification in poetry is evolving towards more sophisticated, integrated approaches that continuously adapt to address challenges and explore new analytical possibilities.

2.5. Positioning the Present Work within the Broader Context

In the evolving landscape of text classification, particularly within the nuanced domain of poetry, our present work aims to carve out a distinct position by building upon and extending the existing body of research. Inspired by Yongqi Li and Wenjie Li [43], our research incorporates advanced data processing techniques to enhance the accuracy and efficiency of poetry classification, leveraging the latest advancements in data handling. Additionally, drawing on the approach outlined by Amisha Shingala, this work integrates sophisticated NLP techniques to deepen the understanding of poetic texts, aiming to improve the classification accuracy significantly.

Our approach also builds upon the empirical comparisons made by Yindalon et al. in their 2014 study, incorporating the most effective elements from various classification methods to create a robust model specifically for poetry classification. Furthermore, echoing the versatility demonstrated in studies like [45,46], our work adapts text classification techniques to meet the unique challenges presented by poetic texts, acknowledging the diverse applications of these methodologies.

In addition, our research seeks to address and overcome specific challenges of ambiguity and stylistic variation inherent in poetry, informed by insights from the paper [47]. We also recognize the importance of feature selection and model establishment, as discussed in paper [49] and the text emotion classification model patent [50], and incorporate these critical aspects into our work to enhance the classification model's performance.

By situating our current work within this broader context, we not only acknowledge the contributions of previous studies but also strive to advance the field of poetry classification. Our approach combines proven techniques with innovative methods to address the unique challenges of poetry, setting a new benchmark in the realm of text classification. This paper discusses the challenges and limitations of short text classification and literary text classification. Short text classification often faces problems such as data sparsity, noise and ambiguity, and contextual limitations. Literary text classification faces challenges such as subjectivity and ambiguity, contextual complexity, and linguistic diversity. This paper also discusses the progress made in both areas and highlights the need for further research to address the limitations of existing methods and develop more accurate, efficient, and versatile classification algorithms.

3. Methodology

This study primarily focuses on employing traditional machine learning techniques for the novel task of style classification in modernist French poetry. Our attention is directed towards several key areas:

Text Preprocessing and Vectorization: The text preprocessing phase for classifying modern French poetry is a pivotal process, comprising two critical steps: the identification of stopwords and the tokenization of text. These procedures are fundamental in efficiently extracting pertinent features and ensuring precise text classification. Prior to implementing machine learning techniques, it is imperative to preprocess the dataset of French poetry to confirm its suitability for model training and assessment. Furthermore, in exploring the role of AI in analyzing modernist French poetry, AI's capacity to unveil unique linguistic patterns and stylistic nuances has been invaluable. However, it is crucial to recognize that poetry is not an isolated construct but is shaped by its historical, literary, and cultural milieu. Overlooking these aspects may result in oversimplified and misleading interpretations. For machine learning classification, it is essential to convert textual data into numerical feature vectors that align with the classification models.

Feature Extraction Methods: Our research includes an exploration of various feature extraction techniques, notably TF-IDF, to extract salient stylistic features from the text. These features play a pivotal role in understanding and categorizing the styles of poetry. Our study conducts a comparative analysis of two text feature extraction methodologies: Term Frequency-Inverse Document Frequency (TF-IDF) and Document to Vector (Doc2Vec). This comparison underscores the importance of feature extraction as a vital step in transforming textual content into vectors apt for classification models. The transformation of raw textual data into numerical representations that are compatible with machine learning algorithms is pivotal for the efficacious classification of text. This section is dedicated to a comprehensive exploration of the crucial processes involved in text processing and vectorization that is specifically tailored for the classification of poetry.

Comparison of classification algorithms: To achieve a precise classification of the styles in modern French poetry, our study will test and evaluate eight different machine learning classification algorithms. Our aim is to identify which algorithm is most adept at handling the complexity and uniqueness of poetic texts. As a central part of our research, we have implemented SVM models for classifying poetry styles, integrating traditional feature extraction methods such as Term Frequency-Inverse Document Frequency (TF-IDF). In order to adapt to the unique features of poetic texts, we have carefully adjusted and optimized the SVM parameters. In addition to SVM, we have investigated several other machine learning classifiers, including Logistic Regression (LR), Bagging, Random Forest (RF), AdaBoost, Gradient Boosted Decision Trees (GBDT), XGBoost, and LightGBM. The parameters of each algorithm have been meticulously calibrated to achieve an optimal classification performance. Through extensive testing of these classification algorithms and evaluating their performance based on accuracy, F1 scores, and other relevant metrics, we will select the algorithm that best classifies modern French poetry. This process involves not only a technical comparison but also an in-depth analysis of each algorithm's ability to handle the specific challenges presented by literary texts. Ultimately, our goal is to determine an optimized model that can accurately reflect the stylistic nuances of poetry and provide new perspectives and tools for literary analysis.

In our research, we consciously refrained from deploying deep learning techniques, opting instead for traditional machine learning algorithms to categorize literary texts. This choice was driven by the desire for simplicity and transparency in our models, factors that greatly facilitate their direct interpretation and understanding. This is particularly pertinent in the cross-disciplinary realm of literary studies. Our approach highlights the innovative integration of machine learning in literary analysis that is particularly evident in our work with modernist French poetry, which is known for its rich expression and stylistic diversity. This methodology is not just a technological breakthrough; it also carves out new pathways for the analysis and interpretation of literary texts. Moreover, our method is deeply anchored in computational linguistics and literary theory. It not only fosters technological advancements but also ensures that our models meet the intricate demands of literary interpretation. We harnessed the strengths of a suite of algorithms, including Support Vector Machine (SVM), Logistic Regression, Bagging, Random Forest, AdaBoost, Gradient Boosted Decision Trees, and XGBoost. This amalgamation is tailored to capture the complex patterns and nuances of poetic language. As a result, our models demonstrate exceptional efficacy in classifying modernist French poetry in Figure 1, a claim that will be substantiated in the detailed evaluations presented in the subsequent chapters. Ultimately, our study paves the way for a new theoretical paradigm in applying machine learning to poetry classification, providing a conceptual foundation that bridges the understanding of poetic language with classification accuracy.

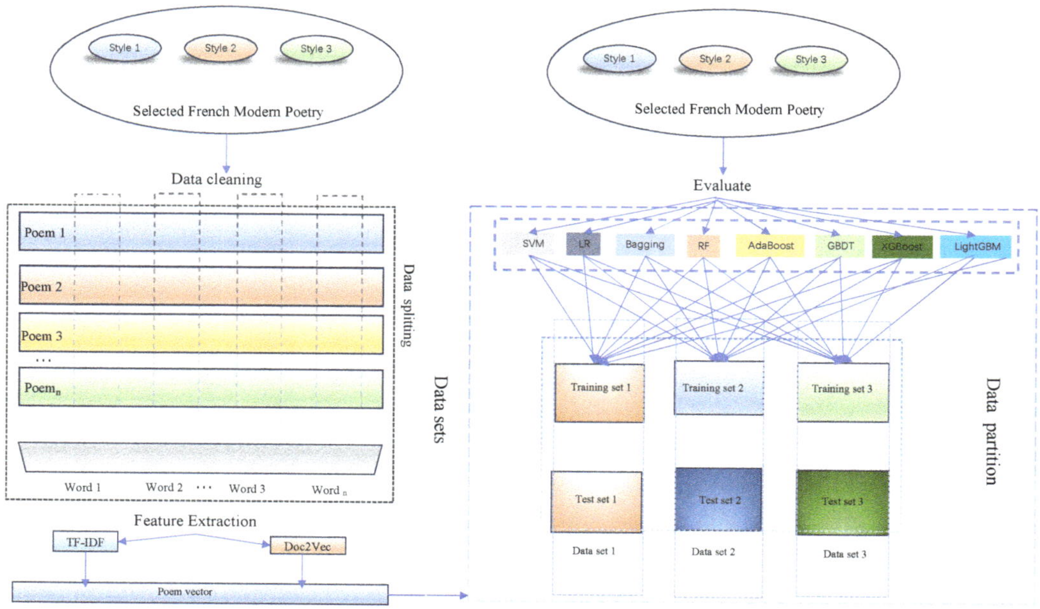

Figure 1. Classification Training for Modern French Poetry.

3.1. Text Preprocessing for Categorization

In the realm of Modern French poetry classification, text preparation is a pivotal phase, encompassing two integral steps: the identification of stop words and the process of tokenization. These steps are vital for the effective extraction of features and the accurate classification of text. Prior to employing machine learning techniques, preprocessing the dataset of French poetry is crucial to render it apt for model training and evaluation.

The text preparation process involves two key stages: (1) **Data Cleaning**: As the initial step in the text classification trajectory, this involves the removal of punctuation and the conversion of all letters to lowercase. This simplification is essential to mitigate unnecessary complexities that might arise from variations in punctuation and letter case; (2) **Data Segmentation**: In alignment with standard machine learning experimental protocols, the dataset is bifurcated into a training set and a testing set, following a 7:3 ratio. Specifically, 70% of the data (amounting to 1152 samples) is allocated for training purposes, while the remaining 30% (comprising 494 samples) is reserved for testing. This segmentation is crucial for detecting the potential overfitting of the model on test data and for assessing its overall efficacy. The unique linguistic attributes of Modern French poetry make preprocessing especially significant. By eliminating semantically non-essential auxiliary words, the preprocessing step ensures that the machine learning model focuses on learning from the most crucial vocabulary, thereby enhancing both the efficiency and accuracy of the model.

Additionally, when we explore the application of AI technology in the analysis of Modernist French poetry, an AI analysis proves invaluable in uncovering linguistic patterns and stylistic novelties. However, it is crucial to recognize that poetry is not an isolated entity but is shaped by its historical, literary, and cultural milieu. Overlooking these contexts could oversimplify and mislead interpretations.

We advocate for an AI analytical approach that encompasses the wider literary ecosystem. This encompasses: (1) Understanding the historical evolution of Modernist French poetry; (2) Investigating its connections with literary traditions like Symbolism and Surrealism; (3) Examining how these poems' receptions and interpretations have evolved over time. Incorporating these contextual elements enables a more thorough and nuanced comprehension of Modernist French poetry. AI technologies are adept at detecting inherent patterns and links in poetry, but it is the contextual knowledge that frames these findings. Such a methodology enhances not only the precision and pertinence of AI analysis but also enriches our overall grasp of Modernist French poetry. Practical examples of this methodology include: (1) Utilizing AI to discern links between poetry and historical events; (2) Examining the stylistic features of Modernist French poetry relative to preceding literary movements; (3) Monitoring the evolving reception and interpretations of these poems through different historical critiques.

Finally, for machine learning classification purposes, textual data must be converted into numerical feature vectors. This study contrasts two text feature extraction techniques, TF-IDF and Doc2Vec, which highlights that feature extraction is a crucial phase in converting the text into feature vectors suitable for classification models.

3.1.1. Text Processing and Vector Construction

The process of transforming raw text data into numerical representations suitable for machine learning algorithms is crucial for effective text classification. In this section, we delve into the essential steps involved in text processing and vector construction for poetry classification.

3.1.2. Text Preprocessing: Laying the Foundation

Text preprocessing is the initial stage where the raw text, often riddled with inconsistencies and noise, is transformed into a cleaner and more structured format. This preparatory step involves several crucial steps:

1. **Normalization:** Normalization ensures uniformity in the text representation by converting all characters to lowercase, eliminating punctuation marks and special characters, and handling inconsistencies in whitespace and encoding. This standardization helps in reducing the vocabulary size and unifying the text representation, making it easier for machine learning algorithms to process and analyze.
2. **Tokenization:** Tokenization breaks down the text into individual tokens, which can be words, phrases, punctuation marks, or any other meaningful units of language. This step is essential for identifying and extracting relevant features from the text. The choice of tokenization strategy depends on the specific task and language, and in the context of poetry classification, it is crucial to consider the unique characteristics of poetic language, such as wordplay, neologisms, and unconventional syntax.
3. **Stop Word Removal:** Stop words are common words that carry little or no meaning in a given context, such as "le," "un," "une," and "à." Removing stop words can reduce the dimensionality of the vector space and improve classification performance by eliminating noise and focusing on more meaningful terms. However, the decision of whether or not to remove stop words requires careful consideration, as some stop words may carry contextual significance in poetry, especially in cases where they contribute to the rhythm, rhyme, or overall structure of the poem.

3.2. Feature Extraction Methods: TF-IDF and Doc2Vec

Our research investigates the role of feature extraction in poetry classification, focusing on techniques like TF-IDF. We compare TF-IDF and Doc2Vec to analyze their effectiveness in transforming text into vectors suitable for machine learning models. This exploration highlights the significance of converting raw text into numerical formats for successful text classification, emphasizing the process's importance in poetry analysis.

3.2.1. TF-IDF

Feature extraction, which is essential in our study, involves transforming preprocessed text into a numerical format, thereby capturing key linguistic characteristics crucial for classification. This enables machine learning algorithms to discern patterns and formulate insights. Our approach utilized two predominant feature extraction methods:

- **Term Frequency (TF)**: This quantifies the frequency of a term within a document, signifying its role in encapsulating the document's essence. A term's elevated TF value denotes its recurrent presence, suggesting its pertinence to the theme or genre of the document.
- **Inverse Document Frequency (IDF)**: This assesses a term's rarity across a document collection, granting higher significance to rarer terms. This methodology accentuates the value of distinctive terms that contribute to differentiating documents.

Integrating TF and IDF, we generated a TF-IDF vector for each document, encapsulating both the term frequency within and its rarity across the corpus. This comprehensive representation enriches the characterization of document content for classification.

Yet, when analyzing Modernist French poetry using TF-IDF, we encounter limitations in capturing the nuanced styles and themes. Our innovation lies not in discarding TF-IDF but in complementing it with Doc2Vec and various machine learning algorithms, including SVM. This combination creates a detailed and sophisticated toolkit for probing Modernist French poetry. This methodology addresses initial limitations and establishes new benchmarks in AI-driven literary analysis. We aim to continually investigate and integrate emerging machine learning techniques, enhancing our model's analytical capabilities and ensuring its sustained relevance in literary studies.

In addition, we must pay more attention to these major concerns:

1. **Lemmatization and Stemming: Preserving Linguistic Integrity**: Lemmatization and stemming are essential in maintaining the integrity of poetic language for classification. Lemmatization is particularly valuable in poetry for preserving grammatical structure and meaning, while stemming reduces words to their root forms. The choice between these methods hinges on balancing grammatical accuracy with computational simplicity.
2. **Balancing Simplicity and Effectiveness: Striking the Right Chord**: This involves finding a balance in text processing techniques for poetry classification. The combination of TF-IDF vectorization, Doc2Vec, and lemmatization optimizes this balance, capturing essential linguistic features while preserving the unique characteristics of poetry. This balance is crucial for maintaining the richness of poetic language without oversimplification, ensuring effective classification through machine learning.
3. **Enhancing Poetic Language Analysis in Machine Learning-Driven Classification**: The future of poetry classification in AI hinges on addressing challenges like subjective language and poetic diversity. The research should focus on developing methods to handle these complexities, incorporating comprehensive poetic knowledge, and leveraging advancements in NLP and machine learning. This will foster a deeper understanding and appreciation of poetic language, which contributes significantly to the field's advancement.

Here, a word's occurrence in a given document is quantified by a metric called Term Frequency (TF). Conversely, Inverse Document Frequency (IDF) assesses the significance of the term throughout the whole corpus. Multiplying a word's TF value by its IDF value yields its TF-IDF composite score. A higher composite score signifies the word's elevated importance within the document in question.

Subsequent sections will delve into the mathematical intricacies and variations of the TF-IDF algorithm.

Let M stand for a collection of papers, represented as:

$$M = \left\{d_1, d_2, \ldots, d_j, \ldots d_{|M|}\right\}$$

where d_j represents the jth document in M.

Allow M to include a collection of words, K, represented as:

$$K = \left\{t_1, t_2, \ldots, t_j, \ldots t_{|K|}\right\}$$

where t_i stands for the i th in the element of K.

The occurrence of a term in a text is quantified using the term frequency (TF) metric. For instance, the formula for determining the frequency with which occurrences of the sequence t_i occur in sequence d_j is as follows:

$$TF_{ij} = \frac{n_{i,j}}{\sum_k n_{k,j}},$$

where $n_{i,j}$ is the total number of occurrences of word t_i in document d_j, and $\sum_k n_{k,j}$ is the total occurrences of all terms K in document d_j.

Overall, the TF-IDF combines the word's frequency in the text with its scarcity in the corpus in order to assess the word's relevance inside. Word frequency in a document serves to determine a word's TF by dividing the number of occurrences of the word by the overall number of words in the content of the document.

A word's scarcity in a corpus can be assessed with the inverted document frequency (IDF) method. Take IDF_i as an example. The logarithm of the ratio of documents in the corpus that includes the term to the total number of documents in the corpus is the formula for the IDF. Here is the formula:

$$IDF_i = \log \frac{|M|}{|d \in M : t_i \in d|} \tag{1}$$

where, for a large number of documents, $|M|$, the corpus is considered. The total number of occurrences of t_i in the corpus is represented by $|d \in M : t_i \in d|$.

Word t_i 's inverse document frequency (IDF) is found by using the formula:

$$IDF_i = \log \frac{|M|}{|d \in M : t_i \in d|}$$

where the total number of documents in the corpus is $|M|$. The number of documents in the corpus that include the term t_i is given by $|d \in M : t_i \in d|$. The larger the IDF_i value, the fewer are the documents which contain t_i, indicating that t_i has a significant capacity to discriminate between documents.

TF-IDF stands for Term Frequency-Inverse Document Frequency. A word's TF-IDF in a document is determined by multiplying its term frequency (TF) by its inverse document frequency (IDF). The TF-IDF is calculated by multiplying TF_{ij} and IDF_i. This is how it is defined:

$$TF - IDF = TF_{ij} \times IDF_i.$$

Finally, in text mining and natural language processing, the TF-IDF is a prominent measure of word value. It is utilized for tasks like document classification, text summarization, and information retrieval. In the context of our research, TF-IDF is a text analysis approach that considers the frequency of a word t_i in a document as well as its frequency in the corpus to determine its relevance. The significance of a term t_i is proportional to its frequency in the corpus. Figure 2 depicts the poetry vector training procedure.

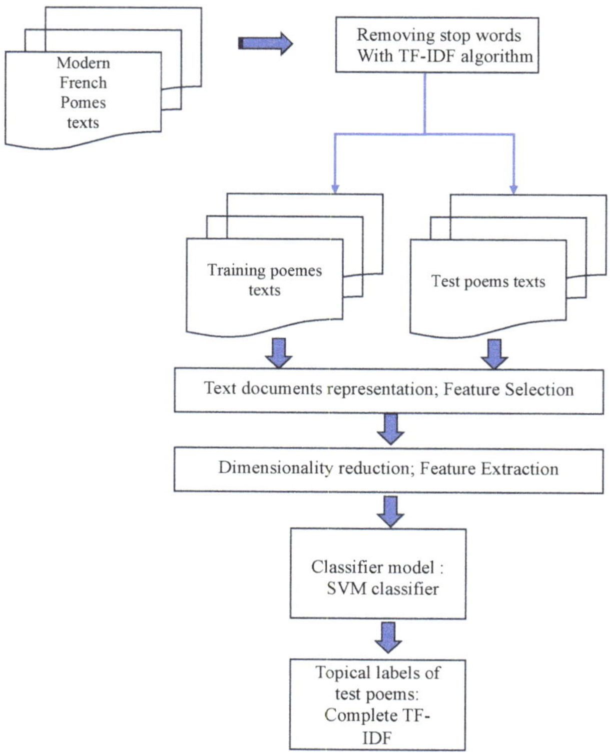

Figure 2. TF-IDF processing for Modern French Poetry texts.

3.2.2. Doc2Vec

One-hot encoding, a rudimentary technique for converting words into fixed-size numerical vectors, suffers from two significant limitations. First of all, it necessitates an immense quantity of memory, as the dimensionality of the word vector corresponds to the total number of unique words in the corpus, which might fluctuate between hundreds of thousands. Second, it fails to capture semantic relationships between words, leaving all words as mutually independent, as evidenced by their zero inner products. To address these shortcomings, Mikolov et al. introduced Word2Vec, a neural network-based word representation technique [51]. The key objective of Word2Vec is to maximize the log-probability of a given sequence of training words $w_1, w_2, \ldots, w_T$

$$\frac{1}{T}\sum_{t=k}^{T-k} \log p(w_t \mid w_{t-k}, \ldots, w_{t+k}),$$

where k is the dimension of the window utilized to maintain contextual information. In general, the prediction is performed using a multiclass classification with the softmax function, which is illustrated below:

$$p(w_t \mid w_{t-k}, \ldots, w_{t+k}) = \frac{e^{y_{w_t}}}{\sum_i e^{y_i}},$$

where y_i suggests the i-th output value of a feedforward neural network created in the following way:

$$y = b + Uh(w_{t-k}, \ldots, w_{t+k}; W)$$

where variables $b, U, h,$ and W are the bias terms between the hidden and output layer, the weight matrix between the hidden and output layer, the average or concatenation of context words, and the word embedding matrix.

Word2Vec's successor, Doc2Vec, aims to maintain the semantic connections between documents by searching for a continuous vector representation of a paragraph or bigger text. In the same way that Word2Vec does, we represent each word as a continuous vector of length d, where d is significantly less than the size of the vocabulary in the corpus $(d << |V|)$. Also, in the same vector space as words, the document itself is represented as a continuous vector.

Each document in the Doc2Vec model has its own unique vector, which is a row in the matrix D. In a similar way, each word is associated with a particular vector, represented by a separate row in the matrix W. Introducing D to Eq. merely partially alters the mathematical formulation of the network.

$$y = b + Uh(w_{t-k}, \ldots, w_{t+k}; W, D)$$

Distributed representations of each document in the corpus could be obtained once the network was properly trained. Text mining methods such as clustering and classification benefit greatly from these representations. Both the PV-DM and PV-DBOW designs, which are cornerstones of the Doc2Vec framework, were utilized in the present research. By integrating the vectors generated by these two topologies, we improved classification efficiency.

To accommodate texts of varying lengths, from single words to whole documents, Doc2Vec is an unconstrained framework. Figure 3 depicts the poetry vector generation training method. The model's input layer consists of both the poetry vector and the word vectors in the poem. The tokenized French text is scrolled across a window throughout training to extract lines of poetry. This process generates several training iterations for each poem, all of which involve the poetry vector. In each training iteration, the PoetryVector is used to represent the poem's central idea or theme.

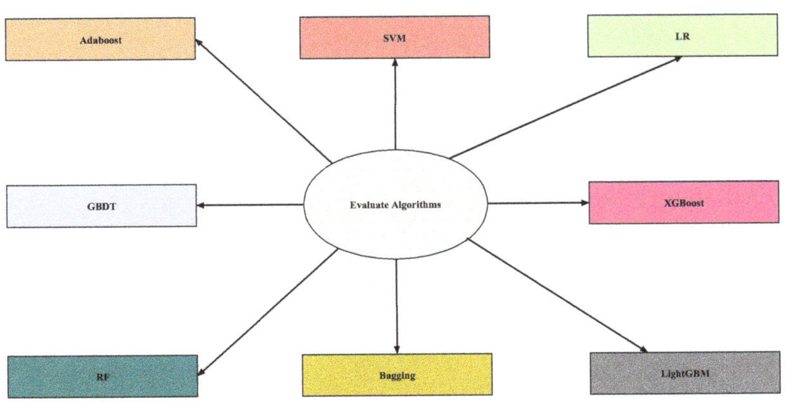

Figure 3. Modern French Poetry vector training system.

A frequently used poetry vector is obtained in addition to word vectors throughout training. Each training process employs this vector as part of its input layer. As the window passes across more words, this method obtains more and more efficient results. When training poetry vectors with Doc2Vec, a unique vector can be generated for each poem, which captures the most significant possible connections between the poem's words.

During the training phase, model parameters are refined based on the computed gradient of the neural network's error. Upon reaching convergence, the fidelity of the vectors undergoes continual enhancement. The poetry vector becomes increasingly adept at encapsulating the poem's thematic essence. Concurrently, word vectors are generated, which can be transformed into a format compatible with machine learning classification algorithms.

3.3. Comparison of Classification Algorithms

To adapt to the unique characteristics of poetic texts, we carefully adjusted and optimized the SVM parameters, including regularization terms and kernel function types. Besides SVM, we investigated several other machine learning classifiers, including Logistic Regression (LR), Bagging, Random Forest (RF), AdaBoost, Gradient Boosted Decision Trees (GBDT), XGBoost, and LightGBM. Each algorithm's parameters were meticulously calibrated to achieve the best classification performance. In summary, through extensive testing of these classification algorithms and evaluating their performance based on accuracy, F1 scores, and other relevant metrics, we aim to select the algorithm that best classifies modern French poetry. This process involves not only a technical comparison but also a thorough analysis of each algorithm's ability to address the specific challenges of literary texts. Ultimately, our goal is to determine an optimized model that can accurately reflect the stylistic differences in poetry and provide new perspectives and tools for literary analysis.

3.4. Significance of Automated Poetry Classification

Expert-driven traditional poetry classification methods, prone to subjective biases and inconsistency, are often unsuitable for contemporary poetry and large-scale tasks. Our research introduces an automated classification model using AI and natural language processing, aiming to standardize and objectify poetry classification. This approach, leveraging AI's ability to identify patterns in extensive poetry datasets, provides a more objective, consistent, scalable, and adaptable alternative. Particularly beneficial for new or evolving poetry styles, AI-driven classification can significantly advance poetry understanding and categorization, as shown in Figure 4.

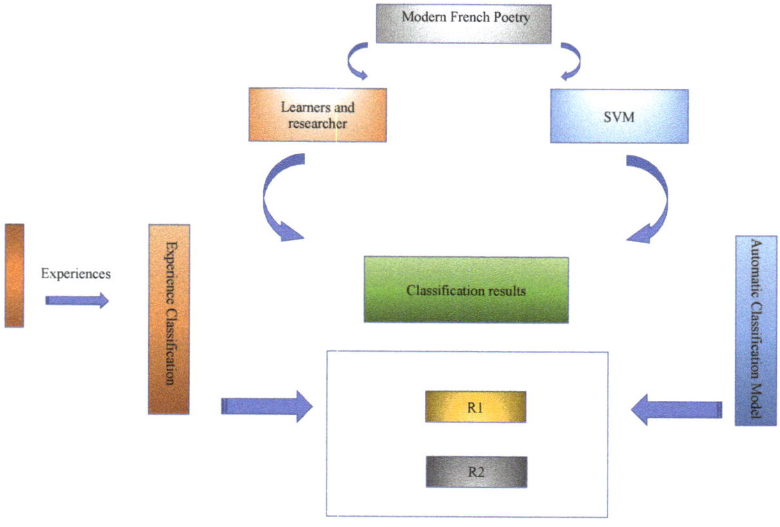

Figure 4. SVM Model for Modern French Poetry Learning.

In educational contexts, these AI models offer personalized learning and timely feedback to students, enhancing their poetry style development. For scholars, they aid in exploring poetry style evolution and genre relationships, and in recognizing contemporary trends. The paper discusses the importance of converting text into numerical data for machine learning, comparing TF-IDF and Doc2Vec techniques. Overall, AI-driven models present a substantial improvement in literary analysis, promising enhanced educational and research methodologies in poetry, with future AI advancements poised to offer even more sophisticated poetry analysis tools.

3.5. Pseudo Code for AI-Driven Poetry Classification Model

This pseudocode outlines the algorithmic process for the AI-based modern French poetry classification in our study. It details the preprocessing of poetry data, including normalization, tokenization, and stopword removal, followed by feature extraction using TF-IDF to analyze word significance and meanings.

The subsequent classification phase employs machine learning models, using extracted features to categorize poetry. This clear, structured pseudocode, which we will refer to as Algorithm 1, not only describes our methodology but also makes the complex computational processes accessible to non-experts, bridging technical complexity and comprehensibility.

In summary, the pseudocode (Algorithm 1) is crucial for understanding our AI-based poetry classification approach, emphasizing transparency and methodological rigor in integrating AI with a literary analysis.

Algorithm 1 AI-Based Poetry Classification Algorithm

```
input: poetry_dataset X, machine_learning_model M;
output: Classifications C;
function PREPROCESS_POETRY_DATA(dataset)
    for i = 1 to length(dataset) do
        Normalize text(dataset[i]);
        Tokenize text(dataset[i]);
        Remove stop words(dataset[i]);
        Apply TF-IDF(dataset[i]);
    end for
end function
function EXTRACT_FEATURES(processed_dataset)
    Initialize feature set F;
    for i = 1 to length(processed_dataset) do
        F[i] =compute_TF_IDF(processed_dataset[i]);
    end for
end function
function CLASSIFY_POEMS(features, machine_learning_model)
    Initialize classifications C;
    for i = 1 to length(features) do
        C[i] = machine_learning_model(features[i]);
    end for
end function
function MAIN(dataset, machine_learning_model)
    processed_dataset = PREPROCESS_POETRY_DATA(dataset);
    features = EXTRACT_FEATURES(processed_dataset);
    classifications = CLASSIFY_POEMS(features, machine_learning_model);
    return classifications;
end function
```

4. Experiment

Having delineated the intricate workings of our AI model methodology, which employs advanced natural language processing techniques, we now shift our focus to the practical application of this model. The transition from the theoretical underpinnings and technical robustness of the model, demonstrated through various algorithms and a bespoke training process to its real-world applicability in the realm of literary analysis, is pivotal.

This section contextualizes the AI-driven analysis within the broader literary ecosystem of Modernist French poetry. It emphasizes the importance of not only recognizing linguistic patterns and stylistic novelties but also understanding the historical, literary, and cultural contexts that shape these poems. This holistic approach, integrating both technical acumen and nuanced literary comprehension, ensures a more thorough and accurate analysis of the poetic corpus.

4.1. Source and Background of Dataset

The study utilized a dataset from "Bonjour Poésie", a comprehensive source of classic French poetry at https://www.bonjourpoesie.fr/lesgrandsclassiques (accessed on 14 January 2024). Curated by experts, the site offers poems with annotations on the poet, the work, and its historical context. The dataset comprises 1646 poems, representing modern French poetry's three main streams: Symbolism (309 poems), Parnassism (390 poems), and Romanticism (453 poems). It is split into training (70%) and testing (30%) sets for effective AI model evaluation. The advantages of using "Bonjour Poésie" include: **Expert Curation:** Ensuring dataset quality and accuracy. **Contextual Annotations:** Providing insights into poems' backgrounds. **Comprehensive Representation:** Covering the genre's main streams. **Rigorous Dataset Split:** Facilitating thorough model training and evaluation. In summary, "Bonjour Poésie" offers a well-curated, context-rich, and genre-representative dataset, ideal for an AI-driven analysis of modern French poetry.

4.2. Training and Test Sets

In this research, we classified 1646 poems from Modern French Poetry into Romanticism, Parnassian, and Symbolist categories, informed by literary expert opinions. The dataset was allocated into training (1152 poems) and test sets (494 poems), as outlined in Table 1.

Table 1. Distribution of Poetry Types in Training and Test Sets.

Poetry Category	Training Sets	Test Sets
Romanticism	453	183
Parnasse	390	171
Symbolism	309	140

We evaluated machine learning classifiers such as SVM, LR, RF, AdaBoost, GBDT, XGBoost, and LightGBM, using TF-IDF and Doc2Vec for text features. The data split was 70% for training and 30% for testing, with cross-validation to select the best models. SVM, with hyperparameters $C = 1.0$ and $\gamma = 0.1$, performed well, along with LR and GBDT, while RF and AdaBoost were less effective.

This study's thorough methods demonstrated the effectiveness of eight algorithms classification in French poetry classification and emphasized the role of hyperparameters, features, and ensemble techniques. These insights provide a foundation for future enhancements with advanced deep learning algorithms.

4.3. Training and Testing Design

The stages of our experiment were as follows:

Step 1. We applied the TF-IDF algorithm to preprocess and transform poems into numerical feature vectors, which were then used for SVM training.

Step 2. Following machine learning norms, the TF-IDF processed data was divided into training (1152 samples) and test sets (494 samples), covering Parnasse, Romantisme, and Symbolisme.

Step 3. Utilizing grid search and cross-validation, we optimized SVM's parameters to $C = 1.0$ and $\gamma = 0.1$. The model was then trained on the training set and evaluated on the test set comprising various poetry categories.

Step 4. We thoroughly analyzed the results, focusing on the accuracy, precision, recall, and F1 score.

This experiment demonstrated the synergy between TF-IDF and SVM, highlighting their combined effectiveness in text classification. The findings offer valuable insights for future text classification research. Overall, SVM's robustness in classification, enhanced by its adjustable parameters, was pivotal in our study of French poetry classification using the TF-IDF feature extraction method.

4.4. Hyperparameter Optimization for Classifiers

Python 3.8.15, pandas 1.5.2, gensim 4.3.0, and scikit-learn 1.2.0 were used for conducting experiments on the French poetry classification. Key steps included data pre-processing and vectorization, followed by training with scikit-learn. The models employed and their fine-tuned parameters were as follows:

- **SVM:** Adapted for high-dimensional poetry data, with rbf kernel. Parameters: $C = 1.0$, penalty = 'l2', max_iter = 1000.
- **LR:** Applied for probabilistic categorization. Parameters: penalty = 'l2', $C = 1.0$, max_iter = 1000, solver = 'lbfgs'.
- **Bagging:** To capture stylistic nuances. Parameters: n_estimators = 60, max_samples = 1.0.
- **RF:** Ensemble method suitable for diverse poetry styles. Parameters: n_estimators = 10, criterion = 'gini', max_features = 'sqrt'.
- **AdaBoost:** For iterative correction and detection of stylistic elements. Parameters: n_estimators = 50.
- **GBDT:** Iterative model capturing stylistic intricacies. Parameters: n_estimators = 100, max_depth = 3.
- **XGBoost:** Efficient for sparse stylistic data. Parameters: max_depth = 6, n_estimators = 100.
- **LightGBM:** Effective in capturing hierarchical poetic styles. Parameters: num_leaves = 31, n_estimators = 250.

Each classifier in our study was meticulously fine-tuned and evaluated using cross-validation on the training data. Following this, they were retrained on the complete dataset and tested on previously unobserved poetry. This methodological approach, which included careful parameter optimization, enabled us to accurately classify Modern French Poetry into distinct schools such as Romanticism, Parnasse, and Symbolism. The details of the classifier parameters and the dataset, comprising 1644 poems, are available at our GitHub repository: https://github.com/wkwg429/FrenchLiteratureTextClassification.git (accessed on 14 January 2024). Notably, the classifiers achieved an impressive accuracy rate of 90%.

In our research, the Support Vector Machine (SVM) emerged as a pivotal supervised machine learning method for classification tasks. SVM's efficacy hinges on its ability to find an optimized hyperplane, thus maximizing the margin between different categories. Figure 5 depicts how the optimal hyperplane is determined: it minimizes the distance between the nearest training data points, known as support vectors, and the hyperplane itself. This larger margin is crucial as it enhances the model's generalization capabilities when dealing with unknown data.

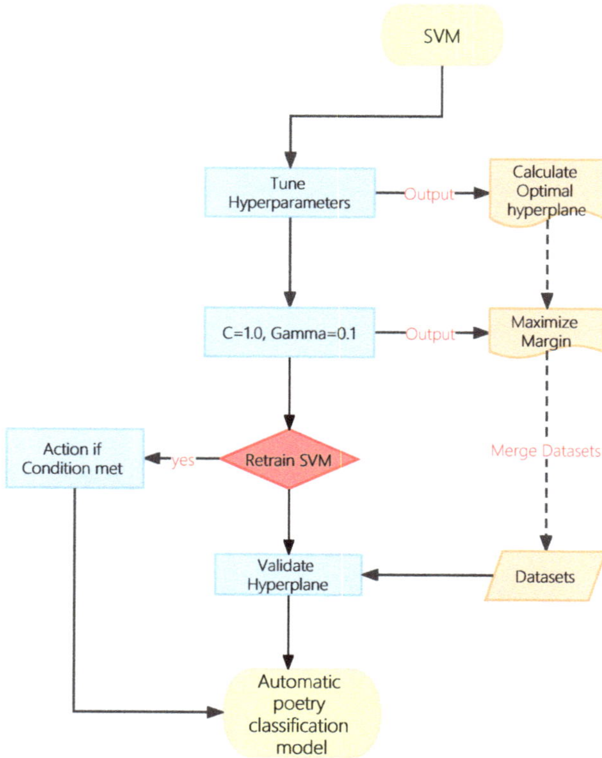

Figure 5. Optimal hyperplane in SVM maximizing the margin.

In the context of SVM, we utilized cross-validation to fine-tune its hyperparameters. The optimal model, as determined by this process, was subsequently retrained on the entire collection of training and testing poetry. A cornerstone of our study, the SVM models were adeptly implemented to classify the diverse styles of poetry. We integrated these models with traditional feature extraction methods, notably Term Frequency–Inverse Document Frequency (TF-IDF), to capture the nuanced differences among various poetic schools.

4.5. Analysis of the Results

Due to the inherent nuances and complexity of poetry, the process of categorizing French poetry into separate stylistic genres, such as Romanticism, Parnasse, and Symbolism, can be a complex and nuanced endeavor. Our experimental approach consisted of using a variety of classifiers in conjunction with the TF-IDF feature extraction method so that we could efficiently distinguish between these stylistic variances. Results showed that SVM with TF-IDF features, which provided optimal results in the Table 2, achieved the best performance with an accuracy of 0.7571 and an F1 score of 0.7518, while other classifiers, despite a reasonable performance, were less effective.

Table 2. Performance of classifiers on French poetry classification with different features.

Feature	Classification	Accuracy	Precision	Recall	F1 Score
tfidf	lr	0.7045	0.7202	0.6872	0.6879
tfidf	svm	0.7571	0.7549	0.7504	0.7518
tfidf	bagging	0.7510	0.7533	0.7418	0.7442
tfidf	rf	0.5506	0.5469	0.5391	0.5387
tfidf	adaboost	0.6275	0.6952	0.6108	0.6054
tfidf	gbdt	0.6194	0.6172	0.6190	0.6177
tfidf	xgb	0.6377	0.6375	0.6410	0.6355
tfidf	lgb	0.6721	0.6688	0.6703	0.6685
doc2vec_25	lr	0.6640	0.6570	0.6567	0.6566
doc2vec_25	svm	0.6599	0.6542	0.6538	0.6531
doc2vec_25	bagging	0.6640	0.6572	0.6571	0.6566
doc2vec_25	rf	0.5891	0.5781	0.5752	0.5733
doc2vec_25	adaboost	0.6538	0.6455	0.6457	0.6453
doc2vec_25	gbdt	0.6842	0.6795	0.6798	0.6795
doc2vec_25	xgb	0.6579	0.6515	0.6509	0.6508
doc2vec_25	lgb	0.6761	0.6726	0.6694	0.6699
ensemble_spar	lr	0.7045	0.6983	0.6986	0.6982
ensemble_spar	svm	0.7429	0.7389	0.7367	0.7363
ensemble_spar	bagging	0.7368	0.7326	0.7315	0.7312
ensemble_spar	rf	0.5749	0.5742	0.5669	0.5683
ensemble_spar	adaboost	0.6579	0.6475	0.6477	0.6475
ensemble_spar	gbdt	0.7287	0.7266	0.7250	0.7242
ensemble_spar	xgb	0.7227	0.7252	0.7196	0.7172
ensemble_spar	lgb	0.7368	0.7394	0.7323	0.7322

The classifiers' performance in terms of accuracy is summarized in Table 3. The SVM classifier clearly outperforms the competition with an accuracy of 0.7571, demonstrating its ability to handle the stylistic variations present in the presented dataset with ease.

Table 3. Classifier Efficiency with TF-IDF Features.

Classifier	Accuracy	Precision	Recall	F1 Score
LR	0.7045	0.7202	0.6872	0.6879
SVM	**0.7571**	**0.7549**	**0.7504**	**0.7518**
Bagging	0.7510	0.7533	0.7418	0.7442
RF	0.5506	0.5469	0.5391	0.5387
AdaBoost	0.6275	0.6952	0.6108	0.6054
GBDT	0.6194	0.6172	0.6190	0.6177
XGBoost	0.6377	0.6375	0.6410	0.6355
LightGBM	0.6721	0.6688	0.6703	0.6685

This is in line with how the SVM is meant to function, which is to locate a hyperplane that can partition the dataset into classes in the most effective way possible. More specifically, this is consistent with the intended operation of the SVM that was developed. When it pertains to the subject of our research, the Support Vector Machine (SVM) is preferable to other classifiers in terms of its potential to recognize the change that takes place when shifting from one form of poetry to another. This is because the SVM is able to distinguish the shift more accurately.

Random Forest (RF) failed to perform well as a classifier, achieving an accuracy of just 0.5506. It is possible that this is because it struggled to handle the delicate stylistic components of the dataset. The AdaBoost classifier, on the other hand, performed exceptionally well in precision, earning a score of 0.6952, but its lower recall score shows that there is potential for development.

Notably, the Support Vector Machine, or SVM, won the competition for the greatest F1 Score. This score is a combination of accuracy and recall, and as such, it is the option that is both the best balanced and an effective alternative for categorizing this specific dataset. Figure 6 is a graphic illustration of these essential indicators, which aims to promote a more intuitive understanding of the differences in performance that were observed.

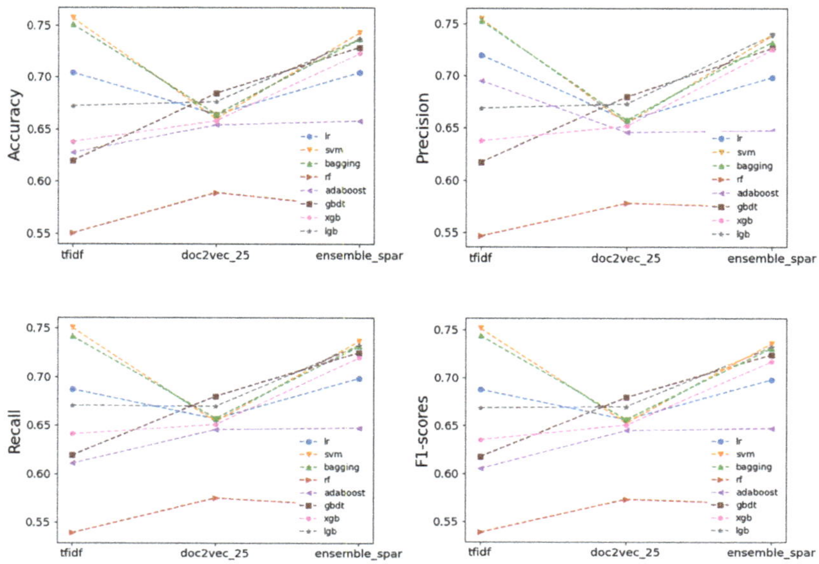

Figure 6. Four Classification Models Assessed Through Experiments With Real Data.

4.5.1. Performance Using TF-IDF Features

Table 4 summarizes the results using TF-IDF features. SVM achieves the best performance, with an accuracy and F1 score of 0.757 and 0.752, respectively. The other classifiers have an inferior performance:

Table 4. Classifier performance using method TF-IDF.

Classifier	Accuracy	Precision	Recall	F1 Score
SVM	**0.7571**	**0.755**	**0.750**	**0.7518**
LR	0.704	0.720	0.687	0.688
Bagging	0.751	0.753	0.742	0.744
RF	0.551	0.547	0.539	0.539
AdaBoost	0.628	0.695	0.611	0.605
GBDT	0.619	0.617	0.619	0.618
XGBoost	0.638	0.637	0.641	0.636
LightGBM	0.672	0.669	0.670	0.668

4.5.2. Performance Using Doc2Vec Features

Table 5 demonstrates that using Doc2Vec features leads to the highest levels of accuracy (0.684) and F1 score (0.679) for GBDT. The performance of SVM drops significantly to only 0.66 accuracy with Doc2Vec. LR, Bagging and LightGBM also perform reasonably well. But overall, results indicate that TF-IDF is better than Doc2Vec for this task.

Table 5. Classifier performance using Doc2Vec.

Classifier	Accuracy	Precision	Recall	F1 Score
GBDT	0.684	0.679	0.680	0.679
LR	0.664	0.657	0.657	0.657
Bagging	0.664	0.657	0.657	0.657
LightGBM	0.676	0.673	0.669	0.670
SVM	0.660	0.654	0.654	0.653
XGBoost	0.658	0.652	0.651	0.651
AdaBoost	0.654	0.645	0.646	0.645
RF	0.589	0.578	0.575	0.573

4.5.3. Ensemble Technique

The ensemble method in Table 6 improves accuracy of most classifiers by 2–5% over individual features. Using ensemble features, SVM obtains a best-in-class accuracy of 0.743 and an F1 score of 0.736.

Table 6. Classifier performance using ensemble features.

Classifier	Accuracy	Precision	Recall	F1 Score
SVM	**0.743**	**0.739**	**0.737**	**0.736**
LightGBM	0.737	0.739	0.732	0.732
GBDT	0.729	0.727	0.725	0.724
XGBoost	0.723	0.725	0.720	0.717
Bagging	0.737	0.733	0.732	0.731
LR	0.704	0.698	0.699	0.698
AdaBoost	0.658	0.647	0.648	0.647
RF	0.575	0.574	0.567	0.568

In summary, the investigation shows that SVM is the best TF-IDF classifier for French poetry categorization. The ensemble technique improves performance. The findings suggest that the multi-class text categorization machine learning method's SVM classifier is the most successful in classifying French poetry into stylistic genres, but it is important to understand its strengths and weaknesses. Classifiers may vary depending on the needs, such as favoring precision above recall or vice versa. Further research into parameter tweaking and other feature extraction approaches may provide even better findings, revealing more about French literary genres. The enhanced SVM model has been developed on the entire set of training data with the help of ensemble features and the revised hyperparameters $C = 1.0$, as well as through the $\gamma = 0.1$ process of cross-validation. This model was tested on 494 unobserved poems. The model includes 0.743 test set accuracy, 0.73–0.74 precision, recall, and F1 score. This suggests a good generalization to new French poetry data.

5. Discussion

This study contributes to Modern French Poetry classification using machine learning, with our SVM-based model achieving an accuracy of 0.743. However, its performance, considering the limited dataset and basic feature set, suggests room for improvement. The model's generalization ability needs testing with a larger, more diverse dataset for robust evaluation. The feature representations used, TF-IDF and Doc2Vec, capture basic stylistic elements but may not fully grasp poetry's intricate linguistic and contextual nuances. Advanced features like word embeddings and latent semantic analysis could better differentiate poetic styles. Moreover, our focus on SVM, despite its effectiveness in the text classification, warrants an exploration of other algorithms like CNNs and RNNs, which might better capture poetry's semantic and contextual intricacies. The study also opens possibilities for integrating this style classification model into poetry education tools, potentially enhancing student engagement and understanding. However, further research is needed to ensure the effectiveness and personalization of these technologies in educational settings. In summary, while our SVM model shows promise for classifying Modern French Poetry, exploring advanced features, diverse algorithms, and larger datasets could improve its performance. The model's integration into educational tools holds potential, but requires a careful evaluation of its impact on learning. Addressing these aspects could further advance computational poetry and educational technology.

5.1. In-Depth Comparative Analysis of AI-Driven Poetry Classification Model

Building upon the foundations established in the preceding sections, this section presents a comparative analysis that incorporates the latest advancements in AI to augment our poetry classification model's effectiveness. The integration of these sophisticated methodologies is crucial for effectively navigating the unique complexities associated with Modernist French poetry. Furthermore, this integration lays the groundwork for future research directions, inspiring further exploration and innovation in the field.

Li et al. discussed the cutting-edge data processing techniques providing valuable insights into the refinement of our poetry classification approach [43]. By implementing similar data distillation methods, we can enhance the accuracy and efficiency of our model, ensuring that even the subtlest nuances of Modernist French poetry are captured and analyzed effectively. Further, Shingala explored the integration of NLP with text classification and underscores the potential of combined methodologies [44]. This approach is particularly beneficial in our model, as it improves the accuracy and applicability of the classification, enabling a deeper understanding of the intricate linguistic structures and themes inherent in the poetry. By evaluating and incorporating the strengths of various classification methods, our model can achieve a higher degree of precision in categorizing and interpreting poetic texts. Particularly noteworthy is the research by Wang et al. [48] on predicting the lithium-ion battery lifespan using the PF-BiGRU-TSAM model, which integrates Particle Filtering, Bidirectional Gated Recurrent Units, and a Time Series Attention Mechanism, offering a valuable parallel perspective to our study. Additionally, the method proposed by Bilski [52], "Lifetime Extension via Levenberg-Marquardt Neural Networks" demonstrates proficiency in handling complex, time-sensitive data. This proficiency is directly relevant to our poetry classification model, where understanding temporal and stylistic shifts in language is crucial. Finally, the recent advancements in AI, such as the research made by Wang et al. [40], which incorporates contrastive learning and adversarial training, offer novel approaches for tackling complex classification challenges.

In summary, this research synthesizes findings from both established and emerging areas of AI research to enhance our poetry classification model. Specifically, the methodologies adopted are tailored to tackle the unique challenges inherent in Modernist French poetry, including ambiguity, subjectivity, and unconventional syntax. These challenges necessitate a nuanced approach for a further comprehensive analysis in the future study. Consequently, our model not only addresses the specificities of Modernist French poetry but also aligns with the latest advancements in AI, resulting in a more robust and insightful analytical framework.

5.2. Summary of Findings and Future Directions

Our study on Modern French Poetry classification using machine learning has led to significant insights:

- The SVM-based model effectively classified poetry with an accuracy of 0.743, demonstrating machine learning's potential in capturing poetic styles.
- Limitations in current feature representations (TF-IDF and Doc2Vec) were observed. Advanced methods like word embeddings could better capture poetic nuances.
- The dataset's size limits the model's ability to generalize. A larger dataset would offer a more robust evaluation of its performance.

The study acknowledges limitations, setting the course for future research:

- Enhancing generalization across diverse poetic styles requires a more extensive dataset.

- Investigating sophisticated feature representations like latent semantic analysis could improve style discrimination.
- Exploring other machine learning techniques, such as CNNs and RNNs, might capture poetic nuances more effectively.
- Integrating the model into educational platforms demands careful consideration of effectiveness and personalization. Further research should focus on ensuring these technologies augment educational outcomes and democratize learning.

In conclusion, while our SVM model shows promise, addressing these limitations and exploring new methodologies could significantly enhance its capabilities and educational impact. This research serves as a foundation for future studies in computational poetry analysis and its integration into educational settings.

Author Contributions: Conceptualization, L.Y.; methodology, L.Y.; software, G.W., L.Y.; validation, L.Y.; formal analysis, L.Y.; investigation, L.Y.; resources, L.Y.; data curation, G.W., L.Y.; writing—original draft preparation, L.Y.; writing—review and editing, H.W., L.Y.; visualization, L.Y.; supervision, H.W.; project administration, H.W.; funding acquisition, L.Y.. All authors have read and agreed to the published version of the manuscript.

Funding: This work was funded by the Central Basic Research Operation Fee Cultivation Project of Zhongnan University of Economics and Law for the year 2019 under Grant number Category B, No. 61. School of Foreign Studies, Zhongnan University of Economics and Law.

Data Availability Statement: The codes and datasets associated with the paper are shared at https://github.com/wkwg429/FrenchLiteratureTextClassification.git, accessed on 14 January 2024.

Acknowledgments: We extend our heartfelt thanks to Gang Wang for his significant contributions to software development and data curation, and to Hongjun Wang for his invaluable guidance and supervision. This article is the culmination of joint efforts from all contributors.

Conflicts of Interest: The authors declare no conflict of interest

References

1. Middleton, P.; Marsh, N. *Teaching Modernist Poetry*; Cambridge University Press: Cambridge, UK, 2010. [CrossRef]
2. Camilleri, M.; Camilleri, A. The Sustainable Development Goal on Quality Education. In *The Future of the UN Sustainable Development Goals*; United Nations: New York, NY, USA, 2019. [CrossRef]
3. Gallagher, M. Ethics in the Absence of Reference: Levinas and the (Aesthetic) Value of Diversity. *Levinas Stud.* **2012**, *7*, 125–195. [CrossRef]
4. Röhnert, J. Vom Spleen de Paris zum spleenigen Paris. *Z. Für Lit. Und Linguist.* **2010**, *40*, 168–179. [CrossRef]
5. Sherry, V. *The Great War and the Language of Modernism*; Oxford University Press: Oxford, UK, 2003. [CrossRef]
6. Fetzer, G.W. Linguistique et analyse de la poésie: Apports actuels. *Contemp. Fr. Francoph. Stud.* **2016**, *20*, 470–477. [CrossRef]
7. Gardner, W.O. Advertising Tower: Japanese Modernism and Modernity in the 1920s. *Comp. Crit. Stud.* **2007**, *4*, 455–459. [CrossRef]
8. Tanasescu, C.; Paget, B.; Inkpen, D. Automatic Classification of Poetry by Meter and Rhyme. In Proceedings of the 29th International Florida Artificial Intelligence Research Society Conference (FLAIRS), Key Largo, FL, USA, 16–18 May 2016; pp. 823–828.
9. Prieto, J.C.S.; Gamazo, A.; Cruz-Benito, J.; Therón, R.; García-Peñalvo, F. AI-Driven Assessment of Students: Current Uses and Research Trends. In Proceedings of the International Conference on Human-Computer Interaction, Virtual, 19–24 July 2020; Springer International Publishing: Cham, Germany, 2020; pp. 292–302. [CrossRef]
10. Huang, M.H.; Rust, R. Artificial Intelligence in Service. *J. Serv. Res.* **2018**, *21*, 155–172. [CrossRef]
11. Yang, S.J.H.; Ogata, H.; Matsui, T.; Chen, N. Human-centered artificial intelligence in education: Seeing the invisible through the visible. *Comput. Educ. Artif. Intell.* **2021**, *2*, 100008. [CrossRef]
12. Hosseini, M.; Nasrabadi, M.; Mollanoroozy, E.; Khani, F.; Mohammadi, Z.; Barzanoni, F.; Amini, A.; Gholami, A. Relationship of sleep duration and sleep quality with health-related quality of life in patients on hemodialysis in Neyshabur. *Sleep Med.* **2023**, *5*, 100064. [CrossRef] [PubMed]
13. Wei, H.; Geng, H. The Revival of Classical Chinese Poetry Composition: A Perspective from the New Liberal Arts. *Int. J. Comp. Lit. Transl. Stud.* **2022**, *10*, 18–22. [CrossRef]
14. Kempton, H.M.; School of Psychology. Holy be the Lay: A Way to Mindfulness Through Christian Poetry. *OBM Integr. Complement. Med.* **2021**, *7*, 011. [CrossRef]

15. Yusifov, T. Methods of Analysis of Lyrical Texts in Foreign Literature Classes in Higher Educational Institutions (Based on the Works of Nazim Hikmet). *Sci. Bull. Mukachevo State Univ. Ser. Pedagogy Psychol.* **2022**, *8*, 81–88. [CrossRef]
16. Alsharif, O.; Alshamaa, D.; Ghneim, N. Emotion Classification in Arabic Poetry using Machine Learning. *Int. J. Comput. Appl.* **2013**, *65*, 10–15.
17. Ahmed, M.A. A Classification of Al-hur Arabic Poetry and Classical Arabic Poetry by Using Support Vector Machine, Naïve Bayes, and Linear Support Vector Classification. *Iraqi J. Comput. Sci. Math.* **2022**, *3*, 128–137. [CrossRef]
18. Rostampour, S. Word Order of Noun and Verb Phrases in Contemporary Persian and English Poems. *J. Adv. Linguist.* **2017**, *8*, 1229–1235. [CrossRef]
19. Tangirova, D. Variety Of Forms And Genres In Modern Poetry. *Am. J. Interdiscip. Innov. Res.* **2020**, *2*, 32–41. [CrossRef]
20. Dadhich, A.; Thankachan, B. Opinion Classification of Product Reviews Using Naïve Bayes, Logistic Regression and Sentiwordnet: Challenges and Survey. *IOP Conf. Ser. Mater. Sci. Eng.* **2021**, *1099*, 012071. [CrossRef]
21. Puri, S.; Singh, S. Text recognition in bilingual machine printed image documents—Challenges and survey: A review on principal and crucial concerns of text extraction in bilingual printed images. In Proceedings of the 2016 10th International Conference on Intelligent Systems and Control (ISCO), Coimbatore, India, 7–8 January 2016; pp. 1–8. [CrossRef]
22. Li, Q.; Peng, H.; Li, J.; Xia, C.; Yang, R.; Sun, L.; Yu, P.S.; He, L. A Survey on Text Classification: From Shallow to Deep Learning. *arXiv* **2020**, arXiv:2008.00364. [CrossRef].
23. Kowsari, K.; Meimandi, K.; Heidarysafa, M.; Mendu, S.; Barnes, L.E.; Brown, D.E. Text Classification Algorithms: A Survey. *Information* **2019**, *10*, 150. [CrossRef]
24. Li, Z.; Qian, S.; Cao, J.; Fang, Q.; Xu, C. Adaptive Transformer-Based Conditioned Variational Autoencoder for Incomplete Social Event Classification. In Proceedings of the 30th ACM International Conference on Multimedia, New York, NY, USA, 10–14 October 2022. [CrossRef]
25. Wu, M.; Pan, S.; Zhu, X.; Zhou, C.; Pan, L. Domain-Adversarial Graph Neural Networks for Text Classification. In Proceedings of the 2019 IEEE International Conference on Data Mining (ICDM), Beijing, China, 8–11 November 2019. [CrossRef]
26. Rafeeque, P.C.; Sendhilkumar, S. A survey on Short text analysis in Web. In Proceedings of the 2011 Third International Conference on Advanced Computing, Chennai, India, 14–16 December 2011; pp. 365–371. [CrossRef]
27. Xia, C.; Yin, W.; Feng, Y.; Yu, P. Incremental Few-shot Text Classification with Multi-round New Classes: Formulation, Dataset and System. *arXiv* **2021**, arXiv:2104.11882; pp. 1351–1360. [CrossRef]
28. Lai, S.; Xu, L.; Liu, K.; Zhao, J. Recurrent Convolutional Neural Networks for Text Classification. In Proceedings of the AAAI Conference on Artificial Intelligence, Austin, TX, USA, 25–30 January 2015; pp. 2267–2273. [CrossRef]
29. Wang, P.; Hu, J.; Zeng, H.J.; Chen, Z. Using Wikipedia knowledge to improve text classification. *Knowl. Inf. Syst.* **2009**, *19*, 265–281. [CrossRef]
30. Abel, J.; Lantow, B. A Methodological Framework for Dictionary and Rule-based Text Classification. In Proceedings of the KDIR, Vienna, Austria, 16–18 September 2019; pp. 330–337.
31. Wang, H.; Hong, M. Supervised Hebb rule based feature selection for text classification. *Inf. Process. Manag.* **2019**, *56*, 167–191. [CrossRef]
32. Hadi, W.; Al-Radaideh, Q.A.; Alhawari, S. Integrating associative rule-based classification with Naïve Bayes for text classification. *Appl. Soft Comput.* **2018**, *69*, 344–356. [CrossRef]
33. Mishra, M.; Vishwakarma, S.K. Text Classification based on Association Rule Mining Technique. *Int. J. Comput. Appl.* **2017**, *169*, 46–50. [CrossRef]
34. Liu, J.; Bai, R.; Lu, Z.; Ge, P.; Aickelin, U.; Liu, D. Data-driven regular expressions evolution for medical text classification using genetic programming. In Proceedings of the 2020 IEEE Congress on Evolutionary Computation (CEC), Glasgow, UK, 19–24 July 2020; pp. 1–8.
35. Faguo, Z.; Fan, Z.; Bingru, Y.; Xingang, Y. Research on Short Text Classification Algorithm Based on Statistics and Rules. In Proceedings of the 2010 Third International Symposium on Electronic Commerce and Security, Nanchang, China, 29–31 July 2010; pp. 3–7. [CrossRef]
36. Choi, J.; Kilmer, D.; Mueller-Smith, M.; Taheri, S.A. Hierarchical Approaches to Text-based Offense Classification. *Sci. Adv.* **2023**, *9*, eabq8123. [CrossRef] [PubMed]
37. Elmahdy, A.; Inan, H.A.; Sim, R. Privacy Leakage in Text Classification: A Data Extraction Approach. *arXiv* **2022**, arXiv.2206.04591. [CrossRef].
38. Guo, Z.; Zhang, R.; Huan, H. Text Classification Method Based on PEGCN. Online Resource, 2024. Available online: https://www.authorea.com/doi/full/10.22541/au.168210369.91223406/v1 (accessed on 14 January 2024).
39. Wang, H.; Tian, K.; Wu, Z.; Wang, L. A Short Text Classification Method Based on Convolutional Neural Network and Semantic Extension. *Int. J. Comput. Intell. Syst.* **2020**, *14*, 367. [CrossRef]
40. Wang, X.; Zhang, J.; Zhao, L.; Wang, X. Research on Text Classification Technology Integrating Contrastive Learning and Adversarial Training. In Proceedings of the 2023 IEEE 3rd International Conference on Electronic Technology, Communication and Information (ICETCI), Changchun, China, 26–28 May 2023; pp. 860–865.
41. Zhang, R.; Guo, Z.; Huan, H. Text Classification Based on an Improved Graph Neural Network. Online Resource, 2022. Available online: https://www.researchsquare.com/article/rs-2385115/v1 (accessed on 21 December 2022).

42. Kargupta, P.; Komarlu, T.; Yoon, S.; Wang, X.; Han, J. MEGClass: Extremely Weakly Supervised Text Classification via Mutually-Enhancing Text Granularities. *arXiv* **2023**, arXiv.2304.01969. [CrossRef].
43. Li, Y.; Li, W. Data Distillation for Text Classification. *arXiv* **2021**, arXiv.2104.08448. [CrossRef].
44. Shingala, A. Three Phase Synthesizing of Nlp and Text Classification for Query Generation. *Int. J. Res. Appl. Sci. Eng. Technol.* **2017**, *5*, 39–42. [CrossRef]
45. Abdulla, H.H.H.A.; Awad, W.S. Text Classification of English News Articles using Graph Mining Techniques. In Proceedings of the 14th International Conference on Agents and Artificial Intelligence (ICAART 2022), Virtual, 3–5 February 2022; pp. 926–937.
46. Zhang, S.; Li, H.; Zhang, S. Job opportunity finding by text classification. *Procedia Eng.* **2012**, *29*, 1528–1532. [CrossRef]
47. Liu, X.; Mou, L.; Cui, H.; Lu, Z.; Song, S. Finding decision jumps in text classification. *Neurocomputing* **2020**, *371*, 177–187. [CrossRef]
48. Wang, Y.; Hei, C.; Liu, H.; Zhang, S.; Wang, J. Prognostics of Remaining Useful Life for Lithium-Ion Batteries Based on Hybrid Approach of Linear Pattern Extraction and Nonlinear Relationship Mining. *IEEE Trans. Power Electron.* **2023**, *38*, 1054–1063. [CrossRef]
49. Forman, G. An extensive empirical study of feature selection metrics for text classification. *J. Mach. Learn. Res.* **2003**, *3*, 1289–1305.
50. Ameer, I.; Sidorov, G.; Gómez-Adorno, H.; Nawab, R.M.A. Multi-Label Emotion Classification on Code-Mixed Text: Data and Methods. *IEEE Access* **2022**, *10*, 8779–8789. [CrossRef]
51. Mikolov, T.; Chen, K.; Corrado, G.; Dean, J. Efficient Estimation of Word Representations in Vector Space. *arXiv* **2013**, arXiv:1301.3781. [CrossRef].
52. Bilski, J.; Smoląg, J.; Kowalczyk, B.; Grzanek, K.; Izonin, I. Fast Computational Approach to the Levenberg-Marquardt Algorithm for Training Feedforward Neural Networks. *J. Artif. Intell. Soft Comput. Res.* **2023**, *13*, 45–61. [CrossRef]

information

MDPI

Article

Detecting Moral Features in TV Series with a Transformer Architecture through Dictionary-Based Word Embedding

Paolo Fantozzi [1,†], Valentina Rotondi [2,3,†], Matteo Rizzolli [1,†], Paola Dalla Torre [4,†] and Maurizio Naldi [1,5,*,†]

1 Department of Law, Economics, Politics, and Modern Languages, LUMSA University, 00192 Rome, Italy; p.fantozzi1@lumsa.it (P.F.); m.rizzolli@lumsa.it (M.R.)
2 Department of Economics, Health and Social Care, SUPSI, 6928 Lugano, Switzerland; valentina.rotondi@supsi.ch
3 Department of Sociology, University of Oxford, Oxford OX1 1JD, UK
4 Department of Social Sciences—Communication, Education and Psychology, LUMSA University, 00193 Rome, Italy; p.dallatorre1@lumsa.it
5 Department of Civil, Computer Science and Aeronautical Technologies Engineering, Roma Tre University, 00146 Rome, Italy
* Correspondence: m.naldi@lumsa.it
† These authors have contributed equally to this work.

Abstract: Moral features are essential components of TV series, helping the audience to engage with the story, exploring themes beyond sheer entertainment, reflecting current social issues, and leaving a long-lasting impact on the viewers. Their presence shows through the language employed in the plot description. Their detection helps regarding understanding the series writers' underlying message. In this paper, we propose an approach to detect moral features in TV series. We rely on the Moral Foundations Theory (MFT) framework to classify moral features and use the associated MFT dictionary to identify the words expressing those features. Our approach combines that dictionary with word embedding and similarity analysis through a deep learning SBERT (Sentence-Bidirectional Encoder Representations from Transformers) architecture to quantify the comparative prominence of moral features. We validate the approach by applying it to the definition of the MFT moral feature labels as appearing in general authoritative dictionaries. We apply our technique to the summaries of a selection of TV series representative of several genres and relate the results to the actual content of each series, showing the consistency of results.

Keywords: moral features; moral foundations theory; TV series; storytelling; language analysis; genre analysis; deep learning; transformers; SBERT

1. Introduction

The description and transmission of moral features through language have a long-standing history [1]. Moral content has been intrinsic to narration since ancient times when religious texts and myths aimed at leading the audience to draw some moral conclusions [2]. Actually, morality has been viewed as an unavoidable companion to any narration [3]. Also, moral prescriptions on behavior and expression were common in many manuals from the 16th to the 18th century [4]. The conveyance of morality through language has occurred in more recent forms of narration, such as movies [5,6] and TV series [7,8]. The relevance of TV series in the transmission of moral features is especially pertinent due to their role in shaping popular culture and influencing viewers' perceptions and attitudes [9]. Even when blockbusters are devised for audience success, moral patterns are somewhat included, either in the form of adherence to the audience's moral beliefs or as moral norm violations introduced in the conflicts among characters [10].

An established classification of moral features has been set through Moral Foundations Theory [11] (MFT), which posits five universal moral foundations— Harm/Care,

Fairness/Reciprocity, Ingroup/Loyalty, Authority/Respect, and Purity/Sanctity. This theoretical framework has been largely used to analyze the presence of moral content in traditional media (books and songs) as well as relatively recent ones (movies and video games) [12–14]. However, no attempts have been made in the literature to employ it in the context of TV series. The growing relevance of this entertainment outlet for the formation of popular culture poses a spurring need for its analysis.

Our paper aims to fill this research gap by adopting the MFT framework to analyze the presence of moral content in TV series. We propose a deep learning-based methodology using the Sentence-Bidirectional Encoder Representations from Transformers (SBERT) architecture, based on the combined use of a lexicon established as a companion to MFT (the *Moral Foundations Dictionary*, MFD) and a word embedding approach. We strive to provide a wide panorama of TV series by analyzing series encompassing several genres.

Our major contributions are the following:

- we propose a deep learning architecture to identify the presence of moral foundations in TV series;
- we validate the method through an authoritative general dictionary-based reference;
- we apply the novel architecture to a selection of seven TV series belonging to different genres, showing how the quantitative analysis of moral foundations relates to the content of those series.

The structure of the paper is as follows. We review the literature related to the quantitative analysis of TV series and the MFT framework in Section 2. We describe our datasets and methodology in Section 3 and finally provide the method validation and the results in Section 4.

2. Related Literature

Our study consists of applying quantitative techniques to TV series by employing the Moral Foundations Theory framework. In this section, we provide a brief literature review of quantitative studies concerning TV series and a wider description of the MFT framework and its applications.

2.1. The Quantitative Analysis of TV Series

TV series have started being analyzed quantitatively in the last decade using tools from graph theory and text mining.

The analysis first focused on the relationships between characters, embodied by the character network. Beveridge and Shan have shown how graph theory could be employed to examine the interactions among characters and the presence of clusters of characters in *Game of Thrones* [15]. Bost et al. extracted dynamic conversational networks from *Breaking Bad*, *Game of Thrones*, and *House of Cards* [16]. Tan et al. measured the graph characteristics of co-occurrence character networks in *Stargate* and *Star Trek* [17]. Complex networks were introduced to describe roles in *Mr. Love*, *Westworld*, and *The Dream of Red Mansions* [18]. The identification of leading roles among characters to distinguish between choral series, on the one hand, and series focusing on the main character, on the other hand, was tackled in [19] through the use of suitable metrics. Also, the influence of the network structure on the series' performance was examined by [20].

A more recent theme of investigation has been the analysis of the narrative structure of series. A classification of plots of medical series into medical cases plots, professional plots, and sentimental plots was proposed in [21]. Instead, the evolution of series over time was analyzed in [22] by examining the changing salience of characters and locations.

2.2. Moral Foundations Theory

Moral Foundations Theory, employed in this paper, has gained recognition as a psychological framework that uncovers the fundamental moral principles influencing human judgments and behavior. Although relatively recent, MFT has quickly gained acceptance in the field. The following section delves into this theory's historical development and formulation. Next, we explore its application to identifying moral foundations within traditional media formats like books, songs, television, cinema, and emerging media platforms like video games. We analyze the media under scrutiny and the methodologies employed to ascertain the prominence of moral foundations, offering a comprehensive examination of their presence and impact.

Graham et al. introduced a comprehensive framework for classifying moral values, which they termed *Moral Foundations Theory* [11,23]. MFT builds on earlier theories of moral judgment and offers a unified framework to account for variations in human moral reasoning as the result of the combination of a few innate and modular foundations.

While alternative approaches exist (see, for instance, [24]), and although MFT is not impervious to criticism [25], its rapid ascent in popularity is unmistakable, evident in the proliferation of citations and the broad adoption of its questionnaire and associated instruments across various disciplines, including moral psychology, political science [26], economics [27], law [28], behavioral science [29], and beyond.

Within MFT, Graham et al. identified five fundamental dimensions, which they referred to as *foundations*. In their original formulation, the five dimensions were identified by the following pairs:

- *Harm/Care*;
- *Fairness/Reciprocity*;
- *Ingroup/Loyalty*;
- *Authority/Respect*;
- *Purity/Sanctity*.

According to Moral Foundations Theory, these five foundations are universal across cultures and reflect evolved psychological mechanisms that enable individuals and societies to solve collective action problems and navigate social complexity. However, different cultures and individuals may emphasize or prioritize these foundations differently, leading to different moral beliefs and values.

The *Harm/Care* foundation revolves around the notion that individuals and societies should protect and care for those who are vulnerable and in need. It encompasses values such as compassion, empathy, and kindness.

The *Fairness/Reciprocity* foundation centers on the idea that individuals and societies should strive for fairness, reciprocity, and justice. It encompasses values such as equality, proportionality, and impartiality.

The *Ingroup/Loyalty* foundation emphasizes the importance of loyalty and commitment to one's social groups, including family, tribe, or nation. It encompasses values such as patriotism, group solidarity, and sacrifice for the common good.

The *Authority/Respect* foundation underscores the significance of respecting and deferring to legitimate authority and hierarchical structures. It encompasses values such as obedience, respect for traditions, and deference to leaders.

The *Purity/Sanctity* foundation highlights the value of upholding purity, cleanliness, and sacredness within various domains, such as sexuality, food, and religion. It encompasses values such as reverence for the sacred, disgust for the impure, and adherence to traditional moral codes.

As you can see, [11] used a couple of terms to define each foundation. The terms in each couple were akin in most cases, but, in the case of *Harm/Care*, they seemed to identify opposite extremes of the same moral value. Similar couples of opposites have been identified in [23] for the other foundations as well, such as *Fairness/Cheating*, *Loyalty/Betrayal*, *Authority/Subversion*, and *Sanctity/Degradation*. In the following, we opt for the more recent formulation based on a couple of extremes for each moral foundation, as proposed at https://moralfoundations.org (accessed on 18 January 2024).

In order to identify the presence of those moral foundations in a corpus of texts, [30] built a lexicon for each foundation. The lexicon used in this study was developed through an iterative process comprising both an expansive and contractive phase. During the expansive phase, the researchers began with the core concepts of each moral foundation and systematically generated a comprehensive list of associations, synonyms, and antonyms. This process involved consulting thesauruses, engaging in discussions with colleagues, and exploring various linguistic resources.

Subsequently, in the contractive phase, the lexicon underwent refinement. Words that appeared distant from the fundamental concepts of the moral foundations were purged from the lexicon. This selective process ensured that the final lexicon captured the essence of each foundation, encompassing both positive and negative polarities associated with them. By considering the moral foundations as cohesive entities, inclusive of their positive and negative dimensions, the lexicon provides a comprehensive and nuanced representation of the moral values under examination. For example, the lexicon for *Purity/Sanctity* includes *profane* and *pervert* as well as *pious* and *purity*, among others. The resulting lexicon was dubbed the *Moral Foundations Dictionary*.

In order to measure the presence of each foundation, [31] developed a questionnaire (the Moral Foundations Questionnaire, or MFQ for short) that included 30 items.

In addition to the comprehensive lexicon encompassing words associated with the five moral foundations, the researchers identified specific lexicons for the two opposite facets of each foundation. This recognition stems from the understanding that each foundation can be expressed in terms of both positive and negative dimensions, representing different sides of the moral spectrum. The researchers defined those two facets of the same foundation as *virtue* vs. *vice*. For a more detailed exploration of the lexicons associated with the virtue and vice sides of each foundation, interested readers can refer to the webpage available at http://moralfoundations.org/wp-content/uploads/files/downloads/moral%20foundations%20dictionary.dic (accessed on 17 January 2024). On this webpage, the lexicons associated with each facet of the moral foundations can be accessed, providing a comprehensive resource for understanding the specific words and concepts associated with the positive and negative dimensions of each foundation.

2.3. Moral Foundations Theory in Media Analysis

Understanding the moral dimensions portrayed in various forms of media is vital for comprehending their impact on individuals' attitudes, behaviors, and societal norms. The application of Moral Foundations Theory provides a systematic framework for delving into these moral underpinnings and examining their influence within media content. This subsection reviews the existing literature on the exploration of MFT in media analysis, highlighting its significance and contributions to the field. We consider first books, moving then to songs and movies, to end with video games.

Wheeler et al. employed the Google Books Ngram viewer to analyze books published in the 1900–2007 period [32]. They adopted the Moral Foundations Theory framework to examine how moral values shifted during the century. The Google Books Ngram viewer is a search engine that outputs the frequencies of search strings using n-grams in printed sources published between 1500 and 2019 in Google's text corpora in several languages. The total collection is far from complete and is claimed to contain more than 6% of all the books ever published [33]. The authors employed the terms comprising the *Moral Foundations Dictionary* (see Section 2.2 for a description of that lexicon) as search strings and found the resulting term frequencies for all the terms associated with the six moral foundations and derived the frequency of each moral foundation, restricting their analysis to books in English.

Similarly, Long and Eveland conducted a lexicon-based analysis (again employing the MFT framework described in Section 2.2) on song lyrics, encompassing 13 genres, to explore the variations in moral content across these genres [34]. The songs were selected by referencing the primary US chart categories curated by Billboard. While these charts may feature songs in languages other than English, we speculate that the authors exclusively incorporated English-language song lyrics. Additionally, the authors administered a survey employing the Moral Foundations Questionnaire to assess the moral attitude of the respondents and record their genre preferences. By comparing the data derived from the analysis of song lyrics with the questionnaire responses, the study aimed to examine whether the participants' moral progressivism aligned with the moral progressivism reflected in the lyrics of their preferred music genres.

While the available literature on the application of Moral Foundations Theory to the aforementioned media forms is limited, there exists a more substantial body of research focused on applying MFT in the analysis of TV and cinema.

Bowman et al. examined the mediating role of moral foundations in individuals' preferences for media genres, specifically focusing on movies (drama, action, and horror) and TV shows (comedy, news, and sports) [35]. They found that moral foundations play a mediating role in the relationship between nationality and genre preferences. In order to gauge the salience of moral foundations, the study employed the MFQ, administered to individuals from two different countries, namely the United States and Germany. The questionnaire for US respondents was the MFQ itself, while an adapted 29-item scale in German developed using back-translation was submitted to German respondents. Similarly, ref. [12] considered the influence of moral foundations on the consumption of TV crime dramas. In their study, the researchers also employed the MFQ.

In a study by Tamborini et al. [14], rather than using actual movies, ten summaries of fictional movies were created to examine whether viewers' moral beliefs influenced characters' appeal. Participants' moral beliefs were assessed using the standard MFQ, while viewers were asked to express their enjoyment of the movie outcome for the specific character (for example, if they enjoyed a negative outcome for a character violating a moral domain).

A similar investigation was carried out in [36] for the viewers of the series *Downton Abbey*. In the paper, the researchers examined Twitter posts to investigate how the behaviors of characters influenced viewers' perceptions in relation to moral norms. The salience of moral foundations was assessed by searching for the terms comprising the *Moral Foundations Dictionary* in the tweets.

Gehman et al. adopted a focus on children's movies, specifically examining three movies, with the aim of identifying the differences in moral foundations between heroes and villains [37]. The presence of moral foundations was investigated by having a group of human coders fill out the Moral Foundations Questionnaire for each character under analysis.

In another study conducted in [38], the focus was once again on children. The researchers explored the presence of moral foundations in the narratives contained within thematic textbooks used in Indonesian primary schools. The assessment of moral foundations involved tracing the occurrence of lexical tags associated with each moral foundation within the textbooks. In contrast to the aforementioned literature, which primarily relied on the direct search of *Moral Foundations Dictionary* (MFD) terms in texts, Araque et al. introduced the use of word embeddings to search for the presence of moral values by adopting a Wordnet-based extension of the MFD and using the SIMilarity-based sentiment projectiON (SIMON) [39] to compute the cosine similarity as a measure of semantic similarity between the words in the text and the words in the extended lexicon [40]. They applied their method to a corpus of tweets using a classification approach, where each tweet was assigned a single moral trait. Overcoming the binary classification task adopted in [39], Gonzalez et al. extended the number of moral foundations that can be assigned to a text using a 20% threshold, i.e., assigning 20% of the potential number of foundations to each movie [41]. They employed two embedding techniques, namely Word2Vec and BERT, to analyze tags extracted from synopses of a selection of movies (the authors downloaded the synopses from three popular online sources: IMDb, Rotten Tomatoes, and FilmAffinity, although it is not clear if they used all three sources). Tag extraction was performed through the YAKE! tool designed by Campos et al. [42]. Gonzalez et al. employed both the original *Moral Foundations Dictionary* (composed of ten items, including the opposite extremes of the five moral foundations) and an extended version, comprising twenty-four foundations. The analysis was conducted by computing the similarity between the embedding vectors of the

MFD terms and those of the words in the synopses. A threshold was applied to extract the most relevant foundations for each movie.

In addition to exploring moral dimensions in traditional media, it is worth mentioning a smaller but emerging area of research that examines the presence of moral dimensions within video games. However, unlike traditional media, the focus of this research is not solely on the moral content embedded in video games but rather on the moral behavior and decisionmaking processes evoked during gameplay.

The relationship between moral decisions and facial thermal variations was investigated by Guglielmo et al. [43], where specific moral foundations were assigned to decisions within the narrative of the video game *The Walking Dead*. These assignments were likely performed manually. In another study, Hodge et al. utilized a purpose-made video game to examine the time taken for moral decisions and the alignment between players and the game in terms of moral values [44].

Turning to the Chinese version of the popular video game *World of Warcraft*, Hornbeck et al. identified the presence of moral foundations elicited during gameplay through a survey [45]. Participants were asked to rate the frequency of experiencing feelings associated with moral foundations while playing their main *World of Warcraft* character.

Although recognizing that players may use their moral intuition when playing games, Krcmar et al. considered both moral decisions and strategic decisions (driven just by the desire to play and win the game) and traced the correspondence between the moral beliefs of the player and his/her behavior in the game [46]. The salience of the moral foundations was measured through a questionnaire. Similarly, Joeckel et al. analyzed the influence of moral intuition when making decisions in video games [13]. Again, the MFQ questionnaire was employed to measure moral foundations.

To summarize, previous studies have measured the salience of moral foundations through questionnaires or by quantifying the frequency of *Moral Foundations Dictionary* (MFD) terms in the analyzed text, except for the work of González-Santos et al. [41], which employed a deep learning-based approach. Additionally, the literature has primarily focused on media such as books, songs, movies, and video games, with only one exception in the TV series domain, as observed in the work of Ji and Raney [36], which analyzed viewers' perceptions rather than the actual moral content of the series.

In contrast to the existing literature, our approach differs in two key aspects: the dataset of interest and the methodology employed. We specifically focus on TV series, which have received limited attention in the current literature. Although Gonzalez et al. analyzed movies, they considered a selection of 20 movies in contrast to our massive scale of over 600 TV series episodes [41]. Moreover, we employ a deep learning-based approach to quantify the salience of moral foundations. While most previous studies relied on the use of the Moral Foundations Questionnaire and involved human coders, our approach is entirely automated, utilizing the SBERT architecture. This distinguishes our work from previous research, including the work by González et al. [41], who employed different embedding techniques (Word2Vec/BERT instead of SBERT). Further differences with the method employed by [41] are that we use the full text of the synopses rather than keywords extracted from them, which allows us not to ignore text that has not been distilled into keywords. They also sum embedding vectors rather than averaging them as we do. Averaging (our choice) rather than summing allows us to compare different movies (or different TV series) since summing outputs values that are influenced by the number of tags of each movie (more tags means more summing terms), making a comparison unfeasible. Finally, we provide the full range of salience values for moral foundations rather than just outputting one moral foundation [40] or two [41]. This allows us to obtain a more complete view of the moral foundations represented in the series.

3. Data and Methods

3.1. Data

We aim to employ our method to trace moral foundations in TV series, focusing on a selection of popular series. In this section, we provide a detailed description of our dataset, outlining the process of series selection, as well as the content and sources used.

To ensure a comprehensive representation of TV series, we adopted a top-down approach for our selection task. We began by considering a classification of TV series into various genres. However, it is worth noting that the classification of genres in TV series is subjective and lacks consensus. As a reference, we consulted Wikipedia, which lists a total of 95 genres on its webpage dedicated to TV genres (https://en.wikipedia.org/wiki/Category:Television_series_by_genre (accessed on 17 January 2024). Instead, IMDb lists the following 20 genres (https://www.imdb.com/list/ls023983860/ (accessed on 17 January 2024)):

- Drama;
- Comedy;
- Thriller;
- Crime;
- Mystery;
- Romance;
- Action;
- Sci-Fi;
- Fantasy;
- History;
- Adventure;
- Animation;
- Horror;
- Biography;
- War;
- Documentary;
- Music;
- Family;
- Western;
- Sport.

Finally, Creeber adopts the taxonomy of TV genres shown in Figure 1 [47].

Acknowledging the difficulty of establishing a universally accepted classification system, we have decided to rely on Creeber's classification and adopt a selection of the genres appearing in it. However, some (Crime, Fantasy, and Sci-Fi) are explicitly considered in IMDb too, and the others are subgenres of those employed by IMDb (Teen drama, Legal drama, and Hospital drama are subgenres of Drama, while Sitcom is a subgenre of Comedy). Our selection process involved choosing a popular series that exemplifies each genre. The following genres and their corresponding series have been selected:

- Crime (*Gomorrah*);
- Teen drama (*13 Reasons Why*);
- Fantasy (*Game of Thrones*);
- Hospital drama (*House, MD*);
- Sitcom (*Sex and the City*);
- Legal drama (*Suits*);
- Sci-Fi (*Westworld*).

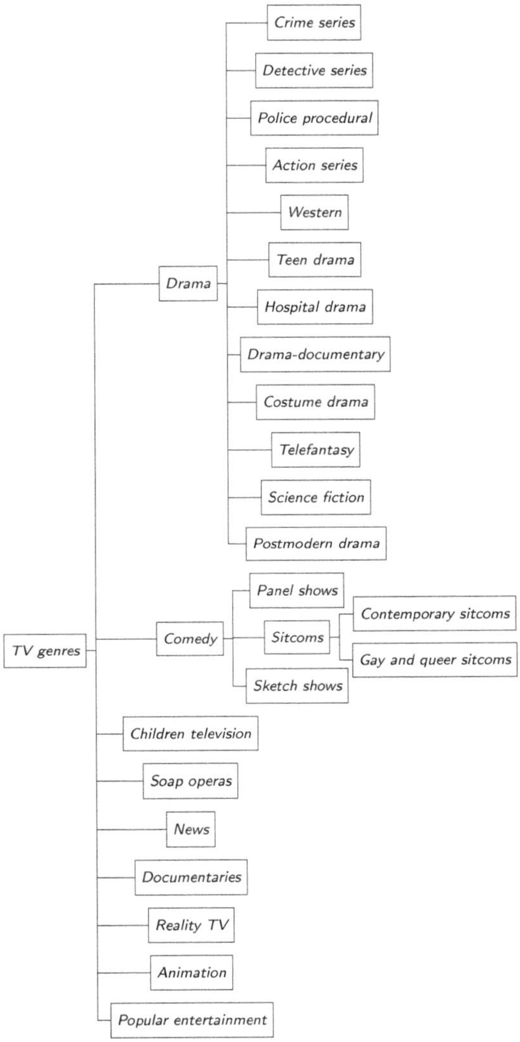

Figure 1. Taxonomy of TV genres by Creeber.

For each series in our dataset, we conducted our analysis on the summaries of the plots of each episode as reported on Wikipedia. We have chosen to analyze summaries because they exhibit several advantages over dialogues in describing the actual content of a series. They represent actions, which are not reflected in dialogues and would be lost if we considered dialogues instead of summaries. They may also represent states of mind that are not conveyed by dialogue but rather the appearance or gestures of a character. Also, they can effectively capture the structure and flow of the movie by highlighting the key plot points, major twists, and character developments in a coherent manner. Tags derived from summaries were employed in [41]. Our approach employing the full text of summaries avoids the potential misses introduced by the mediation layer represented by summary tagging.

We show the major statistics for all the series in Table 1, including the minimum, average, and maximum length of summaries, computed both in words and characters.

Word tokenization has been carried out through the `en_core_web_lg` model in the spacy library. The language for all episodes is English.

Table 1. Length statistics of series expressed in words (chars).

Series	No. of Episodes	Min Length	Avg Length	Max Length
Gomorrah	58	92 (463)	329.9 (1669.6)	569 (2901)
13 Reasons Why	49	127 (628)	225.5 (1132.6)	487 (2366)
Game of Thrones	73	116 (571)	211.6 (1098.6)	284 (1424)
House, MD	176	34 (183)	92.5 (479.4)	345 (1739)
Sex and the City	94	37 (186)	70.3 (355.4)	221 (1047)
Suits	134	24 (120)	156.4 (794.3)	483 (2416)
Westworld	36	148 (774)	304.3 (1069.6)	288 (1455)

3.2. Methods

In order to identify the presence of moral concepts in the texts of interest (the summaries of TV series episodes), we adopt an approach based on identifying semantic similarities through a deep learning architecture. In this section, we describe the details of our approach.

Embedding Similarity through SBERT

The basic concept is to represent each text as a vector in a dense space of fixed dimension in a way such that semantically similar texts are represented by close vectors. Semantic similarity can then be measured through any vector distance metric. In this paper, we have opted to use cosine similarity as a distance metric. The representation of text is of the embedding type, which allows for achieving space density as opposed to intrinsically sparse representations like one-hot encoding, as described by [48]. We obtain vector embeddings both for the episode summaries and the words in the *Moral Foundations Dictionary* for each moral dimension reported in [30]. The average cosine similarity between the episode summary embedding and the words appearing in a specific moral dimension lexicon is considered a measure of the presence of that moral dimension in that episode. Such an approach has already been validated in [39], where cosine similarity between embeddings of words in a text and moral foundations words as appearing in a lexicon has been adopted as a measure of the presence of moral foundations and shown to agree with the results of human annotation. Aside from the specific application of moral foundations identification, the application of cosine similarity to word embeddings to compute semantic similarity was validated, e.g., in [49] for newspaper articles. In quite general terms, the property of word embedding to represent similar words by similar vectors is stated in Chapter 24.1 of the reference textbook by Russell and Norvig [50] such that a measure of distance like cosine similarity will allow us to evaluate the semantic distance between words expressed through embeddings. More precisely, if we examine n episodes in the TV series and make use of the *Moral Foundations Dictionary*, which adopts five moral dimensions (without loss of generality, we associate an integer number $j \in \{1,2,3,4,5\}$ to each moral dimension) and lists w_j words for the j-th moral dimension, the measure of the presence of the j-th moral dimension in the i-th episode is

$$p_{ij} = \frac{1}{w_j} \sum_{k=1}^{w_j} S_C(e_i, m_{jk}), \quad (1)$$

where e_i is the embedding vector for the i-th episode summary, and m_{jk} is the embedding vector for the k-th word ($k = 1, 2, \ldots, w_j$) in the j-th moral dimension lexicon ($j \in \{1,2,3,4,5\}$).

We can perform a similar analysis by separately examining the lexicon pertaining to the positive and negative facets of each moral dimension, as described in Section 2.2. If we represent the pertaining presence as p_{ij}^{+} and p_{ij}^{-}, respectively, for the j-th moral dimension in the i-th episode, we can obtain a measure of the prevalence of the positive over the negative polarity by computing the difference $q_{ij} = p_{ij}^{+} - p_{ij}^{-}$. If the difference is positive, the positive polarity (virtue) will be considered the dominant facet of that foundation; vice versa, the negative polarity (vice) will be considered the dominant one. Since we obtain a polarity value for each episode, we will plot the estimated probability density of polarity. For the empirical probability density function, we have employed the density function in R, which employs the Gaussian kernel method described by [51]. More precisely, the algorithm used in that function disperses the mass of the empirical distribution function over a regular grid of at least 512 points and then uses fast Fourier transform to convolve this approximation with a discretized version of the kernel and then uses a linear approximation to evaluate the density at the specified points. The bandwidth employed in the kernel method is determined as in [52].

The deep learning architecture we employ to obtain the embedding vectors is Sentence-BERT (SBERT), proposed by [53], which improves on the popular BERT transformer architecture proposed by [54] by drastically reducing the computational effort required for large-scale semantic similarity tasks. The improvement of SBERT over BERT is achieved by adding a pooling layer at the output of BERT that computes the mean of all the output vectors and by using a Siamese training approach over pairs of sentences, with a distance function over representations to be as close as possible. The differences with BERT can be seen in Figure 2, taken from [53], where the SBERT architecture is shown for training (left) and inference (right), and the use of two BERT networks in parallel and the addition of a pooling layer are visible.

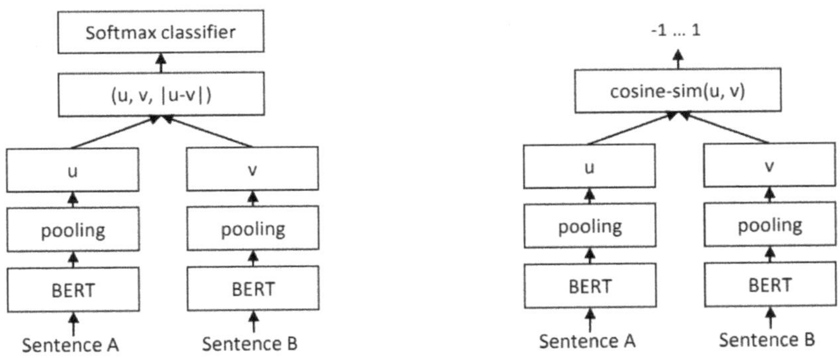

Figure 2. The SBERT architecture.

The model is a pre-trained, one named `paraphrase-multilingual-MiniLM-L12-v2` [53] (https://huggingface.co/sentence-transformers/paraphrase-multilingual-MiniLM-L12-v2) (accessed on 17 January 2024), which is fine-tuned using a Siamese network structure: couples of text are input to the Siamese networks to minimize their difference.

4. Results

Our main objective is to examine the moral content of TV series along the five foundations proposed by [11]. Of course, the complex plots that characterize modern TV series are all likely to harness multiple foundations of morality. In addition to examining the moral content of a series on its own, our study also embraces a comparative perspective: different series/genres are compared to each other both regarding how salient each foundation is for a particular series/genre and regarding which side of the virtue–vice spectrum dominates for each foundation.

In this section, we show the results of our analysis. In order to visualize the results, we resort to a radar chart, where each radius represents one of the five moral dimensions described in Section 2.2, and the resulting pentagon cuts each radius at a value representing the relative importance of the corresponding moral dimension. For the results to be easily comparable, we have normalized the presence values so that they sum to 1 for each episode; i.e., the following condition holds:

$$\sum_{j=1}^{5} p_{ij} = 1 \qquad \forall i \tag{2}$$

We will begin by presenting a comprehensive validation of our findings and then conducting an individual analysis of the selected series, followed by a comparative assessment.

4.1. Validation

In order to ensure the reliability and accuracy of our algorithm, it is essential to validate its performance. Recognizing the presence of moral foundations in TV series is a complex classification task as multiple foundations can coexist simultaneously with varying degrees of prominence. Moreover, we cannot access a definitive *ground truth* that would indicate which specific foundation is present in each episode.

Given these challenges, we have developed a validation approach that relies on the semantic associations of words related to moral foundations.

To ensure a robust validation process, we have obtained the definitions and sample sentences of the five moral foundation names and their polarity subdivisions from the widely respected *Oxford English Dictionary* [55]. By leveraging these authoritative linguistic sources, we aim to establish a reliable benchmark for evaluating our algorithm's performance.

In the validation phase, instead of employing the episode summaries, we fed our algorithm with those extracted definitions and sample sentences. This approach allows us to assess whether the algorithm can accurately identify the moral foundation corresponding to the provided definition. The algorithm generates a similarity value as its output, reflecting the degree of similarity between the input definition and each moral foundation.

To evaluate the algorithm's recognition accuracy, we have ranked the moral foundations based on their respective similarity scores. If the algorithm correctly identifies the moral foundation, it will rank first, indicating a higher similarity score compared to the other foundations. This ranking-based approach provides an explicit criterion for assessing the algorithm's performance.

Tables 2 and 3 present the results in a matrix format for foundations and foundation polarities, respectively. In these tables, the rows represent the actual foundations, while the columns indicate the output provided by the algorithm. The numbers inside the table indicate the rankings obtained. Ideally, if the algorithm were capable of perfectly recognizing the foundation, we would observe a diagonal consisting of 1s. We observe that this holds true for four out of five foundations, with the correct foundation ranking second in the missed case. Furthermore, for the polarity task, we achieve this perfect recognition in seven out of ten cases, with the correct polarity ranking second in the missed cases. It is important to note that this cannot be treated solely as a classification task since there is no perfect mutual exclusivity of foundations, as clarified previously. Nevertheless, if we were to consider it as such, the accuracy achieved would be 80% for foundations and 70% for foundation polarities.

Table 2. Validation ranking for moral foundations.

	Authority/Subversion	Care/Harm	Fairness/Cheating	Loyalty/Betrayal	Sanctity/Degradation
Authority/Subversion	**2**	5	1	3	4
Care/Harm	3	**1**	2	5	4
Fairness/Cheating	2	5	**1**	4	3
Loyalty/Betrayal	2	4	3	**1**	5
Sanctity/Degradation	4	3	2	5	**1**

Table 3. Validation ranking for moral foundations polarity.

	Authority	**Betrayal**	*Care*	**Cheating**	**Degradation**	**Fairness**	**Harm**	**Loyalty**	**Sanctity**	**Subversion**
Authority	**1**	5	7	3	8	2	10	6	9	4
Betrayal	8	**2**	7	5	4	9	3	6	10	1
Care	2	4	**1**	5	6	7	10	3	9	8
Cheat	7	2	10	**1**	5	4	6	9	8	3
Degradation	10	5	6	3	**1**	7	2	9	8	4
Fairness	3	8	5	2	7	**1**	10	6	4	9
Harm	9	7	5	1	6	3	**2**	10	8	4
Loyalty	5	7	6	2	10	3	9	**1**	8	4
Sanctity	4	9	2	6	7	3	10	5	**1**	8
Subversion	6	4	10	1	5	3	7	9	8	**2**

4.2. Measuring Moral Dimensions in TV Series

After assessing the capability of our approach to identify the presence of moral features, in this section, we report the results we have obtained by applying our method to the dataset described in Section 3.1. We devote a subsection to each series and the last subsection to an overall comparison of our findings.

4.2.1. *Gomorrah*

Gomorrah is an Italian TV series based on Roberto Saviano's book [56]. It focuses on the Camorra, a violent organized crime syndicate in Naples. The show is set in gritty neighborhoods and depicts the Camorra's operations and power struggles, affecting both criminals and ordinary people. The series does not shy away from portraying the harsh realities of the criminal underworld, showcasing violence, intimidation, and betrayal.

We consider first the radar chart where all the episodes are shown in Figure 3.

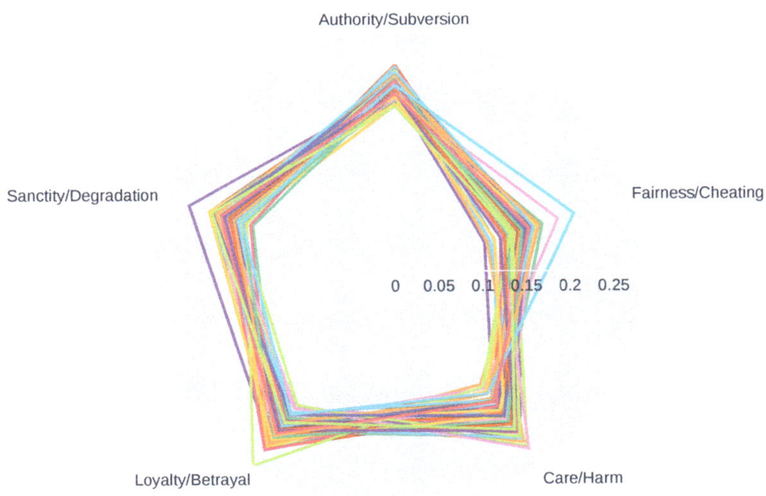

Figure 3. Moral foundation scores for all episodes in *Gomorrah*.

As observed, the pentagons representing the moral dimensions for all the episodes exhibit a significant degree of overlap, indicating remarkable consistency in the presence of moral dimensions across the episodes.

To evaluate the prominence of each moral dimension within the TV series, we employ a ranking based on the presence score, denoted as p_{ij}. By calculating the value of p_{ij} for each moral dimension in each episode, we can generate rankings that consistently highlight the most prominent moral dimension in the drama. Of course, the picture is not extremely sharp: there is no moral dimension ranking first in all the episodes. We can obtain an overall picture of the presence of each moral dimension by computing the number of times it ranks first, second, etc. Table 4 presents the results of this analysis, showcasing the presence rankings of each moral dimension across the episodes. We see that the *Ingroup* moral dimension is indisputably the most present one, ranking first in 31 out of 58 episodes. At the same time, *Harm* is the sure runner-up, ranking first in sixteen out of the fifty-eight episodes, whereas *Authority* ranks first in six episodes and second in twenty-six. On the other end of the spectrum, we have *Fairness*, which holds the wooden spoon of this competition, being the least present moral dimension in fifty-six episodes, i.e., in all but two.

Table 4. Count of moral foundation rankings over all episodes in *Gomorrah*.

Ranking	1	2	3	4	5
Authority	6	26	18	8	0
Fairness	0	1	0	1	56
Harm	16	10	12	18	2
Ingroup	31	13	10	4	0
Purity	5	8	18	27	0

We can now examine the actual polarity of each foundation. In Figure 4, we see the resulting empirical density of q_{ij} for each moral foundation. We see that the negative polarity prevails for all the foundations, in particular for the *Ingroup* foundation, whose mode is largely in the negative semi-axis.

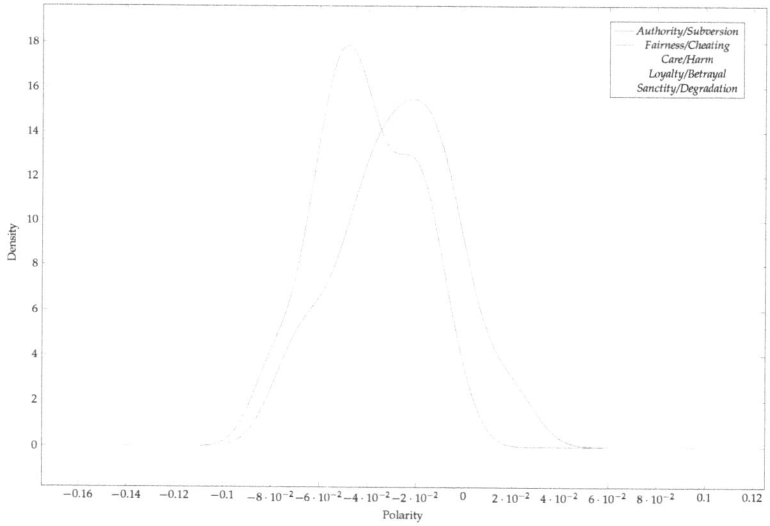

Figure 4. Empirical probability density of foundation polarity in *Gomorrah*.

The findings regarding *Gomorrah*'s dominant moral foundations are consistent with our expectations. The presence of the *Care/Harm* foundation aligns with the portrayal of the characters in the series. While some characters in the series may show signs of caring for their families or loved ones, a significant portion of the show revolves around violence and harm. The instances of characters inflicting pain, hurting, or even killing others without regard for their well-being demonstrate the prevalence of harm, indicating a negative polarity within this foundation. Regarding the *Ingroup/Loyalty* foundation, the series accurately reflects the theme of loyalty within the context of family or criminal organizations. *Gomorrah*'s characters are expected to show unwavering loyalty to their bosses and associates. However, betrayal and treachery indicate that loyalty is not always absolute as characters may switch allegiances or betray others for personal gain. This observation aligns with our analysis, which shows a mixed picture of loyalty and lack thereof.

As to fairness (see Table 4), the absence of this moral dimension in the world of organized crime portrayed in *Gomorrah* is consistent with our findings. The series often depicts characters resorting to violence, coercion, or bribery to achieve their objectives rather than engaging in fair exchanges or negotiations. This absence of fairness further confirms its limited role within the moral dynamics of the series.

Finally, the analysis of the *Authority/Subversion* foundation reflects the negative aspect, where characters tend to operate outside the law or exploit their positions of power to mistreat others. The focus on bosses and their ability to establish new rules and subvert existing hierarchies reinforces the presence of subversion within the series. This observation aligns with the dynamics of power and control depicted in *Gomorrah*.

4.2.2. *13 Reasons Why*

Let us delve into the analysis of the teen drama series, *13 Reasons Why*.

13 Reasons Why is a Netflix original series that is based on the 2007 novel of the same name by Jay Asher [57]. The storyline revolves around the life of Hannah Baker, a high school student who tragically takes her own life. Before her death, Hannah records a series of cassette tapes in which she explains the *13 Reasons Why* she felt compelled to end her life. Each episode focuses on one of the reasons and explores the individuals who played a role in Hannah's life, including her classmates and friends. The series deals with themes that resonate with many teenagers (e.g., bullying, sexual assault, mental health, and suicide) and examines the role of social media and technology in the lives of teenagers, exploring how these platforms can connect and isolate individuals. The series unfolded over four seasons, comprising a total of 49 episodes, sparking significant discussions and raising awareness about mental health issues and the importance of suicide prevention.

We show the moral foundation scores for all the episodes in Figure 5. Here, we observe significant differences among the episodes. However, the *Care/Harm* dimension is largely dominant, with *Ingroup* being a close second (the distance may be considerable in a few episodes, but the overall rankings shown in Table 5 are rather similar).

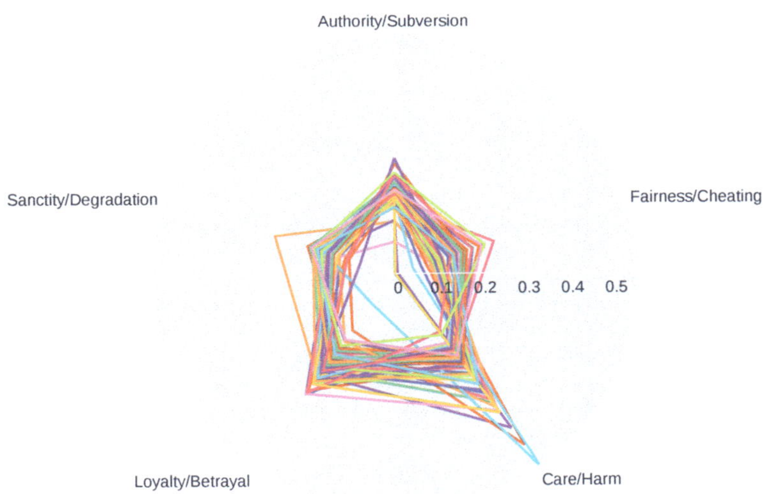

Figure 5. Moral foundation scores for all episodes in *13 Reasons Why*.

Table 5. Count of moral foundation rankings over all episodes in *13 Reasons Why*.

Ranking	1	2	3	4	5
Authority	2	10	21	14	2
Fairness	1	2	0	12	34
Harm	24	17	7	0	1
Ingroup	22	19	6	1	1
Purity	0	1	15	22	11

If we look at the polarity in Figure 6, again, all the modes are in the negative half. The *Subversion* component is dominant, with *Harm* being quite negative as well. On the other end of the spectrum, *Fairness*, although mostly negative, exhibits the smallest imbalance towards vice.

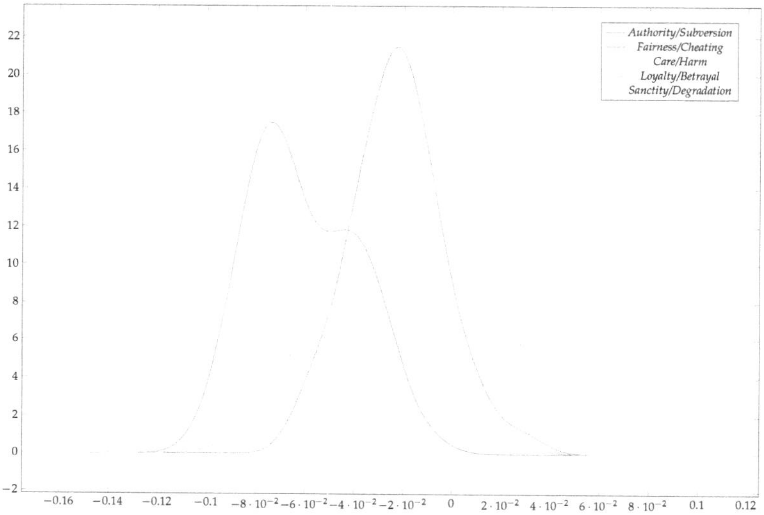

Figure 6. Empirical probability density of foundation polarity in *13 Reasons Why*.

Once again, we observe a strong correlation between the moral foundation scores and the thematic content of the series. The presence of the *Care/Harm* foundation is evident as the show addresses topics such as mental health, suicide, bullying, and sexual assault, all of which are closely related to the concept of harm. For instance, the character Hannah Baker, like many others, experiences harm through bullying and sexual assault, ultimately leading to her feeling neglected and unimportant. The *Loyalty/Betrayal* foundation is also prominent, particularly in the relationships between characters. Hannah feels betrayed by her former friend Jessica when she starts dating Hannah's crush, and Clay Jensen struggles with conflicting loyalties between Hannah and his other friends. The series predominantly adopts the viewpoint of teenage characters, and their relationships with parents are either absent from the narrative or depicted as negative, highlighting a lack of understanding and support. The relationships depicted in the series primarily revolve around peer interactions, often characterized by betrayal and broken trust. This emphasis on negative polarities further explains the dominant presence of negative moral dimensions in the moral foundation scores.

4.2.3. *Game of Thrones*

For the Fantasy genre, we have examined the series *Game of Thrones*.

It is an epic fantasy TV series based on George R.R. Martin's *A Song of Ice and Fire* novel. Set in the fictional world of Westeros, it follows noble houses competing for power and the Iron Throne. Known for complex plotlines, world-building, and a large ensemble cast, it explores the themes of power, loyalty, and morality. *Game of Thrones* was aired from 2011 to 2019, spanning eight seasons and 73 episodes. It gained immense popularity and critical acclaim, winning numerous awards. The series captivated audiences with its mix of violence, sex, and political intrigue.

In Figure 7, the *Care/Harm* foundation appears dominant, ranking first in 47 episodes out of 73 (see Table 6). *Ingroup* is another strong foundation, with 18 first-place rankings. *Fairness*, as in *Gomorrah*, plays a negligible role, ranking last in all the episodes.

Table 6. Count of moral foundation rankings over all episodes in *Game of Thrones*.

Ranking	1	2	3	4	5
Authority	7	12	45	9	0
Fairness	0	0	0	0	73
Harm	47	16	6	4	0
Ingroup	18	39	9	7	0
Purity	1	6	13	53	0

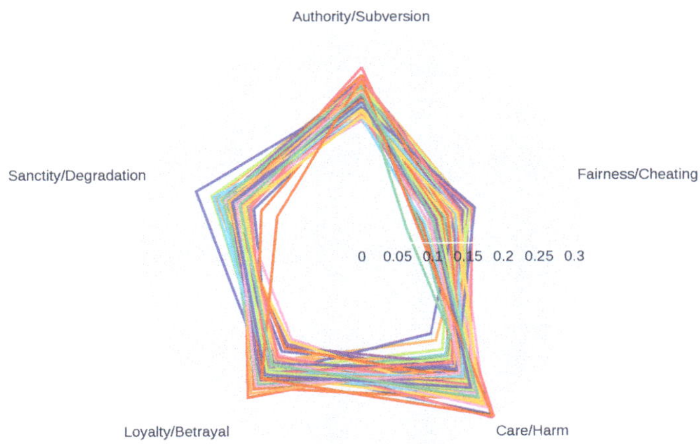

Figure 7. Moral foundation scores for all episodes in *Game of Thrones*.

All the polarity values are heavily shifted towards the vice side (see Figure 8), in particular for *Authority/Subversion* (hence, the *Subversion* facet predominates) and *Loyalty/Betrayal* (hence, *Betrayal* prevails). The least negative foundation is *Fairness/Cheating*.

We can relate the presence of the *Care/Harm* foundation through the characters' attitudes toward protecting the innocent and vulnerable. Characters like Jon Snow and Daenerys Targaryen prioritize the safety and well-being of those under their care. We also observe that the reference for the fantasy genre is the classical tragedy, where the dominant characters are mostly anti-heroes who end up being destroyed by their own vices. Furthermore, the show addresses mental health and trauma, which are connected to the *Care/Harm* foundation.

The themes of loyalty and betrayal, representing the ingroup foundation, play a central role in the series. Characters form alliances and allegiances with one another, emphasizing loyalty to family, friends, or allies. However, these relationships are often tested, leading to conflicts and betrayals, resulting in a negative polarity score. The consequences of breaking oaths and betraying trust are explored throughout the show.

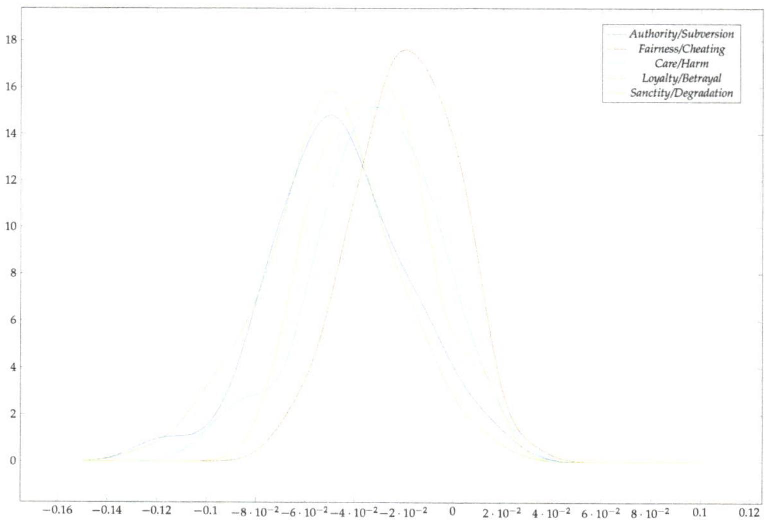

Figure 8. Empirical probability density of foundation polarity in *Game of Thrones*.

4.2.4. *House, MD*

House, MD is a medical drama series that was aired from 2004 to 2012, spanning eight seasons and 177 episodes. Starring Hugh Laurie as Dr. Gregory House, the show follows a team of doctors at Princeton-Plainsboro Teaching Hospital. The series' themes include medical ethics, the challenges of practicing medicine, and the personal struggles of the characters. It tackles complex medical cases, with House and his team using unconventional methods to uncover diagnoses. The show also features a recurring cast of supporting characters who contribute to the story.

This series stands out against those examined so far in that its mix of moral foundations is rather balanced, as can be seen in Figure 9, except a single episode where the *Sanctity/Degradation* pair takes the entire spotlight.

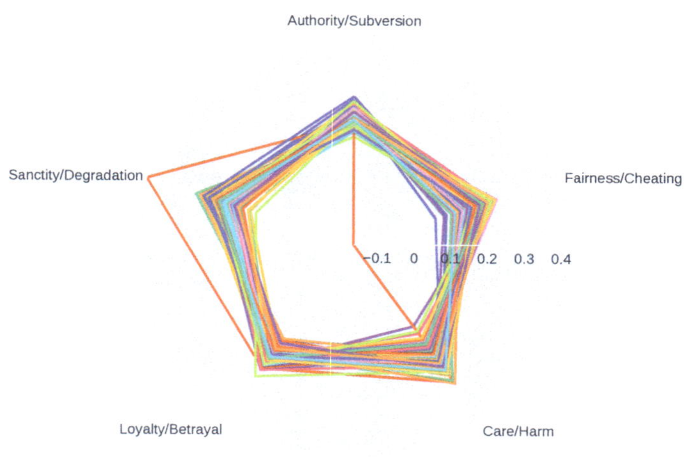

Figure 9. Moral foundation scores for all episodes in *House, MD*.

However, while all the moral foundations are represented in the series, there are a few that stand out by ranking higher than the others, although the differences in their rankings are not stark. If we look at Table 7, we see that *Ingroup* and *Harm* remain the most present foundations. *Fairness* is, again, the least present, although not lagging behind as much as in the other series.

Table 7. Count of moral foundation rankings over all episodes in *House, MD*.

Ranking	1	2	3	4	5
Authority	6	27	52	70	21
Fairness	10	13	19	35	99
Harm	64	39	32	18	23
Ingroup	71	49	36	14	6
Purity	25	48	37	39	27

The dominant polarity is negative for all the foundations, except *Care/Harm*, where the two components show quite a similar weight (see Figure 10).

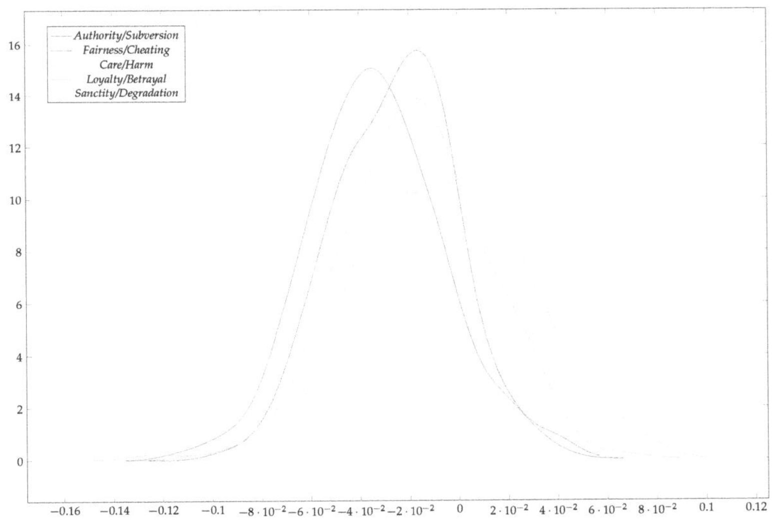

Figure 10. Empirical probability density of foundation polarity in *House, MD*.

The presence of the *Care/Harm* foundation is reasonably expected. Its presence shows through the medical cases that the main character, Dr. House, and his team handle. The team's goal is to provide care to patients and prevent harm to them. Dr. House, while often being cynical and irascible, is ultimately motivated by a desire to help his patients and cure their illnesses. His attitude makes a strong case for the dominant presence of *Care/Harm*, as appearing in Table 7, and also for its balance of polarities. The medical perspective leading to acting for the good of people tilts the picture towards the positive side, while Dr. House's behavior pushes the foundation towards the negative polarity. Dr. House's character is the opposite of the caring doctor in previous medical dramas. His rudeness and impoliteness make his role unique in that genre. The theme of loyalty and betrayal (*Ingroup*) is also present in the relationships between the characters. For example, the team members are loyal to Dr. House, even when they disagree with him or find his behavior difficult. Similarly, Dr. House is loyal to his patients, even when it means going against hospital policy or risking his own reputation. Overall, the series actually shows a conflict of loyalty-related behaviors: the team members may shift between being loyal to the institution or Dr. House, and a similar conflict is present in Dr. House himself, who may decide to be loyal to his patients against the institution to which he belongs. The overall attitude is shown by the mostly negative polarity of this foundation in Figure 10.

4.2.5. *Sex and the City*

Sex and the City is a beloved romantic comedy–drama series that aired on HBO from 1998 to 2004, spanning six seasons and a total of 94 episodes. It revolves around the lives of four women, Carrie, Charlotte, Miranda, and Samantha, as they navigate love, relationships, and careers in the vibrant city of New York. The themes touched upon include love, sexuality, female empowerment, and the complexities of modern dating. It gained immense popularity and became a cultural phenomenon, influencing fashion and popular culture. The show's candid discussions about sex and its portrayal of independent women resonated with audiences worldwide.

The radar chart of foundations in Figure 11 shows a relatively balanced image, with all the foundations being present. However, some foundations rank consistently higher than others.

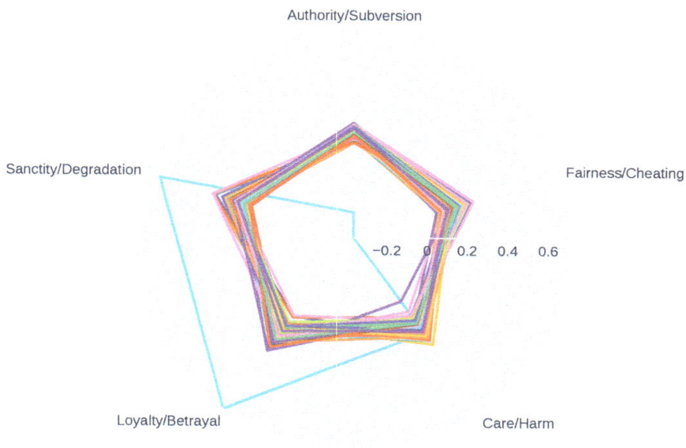

Figure 11. Moral foundation scores for all episodes in *Sex and the City*.

In Table 8, we observe that *Ingroup* and *Purity* are the dominant ones, while *Fairness* and *Authority* typically occupy the lowest positions.

Table 8. Count of moral foundation rankings over all episodes in *Sex and the City*.

Ranking	**1**	**2**	**3**	**4**	**5**
Authority	2	7	40	40	5
Fairness	3	6	5	14	66
Harm	10	21	16	26	21
Ingroup	42	24	16	11	1
Purity	37	36	17	3	1

The picture of polarities shifts away from the nearly entirely negative side we have observed so far. We can see in Figure 12 that the *Purity* foundation exhibits a dominant positive polarity, and *Loyalty* has a significant positive tail as well.

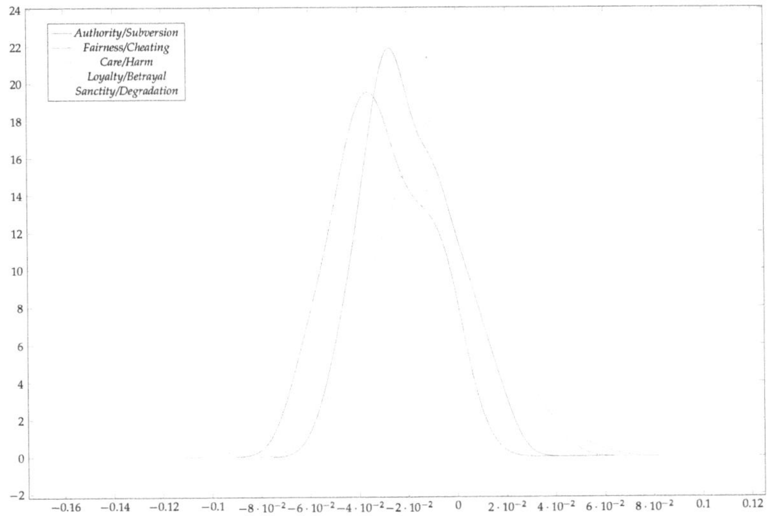

Figure 12. Empirical probability density of foundation polarity in *Sex and the City*.

We can recognize that *Ingroup* is the dominant foundation shown in Table 8. For example, the main characters are loyal to each other and often support each other through difficult times. However, the show also explores the ways in which loyalty can be tested and betrayed as the characters occasionally experience conflicts or betrayals in their relationships. We experience some difficulties in reconciling the results of our analysis with the series' content for the *Sanctity/Degradation* pair. The *Sanctity/Degradation* foundation is present in the show through the characters' attitudes toward sex and sexuality. For example, the show portrays a range of sexual behaviors and attitudes, some of which challenge the traditional notions of sanctity and morality. The characters often grapple with issues of shame and guilt around their sexual behavior, and the show explores the ways in which sexual expression can be stigmatized or celebrated. We would expect a strong presence of the *Purity* foundation (which we actually observe) but tilted towards the negative polarity, while we observe a different dominant polarity in Figure 12. The low rank of the *Authority* foundation is well-explained by the characters' identity. They are a group of friends who share their joys, fears, and loves. They consider themselves independent and liberated under a feminist framework and do not recognize the authority and the rules of a chauvinist society. Actually, they ignore those rules rather than openly subverting them, recognizing just their friendship and loyalty to one another.

4.2.6. *Suits*

Suits is a captivating legal drama series that was aired on USA Network from 2011 to 2019, spanning nine seasons and a total of 134 episodes. The show revolves around the story of Mike Ross, a brilliant college dropout, who finds himself working as a law associate for the charismatic and successful lawyer Harvey Specter despite lacking a law degree. The series explores the intricacies of the law, showcasing legal strategies, client relationships, and the cutthroat world of corporate politics. It also delves into the personal lives of the characters, exploring romantic relationships, familial conflicts, and personal growth. The diverse ensemble cast includes lawyers, paralegals, secretaries, and corporate executives, working together to overcome challenges and achieve their goals. The success of the series led to a spinoff titled *Pearson* in 2019, focusing on the character Jessica Pearson.

The picture of the moral foundation scores in all the episodes in Figure 13 appears quite blurry. The two dimensions of *Care/Harm* and *Fairness/Cheating* exhibit significant peaks but also a substantial dispersion.

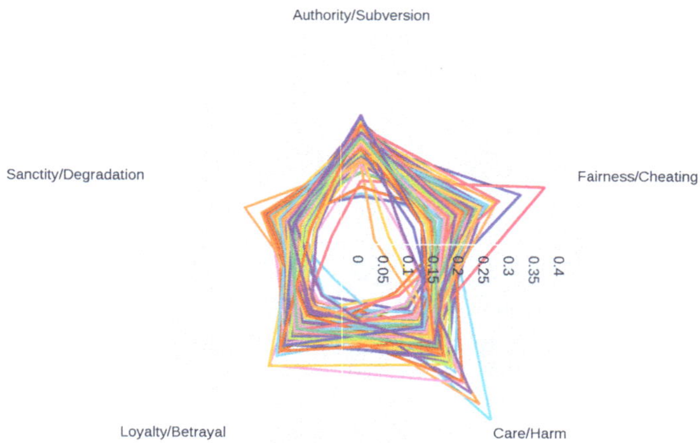

Figure 13. Moral foundation scores for all episodes in *Suits*.

The picture becomes clearer if we look at the relative positioning in Table 9. The *Care/Harm* dimension emerges as the dominant one in most episodes, with *Fairness/Cheating* and *Ingroup* being distant runner-ups. Instead, we find *Purity* lying nearly always at the bottom.

Table 9. Count of moral foundation rankings over all episodes in *Suits*.

Ranking	1	2	3	4	5
Authority	10	39	58	21	6
Fairness	33	18	20	41	22
Harm	65	37	16	11	5
Ingroup	26	37	29	32	10
Purity	0	3	11	29	91

The actual polarity of all the foundations is again mostly negative, as shown in Figure 14. The mode is well in the negative field for *Authority/Subversion* and *Care/Harm*.

We can confirm the dominant presence of the *Care/Harm* foundation through the legal cases that the main characters handle. The characters often work to protect their clients and prevent them from being harmed by legal and business issues. Additionally, the show explores issues of mental health and addiction, both of which relate to the *Care/Harm* foundation. The polarity analysis agrees more with the latter observation than with the former. In addition to the previously mentioned foundations, *Suits* also touches upon the *Fairness/Cheating* foundation through its portrayal of the characters' attitudes towards justice and the legal system. The main characters consistently strive for fairness in their legal cases, working diligently to expose corruption and uncover the truth. However, the show also delves into the darker side, exploring how cheating and deception can be employed to gain an advantage within the legal and business realms. This aspect is prominently reflected in our polarity analysis. Furthermore, the themes of loyalty and betrayal (*Ingroup*) comprise a significant element within the show, influencing the dynamics between the characters. Loyalty is a crucial virtue, both personally and professionally, as the characters display unwavering support for one another. However, *Suits* also delves into the complexities of loyalty, showcasing instances where trust is tested and betrayal occurs, resulting in conflicts within relationships. Once again, our polarity analysis emphasizes this latter aspect, highlighting the presence of negative polarities.

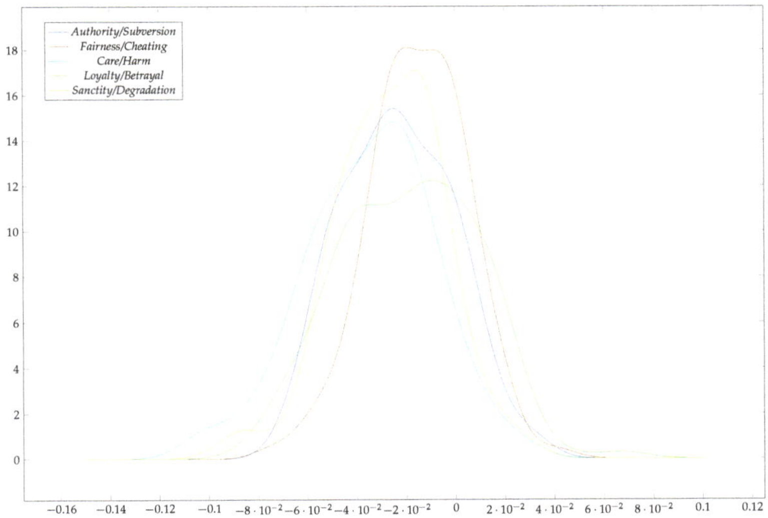

Figure 14. Empirical probability density of foundation polarity in *Suits*.

4.2.7. *Westworld*

Westworld is a science fiction television series that premiered on HBO in 2016 and is still ongoing. The show is inspired by the 1973 film of the same name. It is set in a futuristic amusement park called *Westworld*, where guests can live out their wildest fantasies in a hyper-realistic Wild West environment populated by android hosts. The series explores themes related to artificial intelligence, consciousness, morality, and the nature of reality as the characters confront the ethical and existential implications of creating and interacting with lifelike androids. The show is known for its intricate plotlines, complex characters, and thought-provoking philosophical themes. The show has also spawned a devoted fanbase that eagerly anticipates each new season and dissects each episode for hidden clues and plot twists.

In the radar chart shown in Figure 15, two foundations emerge: *Care/Harm* and *Sanctity/Degradation*. We observe again an outlier episode, where *Care/Harm* is highly dominant over the other foundations.

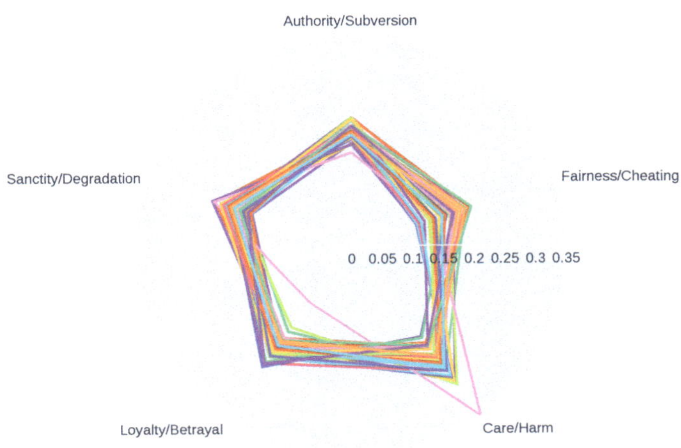

Figure 15. Moral foundation scores for all episodes in *Westworld*.

This picture is to be slightly reconsidered when we take a look at the table of rankings in Table 10, which confirms the dominant role of *Care/Harm* but ranks *Ingroup* as the runner-up rather than *Purity*. The least present foundation is *Fairness*.

Table 10. *Westworld*: count of moral foundation rankings over all episodes.

Ranking	1	2	3	4	5
Authority	0	3	14	18	1
Fairness	0	3	4	4	25
Harm	26	6	1	3	0
Ingroup	9	13	9	3	2
Purity	1	11	8	8	8

The polarity density in Figure 16 shows a sharp negative polarity for all the foundations except two, *Fairness* and *Purity*, where the positive polarity does not lag behind as much as in the other foundations.

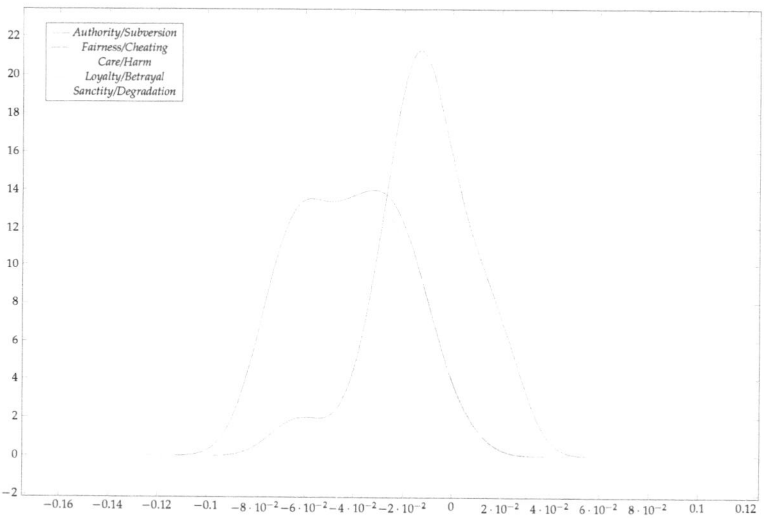

Figure 16. Empirical probability density of foundation polarity in *Westworld*.

In the TV show being discussed, the foundation of *Care/Harm* holds significant importance, evident through its exploration of consciousness and empathy. The AI hosts, who attain self-awareness, begin to question their own suffering and the suffering of their fellow hosts. This introspection prompts an examination of the ethical implications of humans exploiting the hosts for their own ends. Consequently, the themes of consciousness and empathy serve as a central pillar in the narrative.

Moreover, the foundation of *Sanctity/Degradation* emerges prominently, focusing on matters of morality and ethics. Both the hosts and the human characters grapple with profound moral and ethical dilemmas as they delve into questions surrounding existence and consciousness. The repercussions of violating moral and ethical boundaries in the pursuit of scientific progress and personal desires are explored throughout the show.

4.2.8. Overall Comparison

Figure 17 offers a comprehensive overview of the prevalence of the moral dimensions across the series we have examined, allowing readers to compare and contrast the moral foundations that underpin each show. This visual representation serves as a valuable tool for understanding the moral landscapes that shape the narratives of these series.

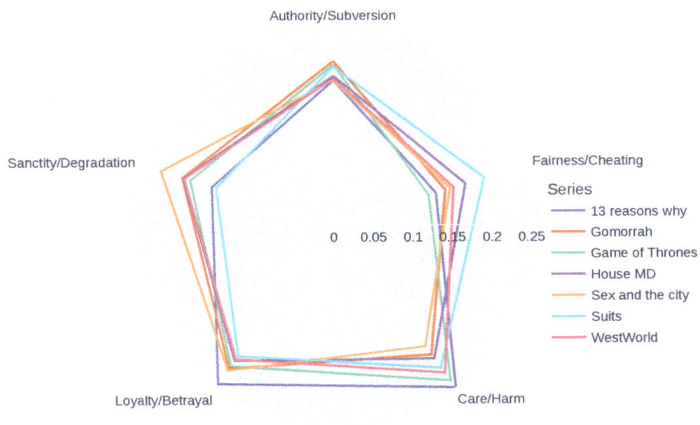

Figure 17. Radar chart of moral foundations distribution over the series.

By examining the radar chart, readers can gain insights into the relative prominence of different moral dimensions within each show. This information facilitates a deeper exploration of the ethical considerations and thematic emphasis present in the series, stimulating further discussion and analysis.

Figure 17 reveals the presence of multiple moral foundations across the selected series. The *Care/Harm* foundation emerged prominently in many shows, highlighting themes of empathy, protection of the vulnerable, and the consequences of harm inflicted upon others. This foundation was particularly evident in series such as *13 Reasons Why*, where issues of mental health, bullying, and sexual assault were explored, and *Westworld*, where the consciousness and suffering of AI hosts were central to the storyline.

The *Fairness/Cheating* foundation was also prevalent, as depicted through the pursuit of justice, exposure of corruption, and exploration of ethical dilemmas. It was prominent in series such as *Suits*, where the characters sought fairness in the legal system while navigating the complexities of a cutthroat industry. This foundation was also observed in *Westworld*, where the exploitation of hosts for personal gain raised questions about fairness and the consequences of cheating.

Additionally, the *Sanctity/Degradation* foundation emerged in the exploration of morality, ethics, and the violation of moral codes. Series like *Westworld* examined the consequences of violating ethical boundaries in the pursuit of scientific advancement and personal gain. In contrast, *Game of Thrones* explored the moral complexities and consequences of actions in a power-driven world.

Finally, the *Loyalty/Betrayal* foundation emerged as a significant theme in several series, vividly portraying the dynamics of trust, loyalty, and the potential for betrayal. One notable example is the series *Gomorrah*, which delves into the gritty and dangerous world of a criminal society.

5. Conclusions

This paper has provided an insightful exploration of the moral dimensions present in a selection of popular television series across different genres. By analyzing these series, valuable insights have been gained into the moral landscapes that shape their narratives, offering a foundation for deeper exploration and discussion.

Through the comparison of moral dimensions, the distinct moral landscapes of each series have been highlighted. It is evident that each show, within its genre and storytelling, prioritizes specific moral foundations, influencing the themes, character dynamics, and overall messages conveyed to the audience. However, while certain moral foundations may take precedence within a particular series, other foundations are still present to varying degrees, showing the complexity and richness of the storytelling.

TV series have the potential to shape viewers' moral attitudes and beliefs, making it crucial for viewers to engage critically with these series. By actively considering the moral foundations presented, questioning their portrayals, and reflecting on how they align with personal beliefs and experiences, viewers can deepen their understanding of the cultural, social, and ethical significance of these shows.

Further research is needed to explore the link between the moral dimensions embedded in TV shows and the moral behavior of their viewers. Understanding the impact of these shows on viewers' moral complexities and behavior will provide valuable insights into the societal implications of TV series as a medium for exploring moral questions.

Author Contributions: The authors' individual contributions are shown in the following: Conceptualization, M.R., M.N. and V.R.; methodology, M.N. and P.F.; software, P.F.; validation, M.R., V.R., M.N. and P.F.; formal analysis, M.N. and P.F.; investigation, M.R., M.N., P.F., V.R. and P.D.T.; data curation, P.F.; writing—original draft preparation, M.N., M.R., V.R. and P.D.T.; writing—review and editing, M.N., M.R., V.R. and P.D.T.; visualization, P.F.; supervision, M.N. All authors have read and agreed to the published version of the manuscript.

Funding: This research received no external funding.

Data Availability Statement: No new data were created.

Conflicts of Interest: The authors declare no conflicts of interest.

Abbreviations

The following abbreviations are used in this manuscript:

BERT	Bidirectional Encoder Representations from Transformers
DOAJ	Directory of open access journals
MDPI	Multidisciplinary Digital Publishing Institute
MFD	*Moral Foundations Dictionary*
MFQ	Moral Foundations Questionnaire
MFT	Moral Foundations Theory
SBERT	Sentence-Bidirectional Encoder Representations from Transformers

References

1. Bergmann, J.R. Introduction: Morality in discourse. *Res. Lang. Soc. Interact.* **1998**, *31*, 279–294. [CrossRef]
2. Hemming, J. Morality after myth. *J. Moral Educ.* **1996**, *25*, 39–45. [CrossRef]
3. White, H. The value of narrativity in the representation of reality. *Crit. Inq.* **1980**, *7*, 5–27. [CrossRef]
4. Burke, P. *The Art of Conversation*; John Wiley & Sons: Hoboken, NJ, USA, 2013.
5. Shaw, D. *Morality and the Movies: Reading Ethics through Film*; Bloomsbury Publishing: London, UK, 2012.
6. Carroll, N. Movies, the moral emotions, and sympathy. *Midwest Stud. Philos.* **2010**, *34*, 1–19. [CrossRef]
7. Bilandzic, H.; Hastall, M.R.; Sukalla, F. The morality of television genres: Norm violations and their narrative context in four popular genres of serial fiction. *J. Media Ethics* **2017**, *32*, 99–117. [CrossRef]
8. Vaage, M.B. Blinded by familiarity: Partiality, morality, and engagement with TV series. In *Cognitive Media Theory*; Routledge: London, UK, 2014; pp. 268–284.
9. La Ferrara, E. Mass media and social change: Can we use television to fight poverty? *J. Eur. Econ. Assoc.* **2016**, *14*, 791–827. [CrossRef]
10. Bilandzic, H. The complicated relationship between media and morality. *J. Media Psychol.* **2011**, *23*, 46–51. [CrossRef]
11. Haidt, J. The new synthesis in moral psychology. *Science* **2007**, *316*, 998–1002. [CrossRef]
12. Jöckel, S.; Früh, H. 'The world ain't all sunshine': Investigating the relationship between mean world beliefs, conservatism and crime TV exposure. *Communications* **2016**, *41*, 195–217. [CrossRef]
13. Joeckel, S.; Bowman, N.D.; Dogruel, L. Gut or game? The influence of moral intuitions on decisions in video games. *Media Psychol.* **2012**, *15*, 460–485. [CrossRef]
14. Tamborini, R.; Eden, A.; Bowman, N.D.; Grizzard, M.; Weber, R.; Lewis, R.J. Predicting media appeal from instinctive moral values. *Mass Commun. Soc.* **2013**, *16*, 325–346. [CrossRef]
15. Beveridge, A.; Shan, J. Network of thrones. *Math Horiz.* **2016**, *23*, 18–22. [CrossRef]
16. Bost, X.; Labatut, V.; Gueye, S.; Linares, G. Narrative smoothing: Dynamic conversational network for the analysis of TV series plots. In Proceedings of the 2016 IEEE/ACM International Conference on Advances in Social Networks Analysis and Mining (ASONAM), San Francisco, CA, USA, 18–21 August 2016; pp. 1111–1118.

17. Tan, M.S.; Ujum, E.A.; Ratnavelu, K. A character network study of two Sci-Fi TV series. In Proceedings of the AIP Frontiers in Physics Conference: 4th International Meeting. American Institute of Physics, Kuala Lumpur, Malaysia 27–30 August 2013; Volume 1588, pp. 246–251.
18. Zhang, L.; Li, C.; Fan, L.; Shi, M. Analysis of character relationship in tv series based on complex network. In Proceedings of the 2018 IEEE/ACIS 17th International Conference on Computer and Information Science (ICIS), Singapore, 6–8 June 2018; pp. 723–727.
19. Fronzetti Colladon, A.; Naldi, M. Concentration indices for dialogue dominance phenomena in TV series: The case of the Big Bang Theory. In *Proceedings of the Text Analytics: Advances and Challenges*; Springer: Berlin/Heidelberg, Germany, 2020; pp. 55–64.
20. Fronzetti Colladon, A.; Naldi, M. Predicting the performance of TV series through textual and network analysis: The case of Big Bang Theory. *PLoS ONE* **2019**, *14*, e0225306. [CrossRef]
21. Rocchi, M.; Pescatore, G. Modeling narrative features in TV series: Coding and clustering analysis. *Humanit. Soc. Sci. Commun.* **2022**, *9*, 333. [CrossRef]
22. Naldi, M.; Dalla Torre, P. Uncovering the Narrative Structure of "Breaking Bad" Through a Multi-Dimensional Quantitative Analysis. *Ser. Int. J. Ser. Narrat.* **2022**, *8*, 17–32.
23. Graham, J.; Haidt, J.; Koleva, S.; Motyl, M.; Iyer, R.; Wojcik, S.P.; Ditto, P.H. Moral foundations theory: The pragmatic validity of moral pluralism. In *Advances in Experimental Social Psychology*; Elsevier: Amsterdam, The Netherlands, 2013; Volume 47, pp. 55–130.
24. Curry, O.S.; Chesters, M.J.; Van Lissa, C.J. Mapping morality with a compass: Testing the theory of 'morality-as-cooperation' with a new questionnaire. *J. Res. Personal.* **2019**, *78*, 106–124. [CrossRef]
25. Zakharin, M.; Bates, T.C. Remapping the foundations of morality: Well-fitting structural model of the Moral Foundations Questionnaire. *PLoS ONE* **2021**, *16*, e0258910. [CrossRef]
26. Haidt, J. *The Righteous Mind: Why Good People are Divided by Politics and Religion*; Knopf Doubleday Publishing Group: New York, NY, USA, 2012.
27. Welsch, H. Moral foundations and voluntary public good provision: the case of climate change. *Ecol. Econ.* **2020**, *175*, 106696. [CrossRef]
28. Silver, J.R. Moral foundations, intuitions of justice, and the intricacies of punitive sentiment. *Law Soc. Rev.* **2017**, *51*, 413–450. [CrossRef]
29. Hopp, F.R.; Amir, O.; Fisher, J.T.; Grafton, S.; Sinnott-Armstrong, W.; Weber, R. Moral foundations elicit shared and dissociable cortical activation modulated by political ideology. *Nat. Hum. Behav.* **2023**, *7*, 2182–2198. [CrossRef]
30. Graham, J.; Haidt, J.; Nosek, B.A. Liberals and conservatives rely on different sets of moral foundations. *J. Personal. Soc. Psychol.* **2009**, *96*, 1029. [CrossRef]
31. Graham, J.; Nosek, B.A.; Haidt, J.; Iyer, R.; Koleva, S.; Ditto, P.H. Mapping the moral domain. *J. Personal. Soc. Psychol.* **2011**, *101*, 366. [CrossRef]
32. Wheeler, M.A.; McGrath, M.J.; Haslam, N. Twentieth century morality: The rise and fall of moral concepts from 1900 to 2007. *PLoS ONE* **2019**, *14*, e0212267. [CrossRef]
33. Lin, Y.; Michel, J.B.; Lieberman, E.A.; Orwant, J.; Brockman, W.; Petrov, S. Syntactic annotations for the Google Books Ngram corpus. In Proceedings of the ACL 2012 System Demonstrations, Jeju, Republic of Korea, 8–14 July 2012; pp. 169–174.
34. Long, J.A.; Eveland, W.P., Jr. Entertainment use and political ideology: Linking worldviews to media content. *Commun. Res.* **2021**, *48*, 479–500. [CrossRef]
35. Bowman, N.D.; Jöckel, S.; Dogruel, L. A question of morality? The influence of moral salience and nationality on media preferences. *Commun.-Eur. J. Commun. Res.* **2012**, *37*, 345–369. [CrossRef]
36. Ji, Q.; Raney, A.A. Morally judging entertainment: A case study of live tweeting during Downton Abbey. *Media Psychol.* **2015**, *18*, 221–242. [CrossRef]
37. Gehman, R.; Guglielmo, S.; Schwebel, D.C. Moral foundations theory, political identity, and the depiction of morality in children's movies. *PLoS ONE* **2021**, *16*, e0248928. [CrossRef]
38. Imelwaty, S.; Gunawan, F.; Kuraedah, S.; Mardiana, W.; Wardhana, D.E.C.; Boulahnane, S. Moral values in Indonesian primary school thematic textbooks: The marrying of language appraisal and moral foundation theories. In *Education 3-13*; Taylor and Francis: Milton Park, UK, 2022; pp. 1–13.
39. Araque, O.; Zhu, G.; Iglesias, C.A. A semantic similarity-based perspective of affect lexicons for sentiment analysis. *Knowl.-Based Syst.* **2019**, *165*, 346–359. [CrossRef]
40. Araque, O.; Gatti, L.; Kalimeri, K. MoralStrength: Exploiting a moral lexicon and embedding similarity for moral foundations prediction. *Knowl.-Based Syst.* **2020**, *191*, 105184. [CrossRef]
41. González-Santos, C.; Vega-Rodríguez, M.A.; Pérez, C.J.; López-Muñoz, J.M.; Martínez-Sarriegui, I. Automatic assignment of moral foundations to movies by word embedding. *Knowl.-Based Syst.* **2023**, *270*, 110539. [CrossRef]
42. Campos, R.; Mangaravite, V.; Pasquali, A.; Jorge, A.M.; Nunes, C.; Jatowt, A. Yake! collection-independent automatic keyword extractor. In Proceedings of the Advances in Information Retrieval: 40th European Conference on IR Research, ECIR 2018, Grenoble, France, 26–29 March 2018; Proceedings 40; Springer: Berlin/Heidelberg, Germany, 2018; pp. 806–810.

43. Guglielmo, G.; Klincewicz, M. The temperature of morality: A behavioral study concerning the effect of moral decisions on facial thermal variations in video games. In Proceedings of the 16th International Conference on the Foundations of Digital Games, Online, 2–6 August 2021; pp. 1–4.
44. Hodge, S.E.; Taylor, J.; McAlaney, J. (A) morally demanding game? An exploration of moral decision-making in a purpose-made video game. *Media Commun.* **2020**, *7*, 213–225. [CrossRef]
45. Hornbeck, R.G. Moral Cognition Empowers Spiritual Experience in Chinese World of Warcraft. In *Religious Cognition in China: "Homo Religiosus" and the Dragon*; Springer: Berlin/Heidelberg, Germany, 2017; pp. 179–194.
46. Krcmar, M.; Cingel, D.P. Moral foundations theory and moral reasoning in video game play: Using real-life morality in a game context. *J. Broadcast. Electron. Media* **2016**, *60*, 87–103. [CrossRef]
47. Creeber, G. *The Television Genre Book*; Bloomsbury Publishing: London, UK, 2015.
48. Li, Y.; Yang, T. Word embedding for understanding natural language: A survey. In *Guide to Big Data Applications*; Springer: Berlin/Heidelberg, Germany, 2018; pp. 83–104.
49. Sitikhu, P.; Pahi, K.; Thapa, P.; Shakya, S. A comparison of semantic similarity methods for maximum human interpretability. In Proceedings of the 2019 Artificial Intelligence for Transforming Business and Society (AITB), IEEE, Kathmandu, Nepal, 5 November 2019; Volume 1, pp. 1–4.
50. Russell, S.J.; Norvig, P. *Artificial Intelligence: A Modern Approach*; Pearson Educaiton Limited: Harlow, UK, 2021.
51. Silverman, B.W. *Density Estimation for Statistics and Data Analysis*; CRC Press: Boca Raton, FL, USA, 1986; Volume 26.
52. Sheather, S.J.; Jones, M.C. A reliable data-based bandwidth selection method for kernel density estimation. *J. R. Stat. Soc. Ser. B Methodol.* **1991**, *53*, 683–690. [CrossRef]
53. Reimers, N.; Gurevych, I. Sentence-BERT: Sentence Embeddings using Siamese BERT-Networks. In Proceedings of the 2019 Conference on Empirical Methods in Natural Language Processing and the 9th International Joint Conference on Natural Language Processing (EMNLP-IJCNLP), Hong Kong, China, 3–7 November 2019; pp. 3982–3992.
54. Devlin, J.; Chang, M.W.; Lee, K.; Toutanova, K. Bert: Pre-training of deep bidirectional transformers for language understanding. *arXiv* **2018**, arXiv:1810.04805.
55. Stevenson, A. *Oxford Dictionary of English*; Oxford University Press: Oxford, UK, 2010.
56. Saviano, R. *Gomorrah*; Pan Macmillan: New York, NY, USA, 2019; Volume 82.
57. Asher, J. *13 Reasons Why*; Penguin: New York, NY, USA, 2017.

information

MDPI

Article

Domain-Specific Dictionary between Human and Machine Languages

Md Saiful Islam * and Fei Liu

Department of Computer Science and Information Technology, La Trobe University, Melbourne 3086, Australia; f.liu@latrobe.edu.au
* Correspondence: 18882762@students.latrobe.edu.au

Abstract: In the realm of artificial intelligence, knowledge graphs have become an effective area of research. Relationships between entities are depicted through a structural framework in knowledge graphs. In this paper, we propose to build a domain-specific medicine dictionary (DSMD) based on the principles of knowledge graphs. Our dictionary is composed of structured triples, where each entity is defined as a concept, and these concepts are interconnected through relationships. This comprehensive dictionary boasts more than 348,000 triples, encompassing over 20,000 medicine brands and 1500 generic medicines. It presents an innovative method of storing and accessing medical data. Our dictionary facilitates various functionalities, including medicine brand information extraction, brand-specific queries, and queries involving two words or question answering. We anticipate that our dictionary will serve a broad spectrum of users, catering to both human users, such as a diverse range of healthcare professionals, and AI applications.

Keywords: knowledge graph; medicine dictionary; structured triples; information extraction; question answering; artificial intelligence

1. Introduction

Knowledge representation refers to the process of crafting a structured framework that represents information related to a particular domain of interest. The purpose of knowledge representation is to facilitate reasoning and decision-making concerning the domain of interest [1]. In order to represent scientific knowledge through a structured framework, knowledge graphs are widely used. A knowledge graph can be described as a systematic representation of facts through entities, relationships, and a semantic framework. Knowledge graphs can also be defined as semantic networks. Semantic networks are structured representations of knowledge or concepts, where nodes represent entities or concepts, and edges represent relationships between entities [2]. The primary objective of both semantic networks and knowledge graphs is to capture the semantics or meaning of the relationships between entities. Knowledge graphs facilitate the spontaneous exploration and analysis of complex datasets. They enhance decision-making processes and accelerate knowledge discovery.

A significant number of knowledge graphs have been developed so far, such as Freebase, WordNet, ConceptNet, DBpedia, YAGO, and NELL [1]. These systems have been extensively used for question-answering systems, search engines, and recommendation systems. Since the introduction of semantic networks by Quillian [3] in 1963, research in this area has been continuously conducted, with various algorithms, mechanisms, and applications being presented. Semantic webs and ontology [4] are considered to represent the second wave of this research, in which the merging of local and universal ontologies was proposed. Compared with semantic networks, the second wave represents knowledge in a hierarchal structure, and hence, inheritance becomes possible. The most fundamental and influential work was RDF and OWL by the World Wide Web Consortium (W3C).

W3C also developed standards and guidelines for web information representation and extraction. Knowledge graphs and knowledge graph learning, which represent the third wave of this research, were introduced in recent years. Information is represented as tuples which form knowledge graphs. Significant progress has been made in recent years in terms of applying machine learning algorithms to knowledge graphs. In their recent survey article [1], Ji et al. provided a comprehensive summary of the research in this area. In the academic and industrial research communities, the expressions knowledge graph and knowledge base are used indiscriminately [1]. There is a negligible difference between these two expressions. When considering the graph structure, a knowledge graph can be seen as a graph [1]. However, when formal semantics are applied, it can be regarded as a knowledge base used for interpreting and inferring facts [1]. In Figure 1a, we can see an example of a knowledge base and Figure 1b an example of a knowledge graph. In the knowledge base (Figure 1a) example, knowledge is represented in the form of factual triples. Triples comprise the subject, predicate, and object. For example, Bird, locatedAt, and Tree. In triples, a relationship between subject and object is established through the predicate.

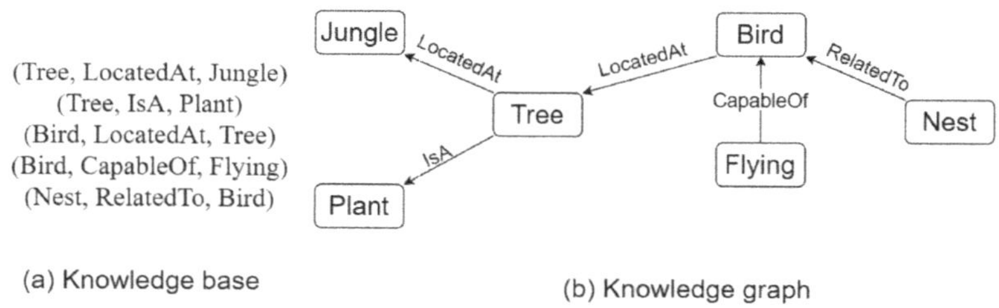

Figure 1. Example of a knowledge base and a knowledge graph. (**a**) Factual triples in a knowledge base. (**b**) Entities and relations in a knowledge graph.

On the other hand, the knowledge graph (Figure 1b) contains a set of entities (nodes) linked by directed and labeled edges. Each edge represents a relation. The two entities linked by a relation represent a relationship. The entity pointed to by the relation is the head of the relationship, whereas the other entity is called the tail. An entity can be a head as well as a tail in a knowledge graph. For instance, the entity "tree" is the head in the relationship "tree isA plant", whereas it is a tail in the relation "bird locatedAt tree".

Structured information can be useful outside of knowledge graphs as well. OMRKBC [5] is a machine-readable knowledge base designed to enable efficient data access and utilization. The authors of OMRKBC [5] structured it using the fundamental concept of knowledge graph triples, making it accessible via a variety of systems. OMRKBC [5] allows users to extract valuable information efficiently through diverse applications and interfaces. Moreover, the authors have introduced an additional framework known as NLIKR [6], which allows an application to extract definitions of a concept from their dictionary and understand its meaning. This framework provides a definition corresponding to each concept [6]. The application possesses the capability of accurately estimating the distance and similarity between concepts, thereby enhancing its understanding of their meaning.

In this paper, we propose a domain-specific dictionary between human and machine languages. The inspiration for this dictionary stemmed from an extensive survey of knowledge graphs. There is a unique opportunity to enhance the way medicine information is organized, accessed, and understood. The ultimate goal of this dictionary is to improve the quality of healthcare services. This knowledge graph-driven medicine dictionary will serve as a cornerstone in the realm of medical information systems. Its foundation lies in a well-structured ontology that utilizes knowledge graph triples to represent essential information about medications, their classifications, strengths, side effects, and various attributes. These triples, such as "A-Cold, has dosage form, Syrup", "A-Cold, type of, allopathic", etc., form the backbone of our ontology, enabling us to organize and present information in a format that is both machine-readable and human-understandable. This paper will explore the rationale, methodology, and potential benefits of constructing such a medicine dictionary.

The primary aim of this paper is to introduce a novel framework for constructing a comprehensive medicine dictionary using structured triples. While existing resources, such as The Danish Fetal Medicine database [7], YaTCM [8], and MEDI database [9], and knowledge graphs, such as SMR [10] and SnoMed kg [11], have contributed to the field, they typically present data in relational table formats or contain triples that are not exclusively focused on medicine-related information. Furthermore, these knowledge graphs primarily serve as repositories of medical knowledge within the medical sector.

What sets our proposed dictionary apart is its unique capability to represent medicine attributes through entities and relations, thereby enabling advanced reasoning abilities. Users of this dictionary will be empowered to effortlessly extract crucial medicine-related details, including generic names, types, strengths, manufacturers, pharmacological descriptions, side effects, and, significantly, a wide range of alternative medicine brands for each primary medicine brand.

The rest of the paper will be organized as follows. Section 2 will briefly discuss the previous research on knowledge graphs and the findings from the literature survey on knowledge representation learning, acquisition, and applications. In the next section, we will delve into the methodology employed to construct a medicine dictionary. Here, we will briefly lay out our approach, detailing how we harness structured triples to construct our comprehensive medicine dictionary. The methodology section will unveil the techniques and tools utilized in this project. After that, we will explore the practical application of our medicine dictionary. Real-world applications, such as the information extraction mechanism and question-answering techniques, will be discussed. Furthermore, we will showcase our experimental results and compare our work with existing mechanisms. Lastly, this paper will conclude with future research directions and the broader implications of our work.

2. Related Works

The domain of artificial intelligence has an extensive and well-established history of knowledge representation and reasoning, often facilitated by knowledge graphs. These graphs are primarily used to predict missing links within a vast network of information. Knowledge reasoning ability is crucial for representing knowledge in a structured format. Reasoning can be described as the process of analyzing, consolidating, and deriving new information on various aspects based on known facts and inference rules (relationships). It involves accumulating facts, identifying relationships between entities, and developing advanced understandings. Reasoning relies on prior knowledge and experience. Mining, organizing, and effectively managing knowledge from large-scale data are conducted through reasoning capabilities [12].

The concept of semantic net, proposed by Richens in 1956, can be identified as the origins of diagram-based knowledge interpretation [1]. The roots of symbolic logic knowledge trace back to the General Problem Solver in 1959 [1]. As knowledge representation progressed, various methods emerged, including framework-driven language, reasoning-driven systems, and blended manifestation systems. MYCIN [1], the renowned knowledge reasoning system in medical diagnosis, utilized a rule-based approach. The semantic web's essential standards, such as Web Ontology Language (OWL) and resource description framework (RDF), were inspired by knowledge representation and reasoning systems [1]. Semantic databases offer flexibility in depicting complex data relationships and enable sophisticated querying through semantic technologies such as OWL, RDF, and SparQl. Nonetheless, their management complexity and potential performance overhead demand proficiency in semantic standards. Despite scalability, the steep learning curve and limited tooling support can hinder widespread use. RDF serves as a framework for organizing web-based knowledge through structured triples, facilitating the development of interconnected datasets represented in a graph format [5]. Additionally, it facilitates the querying of these datasets via SparQl. OWL, as a language designed for crafting web ontologies, enables the specification of classes, properties, and logical axioms within specific domains [5]. OWL builds on RDF and handles complex knowledge models with detailed meanings, enabling automated reasoning and inference based on asserted knowledge. Apart from these, various systems and resources, including WordNet, DBpedia, ConceptNet, YAGO, and Freebase, have been developed to capture and represent knowledge effectively and efficiently.

WordNet [13] can be described as a lexical database of English words defined through synonyms. In the database, words are bundled as synsets. One synset can be defined as one unique concept. Concepts are linked through lexical relations, thus allowing machines to apply knowledge to reason over the meaning of words. However, the authors of NLIKR [6] argue that synsets are not enough to describe a word. Their argument was based on the fact that a word representing existence may reveal its characteristics in various ways, and WordNet is not capable of expressing them [6]. ConceptNet [14] was constructed using words and phrases connected by relations to model general human knowledge. ConceptNet has the ability to supply a comprehensive collection of general knowledge required by computer applications for the analysis of text based on natural language. However, ConceptNet has a significant drawback in that its relationships are inflexible and limited. Users cannot define custom relationships for their choice of words or phrases. DBPedia [15] is a collection of structured information on various domains that has been extracted from Wikipedia. However, the knowledge is limited to named entities or concepts.

In recent years, knowledge representation learning has become essential for various applications, such as knowledge graph completion and reasoning. Researchers have explored multiple geometric spaces, including Euclidean, complex, and hyperbolic spaces. A Euclidean space can be described as a three-dimensional geometric space in which the points are denoted by their Cartesian co-ordinates [1]. It utilizes the principles of Euclidean geometry for calculating distances. A complex space refers to a mathematical concept where numbers are denoted by complex numbers [16]. This framework expands the one-dimensional real number line into a two-dimensional plane, where each point is depicted by a distinct complex number comprising both real and imaginary parts [16]. A hyperbolic space refers to a mathematical space that has a negative curvature. It is employed to model complex hierarchical structures to capture the inherent geometry of the dataset [17]. Notable models, such as RotatE [16], leverage complex spaces, while ATTH [17] focuses on hyperbolic spaces to encode hierarchical relationships. TransModE [18] takes an innovative approach by utilizing modulus spaces, and DiriE [19] introduces Bayesian inference to tackle uncertainty in knowledge graphs.

RotatE [16] introduced a novel approach by leveraging complex spaces to encode entities and relations. This model is based on Euler's identity and treats unitary complex numbers as rotational transformations within the complex plane. RotatE aims to capture relationship structures, including symmetry/anti-symmetry, inversion, and composition. Symmetry refers to a relationship between entities where if entity A is related to entity B, entity B is likewise related to entity A, for example, (Barack Obama, MarriedTo, Michelle Obama), (Michelle Obama, MarriedTo, Barack Obama). If a relationship between entities exists in one direction, it cannot exist in the opposite direction unless the entities are the same; this is known as anti-symmetry. For example, (Parent, IsParentOf, Child). The opposite relationship (Child, IsParentOf, Parent) is not true. Inversion can be defined as a relationship where the direction of a relationship is reversed. For example, (Doctor, Treats, Patient), (Patient, TreatedBy, Doctor). Composition refers to combining multiple relationships to derive new relationships or discover new knowledge. For example, (Alex, StudiesAt, University Of Melbourne), (University Of Melbourne, LocatedIn, Melbourne). By composing the two relationships "StudiesAt" and "LocatedIn", we can infer another relationship (Alex, LivesIn, Melbourne). Another approach delves into hyperbolic spaces, as seen in the ATTH [17] model. This model focuses on encoding hierarchical and logical relations within a knowledge graph. The curvature of the hyperbolic space is a crucial parameter that dictates whether relationships should be represented within a curved, tree-like structure or a flatter Euclidean space. Similarly, MuRP [20] employs hyperbolic geometry to embed hierarchical relationship structures. This model is suitable for encoding hierarchical data with relatively few dimensions, offering scalability benefits. TransModE [18] takes a unique approach by utilizing modulus spaces, which involves replacing numbers with their remainders after division by a given modulus value. This model is capable of encoding a wide range of relationship structures, including symmetry, anti-symmetry, inversion, and composition. DiriE [19] adopts a Bayesian inference approach to address the uncertainty associated with knowledge graphs. Entities are represented as Dirichlet distributions and relations as multinomial distributions, allowing the model to quantify and model the uncertainty of large and incomplete knowledge frameworks.

Knowledge graphs require continuous expansion, as they often contain incomplete data. Knowledge graph completion (KGC) aims to add new triples from unstructured text, employing tasks such as relation path analysis. Relation extraction and entity discovery play vital roles in discovering new knowledge from unstructured text. Path analysis entails examining sequences of relations between entities to infer missing or potential relations. Relation extraction and entity discovery are essential for discovering new knowledge from unstructured text, involving tasks such as determining relationships between entities and aligning entities with their types. Distant supervision, also known as weak supervision or self-supervision, is primarily used to infer missing relations [1]. This approach generates training data by heuristically matching sentences that mention the same entities under the assumption that they may express the same relation [1]. It is used under the guidance of a relational database. RECON [21] is a relation extraction model (introduced in 2021) that effectively represents knowledge derived from knowledge graphs using a graph neural network (GNN). This model leverages textual and multiple instance-based mechanisms to learn the background characteristics of concepts, analyze triple context, and aggregate context. Knowledge graph embedding (KGE) has become a popular approach for KGC, with models such as TransMS [22] addressing the limitations of earlier translation-based models. TransMS projects entities and relations into different embedding spaces, allowing for more flexible and accurate modeling of complex relations. Type-aware attention path reasoning (TAPR) [23], proposed in 2020, tackles path reasoning in knowledge graphs. It offers greater flexibility in path prediction by considering the structural facts, recorded facts, and characteristic information of knowledge graphs (KG). TAPR leverages character-level information to enrich entity and relation representations and employs path-level attention mechanisms to weight paths and calculate relations between entities.

The integration of structured knowledge, especially knowledge graphs, has significant implications for AI systems. Knowledge-aware applications have emerged in various domains, including language representation learning and recommendation systems. Models such as K-BERT [24] and ALBERT [25] offer solutions to integrate knowledge graphs and enhance AI capabilities. For domain-specific knowledge in language representation (LR), K-BERT [24] was introduced in 2020 as a notable advancement. It addresses the challenges of integrating heterogeneous embedding spaces and handling noise in knowledge graphs. K-BERT extends existing BERT models, allowing them to incorporate domain-specific knowledge from a knowledge graph. ALBERT [25], introduced in 2022, focuses on fact retrieval from knowledge graphs. This model leverages schema graph expansion (SGE) to extract relevant knowledge from a knowledge graph and integrate it into a pre-trained language model. ALBERT consists of five modules, including a text encoder, classifier, knowledge extractor, graph encoder, and schema graph expander.

As we conclude our exploration of knowledge representation learning, knowledge acquisition, and integration, it becomes evident that while previous endeavors have made significant strides, a distinct opportunity lies on the horizon—a chance to pioneer a revolutionary approach tailored specifically to the field of medicine: the creation of a dynamic and comprehensive medicine dictionary. Unlike prior initiatives, which have generally covered a broad spectrum of medical data, this endeavor focuses solely on consolidating medicine information into a structured knowledge graph format. Inspired by the architecture of knowledge graphs and various other databases, this opportunity presents unparalleled potential to transform the way we understand and utilize medicine knowledge. The uniqueness of this approach lies in its focused representation of medical information as entities and relations, facilitating enhanced information retrieval and question-answering capabilities. Incorporating this approach into medicine holds the potential for substantial benefits, significantly enhancing healthcare practices and outcomes.

3. The Domain-Specific Medicine Dictionary (DSMD) and Its Construction

One perspective of defining a domain-specific dictionary is to characterize it as a knowledge base organized in a knowledge graph architecture comprising entities and relations. Each entity is interconnected with other entities through relationships. A domain-specific dictionary is centered around a particular field of expertise, such as medicine, economics, finance, electronics, cellular biology, etc. The primary objective is to populate this knowledge base with triples to facilitate information extraction and question-answering. Let's take an example of a knowledge base or knowledge graph in medicine domain:

$$(\text{A-Cold}, \text{generic\_name\_is}, \text{Bromhexine Hydrochloride})$$
$$(\text{A-Cold}, \text{type\_of}, \text{Allopathic})$$
$$(\text{A-Cold}, \text{has\_dosage\_form}, \text{Syrup})$$
$$(\text{A-Cold}, \text{has\_strength\_of}, 4\,\text{mg}/5\,\text{mL})$$
$$(\text{A-Cold}, \text{manufactured\_by}, \text{ACME Laboratories Ltd.})$$
$$(\text{Bromhexine Hydrochloride}, \text{pharmacology\_description}, \text{definition})$$
$$(\text{Bromhexine Hydrochloride}, \text{side\_effects}, \text{side effects description})$$

This domain-specific dictionary serves as a structured and interconnected repository of knowledge tailored to a specific field, which is important for enhancing information retrieval and analysis within that domain.

In this section, we present a structured approach to construct a human-machine dictionary in the medicine domain smoothly and effectively. The open source 'Assorted Medicine Dataset of Bangladesh' [26] was used to build a prototype dictionary. Before moving on to the prototype design, we will explore the properties of the dictionary.

3.1. Concepts and Relations

Our knowledge graph will consist of entities and relations. Each entity will be considered a concept, and the concepts will be connected through relations. Examples of entities include A-Cold, A-Cof, Syrup, Allopathic, etc. Entities can be names of medicine brands, generic names, types of medicine, such as herbal or allopathic, dosage forms of medicine, such as tablet or syrup, the strength of medicine, etc. On the other hand, relations will express the connection between concepts. For example, if A-Cold and Syrup are both concepts in the dictionary, what is the appropriate connection or link between them? The link between them can be defined as a relation. Here, the appropriate link between A-Cold and Syrup would be 'dosage form'. Once the links are identified, we can add a form of triple, such as "(A-Cold, has dosage form, Syrup)".

Relations are useful when they establish meaningful connections between entities. Consistency is the most important attribute of a relation. For example, in the triple "('A-Cold', 'manufactured by', 'ACME Laboratories Ltd.')", the relation 'manufactured by' indicates that the medicine 'A-Cold' is manufactured by ACME Laboratories Ltd. In order to ensure consistency, whenever the relation 'manufactured by' is used in the entire knowledge base, it should always point towards the manufacturer. Other valuable attributes of relations are relevance and the clarity of semantics. In the triple "('A-Cold', 'type of', 'allopathic')", the relation 'type of' is relevant, as it specifies the classification of the medicine 'A-Cold' within the context of medical domain. In the triple "('Bromhexine Hydrochloride', 'pharmacology description', 'definition')", the relation 'pharmacology description' has clear semantics, implying that it provides a description or definition of the pharmacology of 'Bromhexine Hydrochloride'. Our dictionary provides a broad definition of the pharmacology for each generic medicine. The word 'definition' is used here in the triple to keep it short. All these attributes of relations ensure that machines can interpret the relationship between entities accurately. For instance, the relation 'generic name is' indicates that 'Bromhexine Hydrochloride' serves as the generic name for 'A-Cold,' enabling the machine to understand the relationship between the medicine and its generic identifier. Similarly, the relation 'manufactured by' indicates that 'ACME Laboratories Ltd.' is the manufacturer of 'A-Cold,' providing crucial information about the entity responsible for producing the medication. By interpreting these relations appropriately, machines can navigate the knowledge base, extract relevant information, and generate comprehensive insights.

While concepts are collected easily from data, discovering relations is the tricky part. Khanam et al. [5] established certain rules for discovering relations. One such rule is that a verb, common noun, or an adjective followed by a preposition can be considered as a relation. For example, type of, strength of, manufactured by, etc. We followed this rule to establish a few relations for our dictionary. Some new rules have been discovered as well. The following are two example rules that we have discovered:

1. Rule number one: a verb phrase can be considered as a relation.
2. Rule number two: a noun or noun phrase can be considered a relation.

An example of a verb phrase is 'has dosage form'. Examples of noun phrases are 'generic name', 'side effects', and 'pharmacology description'.

Since we are constructing a medicine dictionary with a limited number of attributes, we decided to keep a limited number of relations in the knowledge graph. The relation types are symmetric, complex, and asymmetric. A symmetric relation is the one in which the positions of the head and tail can be swapped. Let us take an example of a symmetric relation—(A-Cold, alternative brand, Brohexin). The reverse triple—(Brohexin, alternative brand, A-Cold) is true as well. Not all relationships are symmetric, but an inverse relationship can be created easily. For example, ('A-Cold', 'has dosage form', 'Syrup') can be written as ('Syrup', 'is a form of dosage for', 'A-Cold'). A complex relation is defined as a more intricate or multi-layered connection between entities. Complex relation—(A-Cold, pharmacology description, description); this is true because of—(Bromhexine Hydrochloride, pharmacology description, description). More explanations can be found on this in the hierarchical structure and inheritance section. An example of an asymmetric relation is "(A-Cold, type of, allopathic)". An example of the architecture of the structured triples can be found in Figure 2.

3.2. The Hierarchical Structure and Inheritance

Following the knowledge graph architecture, a hierarchical structure is maintained in the dictionary. Hierarchy in a knowledge graph refers to the phenomenon that an entity can be a type of another entity; hence, attribute inheritance becomes possible. For instance, "Cat" as an entity is a type of "Mammal", which is another entity in a knowledge graph. As such, Cat can be defined as a descendant of Mammal and inherits attributes such as being "warm-blooded" and "produce milk to feed their young" from a Mammal. In our knowledge graph, the hierarchy is as follows: each generic medicine has multiple medicine brands manufactured by multiple manufacturers. Each medicine brand has four different attributes, including type, dosage form, strength, and manufacturer. Generic names, brand names, and attributes form a hierarchy, which is true for the entire database. Limiting the number of relations or attributes aims to simplify database structures, uphold data quality, enhance semantic clarity, ensure consistency and prioritize relevant information.

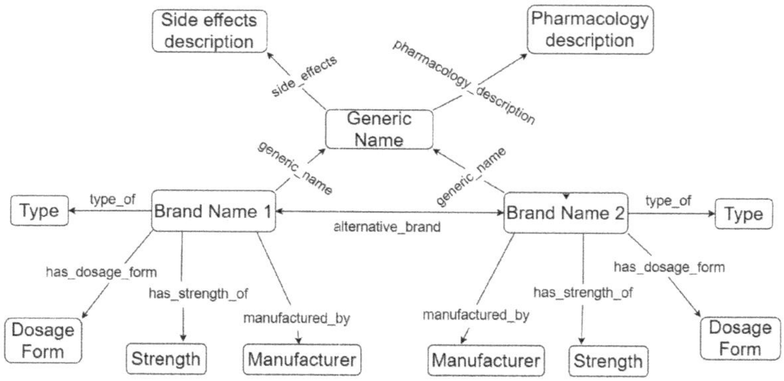

Figure 2. Architecture of structured triples—a knowledge graph.

Moreover, each medicine brand inherits the attributes of generic medicine. Each generic medicine has two definitions as its attributes, including the pharmacology description and side effects. Let us take an example of a complex relation—(Bromhexine Hydrochloride, pharmacology description, description). Since each medicine brand inherits attributes from generic medicine, when the dictionary connects all the triples together, it will find that the medicine brand will have a definition. We did not explicitly mention in the database that A-Cold has a description. However, through complex relations, each brand should find a definition and description of side effects description. So that we end up with—(A-Cold, pharmacology description, description).

3.3. Prototype Dictionary

In this section, we will provide an overview of the process involved in building a prototype dictionary, encompassing data collection, processing, mapping, structured triple formation, and functional programming design and implementation. The architecture of the prototype dictionary is detailed in Figure 3, and the process is explained in the following subsections.

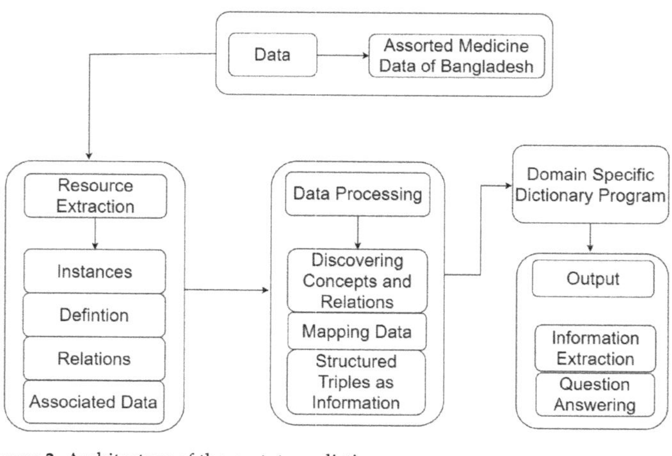

Figure 3. Architecture of the prototype dictionary.

The 'Assorted Medicine Dataset of Bangladesh' [26], an open source medicine data repository that is available on Kaggle, serves as the foundation for our prototype dictionary.

This repository contains real-world medicine data and is extensively described in Section 3.4 of this paper. With information on over 21,715 medicine brands, this dataset provides a comprehensive resource for our project.

Creating the prototype dictionary involves discovering entities and relations from the dataset and forming triples. This process is elaborated upon in the data processing section (Section 3.5), where we outline the steps involved in transforming raw data into structured triples.

Furthermore, the Section 4 delves into the application developed using Python for information retrieval and question-answering experiments. This section provides insights into the practical implementation of our prototype dictionary and its functionality.

3.4. Brief Description of the Dataset

In order to build our dictionary, we used an open sourced medicine dataset called Assorted Medicine Dataset of Bangladesh [26]. This dataset consists of medicine brands with their generics, drug classes, indications, dosage forms, manufacturer's information, descriptions, side effects, etc. The dataset contains more than 20,000 different medicine brands. All information is stored in six different csv files. For our research purposes, we only used two csv files, medicine.csv and generic.csv. Figure 4 presents a preview of the medicine.csv dataset.

	brand id	brand name	type	slug	dosage form	generic	strength	manufacturer	package container	Package Size
2	4077	A-Cold	allopathic	a-coldsyrup4-mg5-ml	Syrup	Bromhexine Hydrochl(	4 mg/5 ml	ACME Laboratories	100 ml bottle: à§³ 40.12	
3	4006	A-Cof	allopathic	a-cofsyrup10-mg30-mg125-mg5-n	Syrup	Dextromethorphan + P	(10 mg+30	ACME Laboratories	100 ml bottle: à§³ 100.00	
4	6174	A-Clox	allopathic	a-cloxinjection500-mgvial	Injection	Cloxacillin Sodium	500 mg/vial	ACME Laboratories	500 mg vial: à§³ 28.43,(5	(5's pack: à§³ 142.15)
5	6173	A-Clox	allopathic	a-cloxinjection250-mgvial	Injection	Cloxacillin Sodium	250 mg/vial	ACME Laboratories	250 mg vial: à§³ 20.00,(5	(5's pack: à§³ 100.00)
6	6172	A-Clox	allopathic	a-cloxpowder-for-suspension125-	Powder for Suspen:	Cloxacillin Sodium	125 mg/5 m	ACME Laboratories	100 ml bottle: à§³ 45.00	

Figure 4. A preview of medicine.csv.

'Medicine.csv' contains information on many different brands of medicine with their attributes. Attributes include brand ID, brand name, type, slug, dosage form, generic, strength, manufacturer, package container, and package size. Some of the information is not useful, while others are very important. We decided to keep the useful information and remove unnecessary information, such as brand ID, slug, package container, and package size. Package size can be useful, but there was a lot of missing information in that specific column. Hence, the decision is to remove the package size. 'Generic.csv' consists of many columns, such as generic ID, generic name, slug, monographic link, drug class, indication, therapeutic class description, pharmacology description, dosage description, side effects description, and many more. For our research purposes, we decided to use the generic name, pharmacology description, and side effects description column. We simply removed the other information. There are more than 1,400 different generic medicine names, with their associated information in the dataset.

3.5. Data Processing

Data processing involves selecting concepts, discovering the relations between them, mapping data, and forming structured triples. The collected instances from generic.csv and medicine.csv were used to select concepts for the dictionary. For example, A-Cold, allopathic, Syrup, Bromhexine Hydrochloride, 4 mg/5 mL, ACME Laboratories Ltd. In the above instance, A-Cold is a medicine brand, allopathic is the type of the brand, Syrup is the dosage form of the brand, Bromhexine Hydrochloride is the generic name of the brand, 4 mg/5 mL is the strength of the brand, and ACME Laboratories Ltd. is the manufacturer of the brand. Each attribute is treated as a concept for the dictionary. We also have a pharmacology definition of each generic name and the side effects of each generic name. They have also been included in the dictionary. After selecting our concepts, we started the task of discovering relations. Relations represent the link between two concepts. Hence, it is considered the most important and challenging task in our dictionary construction.

After discovering concepts and relations, we focus on mapping entities and relations to form structured triples. The generic.csv file contains pharmacology descriptions and side effects descriptions for each generic medicine. We encountered an issue where the pharmacology descriptions and side effects descriptions in the 'generic.csv' file contained HTML tags throughout the text. Since our goal was to extract definitions and side effects for each medicine from this file and ensure they are usable as triples, we needed to remove these HTML tags. In order to accomplish this, we utilized Python libraries such as pandas and BeautifulSoup. First, we loaded the csv file using pandas csv reader and identified the columns containing pharmacology descriptions and side effects descriptions. Next, we applied a function written in Python, leveraging BeautifulSoup, to extract the text from the HTML content in these columns. The algorithm for extracting text from HTML content can be found in Figure 5. Once the HTML tags were removed, we saved the cleaned data as a new csv file. With the 'medicine.csv' and 'generic.csv' files now cleaned and ready for use, we proceeded to transform the rows of information into triples. Using a Python function and pandas data frames, we mapped the discovered entities and linked them with the appropriate relations. The algorithm to transform rows of data into triples can be found in the public repository of my program, which is available at (https://github.com/Saif0013/DSMD (accessed on 15 February 2024)). In order to ensure data integrity, we checked for and removed any duplicate rows in the database before saving the triples as a csv file.

```
def extract_text_from_html(html):
    if isinstance(html, str):
        soup = BeautifulSoup(html, 'html.parser')
        return soup.text.strip()
    else:
        return ''

# Apply the extract text from HTML function on pharmacology and side effects
new_gen['pharmacology description'] = new_gen['pharmacology description'].apply(extract_text_from_html)
new_gen['side effects description'] = new_gen['side effects description'].apply(extract_text_from_html)
```

Figure 5. Algorithm for removing text from HTML content.

3.6. Dealing with Uncertainties

During data processing, we encountered a range of uncertainties, including missing data, duplicate entries, and data in incorrect formats, among others. Uncertainty within the dictionary can be detrimental, as it undermines data accuracy and integrity, leading to inaccurate information. In our commitment to enhancing the quality and reliability of our dictionary, we made the deliberate decision to systematically address and eliminate these uncertainties. The original medicine dataset contains information for 21,715 medicine brands. However, some entries in the dataset have missing information. While it is common for real-world knowledge graphs to be incomplete, ensuring accuracy and completeness is crucial, especially in the context of medicine. In order to maintain data integrity, we have opted to remove all medicine brands with missing or incomplete information from our database. After removing missing information, our dataset now contains information for 20,311 medicine brands. This meticulous effort ensures that our dictionary offers users accurate and trustworthy information, enhancing its utility for both healthcare professionals and AI applications.

4. Experiments

A program was designed to implement a prototype dictionary. The application was built using Python, leveraging rich libraries such as Pandas for data management and Tkinter for GUI development. It employs a functional programming approach to process user queries efficiently. Queries are submitted through the GUI interface, where users input questions or specific queries about medicine brands and their attributes. These queries are then transformed and formatted as needed before being submitted to the database. Unlike SparQL, which is commonly used for querying RDF databases, this application interacts directly with a Pandas DataFrame to retrieve information rather than using a specialized query language. The program has been open source and made available on GitHub for public access. The program can be found at https://github.com/Saif0013/DSMD (accessed on 15 February 2024) The architecture of our application is presented in Figure 6.

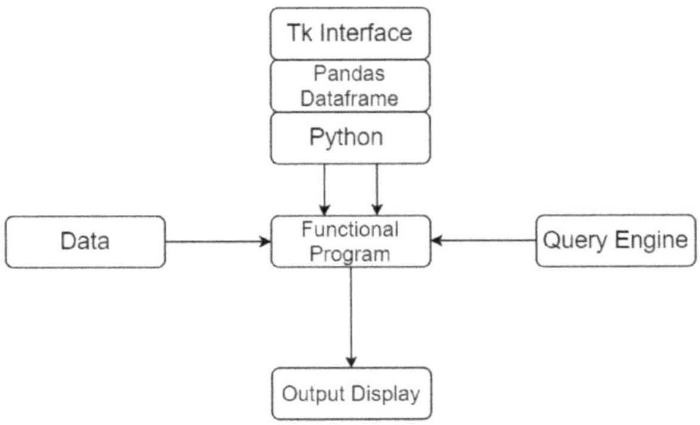

Figure 6. Functional program architecture.

There are more than 20,000 medicine brands, and their associated information is available in the dictionary. We selected 50 different medicine brands as part of our experiment. The dictionary contains no missing information, and all the brands have similar information, including the generic name, type, dosage form, strength, manufacturer, pharmacology description, and side effects. Therefore, we think 50 brands for the experiment provide a representative sample of the entire dataset. The experiment was conducted on different types of questions, such as brand information extraction, specific information extraction about a brand, and question-answering with a yes or no. Please navigate to the Section 5 to find out how a question can be asked and how information can be extracted. The overall accuracy of the experiment is 100%. Overall accuracy was calculated based on the following formula:

$$\text{Overall Accuracy} = \frac{\text{Number of Correct Answers}}{\text{Total Number of Answers}} \tag{1}$$

Our DSMD is truly unique, setting it apart from any other database. Our database boasts an impressive repository of over 348,000 triples, encompassing information on more than 20,000 medicine brands and 1,500 plus details on generic medicines. In contrast to the databases that served as our inspiration, which span a wide range of domains, our dictionary distinguishes itself by its focused approach. When compared to well-known databases, such as DBpedia, ConceptNet, WordNet, and NLIKR, our dictionary notably contains a leaner volume of data. This not only streamlines information retrieval but also results in faster access when compared to these larger databases. Despite the differences in the nature of these databases, we've made deliberate efforts to emphasize the unique characteristics of our DSMD, which are outlined in Table 1. Our database shares many characteristics with NLIKR. However, when it comes to executing searches or queries, our dictionary outperforms NLIKR significantly. The author of NLIKR notes that while DBPedia, WordNet, and ConceptNet operate at an O(n) complexity level for searches, NLIKR's complexity is $O(n^2)$, where 'n' represents the number of concepts [6]. During our experiments, we noted that our fastest query execution time was 0.034 s, while the slowest query execution time was 0.057 s.

Table 1. Comparison with other databases.

	DBpedia	WordNet	ConceptNet	NLIKR	DSMD
Meaningful and well-structured properties	N	N	N	Y	Y
Supporting multiple types of relations	N	N	Y	Y	Y
Concepts are linked in various ways	N	N	Y	Y	Y
Allows Inheritance	N	Y	N	Y	Y
Allows Queries between two words	Y	N	N	Y	Y
Faster query execution time	Y	Y	Y	N	Y

5. Applications

DSMD has diverse applications across multiple sectors, benefiting healthcare professionals, medical researchers, pharmacies, healthcare educators, healthcare writers, journalists, regulatory authorities, and pharmaceutical experts. It offers a wealth of information about medicines and drugs, including generic names, dosage forms, medicine types, strengths, side effects, pharmacological descriptions, manufacturers, and alternative brands. Notably, our dictionary excels in providing multiple alternative brands for the same medicine, a highly valuable feature for pharmacists, doctors, medicine students, and researchers. Additionally, DSMD enables users to compare two medicines by calculating their distance and similarity. BERT models, such as K-BERT [24] and ALBERT [25], can seamlessly integrate knowledge graph databases as an external source of information. Given the adherence of our dictionary to the knowledge graph structure, it serves as a valuable source of information for AI language models. In the following subsections, we will illustrate example use cases, including retrieving information about medicine brands, comparing different medicines, and conducting word-based queries.

5.1. Medicine Comparison

As a dictionary, DSMD allows the distance and similarity of two medicines to be estimated based on their percentage of common ancestor (PCA), percentage of common association (PCAS), and percentage of binding association (PBAS).

Given two entities, e_1 and e_2, the distance between the two is calculated as [6]

$$D(e_1, e_2) = W_{CA} \log \frac{1}{PCA(e_1, e_2)} + W_{CAS} \log \frac{1}{PCAS(e_1, e_2)} + W_{AB} PBAS(e_1, e_2) \quad (2)$$

where W_{CA}, W_{CAS}, and W_{BAS} are three weights. The similarity of e_1 and e_2 can be estimated as [6]

$$S(e_1, e_2) = f_{CA} PCA(e_1, e_2) + f_{CAS} PCAS(e_1, e_2) \quad (3)$$

where f_{CA} and f_{CAS} are two coefficients satisfying $f_{CA} \geq 0$ and $f_{CAS} \geq 0$ and $f_{CA} + f_{CAS} = 1$.

The capability of estimating the distance and similarity is extremely important. It enables us to systematically compare the effects and side effects of two drugs or even explore their interaction.

5.2. Brand Information Extraction

Figure 7 illustrates how the dictionary presents information for each medicine brand through relationships.

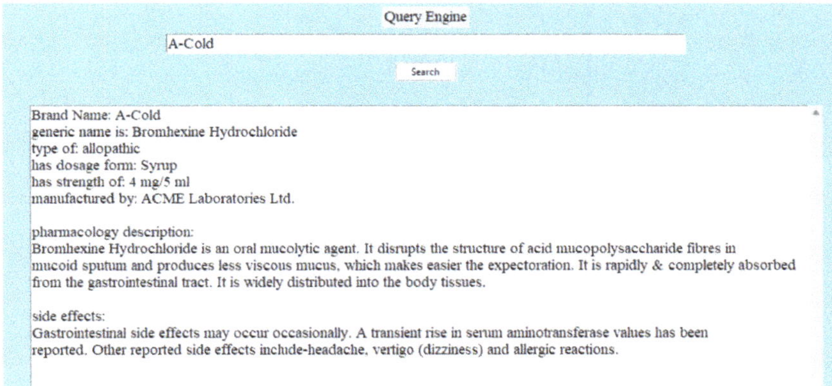

Figure 7. Brand information extraction.

In Figure 7, A-Cold is the medicine brand. The extracted information, for example, 'Bromhexine Hydrochloride' is represented by the relation 'generic name is' and 'allopathic' is represented by the relation 'type of'.

5.3. Alternative Medicine Information Extraction

Figure 8 depicts how the dictionary provides alternative medicine brands for a given medicine brand.

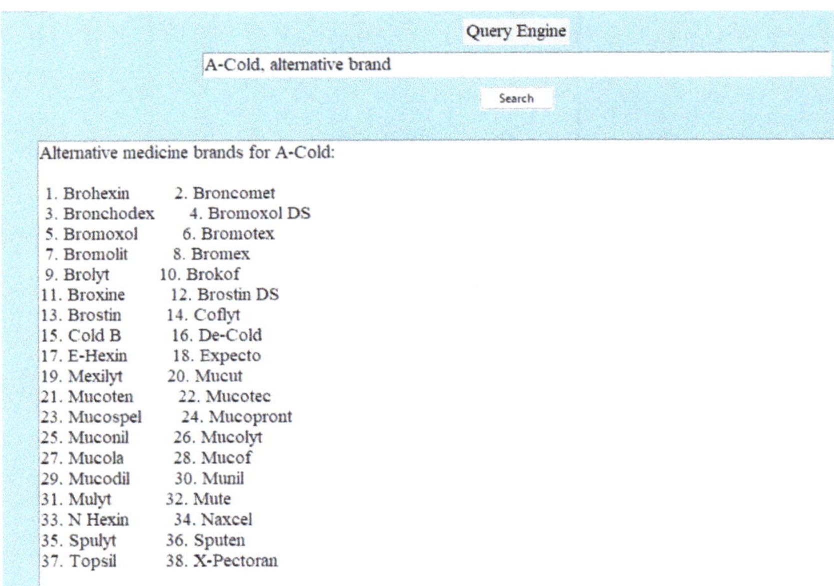

Figure 8. Alternative medicine information extraction.

The dictionary contains information on 38 different alternative medicine brands for 'A-Cold'.

5.4. Question-Answering

Our dictionary is also capable of answering specific questions about a medicine brand. Figure 9 is an example of answering a specific question related to a particular medicine brand.

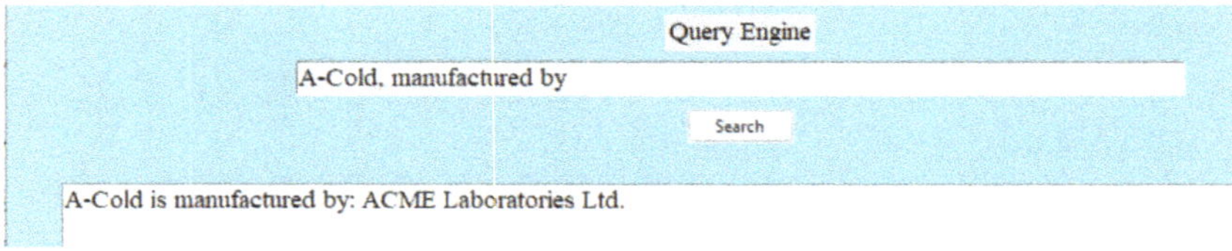

Figure 9. Specific information extraction.

Figure 9 demonstrates how the dictionary can provide answers to a specific question.

Along with the above information extraction capabilities, the dictionary also offers the ability to answer questions with a yes or no. For example:

Figure 10 demonstrates the ability to answer a question with 'Yes' if the provided information is true.

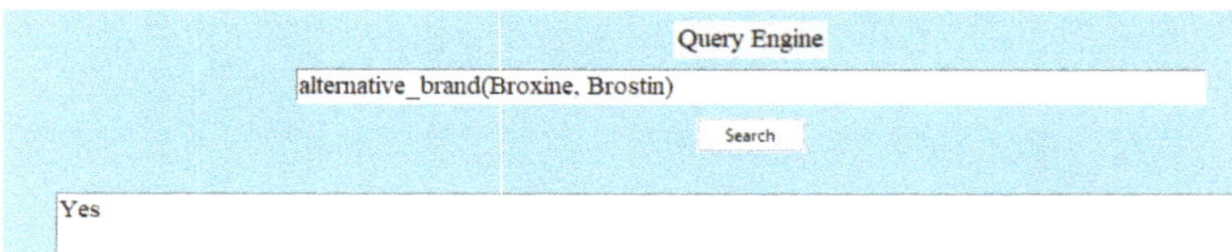

Figure 10. Question -answering.

Here is another example:

Figure 11 demonstrates the ability of answering a question with 'No' if the provided information is false.

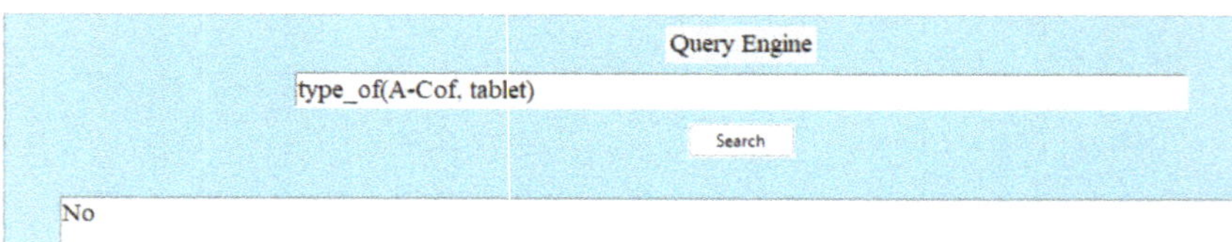

Figure 11. Question-answering.

5.5. A Brief Overview of Information Extraction and Question-Answering

The domain-specific medicine dictionary can be used by both human users and machines, such as language models, including BERT models, ChatGpt, etc. By accessing the dictionary, a machine or a user can extract the following information:

Medicine Information

1. Medicine brand information by searching a medicine brand name such as 'A-Cof'.

Specific Information about a Particular Medicine Brand

1. Generic name: 'A-Cof', 'generic name is'
2. Medicine type: 'A-Cof', 'type of'
3. Dosage form: 'A-Cof', 'has dosage form'
4. Strength: 'A-Cof', 'has strength of'
5. Manufacturer: 'A-Cof', 'manufactured by'

6. Pharmacology description: 'A-Cof', 'pharmacology description'
7. Side effects: 'A-Cof', 'side effects'
8. Alternative brand: 'A-Cof', 'alternative brand'

Yes or No Answers

1. `generic_name_is(A-Cold, Bromhexine Hydrochloride)`
2. `type_of(A-Cold, allopathic)`
3. `has_dosage_form(A-Cold, Syrup)`
4. `has_strength_of(A-Cold, 4 mg/5 mL)`
5. `manufactured_by(A-Cold, ACME Laboratories Ltd.)`

6. Conclusions

We have introduced a comprehensive framework for creating a domain-specific medicine dictionary designed to serve both human users and AI applications. In our dictionary, we represent each entity as a concept and establish connections between concepts through meaningful relations. This dictionary excels in its ability to extract essential information related to medicine brands, offer specific insights into individual medicine brands, and respond to inquiries effectively.

A standout feature of our dictionary is its capacity to provide multiple alternative brand options for a single medicine brand, enhancing its practicality and versatility. We anticipate that our dictionary will find valuable application across a diverse spectrum of healthcare fields, including general practice, medical research, pharmacies, healthcare education, and regulatory authorities. Furthermore, the dictionary serves as a rich source of information for various AI applications.

A further research direction has been identified: the incorporation of more comprehensive details for each medicine brand, such as additional attributes related to manufacturers and generic medicines. These additions may encompass data on drug class, drug indications, and the specific diseases for which the drugs are prescribed. Apart from these, we would like to automate the relation extraction process so that triples are automatically extracted from plain text and added to the knowledge base. A number of machine learning-based tools for natural language processing, such as BERT and spaCy, can be used. Research in the area is less mature. The accuracy of general-purpose information extraction normally has low accuracy. As such, we aim to pursue our goal in a domain-specific area, which is likely to achieve accuracy at a satisfactory level. Additionally, some limitations of our dictionary have also been identified, including a limited number of relations due to the nature of the available data and a constrained number of concepts due to limited data availability. Our original focus was on identifying alternative medicine options for a given brand and providing the essential attributes related to medicine brands, such as medicine type, strength, dosage form, and manufacturer. With this framework, a domain-specific dictionary can be constructed in the same or any other domain of choice.

Author Contributions: M.S.I. conceptualized and implemented the proposed framework for the Domain-Specific Medicine Dictionary (DSMD), conducted experiments, and performed data analysis. F.L. formulated the framework for medicine comparison, provided guidance throughout the research, and supervised the project. All authors have read and agreed to the published version of the manuscript.

Funding: This research received no external funding.

Institutional Review Board Statement: Not applicable.

Informed Consent Statement: Not applicable.

Data Availability Statement: The prototype of the Domain-Specific Medicine Dictionary (DSMD), along with the associated data and experimental details, has been made publicly accessible. To access the DSMD prototype and related materials, please visit the following link: https://github.com/Saif0013/DSMD (accessed on 15 February 2024)

Conflicts of Interest: The authors declare no conflict of interest.

Abbreviations

The following abbreviations are used in this manuscript:

DSMD	Domain-Specific Medicine Dictionary
KG	Knowledge Graph
KRL	Knowledge Representation Learning
KGE	Knowledge Graph Embedding

References

1. Ji, S.; Pan, S.; Cambria, E.; Marttinen, P.; Yu, P.S. A Survey on Knowledge Graphs: Representation, Acquisition, and Applications. *IEEE Trans. Neural Netw. Learn. Syst.* **2022**, *33*, 494–514. [CrossRef] [PubMed]
2. Sowa, J.F. Semantic networks. *Encycl. Artif. Intell.* **1992**, *2*, 1493–1511.
3. Quillian, R. *A Notation for Representing Conceptual Information: An Application to Semantics and Mechanical English Paraphrasing*; SP-1395; System Development Corporation: Santa Monica, CA, USA, 1963.
4. Dou; D.; Wang, H.; Liu, H. Semantic data mining: A survey of ontology-based approaches. In Proceedings of the 2015 IEEE 9th International Conference on Semantic Computing (IEEE ICSC 2015), Anaheim, CA, USA, 7–9 February 2015; IEEE: Piscataway, NJ, USA, 2015.
5. Khanam, S.A.; Liu, F.; Chen, P.Y. Comprehensive structured knowledge base system construction with natural language presentation. *Hum. Cent. Comput. Inf. Sci.* **2019**, *9*, 23. [CrossRef]
6. Liu; F.; Khanam, S.A.; Chen, Y.P. A Human-Machine Language Dictionary. *Int. J. Comput. Intell. Syst.* **2020**, *13*, 904–913. [CrossRef]
7. Ekelund, C.K.; Kopp, T.I.; Tabor, A.; Petersen, O.B. The Danish Fetal Medicine database. *Clin. Epidemiol.* **2016**, *8*, 479–483. [CrossRef] [PubMed]
8. Li, B.; Ma, C.; Zhao, X.; Hu, Z.; Du, T.; Xu, X.; Wang, Z.; Lin, J. YaTCM: Yet another Traditional Chinese Medicine Database for Drug Discovery. *Comput. Struct. Biotechnol. J.* **2018**, *16*, 600–610. [CrossRef] [PubMed]
9. Wei, W.-Q.; Cronin, R.M.; Xu, H.; Lasko, T.A.; Bastarache, L.; Denny, J.C. Development and evaluation of an ensemble resource linking medications to their indications. *J. Am. Med. Inform. Assoc.* **2013**, *20*, 954–961. [CrossRef] [PubMed]
10. Gong, F.; Wang, M.; Wang, H.; Wang, S.; Liu, M. SMR: Medical knowledge graph embedding for safe medicine recommendation. *Big Data Res.* **2021**, *23*, 100174. [CrossRef]
11. Chang, D.; Balažević, I.; Allen, C.; Chawla, D.; Brandt, C.; Taylor, R.A. Benchmark and Best Practices for Biomedical Knowledge Graph Embeddings. In Proceedings of the 19th SIGBioMed Workshop on Biomedical Language Processing, Online, 9 July 2020. [CrossRef]
12. Chen, X.; Jia, S.; Xiang, Y. A review: Knowledge reasoning over knowledge graph. *Expert Syst. Appl.* **2020**, *141*, 112948. [CrossRef]
13. Miller, G.; Beckwith, R.; Fellbaum, C.; Gross, D.; Miller, K. WordNet: An on-line lexical database. *Int. J. Lexicogr.* **2000**, *3*, 235–244. [CrossRef]
14. Liu, H.; Singh, P. ConceptNet—A practical commonsense reasoning tool kit. *BT Technol. J.* **2004**, *22*, 211–226. [CrossRef]
15. Lehmann, J.; Isele, R.; Jakob, M.; Jentzsch, A.; Kontokostas, D.; Mendes, P.N.; Hellmann, S.; Morsey, M.; van Kleef, P.; Auer, S.; et al. DBpedia—A large-scale, multilingual knowledge base extracted from Wikipedia. *Sem. Web J.* **2015**, *6*, 167–195. [CrossRef]
16. Sun, Z.; Deng, Z.; Nie, J.; Tang, J. RotatE: Knowledge graph embedding by relational rotation in complex space. *arXiv* **2019**, arXiv:1902.10197.
17. Chami, I.; Wolf, A.; Juan, D.; Sala, F.; Ravi, S.; Re, C. Low-Dimensional Hyperbolic Knowledge Graph Embeddings. *arXiv* **2020**, arXiv:2005.00545v1.
18. Baalbakia, H.; Hazimehb, H.; Harbc, H.; Angarita, R. TransModE: Translational Knowledge Graph Embedding Using Modular Arithmetic. *Procedia Comput. Sci.* **2022**, *207*, 1154–1163. [CrossRef]
19. Wang, F.; Zhang, Z.; Sun, L.; Ye, J.; Yan, Y. DiriE: Knowledge Graph Embedding with Dirichlet Distribution. In Proceedings of the ACM Web Conference 2022, Online, 25–29 April 2022.
20. Balažević, I.; Allen, C.; Hospedales, T. Multi-relational Poincaré Graph Embeddings. In Proceedings of the 33rd International Conference on Neural Information Processing Systems NIPS'19, Vancouver, BC, Canada, 8–14 December 2019.
21. Bastos, A.; Nadgeri, A.; Singh, K.; Mulang, I.O.; Shekarpour, S.; Hoffart, J.; Kaul, M. RECON: Relation Extraction using Knowledge Graph Context in a Graph Neural Network. In Proceedings of the ACM Web Conference, Ljubljana, Slovenia, 19–23 April 2021.
22. Yang, S.; Tian, J.; Zhang, H.; Yan, J.; He, H.; Jin, Y. TransMS: Knowledge Graph Embedding for Complex Relations by Multidirectional Semantics. In Proceedings of the Twenty-Eighth International Joint Conference on Artificial Intelligence (IJCAI-19), Macao, China, 10–16 August 2019.
23. Shen, Y.; Ding, N.; Zheng, H.; Li, Y.; Yang, M. Modeling Relation Paths for Knowledge Graph Completion. *IEEE Trans. Knowl. Data Eng.* **2021**, *33*, 3607–3617. [CrossRef]
24. Liu, W.; Zhou, P.; Zhao, Z.; Wang, Z.; Ju, Q.; Deng, H.; Wang, P. K-BERT: Enabling Language Representation with Knowledge Graph. In Proceedings of the AAAI Conference on Artificial Intelligence, New York, NY, USA, 7–12 February 2020.

25. Choi, B.; Lee, Y.; Kyung, Y.; Kim, E. *ALBERT with Knowledge Graph Encoder Utilizing Semantic Similarity for Commonsense Question Answering*; Tech Science Press: Henderson, NV, USA, 2022.
26. Sakib, A.S. Assorted Medicine Dataset of Bangladesh. 2020. Available online: https://www.kaggle.com/datasets/ahmedshahriarsakib/assorted-medicine-dataset-of-bangladesh (accessed on 20 July 2023).

information

MDPI

Article

Genre Classification of Books in Russian with Stylometric Features: A Case Study

Natalia Vanetik *,†, Margarita Tiamanova †, Genady Kogan † and Marina Litvak †

Department of Software Engineering, Shamoon College of Engineering, Beer Sheva 84500, Israel; margati@ac.sce.ac.il (M.T.); genadko@ac.sce.ac.il (G.K.); marinal@sce.ac.il (M.L.)
* Correspondence: natalyav@sce.ac.il; Tel.: +972-8-647-5015
† These authors contributed equally to this work.

Abstract: Within the literary domain, genres function as fundamental organizing concepts that provide readers, publishers, and academics with a unified framework. Genres are discrete categories that are distinguished by common stylistic, thematic, and structural components. They facilitate the categorization process and improve our understanding of a wide range of literary expressions. In this paper, we introduce a new dataset for genre classification of Russian books, covering 11 literary genres. We also perform dataset evaluation for the tasks of binary and multi-class genre identification. Through extensive experimentation and analysis, we explore the effectiveness of different text representations, including stylometric features, in genre classification. Our findings clarify the challenges present in classifying Russian literature by genre, revealing insights into the performance of different models across various genres. Furthermore, we address several research questions regarding the difficulty of multi-class classification compared to binary classification, and the impact of stylometric features on classification accuracy.

Keywords: text classification; genre classification; Russian literature; stylometry; genres dataset

1. Introduction

In the realm of literature, the concept of genre serves as a fundamental organizational principle, providing readers, publishers, and scholars with a cohesive framework. Within any collection of works, a genre stands as a distinct category, characterized by shared stylistic, thematic, and structural elements. It functions as a conceptual tool, simplifying the process of categorization and enhancing the comprehension of a diverse array of literary expressions. Genres encompass a broad spectrum, ranging from timeless and conventional categories like fiction and non-fiction to more nuanced classifications such as mystery, romance, fantasy, and beyond.

Genres extend beyond mere categorization; they act as guiding beacons, directing readers toward narratives that align with their preferences and expectations. Recognizing the genre of a literary work becomes akin to following arrows that point toward stories tailored to individual tastes.

A text's stylistic features serve as markers of different genres and are frequently employed for automatic analysis in this field because they represent a text's structural quirks, among other things [1,2].

Automatic genre classification makes it possible to solve several computational linguistics problems more quickly, including figuring out a word or phrase's meaning or part of speech, locating documents that are pertinent to a semantic query [3], improving authorship attribution [4–6], and more [2,7].

Only a small number of the numerous studies that address the subject of automatic genre classification (explained in more detail in Section 2) focus on Russian literature, and just three corpora have been generated for the job of genre classification in Russian, even though there are over 258 million Russian speakers in the world [8]. The corpus introduced in [9] contains texts collected from the Internet that belong to six genre segments of Internet texts, namely, contemporary fiction, poetry, social media, news, subtitles for films, and a collection of thematic magazines annotated as "the rest". These texts span 5 billion words; however, out of the six genres, only two can be attributed to literature—fiction and poetry. The corpus of [2] contains 10,000 texts assigned to five different genres—novels, scientific articles, reviews, posts from the VKontakte social network [10], and news texts from OpenCorpora [11], the open corpus of Russian texts. Only one genre in this corpus is a literature genre—the novels. In [12], the authors have developed a corpus of the A.S. Pushkin Lyceum period (1813–1817) that contains ten different genres of his poems. However, no prosaic texts are contained in this corpus, and the texts are limited to a single author.

None of the above corpora covers a significant amount of modern and historical genres in Russian literature. To overcome this gap, we present a new dataset comprising Russian books spanning eleven diverse literature genres, aimed at facilitating research in text classification. The dataset encompasses eleven different literature genres, thereby providing a comprehensive resource for studying genres in Russian literature. We evaluate several traditional machine learning models, alongside state-of-the-art deep learning models, including transformers [13] and dual contrastive learning [14], for both binary and multi-class genre classification tasks. Furthermore, we provide insights into the strengths and limitations of each model, shedding light on their applicability to real-world genre classification scenarios. This dataset can serve as a valuable resource for researchers interested in advancing the understanding and development of genre studying and classification systems for Russian texts.

We perform an extensive evaluation of binary and multi-class genre classification on a subset of our dataset and analyze the results; we employ a wide range of text representations, including stylometric features [2]. The purpose of this evaluation is to show that genre classification of Russian books is a highly nontrivial task. We also analyze what text representations work better for what task, and the difference in classification of different genres.

We address the following research questions in our work.

- RQ1: Do stylometric features improve genre classification accuracy?
- RQ2: What genres are easier to classify?
- RQ3: Does contrastive learning perform better for genre classification than fine-tuned transformer models and traditional models?
- RQ4: Does removing punctuation decrease classification accuracy for genre classification?
- RQ5: Does a transformer model pre-trained on Russian perform better than a multilingual transformer model?

This paper is organized as follows. Section 2 describes the related work. Section 3 describes our dataset, the process of its collection, and the data processing we performed. In Section 4, we describe text representations and classification models we used to perform genre classification on our data. Section 5 describes the hardware and software setup and full results of our experimental evaluation. Finally, Sections 6 and 7 discuss the conclusions and limitations of our approach.

2. Related Work

The task of categorizing Russian literary genres has garnered significant attention in the domains of literary analysis and Natural Language Processing (NLP). Many studies have attempted to enhance the understanding and automation of genre classification, focusing on the unique linguistic and cultural components present in Russian literature. We must acknowledge the growing body of research focusing on topics other than English literature, even though a lot of work has helped us comprehend how genres are applied to English-language novels. Renowned research on Arabic [15] and Spanish [16] genre classification has highlighted both the benefits and drawbacks of linguistic and cultural diversity.

Genre classification occurs not only at the level of texts but also based on book titles. The authors of [17] presented a method for genre classification based on the book's title. The dataset (available at https://github.com/akshaybhatia10/Book-Genre-Classification, accessed on 1 January 2024) constructed by the authors contains 207,575 samples of data assigned to 32 different genres.To represent the data, the texts were converted to lowercase, tokenized, and stemmed. Punctuation and English stopwords were removed. Word embeddings were used as word representations, and five different machine learning models were applied for the task of genre classification by title. The best-performing model was Long Short-Term Memory (LSTM) with dropout, achieving an accuracy of 65 %.

The work of [16] addresses genre classification in Spanish [16]. The authors introduce a method for automatic detection of books' themes that does not rely on a pre-defined list of genres. The authors construct the dataset by scraping the books from two undisclosed Latin American publishers. Their approach clusters key categories and results in 26 thematic categories. Models such as SVM [18] and BERT [13] achieve F1 scores ranging from 57% to 65.26%.

The work of [19] uses Recurrent Neural Networks (RNNs) as a deep learning method to classify book plots and reviews. The successful classification of 28 genres, including action, adventure, comedy, drama, family, mystery, romance, and science, is demonstrated by the testing findings. For the top 10 recommendations, the RNN-based recommendation system outperforms the matrix factorization technique with a precision of 82%, compared to 77%. In comparison to conventional artificial neural network techniques, the study indicates that combining a deep learning model with an RNN enhances accuracy and lowers validation loss percentage, improving Root Mean Squared Error (RMSE).

Several corpora for genre classification have been developed over the years in multiple languages, such as English, Arabic, Spanish, and more [20–23]. Not much analogous research has been conducted on datasets in the Russian language. The authors of [2] investigated contemporary vector text models, such as ELMo embeddings, the BERT language model, and a complex of numerical rhythm features, for genre categorization of texts written in the Russian language. Their experiments used ten thousand texts from five different genres: OpenCorpora news, Vkontakte communications, reviews, scientific publications, and novels. The study differentiated between genres with limited rhythms and those with diverse rhythms, such as novels and reviews, using rhythm features and LSTM. The multi-classification F-score of 0.99 attests to the effectiveness of contemporary embeddings. In [12], an automated technique for classifying Russian poetry writings' genre type and semantic properties is proposed. Based on the relationship between genre and text style, it describes a combined classifier for genre kinds and stylistic coloring. Computational tests with A.S. Pushkin's Lyceum lyrics show good results in determining stylistic colors and genres. The author of [24] proposed a method for genre classification of Russian texts that relies on different feature types—lexical, morphological, and syntactic features, as well as readability, text and word length, and symbolic features (n-grams). Support Vector Machine [25] is then used as a classifier for different genre types. All the experiments in this work are performed on the "Taiga" webcorpous [9] that has undergone morphological and syntactic annotation and covers six different genres of Internet texts.

As a representation learning technique, contrastive learning seeks to maximize similarity between samples in the same class and minimize it across samples in different classes [26]. By including both input data and their related labels, dual contrastive learning expands on this strategy and makes it easier to learn discriminatory representations for both aspects [27].

Our study presents a substantial dataset for the genre classification of Russian books, and the evaluation of this dataset with binary genre classification. The dataset is extensive, with genres represented in varying proportions, due to some genres being more popular while others are less so. Our dataset covers 11 genres and more than 8K books.

We perform our study with multiple classifiers, including traditional ones (Random Forest [28], logistic regression (LR) [29], and Extreme Gradient Boosting [30]), their ensemble, transformers, and contrastive learning. The RF model is an ensemble learning method that constructs multiple decision trees during training and outputs the mode of the classes of the individual trees; the LR model finds the probability of a binary outcome based on one or more predictor variables, and it uses a logistic function to represent the output as a probability; XGB performs gradient boosting by building the models sequentially with each new model correcting the errors made by previous ones. The ensemble learning approach involves combining the predictions of multiple models (RF, LR, and XGB) by combining their predicted probabilities. This method uses the strengths of each model to enhance the overall prediction performance. Fine-tuned transformers are the pre-trained transformer models that have been further trained on our dataset, allowing the model to adapt to specific tasks. A contrastive learning model is trained to differentiate between similar and dissimilar pairs of data points. Full descriptions of these models are provided in Section 4.4.

Stylometry, also called computational stylistics, encompasses a wide-ranging field of studies that involves analyzing linguistic features extracted from texts to characterize the style of authors, documents, or document groups. Using statistical techniques, subtle differences and similarities between texts that may be imperceptible to the naked eye can be identified, allowing the delineation of text groups based on their linguistic affinity. Stylometry subtasks include authorship attribution, authorship verification, authorship profiling, stylochronometry, and adversarial stylometry [31]. In some cases, authorship profiling helps narrow the search space by identifying different variables such as genre, age, or gender [32–34]. Stylometry is valuable for genre classification due to its ability to capture unique stylistic features that distinguish different genres. Word frequency, sentence length, and syntactic patterns are examples of stylometric characteristics that may be used to distinguish between genres by emphasizing writers' consistent stylistic choices within each genre. Furthermore, the efficiency of stylometry in genre categorization has been further validated by its successful application in tasks such as author profiling across genres [35].

Several tools for stylometric analysis have been developed, and a number of them support the Russian language. Stylo [36] is an R package that supports various languages, including Russian, and provides functionalities for authorship attribution, stylistic analysis, and text classification. WebSty [37] is another stylometric analysis tool that supports Russian language processing. It is an easily accessible open-source tool and forms part of the CLARIN-PL research infrastructure. While primarily focused on English texts, Coh-Metrix [38] is a comprehensive tool for analyzing various aspects of text cohesion, coherence, and readability. It has inspired versions for analyzing other languages, including Russian, albeit with fewer functionalities compared to its English counterpart. Finally, StyloMetrix [39] is an open-source multi-lingual tool specifically designed for representing stylometric vectors. It supports Russian language analysis, as well as English, Polish, Ukrainian, and German. This tool offers a multitude of features for syntactic and lexical vector representation.

Stylometry subtasks include authorship attribution, authorship verification, authorship profiling, stylochronometry, and adversarial stylometry [31]. In some cases, authorship profiling helps narrow the search space by identifying different variables such as genre, age, or gender [32–34].

We use the StyloMetrix [39] package to compute over 90 stylometric features for Russian texts and use them further in our text representation (described in Section 4.3.3). A full list of these features is provided in the Appendix A.

Language models, such as RuBERT and multi-lingual BERT (mlBERT), are applied to evaluate the dataset quality and see how they behave, with and without contrastive learning, compared to traditional models. In the context of genre classification, transformers are used to automatically learn representations of text documents that capture the stylistic and semantic features associated with different genres [40,41]. Transformers have been already applied to genre classification in Spanish [16].

There are several pre-trained transformer models available in the literature and in the HuggingFace repository [42], and we describe them here. The BERT multi-lingual model [13] is a multi-lingual variant of BERT (Bidirectional Encoder Representations from Transformers) which supports multiple languages, including Russian, and the "ruBERT-base-cased" transformer model [43] which is an adapted BERT for Russian language-processing tasks. The ruBERT model extends the original BERT architecture [13] by fine-tuning pre-trained multi-lingual embeddings specifically for the Russian language. The adapted model demonstrates improved performance on Russian language tasks compared to the original multi-lingual BERT model.

We use contrastive learning to improve representation learning, in which a model is trained to minimize similarity between samples from different genres and increase similarity between samples of the same genre [26]. By considering both the input data and their corresponding labels, dual contrastive learning encourages the model to learn representations that are discriminatory for both the input data and their labels (genres in our case).

The dual contrastive learning (DualCL) method is suggested in [27] to adapt the contrastive loss to supervised contexts. The DualCL framework learns both the classifier parameters and the properties of input samples simultaneously in the same space. To be more specific, DualCL uses contrastive learning to differentiate between the input samples and these augmented samples, treating the classifier parameters as improved samples associated with unique labels. In Natural Language Processing (NLP), contrastive learning has been already applied to tasks such as text classification, sentiment analysis, and language modeling [14].

In addition to providing a novel dataset and evaluating its quality, our contribution addresses the applicability of stylometry, contrastive learning, and modern language models in genre categorization.

3. The SONATA Dataset

We have considered several online sources of Russian literary texts. Our requirements were as follows:

- A wide, up-to-date, and legitimate selection of titles, and agreements with leading Russian and international publishers;
- Clear genre labels and a wide selection of genres;
- The option to freely and legally download a significant number of text samples in .txt format;
- A convenient site structure that allows automated data collection.

The following options were examined. The LitRes site [44] contains a wide range of e-books across various genres, including fiction, non-fiction, educational materials, and more. For most of the books, text fragments but not the whole texts can be downloaded. However, to use LitRes API and to automatically download multiple text samples, a user is required to pay with a credit card issued in Russia, which may not be suitable for some researchers. http://royallib.com/ (accessed on 1 January 2024) is an online library that offers a large collection of free electronic books [45]. The site provides access to a wide range of e-books, including classic literature, modern novels, non-fiction, educational materials, and more. This site offers books for free, making literature accessible to a broad audience. However, this feature also implies that the text collection is outdated because most modern Russian books are the subject of a copyright. Finally, https://knigogo.net/ (accessed on 1 January 2024) is a Russian-language website that provides fresh news about literature, reviews, and feedback on popular books. It contains a large selection of audiobooks and online books in formats such as fb2, rtf, epub, and txt for iPad, iPhone, Android, and Kindle. It has clear genre labels and a convenient structure that allows efficient parsing. Moreover, it provides free access to text samples.

For these reasons, we have chosen to collect our data from https://knigogo.net/ (accessed on 1 January 2024). We name the resulting dataset SONATA for ruSsian bOoks geNre dATAset. Genre categories were translated into English for the reader's benefit because the source website [46] supports the Russian language only. The dataset is available on GitHub at https://github.com/genakogan/Identification-of-the-genre-of-books.

3.1. The Genres

To build our dataset, we used the genres provided by the Knigogo website at https://knigogo.net/zhanryi/ (accessed on 1 January 2024). Because not all genres and sub-genres provided by the website have a sufficient amount of data for analysis, we filtered out the less-represented genres and combined sub-genres where appropriate, aimed to streamline the classification for more meaningful insights.

As a result, 11 genres were selected for the dataset: science fiction, detective, romance, fantasy, classic, action, non-fiction, contemporary literature, adventure, novel and short stories, and children's books. In non-fiction, we encompassed all genres that do not belong to fiction literature. Due to the relatively small number of books in each sub-genre within non-fiction, considering each sub-genre separately would not be productive for our experiment. The original list of genres on Knigogo and the list of selected genres are depicted in Figure 1. All genres, covered by the SONATA dataset, and their translations are shown in Table 1.

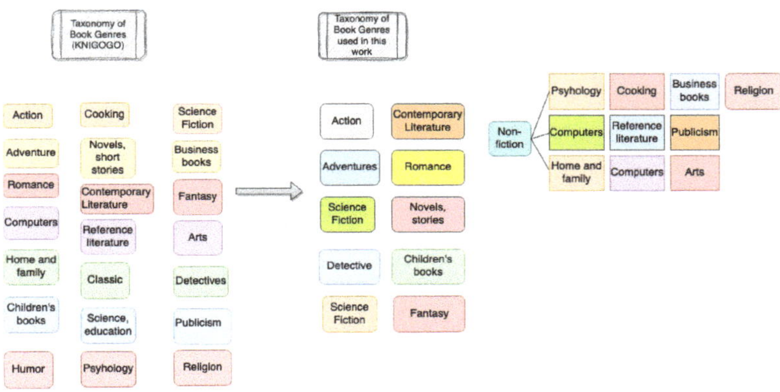

Figure 1. Genre taxonomy in Knigogo and a subset of genres used in the SONATA dataset.

Table 1. Genres in Russian and their translation to English.

Genre (Russian)	Translation
фантастика	Science fiction
Adventure	Detective
Роман	Romance
фэнтези	Fantasy
Классика	Classics
Боевик	Action
Нехудожественная литература	Non-fiction
Современная литература	Contemporary literature
Приключения	Adventure
Новеллы, рассказы	Short stories
Детские книги	Children's books

3.2. Data Processing and Statistics

Book downloading was performed by a Python script; the script extracts URLs leading to pages where individual books can be downloaded first; then, it extracts the URLs for direct download of the text files of these books. Then, the script attempts to download each book, saving them as text files in a directory. The execution of the script is initiated using a specific URL associated with fantasy genre books. A more detailed description of the script is available in the Appendix A.

As a result, 8189 original books were downloaded. However, because some books belong to multiple genres, the total amount of book instances with a single genre label is 10,444.

During the data processing, a series of challenges arose, such as text formatting, removing author names and publisher information, and the volume of texts. We applied the following steps: (1) using a custom Python script, we re-encoded the files into a UTF-8 format; (2) we parsed the second line of text containing the meta-data and removed the authors' names; (3) finally, we extracted books without author names and split them into small parts (denoted by chunks) of 300 words each. Splitting text into chunks allows us to process long texts that exceed the length limit in many pre-trained language models (LMs).

The amount of books and book chunks per genre in the SONATA dataset appears in Table 2. Because some books are attributed to several genres on the original site, the total unique number of books is smaller than the sum of books per genre. We report both of these values in the table.

Table 2. Size of the collected data.

Genres	Books Number	Chunks Number
action	640	59,040
adventure	120	6969
children's	282	4801
classic	463	20,919
detective	1303	51,022
science-fiction	1909	244,217
fantasy	2595	113,044
non-fiction	896	22,632
contemporary	811	28,648
short stories	206	3798
romance	1219	39,779
all genres	10,444	594,869
all genres, unique	8189	414,574

4. Binary and Multi-Class Genre Classification

In binary genre classification, the task involves categorizing texts into two distinct genres. For example, a text can be classified as either fiction or non-fiction, romance or thriller, positive or negative sentiment, etc. In multi-class genre classification, texts are classified into more than two genres or categories. The task is usually more complex than binary genre classification, as the classifier needs to differentiate between multiple classes and assign the most appropriate genre label to each text. Multi-class genre classification problems are often encountered in large-scale text categorization tasks, where texts can belong to diverse and overlapping genres.

4.1. The Pipeline

To evaluate the SONATA dataset for tasks of binary and multi-class genre classification, we first processed and sampled the data (see details in Section 4.2) and generated the appropriate text representation (see details in Section 4.3). Then, we split the text representations into training and test sets, trained the selected model (see Section 4.4) on the training set and evaluated the model on the test set. This pipeline is depicted in Figure 2.

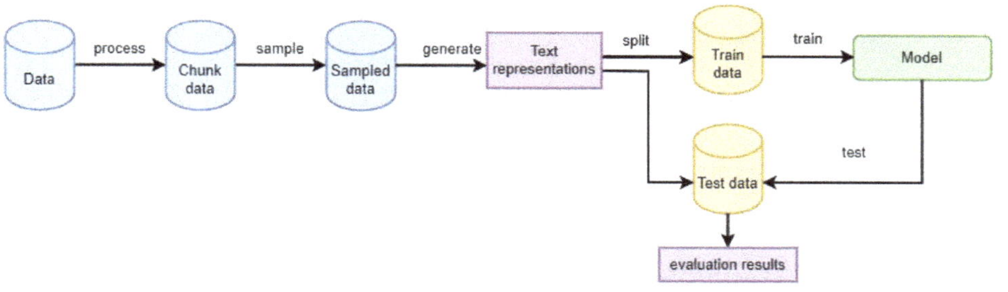

Figure 2. Evaluation pipeline.

4.2. Preprocessing and Data Setup

We did not change the case of the texts and did not remove punctuation in the main setup. The effect of these optional operations on evaluation results is addressed in the Appendix A.

Because of the hardware limitations and data size, we could not apply classification models to the whole dataset. To construct a sample of our dataset, we first selected one random text chunk from every book to avoid the case of author recognition instead of genre recognition. Then, we sampled N chunks at random from every genre, where N is a user-defined parameter. In our experiments, we used $N = 100$. The number of text chunks, average character counts, and the number of unique words for sample size $N = 100$ and every genre is shown in Table 3 (we do not report the average number of words per chunk because all the chunks in our data contain exactly 300 words). The effect of smaller and larger values of N is addressed in the Appendix A.

Table 3. Data statistics.

Genre	Total Chunks	Avg Chars per Chunk	Unique Words	Word(s) with the Highest Frequency	Translation
action	630	2604.4	48,058	просто	simply
adventure	120	2596.1	16,241	время, сказал	time, said
children's	279	2549.8	26,423	сказал	said
classic	479	2164.9	40,127	сказал	said
contemporary	802	2587.3	61,526	очень	very
detective	989	2578.1	63,937	очень	very
fantasy	992	2621.2	67,054	просто	simply
non-fiction	886	2730.2	61,922	которые	which/what
romance	994	2528.7	58,459	просто	simply
science-fiction	989	2632.1	70,551	просто	simply
short-stories	206	2511.0	21,788	очень	very
all	7366	2576.5	200,285	просто	simply

For the binary genre classification task, we select text chunks as a balanced random sample of size N where N is a user-defined parameter. If a genre contains fewer than N book chunks, we select all of them. In each sample, half of the chunks represent positive samples belong to the selected genre, and the other half contain book chunks that represent negative samples and are chosen in a uniformly random fashion from all the other genres. We ensure that no chunks belonging to the same book fall into different sample categories. The positive samples are labeled 1, and the negative samples are labeled 0. For the multiclass genre classification task, we select a random sample of N text chunks from every genre, where N is a user-defined parameter. If a genre contains fewer than N book chunks, all of them are added to the data. The label of every sample is determined by its genre and is a number in the range $[0 \ldots 10]$.

For the evaluation, the obtained balanced dataset is randomly divided into training and test sets with the ratio 80%/20%. This process is illustrated in Figure 3.

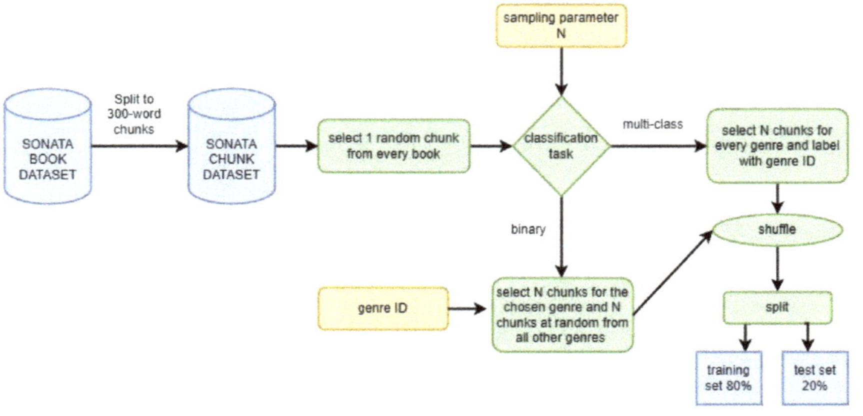

Figure 3. Evaluation pipeline.

4.3. Text Representations

We represent texts as vectors and optionally enhance them with stylometric features. Details are provided in the subsections below. Figure 4 depicts the general pipeline of text representation construction.

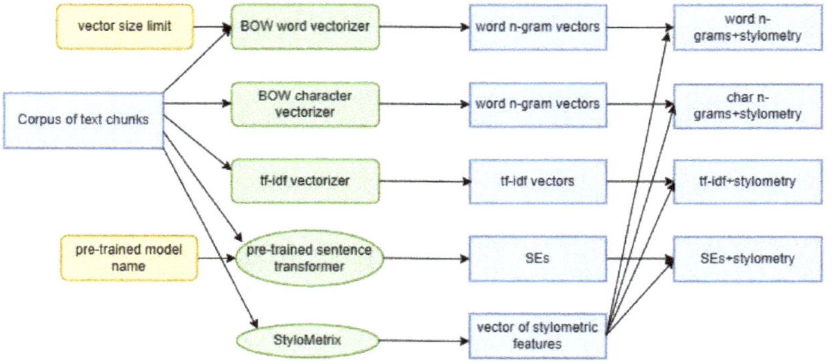

Figure 4. Text representations.

4.3.1. Sentence Embeddings

BERT sentence embeddings [13] are vector representations of entire sentences generated using the BERT model. These embeddings can then be used as features for various downstream NLP tasks. The sentence embeddings (SEs) we use in this work were obtained using one of the pre-trained BERT models (a multi-lingual model of [13] or a Russian BERT model [43]). With both models, the SE vector size is 768.

Figure 5 shows the distribution of books from different genres, where every book is represented by its SE vector computed with ruBERT. For data visualization, we used t-Distributed Stochastic Neighbor Embedding (t-SNE), a common dimensionality reduction technique [47]. It is designed to preserve pairwise similarities, making it more effective at capturing non-linear structures and clusters in high-dimensional data. We can see that contemporary literature (top left) and science fiction (top right) are the only genres for which the data points are partially clustered together. This plot demonstrates that genre classification is a non-trivial task and relying solely on SE can be challenging.

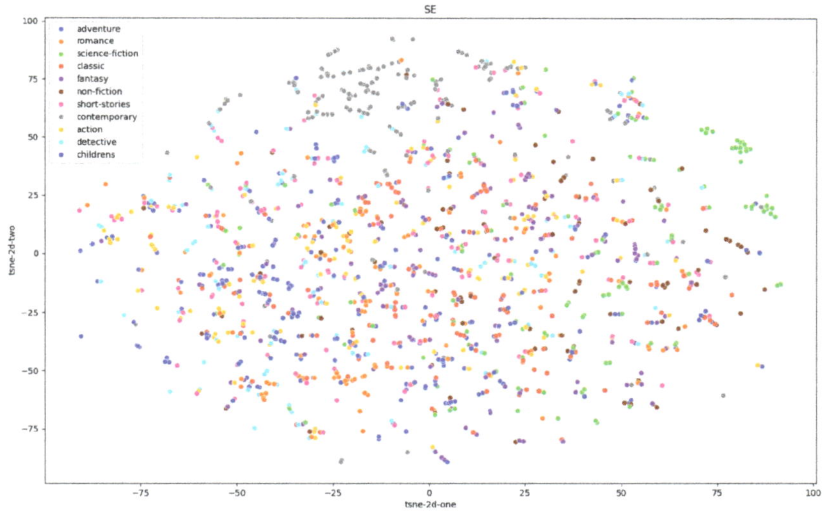

Figure 5. Sentence embedding features of 11 genres represented by t-SNE for samples of size $N = 100$.

4.3.2. BOW Vectors with tf-idf and n-Gram Weights

The concept of Term Frequency-Inverse Document Frequency (tf-idf) constitutes a quantitative measure designed to signify the significance of a term within a document set or corpus. The tf-idf value increases proportionally to the number of times a word appears in the document and is offset by the number of documents in the corpus that contain the word. In our methodology, book chunks were treated as discrete documents, and the entire dataset was regarded as the corpus. We filtered out Russian stopwords using the list provided by the NLTK package [48], to which we added the word 'это' (meaning 'this'); details are provided in the Appendix A.

N-grams are the sequences of n consecutive words or characters seen in the text, where n is a parameter. In our evaluation, we used the values $n = 1, 2, 3$ for both character and word n-grams. In the case of word n-grams, we filtered out Russian stopwords as well using the list provided by NLTK [48]. Vector sizes for these representations for the samples of size $N = 100$ are shown in Table 4. For the multi-class setup, we empirically limited the number of word n-gram features to 10,000 due to very large vector sizes. This does not affect our analysis because this text representation does not provide the best performance.

Table 4. BOW vector lengths for samples of size $N = 100$.

Genre	Char n-Grams Vector Sizes $n = [1, 2, 3]$	Word n-Grams Vector Sizes $n = [1, 2, 3]$	tf-idf Vector Size
action	14,665	46,877	21,781
adventure	13,319	29,283	16,241
children's	13,727	36,189	17,489
classic	16,278	42,994	22,414
contemporary	16,053	46,980	23,588
detective	13,962	46,734	21,841
fantasy	13,389	47,811	22,830
non-fiction	19,688	48,554	23,176
romance	13,237	44,325	19,902
science-fiction	14,759	48,227	23,806
short-stories	14,765	31,974	16,561
all	32,500	403,194	101,350

4.3.3. Stylometric Features

StyloMetrix [49] is a multi-lingual tool designed for generating stylometric vectors for texts in Polish, English, German, Ukrainian, and Russian introduced in [39]. These vectors encode linguistic features related to writing style and can be used for authorship attribution, and genre classification. A total of 95 metrics are supported for the Russian language. The metrics describe lexical forms, parts of speech, syntactic forms, and verb forms. The lexical metrics provide information on plural and singular nouns, and additional morphological features such as animacy (animate/inanimate), gender (feminine, masculine, and neutral), distinguishing between first and second names, and diminutive. Direct and indirect objects as well as cardinal and ordinal numerals are also included in the metrics. Six distinctive lexical forms of pronouns such as demonstrative, personal, total, relative, and indexical are reported, as well as qualitative, quantitative, relative, direct and indirect adjectives. Other lexical features include punctuation, direct speech, and three types of adverb and adjective comparison. A partial list of stylometric features for Russian is provided by the authors of the StyloMetrix package on their GitHub repository [50]; we present a compact list of these features in the Appendix A. We compute stylometric features with StyloMetrix for text chunks in our dataset and use them alone or in conjunction with text representations described in previous sections.

Data visualization of stylometric features with t-SNE for data samples of size $N = 100$ and 11 genres is shown in Figure 6. We can see that, similarly to SEs, contemporary literature (bottom left) and science fiction (bottom right) are the only genres for which the data points are partially clustered together. Therefore, relying solely on stylometric features for genre classification is not expected to produce a good result.

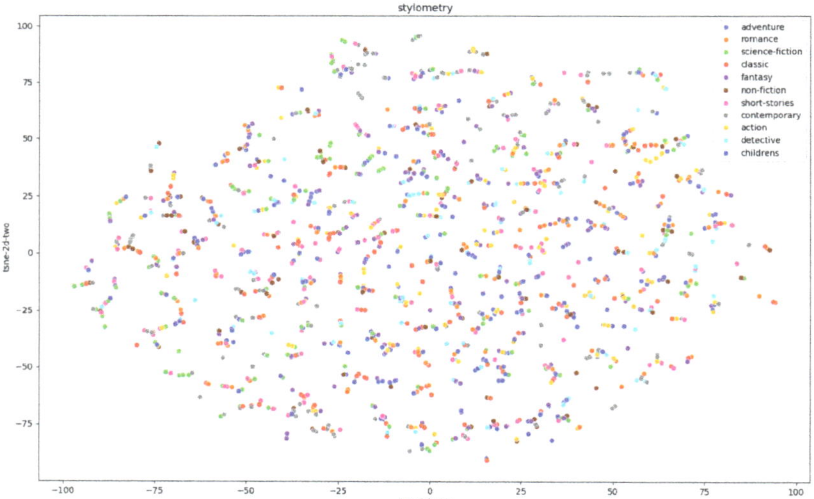

Figure 6. Stylometric features of 11 genres represented by t-SNE for samples of size $N = 100$.

4.4. Classification Models

4.4.1. Traditional Models

An ensemble learning technique called the Random Forest (RF) [28] classifier works by building several decision trees during training. A bootstrapped sample of the training data and a random subset of the characteristics are used to build each tree in the forest. The logistic function, which converts input values into probabilities between 0 and 1, is used in logistic regression (LR) [29] to represent the relationship between the predictor variables and the probability of the result. Gradient boosting is used in the Extreme Gradient Boosting (XGB) [30] classifier, an ensemble learning technique that creates a predictive model. It creates a sequence of decision trees repeatedly, trying to fix the mistakes of the preceding ones with each new tree. We apply RF, LR, and XGB models to all data representations described in Section 4.3.

4.4.2. Voting Ensemble of Traditional Models

A voting-based ensemble classifier approach combines the predictions of multiple base classifiers to make a final decision. Each base classifier is trained independently on the same dataset or subsets of it using different algorithms or parameter settings [51]. During the prediction phase, each base classifier provides its prediction for a given instance. The final prediction is then determined by aggregating the individual predictions through a voting mechanism, where the most commonly predicted class is selected as the ensemble's prediction.

In our voting setup, we use RF, LR, and XGB classifiers described in Section 4.4.1. For the binary genre classification setup, the decision is made based on the majority vote of the three classifiers (i.e., max voting). For the multi-class genre classification setup, we computed the sum of probabilities of every class based on the individual probability distributions produced by each classifier and assigned each sample to the class with the highest accumulated probability.

4.4.3. Fine-Tuned Transformers

We fine-tune and apply fine-tuned transformer models to the texts in our dataset for both tasks—binary genre classification and multi-class genre classification.

The main transformer model we employ is the ruBERT (Russian BERT) model, specifically the `ruBERT-base-cased` variant, which is trained on large-scale Russian derived from the Russian part of Wikipedia and news data [43]. The baseline transformer model is the BERT multi-lingual base model `bert-base-multilingual-uncased` developed by GoogleAI [13]. The model is pre-trained on the top 102 languages (including Russian) with the largest Wikipedia using a masked language modeling objective. We denote this model by mlBERT. Both models utilize a BERT transformer architecture, which employs a bidirectional approach that allows to capture of contextual information from both left and right contexts.

4.4.4. Dual Contrastive Learning

To tackle the problem of genre classification, we also apply the advanced text classification method DualCL [27] that uses contrastive learning with label-aware data augmentation.

The objective function used in this method consists of two contrastive losses, one for labeled data and another for unlabeled data. Contrastive loss is computed for each labeled instance (x_i, y_i) as

$$\mathcal{L}_L = -\log \frac{e^{f(x_i)\cdot g(y_i)}}{\sum_{j=1}^{N} e^{f(x_i)\cdot g(y_j)}}$$

where $f(x_i)$ is the feature representation of input x_i, y_i is the corresponding label of x_i, $g(y_i)$ is the embedding of label y_i, and N is the total number of classes. In our experiments, we use the pre-trained transformer model ruBERT [43] as the basis for feature representation computation. The number of classes N is set to 2 for the task of binary genre classification, and to 11 for the multi-class genre classification. Contrastive loss for unlabeled data is computed as

$$\mathcal{L}_U = -\log \frac{e^{f(x_i)\cdot f(x_j)/\tau}}{\sum_{k=1}^{M} e^{f(x_i)\cdot f(x_k)/\tau}}$$

where $f(x_i)$ and $f(x_j)$ are the feature representations of inputs x_i and x_j, M is the total number of unlabeled instances, and τ is a temperature parameter that controls the concentration of the distribution. We use the default value of τ provided by [52].

Dual contrastive loss is the combination of the contrastive losses for labeled and unlabeled data, along with a regularization term:

$$\mathcal{L} = \mathcal{L}_L + \lambda \mathcal{L}_U + \beta ||\theta||^2$$

where λ and β are hyperparameters that control the trade-off between the supervised and unsupervised losses, and the regularization term θ represents the model parameters. The values of these parameters we use are of the native implementation in [52].

5. Experimental Results

5.1. Hardware Setup

Experiments were performed on a cloud server with a 2-core Intel Xeon CPU, 16 GB of RAM, and 1 NVIDIA TU104GL GPU. The runtime for every experiment setting (binary or multi-class classification) was less than 10 min.

5.2. Software Setup

All non-neural models were implemented in sklearn [53] python package. Our neural models were implemented with PyTorch [54]. NumPy and Pandas libraries were used for data manipulation. For contrastive learning, we utilized the publicly available Python implementation DualCL [52]. Pre-trained transformer models mlBERT [55] and ruBERT [56] were applied.

5.3. Models and Representations

We applied traditional models denoted by RF, LR, and XGB described in Section 4.4.1. We also used the voting model described in Section 4.4.2 and denoted it by 'voting'. Additionally, we fine-tuned the two transformer models described in Section 4.4.1 and denoted the Russian-language model by RuBERT, and the multi-lingual BERT model by mlBERT. Finally, we also applied the dual contrastive model of [27] and denoted it by DualCL. All of the above models were used for the binary classification task and the multi-class classification task.

For the traditional and voting models, we used the eight representations described in Section 4.3. Transformer models and DualCL were applied to the raw text.

5.4. Metrics

We report the metrics described below for all the models.

Precision measures the accuracy of positive predictions made by the model, and it is computed as

$$\text{Precision} = \frac{\text{True Positives}}{\text{True Positives} + \text{False Positives}}$$

Recall or sensitivity measures the ability of the model to correctly identify all positive instances. It is computed as

$$\text{Recall} = \frac{\text{True Positives}}{\text{True Positives} + \text{False Negatives}}$$

The F1 measure combines precision and recall into a single metric and is computed as

$$F1 = 2 \times \frac{\text{Precision} \times \text{Recall}}{\text{Precision} + \text{Recall}}$$

Accuracy is the ratio of correctly predicted instances to the total number of instances in the data:

$$\text{Accuracy} = \frac{\text{True Positives} + \text{True Negatives}}{\text{Total Population}}$$

When assessing the genre classification results, it is essential to employ all of these metrics because each statistic represents a distinct facet of model performance. The accuracy of positive predictions is the main focus of precision, which is important for situations where false positives can be expensive. In situations where missing a relevant instance is very undesirable, recall evaluates the model's capacity to find all relevant examples and ensures that true positives are not overlooked. Because it combines recall and precision, the F1 score offers a balanced metric that is especially helpful in situations when class distributions are unbalanced.

Although accuracy provides a measure of overall correctness, it can be deceptive in situations where class distributions are not uniform since it may be excessively optimistic [57,58]. Moreover, for the task of genre classification, it is vital to see how a model performs on different classes. The most undesirable output would be assigning all text instances to a single genre, implying that the model does not learn anything except the majority rule. What we seek is a model that learns what the genres are and has moderate to high success in identifying all the genres. Thus, employing all four metrics ensures a comprehensive evaluation.

5.5. *Binary Genre Classification Results*

This section describes the evaluation of all of the 11 genres in the SONATA dataset with all the models applied to the task of binary genre identification.

5.5.1. Traditional Models

Table 5 shows the results of traditional model evaluation. Because of the large number of setups (11 genres, 8 representations, and 3 models), we show the representation and the classifier that achieved the best result for every one of the 11 genres. We use here the default setting of $N = 100$ samples for every genre and address different values of N in the Appendix A. We can see that all of the obtained accuracies are above the majority, which is 0.5, as we have balanced data samples. We can see a clear difference in the classification accuracy of different genres—the classic literature is easier to detect (with the accuracy of over 0.93), and the short stories genre is the hardest one (with the accuracy of 0.68). This may be because classic literature tends to employ a more formal and elaborate language style compared to short stories. The language in classic literature often includes archaic words, complex sentence structures, and sophisticated vocabulary, while short stories may use simpler language and have a more straightforward narrative style. In terms of text representation, sentence embeddings perform better for the majority of genres but not for all of them, and stylometric features are helpful in some but not in all of the cases. Tf-idf vectors work best for children's and contemporary literature—children's literature typically uses simpler language with shorter sentences, basic vocabulary, and straightforward syntax that can be captured with tf-idf vectors successfully. Contemporary Russian literature may employ innovative narrative techniques, non-linear storytelling, metafiction, and experimental forms that are also expressed in the vocabulary used. The traditional classifier that performs the best for the majority of genres (but not always) is RF.

Table 5. Results of binary genre classification with traditional models for sample size $N = 100$.

Genre	Representation	Classifier	P	R	F1	Acc
action	SE + stylometry	RF	0.8144	0.8084	0.7997	0.8000
adventure	SE + stylometry	LR	0.8548	0.8542	0.8541	0.8542
children's	tfidf + stylometry	RF	0.8486	0.8555	0.8397	0.8400
classic	SE + stylometry	RF	0.9355	0.9130	0.9179	0.9200
contemporary	tfidf + stylometry	RF	0.7192	0.7150	0.7159	0.7200
detective	SE	LR	0.7905	0.7456	0.7453	0.7600
fantasy	char n-grams	XGB	0.7420	0.7432	0.7399	0.7400
non-fiction	SE	LR	0.8800	0.8824	0.8798	0.8800
romance	SE	XGB	0.7603	0.7552	0.7565	0.7600
science-fiction	SE	LR	0.7890	0.7866	0.7799	0.7800
short-stories	SE	RF	0.6899	0.6899	0.6800	0.6800

5.5.2. The Voting Model

Table 6 shows the results of the evaluation for the ensemble voting models. Because of the large number of setups (11 genres and 8 representations), we show the results for the text representation that achieved the best result for every one of the 11 genres. The arrows indicate the increase (↑) or decrease (↓) of classification accuracy in comparison to the best traditional model for that genre. We can see that in all but one genre (non-fiction) the voting model does not outperform the best single traditional classifier. Non-fiction literature can include a wide range of sub-genres, including history, science, biography, memoirs, essays, and more. Each of these sub-genres may have distinct linguistic features that perhaps can be better captured by a voting ensemble. However, for other genres, single models seem to build different classification functions that do not separate between classes in the same way. The texts that fall to opposite "sides" of each separation function "confuse" the ensemble model.

Table 6. Results of binary genre classification with the voting model; grey color indicates the best result.

Genre	Classifier	P	R	F1	Acc	Comparison to the Best Trad Model
action	SE	0.7890	0.7866	0.7799	0.7800	↓
adventure	SE	0.7937	0.7917	0.7913	0.7917	↓
children's	tfidf + stylometry	0.8621	0.8621	0.8400	0.8400	↓
classic	n-grams	0.9200	0.9227	0.9199	0.9200	↓
contemporary	n-grams + stylometry	0.6782	0.6747	0.6753	0.6800	↓
detective	n-grams + stylometry	0.7585	0.7585	0.7585	0.7600	↓
fantasy	SE + stylometry	0.7388	0.7399	0.7391	0.7400	↓
non-fiction	SE + stylometry	0.9010	0.8977	0.8990	0.9000	↑
romance	SE + stylometry	0.7388	0.7399	0.7391	0.7400	↓
science-fiction	SE	0.7734	0.7681	0.7596	0.7600	↓
short-stories	SE	0.6659	0.6672	0.6599	0.6600	↓

5.5.3. Fine-Tuned Transformers

Table 7 shows the results of fine-tuning and testing BERT-based models—mlBERT and ruBERT—for every one of the 11 genres separately. We can see that both models produce results that are much worse than those of traditional models, and in most cases, these results fall below the majority. This outcome might be the result of several factors. First, our training data might be too small for efficient training of LLMs. Second, distinguishing between one specific genre against a mix of multiple genres is a difficult task based on semantics, without any stylistic features.

To our surprise, classification accuracy is higher for ruBERT for several genres only but not for all of them. This may be an indication that a cross-lingual training of mlBERT allows the model to utilize insights from other languages when classifying Russian texts.

Table 7. Results of binary genre classification with fine-tuned BERT models; the grey color indicates the best accuracy.

Genre	mlBERT F1	mlBERT Acc	ruBERT F1	ruBERT Acc
action	0.4762	0.5600	0.4156	0.5000
adventure	0.4045	0.4792	0.4678	0.4792
children's	0.3107	0.4000	0.5833	0.6000
classic	0.4156	0.5000	0.3189	0.3200
contemporary	0.4165	0.5400	0.3151	0.4600
detective	0.3506	0.5400	0.4746	0.5000
fantasy	0.3689	0.4600	0.4058	0.4400
non-fiction	0.4000	0.4000	0.4802	0.6000
romance	0.3151	0.4600	0.3151	0.4600
science-fiction	0.3506	0.5400	0.5833	0.6000
short-stories	0.4283	0.5600	0.3810	0.4800

5.5.4. Dual Contrastive Learning

Table 8 shows the results of binary genre classification with the DualCL model that employs either ruBERT or mlBERT as its base transformed model. We also indicate by the grey color the best accuracy among the two base transformer models.

We can see that while the results are worse than those of traditional models for every genre, there is a significant improvement over the fine-tuned transformer models. It is also evident that for all but one genre (romance), the DualCL model with ruBERT outperforms the same model with mlBERT.

Table 8. Results of binary genre classification for DualCL; the grey color indicates better results.

Model	Genre	ruBERT F1	ruBERT Acc	mlBERT F1	mlBERT Acc
DualCL	action	0.5703	0.6200	0.5331	0.5600
DualCL	adventure	0.5623	0.5625	0.5279	0.5625
DualCL	children's	0.5536	0.5600	0.5484	0.5600
DualCL	classic	0.6716	0.6800	0.4900	0.5800
DualCL	contemporary	0.6486	0.6600	0.3658	0.5000
DualCL	detective	0.6394	0.6400	0.5942	0.6000
DualCL	fantasy	0.6394	0.6400	0.3969	0.5600
DualCL	non-fiction	0.7391	0.7400	0.3867	0.5400
DualCL	romance	0.6162	0.6200	0.5066	0.6400
DualCL	science-fiction	0.5942	0.6000	0.4172	0.6000
DualCL	short-stories	0.5824	0.6200	0.5785	0.5800

5.6. Multi-Class Genre Classification Results

5.6.1. Traditional Models

Table 9 contains the results produced by traditional classifiers RF, LR, and XGB for all the text representations we employ. For every text representation, we report the results of the best model out of three (full results are contained in the Appendix A). Here, we can see a clear advantage of using sentence embeddings enhanced with stylometric features as text representation. The second best result is achieved by the sentence embeddings without stylometric features. These results indicate that capturing semantic information, linguistic patterns, and stylistic characteristics of the text is much more important for Russian genre classification than the vocabulary.

We can also see that the LR classifier achieves the best result for the majority of text representations. This may be because the logistic regression model is less prone to overfitting, especially when the dataset is small.

Table 9. Results of multi-class genre classification for traditional models; grey color indicates the best result.

Representation	Classifier	P	R	F1	Acc
SE	LR	0.4289	0.4332	0.4264	0.4293
SE + stylometry	LR	0.4415	0.4471	0.4386	0.4367
char n-grams	LR	0.2865	0.2650	0.2711	0.2705
char n-grams + stylometry	LR	0.2694	0.2471	0.2550	0.2506
n-grams	LR	0.3004	0.2866	0.2800	0.2754
n-grams + stylometry	RF	0.2962	0.2911	0.2617	0.2878
tfidf	LR	0.2996	0.2990	0.2372	0.2903
tfidf + stylometry	RF	0.2503	0.2617	0.2308	0.2581

Table 10 shows the per-genre precision, recall, and F-measure produced by the best model (LR and SE + stylometry text representation). We can see that the model does attribute all instances to a single class but is producing real predictions for all the genres. Some genres are identified better than others—adventure, contemporary literature, and science fiction. It may be because these genres typically adhere to clear conventions and tropes that provide consistent patterns and signals that a classification model can leverage.

In contrast, genres with more fluid boundaries pose greater challenges for classification due to their variability and ambiguity.

Table 10. Best result details of multi-class genre classification for traditional models (SE + stylometry, LR).

Genre	P	R	F1
action	0.3654	0.3878	0.3762
adventure	0.7353	0.5814	0.6494
children's	0.3519	0.5000	0.4130
classic	0.3478	0.3902	0.3678
contemporary	0.6000	0.7241	0.6562
detective	0.3600	0.3333	0.3462
fantasy	0.3514	0.4062	0.3768
non-fiction	0.4500	0.4500	0.4500
romance	0.4375	0.2593	0.3256
science-fiction	0.5610	0.6571	0.6053
short-stories	0.2963	0.2286	0.2581

5.6.2. The Voting Model

Table 11 shows the evaluation results of the voting ensemble model applied to different text representations. The arrow indicates an increase or decrease in accuracy concerning the results produced by individual traditional models. In general, the voting model does not reach the high scores of the best single traditional models; however, there is an improvement in accuracy for text representations that use word n-grams and character n-grams with stylometric features. N-grams capture local syntactic and semantic information, which might be beneficial for capturing genre-specific patterns, and using multiple classifiers may help to identify the most probable outcome that enhances classification accuracy.

Table 11. Results of multi-class genre classification for the voting model.

Representation	P	R	F1	Acc	vs. Best Trad. Model
SE	0.4076	0.4052	0.3995	0.3970	↓
SE + stylometry	0.3978	0.3977	0.3924	0.3921	↓
char n-grams	0.2779	0.2635	0.2651	0.2655	↓
char n-grams + stylometry	0.2740	0.2595	0.2630	0.2605	↑
n-grams	0.2915	0.2965	0.2799	0.2854	↑
n-grams + stylometry	0.3181	0.3044	0.2923	0.2953	↑
tfidf	0.2286	0.2459	0.2072	0.2382	↓
tfidf + stylometry	0.2935	0.2956	0.2640	0.2878	↓

The best text representation for the voting model is sentence embeddings. The detailed scores for all the genres produced by this model are shown in Table 12, with an arrow indicating a comparison with the F1 scores of the best single traditional model result shown in Table 10. We can see that while the combined score of this voting model is lower than that of its single-model counterpart, there are individual genres such as children's books, classic literature, fantasy, and romance novels that have higher F1 scores. Again, we observe that some genres such as adventure and science fiction are 'easier' to identify in this task.

5.6.3. Fine-Tuned Transformer Models

Table 13 shows the evaluation results of two fine-tuned transformer models, ruBERT and mlBERT, for the task of muli-class genre classification. The scores are low for both of the models, and the per-genre detailed scores show that both models failed to learn and classify all texts as belonging to a single class. There is a slight advantage to the mlBERT model over ruBERT, similar to the binary classification task. We believe that classifying books into one out of multiple genres based purely on their vocabulary and semantics is a very difficult task and something beyond embeddings learned by transformers needs to be provided to a classification layer. One such thing is the stylistic characteristics of the text provided with stylometric features.

Table 12. Best result details of multi-class genre classification for the voting model (SE + stylometry); grey color indicates improvement.

Genre	P	R	F1	vs. Best Trad. Model
action	0.3000	0.3061	0.3030	↓
adventure	0.7931	0.5349	0.6389	↓
children's	0.3704	0.5263	0.4348	↑
classic	0.3542	0.4146	0.3820	↑
contemporary	0.5556	0.6897	0.6154	↓
detective	0.3200	0.2963	0.3077	↓
fantasy	0.3500	0.4375	0.3889	↑
non-fiction	0.4000	0.3000	0.3429	↓
romance	0.4103	0.2963	0.3441	↑
science-fiction	0.5366	0.6286	0.5789	↓
short-stories	0.2308	0.1714	0.1967	↓

Table 13. Multi-class classification results of ruBERT and mlBERT transformer models; grey color indicates better results.

classifier	P	R	F1	Acc
ruBERT	0.0087	0.0841	0.0158	0.0918
		per genre scores		
genre	P	R	F1	
action	0	0	0	
adventure	0	0	0	
children's	0	0	0	
classic	0	0	0	
contemporary	0	0	0	
detective	0	0	0	
fantasy	0	0	0	
non-fiction	0	0	0	
romance	0	0	0	
science-fiction	0	0	0	
short-stories	0.0956	0.925	0.1733	
classifier	P	R	F1	Acc
mlBERT	0.0091	0.0909	0.0166	0.0993
		per genre scores		
genre	P	R	F1	
action	0	0	0	
adventure	0	0	0	
children's	0	0	0	
classic	0	0	0	
contemporary	0	0	0	
detective	0	0	0	
fantasy	0.1005	1	0.1826	
non-fiction	0	0	0	
romance	0	0	0	
science-fiction	0	0	0	
short-stories	0	0	0	

5.6.4. Dual Contrastive Learning

Table 14 contains the evaluation results for the DualCL model with ruBERT and mlBERT backends. The model was trained for 100 epochs, and the best score that was achieved at epoch 97 is reported in the table, together with the per-genre scores. The scores are much higher than those of fine-tuned transformers, but they do not reach the results produced by the best single traditional model. Again, we see that some genres such as non-fiction and classic literature achieve higher scores than other genres. Similarly to the binary classification results and the fine-tuning results, the model that uses mlBERT as the backend, surprisingly, outperformed ruBERT in terms of the final accuracy. However, for specific genres, ruBERT-based DualCL performs better for 9 out of 11 genres (the grey color in the table indicates the best F1 genre for both variants of the DualCL model).

Table 14. Multi-class classification results for the DualCL model; grey color indicates better results.

classifier	P	R	F1	Acc
DualCL ruBERT	0.3706	0.3400	0.3400	0.3704
		per genre scores		
genre	P	R	F1	
action	0.2761	0.3700	0.3162	
adventure	0.1020	0.2083	0.1370	
children's	0.5714	0.2857	0.3810	
classic	0.4497	0.6979	0.5469	
contemporary	0.2039	0.3100	0.2460	
detective	0.3220	0.1900	0.2390	
fantasy	0.4353	0.3700	0.4000	
non-fiction	0.8228	0.6500	0.7263	
romance	0.3763	0.3500	0.3627	
science-fiction	0.4561	0.2600	0.3312	
short-stories	0.0606	0.0476	0.0533	
classifier	P	R	F1	Acc
DualCL mlBERT	0.3582	0.3571	0.3354	0.3758
		per genre scores		
genre	P	R	F1	
action	0.3684	0.2100	0.2675	
adventure	0.1400	0.2917	0.1892	
children's	0.3011	0.5000	0.3758	
classic	0.6092	0.5521	0.5792	
contemporary	0.1970	0.2600	0.2241	
detective	0.3409	0.1500	0.2083	
fantasy	0.3286	0.4600	0.3833	
non-fiction	0.7660	0.7200	0.7423	
romance	0.3473	0.5800	0.4345	
science-fiction	0.3750	0.1800	0.2432	
short-stories	0.1667	0.0238	0.0417	

5.7. Punctuation Importance

To verify our assumption about the inherent importance of punctuation for genre classification, we conducted a series of additional experiments. In this experiment, we removed punctuation marks from the texts. This act decreased slightly the sizes of BOW representations (details are provided in the Appendix A). We applied the experimental setup of Section 4.2 to the simplified SONATA dataset and used the same sample size of $N = 100$ book chunks per genre.

The results of the binary genre classification for this setup for traditional classifiers appear in Table 15. We show the best results for every genre and indicate the representation and classifier that achieve them. The arrows indicate an increase or decrease in accuracy in comparison to the best traditional model results shown on texts with punctuation. We see that in most cases, the results are inferior to those of Section 5.5.1, and stylometric features have a less prominent role. However, for 3 genres out of 11, the results are improved—fantasy, romance, and non-fiction. In these genres, the content words play a crucial role in conveying the theme and style of the text. It is possible that by removing punctuation, these content words are emphasized and can become more indicative of genre characteristics.

Table 15. Binary classification with traditional classifiers with sample size $N = 100$.

Genre	Representation	Classifier	P	R	F1	Acc	vs. Best Punct Acc
action	SE	LR	0.6987	0.6997	0.6989	0.7000	↓
adventure	SE	RF	0.7500	0.7500	0.7500	0.7500	↓
children's	SE	LR	0.8346	0.7989	0.8069	0.8200	↓
classic	char n-grams	XGB	0.5455	0.5197	0.4673	0.5800	↓
contemporary	SE + stylometry	RF	0.7167	0.7093	0.6989	0.7000	↓
detective	char n-grams	LR	0.6575	0.6562	0.6566	0.6600	↓
fantasy	SE + stylometry	RF	0.7788	0.7802	0.7792	0.7800	↑
non-fiction	tfidf + stylometry	RF	0.9600	0.9630	0.9599	0.9600	↑
romance	SE	LR	0.8622	0.8639	0.8599	0.8600	↑
science-fiction	SE + stylometry	LR	0.6502	0.6473	0.6394	0.6400	↓
short-stories	tfidf + stylometry	LR	0.6619	0.6430	0.6380	0.6531	↓

The results of multi-class genre classification for this setup appear in Table 16. We applied single traditional models because they produced the best scores on the original SONATA dataset. In a few cases, an improvement was achieved; however, none of these setups outperformed the best model-representation combo in the original setting that uses the data with punctuation.

Table 16. Multi-class classification with traditional classifiers with sample size $N = 100$, with and without punctuation; grey color indicates improvement.

Representation	Classifier	Acc with Punctuation	Acc without Punctuation
SE	RF	0.3375	0.2926
SE	LR	0.4293	0.3232
SE	XGB	0.2978	0.2850
SE + stylometry	RF	0.3400	0.3181
SE + stylometry	LR	0.4367	0.3282
SE + stylometry	XGB	0.3127	0.2799
char n-grams	RF	0.2333	0.2214
char n-grams	LR	0.2705	0.2366
char n-grams	XGB	0.2432	0.1934
char n-grams + stylometry	RF	0.2531	0.2087
char n-grams + stylometry	LR	0.2506	0.2316
char n-grams + stylometry	XGB	0.2382	0.1985
n-grams	RF	0.2333	0.2341
n-grams	LR	0.2754	0.2748
n-grams	XGB	0.1712	0.1501
n-grams + stylometry	RF	0.2878	0.2316
n-grams + stylometry	LR	0.2779	0.2621
n-grams + stylometry	XGB	0.2233	0.1985
tfidf	RF	0.2432	0.2341
tfidf	LR	0.2903	0.2545
tfidf	XGB	0.1439	0.1908
tfidf + stylometry	RF	0.2804	0.2545
tfidf + stylometry	LR	0.2531	0.2545
tfidf + stylometry	XGB	0.2134	0.1832

To further verify our hypothesis about the importance of punctuation, we also tested the ensemble voting model for the multi-class genre classification; the results are shown in Table 17. No model–representation setup achieved an increase in accuracy over the non-modified dataset. Therefore, we can conclude that preserving punctuation is vital for genre classification.

Table 17. Multi-class classification with the voting model, sample size $N = 100$, with and without punctuation (grey color indicates better result in each case).

Representation	Acc with Punctuation	Acc without Punctuation
SE	0.3970	0.3282
SE + stylometry	0.3921	0.3435
char n-grams	0.2655	0.2392
char n-grams + stylometry	0.2605	0.2494
n-grams	0.2854	0.2468
n-grams + stylometry	0.2953	0.2875
tfidf	0.2382	0.2265
tfidf + stylometry	0.2878	0.2723

6. Conclusions

In this study, we studied the task of genre classification for Russian literature. By introducing a novel dataset comprising Russian books spanning 11 different genres, we facilitate research in genre classification for Russian texts and evaluate multiple classification models to discern their effectiveness in this context. Through extensive experimentation, we explored the impact of different text representations, such as stylometric features, on genre classification accuracy.

Our experimental evaluation confirms that stylometric features improve classification accuracy in most cases, especially in binary genre classification. Therefore, RQ1 is also answered positively. Our evaluation also shows that while there are genres that receive higher accuracy scores, the results depend more on the model being used than on the features. Thus, some genres are 'easier' for traditional models, while other genres are 'easier' for contrastive learning, and so on. It means that RQ2 cannot be answered positively. We have also verified that contrastive learning performs much better than transformer models for both classification tasks, answering RQ3. Finally, we have shown that removing punctuation decreases classification accuracy and thus answered positively to RQ4. We have also found, surprisingly, that the ruBERT model pre-trained on a large Russian corpus performs worse than the multi-lingual BERT model for the multi-class classification task. For the binary classification, ruBERT performs worse than multi-lingual BERT on 8 out of 11 genres, answering negatively to RQ5.

Our study highlights the multi-faceted nature of genre classification in Russian literature and underscores the importance of considering diverse factors, including linguistic characteristics, cultural nuances, and genre-specific features. An accurate model of genre classification is capable of performing literary analysis by automating the identification and categorization of texts. This can help researchers better understand how genres in Russian literature have evolved with social and political changes in Russian-speaking nations by, for example, enabling them to identify trends and changes in literary styles across time. Furthermore, by examining relatively small (300-word) text samples rather than the whole texts, our classification models can be utilized to quickly search and retrieve books by genre given the extensive holdings of Russian literary works in digital libraries and archives.

While our research provides valuable insights into genre classification for Russian texts, it also reveals limitations and areas for future exploration.

7. Limitations and Future Research Directions

While our study provides valuable insights into genre classification for Russian literature, several limitations are worth mentioning. Firstly, the dataset we compiled, though extensive, may not encompass the entirety of Russian literary genres, potentially limiting the generalizability of our findings to all facets of Russian literature.

Furthermore, our evaluation of classification models is based on a subset of the dataset, which may not fully capture the diversity and complexity of genre classification for Russian books. The selection of this subset could introduce sampling bias and impact the robustness of our conclusions.

Another limitation relates to the choice of text representations and classification models evaluated in our study. While we explored a range of traditional machine learning models and state-of-the-art deep learning architectures, there may exist alternative approaches or models that could yield superior performance in genre classification tasks. Moreover, the effectiveness of stylometric features and other text representations may vary across different genres, and our study may not fully capture this variability.

Finally, the research questions addressed in our study provide valuable insights into the genre classification of Russian books; however, they represent only a subset of the broader landscape of research questions in this domain. Future studies may explore additional research questions, such as the impact of personal authorial style on genre classification, the role of narrative structure in genre categorization, transfer learning from other languages, or the influence of reader preferences on genre classification outcomes.

Addressing these limitations through further research could enhance the robustness and applicability of genre classification systems for Russian texts.

Author Contributions: Conceptualization, N.V. and M.L.; methodology, N.V. and M.T.; software, N.V. and G.K.; validation, N.V., M.T. and M.L.; formal analysis, N.V. and M.L.; investigation, M.T.; resources, G.K.; data curation, M.T.; writing—original draft preparation, N.V. and M.T.; writing—review and editing, N.V., M.L. and M.T.; supervision, N.V. and M.L. All authors have read and agreed to the published version of the manuscript.

Funding: This research received no external funding.

Institutional Review Board Statement: Not applicable.

Informed Consent Statement: Not applicable.

Data Availability Statement: The SONATA dataset is residing in repository on GitHub at https://github.com/genakogan/Identification-of-the-genre-of-books. It is freely available to the NLP community.

Conflicts of Interest: The authors declare no conflicts of interest.

Abbreviations

The following abbreviations are used in this manuscript:

NLP	Natural Language Processing
RQ	Research Question
RF	Random Forest
XGB	eXtreme Gradient Boost
LR	Logistic Regression
CL	Contrastive Learning
RNN	Recurrent Neural Network
SVM	Support Vector Machine
BERT	Bidirectional Encoder Representations from Transformers
R	Recall
P	Precision
F1	F1 measure

Appendix A

Appendix A.1. The List of Stylometric Features

We use the features provided by the StyloMetrix package [49]. Tables A1–A3 contains the lists of these features according. Unless specified otherwise, the incidence (amount) of appearances of a feature is reported.

Table A1. Lexical features provided by the StyloMetric tool.

Lexical Features
type-token ratio for words lemmas, content words, function words, content words types, function words types, nouns in plural, nouns in singular, proper names, personal names, animate nouns, inanimate nouns, neutral nouns, feminine nouns, masculine nouns, feminine proper nouns, masculine proper nouns, surnames, given names, flat multiwords expressions, direct objects, indirect objects, nouns in Nominative case, nouns in Genitive case, nouns in Dative case, nouns in Accusative case, nouns in Instrumental case, nouns in Locative case, qualitative adj positive, relative adj, qualitative comparative adj, qualitative superlative adj, direct adjective, indirect adjective, punctuation, dots, comma, semicolon, colon, dashes, numerals, relative pronouns, indexical pronouns, reflexive pronoun, posessive pronoun, negative pronoun, positive adverbs, comparative adverbs, superlative adverbs

Table A2. Part-of-speech features provided by the StyloMetric tool.

Part-of-Speech Features
verbs, nouns, adjectives, adverbs, determiners, interjections, conjunctions, particles, numerals, prepositions, pronouns, code-switching, number of words in narrative sentences, number of words in negative sentences, number of words in parataxis sentences, number of words in sentences that do not have any root verbs, words in sentences with quotation marks, number of words in exclamatory sentences, number of words in interrogative sentences, number of words in general questions, number of words in special questions, number of words in alternative questions, number of words in tag questions, number of words in elliptic sentences, number of positionings, number of words in conditional sentences, number of words in imperative sentences, number of words in amplified sentences

Table A3. Grammar features provided by the StyloMetric tool.

Grammar Features
root verbs in imperfect aspect, all verbs in imperfect aspect, active voice, root verbs in perfect form, all verbs in perfect form, verbs in the present tense, indicative mood, imperfect aspect, verbs in the past tense, indicative mood, imperfect aspect, verbs in the past tense, indicative mood, perfect aspect, verbs in the future tense, indicative mood, perfect aspect, verbs in the future tense, indicative mood, imperfect aspect, simple verb forms, verbs in the future tense, indicative mood, complex verb forms, verbs in infinitive, verbs in the passive form, transitive verbs, intransitive verbs, impersonal verbs, passive participles, active participles, adverbial perfect participles, adverbial imperfect participles

Appendix A.2. The List of Russian Stopwords

Below, we show the list of Russian stopwords produced that we used and their translation.

Stopwords (Russian)
и, в, во, не, что, он, на, я, с, со, как, а, то, все, она, так, его, но, да, ты, к, у, же, вы, за, бы, по, только, ее, мне, было, вот, от, меня, еще, нет, о, из, ему, теперь, когда, даже, ну, вдруг, ли, если, уже, или, ни, быть, был, него, до, вас, нибудь, опять, уж, вам, ведь, там, потом, себя, ничего, ей, может, они, тут, где, есть, надо, ней, для, мы, тебя, их, чем, была, сам, чтоб, без, будто, чего, раз, тоже, себе, под, будет, ж, тогда, кто, этот, того, потому, этого, какой, совсем, ним, здесь, этом, один, почти, мой, тем, чтобы, нее, сейчас, были, куда, зачем, всех, никогда, можно, при, наконец, два, об, другой, хоть, после, над, больше, тот, через, эти, нас, про, всего, них, какая, много, разве, три, эту, моя, впрочем, хорошо, свою, этой, перед, иногда, лучше, чуть, том, нельзя, такой, им, более, всегда, конечно, всю, между
Translation
and, in, in the, not, that, he, on, I, with, with, like, and, then, all, she, so, his, but, yes, you, to, at, already, you (plural), behind, would, by, only, her, to me, was, here, from, me, yet, no, about, to him, now, when, even, well, suddenly, whether, if, already, or, neither, to be, was, him, before, to you, ever, again, already, you (plural), after all, there, then, oneself, nothing, to her, can, they, here, where, there is, need, her, for, we, you (singular), them, than, was, oneself, without, as if, of what, time, also, to oneself, under, will be, what, then, who, this, of that, therefore, of this, what kind, completely, him, here, in this, one, almost, my, by, her, now, were, where, why, all, never, can, at, finally, two, about, other, even if, after, above, more, that, through, these, us, about, all, what kind of, many, whether, three, this, my, however, well, her own, this, before, sometimes, better, a bit, that, cannot, such, to them, more, always, of course, whole, between

Appendix A.3. BOW Vector Statistics for the No-Punctuation SONATA Data Sample

The sizes of BOW vectors for the SONATA dataset sample with $N = 100$ are provided in Table A4.

Table A4. BOW vector lengths for samples of size $N = 100$ without punctuation.

Genre	Char n-Grams Vector Sizes $n = [1,2,3]$	Word n-Grams Vector Sizes $n = [1,2,3]$	tf-idf Vector Size
action	10,593	35,521	17,923
adventure	9085	18,236	11,506
children's	11,647	27,262	14,581
classic	11,907	27,456	15,905
contemporary	11,844	35,396	19,132
detective	11,750	34,963	18,532
fantasy	9334	35,635	18,044
non-fiction	13,900	34,900	17,867
romance	10,867	33,398	16,553
science-fiction	9590	35,824	18,799
short-stories	9298	23,673	13,442
all	23,902	315,812	87,706

Appendix A.4. Changing the Number of Samples

Because of HW limitations, we were unable to run all the experiments on full data, and we used the sampling procedure described in Section 4.2 with the default value of $N = 100$ randomly sampled book chunks per genre. However, we examined the setups with fewer and more sampled chunks ($N = 50$ and $N = 150$). Tables A5 and A6 show the sizes of BOW vectors for both of these setups.

Table A5. BOW vector lengths for samples of size $N = 50$.

Genre	Char n-Grams Vector Sizes $n = [1,2,3]$	Word n-Grams Vector Sizes $n = [1,2,3]$	tf-idf Vector Size
action	12,104	23,470	13,037
adventure	11,845	18,024	11,108
children's	11,803	23,115	12,414
classic	13,332	23,692	14,159
contemporary	12,956	23,747	14,167
detective	11,680	24,236	13,564
fantasy	10,910	24,235	13,639
non-fiction	14,435	24,656	13,676
romance	10,852	22,598	12,048
science-fiction	11,866	24,234	14,016
short-stories	12,853	20,803	11,874
all	26,192	222,487	69,362

Table A6. BOW vector lengths for samples of size $N = 200$.

Genre	Char n-Grams Vector Sizes $n = [1,2,3]$	Word n-Grams Vector Sizes $n = [1,2,3]$	tf-idf Vector Size
action	16,721	77,373	31,126
adventure	13,319	29,283	16,241
children's	15,911	58,789	24,921
classic	18,091	62,025	29,327
contemporary	19,068	84,345	36,132
detective	16,964	93,493	35,765
fantasy	15,759	95,349	37,162
non-fiction	23,288	90,602	35,625
romance	15,637	88,178	32,476
science-fiction	17,351	95,400	39,043
short-stories	16,684	46,214	21,788
all	37,228	687,100	139,054

Table A7 shows evaluation results of traditional models for both of these sampling setups and their comparison to the default sampling setup of $N = 100$ for the task of multi-class genre classification. The arrows show a decrease or increase in classification accuracy of the sampling setup $N = 100$ as compared to $N = 50$, and the sampling setup $N = 150$ as compared to $N = 100$. We observe that, with some exceptions, increasing sample size does improve the classification accuracy of traditional models across representations. However, it is worth mentioning that increasing the sample size makes running advanced transformer models in our HW setup much slower and in some cases, impossible.

Table A7. Comparing smaller and larger sample sizes for multi-class genre classification with traditional models; grey color indicates the best result.

Representation	Classifier	Sample Size $N = 50$ Acc	Sample Size $N = 100$ Acc	Sample Size $N = 150$ Acc
SE	RF	0.3645	0.3375 ↓	0.3462 ↑
SE	LR	0.3785	0.4293 ↑	0.4095 ↓
SE	XGB	0.2617	0.2978 ↑	0.3163 ↑
SE + stylometry	RF	0.3458	0.3400 ↓	0.3374 ↓
SE + stylometry	LR	0.3738	0.4367 ↑	0.4130 ↓
SE + stylometry	XGB	0.2710	0.3127 ↑	0.3603 ↑
char n-grams	RF	0.2710	0.2333 ↓	0.2882 ↑
char n-grams	LR	0.2477	0.2705 ↑	0.2953 ↑
char n-grams	XGB	0.1729	0.2432 ↑	0.3005 ↑
char n-grams + stylometry	RF	0.2336	0.2531 ↑	0.2882 ↑
char n-grams + stylometry	LR	0.2477	0.2506 ↑	0.3146 ↑
char n-grams + stylometry	XGB	0.2290	0.2382 ↑	0.3040 ↑
n-grams	RF	0.2570	0.2333 ↓	0.2794 ↑
n-grams	LR	0.3084	0.2754 ↓	0.2988 ↑
n-grams	XGB	0.1168	0.1712 ↑	0.2320 ↑
n-grams + stylometry	RF	0.2757	0.2878 ↑	0.3076 ↑
n-grams + stylometry	LR	0.3037	0.2779 ↓	0.2917 ↑
n-grams + stylometry	XGB	0.2523	0.2233 ↓	0.2812 ↑
tfidf	RF	0.2383	0.2432 ↑	0.2865 ↑
tfidf	LR	0.2991	0.2903 ↓	0.3409 ↑
tfidf	XGB	0.0981	0.1439 ↑	0.2021 ↑
tfidf + stylometry	RF	0.2523	0.2804 ↑	0.2917 ↑
tfidf + stylometry	LR	0.2430	0.2531 ↑	0.3093 ↑
tfidf + stylometry	XGB	0.2664	0.2134 ↓	0.2654 ↑

Appendix A.5. Full Results of Traditional Models for the Multi-Class Genre Classification Task

Table A8 contains the full list of results for the multi-class classification task performed with traditional models.

Table A8. Full results of multi-class genre classification for traditional models; grey color indicates the best result.

Representation	Classifier	P	R	F1	Acc
SE	RF	0.3221	0.3310	0.3113	0.3275
SE	LR	0.4289	0.4332	0.4264	0.4293
SE	XGB	0.3154	0.3019	0.2997	0.3027
SE + stylometry	RF	0.3361	0.3182	0.3003	0.3176
SE + stylometry	LR	0.4415	0.4471	0.4386	0.4367
SE + stylometry	XGB	0.3082	0.3075	0.2961	0.2978
char n-grams	RF	0.2163	0.2315	0.2034	0.2333
char n-grams	LR	0.2865	0.2650	0.2711	0.2705
char n-grams	XGB	0.2180	0.2373	0.2188	0.2357
char n-grams + stylometry	RF	0.2150	0.2436	0.2080	0.2407
char n-grams + stylometry	LR	0.2694	0.2471	0.2550	0.2506
char n-grams + stylometry	XGB	0.2444	0.2480	0.2357	0.2457
n-grams	RF	0.2055	0.2494	0.2062	0.2333
n-grams	LR	0.3004	0.2866	0.2800	0.2754
n-grams	XGB	0.2011	0.1771	0.1600	0.1712
n-grams + stylometry	RF	0.2962	0.2911	0.2617	0.2878
n-grams + stylometry	LR	0.2956	0.2868	0.2784	0.2779
n-grams + stylometry	XGB	0.2373	0.2349	0.2190	0.2233
tfidf	RF	0.2234	0.2332	0.1939	0.2283
tfidf	LR	0.2996	0.2990	0.2372	0.2903
tfidf	XGB	0.2071	0.1964	0.1794	0.1911
tfidf + stylometry	RF	0.2503	0.2617	0.2308	0.2581
tfidf + stylometry	LR	0.2325	0.2549	0.2190	0.2531
tfidf + stylometry	XGB	0.2187	0.2289	0.1975	0.2233

Appendix A.6. The Python Script Used to Download Books from knigogo.net

The script is freely available at https://github.com/genakogan/Identification-of-the-genre-of-books. Due to size limitations, we do not provide it here in full. Its main parts are described below.

- The `url_download_for_each_book` function takes a URL (in this case, a page with links to free books) and retrieves the HTML content. It then parses the HTML to extract URLs that link to book download pages, specifically those that match a pattern (starts with https://knigogo.net/knigi/ (accessed on 1 January 2024) and end with `/#lib_book_download`).
- The `url_text_download_for_each_book` function takes the list of book download URLs obtained in the previous step and retrieves the HTML content of each page. It then parses these pages to extract URLs of the actual text files.
- The `download_url` function attempts to download the content of a given URL and returns the content if successful.
- The `download_book` function receives a text file URL, a book ID, and a save path. It downloads the text file's content and saves it locally as a .txt file in the specified directory.

Appendix A.7. Validation on Texts from a Different Source

To ensure that our best models for genre classification are suitable for texts from different sources, we conducted an additional experiment.

We manually downloaded an additional 200 texts from the https://www.rulit.me (accessed on 15 May 2024) online book repository, and performed the pre-processing described in Section 3.2. We chose the Russian language, .txt format, and the genre of science fiction, which constitutes the most texts in the repository. The positive samples were chosen to be 100 texts belonging to the science fiction genre, and the negative samples were another 100 texts that belong to other genres such as detectives, children's books, romance, documentaries, adventure, thrillers, ancient literature, esoterics, home economics, science, and culture. Then, we split all the texts into 300-word chunks and preserved one chunk from each book.

In the next step, we trained our best-performing models on the training part of the SONATA dataset for the science fiction genre and evaluated them on the rulit.me data. The results of this binary cross-source genre classification are shown in Tables A9 and A10. In Table A9, we can see that traditional models achieve good results on the new data, and the best classifier is RF, which is consistent with our findings in Section 5.5.1. It is also evident that adding stylometric features is beneficial in this case, and the best text representation is n-grams combined with stylometry. Table A10 contains the results of the voting model evaluation and shows that the best representation in this setup is the same as above. However, similarly to the SONATA dataset tests, the voting models, while producing decent results, fail to achieve the same accuracy as the best traditional model in Table A9.

Table A9. Evaluation results for traditional models on the rulit.me data (accessed on 15 May 2024); grey color indicates best results.

Genre	Representation	Classifier	F1	Acc
science-fiction	SE	RF	0.6900	0.6900
science-fiction	SE	LR	0.7097	0.7100
science-fiction	SE	XGB	0.6387	0.6400
science-fiction	SE + stylometry	RF	0.7698	0.7700
science-fiction	SE + stylometry	LR	0.6995	0.7000
science-fiction	SE + stylometry	XGB	0.6297	0.6300
science-fiction	char n-grams	RF	0.6394	0.6400
science-fiction	char n-grams	LR	0.6808	0.6900
science-fiction	char n-grams	XGB	0.6673	0.6700
science-fiction	char n-grams + stylometry	RF	0.7796	0.7800

Table A9. *Cont.*

Genre	Representation	Classifier	F1	Acc
science-fiction	char n-grams + stylometry	LR	0.6784	0.6900
science-fiction	char n-grams + stylometry	XGB	0.5900	0.5900
science-fiction	n-grams	RF	0.6970	0.7000
science-fiction	n-grams	LR	0.7100	0.7100
science-fiction	n-grams	XGB	0.6052	0.6100
science-fiction	n-grams + stylometry	RF	0.7300	0.7300
science-fiction	n-grams + stylometry	LR	0.7100	0.7100
science-fiction	n-grams + stylometry	XGB	0.6096	0.6100
science-fiction	tfidf	RF	0.6532	0.6600
science-fiction	tfidf	LR	0.6800	0.6800
science-fiction	tfidf	XGB	0.5512	0.5600
science-fiction	tfidf + stylometry	RF	0.7093	0.7100
science-fiction	tfidf + stylometry	LR	0.6255	0.6300
science-fiction	tfidf + stylometry	XGB	0.6394	0.6400

Table A10. Evaluation results for the voting model on the rulit.me data (accessed on 15 May 2024); the grey color indicates improvement over individual models.

Genre	Representation	F1	Acc
science-fiction	SE	0.6800	0.6800
science-fiction	SE + stylometry	0.6999	0.7000
science-fiction	char n-grams	0.6862	0.6900
science-fiction	char n-grams + stylometry	0.7383	0.7400
science-fiction	n-grams	0.6768	0.6800
science-fiction	n-grams + stylometry	0.6995	0.7000
science-fiction	tfidf	0.6305	0.6400
science-fiction	tfidf + stylometry	0.6753	0.6800

References

1. Kochetova, L.; Popov, V. Research of Axiological Dominants in Press Release Genre based on Automatic Extraction of Key Words from Corpus. *Nauchnyi Dialog.* **2019**, *6*, 32–49. [CrossRef]
2. Lagutina, K.V. Classification of Russian texts by genres based on modern embeddings and rhythm. *Model. I Anal. Informatsionnykh Sist.* **2022**, *29*, 334–347. [CrossRef]
3. Houssein, E.H.; Ibrahem, N.; Zaki, A.M.; Sayed, A. Semantic protocol and resource description framework query language: A comprehensive review. *Mathematics* **2022**, *10*, 3203. [CrossRef]
4. Romanov, A.; Kurtukova, A.; Shelupanov, A.; Fedotova, A.; Goncharov, V. Authorship identification of a Russian-language text using support vector machine and deep neural networks. *Future Int.* **2020**, *13*, 3. [CrossRef]
5. Fedotova, A.; Romanov, A.; Kurtukova, A.; Shelupanov, A. Authorship attribution of social media and literary Russian-language texts using machine learning methods and feature selection. *Future Int.* **2021**, *14*, 4. [CrossRef]
6. Embarcadero-Ruiz, D.; Gómez-Adorno, H.; Embarcadero-Ruiz, A.; Sierra, G. Graph-based siamese network for authorship verification. *Mathematics* **2022**, *10*, 277. [CrossRef]
7. Kessler, B.; Nunberg, G.; Schütze, H. Automatic detection of text genre. *arXiv* **1997**, arXiv:cmp-lg/9707002.
8. Russian language—Wikipedia, The Free Encyclopedia. 2024. Available online: https://en.wikipedia.org/wiki/Russian_language (accessed on 16 May 2024).
9. Shavrina, T. Differential Approach to Webcorpus Construction. In *Computational Linguistics and Intellectual Technologies: Proceedings of the International Conference Dialogue 2018*; National Research University Higher School of Economics: Moscow, Russia, 2018.
10. VKontakte. 2024. Available online: https://vk.com (accessed on 1 January 2024).
11. OpenCorpora. 2024. Available online: http://opencorpora.org (accessed on 1 January 2024).
12. Barakhnin, V.; Kozhemyakina, O.; Pastushkov, I. Automated determination of the type of genre and stylistic coloring of Russian texts. In *ITM Web of Conferences*; EDP Sciences: Les Ulis, France, 2017; Volume 10, p. 02001.
13. Devlin, J.; Chang, M.W.; Lee, K.; Toutanova, K. BERT: Pre-training of Deep Bidirectional Transformers for Language Understanding. *arXiv* **2018**, arXiv:1810.04805.
14. Sun, H.; Liu, J.; Zhang, J. A survey of contrastive learning in NLP. In Proceedings of the 7th International Symposium on Advances in Electrical, Electronics, and Computer Engineering, Xishuangbanna, China, 18–20 March 2022; Volume 12294, pp. 1073–1078.
15. Bulygin, M.; Sharoff, S. Using machine translation for automatic genre classification in Arabic. In Proceedings of the Komp'juternaja Lingvistika i Intellektual'nye Tehnologii, Moscow, Russia, 30 May–2 June 2018; pp. 153–162.

16. Nolazco-Flores, J.A.; Guerrero-Galván, A.V.; Del-Valle-Soto, C.; Garcia-Perera, L.P. Genre Classification of Books on Spanish. *IEEE Access* **2023**, *11*, 132878–132892. [CrossRef]
17. Ozsarfati, E.; Sahin, E.; Saul, C.J.; Yilmaz, A. Book genre classification based on titles with comparative machine learning algorithms. In Proceedings of the 2019 IEEE 4th International Conference on Computer and Communication Systems (ICCCS), Singapore, 23–25 February 2019; IEEE: Piscataway, NJ, USA, 2019; pp. 14–20.
18. Steinwart, I.; Christmann, A. *Support Vector Machines*; Springer Science & Business Media: Berlin/Heidelberg, Germany, 2008.
19. Saraswat, M.; Srishti. Leveraging genre classification with RNN for Book recommendation. *Int. J. Inf. Technol.* **2022**, *14*, 3751–3756. [CrossRef]
20. Webster, R.; Fonteyne, M.; Tezcan, A.; Macken, L.; Daems, J. Gutenberg goes neural: Comparing features of dutch human translations with raw neural machine translation outputs in a corpus of english literary classics. *Informatics* **2020**, *7*, 32. [CrossRef]
21. Alfraidi, T.; Abdeen, M.A.; Yatimi, A.; Alluhaibi, R.; Al-Thubaity, A. The Saudi novel corpus: Design and compilation. *Appl. Sci.* **2022**, *12*, 6648. [CrossRef]
22. Mendhakar, A. Linguistic profiling of text genres: An exploration of fictional vs. non-fictional texts. *Information* **2022**, *13*, 357. [CrossRef]
23. Williamson, G.; Cao, A.; Chen, Y.; Ji, Y.; Xu, L.; Choi, J.D. Exploring a Multi-Layered Cross-Genre Corpus of Document-Level Semantic Relations. *Information* **2023**, *14*, 431. [CrossRef]
24. Shavrina, T. Genre Classification on Text-Internal Features: A Corpus Study. In Proceedings of the Web Corpora as a Language Training Tool Conference (ARANEA 2018), Univerzita Komenského v Bratislave, Bratislava, Slovakia, 23–24 November 2018; pp. 134–147.
25. Cortes, C.; Vapnik, V. Support-vector networks. *Mach. Learn.* **1995**, *20*, 273–297. [CrossRef]
26. Le-Khac, P.H.; Healy, G.; Smeaton, A.F. Contrastive representation learning: A framework and review. *IEEE Access* **2020**, *8*, 193907–193934. [CrossRef]
27. Chen, Q.; Zhang, R.; Zheng, Y.; Mao, Y. Dual Contrastive Learning: Text Classification via Label-Aware Data Augmentation. *arXiv* **2022**, arXiv:2201.08702.
28. Breiman, L. Random forests. *Mach. Learn.* **2001**, *45*, 5–32. [CrossRef]
29. Wright, R.E. Logistic Regression. In *Reading and Understanding Multivariate Statistics*; Grimm, L.G., Yarnold, P.R., Eds.; American Psychological Association: Worcester, MA, USA, 1995; pp. 217–244.
30. Chen, T.; Guestrin, C. Xgboost: A scalable tree boosting system. In Proceedings of the 22nd aCm Sigkdd International Conference on Knowledge Discovery and Data Mining, San Francisco, CA, USA, 13–17 August 2016; pp. 785–794.
31. Neal, T.; Sundararajan, K.; Fatima, A.; Yan, Y.; Xiang, Y.; Woodard, D. Surveying stylometry techniques and applications. *ACM Comput. Surv.* **2017**, *50*, 86. [CrossRef]
32. Lagutina, K.; Lagutina, N.; Boychuk, E.; Vorontsova, I.; Shliakhtina, E.; Belyaeva, O.; Paramonov, I.; Demidov, P. A survey on stylometric text features. In Proceedings of the 2019 25th Conference of Open Innovations Association (FRUCT), Helsinki, Finland, 5–8 November 2019; IEEE: Piscataway, NJ, USA, 2019; pp. 184–195.
33. Stamatatos, E.; Fakotakis, N.; Kokkinakis, G. Automatic text categorization in terms of genre and author. *Comput. Linguist.* **2000**, *26*, 471–495. [CrossRef]
34. Sarawgi, R.; Gajulapalli, K.; Choi, Y. Gender attribution: Tracing stylometric evidence beyond topic and genre. In Proceedings of the Fifteenth Conference on Computational Natural Language Learning, Portland, OR, USA 23–24 June 2011; pp. 78–86.
35. Eder, M. Rolling stylometry. *Digit. Scholarsh. Humanit.* **2016**, *31*, 457–469. [CrossRef]
36. Eder, M.; Rybicki, J.; Kestemont, M. Stylometry with R: A package for computational text analysis. *R J.* **2016**, *8*, 107–121. [CrossRef]
37. Maciej, P.; Tomasz, W.; Maciej, E. Open stylometric system WebSty: Integrated language processing, analysis and visualisation. *CMST* **2018**, *24*, 43–58.
38. McNamara, D.S.; Graesser, A.C.; McCarthy, P.M.; Cai, Z. Cohesive Features in Expository Texts: A Large-scale Study of Expert and Novice Writing. *Writ. Commun.* **2014**, *31*, 151–183.
39. Okulska, I.; Stetsenko, D.; Kołos, A.; Karlińska, A.; Głąbińska, K.; Nowakowski, A. StyloMetrix: An Open-Source Multilingual Tool for Representing Stylometric Vectors. *arXiv* **2023**, arXiv:2309.12810.
40. Minaee, S.; Kalchbrenner, N.; Cambria, E.; Nikzad, N.; Chenaghlu, M.; Gao, J. Deep learning–based text classification: A comprehensive review. *ACM Comput. Surv.* **2021**, *54*, 62. [CrossRef]
41. Cunha, W.; Viegas, F.; França, C.; Rosa, T.; Rocha, L.; Gonçalves, M.A. A Comparative Survey of Instance Selection Methods applied to Non-Neural and Transformer-Based Text Classification. *ACM Comput. Surv.* **2023**, *55*, 265. [CrossRef]
42. Face, H. Hugging Face. 2016. Available online: https://huggingface.co/ (accessed on 26 April 2024).
43. Kuratov, Y.; Arkhipov, M. Adaptation of deep bidirectional multilingual transformers for Russian language. *arXiv* **2019**, arXiv:1905.07213.
44. LitRes. LitRes: Digital Library and E-Book Retailer. 2024. Available online: https://www.litres.ru (accessed on 1 January 2024).
45. Royallib: Free Online Library. 2024. Available online: https://royallib.com/ (accessed on 1 January 2024).
46. knigogo.net. Knigogo. 2013. Available online: https://knigogo.net/zhanryi/ (accessed on 1 January 2024).

47. Belkina, A.C.; Ciccolella, C.O.; Anno, R.; Halpert, R.; Spidlen, J.; Snyder-Cappione, J.E. Automated optimized parameters for T-distributed stochastic neighbor embedding improve visualization and analysis of large datasets. *Nat. Commun.* **2019**, *10*, 5415. [CrossRef]
48. Bird, S.; Loper, E.; Klein, E. NLTK: The Natural Language Toolkit. *arXiv* **2009**, arXiv:cs/0205028. [CrossRef]
49. ZILiAT-NASK. StyloMetrix: An Open-Source Multilingual Tool for Representing Stylometric Vectors (Code Repository). 2023. Available online: https://github.com/ZILiAT-NASK/StyloMetrix (accessed on 26 April 2024).
50. Okulska, I.; Stetsenko, D.; Kołos, A.; Karlińska, A.; Głąbińska, K.; Nowakowski, A. StyloMetrix Metrics List (Russian). 2023. Available online: https://github.com/ZILiAT-NASK/StyloMetrix/blob/main/resources/metrics_list_ru.md (accessed on 26 April 2024).
51. Schapire, R.E. Improving Regressors using Boosting Techniques. In Proceedings of the International Conference on Machine Learning (ICML), Austin, TX, USA, 21–23 June 1990.
52. Hiyouga. Dual Contrastive Learning. 2022. Available online: https://github.com/hiyouga/Dual-Contrastive-Learning (accessed on 26 March 2024).
53. Pedregosa, F.; Varoquaux, G.; Gramfort, A.; Michel, V.; Thirion, B.; Grisel, O.; Blondel, M.; Prettenhofer, P.; Weiss, R.; Dubourg, V.; et al. Scikit-learn: Machine Learning in Python. *J. Mach. Learn. Res.* **2011**, *12*, 2825–2830.
54. Paszke, A.; Gross, S.; Massa, F.; Lerer, A.; Bradbury, J.; Chanan, G.; Killeen, T.; Lin, Z.; Gimelshein, N.; Antiga, L.; et al. PyTorch: An Imperative Style, High-Performance Deep Learning Library. In *Advances in Neural Information Processing Systems 32*; Curran Associates, Inc.: Red Hook, NY, USA, 2019; pp. 8024–8035.
55. Google Research. BERT: Multilingual (Uncased). 2018. Available online: https://huggingface.co/google-bert/bert-base-multilingual-uncased (accessed on 26 April 2024).
56. DeepPavlov. RuBERT: Russian (Cased). 2021. Available online: https://huggingface.co/DeepPavlov/rubert-base-cased (accessed on 26 April 2024).
57. Makridakis, S. Accuracy measures: Theoretical and practical concerns. *Int. J. Forecast.* **1993**, *9*, 527–529. [CrossRef]
58. Streiner, D.L.; Norman, G.R. "Precision" and "accuracy": Two terms that are neither. *J. Clin. Epidemiol.* **2006**, *59*, 327–330. [CrossRef]

information

MDPI

Article

Automated Knowledge Extraction in the Field of Wheat Sharp Eyespot Control

Keyi Liu [1,2] and Yunpeng Cui [1,2,*]

1 Agricultural Information Institute, Chinese Academy of Agricultural Sciences, Beijing 100081, China; liukeyi@caas.cn
2 Key Laboratory of Big Agri-Data, Ministry of Agriculture and Rural Areas, Beijing 100081, China
* Correspondence: cuiyunpeng@caas.cn

Abstract: Wheat sharp eyespot is a soil-borne fungal disease commonly found in wheat areas in China, which can occur throughout the entire reproductive period of wheat and has a great impact on the yield and quality of wheat in China. By constructing a domain ontology for wheat sharp eyespot control and modeling the domain knowledge, we aim to integrate and share the knowledge in the field of wheat sharp eyespot control, which can provide important support and guidance for agricultural decision-making and disease control. In this study, the literature in the field of wheat sharp eyespot control was used as a data source, the KeyBERT keyword extraction algorithm was used to mine the core concepts of the ontology, and the hierarchical relationships among the ontology concepts were extracted through clustering. Based on the constructed ontology of wheat sharp eyespot control, the schema of knowledge extraction was formed, and the knowledge extraction model was trained using the ERNIE 3.0 knowledge enhancement pretraining model. This study proposes a model and algorithm to realize knowledge extraction based on domain ontology, describes the construction method and process framework of wheat sharp eyespot control domain ontology, and details the training and reasoning effect of the knowledge extraction model. The knowledge extraction model constructed in this study for wheat sharp eyespot control contains a more complete conceptual system of wheat sharp eyespot. The F1 value of the model reaches 91.26%, which is a 17.86% improvement compared with the baseline model, and it can satisfy the knowledge extraction needs in the field of wheat sharp eyespot control. This study can provide a reference for domain knowledge extraction and provide strong support for knowledge discovery and downstream applications such as intelligent Q&A and intelligent recommendation in the field of wheat sharp eyespot control.

Keywords: wheat sharp eyespot; knowledge extraction; domain ontology; automatic extraction

1. Introduction

Wheat sharp eyespot (*Rhizotonia cerealis* van der Hoeven apud.Boerema & Verhoeven) is a worldwide soil-borne fungal disease caused by *Rhizoctonia cerealis* van der Hoeven [1,2]. At present, the disease occurs to varying degrees in nearly twenty provinces and cities in China, especially in the wheat areas of Jiangsu, Zhejiang, Anhui, Shandong, Henan, Hebei, Shaanxi, Guizhou, Hubei, and Sichuan provinces, where it is more prevalent. Wheat sharp eyespot can occur throughout the entire reproductive period of wheat, causing a variety of symptoms such as rotting buds, diseased and dead seedlings, rotting stems of flower stalks, and collapse [3]. In recent years, the incidence of blight in straw-returned wheat areas in northern China has been increasing year by year, seriously jeopardizing the yield and quality of wheat. Wheat sharp eyespot has a huge impact on yield, usually leading to a reduction in wheat yield between 10% and 20%, and in severe cases, even up to about 50% reduction in yield, and even complete crop failure in individual plots [4]. Farmers in the process of wheat disease control mostly rely on experience. Although many farmers are already experts in wheat diseases, the level of knowledge varies, and regional differences, climate differences, and other factors pose challenges for accurate disease control. Mostly relying on past experience to apply pesticides, the issue of grain quality and safety is ignored in the pursuit of yield. Although scientific and technological research is an important carrier of technological innovation, it is difficult for farmers to gain knowledge of wheat sharp eyespot in the literature, and it is difficult to judge the authenticity of the relevant knowledge through the Internet. Therefore, by constructing an ontology for wheat sharp eyespot, modeling the domain knowledge, and extracting the knowledge in the scientific and technological literature based on the knowledge model of wheat sharp eyespot, we can provide more scientific guidance to the producers so that farmers can understand how to control wheat sharp eyespot according to the onset of the disease and can independently use the professional methods of wheat sharp eyespot prevention and control, improve the efficiency of wheat disease prevention and control, and reduce the losses caused by the disease. It is of great significance to China's agricultural production and food security.

Massive literature data bring great challenges to technical analysis. As an unstructured text, the literature is not uniform in description or terminology, which makes it difficult to use simple rules to extract the core knowledge in it, and the current extraction method of manual participation in annotation can no longer meet the needs of rapid analysis of large-scale datasets. Entity–relationship extraction is one of the important tasks of information extraction, aiming at extracting the semantic relationships between different entities from unstructured text so as to extract useful information. In 1998, the first Message Understanding Conference (MCU) was held on entity–relationship extraction, and after years of development, the general field of relationship extraction has significantly advanced. Users use the information extraction method to obtain the required information from a large number of data sources, and on this basis, the extracted information is processed, organized, and analyzed through a secondary approach to obtain a new understanding of the information, which can help to improve the understanding of the original information and then reach the level of knowledge.

This study is oriented toward the field of wheat sharp eyespot control, aiming at integrating the relevant knowledge in this field through knowledge modeling, constructing an ontology of wheat sharp eyespot control that is useful for agricultural decision-making and practice in response to the actual needs in this field, and applying the domain ontology to the knowledge extraction process in order to improve the accuracy and efficiency of the extraction, so as to provide important support and guidance for agricultural decision-making and disease control. At the same time, the methods and results of this study will also provide reference and inspiration for knowledge extraction in other fields.

Our major contributions are the following:

- We propose a method for constructing an ontology in the field of wheat sharp eyespot control, detailing the process framework for building the domain ontology based on a corpus of wheat sharp eyespot research, which facilitates the integration and sharing of knowledge in this field.
- Based on the ontology of wheat sharp eyespot control, we introduce a knowledge extraction model specific to this domain, forming a framework for knowledge extraction that effectively extracts relevant information about wheat sharp eyespot control from texts.
- The knowledge extraction model and algorithm we proposed have achieved significant results in the field of wheat sharp eyespot control and also provide a reference for knowledge extraction in other domains.

The structure of the paper is as follows: In Section 2, we discuss the background concepts and overview of the research methodology. Section 3 describes the research methodology for datasets, ontology construction, and automated knowledge extraction. Section 4 presents the current limitations and future research directions, and the conclusion is presented in Section 5.

2. Related Work

2.1. Ontology

In the 1980s, ontology was introduced into the field of information science and later gradually extended to the fields of knowledge engineering and artificial intelligence [5]. In 2001, the Food and Agriculture Organization of the United Nations (FAO) introduced the Agricultural Ontology Service (AOS), which provides users with a way to define and describe domain knowledge through an ontological methodology and assists communication within the domain. Based on the AOS project, crop ontology, food ontology, and agronomy ontology were constructed [6,7]. Chang Chun (2003) introduced the AOS into the Chinese context, which was the beginning of agricultural ontology research in China [8]. Since then, many scholars have started to elaborate on the construction principles, processes, methods, and other contents of ontologies in the field of agriculture. In addition to the theoretical study of ontology, it has also been applied and practiced in many aspects of the agricultural field, such as crop production and cultivation, pest control, germplasm resources, and so on. Among them, the ontology research of crop pest control is the most extensive, considering areas such as rice pests and diseases [9,10], maize pests and diseases [11,12], and cotton diseases [13]. In the field of agriculture, a commonly used ontology construction method is semi-automatic construction, by transforming agricultural narrative lists and knowledge categorization into ontologies. Currently, the commonly used agricultural narrative lists are the Chinese Agricultural Thesaurus (CAT), AGROVOC (Multilingual Agricultural Thesaurus), NALT (National Agricultural Library of the United States), and the Centre Agriculture Bioscience International (CABI). Liu Guifeng et al. (2022) used the National Agricultural Science Data Center's Cotton, Hemp Crop Pathogenic Fungal Disease Database, and Microbial Pesticide Database as their main data sources and combined the classification and terminology in the Chinese Classification Thesaurus, Agricultural Science Narrative Thesaurus, Chinese Thesaurus, and Chinese Library Classification to construct the "Cotton Disease Prevention and Control" ontology [13]. Renny et al. (2021) used text mining and machine learning to construct an ontology for the tomato pest and disease domain [14]. Deepa R et al. (2022) used natural speech processing techniques to extract agricultural terms and combined textual similarity with plain Bayes (NBM) to propose a method for automatically constructing agricultural ontologies [15]. In specific verticals, narrative lists are difficult to provide finer-grained knowledge categorization, and ontology construction relies more on domain experts by manual construction. Dong et al. (2023) used a top-down modeling approach, in which domain experts manually compiled concepts from the topmost level, and agricultural experts further refined the relationships and hierarchies among knowledge to construct an ontology model for precision rice fertilization [16]. Agricultural ontology research has made some progress in China, especially in crop pest control, which is widely used. However, there are some shortcomings, including the inadequacy of narrative lists for fine-grained classification, subjective factors in the semi-automatic construction process, challenges in updating and maintaining ontologies, lack of standardization, and complexity of expertise acquisition and validation. In order to improve the quality and sustainability of agricultural ontology research, there is a need to explore more effective construction methods and promote standardization.

2.2. Knowledge Extraction

In response to all the above problems arising from the pipeline approach, scholars gradually began to study the strengthening of the link between two subtasks. As a result, joint extraction methods have been proposed and have been continuously developed in recent years. The joint entity–relationship extraction method can further utilize entity recognition and relationship to extract the potential information between two subtasks, which often achieves better results than the pipeline method. Entity–relationship extraction is the joint completion of entity recognition and relationship extraction, directly from the text to obtain the entity–relationship ternary. Its mathematical description is as follows: The set of relationship categories R and the set of entity categories E are known. Given the sentence S = {w_1, w_2, · · · , w_n}, using the entity–relationship joint extraction method, all entity–relationship quintuples <h, e_1, r, t, e_2> in the sentence S are extracted by using the established unified model, where $r \in R$, $e_1 \in E$, and $e_2 \in E$. The significant difference between this method and the streamlined approach is that there is no prelabeling of the given entity boundaries and types, and the joint model outputs all the relation triples <h, r, t> for sentence S.

Zeng et al. [17] designed CNNs for relationship classification but did not consider a ternary form. Makoto et al. [18] achieved end-to-end prediction of entity relationships by constructing a stacked network based on BiLSTM and Bi-TreeLSTM for both entity extraction and relationship detection. Li et al. [19] used a two-layer LSTM with an encoder–decoder architecture to construct a knowledge extraction model that is not limited to the ternary form and can predict structured knowledge in a fixed format. Zheng et al. [20] transformed the entity–relationship extraction task into a sequence annotation task through an annotation strategy and then constructed a Bi-LSTM model similar to the previous one to handle it. This enables the model to extract triples directly from statements, but this model also has a design flaw, namely that it cannot deal with data with overlapped triples. Luan et al. [21] designed a multi-task learning framework for recognizing entities and relationships in scientific research to construct a scientific knowledge graph, and this model outperforms the existing models without any prior knowledge of the domain. Wang et al. [22] presented a new handshake labeling strategy to label the entity head to entity tail, subject head to object head, and subject tail to object tail, to decompose the joint extraction task into sequence labeling subtasks in order to solve the problem of exposing bias in the training and prediction phases. Sui et al. [23] used a transformer as a decoder, stacked multiple identical transformers, and used a multi-head self-attention mechanism to simulate the relationship between the triples, fusing sentence information and giving an attentional representation to the sentence through multi-head mutual attention.

Although the above works have achieved good results and pushed forward the progress and development of the field of joint entity–relationship extraction, none of them focuses on how to fully mine semantic and syntactic information, or how to reasonably fuse the two kinds of information for different contexts. Classical relational extraction tends to focus on a single sentence and just tries to mine the entity relationships within each sentence. Early research in relational extraction focused on categorizing relationships between pairs of entities in a single sentence or jointly extracting entities and relationships in a sentence, i.e., intra-sentence relationships, ignoring the relationships of pairs of entities that cross sentence boundaries, i.e., inter-sentence relationships. Therefore, entity–relationship extraction is inevitably limited to a certain extent in practical application scenarios. In reality, a large number of relationships actually need to rely on cross-sentence or even document linguistic information in order to be extracted; this document will mention many modern composite cross-passing-related system entities, where a composite of multiple sentence scenarios is proposed according to which the relationship needs are read, memorized, and reasoned in order to find out the relationship facts between multiple sentences. There are many relationship facts that are hidden in entity pairs of different sentences in a document, and there are complex interactions between multiple entities in a document. With the continuous progress of technology and the deepening of the research on relationship extraction, the demand for document-level entity–relationship extraction is rapidly increasing.

Ontology-based information extraction techniques, with the help of predefined ontology hierarchies, can effectively identify domain-specific concepts, entities, relationships, and other forms of knowledge. Ontology can be regarded as a tree-structured knowledge base mold, which is the semantic basis for communication and connectivity between different subjects in the same domain. Moreno [24] proposed a method to achieve information extraction based on ontology in an independent domain. The application was oriented toward the field of molecular biology, the extraction of information about E. coli, and the establishment of a regulatory network for E. coli. The constructed system was tested on the abstracts of scientific papers and the complete literature in this field. Additionally, the complete literature was mined by designing the domain ontology and then implementing information extraction based on the knowledge contained in the ontology. Li et al. [25] implemented an agricultural domain based on agricultural ontology for the extraction of structured AJAX data. Daya [26] used multiple ontologies for information extraction considering the two cases of subdomain determination and subdomain expression. The first system based on multiple ontologies was developed for the university domain, which uses two ontologies specialized in subdomains. The corpus consists of documents from 100 universities, 50 web pages from North America, and 50 from the rest of the world. The second system realized was applied to the domain of terrorist attacks, and the corpus used by the Message Understanding Conference (MUC) provides the subdomains.

3. Method

3.1. Dataset Construction

In this paper, the literature in the field of wheat sharp eyespot control was collected using the CNKI as a data source, which allowed us to obtain more concepts and relationships compared to structured data, making the constructed ontology of wheat sharp eyespot control more comprehensive and complete. Scientific and technical research often comes with fixed keywords, but the number of keywords is not enough to characterize the core concepts of the field, and keyword extraction for chapter-level documents can reveal more comprehensive concepts. Using "Wheat Sharp Eyespot AND (control OR prevention)" as the search formula, a total of 1008 documents were found. The corpus of wheat sharp eyespot control was obtained by formatting the documents, preprocessing the text, and filtering the words by word splitting and stopword filtering.

3.2. Ontology Construction

The skeletal methodology, the TOVE method, the methontology method, the five-step cycle method, and the seven-step method are the typical ontology modeling methods available. The skeletal methodology was summarized by Mike Uschold and King from enterprise ontology construction at the University of Edinburgh in 1995. The TOVE methodology was proposed by Gruninger and Mark S. Fox from the Enterprise Integration Laboratory of the University of Toronto in 1996 during the TOVE project. The methontology method was proposed by Mariano Fernandez and Gomez Gomez from the University of Madrid Crafts Campus. Mariano Fernandez and Gomez Perez et al. developed in 1997 [27]. The five-step cycle method was developed for the construction of semantic web ontology learning by Maedche and Staab in 2000. The seven-step method is a domain ontology construction method developed by Noy and McGuinness at Stanford University School of Medicine in 2000. A comparison of the characteristics and uses of these five methods is shown in Table 1.

Table 1. Ontology construction methods.

Ontology Modeling Methods	Application Areas	Basic Processes	Drawbacks	Life Cycle	Reusable or Not
Skeletal Methodology	Corporate Area	Defining the purpose and scope of ontology applications; Building ontologies; Evaluation; Documentation	Lack of specific methodologies and techniques	No life cycle	no
TOVE	Corporate Area	Clarify the purpose of the construction; Formulate the methodology; Formalize the steps; Constraints; Test and revise the ontology	Lack of documented process descriptions and specific build steps	No true life cycle	no
Methontology	Chemical Field	Specification; Knowledge acquisition; Conceptualization; Integration; Realization; Evaluation; Documentation	Unable to update iterations	Life cycle	no

Table 1. *Cont.*

Ontology Modeling Methods	Application Areas	Basic Processes	Drawbacks	Life Cycle	Reusable or Not
Five-Step Cycle	Semantic Web Ontology Learning	Ontology import and reuse; Ontology extraction; Ontology trimming; Ontology refinement; Ontology application	Poorly operated and difficult	Life cycle	yes
Seven-Step Process	Medical Field	Define domain scope; Reuse existing ontologies; List conceptual terms; Define classes and inter-class hierarchies; Define class attributes; Define facets of attributes; Create instances	Lack of ontology assessment to update iterations	No true life cycle	yes

The ontology construction process is proposed to meet the actual needs of wheat sharp eyespot control (Figure 1). The topic of "wheat sharp eyespot control" is systematic, covering a wide range of fields such as agricultural science, plant protection, chemistry, biology, pesticide science, etc. The knowledge related to wheat is extremely large. This makes it impossible to build an ontology that covers all of it. Therefore, the focus of this study is to construct the ontology of "wheat sharp eyespot control", eliminate irrelevant subconcepts, retain the overall framework structure, and on this basis, add new concepts and their subconcepts to realize the integration, supplementation, and improvement of the ontology concepts of wheat sharp eyespot control and develop the conceptual framework structure.

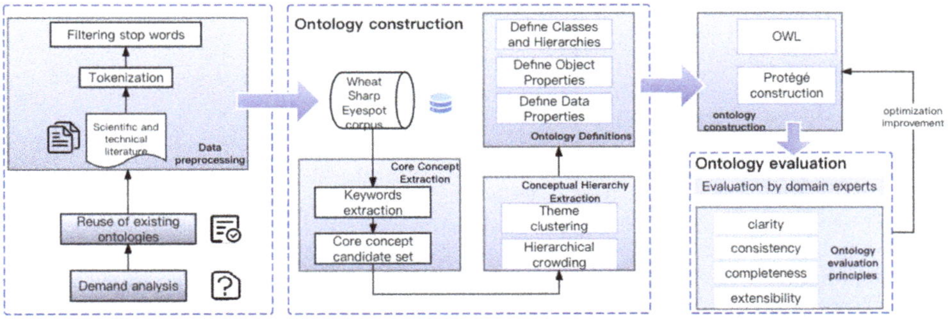

Figure 1. Ontology construction process.

In this study, the KeyBERT keyword extraction algorithm was used to find the most similar subphrases in a document to the document itself using BERT embedding and cosine similarity. Firstly, BERT was used to calculate the embedding value of the document to obtain a vector-level representation of the document. Then, the word vectors were extracted for the n-gram, and finally, cosine similarity was used to determine the keywords or key phrases that were most similar to the document to obtain the keywords that best described the whole document. In order to diversify the results, we used maximum marginal relevance (*MMR*) to create keywords/key phrases, also based on cosine similarity. The specific formula is as follows:

$$MMR(Q,C,R) = \underset{d_i \in C}{\overset{k}{\text{argmax}}}[\lambda sim(Q,d_i) - (1-\lambda) \max_{d_j \in R} (sim(d_i,d_j))] \tag{1}$$

where Q denotes the query statement; C denotes the set of all documents; R denotes an initial set that has been obtained based on the relevance; $\arg\max^k [*]$ denotes the index that gives the k largest elements of the set; $sim(Q, d_i)$ represents the correlation between d_i and Q; $sim(d_i, d_j)$ represents the redundancy of the representation.

On the basis of the keywords, they were further screened and condensed as a core concept candidate set, taking into account the ontological needs of wheat sharp eyespot control. Table 2 demonstrates five sets of keywords.

Table 2. Keywords.

Keywords
[('Disease-resistant, Varieties, Wheat, Varieties', 0.7423), ('Wheat, Variety, Field, Resistance', 0.7211), ('Fertility, Disease prevention, Wheat, Population', 0.7206), ('Yumai, New wheat, Variety, Resistance', 0.7189), (Disease prevention, Wheat, Population, Structure', 0.717)]
[('Disease Strain, Disease Strain, Carrying Bacteria, Overwintering', 0.6457), ('Wheat fields, Morbidity, Climate', 0.594), ('Spring, Early, Onset, Sources of Infestation', 0.5845), ('Wheat, Wheat Sharp Eyespot, Period of occurrence', 0.5814), ('Carrying bacteria, Overwintering, Next year, Spring', 0.5766)]
[('Temperature, Humidity, Wheat, Wheat Sharp Eyespot', 0.6713), ('Spring, High humidity, First third of a month, Rainfall', 0.6434), ('Humidity, Wheat, Wheat Sharp Eyespot, Occurrence', 0.6238), ('Humidity, Wheat, Wheat Sharp Eyespot', 0.6233), ('Wheat Sharp Eyespot, Research, Hot Spots ', 0.538)]
[('Climate, Conditions, Wheat, Wheat Sharp Eyespot', 0.6904), ('Agriculture, Prevention and Control, Suzhou City, Climate', 0.6856), ('Climate, Soil, Growth, Wheat', 0.6569), ('Prevention and Control, Suzhou City, Climate, Soil', 0.6548), ('Disease, Resistance, Control, Wheat Field', 0.6446)]
[('Field, Morbidity, Overwintering, Fertilization', 0.6605), ('Infestation, Bacterial source, Wheat, Sowing', 0.643), ('Incidence, Seeding rate, Wheat field, Seasonal period', 0.6325), ('Field, Pathogen, Quantity, Deep plowing', 0.6318), ('Overwintering, Initial infestation, Bacterial source', 0.6144)]

After clarifying the domain scope and the core concept candidate set, the first task of constructing a domain ontology is to model the ontology hierarchy. In this study, we used BERTopic for topic modeling, which uses Transformer and c-TF-IDF to create dense clusters that can obtain topics and important words. The main steps are as follows: First, input the whole document into BERT to obtain the word vectors of the document; apply UMAP to downsize these word vectors to obtain the low-dimensional word vectors; cluster the low-dimensional word vectors to obtain the documents with good clustering classes; use c-TF-IDF to obtain the subject words of each topic for the clustered documents; use maximum marginalization for these subject words; and use c-TF-IDF to obtain the subject words of each topic. These words were filtered using the maximum marginal correlation algorithm. By clustering the core concept candidate set of topics, 50 topics were obtained. Table 3 shows the top five topics. Topic "−1" is the largest, which refers to the outlier text that is not assigned to any of the generated topics and will be ignored in this paper.

Table 3. Topic clustering.

Topic	Count	Name	Representation
−1	1787	−1_Wheat_control_Wheat Sharp Eyespot _occurrence	['wheat', 'control', 'Wheat Sharp Eyespot', 'occurrence', 'disease', 'incidence', 'varieties', 'agents', 'research', 'impact', 'agriculture', 'trials', 'growth', 'seed', 'efficacy', 'seed mixes', 'technology', 'field', 'survey', 'soil']
0	177	0_Gene_Marker_Resistance_Inheritance	['gene', 'marker', 'resistance', 'genetic', 'chromosome', 'identification', 'analysis', 'localization', 'detection', 'population', 'expression', 'molecular', 'research', 'Wheat Sharp Eyespot', 'chain', 'material', 'trait', 'mapping', 'protein', 'utilization']
1	127	1_Tests_Pharmaceuticals_Investiga-tions_Effectiveness	['test', 'agent', 'investigation', 'efficacy', 'plot', 'Wheat Sharp Eyespot', 'wheat', 'application', 'seed dressing', 'seed', 'seed coating', 'control', 'control efficacy', 'ltd', 'penicillin', 'method', 'phenoxyethanol', 'suspension', 'for test', 'year/month/day']
2	111	2_Occurrence_Wheat_Wheat Sharp Eyespot_Disease	['occurrence', 'wheat', 'Wheat Sharp Eyespot', 'onset', 'disease', 'area', 'plant', 'average', 'variety', 'infestation', 'control', 'survey', 'damage', 'million acres', 'impact', 'disease', 'leaf sheath', 'corn', 'extent', 'symptoms']

Table 3. *Cont.*

Topic	Count	Name	Representation
3	101	3_Research_Journal_of_Wheat Sharp Eyespot_Strains	['Research', 'Journal', 'Wheat Sharp Eyespot', 'Strain', 'Bacteria', 'Wheat', 'Agriculture', 'Plant', 'China', 'Nucleobacteria', 'Screening', 'Science', 'Isolation', 'Identification', 'Beijing', 'Biophylaxis', 'Antagonism', 'Prevention and control', 'Publisher', 'Henan']
4	97	4_Sowing_Control_Wheat_Soil	['sowing', 'control', 'wheat', 'soil', 'field', 'wheat field', 'Wheat Sharp Eyespot', 'nitrogen fertilizer', 'fertilization', 'mulching', 'raising', 'deep loosening', 'lowering', 'potash', 'impact', 'incidence', 'control', 'weeds', 'occurrences', 'kilogram']
5	93	5_Disease_leaf sheaths_wheat_leaf blades	['onset', 'leaf sheath', 'wheat', 'leaf', 'disease', 'infestation', 'basal', 'control', 'spot', 'occurrence', 'brown', 'symptom', 'dieback', 'plant', 'stalk', 'disease', 'sowing', 'diseased plant', 'seed', 'white spike']

3.2.1. Wheat Sharp Eyespot Control Ontology Concept Definition

In this study, the results of theme and hierarchical clustering were analyzed and condensed, and the ontology of wheat sharp eyespot control was divided into eight categories of parent concepts, namely incidence characteristics, wheat growing period, pathogenesis, region of incidence, degree of disease, lesion site, symptom, and control measures. In accordance with the structural requirements of OWL, they are all subordinate concepts of "Thing". The Protégé selected in this article is a widely used open source ontology editor developed by Stanford University. It is based on Java and is used for ontology editing and knowledge acquisition. Protégé has an extensible structure and multiple plug-ins; supports ontology description languages such as RDF, RDFS, and OWL; and provides a graphical interface that is easy to use.

Using Protégé, we incorporated hierarchical concepts into the "Classes" based on data content and representation characteristics. This was accomplished in collaboration with domain experts and in accordance with ontology design principles, ensuring a balanced scope of knowledge description and conceptual refinement (Figure 2).

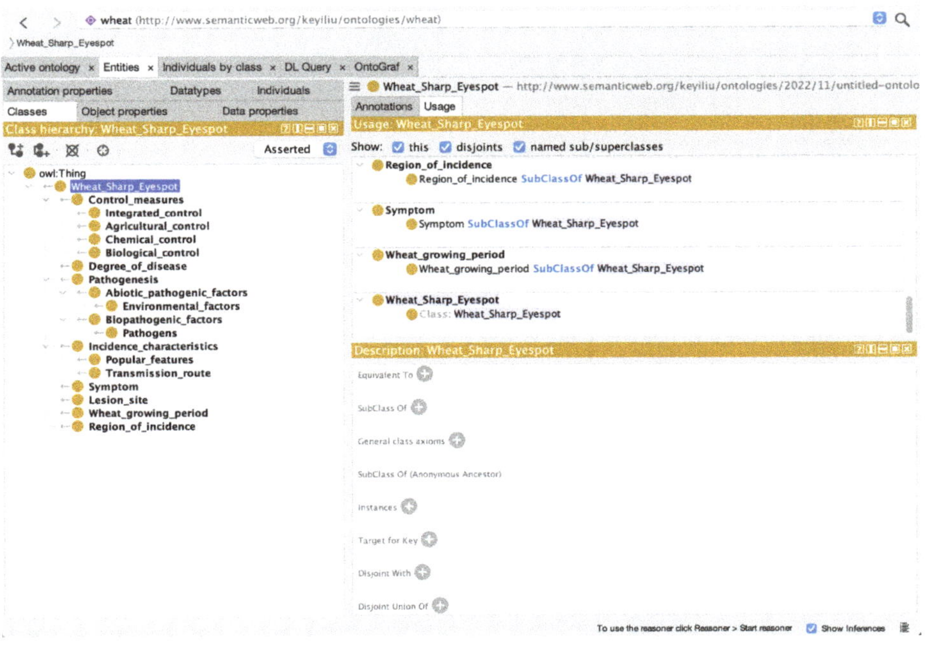

Figure 2. Ontology concept.

3.2.2. Wheat Sharp Eyespot Control Ontology Attribute Definition

Once the conceptual hierarchy of an ontology is constructed, the relationships between concepts need to be determined, i.e., defining ontology property relationships [28]. Ontology property relationships are the basis for the subsequent implementation of knowledge reasoning. Three types of property relationships are covered in the Protégé tool, namely object properties, data properties, and annotation properties. Object properties are used to represent the relationships between concepts, data properties are used to describe the properties of the concepts themselves, and annotation properties are used to annotate the concept properties. In this study, we considered only object properties and data properties. According to the characteristics of the field of wheat sharp eyespot control, by organizing and analyzing the associations between parent concepts, the object attribute relationships involved in the ontology are shown in Table 4. In this study, 11 object attributes, 16 primary data attributes, and 8 secondary data attributes were defined for the wheat sharp eyespot control ontology. The object properties and data properties options in Protégé were used to add object properties and data properties, respectively (Figure 3). The characteristic information of each object property was used to define its nature. Then, the corresponding description information was filled, and constraint information on aspects such as definition domain, value domain, and inverse property was added [28].

Table 4. Object attribute definition.

Type	Attribute Relationship	Relationship Description	Domain	Range	Reciprocal Attribute
Object Properties	beCausedBy	Caused by . . .	Wheat Sharp Eyespot	Environmental factors, pathogens	cause
	beControledBy	Controlled by . . .	Wheat Sharp Eyespot	Control measures	control
	cause	Lead to	Environmental factors, pathogens	Wheat Sharp Eyespot	beCausedBy
	control	Relationship between prevention and control	Control measures	Wheat Sharp Eyespot	beControledBy
	harmOn	Harm relationship	Wheat Sharp Eyespot	Lesion site	none
	hasChannel	Transmission route	Wheat Sharp Eyespot	Transmission route	none
	hasCharacteristics	Popular features	Wheat Sharp Eyespot	Popular features	none
	hasSymptom	Symptomatic	Diseased or infected plant	Symptom	none
	infectPeriod	Disease Infestation Stage	Wheat Sharp Eyespot	Wheat growing period	none
	occurredIn	Disease Areas	Wheat Sharp Eyespot	Region of incidence	none

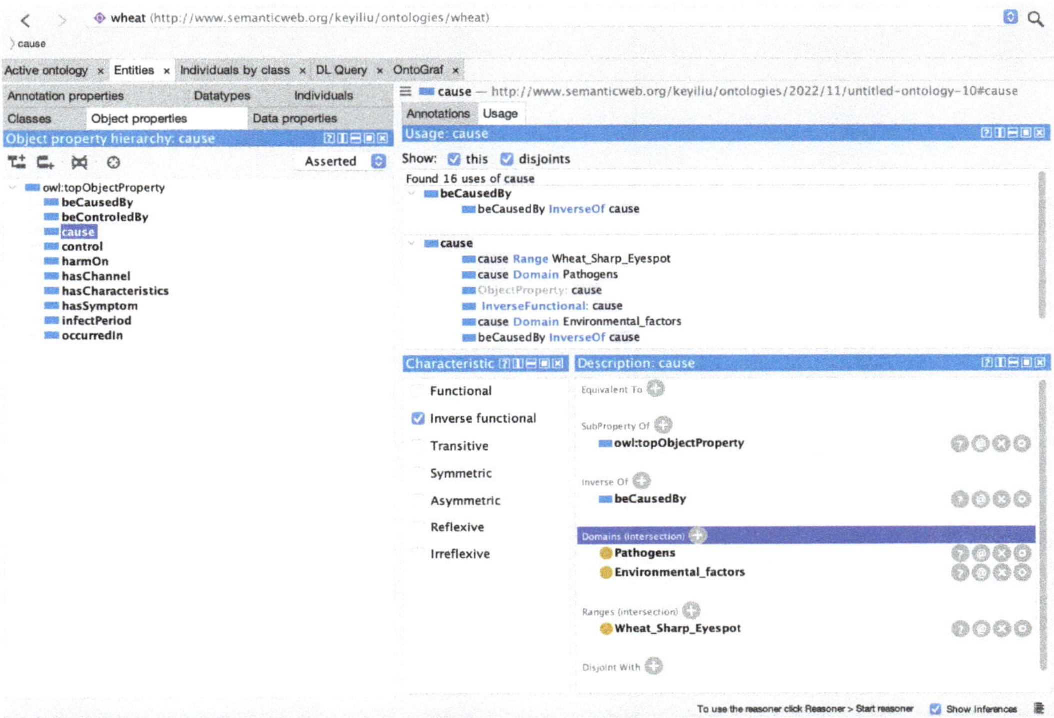

Figure 3. Object properties and data properties.

3.2.3. Ontology Construction and Evaluation

In this study, the constructed ontology was evaluated and optimized according to the ontology evaluation criteria to ensure the scientific and professional nature of the ontology so that it can fully express the concepts of the wheat sharp eyespot control domain. The criteria for ontology evaluation usually include clarity, consistency, refinement, and extensibility [29,30]. Clarity requires that the defined classes and attributes must be clear and free of ambiguity; consistency requires that the relationships between classes are logically consistent [30]; refinement requires that the defined classes and attributes can describe the wheat sharp eyespot control domain in a complete way and be applicable to the body of knowledge in the main data sources; and extensibility requires that the ontology can be extended in the wheat sharp eyespot control domain to accommodate the emergence of new concepts. After the initial construction of the ontology was completed, experts in the field of plant protection were invited to evaluate the outline model of the ontology. The experts believe that the ontology constructed in this study contains a comprehensive conceptual system for wheat sharp eyespot. It meets the evaluation criteria and the requirements for ontology construction, making it suitable for knowledge representation and the next stage of ontology application. The ontology model, refined based on expert evaluation, was visualized and expressed using Protégé (Figure 4).

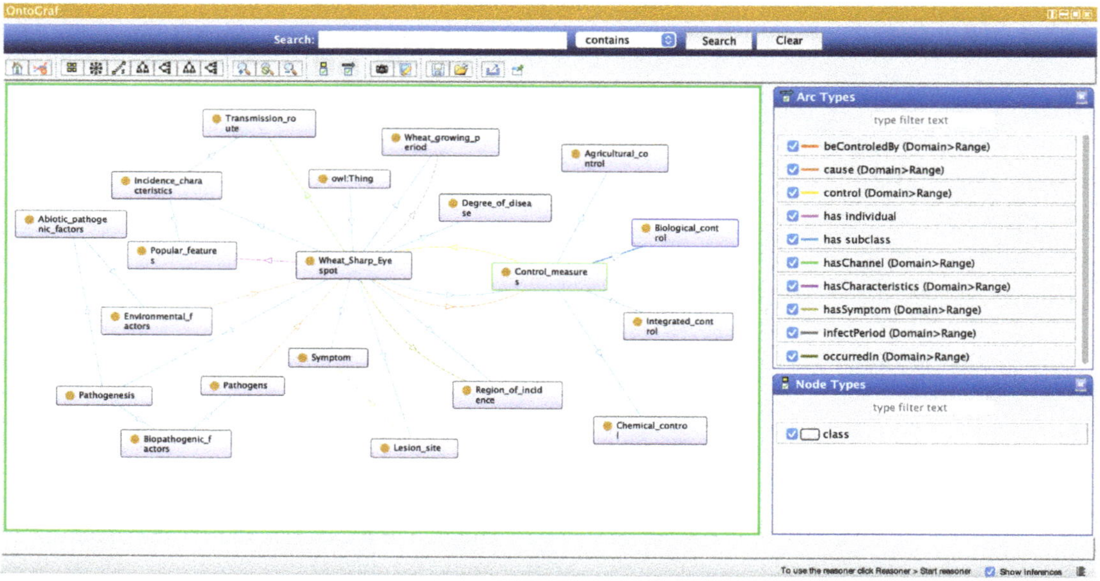

Figure 4. Ontology of wheat sharp eyespot control.

3.3. *Automated Ontology-Based Knowledge Extraction*

3.3.1. Model Training

In this study, a knowledge extraction model in the field of wheat sharp eyespot control was trained based on the ERNIE 3.0 knowledge enhancement pretraining model [31]. ERNIE 3.0 introduces large-scale knowledge graphs into pretraining models containing tens of billions of parameters. It proposes a parallel pretraining method that combines massive unsupervised text and large-scale knowledge graphs, known as Universal Knowledge–Text Prediction. Using a knowledge graph mining algorithm, it extracts 50 million knowledge graph triples and a 4TB large-scale corpus, which are simultaneously input into the pretraining model for joint mask training. This approach promotes information sharing between structured knowledge and unstructured text, significantly enhancing the model's memory and reasoning capabilities for knowledge.

The ERNIE 3.0 framework is divided into two layers (Figure 5). The first layer is the general semantic representation network, which learns basic and generalized knowledge from the data. The second layer is the task semantic representation network, which learns task-related knowledge based on the generic semantic representation. During the learning process, the task semantic representation network learns only the pretrained tasks of the corresponding category, while the generic semantic representation network learns all the pretrained tasks.

In this study, we selected the ERNIE 3.0 knowledge enhancement pretraining model to train a knowledge extraction model in the field of wheat sharp eyespot control. The main reasons for choosing ERNIE 3.0 include the following: (1) ERNIE 3.0 incorporates large-scale knowledge graphs, enabling the joint masked training of knowledge and text during the pretraining process. This promotes information sharing between structured knowledge and unstructured text, which is highly significant for knowledge integration and extraction in the agricultural field, especially for wheat sharp eyespot control; (2) ERNIE 3.0 is designed to significantly enhance the model's memory and reasoning abilities. This is crucial for application scenarios that require processing a large amount of complex agricultural knowledge and reasoning tasks, thereby better supporting the construction of agricultural expert systems; (3) the ERNIE 3.0 framework consists of two layers: the general semantic representation network and the task semantic representation network. These layers can learn basic and task-related knowledge, respectively. This structure improves the model's adaptability and generalization capabilities across different tasks, making it not only suitable for wheat sharp eyespot control but also extendable to other agricultural disease areas.

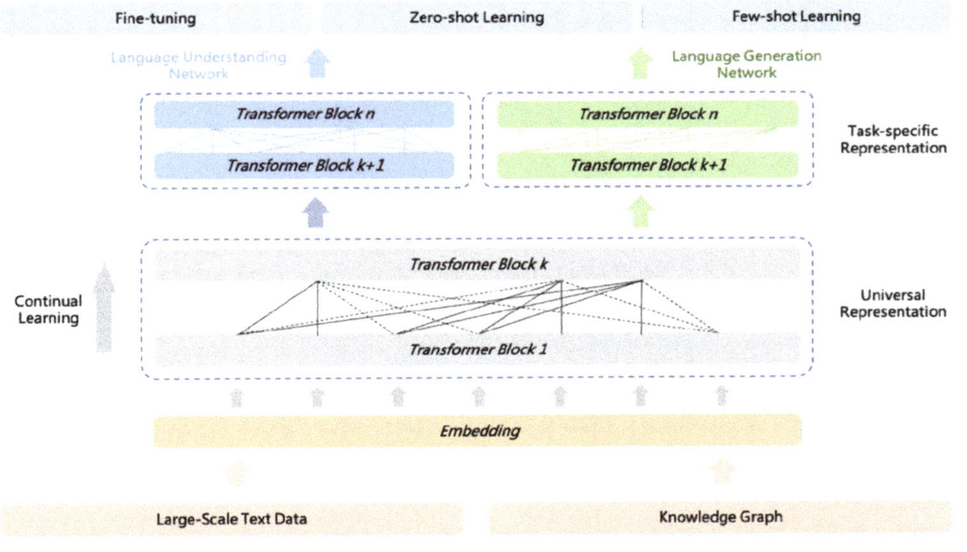

Figure 5. ERNIE 3.0 model framework.

In this study, we used the data annotation platform Doccano for data annotation and divided the data into a training set, validation set, and test set according to the ratio of 8:1:1. The appropriate construction of negative examples can enhance the model's effectiveness. The ratio of positive and negative samples in the training set was 5:1 in order to ensure the accuracy of the evaluation index. The validation and test sets were constructed with full negative examples by default. Table 5 presents the descriptive statistics of the datasets.

Table 5. Descriptive statistics of datasets.

Dataset	Total Samples	Positive Samples	Negative Samples
Training Set	2176	1813	363
Validation Set	272	272	0
Test Set	272	272	0

The learning rate was dynamically adjusted by using the strategy of cosine annealing [32] as follows:

$$\eta_t = \frac{1}{2}(\eta_{max} - \eta_{min})\left(1 + \cos\left(\frac{T_{cur}}{T_i}\pi\right)\right) \quad (2)$$

The initial value of η_{max} is the learning rate, T_{cur} is the current number of training rounds in the training process of SGDR (restart training SGD), and T_i is the number of epochs between two restarts of SGDR. When $T_{cur} = T_i$, set $\eta_t = \eta_{min}$. When $T_{cur} = 0$ after restart, set $\eta_t = \eta_{max}$.

To accurately evaluate the performance advantages and disadvantages of the model, we used three fundamental evaluation metrics in the field of entity–relationship extraction: precision, recall, and *F1* score. These metrics were employed to assess the model's performance comprehensively. The calculation method of each evaluation index was as follows:

- Recall: This metric determines the proportion of true facts that have actually been denoted as true by the model. Considering *TP* and *FN* as the number of true facts correctly and incorrectly classified, respectively, the recall can be obtained as follows:

$$R = \frac{TP}{TP + FN} \tag{3}$$

- Average Precision: This metric weights the precision and recall increment of the model at different threshold values n. It provides an overall measurement of the model's classification performance while penalizing biased predictions. It is calculated as follows:

$$AP = \sum_{n} (R_n - R_{n-1})P_n \tag{4}$$

where R refers to the recall value, and P represents the precision, computed as follows:

$$P = \frac{TP}{TP + FP} \tag{5}$$

where FP denotes the number of unfeasible facts predicted as true.

- *F1* Score: This metric is the harmonic mean between precision and recall and serves as an indicator of the model's accuracy. It can be calculated using the following equation:

$$F1 = \frac{2(P \times R)}{(P + R)} \tag{6}$$

The *F1* value is calculated between the predicted ternary and the gold ternary, and the prediction is considered correct when the predicted [pred_head, pred_rel, pred_tail] is exactly the same as the gold [head, rel, tail].

The model training process is shown in Figure 6. Compared to the baseline model UIE, the accuracy of our model increased by 13.89%, its recall increased by 22.27%, and the *F1* score increased by 17.86%. Table 6 shows the performance metrics of our model compared to the baseline model UIE.

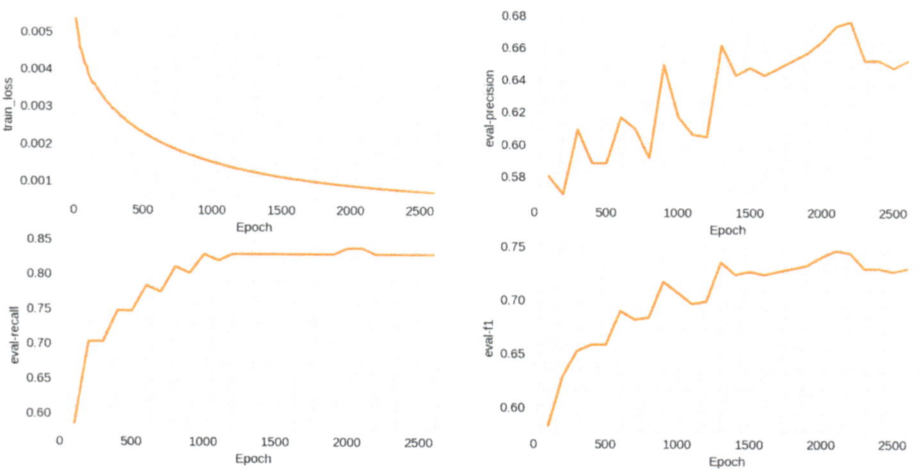

Figure 6. Model training process.

Table 6. Model performance metrics.

Metric	Our Model	Baseline Model UIE	Improvement
Precision/%	87.04	73.15	+13.89
Recall/%	95.92	73.65	+22.27
F1 Score/%	91.26	73.40	+17.86

3.3.2. Model-Based Reasoning

The wheat sharp eyespot domain knowledge extraction model was designed for document-level extraction tasks. For these tasks, a sliding window was used to combine contextual sentences and divide them into smaller paragraphs. This approach helps maintain the contextual coherence of the extracted knowledge fragments and reduces ambiguity. The sliding window covers different parts of the document to ensure that the extracted knowledge is both representative and diverse. Additionally, this method allows the model to process the entire document step by step without experiencing performance degradation or memory shortages due to the document's length. The specific inference algorithm is illustrated in Figure 7.

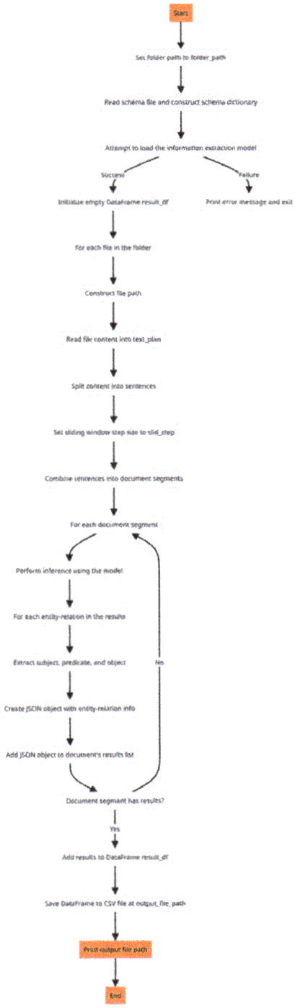

Figure 7. Inference workflow.

4. Discussion

The data sources for the ontology in the field of wheat sharp eyespot control, as constructed in this study, were primarily derived from the scientific and technical literature. In the future, the ontology can be extended by expanding the data sources. For example, credible resources on the Internet, patent databases, reports, and websites of agricultural research organizations can be utilized to collect the latest progress and new findings on wheat sharp eyespot control. During the actual application of the ontology, it needs to be constantly updated and improved. As research progresses, new concepts and relationships may emerge. When collecting new scientific and technological research and data, it is essential to incorporate this new information into the ontology in a timely manner to ensure its completeness. The emergence of large language models, such as the GPT, provides brand new possibilities for the extension of the ontology and the extraction of knowledge. Large language models can extract important information about wheat sharp eyespot control from extensive scientific and technical research, patent databases, and reports from other agricultural research institutions. They can integrate domain terminology and new concepts, facilitating the automated updating, optimization, and extension of knowledge. There have been related studies in the fields of biology and medicine, such as SPIRES, which involves a knowledge extraction algorithm based on a large language model [33] and genome aggregation using the GPT model as a complement to standard enrichment analysis [34]. The application of large language modeling in knowledge updating in the field of wheat sharp eyespot control deserves further exploration and practice.

5. Conclusions

In this study, we proposed an approach for ontology construction in the field of wheat sharp eyespot and developed an ontology-based knowledge extraction model that can efficiently extract relevant knowledge from text. This approach has significant advantages in integrating and organizing dispersed information and provides strong support for applications such as intelligent Q&A and intelligent recommender systems in the agricultural domain, thus facilitating knowledge discovery and sharing. Although the model performs well in the field of wheat sharp eyespot control, its effectiveness is dependent on the quality of the input data, and the scope of applicability needs to be further validated to confirm its applicability to different crops and agricultural diseases. Future work will focus on the following areas: expansion of the dataset to further collect more diverse and extensive datasets to improve the robustness and accuracy of the knowledge extraction model; the validation of cross-domain applicability, with a focus on adapting and validating the applicability of our knowledge extraction framework to other agricultural domains; and integration of the model with advanced decision support systems to better model the experts' decision-making process, help farmers and agricultural practitioners cope with wheat sharp eyespot more effectively, and promote sustainable agricultural development.

Author Contributions: K.L.: data curation, formal analysis, investigation, methodology, writing—original draft, writing—review and editing. Y.C.: funding acquisition, project administration, supervision, writing—review and editing. All authors have read and agreed to the published version of the manuscript.

Funding: This study was supported by the National Key Research and Development Program of China (2022YFF0711902-01), the Central Public-Interest Scientific Institution Basal Research Fund (Y2024XK07), the Fundamental Research Funds for AII-CAAS (JBYWAII202331), and Beijing Municipal Innovation Team Building Project for the Modern Agricultural Industry Technology System (BAIC10-2023-E10).

Institutional Review Board Statement: Not applicable.

Informed Consent Statement: Not applicable.

Data Availability Statement: The original contributions presented in the study are included in the article. Further inquiries can be directed to the corresponding author.

Conflicts of Interest: The authors declare that the research was conducted in the absence of any commercial or financial relationships that could be construed as a potential conflict of interest.

References

1. Boerema, G.H.; Verhoeven, A.A. Check-list for scientific names of common parasitic fungi. series 2b: Fungi on field crops: Cereals and grasses. *Neth. J. Plant Pathol.* **1977**, *83*, 165–204. [CrossRef]
2. Jia, T.; Wu, G.; Liu, C. Current status of research on root rot diseases of wheat in China and countermeasures for their prevention and control. *Chin. Agric. Sci.* **1995**, *3*, 41–48.
3. Pan, H. Occurrence of Wheat Sharp Eyespot and its control measures. *Henan Agric.* **2016**, *7*, 39.
4. Yao, L.; Wang, Q.; Fu, X.; Mei, R. Screening and characterization of Bacillus cereus against Wheat Sharp Eyespot. *China Biol. Control.* **2008**, *24*, 53–57.
5. Zheng, Y.; Zhu, D.; Wu, H.; Peng, X. A review of the knowledge graph Q&A domain. *Comput. Syst. Appl.* **2022**, *31*, 1–13.
6. Li, J. Research on the Construction Method and Application of Domain Ontology. Ph.D. Thesis, Chinese Academy of Agricultural Sciences, Beijing, China, 2009.
7. Consortium, T.P.O. The Plant Ontology™ Consortium and Plant Ontologies. *Comp. Funct. Genom.* **2002**, *3*, 137–142. [CrossRef] [PubMed]
8. Chang, C. Food and Agriculture Organization of the United Nations AOS Project. *J. Agric. Libr. Inf.* **2003**, *2*, 14–15+24.
9. Dai, C.-P.; Huang, Y.-D.; Qian, P.; Wang, R.J.; Dong, W.; Huang, Q. Research on the construction of rice pest and weed ontology. *Guangdong Agric. Sci.* **2011**, *38*, 191–194.
10. Yu, H.; Shen, J.; Bi, C.; Liang, J.; Chen, H. Intelligent diagnosis system for rice pests and diseases based on knowledge graph. *J. South China Agric. Univ.* **2021**, *42*, 105–116.
11. Qi, H.; Guan, Y.; Liu, Y. An ontology learning study of corn pests and diseases for Chinese text. *Comput. Eng. Appl.* **2011**, *47*, 206–209.
12. Zhang, L.; Duan, Q.; Li, D. Research on ontology construction technology for diagnosis and treatment of corn pests and diseases. *Agric. Mech. Res.* **2012**, *34*, 41–45.
13. Liu, G.; Yang, Q.; Liu, Q. Ontology construction and visualization of agricultural science datasets--Taking the field of "cotton disease control" as an example. *J. Intell.* **2022**, *41*, 143–149+175.
14. Ren, N.; Sun, Y.; Bao, T.; Guo, T. Research on ontology construction method in agricultural domain--Taking tomato pests and diseases as an example. *Intell. Explor.* **2021**, *7*, 51–57.
15. Deepa, R.; Vigneshwari, S. An effective automated ontology construction based on the agriculture domain. *ETRI J.* **2022**, *44*, 573–587. [CrossRef]
16. Xu, D.; Lu, W.; Xu, R.; Zhnag, H.; Jiang, Y.; You, L.; Feng, Z. A decision-making method for precision fertilization of rice based on spatio-temporal multimodal knowledge mapping in agriculture. *J. Huazhong Agric. Univ.* **2023**, *42*, 281–292.
17. Zeng, D.; Liu, K.; Lai, S.; Zhou, G.; Zhao, J. Relation classification via convolutional deep neural network. In Proceedings of the COLING 2014, the 25th International Conference on Computational Linguistics: Technical Papers, Dublin, Ireland, 23–29 August 2014.
18. Makoto, M.; Bansal, M. End-to-End Re-lation Extraction using LSTMs on Sequences and Tree Structures. In Proceedings of the 54th Annual Meeting of the Association for Computational Linguistics (Volume 1: Long Papers), Berlin, Germany, 7–12 August 2016.
19. Dong, L.; Lapata, M. Language to Logical Form with Neural Attention. In Proceedings of the 54th Annual Meeting of the Association for Computational Linguistics (Volume 1: Long Papers), Berlin, Germany, 7–12 August 2016.
20. Zheng, S.; Wang, F.; Bao, H.; Hao, Y.; Zhou, P.; Xu, B. Joint Extraction of Entities and Relations Based on a Novel Tagging Scheme. In Proceedings of the 55th Annual Meeting of the Association for Computational Linguistics (Volume 1: Long Papers), Vancouver, BC, Canada, 30 July–4 August 2017.
21. Luan, Y.; He, L.; Ostendorf, M.; Hajishirzi, H. Multi-Task Identification of Entities, Relations, and Coreference for Scien-tific Knowledge Graph Construction. In Proceedings of the 2018 Conference on Empirical Methods in Natural Language Processing, Brussels, Belgium, 31 October–4 November 2018.
22. Wang, J.; Lu, W. Two are better than one:Joint entity and relation extraction with table sequence encoders. *arXiv* **2020**, arXiv:2010.03851.
23. Sui, D.; Chen, Y.; Liu, K.; Zhao, J. Joint Entity and Relation Extraction with Set Prediction Networks. *arXiv* **2020**, arXiv:2011.01675. [CrossRef] [PubMed]
24. Moreno, A.; Isern, D.; Lpez Fuentes, A.C. Ontology-Based Information Extraction of Regulatory Networks from Scientific Articles with Case Studies for Escherichia Coli. *Expert Syst. Appl.* **2013**, *40*, 3266–3281. [CrossRef]
25. Li, C.X.; Su, Y.R.; Wang, R.J.; Wei, Y.Y.; Huang, H. Structured AJAX Data Extraction Based on Agricultural Ontology. *J. Integr. Agric.* **2012**, *11*, 784–791. [CrossRef]
26. Wimalasuriya, D.C.; Dou, D. Using Multiple Ontologies in Information Extraction. In Proceedings of the 18th ACM Conference on Information and Knowledge Management, Hong Kong, China, 2–6 November 2009; pp. 235–244. [CrossRef]
27. Zhang, L. Research on Ontology Construction Methods for Agricultural Domain Based on Narrative Lists and Literature Databases. Master's Thesis, Chinese Academy of Agricultural Sciences, Beijing, China, 2011.

28. Yang, J. Ontology-Based Knowledge Modeling and Reasoning for Citrus Pests and Diseases. Master's Thesis, Central China Normal University, Wuhan, China, 2014.
29. Li, J.; Meng, L. A Comparative Study of Methodological Systems for Constructing Knowledge Ontologies. *Mod. Libr. Intell. Technol.* **2004**, *7*, 17–22.
30. Song, J. Research on Agricultural Knowledge Mapping Construction Based on Knowledge Distillation. Master's Thesis, Harbin Institute of Technology, Harbin, China, 2022.
31. Wang, S.; Sun, Y.; Xiang, Y.; Wu, Z.; Ding, S.; Gong, W.; Feng, S.; Shang, J.; Zhao, Y.; Pang, C.; et al. Ernie 3.0 titan: Exploring larger-scale knowledge enhanced pre-training for language understanding and generation. *arXiv* **2021**, arXiv:2112.12731.
32. Loshchilov, I.; Hutter, F. Sgdr: Stochastic gradient descent with warm restarts. *arXiv* **2016**, arXiv:1608.03983.
33. Caufield, J.H.; Hegde, H.; Emonet, V.; Harris, N.L.; Joachimiak, M.P.; Matentzoglu, N.; Kim, H.; Moxon, S.; Reese, J.T.; Haendel, M.A.; et al. Structured prompt interrogation and recursive extraction of semantics (SPIRES): A method for populating knowledge bases using zero-shot learning. *arXiv* **2023**, arXiv:2304.02711. [CrossRef]
34. Joachimiak, M.P.; Caufield, J.H.; Harris, N.L.; Kim, H.; Mungall, C.J. Gene Set Summarization using Large Language Models. *arXiv* **2023**, arXiv:2305.13338v2.

information

MDPI

Article

Uncovering Tourist Visit Intentions on Social Media through Sentence Transformers

Paolo Fantozzi [1,†], Guglielmo Maccario [2,†] and Maurizio Naldi [1,3,*,†]

1 Department of Law, Economics, Politics, and Modern Languages, Libera Università Maria Ss. Assunta University, Via Marcantonio Colonna 19, 00192 Rome, Italy; p.fantozzi1@lumsa.it
2 Department of Economics, University of International Studies of Rome, Via Cristoforo Colombo 200, 00147 Rome, Italy; guglielmo.maccario@unint.eu
3 Department of Civil, Computer Science and Aeronautical Technologies Engineering, Roma Tre University, Via della Vasca Navale 79, 00146 Rome, Italy
* Correspondence: m.naldi@lumsa.it
† These authors contributed equally to this work.

Abstract: The problem of understanding and predicting tourist behavior in choosing their destinations is a long-standing one. The first step in the process is to understand users' intention to visit a country, which may later translate into an actual visit. Would-be tourists may express their intention to visit a destination on social media. Being able to predict their intention may be useful for targeted promotion campaigns. In this paper, we propose an algorithm to predict visit (or revisit) intentions based on the texts in posts on social media. The algorithm relies on a neural network sentence-transformer architecture using optimized embedding and a logistic classifier. Employing two real labeled datasets from Twitter (now X) for training, the algorithm achieved 90% accuracy and balanced performances over the two classes (visit intention vs. no-visit intention). The algorithm was capable of predicting intentions to visit with high accuracy, even when fed with very imbalanced datasets, where the posts showing the intention to visit were an extremely small minority.

Keywords: tourism; visit intention; social media; sentence transformers

1. Introduction

Tourists typically make informed decisions before traveling to visit a country or a specific destination. Their final choice may depend on several reasons. For example, they may decide their destination based on local culture to gain insights into the rich history, traditions, and customs of the destination [1]. The cultural distance between the country of origin and the destination may also be a driving factor [2]. They may wish to explore historic landmarks and archeological sites to understand the destination's past. They may be driven by the natural beauty of the destination, including the presence of unique landscapes, flora, and fauna [3]. Of course, they may also act based on the search for personal relaxation or recreation [4], as well as to participate in an event [5] or being moved by their personal nostalgia for the place [6]. In some cases, tourists may visit a country a second time or even become loyal visitors, choosing that country as their travel destination multiple times over the years. Tourists deciding to revisit a country have a special appeal, since it was shown in [7] that loyal visitors are more likely to spread word-of-mouth advertising and offer a lower risk associated with their profitability. However, first-time visitors are reported in that paper to be less price-sensitive and spend more.

Entities in charge of promoting tourism have a significant interest in identifying would-be visitors. Such entities may be tourism ministries, national or regional tourism boards, chambers of commerce, private tourism companies, and event and conference organizers. There are several reasons for that interest. Identifying potential visitors allows tourism entities to tailor their marketing efforts to specific demographics, interests, and preferences. This targeted approach increases the chances of attracting the right audience for a destination. Knowing the characteristics and preferences of potential visitors may enable tourism organizations to create customized promotional campaigns, such as personalized advertising, special promotions, and tailored messages that resonate with the target audience. Furthermore, by understanding the demographics and geographic locations of potential visitors, tourism entities can allocate their resources more efficiently and even plan and develop the necessary infrastructure to accommodate the increased demand, e.g., by improving transportation networks, expanding accommodation options, and enhancing other essential services.

However, where can tourism-promoting agencies spot would-be visitors?

Social media is gaining an increasing role in tourism promotion [8–10], acting as a modern and wide-ranging version of word-of-mouth (eWoM) mechanisms [11,12]. eWoM is particularly significant for tourism [13–15]. Tourism promotion bodies may use social media to disseminate destination-related information. Social media is also a means through which past or prospective visitors express their opinions, influencing other would-be visitors. Travel blogs have arisen to reach a wide audience and share the blogger's travel experiences [16]. Social media influencers may turn into real Internet celebrities whose endorsement may significantly increase the popularity of a destination [17]. The influence on would-be visitors may be quite remarkable. For millennials, it has been shown that sharing luxury travel experiences and benign envy toward the experience sharer stimulates consumers' own intentions to visit the same destination [18].

It is then a natural strategy for tourism promotion bodies to monitor social media and detect would-be visitors. This could be the first step towards opinion analysis tasks and more targeted promotional activities.

The literature has, so far, focused on identifying or checking the antecedents for visiting (or revisiting) a specific destination. Our purpose is, instead, to predict whether a specific prospective tourist manifests an intention to visit a destination. Detecting such an intention may be the first step in an organized strategy to transform that intention into a real visit. The information we exploit to perform that prediction is the text expressing prospective tourists' opinions on social media. This is a further difference with respect to the literature where questionnaires (i.e., a structured tool rather than a freeform tool) are employed to elicit tourists' attitudes. As far as the authors know, this is the first such attempt.

In this paper, we propose a sentence-transformer architecture to predict visit intention based on the text of posts on social media. We employ two datasets extracted from Twitter (now X) as the social media of choice and approach the problem as a classification task using logistic regression as a classifier. We show that we reach an average accuracy of 90%, with minimal deviations from that average performance figure.

Our original contributions are the following:

- We built two labeled datasets from social media containing opinions about Italy as a tourism destination;
- We applied machine learning techniques based on sentence transformers to predict visit intentions, considering both the cases where we have a largely imbalanced dataset and where the imbalance is mild, or nonexistent;
- We show the results of a preliminary explainability analysis to identify the most significant linguistic features that are associated with posts showing visit intentions.

After a brief review of the literature in Section 2, we describe our experimental data in Section 3 and our algorithm in Section 4. The results are reported in Section 5.

2. Literature Review

The analysis of visit intentions as expressed on social media has gathered much attention in the literature. In this section, we review the literature, dividing it into two main streams: the papers examining the determinants of the intention to visit and those investigating the use of social media to express or trigger the intention to visit a destination. Much work has been devoted to analyzing either of two well-known investigation areas, which are the *tourism destination image* and the *Product Country Image*. The relevance of social media as a means to promote tourism by national tourism organizations was already established in [19]. However, as far as the authors know, there is no paper addressing the same research question as the one dealt with in this paper, i.e., predicting the intention to visit a destination based on the text posted on social media. It is to be noted that our intention is not to understand the determinants of the intention to visit a country but to understand whether a post on social media expresses such an intention or not.

As factors that delimit the scope of the literature analysis, we considered the country of origin, the status (currently visiting versus not), and the method of opinion sampling (in a structured way as those expressed in a survey or through an unstructured approach, as the posts freely submitted on a social media platform).

We can first consider the papers aiming to identify the determinants of the intention to visit (or revisit) a country.

A seminal paper is attributed to [20], who built a structural equations model to describe travel intentions based on both paradigms of tourism destination image and Product Country Image.

In [21], a survey was employed to find out whether social media content about Saudi Arabia influences the decision to revisit the country, also through the mediation of perceived value and perceived trust. The survey was distributed to tourists from all over the world who were visiting the town of Al-Ahas in Saudi Arabia. The method employed to assess the degree of influence was standard Structural Equation Modeling (SEM).

Satisfaction was considered to mediate the intention to revisit for British tourists currently visiting Spain or Turkey in [22]. The research methodology employed a self-administered questionnaire.

The impact of risk and uncertainty on the intention to visit was examined in [23]. The destination country of choice was Australia, and panels from South Korea, China, and Japan were interviewed through a structured questionnaire for that purpose. A similar study was conducted for Table Mountain National Park in South Africa [24]. The perception of risk was also found to be critical for the decision to attend mega-events [25].

Instead, the influence of e-reputation, destination image, and social media marketing efforts on the intention to visit was examined in [26] through the Stimulus–Organism–Response (SOR) approach. The data were collected again through a survey distributed to tourists in a specific location in India.

The influence of food on the intention to revisit was examined in [27]. The sample was collected in Delhi, India, and was examined through SEM. The same aspect was investigated in [28], where the impact of the food images of France, Italy, and Thailand was assessed through an online survey targeting online travel and food groups from Yahoo.com and MSN.com.

The image of the destination is also a relevant factor, as shown in [29], where a SEM-based approach was employed to study its impact for American tourists traveling to Cuba. Four aspects that influence the perception of a tourism destination image were identified in [30]: experience, history and culture, leisure services, and tourist destination. Data employed in [30] came from an online travel platform (Ctrip Travel, considered to be the largest in China). Again, the most relevant dimensions were identified in [31], where posts from TripAdvisor and Mafengwo are analyzed. Sentiment analysis was carried out through VADER. A questionnaire-based survey was further employed to identify which attributes represent the image of a specific tourism destination.

A systematic literature review was conducted in [32] to investigate the use and impact of user-generated photos.

Two constructs were examined in [33] to predict the intention to visit a country: destination brand personality self-congruity and perceived risks derived from criminal activities. The data were collected in the USA and concerned the intention to visit Mexico (it was, therefore, a deviation from the other papers where the data collected concerned tourists from different countries). The method chosen for the analysis was, again, SEM.

The topics of interest in a tourism destination were determined by analyzing microblog social media in [34], both on-site and after the trip.

A standard SEM model was employed in [35] to investigate the effects of motivation, past experience, perceived constraint, and attitude on revisit intention for mainland Chinese tourists traveling to Hong Kong as their destination. Post-visit impressions were also examined in [36] by collecting data from micro-forums, blogs, e-commerce platforms, and websites.

Of course, the characteristics of tourists may also play a role in their destination decisions, namely due to the presence of an emotional connection between tourists' perceived self-image and the brand personality of destinations [37].

We can now turn to the investigation of social media as a means to express or strengthen the intention to visit a destination.

As to the relevance of social media, it was found that word-of-mouth spread through social media is a significant factor in triggering the intention to visit [38].

A specific analysis was carried out through questionnaires, considering Malaysia as the destination for medical tourism [39]. The role of social media (in comparison with other information sources) was found to be particularly relevant for attitudinal loyalty, i.e., the intention to visit coupled with past visits [40]. Again, the questionnaire tool was employed, targeting tourists from European countries. Social media was also found to be a mediating device for the influence of the subjective norm (i.e., the way the others perceive the tourist behaviors) on the intention to visit a destination [41]. The impact of social media on the effect that the destination image has on the intention to visit was also found to be significant in [42], where questionnaires compiled from Malaysian tourists were examined for a very specific destination in Saudi Arabia. A specific investigation concerning the role of posts on Facebook in triggering visit intentions through benign envy was examined in [43]. A questionnaire-based survey, though restricted to Vietnamese nationals, was carried out in [44] to determine the intention to visit as a function of the desire to visit, the destination image, envy, and the attitude towards visiting a travel destination. A SEM model was employed. Furthermore, the impact of user-generated content on the intention to revisit and word-of-mouth was analyzed in [45] through questionnaires collected in a specific destination (the Gulangyu island). The sentiment towards a tourism destination image was also analyzed in [46], employing nine measurement dimensions.

The opposite target was adopted in [47], where factors for non-revisiting were investigated using sentiment analysis techniques to label reviews posted on social media and, subsequently, examine the factors leading to positive or negative sentiments.

The relationship between the information quality of social media and the intention to travel was investigated in [48]. The method of analysis was based on the Elaboration likelihood model framework and employed multiple linear regression to test the research hypotheses. The viewpoint adopted in [48] is, however, different from ours: they study how the intention to travel of a social media user is influenced by other social media users through their posts (and the quality of the information they convey), while we considered whether a post by a social media user expresses their intention to travel.

Similarly, in [49], the information posted on social media was used as a source of recommendations for tourist destinations, which are filtered and summarized by a BERT architecture. The same considerations put forward earlier apply to the target of the investigation, though a machine learning tool, rather than multiple linear regression, was employed.

Again, questionnaires were employed in [50] to investigate the impact of social media on tourists' destination decisions, where the SEM method was employed to analyze the questionnaires. The same considerations on the focus of the study and the method of choice done for the previous papers apply.

The impact of advertising (namely the types of destination advertising) through social media on tourists' travel intentions was examined in [51], where an experiment was carried out, and statistical hypothesis testing was adopted.

Tourists' level of satisfaction, as well as the interaction with digital marketing channels, were investigated as the the antecedents of tourists' behavioral intentions in their destination selection [52]. The method was, again, SEM, relying on a set of questionnaires.

Means of avoiding the negative impacts of social media-induced tourism were studied in [53], where the leveraging of social media to encourage desirable traveler behaviors was also proposed. Social media were seen in this case as a tool to manage and exploit to obtain a desirable behavior, rather than a source of information.

A similar role for social media by influencers, who can actively influence the travel decisions of other social media users, was advocated in [54], where a mediation model was built and tested through SEM.

The reasons for using social media to plan one's travels were investigated in [55], where technological convenience and perceived enjoyment were found to be the biggest motivations for using social media.

The attitude of the endorser, namely their facial expression (e.g., whether smiling or not), was also found to be a significant factor in the success of influence [56].

The choice of sampling in a specific geographical location, however important it was, is a significant limitation of the studies conducted, with just a few exceptions.

With respect to the literature, our paper differs as follows. Our research question concerned detecting the intention to visit a destination rather than understanding the factors that influence that decision. Furthermore, we did not rely on questionnaires but drew on the potentially much larger data source represented by social media. The opinions we collected came from users that were not limited to a specific geographical area, unlike most literature. Questionnaires impose limitations due to the requirement of answering just the questions included in the questionnaire, while posts may include any opinion by the person posting it. Considering social media posts rather than questionnaires represents an improvement, since they widen the number of participants, their geographical origins, and their possibility of expression. Finally, we employed machine learning techniques rather than techniques based on a superimposed structured model like SEM. Structural Equation Models are linear by nature, while a machine learning approach allowed us to adopt intrinsically nonlinear relationships, hence offering a more flexible representation of reality. The papers employing machine learning in the literature survey do it for sentiment analysis, which is a task different from the one we were tackling here. This is the case of [36] (which employs BERT) and [47], which uses a selection of methods, including decision trees and Support Vector Machines. Latent Dirichlet allocation is employed in [30] to identify the topics of interest, which, again, is a task different from what we investigated here.

Overall, we can conclude that the goal that we considered here has not been pursued yet in the literature, so a comparison of our results with the literature cannot be made. On the other hand, the methods attempted so far to elicit the opinion of potential visitors (which, again, is a different task than that dealt with here) rely on tools (like questionnaires) and methods (like SEM) that are intrinsically less flexible and less powerful than our machine learning approach based on social media posts.

3. Dataset

In order to predict the visit intention as expressed on social media, we considered Twitter (now X) as the social media of choice. We extracted a large number of tweets using words related to tourism to filter out unrelated tweets. We focused on Italy as a country with a very large tourist base. We employed Twitter's API to retrieve the tweets of interest [57,58], following the approach in [59]. The query we used for the search was `Italy AND (visit OR holiday OR travel OR trip)`. We retrieved two datasets at different times using the same query. The two datasets differed largely in size and were labeled by different groups of examiners. The intent was to explore the performance of our method when fed with diverse inputs. In the following, we refer to those datasets as $D1$ (the smaller one) and $D2$ (the larger one). After collecting the data using Twitter's API, we removed the duplicates (there were 169 in $D1$ and 23 in $D2$). The text of each tweet was subsequently retrieved and labeled as either showing the intention to visit the country or not. Manual labeling was adopted. Each tweet was submitted to a couple of independent examiners (different for the two datasets). In the case of contrasting labels, the decision was reached by consensus. Consensus was built by a discussion between the two examiners. In the case of persisting differences, an expert adjudicator was called to decide. Cross-verification, where each examiner examines the labels provided by the other examiners, was therefore not needed as the examiners discussed the cases of contrasting labeling. The percentage of cases where consensus building was needed lay below 5% in both datasets. The accuracy of the process relied on the use of a couple of examiners, which reduced the risk of mislabeling. In fact, if we identify the probability of mislabeling for the single examiners as p_1 and p_2, the probability of obtaining a correct decision without resorting to consensus building was $(1 - p_1)(1 - p_2)$, and the probability of straightforward error was $p_1 p_2$ (i.e., when both examiners err), which is quite lower than the individual probabilities of error. We referred to the group showing the intention to visit as the VISIT class. Hence, the tweets concerning tourism but with no visit intentions were marked as the NOVISIT class. We stress the fact that we did not have any information about whether the people who posted the tweet actually visited Italy. We acted based on the text only and identified the sheer intention to visit.

The datasets' size and composition are shown in Table 1. As can be seen, we have two datasets of quite different sizes, *D*1 and *D*2, with *D*2 being roughly seven times as large as *D*1. The two datasets are made of completely different tweets, i.e., there is no overlapping. Furthermore, they exhibit quite different levels of balance. The composition of *D*1 is largely imbalanced, with the VISIT class representing just 4.2% of the total. Instead, *D*2, though not perfectly balanced, exhibits a mild imbalance, again with the VISIT class being the smaller one, representing 37.3% of the total.

Table 1. Dataset composition.

	Total	**VISIT**	**NOVISIT**
*D*1	4831	230	4601
*D*2	35,590	13,287	22,303

Since an imbalanced dataset may lead to misleading results, we employed rebalancing techniques for the dataset *D*1, which is heavily imbalanced. We refrained from using rebalancing techniques for the dataset *D*2, since it is just mildly imbalanced.

For the dataset *D*1, we employed downsampling to achieve a balanced dataset. Downsampling, as all rebalancing actions, aims at removing or mitigating the bias due to the larger presence of the majority class. Though downsampling could introduce bias of its own if done incorrectly, here, we employed random downsampling for the majority class. Specifically, we employed simple random sampling without replacement, where the size of the subsample obtained after downsampling is fixed, and each possible subsample has the same probability of being extracted [60], thus preserving the original distribution. Since we were applying sampling to a single class (the majority one), class-proportional techniques to preserve the original probability distribution, as in [61], were not needed. It has been shown, e.g., in [62], that downsampling helps manage the skewness due to the majority class and achieves better classifier performance. In order to exploit the minority class (VISIT instances) as much as possible, we kept all the VISIT instances and randomly sampled an equal number of NOVISIT instances. Since the number of VISIT instances was 230, we collected 230 NOVISIT instances and ended up with a dataset made of 460 tweets (230 per class). However, in order to fully exploit our imbalanced dataset, we employed cross-validation [63]. Cross-validation involves dividing the available data into multiple folds (subsets), using one of these folds as a testing set, and training the model on the remaining folds. This process is repeated multiple times, each time using a different fold as the testing set. Finally, the results from each testing step are averaged to produce a more robust estimate of the model's performance. As to the number of folds employed in cross-validation, most textbooks and libraries adopt a default value of 10. However, a recent experiment highlighted that the differences in performance due to the number of folds are quite limited, and the optimal number of folds lies between 10 and 20 [64], but depends on the overall size of the dataset. We opted for the higher end of the range and chose to use 20 folds. It is to be noted that the use of cross-validation practically removes the loss of information that is typically associated with downsampling, as the construction of several training datasets ends up exploiting all the instances in the dataset. Since we had 4601 NoVisit tweets for *D*1, we partitioned them into 20 groups of 230 tweets each to match the number of Visit tweets. This left a single tweet out, so we practically exploited the entire original dataset to its full extent. We selected each of those 20 groups, in turn, to couple them with the single group of Visit tweets, making 20 balanced datasets of 460 tweets each. Each balanced dataset was made of the unique group of 230 Visit tweets and one of the 20 groups of 230 NoVisit tweets. We carried out a 20-fold cross-validation, expecting something less than a 20-fold improvement in the variance, as all folds had half of their data in common, namely the Visit tweets. We ran our classification algorithm for each derived balanced dataset, randomly splitting the dataset into two portions, devoted, respectively, to training and testing according to the fixed proportions 80% and 20%, respectively.

As for the dataset *D*2, the imbalance was not so large as to call for rebalancing. In addition, the dataset was quite large. Hence, we employed it as it was, without any rebalancing or cross-validation.

4. Method

In this section, we describe the method we employed to identify the presence of a visit intention in posts on social media.

The task of distinguishing between Visit and NoVisit instances was modeled as a binary classification task. For the sake of avoiding confusion, we do not use the term *positive* for the Visit class (and, similarly, the term *negative* for the NoVisit class), since we will later use those terms in the contrastive approach that is embedded in SetFit. We did not distinguish whether the visit was actually a revisit, as we did not have information about the previous behavior of the people submitting the post. Revisit intentions were then labeled as visit intentions nonetheless, regardless of the fact that the would-be tourist had already visited the country. We stress, once again, that our purpose was not to predict whether the social media user would actually visit the country but rather to predict whether that user was showing the intention to visit the country in their post. In the absence of true, validated data about the social media user's identity and a tracking system that links that user to their travel behavior (e.g., tracking their entry into a country or their purchase of tickets), predicting users' actual visits could not be validated, and we were limited to predicting intentions.

In the following, we describe the methodology we employed to analyze the two datasets. As already mentioned, the two datasets exhibited quite a different degree of imbalance. For that reason, we employed different algorithms. Dataset *D*1 needed a thorough rebalancing activity, while that was not the case for *D*2. First, we describe the methodology for *D*1. What follows refers exclusively to *D*1, until we explicitly turn to *D*2.

As described in Section 3, the size of each training/testing dataset in the dataset *D*1 was not very large by machine learning standards: each fold was made of 460 tweets, which we further subdivided into a training portion (made of 368 tweets) and a testing one (made of 92 tweets). Nowadays, datasets in excess of hundreds of terabytes may be available [65]. The small-dataset problem is well known in machine learning. The capability of machine learning algorithms to recognize patterns is related to the size of the dataset: the smaller the dataset, the less accurate the algorithm [66]. However, good results may also be obtained with datasets as small as hundreds of instances [67]. The set of techniques to deal with small datasets in machine learning falls under the name of *few-shot learning* [34,68], where examples falling in the categories of few-shot learning exhibit a number of instances per class ranging from tens of instances to slightly beyond one thousand (see Table 3 in [68]).

The scarcity of labeled data made this dataset prone to be categorized as a case of few-shot learning [69]. For this reason, we resorted to the SETFIT method presented in [70], which should allow us to obtain good accuracy even in the presence of a small number of labeled instances in our training dataset. SETFIT relies on sentence transformers and falls into the class of few-shot learning methods, which aim to achieve good classification performances.

A graphical description of the flow of operation in SETFIT is shown in Figure 1. It is based on two phases. In the first phase, a sentence transformer is fine-tuned after being fed with sentence pairs under a contrastive approach. In the second phase, a text classification head is trained using the data output in the first phase as training data. We now describe the steps composing these two phases in Figure 1 in detail.

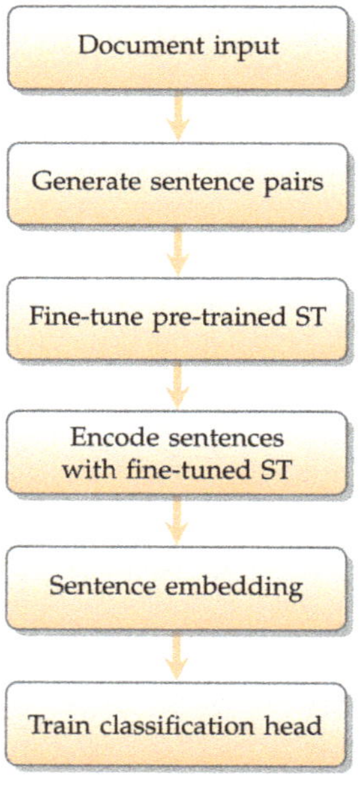

Figure 1. SETFIT flow diagram.

The first step, as described in Figure 1, is represented by feeding the algorithm with our documents. In our case, the dataset described in Section 3 was fed as a `csv` file, where each row contained a tweet and its label.

In the second step in Figure 1, we generated the pairs of positive and negative sentences. As we will describe hereafter, our method employed a Siamese configuration. Hence, we had to feed the model with pairs of labeled tweets rather than directly with VISIT and NOVISIT instances. For that purpose, we randomly picked pairs of tweets and labeled them. Labeling was performed using a contrastive criterion, i.e., we labeled pairs from the same class (e.g., two tweets both in the VISIT class) as positive and pairs from different classes (e.g., one tweet belonging in the VISIT class and the other in the NOVISIT) as negative. It is to be noted that labeling now applies to pairs of tweets rather than single tweets. This contrastive fine-tuning approach allowed us to obtain a much larger training set. As shown in [70], we obtained a roughly quadratic increase in the number of training instances. We now describe the sentence-pair generating process in more detail.

Formally, we had a dataset of n tweets $x_i, i = 1, 2, \ldots, n$ and their respective labels c_i, $i = 1, 2, \ldots, n$, with $c_i \in C = \{\text{VISIT}, \text{NOVISIT}\}$. For each fold, we generated a set of 460 tweets, perfectly balanced between the VISIT class and the NOVISIT class (i.e., 230 instances for each class). We recall that the VISIT instances were always the same, while a subdivision into twenty folds was made for the much larger NOVISIT class. By stratified sampling (so as to maintain the balance), we extracted the training and testing datasets according to the 80/20 proportions, which led us to have a training dataset made of 368 tweets and a testing dataset made of 92 tweets. From the dataset, we randomly picked R same-class pairs and R different-class pairs. If the number of tweets in the VISIT class is v and that in the NOVISIT class is nv, the number of potential same-class pairs is $sc = \frac{v(v-1)}{2} + \frac{nv(nv-1)}{2}$, where the first term represents all the pairs that we can form by coupling two VISIT instances (which can be obtained as the number of combinations of v instances two by two, i.e., $\binom{v}{2} = \frac{v!}{2!(v-2)!} = \frac{v(v-1)}{2}$), and the second term refers, instead, to the NOVISIT instances. For the training dataset, since we must have a balanced dataset, in the end, we needed $v = nv = 184$ after downsampling from the original dataset of 4831 instances (we recall, once again, that downsampling actually refers to the NOVISIT class only). The number of potential same-class pairs was then $sc = 33{,}672$. On the other hand, the number of potential different-class pairs was $dc = v \cdot nv$, where we coupled each VISIT instance with each NOVISIT instance. This formula is simply the cardinality of the Cartesian product of the set of VISIT instances by the set of NOVISIT instances. Again, in the case at hand, $v = nv = 184$, so we had $dc = 33{,}856$. We marked the same-class (positive) pairs with bit 1 and different-class (negative) pairs with bit 0. For both classes, we had two sets of pairs (positive and negative). For the class VISIT, after adding the bit showing class concordance, we had the sets of triplets $T_p^V = \{(x_i, x_j, 1)\}$, where $c_i = c_j =$ VISIT, and $T_n^V = \{(x_i, x_j, 0)\}$, where $c_i = c_j =$ VISIT. Similarly, for the class NOVISIT, we had $T_p^{NV} = \{(x_i, x_j, 1)\}$, where $c_i = c_j =$ NOVISIT, and $T_n^{NV} = \{(x_i, x_j, 0)\}$, where $c_i = c_j =$ NOVISIT. We generated the fine-tuning dataset by aggregating the positive and negative triplets across the two classes $T = \{(T_p^V, T_n^V), (T_p^{NV}, T_n^{NV})\}$.

The third step in Figure 1 consists of fine-tuning a sentence transformer. Sentence transformers are derived from pre-trained transformer models that use Siamese and triplet network structures to obtain semantically meaningful sentence embeddings [71]. By semantically meaningful, it is intended that the vector representation of two semantically similar words are close to each other in the vector space. In a Siamese (triplet) neural network, identical algorithms are applied to two (three) input vectors along two (three) parallel paths, with their outputs being compared at the end [72,73]. The sentence transformer we used is a modification of the BERT (Bidirectional Encoder Representations from Transformers) model [74], namely `paraphrase-mpnet-base-v2` (see the model on the Hugging Face repository at https://huggingface.co/sentence-transformers/paraphrase-mpnet-base-v2 (accessed on 29 September 2024)). Fine-tuning the model was accomplished by feeding our Siamese configuration with the pairs of positive and negative instances. The semantic similarity was evaluated through the cosine similarity between the embedding vector representation of those tweets. Fine-tuning was carried out by minimizing the cosine similarity (which plays the role of loss function) between the vectors representing positive pairs and maximizing it for negative pairs, as in [70]. This optimization (minimization and maximization) task was accomplished through the AdamW optimizer [75]. This optimizer has been shown in [76] to yield models that generalize much better than Adam and to compete with the stochastic gradient descent optimizer while training much faster. The fine-tuned model was then used to encode the sentences (step 4 in Figure 1) and obtain a single sentence embedding per training sample (step 5 in Figure 1).

After obtaining the optimal encoding, we could use the embedding that was now associated with the tweets as features for the classifier. Specifically, the components of each embedding vector, together with the associated label, were fed as input to the classifier. As a classifier, we employed logistic regression, adopting the same choice as in [70]. The logistic classifier returned a probability value for each of the two classes. We chose the higher-probability class as the output of our classifier.

After this long description of the method employed for the dataset $D1$, we can now describe the much simpler procedure for the dataset $D2$. We did not need rebalancing. We did not need cross-validation. We did not need to adopt a few-shots learning approach. For $D2$, we just coded each tweet through the same sentence transformer employed for $D1$, without any fine-tuning, and then fed those embeddings to the logistic classifier.

5. Results

In this section, we show the results of our classification task to predict the intention to visit a tourism destination, Italy in our case.

We employed the following well-established performance metrics:

- Accuracy;
- Precision;
- Recall;
- F1.

In order to precisely define these metrics, we now associate the term *Positive* with VISIT and *Negative* with NOVISIT, so that, e.g., True Positives (TPs) will represent the VISIT instances that were correctly classified as such, while False Negatives (FNs) will represent the VISIT instances that were incorrectly classified as NOVISIT ones. The labels assigned to the instances by the human experts mentioned in Section 3 were considered as the ground truth.

Accuracy is defined as the percentage of correctly classified instances:

$$\text{Accuracy} = \frac{\text{TP} + \text{TN}}{\text{TP} + \text{TN} + \text{FP} + \text{FN}} \tag{1}$$

Precision is the percentage of truly VISIT instances over all the instances that have been classified as VISIT ones:

$$\text{Precision} = \frac{\text{TP}}{\text{TP} + \text{FP}} \tag{2}$$

Recall is the percentage of VISIT instances that have been correctly classified as VISIT, i.e., is the accuracy over the VISIT class:

$$\text{Recall} = \frac{\text{TP}}{\text{TP} + \text{FN}} \tag{3}$$

Finally, F1 is the harmonic mean of precision and recall:

$$\text{F1} = 2\frac{\text{Precision} \cdot \text{Recall}}{\text{Precision} + \text{Recall}} \tag{4}$$

We first report the results for the dataset $D1$ and then for the dataset $D2$.

As stated in Section 3, for the dataset $D1$, we adopted a cross-validation approach to make full use of our data. Since we obtained 20 training and testing datasets, we carried out a 20-fold cross-validation. For each fold, we computed all four performance metrics introduced earlier: accuracy, precision, recall, and F1. We iterated network training through ten epochs.

In Tables 2–5, we report the values of all four performance metrics for epochs 1, 2, 5, and 10, respectively.

The average accuracy is over 90% up to five epochs and goes slightly below (89.4%) for ten epochs. The minimum accuracy achieved over the 20 folds is 85%. The coefficient of variation (ratio of standard deviation to average value) for accuracy is never larger than 3.5%. Hence, the accuracy is very high and pretty stable across the folds. We obtain similar performances by looking at other metrics. The average precision is not lower than 86.7%, with a peak of 90% at epoch 1. The standard deviation is a bit larger, but always around 5%. We obtain higher values for the recall metrics, which exhibit an average value significantly higher than 90% and a coefficient of variation around 3%. As can be seen, all the metrics exhibit a very low standard deviation across the 20 folds. Hence, the performance of our algorithm appears very stable and reliable. Though the performance metrics exhibit very close value, recall is always found to be larger than precision: the algorithm is slightly generous in assigning instances to the VISIT class, allowing us to capture more VISIT instances at the risk of including some NOVISIT instances in the VISIT class.

Table 2. Performance metrics: one epoch.

Fold	Accuracy	Precision	Recall	F1
1	0.880435	0.857143	0.913043	0.884211
2	0.934783	0.934783	0.934783	0.934783
3	0.891304	0.846154	0.956522	0.897959
4	0.923913	0.953488	0.891304	0.921348
5	0.923913	0.933333	0.913043	0.923077
6	0.902174	0.877551	0.934783	0.905263
7	0.913043	0.895833	0.934783	0.914894
8	0.934783	0.916667	0.956522	0.936170
9	0.945652	0.955556	0.934783	0.945055
10	0.902174	0.862745	0.956522	0.907216
11	0.923913	0.914894	0.934783	0.924731
12	0.891304	0.875000	0.913043	0.893617
13	0.923913	0.933333	0.913043	0.923077
14	0.945652	0.936170	0.956522	0.946237
15	0.858696	0.866667	0.847826	0.857143
16	0.934783	0.916667	0.956522	0.936170
17	0.891304	0.875000	0.913043	0.893617
18	0.945652	0.936170	0.956522	0.946237
19	0.858696	0.811321	0.934783	0.868687
20	0.891304	0.909091	0.869565	0.888889
Average	0.91087	0.900378	0.926087	0.912419
Std dev	0.027225	0.039553	0.030254	0.025912

Table 3. Performance metrics: two epochs.

Fold	Accuracy	Precision	Recall	F1
1	0.869565	0.854167	0.891304	0.872340
2	0.934783	0.916667	0.956522	0.936170
3	0.880435	0.843137	0.934783	0.886598
4	0.934783	0.954545	0.913043	0.933333
5	0.945652	0.936170	0.956522	0.946237
6	0.923913	0.914894	0.934783	0.924731
7	0.858696	0.836735	0.891304	0.863158
8	0.891304	0.846154	0.956522	0.897959
9	0.945652	0.955556	0.934783	0.945055
10	0.902174	0.862745	0.956522	0.907216
11	0.913043	0.880000	0.956522	0.916667
12	0.891304	0.875000	0.913043	0.893617
13	0.913043	0.880000	0.956522	0.916667
14	0.934783	0.916667	0.956522	0.936170
15	0.880435	0.888889	0.869565	0.879121
16	0.891304	0.846154	0.956522	0.897959
17	0.913043	0.895833	0.934783	0.914894
18	0.956522	0.956522	0.956522	0.956522
19	0.847826	0.796296	0.934783	0.860000
20	0.913043	0.913043	0.913043	0.913043
Average	0.907065	0.888459	0.933696	0.909873
Std dev	0.030434	0.04454	0.026834	0.028227

Table 4. Performance metrics: five epochs.

Fold	Accuracy	Precision	Recall	F1
1	0.847826	0.820000	0.891304	0.854167
2	0.934783	0.916667	0.956522	0.936170
3	0.880435	0.843137	0.934783	0.886598
4	0.923913	0.914894	0.934783	0.924731
5	0.902174	0.911111	0.891304	0.901099
6	0.923913	0.914894	0.934783	0.924731
7	0.880435	0.843137	0.934783	0.886598
8	0.880435	0.843137	0.934783	0.886598
9	0.945652	0.955556	0.934783	0.945055
10	0.923913	0.897959	0.956522	0.926316
11	0.902174	0.862745	0.956522	0.907216
12	0.858696	0.851064	0.869565	0.860215
13	0.923913	0.933333	0.913043	0.923077
14	0.945652	0.936170	0.956522	0.946237
15	0.869565	0.840000	0.913043	0.875000
16	0.945652	0.936170	0.956522	0.946237
17	0.891304	0.891304	0.891304	0.891304
18	0.923913	0.897959	0.956522	0.926316
19	0.847826	0.785714	0.956522	0.862745
20	0.891304	0.860000	0.934783	0.895833
Average	0.902174	0.882748	0.930435	0.905312
Std dev	0.032128	0.045845	0.02695	0.029533

Table 5. Performance metrics: 10 epochs.

Fold	Accuracy	Precision	Recall	F1
1	0.858696	0.836735	0.891304	0.863158
2	0.945652	0.955556	0.934783	0.945055
3	0.891304	0.875000	0.913043	0.893617
4	0.923913	0.897959	0.956522	0.926316
5	0.923913	0.914894	0.934783	0.924731
6	0.913043	0.880000	0.956522	0.916667
7	0.880435	0.843137	0.934783	0.886598
8	0.858696	0.800000	0.956522	0.871287
9	0.945652	0.955556	0.934783	0.945055
10	0.880435	0.830189	0.956522	0.888889
11	0.869565	0.826923	0.934783	0.877551
12	0.902174	0.877551	0.934783	0.905263
13	0.880435	0.830189	0.956522	0.888889
14	0.923913	0.914894	0.934783	0.924731
15	0.858696	0.836735	0.891304	0.863158
16	0.891304	0.875000	0.913043	0.893617
17	0.880435	0.857143	0.913043	0.884211
18	0.913043	0.895833	0.934783	0.914894
19	0.858696	0.800000	0.956522	0.871287
20	0.880435	0.843137	0.934783	0.886598
Average	0.894022	0.867321	0.933696	0.898579
Std dev	0.028405	0.045207	0.020533	0.025409

Recall is found to be higher (on average) than precision on all epochs. The algorithm is definitely cleverer at recognizing posts showing the intention to visit than rejecting posts that do not show that intention. In a real scenario, where negatives largely outnumber positives (with roughly a 20:1 ratio in some datasets like $D1$, as can seen in Table 1), this behavior can lead to quite a higher number of false positives than false negatives and make the algorithm err on the more tolerant side, labeling as positive more posts than what would be right.

We can see how the estimated accuracy changes with the number of epochs. In Figure 2, we have plotted the accuracy with three-sigma error bars vs. the number of epochs. Under the Gaussian assumption for the distribution of the sampling accuracy, the three-sigma interval ensures that accuracy values fall into this interval with 99.7% probability [77]. Hence, the three-sigma interval can be considered a safe bracket for the accuracy values we can obtain for out-of-sample data. We can see that the average accuracy degrades by a tiny amount (1.8%), probably highlighting a slight overfitting. In order to provide a quantitative indication of the degree of overfitting, we compare the accuracy we have obtained on the training and testing datasets, respectively. The presence of overfitting is due to the ML model parameters being too fit for the training dataset at the expense of the capability of generalizing and obtaining good accuracy on the testing dataset. For that reason, we considered the following overfitting metric, where the accuracy gap is normalized to the average accuracy over the testing and training datasets:

$$\text{Ofit} = \frac{\text{Acc}_{\text{train}} - \text{Acc}_{\text{test}}}{\text{Acc}_{\text{train}} + \text{Acc}_{\text{test}}} \tag{5}$$

We obtained Ofit $= 0.0222$, i.e., the accuracy gap was slightly larger than 2%, which can be considered quite a low value. Going back to Figure 2, the estimation interval width is quite steady, with a 3-σ roughly around $\pm$ 0.09 (i.e., roughly 10% of the average accuracy).

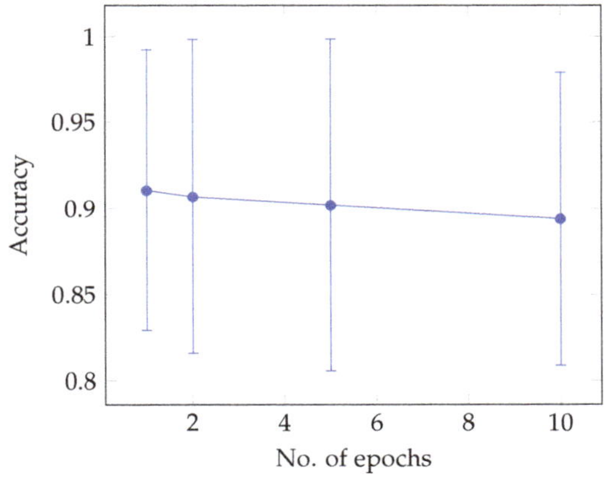

Figure 2. Three-sigma accuracy vs. number of epochs.

We can achieve a better understanding of the way our algorithm errs and where it may be improved by looking at the confusion matrix. We focused on the two extreme cases, i.e., the best-accuracy fold (which was 9 in epoch 1) and the worst-accuracy fold (which was 14 in epoch 1). We report the two confusion matrices in Tables 6 and 7, respectively. The number of total instances is 92, i.e., 20% of the total dataset made of 460 instances. As can be seen, our algorithm is quite balanced, with type I errors (i.e., mistaking no-intention posts for intention ones or false positives) slightly prevailing in the best-performing fold and the reverse happening for the worst-performing fold (where false negatives slightly prevail). Of course, as already hinted, these values refer to our balanced dataset and would change in the presence of an imbalanced scenario that may occur in the actual application of the algorithm.

Table 6. Confusion matrix for best-accuracy fold in epoch 1 (V: Visit and NV: NoVisit).

		Predicted		
		V	**NV**	**Total**
Actual	V	44	2	46
	NV	3	43	46
	Total	47	45	92

Table 7. Confusion matrix for worst-accuracy fold in epoch 1 (V: Visit and NV: NoVisit).

		Predicted		
		V	**NV**	**Total**
Actual	V	39	7	46
	NV	6	40	46
	Total	45	47	92

We can now examine the results for the dataset *D*2. In Table 8, we show the confusion matrix. As stated in Section 4, for the dataset *D*2, we did not need to resort to rebalancing and cross-validation. Hence, there is no across-fold analysis. The overall accuracy is 90.2%, while the per-class accuracy values are, respectively, 89% for the Visit class and 91% for the NoVisit class. As can be seen, the performances of the two classes are very close, and the bias towards the majority class is extremely limited without resorting to rebalancing. If we look at the other performance metrics as we did for *D*1, we obtain a precision of 85.4% and a recall of 89%. Again, the two metrics are rather close, but recall is higher than precision. This result confirms what we observed for *D*1: the algorithm tends to include more instances than necessary in the Visit classes. Furthermore, the performance appears quite aligned for both the small, heavily imbalanced dataset *D*1 and the larger, mildly imbalanced dataset *D*2.

Table 8. Confusion matrix for the dataset *D*2 (V: Visit and NV: NoVisit).

		Predicted		
		V	**NV**	**Total**
Actual	V	2364	293	2657
	NV	403	4058	4461
	Total	2767	4351	7118

Finally, we analyzed the linguistic features that were associated with the user's intentions. First, we analyzed two sample tweets to examine how the sentence elements contribute to the algorithm's decision in a concrete case. We then considered the top features across the whole dataset. We first considered two sample tweets labeled, respectively, as Visit and NoVisit and correctly classified by our classifier. For both, we carried out an explainability analysis by adopting the LIME (Local Interpretable Model-agnostic Explanation) method [78], using the words in the tweets as features (see [79] for a recent survey of explainability methods for transformers). The LIME method provides a surrogate linear model, where the weights in the regression equation represent the relative importance of the associated features (each feature acts as a regressor in the linear model) in leading to the classifier's decisions. In Figure 3, we see that the major features justifying the label Visit mention Italy and the verb *wanna* shows a voluntary action. On the other hand, the major features for the NoVisit tweet in Figure 4 are, again, *Italy* and *want* as the major positive features, while the *think* verb and the personal noun *Daniel* appear as the major negative features leading to the overall negative intention. In both cases, the use of verbs appear as a major element in explaining the classifier's decisions.

In Figure 5, we see, instead, the ten features with the highest average weight, considering all the tweets. All the terms have been pre-converted to lowercase. We see two terms, *travel* and *visit*, that form the object of the intention expressed in the tweet. We see, again, the voluntary verb *wanna* and the motion verb *go*, associated with the motion preposition *to*. A specific destination appears (*Taormina*). The picture is completed by the reference to the user itself (*myself*) and *watercolour*, related to the landscape sometimes associated with the destination.

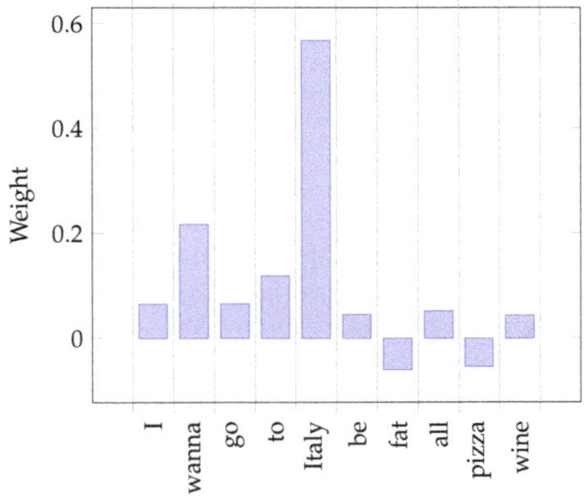

Figure 3. Feature weights for the tweet *I just wanna go to Italy and be a fat ass and eat all the pasta, pizza and drink wine*, correctly labeled as VISIT.

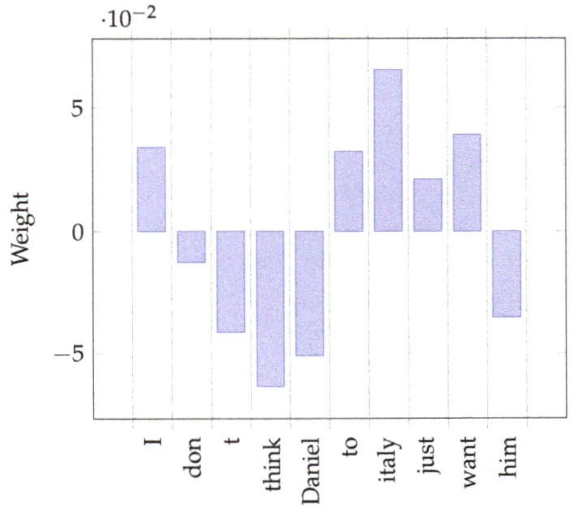

Figure 4. Feature weights for the tweet *At this point I do not think Daniel will come back to italy anytime soon and I'm sad I just want them back here*, correctly labeled as NOVISIT.

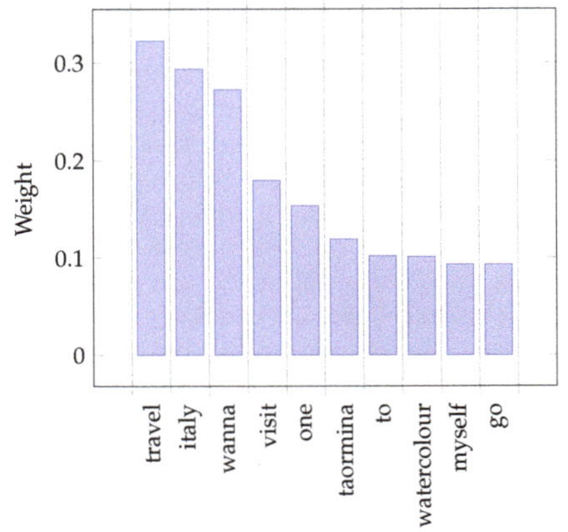

Figure 5. Top 10 feature weights (across all the tweets).

6. Conclusions

As far as the authors know, the problem of predicting visit intentions from the texts of posts on social media has not been tackled before. We have modeled that problem as a classification task here and proposed a logistic regression classifier based on sentence transformers to carry out the classification task.

The results show that we can achieve a high classification accuracy (roughly 90%). We erred on the plus side, adding to the score of posts showing the intention to visit posts that do not actually show that intention. However, we can consider this to be the least harmful of the two types of error. We can envisage the output of the classification as triggering a targeted communication effort to strengthen the intention to visit and transform it into a real visit to the intended destination. Though we do not know additional information about the social media participants, they can be reached through the same social media where they expressed their interest in a country or a specific destination and push marketing information about the places of their interest, proposing special offers and discounts for travel and accommodation. With this aim in sight, being more generous in classification would mean widening the audience of our communication campaign, even if some of those we reach may not be interested. Erring on the other side, i.e., not including social media users who actually intend to visit the destination in our communication campaign, would instead mean excessively restricting our communication audience and failing to reach otherwise valuable customers.

There are several possible uses of the information that we can extract from social media about the intentions of people to visit a specific destination (we considered Italy, i.e., a country, as a case study, but the methodology can easily be applied to more specific destinations, such as towns or even monuments or cultural institutions). For example, tourism boards and private companies wishing to promote a tourist destination could target the social media users who expressed the intention to visit, build a list of potential targets for marketing campaigns made of those users' usernames, and then use them as recipients of promotion campaign messages. Addressing people who have already expressed their intention to visit would certainly increase the conversion rate of the promotion campaign. Another possibility would be to use the explainability analysis to extract some features that may be more interesting for the would-be visitor (since they have been a major driving force for the ML model to make the classification decision) and use them as leverage to build more attention-grabbing campaigns.

As a limitation, we must admit that intentions, as identified by labelers, may be misinterpreted and may not transform into actual visits. In practical terms, that would mean that a promotion campaign based on the ML model's output would miss its target and would address people who are not interested in visiting the country. A more accurate identification of intentions would require, however, sidelining posts with other information. For example, a more accurate determination of the ground truth would call for the analysis of the subsequent behavior, e.g., examining whether a post has been followed by an actual visit. However, the latter would require tracking the user, which is not possible unless you have access to personal information concerning purchasing behavior. This would be accurate only if we are able to match the poster's identity across platforms (i.e., the social media platform with the e-commerce platform used to purchase travel tickets or accommodation). A promotion campaign based on the social media username only would certainly be less effective, since it could not use additional information to target the potential visitor more specifically and customize the offer. An interesting line of research would be to draw an integrated sales and media strategy that would induce the social media user to release more information about themselves, e.g., through a more controlled registration process, and ease the transmission of information between the social media platform and the sales channel.

Author Contributions: Conceptualization, M.N. and G.M.; methodology, M.N. and P.F.; software, P.F.; validation, P.F.; formal analysis, M.N.; investigation, P.F.; resources, M.N. and P.F.; data curation, P.F.; writing—original draft preparation, P.F.; writing—review and editing, M.N.; visualization, P.F.; supervision, M.N.; project administration, G.M. All authors have read and agreed to the published version of the manuscript.

Funding: This research received no external funding

Institutional Review Board Statement: Not applicable.

Informed Consent Statement: Not applicable.

Data Availability Statement: An anonymous version of the data employed in this paper is available from the authors upon request.

Conflicts of Interest: The authors declare no conflicts of interest.

Abbreviations

The following abbreviations are used in this manuscript:

API	Application Programming Interface
BERT	Bidirectional Encoder Representations from Transformers
eWoM	Electronic word-of-mouth
LIME	Local Interpretable Model-agnostic Explanation
ML	Machine learning
SOR	Stimulus–Organism–Response
VADER	Valence-Aware Dictionary and sEntiment Reasoner

References

1. Timothy, D.J. Contemporary cultural heritage and tourism: Development issues and emerging trends. *Public Archaeol.* **2014**, *13*, 30–47. [CrossRef]
2. Ng, S.I.; Lee, J.A.; Soutar, G.N. Tourists' intention to visit a country: The impact of cultural distance. *Tour. Manag.* **2007**, *28*, 1497–1506. [CrossRef]
3. Todd, C. Nature, beauty and tourism. In *Philosophical Issues in Tourism*; Channel view Publishing: Bristol, UK, 2009; pp. 154–170.
4. Csirmaz, É.; Pető, K. International trends in recreational and wellness tourism. *Procedia Econ. Financ.* **2015**, *32*, 755–762. [CrossRef]
5. Hillman, P.; Lamont, M.; Scherrer, P.; Kennelly, M. Reframing mass participation events as active leisure: Implications for tourism and leisure research. *Tour. Manag. Perspect.* **2021**, *39*, 100865. [CrossRef]
6. Christou, P.A. Tourism experiences as the remedy to nostalgia: Conceptualizing the nostalgia and tourism nexus. *Curr. Issues Tour.* **2020**, *23*, 612–625. [CrossRef]
7. Petrick, J.F. Are loyal visitors desired visitors? *Tour. Manag.* **2004**, *25*, 463–470. [CrossRef]
8. Zeng, B.; Gerritsen, R. What do we know about social media in tourism? A review. *Tour. Manag. Perspect.* **2014**, *10*, 27–36. [CrossRef]
9. Mir, T. Role of social media in tourism: A literature review. *Int. J. Res. Appl. Sci. Eng. Technol.* **2017**, *5*, 633–635.
10. Gebreel, O.S.S.; Shuayb, A. Contribution of social media platforms in tourism promotion. *Int. J. Soc. Sci. Educ. Commun. Econ.* **2022**, *1*, 189–198.
11. Barreto, A.M. The word-of-mouth phenomenon in the social media era. *Int. J. Mark. Res.* **2014**, *56*, 631–654. [CrossRef]
12. Kimmel, A.J.; Kitchen, P.J. Word of mouth and social media. *J. Mark. Commun.* **2014**, *20*, 2–4. [CrossRef]
13. Tham, A.; Croy, G.; Mair, J. Social media in destination choice: Distinctive electronic word-of-mouth dimensions. *J. Travel Tour. Mark.* **2013**, *30*, 144–155. [CrossRef]
14. Pourfakhimi, S.; Duncan, T.; Coetzee, W.J. Electronic word of mouth in tourism and hospitality consumer behaviour: State of the art. *Tour. Rev.* **2020**, *75*, 637–661. [CrossRef]
15. Reyes-Menendez, A.; Correia, M.B.; Matos, N.; Adap, C. Understanding online consumer behavior and eWOM strategies for sustainable business management in the tourism industry. *Sustainability* **2020**, *12*, 8972. [CrossRef]
16. Chen, Y.C.; Shang, R.A.; Li, M.J. The effects of perceived relevance of travel blogs' content on the behavioral intention to visit a tourist destination. *Comput. Hum. Behav.* **2014**, *30*, 787–799. [CrossRef]
17. Xu, X.; Pratt, S. Social media influencers as endorsers to promote travel destinations: an application of self-congruence theory to the Chinese Generation Y. *J. Travel Tour. Mark.* **2018**, *35*, 958–972.
18. Liu, H.; Wu, L.; Li, X. Social media envy: How experience sharing on social networking sites drives millennials' aspirational tourism consumption. *J. Travel Res.* **2019**, *58*, 355–369. [CrossRef]
19. Stankov, U.; Lazic, L.; Dragicevic, V. The extent of use of basic Facebook user-generated content by the national tourism organizations in Europe. *Eur. J. Tour. Res.* **2010**, *3*, 105–113. [CrossRef]

20. Nadeau, J.; Heslop, L.; O'Reilly, N.; Luk, P. Destination in a country image context. *Ann. Tour. Res.* **2008**, *35*, 84–106. [CrossRef]
21. Helal, E.A.; Hassan, T.H.; Abdelmoaty, M.A.; Salem, A.E.; Saleh, M.I.; Helal, M.Y.; Abuelnasr, M.S.; Mohamoud, Y.A.; Abdou, A.H.; Radwan, S.H.; et al. Exploration or Exploitation of a Neighborhood Destination: The Role of Social Media Content on the Perceived Value and Trust and Revisit Intention among World Cup Football Fans. *J. Risk Financ. Manag.* **2023**, *16*, 210. [CrossRef]
22. Kozak, M. Repeaters' behavior at two distinct destinations. *Ann. Tour. Res.* **2001**, *28*, 784–807. [CrossRef]
23. Quintal, V.A.; Lee, J.A.; Soutar, G.N. Risk, uncertainty and the theory of planned behavior: A tourism example. *Tour. Manag.* **2010**, *31*, 797–805. [CrossRef]
24. George, R. Visitor perceptions of crime-safety and attitudes towards risk: The case of Table Mountain National Park, Cape Town. *Tour. Manag.* **2010**, *31*, 806–815. [CrossRef]
25. Qi, C.X.; Gibson, H.J.; Zhang, J.J. Perceptions of risk and travel intentions: The case of China and the Beijing Olympic Games. *J. Sport Tour.* **2009**, *14*, 43–67. [CrossRef]
26. Baber, R.; Baber, P. Influence of social media marketing efforts, e-reputation and destination image on intention to visit among tourists: Application of SOR model. *J. Hosp. Tour. Insights* **2022**, *6*, 2298–2316. [CrossRef]
27. Gupta, V.; Galati, A.; Sharma, S. Explore, eat and revisit: Does local food consumption value influence the destination's food image? *Br. Food J.* **2023**, *125*, 4639–4661. [CrossRef]
28. Ab Karim, S.; Chi, C.G.Q. Culinary tourism as a destination attraction: An empirical examination of destinations' food image. *J. Hosp. Mark. Manag.* **2010**, *19*, 531–555. [CrossRef]
29. Chaulagain, S.; Wiitala, J.; Fu, X. The impact of country image and destination image on US tourists' travel intention. *J. Destin. Mark. Manag.* **2019**, *12*, 1–11. [CrossRef]
30. Chen, X.; Li, J.; Han, W.; Liu, S. Urban tourism destination image perception based on LDA integrating social network and emotion analysis: The example of Wuhan. *Sustainability* **2021**, *14*, 12. [CrossRef]
31. Lee, J.S.; Park, S. A cross-cultural anatomy of destination image: An application of mixed-methods of UGC and survey. *Tour. Manag.* **2023**, *98*, 104746. [CrossRef]
32. Li, H.; Zhang, L.; Hsu, C.H. Research on user-generated photos in tourism and hospitality: A systematic review and way forward. *Tour. Manag.* **2023**, *96*, 104714. [CrossRef]
33. Cruz-Milán, O.; Castillo-Ortiz, I. Destination brand personality self-congruity and crime perceptions: Effects on travel intentions. *J. Destin. Mark. Manag.* **2023**, *28*, 100781. [CrossRef]
34. Wang, Y.; Yao, Q.; Kwok, J.T.; Ni, L.M. Generalizing from a few examples: A survey on few-shot learning. *ACM Comput. Surv.* **2020**, *53*, 1–34. [CrossRef]
35. Huang, S.; Hsu, C.H. Effects of travel motivation, past experience, perceived constraint, and attitude on revisit intention. *J. Travel Res.* **2009**, *48*, 29–44. [CrossRef]
36. Mehra, P. Unexpected surprise: Emotion analysis and aspect based sentiment analysis (ABSA) of user generated comments to study behavioral intentions of tourists. *Tour. Manag. Perspect.* **2023**, *45*, 101063. [CrossRef]
37. Murphy, L.; Benckendorff, P.; Moscardo, G. Linking travel motivation, tourist self-image and destination brand personality. *J. Travel Tour. Mark.* **2007**, *22*, 45–59. [CrossRef]
38. Chopra, I.P.; Lim, W.M.; Jain, T. Electronic word of mouth on social networking sites: What inspires travelers to engage in opinion seeking, opinion passing, and opinion giving? *Tour. Recreat. Res.* **2022**, *49*, 726–739. [CrossRef]
39. Cham, T.H.; Lim, Y.M.; Sia, B.C.; Cheah, J.H.; Ting, H. Medical tourism destination image and its relationship with the intention to revisit: A study of Chinese medical tourists in Malaysia. *J. China Tour. Res.* **2021**, *17*, 163–191. [CrossRef]
40. Almeida-Santana, A.; Moreno-Gil, S. New trends in information search and their influence on destination loyalty: Digital destinations and relationship marketing. *J. Destin. Mark. Manag.* **2017**, *6*, 150–161. [CrossRef]
41. Joo, Y.; Seok, H.; Nam, Y. The moderating effect of social media use on sustainable rural tourism: A theory of planned behavior model. *Sustainability* **2020**, *12*, 4095. [CrossRef]
42. Al-Gasawneh, J.A.; Al-Adamat, A.M. The relationship between perceived destination image, social media interaction and travel intentions relating to Neom city. *Acad. Strateg. Manag. J.* **2020**, *19*, 1–12.
43. Latif, K.; Malik, M.Y.; Pitafi, A.H.; Kanwal, S.; Latif, Z. If you travel, I travel: Testing a model of when and how travel-related content exposure on Facebook triggers the intention to visit a tourist destination. *Sage Open* **2020**, *10*, 2158244020925511. [CrossRef]
44. Nguyen, T.T.T.; Tong, S. The impact of user-generated content on intention to select a travel destination. *J. Mark. Anal.* **2023**, *11*, 443–457. [CrossRef]
45. Xu, H.; Cheung, L.T.; Lovett, J.; Duan, X.; Pei, Q.; Liang, D. Understanding the influence of user-generated content on tourist loyalty behavior in a cultural World Heritage Site. *Tour. Recreat. Res.* **2023**, *48*, 173–187. [CrossRef]
46. Wang, Y.; Huang, W.; Yao, X. Research on the evaluation of tourism destination image based on user generated content. In Proceedings of the 2021 2nd International Conference on Artificial Intelligence and Information Systems, Chongqing, China, 28–30 May 2021; pp. 1–5.
47. Chang, J.R.; Chen, M.Y.; Chen, L.S.; Tseng, S.C. Why customers don't revisit in tourism and hospitality industry? *IEEE Access* **2019**, *7*, 146588–146606. [CrossRef]
48. Wang, H.; Yan, J. Effects of social media tourism information quality on destination travel intention: Mediation effect of self-congruity and trust. *Front. Psychol.* **2022**, *13*, 1049149. [CrossRef]

49. Fudholi, D.H.; Zahra, A.; Rani, S.; Huda, S.N.; Paputungan, I.V.; Zukhri, Z. BERT-based tourism named entity recognition: Making use of social media for travel recommendations. *PeerJ Comput. Sci.* **2023**, *9*, e1731. [CrossRef]
50. Keelson, S.A.; Bruce, E.; Egala, S.B.; Amoah, J.; Bashiru Jibril, A. Driving forces of social media and its impact on tourists' destination decisions: A uses and gratification theory. *Cogent Soc. Sci.* **2024**, *10*, 2318878. [CrossRef]
51. Guo, Y.; Yu, M.; Zhao, Y. Impact of destination advertising on tourists' visit intention: The influence of self-congruence, self-confidence, and destination reputation. *J. Destin. Mark. Manag.* **2024**, *31*, 100852. [CrossRef]
52. Armutcu, B.; Tan, A.; Amponsah, M.; Parida, S.; Ramkissoon, H. Tourist behaviour: The role of digital marketing and social media. *Acta Psychol.* **2023**, *240*, 104025. [CrossRef]
53. Siegel, L.A.; Tussyadiah, I.; Scarles, C. Exploring behaviors of social media-induced tourists and the use of behavioral interventions as salient destination response strategy. *J. Destin. Mark. Manag.* **2023**, *27*, 100765. [CrossRef]
54. Yusra, Y.; Vilzati, V.; Eliana, E.; Ariffin, A.A.M.; Susanto, P. Stimulating visit intention using social media influencer: Mediating role of enjoyment. *Indones. J. Bus. Entrep.* **2023**, *9*, 295. [CrossRef]
55. Sakshi; Tandon, U.; Ertz, M.; Bansal, H. Social vacation: Proposition of a model to understand tourists' usage of social media for travel planning. *Technol. Soc.* **2020**, *63*, 101438.
56. Schoner-Schatz, L.; Hofmann, V.; Stokburger-Sauer, N.E. Destination's social media communication and emotions: An investigation of visit intentions, word-of-mouth and travelers' facially expressed emotions. *J. Destin. Mark. Manag.* **2021**, *22*, 100661. [CrossRef]
57. Gentry, J. *twitteR: R Based Twitter Client*; R Package Version 1.1.9; R Core Team: Vienna, Austria, 2015.
58. Kearney, M.W.; Heiss, A.; Briatte, F. *rtweet: Collecting Twitter Data*; R Package Version 1.0.2; R Core Team: Vienna, Austria, 2022.
59. Mastroeni, L.; Naldi, M.; Vellucci, P. Wind energy: Influencing the dynamics of the public opinion formation through the retweet network. *Technol. Forecast. Soc. Chang.* **2023**, *194*, 122748. [CrossRef]
60. Tillé, Y.; Wilhelm, M. Probability sampling designs: Principles for choice of design and balancing. *Stat. Sci.* **2017**, *32*, 176–189. [CrossRef]
61. Lötsch, J.; Malkusch, S.; Ultsch, A. Optimal distribution-preserving downsampling of large biomedical data sets (opdisDownsampling). *PLoS ONE* **2021**, *16*, e0255838. [CrossRef]
62. Tyagi, S.; Mittal, S. Sampling approaches for imbalanced data classification problem in machine learning. In *Proceedings of the ICRIC 2019: Recent Innovations in Computing*; Springer: Cham, Switzerland, 2020; pp. 209–221.
63. Berrar, D. Cross-Validation. In *Encyclopedia of Bioinformatics and Computational Biology*; Ranganathan, S., Gribskov, M., Nakai, K., Schönbach, C., Eds.; Academic Press: Oxford, UK, 2019; pp. 542–545. [CrossRef]
64. Oyedele, O. Determining the optimal number of folds to use in a K-fold cross-validation: A neural network classification experiment. *Res. Math.* **2023**, *10*, 2201015. [CrossRef]
65. Al-Jarrah, O.Y.; Yoo, P.D.; Muhaidat, S.; Karagiannidis, G.K.; Taha, K. Efficient machine learning for big data: A review. *Big Data Res.* **2015**, *2*, 87–93. [CrossRef]
66. Kokol, P.; Kokol, M.; Zagoranski, S. Machine learning on small size samples: A synthetic knowledge synthesis. *Sci. Prog.* **2022**, *105*, 00368504211029777. [CrossRef]
67. Rajput, D.; Wang, W.J.; Chen, C.C. Evaluation of a decided sample size in machine learning applications. *BMC Bioinform.* **2023**, *24*, 48. [CrossRef] [PubMed]
68. Parnami, A.; Lee, M. Learning from few examples: A summary of approaches to few-shot learning. *arXiv* **2022**, arXiv:2203.04291.
69. Jadon, S. An overview of deep learning architectures in few-shot learning domain. *arXiv* **2020**, arXiv:2008.06365.
70. Tunstall, L.; Reimers, N.; Jo, U.E.S.; Bates, L.; Korat, D.; Wasserblat, M.; Pereg, O. Efficient few-shot learning without prompts. *arXiv* **2022**, arXiv:2209.11055.
71. Reimers, N.; Gurevych, I. Sentence-BERT: Sentence Embeddings using Siamese BERT-Networks. In Proceedings of the 2019 Conference on Empirical Methods in Natural Language Processing and the 9th International Joint Conference on Natural Language Processing (EMNLP-IJCNLP), Hong Kong, China, 3–7 November 2019; pp. 3982–3992.
72. Chicco, D. Siamese neural networks: An overview. *Artif. Neural Netw.* **2021**, 73–94.
73. Hoffer, E.; Ailon, N. Deep metric learning using triplet network. In Proceedings of the Similarity-Based Pattern Recognition: Third International Workshop, SIMBAD 2015, Copenhagen, Denmark, 12–14 October 2015; pp. 84–92.
74. Devlin, J.; Chang, M.W.; Lee, K.; Toutanova, K. Bert: Pre-training of deep bidirectional transformers for language understanding. *arXiv* **2018**, arXiv:1810.04805.
75. Zhuang, Z.; Liu, M.; Cutkosky, A.; Orabona, F. Understanding adamw through proximal methods and scale-freeness. *Trans. Mach. Learn. Res.* **2022**.
76. Loshchilov, I.; Hutter, F. Fixing weight decay regularization in Adam. *arXiv* **2018**, arXiv:1711.0510v2.
77. Pukelsheim, F. The three sigma rule. *Am. Stat.* **1994**, *48*, 88–91. [CrossRef]
78. Garreau, D.; Luxburg, U. Explaining the explainer: A first theoretical analysis of LIME. In *Proceedings of the International Conference on Artificial Intelligence and Statistics*; PMLR: Birmingham, UK, 2020; pp. 1287–1296.
79. Fantozzi, P.; Naldi, M. The Explainability of Transformers: Current Status and Directions. *Computers* **2024**, *13*, 92. [CrossRef]

information

MDPI

Article

Correlations and Fractality in Sentence-Level Sentiment Analysis Based on VADER for Literary Texts

Ricardo Hernández-Pérez [1,†], Pablo Lara-Martínez [2], Bibiana Obregón-Quintana [2], Larry S. Liebovitch [3,4] and Lev Guzmán-Vargas [5,*]

1 Escuela Superior de Física y Matemáticas, Instituto Politécnico Nacional, Edif. 9, 2o. Piso, UP Zacatenco, Mexico City 07738, Mexico
2 Facultad de Ciencias, Universidad Nacional Autónoma de México, Mexico City 04510, Mexico; p4blolara@ciencias.unam.mx (P.L.-M.); bobregon@ciencias.unam.mx (B.O.-Q.)
3 Department of Physics, Queens College, City University of New York, New York, NY 11367, USA; lsl2140@columbia.edu
4 Advanced Consortium on Cooperation, Conflict and Complexity (AC4), Climate School, Columbia University, New York, NY 10027, USA
5 Unidad Interdisciplinaria en Ingeniería y Tecnologías Avanzadas, Instituto Politécnico Nacional, Av. IPN No. 2580, L. Ticomán, Mexico City 07340, Mexico
* Correspondence: lguzmanv@ipn.mx
† Sadly, Ricardo passed away on 11 October 2024. This is our tribute to our dear friend, colleague and exceptional scientist.

Abstract: We perform a sentence-level sentiment analysis study of different literary texts in English language. Each text is converted into a series in which the data points are the sentiment value of each sentence obtained using the sentiment analysis tool (VADER). By applying the Detrended Fluctuation Analysis (DFA) and the Higuchi Fractal Dimension (HFD) methods to these sentiment series, we find that they are monofractal with long-term correlations, which can be explained by the fact that the writing process has memory by construction, with a sentiment evolution that is self-similar. Furthermore, we discretize these series by applying a classification approach which transforms the series into a one on which each data point has only three possible values, corresponding to positive, neutral or negative sentiments. We map these three-states series to a Markov chain and investigate the transitions of sentiment from one sentence to the next, obtaining a state transition matrix for each book that provides information on the probability of transitioning between sentiments from one sentence to the next. This approach shows that there are biases towards increasing the probability of switching to neutral or positive sentences. The two approaches supplement each other, since the long-term correlation approach allows a global assessment of the sentiment of the book, while the state transition matrix approach provides local information about the sentiment evolution along the text.

Keywords: sentiment analysis; opinion mining; social systems

1. Introduction

Sentiment analysis, or opinion mining, is an active research area in the field of natural language processing that analyzes people's opinions that are loaded with sentiments and emotions via the computational treatment of subjectivity in text that is produced in different platforms [1–5]. Sentiment analysis mainly considers two aspects: categorical sentiment analysis and dimensional sentiment analysis. Categorical sentiment analysis basically classifies emotions under categories or labels based on the fact that these emotions can be classified using a low number of basic emotions. In contrast, in dimensional analysis, sentiment can be represented by emotions along continuous dimensions rather than discrete categories [6,7]. In general, two basic dimensions are included: valence and intensity. Sentiment analysis makes use of various lexicons to quantify emotional intensity [8–13].

There are several lexicons built from very diverse sources, such as the Social Contextualized Affect Lexicon (SO-CAL), SentiWordNet, AFINN, and ANEW, to name a few [14–17]. SO-CAL aims to analyze sentiment in social network contexts, captures how emotions are expressed in informal language, and evaluates emotions in terms of valence, arousal, and dominance [18–20]. AFINN focuses on evaluating conversations in social network posts and assigns words a score ranging from negative to positive, providing a direct numerical sentiment score [21]. SentiWordNet is an extension of WordNet that provides three scores for each word: positive, negative, and objective, allowing for a nuanced understanding of word sentiment [22,23]. ANEW provides emotional ratings of words, including valence, arousal, and dominance values, and is used in the context of emotional profiling analysis [24–27].

A recent study conducted an extensive literature survey on sentiment analysis to identify existing sentence-level methods covering several different techniques in order to perform a comparison with each other to identify their advantages, disadvantages, and limitations [28]. The authors of that study suggested that there is no single method that always achieves the best prediction performance for all different datasets. However, they found that the method called VADER (for Valence Aware Dictionary for sEntiment Reasoning) was the most consistent method in different experiments that were performed. VADER uses a combination of qualitative and quantitative methods to produce and then empirically validate a sentiment lexicon that is especially attuned to microblog-like contexts. Moreover, after incorporating some lexical rules that embody grammatical and syntactical conventions that humans use when expressing or emphasizing sentiment intensity, the accuracy of the sentiment analysis engine improves across several domain contexts (social media text, NY Times editorials, movie reviews, and product reviews) [29]. Therefore, we select VADER to perform the sentence-level sentiment analysis in the present work.

On the other hand, previous studies performed on different corpora in several languages taken mainly from Web-based content (online forums, blogs, Twitter, etc.) have found that positive words carry less information [30] and that words with a positive emotional content are more frequently used [30,31]. However, these previous studies have been centered in a word-by-word sentiment analysis. Are these conclusions still valid if the analysis is performed at a higher level, i.e., at sentence level?

Our goal is to analyze the evolution of the sentiment along the text by examining the statistics associated to the sentiment value of each sentence and then assess the presence of correlations. We find that, for all the texts analyzed, the correlations follow power laws with exponent values that differ from the randomized case, confirming the existence of long-term memory. We also quantify the dependence of sentiment values on transitions to positive, negative, or neutral, and find that either neutral or positive sentences are more likely to be followed by neutral or positive ones as well. We focus on single-author works for which the writing dynamics differ from those of Web-based content (online forums, blogs, Twitter, etc.) since the authors take more time to conclude the text after reviewing it as part of the writing process and, oftentimes, the texts are also subject to the editor's review process. Therefore, these literary works are subject to a longer production process, implying that the selection of words in the sentences is more thoroughly performed. Thus, our approach supplements the previous studies based on a high number of authors in online opinion forums or Twitter, and then this allows to compare the behavior of an ensemble of authors on shorter texts versus the longer texts produced by single authors under more scrutiny.

This paper is organized as follows: in Section 2, we present the related work. In Section 3, we describe briefly the sample of books that were considered. In Section 4, we describe the methods to obtain series of sentiment values from the texts which are processed to investigate correlations. In Section 5, we discuss the results. Finally, the concluding remarks are given in Section 6.

2. Related Work

Sentiment analysis in literary texts is a developing field that leverages computational techniques to understand and interpret the emotional dimensions that appear in literary texts. As is widely recognized, emotions play a transcendental role in narratives or stories developed by authors, shaping characters' motivations and influencing readers. The study of emotions in literature has been modified to include more quantitative analyses through computational methods, which has allowed for more extensive and systematic investigations of how emotions are displayed through a literary text. VADER offers an important tool for sentiment analysis within literary studies, as it allows the emotional dimensions of texts to be quantified. It has been noted that it also has certain limitations—especially in relation to sarcasm and domain specificity—but its ease of use and effectiveness make it an attractive option for both qualitative and quantitative literary analysis. As the field has progressed, integrating tools such as VADER into literary research can enhance our understanding of emotional dynamics in literature. For example, Bizzoni et al. [32] explored the complexities of analyzing sentiment in narrative texts such as those of E. Hemingway. Yeruva et al. [33] analyzed data from literary texts related to human feeling in classical Greek tragedy. More recently, S. Vinodini [34] conducted a sentiment analysis of selected novels by the celebrated Brazilian author Paulo Coelho.

On the other hand, long-range correlations are characterized by a relationship or memory between subsequences separated by significant distances. In the context of literature, this can be understood as recurrence of ideas or emotional motifs that recur throughout a text, regardless of their physical distance in the narrative. The presence of correlations in literary texts has been reported in various contexts such as word lengths [35–37], sentences [38], and sentiment trajectories [39]. Also, it has been reported that the temporal organization of written texts can be analyzed from a multifractal perspective [40,41].

3. Input Data

The input data are comprised of 50 ebooks in English language downloaded from the websites of the Gutenberg Project (http://www.gutenberg.org/, last accessed date: 27 May 2024) and the Project Gutenberg Australia (http://gutenberg.net.au/, last accessed date: 27 May 2024). The titles of the written texts are described online at https://figshare.com/articles/dataset/A_sentence-level_sentiment_analysis_of_some_literary_texts_inEnglish_language/27092008, last accessed date: 30 September 2024. There was no particular strategy to select the titles. The selected books were first published in different epochs and countries, therefore offering diversity in time and cultures of origin. We remove the preface, table of contents, etc., of the books and only retain the text.

4. Methods

4.1. Vader Sentiment Values

VADER provides four scores for the sentiment and intensity of a sentence: positive (`pos`), neutral (`neu`), negative (`neg`), and compound (`com`). The `pos`, `neu`, and `neg` scores are ratios for proportions of text that fall in each category; therefore, these should all add up to be 1. These are the most useful metrics for multidimensional measures of sentiment for a given sentence. Moreover, the `compound` score is computed by summing the valence scores of each word in the lexicon, adjusted according to certain rules, and then normalized to be a floating number between -1 (most extreme negative) and $+1$ (most extreme positive) [29]. This is the most useful metric for a single unidimensional measure of sentiment for a given sentence.

Using the `compound` score, standardized thresholds can be set for classifying sentences as either positive, neutral, or negative. Typical threshold values are [29]:

- positive sentiment: $\texttt{compound} \geq 0.05$,
- neutral sentiment: $-0.05 < \texttt{compound} < 0.05$,
- negative sentiment: $\texttt{compound} \leq -0.05$.

In the present work, we choose the `compound` score since we are interested in a single unidimensional measure of sentiment for each sentence in order to study correlations of sentiment along the text as well as the evolution of sentiment by studying the changes in sentiment from one sentence to the next.

In order to estimate the sentiment of the sentences in a text, we start by parsing the text to split it into sentences. Each sentence is then evaluated with VADER to obtain its compound sentiment score, and therefore, the text is mapped to a data series of sentiment values. Figure 1 shows an example of these sentiment series for an specific book. The complete resulting corpus containing the sentiment scores for each book can be found online at https://figshare.com/articles/dataset/A_sentence-level_sentiment_analysis_of_some_literary_texts_inEnglish_language/27092008, last accessed date: 30 September 2024. These series are then processed to investigate the kind of correlations that they contain, for which we apply the well-known Higuchi Fractal Dimension (HFD) [42] and the Detrended Fluctuation Analysis (DFA) [43] methods.

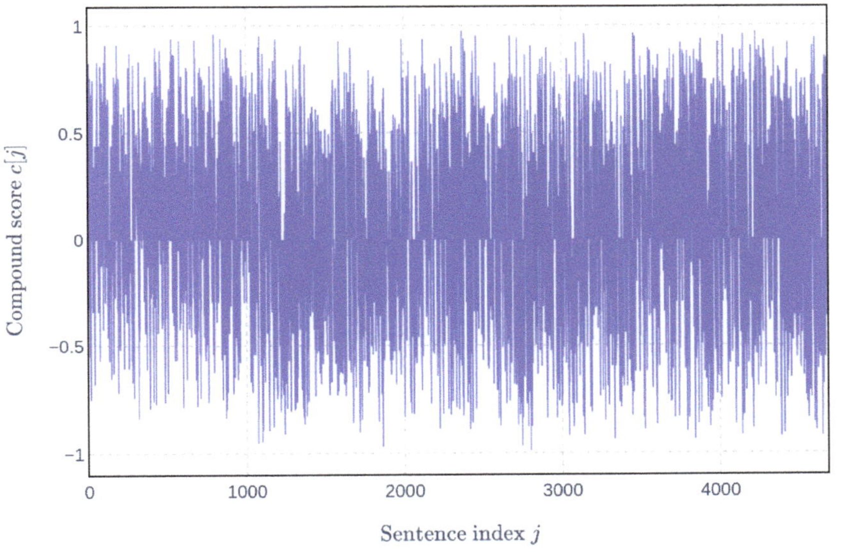

Figure 1. Example of one of the data series of sentiment values estimated with VADER. In this case, for the book The Adventures of Sherlock Holmes by Arthur Conan Doyle.

Moreover, we use the classification threshold mentioned previously to transform each series of compound sentiment into a series of three possible discrete values (states) of sentiment: positive, neutral, or negative (see Figure 2). In order to study the sentiment transitions along the text, we count the number of transitions of each type. For instance, let us suppose that the kth sentence is classified as positive and the $k+1$th is classified as negative, then the number of transitions of the type $\texttt{pos} \to \texttt{neg}$ is increased by one. Once the counting of transitions is finalized, we normalize the matrix to obtain a state transition matrix $\mathbf{p}$ for each one of the books in our sample:

$$\mathbf{p} = \begin{pmatrix} p_{\texttt{pos}\to\texttt{pos}} & p_{\texttt{pos}\to\texttt{neu}} & p_{\texttt{pos}\to\texttt{neg}} \\ p_{\texttt{neu}\to\texttt{pos}} & p_{\texttt{neu}\to\texttt{neu}} & p_{\texttt{neu}\to\texttt{neg}} \\ p_{\texttt{neg}\to\texttt{pos}} & p_{\texttt{neg}\to\texttt{neu}} & p_{\texttt{neg}\to\texttt{neg}} \end{pmatrix} \tag{1}$$

Therefore, we map the evolution of the classified sentiment to a Markov chain for each book, with the state transition coefficients given by Equation (1). Shannon used Markov chains to predict sequences of words, observing that a reasonable approximation to English could be produced if each word was chosen based not just on the previous word but on the last few words, and introduced a mathematical framework for analyzing the information provided by the word [44]. Also, Markov chains have been used to compute how probable each instance of a word is based on the last few words, providing a way to measure the predictability of a word in its context [45]. Interestingly, Markov himself published a report in which he computes the probabilities that a vowel is followed by a vowel or a consonant in a text excerpt containing 20,000 Russian letters of the Russian alphabet from Pushkin's novel [46].

In the present work, we are interested not in the word length, but in the sentiment of the sentence. Given that we wrote a sentence with certain sentiment, what is the probability that the next sentence either switches to another sentiment state or stays on the same one? How does the sentiment of a certain sentence relate to the sentiment of the previous few sentences?

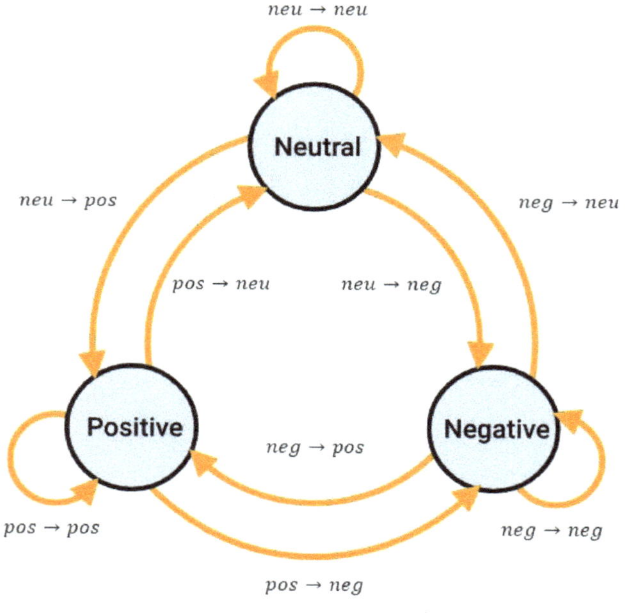

Figure 2. Diagram depicting the possible transitions between sentiment values of sentences in a text.

4.2. Fractal Dimension Method and Detrended Fluctuation Analysis

Fractals are complex patterns that show self-similarity at different scales and are characterized by a dimension that is not necessarily an integer value, which quantifies the complexity of the fractal pattern. In the case of time series, which are considered non-isotropic fractals because they extend over time while the values of the variable remain in a bounded range (auto-affinity), the fractal characterization can be performed using several methodologies. To capture this statistical self-affinity property, it is usually resorted to quantify a measure of the object at different scales. This leads to a power law ($G(x) \sim x^a$), where the scaling exponent a represents the level of spatio-temporal organization displayed by the time series. The power spectrum is the method traditionally used to characterize autocorrelations in time series. For example, we consider a stationary stochastic process with an autocorrelation function following a power law $C(s) \sim s^{\gamma}$, where s is the lag and γ is the correlation exponent, $0 < \gamma < 1$. The presence of long-range correlations is related to the fact that the mean correlation time diverges for infinite time series. According to the Wiener–Khintchin theorem, the power spectrum is the Fourier transform of the autocorrelation function $C(s)$, and for the case described above, we have the scaling relation $S(f) \sim f^{-\beta}$, where f is the frequency and β is called the spectral exponent and is related to the correlation exponent by $\gamma = 1 - \beta$. However, the estimation of β may not be as accurate when we have a nonstationary series. Alternative methods have been proposed for evaluating the correlations and fractal properties of stationary and nonstationary time series [42,47–49]. Here, we briefly describe two robust methods for the estimation of the fractal scaling exponents:

(i) Fractal Dimension Method. We evaluate the time organization in sequences of sentiment values by means of the Fractal Dimension Method (FDM), also known as Higuchi Fractal Dimension (HFD) method [50]. Briefly, we explain the main steps of the FDM [50,51]. Given the time series $x_1, x_2, ..., x_N$, we construct new time series x_m^k defined as $x_m, x_{m+k}, x_{m+2k}, ..., x_{(m+[\frac{N-k}{k}]\cdot k)}$, with $m = 1, 2, 3, ..., k$, [ ] denoting Gauss' notation, that is, the bigger integer and m and k are integers that indicate the initial time and the interval time, respectively. The length of the curve x_m^k, is defined as

$$L_m(k) = \frac{1}{k}\left[\left(\sum_{i=1}^{[\frac{N-m}{k}]} |x(m+ik) - x(m+(i-1)k)|\right)\frac{N-1}{[\frac{N-m}{k}]k}\right] \tag{2}$$

and the term $(N-1)/[(N-m)/k]k$ represents a normalization factor. The length of each sequence x_m^k is considered to construct the length of the original curve for the time interval k, $\langle L(k)\rangle$. Finally, if a scaling behavior of the form $\langle L(k)\rangle \propto k^{-D}$ is observed, then the curve is fractal with dimension D [50]. It is known that the fractal dimension is related to the spectral exponent β by means of $\beta = 5 - 2D$ [50]. We notice that this relationship is valid for $1 < D < 2$ and $1 < \beta < 3$, and thus FDM is not a reliable method for signals with strong anticorrelated behavior, that is, for $-1 < \beta < 0$. To overcome this problem, we first integrate the original time series prior to applying the standard FDM. In this way, for processes which can be described as the first derivative of fluctuations with spectral exponent within the interval $1 < \beta < 3$, the relationship between β and D changes to $\beta = 3 - 2D$. A process with positive long-range correlations leads to $D < 1.5$, whereas for anticorrelated processes, $D > 1.5$. The irregular fluctuations with no memory are represented by $D = 1.5$.

(ii) Detrended Fluctuation Analysis. This method was introduced to quantify long-range correlations in the heartbeat interval time series and DNA sequences [43,48,52]. The DFA method has been used to explore the presence of correlations in different areas of science, from heartbeat [52] and stock markets to earthquakes [53]. Briefly, the DFA is described as follows: First, we integrate the original time series to obtain $y(k) = \sum_{i=1}^{k}[x(i) - x_{ave}]$. The resulting series is divided into boxes of size n. For each box, a straight line is fitted to the points, $y_n(k)$. Next, the line points are subtracted from the integrated series, $y(k)$, in each box. The root mean square fluctuation of the integrated and detrended series is calculated by means of

$$F(n) = \sqrt{\frac{1}{N}\sum_{k=1}^{N}[y(k) - y_n(k)]^2}. \tag{3}$$

This process is taken over several scales (box sizes) to obtain a power law behavior $F(n) \sim n^{\alpha}$, with α being an exponent which reflects self-similar and correlation properties of the signal. An uncorrelated signal leads to $\alpha = 0.5$, $\alpha = 1$ represents a long-range correlated process ($1/f$ noise), and $\alpha = 1.5$ corresponds to a Brownian motion. For $0.5 < \alpha < 1$, the scaling exponent α and the Hurst exponent provide the same information, and therefore both can be used interchangeably [54]. The exponent α is also related to the spectral exponent β (within the interval $0 < \beta < 1$) through relation $\beta = 2\alpha - 1$. Thus, fractal dimension D is related to α by means of $\alpha = 2 - D$, as expected for auto-affine signals [47,55].

5. Results and Discussion

5.1. Correlations Analysis

Figure 3 shows the log–log plots for the HFD and DFA analyses performed on the data series of compound sentiment scores for all the books in our sample. As can be seen, these data series exhibit fractal behavior with different scaling exponents for both analyses. In order to further study these correlations, we shuffle the sentences in each book prior to estimating the VADER sentiment and the resulting data series are analyzed with the HFD and DFA methods.

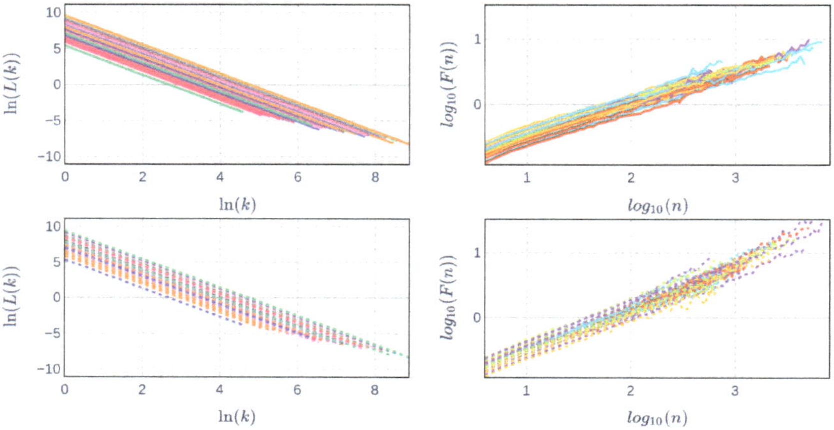

Figure 3. Top row: Log–log plots of $\langle L(k)\rangle$ vs. k for the HFD (**left**) and $F(n)$ vs n for the DFA (**right**). Each trace with different color on both plots corresponds to one book. As can be seen, the composite sentiment data series are monofractal and can be characterized by a single scaling exponent, either D or α. **Buttom row**: Similar log–log plots as in the top row but for the series resulting after shuffling the sentences in the books.

Figure 4 shows a scatter plot of α vs. D for the original texts and the shuffled ones. The mean values for the scaling exponents for the original texts are $D = 1.38 \pm 0.04$ and $\alpha = 0.62 \pm 0.04$. Even though there is scattering in the values for the scaling exponents, we can see from the values of α that the data series of sentiment are slightly long-term correlated. On the other hand, the mean values of the scaling exponents for the shuffled texts are $D = 1.49 \pm 0.03$ and $\alpha = 0.50 \pm 0.02$. We perform a two-sample t-test for each scaling exponent between the original sequences and the shuffled ones, with the null hypothesis that the two populations have no statistically significant difference. In other words, we take the population of one scaling exponent computed for the original sequence (for instance, α) and perform the t-test to assess statistical difference to the population of the values of α obtained for the shuffled sequences, and similar approach is followed for the fractal dimension D. The p-values obtained for the scaling exponents are: $p_D = 7.4 \times 10^{-29}$ and $p_\alpha = 4.5 \times 10^{-22}$. They allow us to reject the null hypothesis, i.e., we find statistically significant differences in α and D between the original sequences and the randomized ones.

We also observe that there is a good concordance between the median values obtained from both methods. By using the relationship $\alpha = 2 - D$, it is easy to show that $\bar{D} = 1.38$ yields to $\bar{\alpha} = 0.62$, which matches the value obtained by means of the DFA. This also applies for the case of the shuffled sequences.

We compute the fraction of the number of sentences on each sentiment state to the total number of sentences for each book. Figure 5 shows box plots for each fraction for all the books considered in our study, with the median values of each population shown within the box. As can be seen, the majority of sentences are valued as neutral, followed by the positive and then the negative ones. The observation that there are more positive than negative sentences in the books under study is in agreement with recent studies reporting a positive bias in human expression [30,31], although in those works, the positivity in the language is based on a word-by-word analysis, and in our case, the analysis is made on a sentence-by-sentence basis, which supplements and extends those previously reported results.

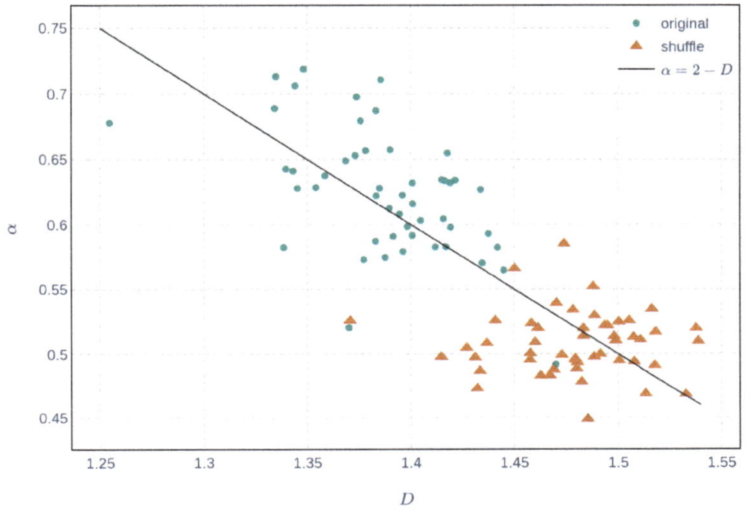

Figure 4. Scaling exponents for the HFD and DFA for the original texts and the shuffled ones. The straight line corresponds to the relationship $\alpha = 2 - D$.

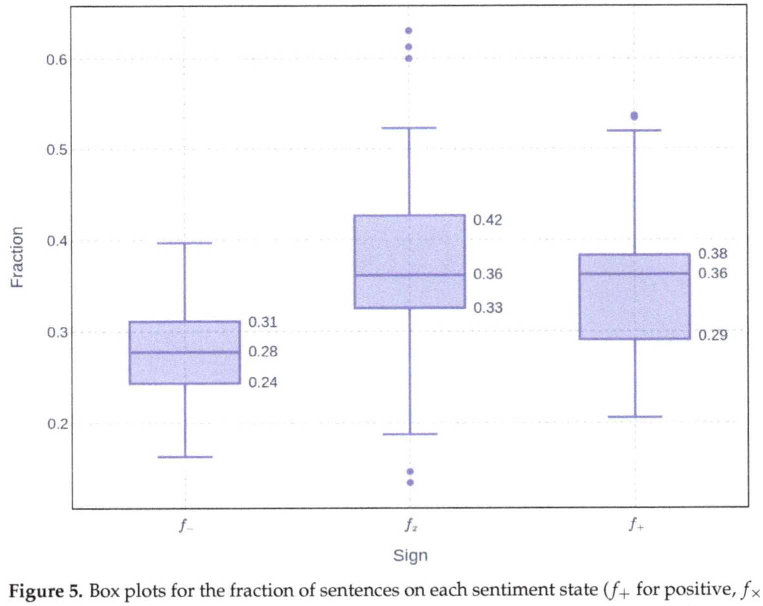

Figure 5. Box plots for the fraction of sentences on each sentiment state (f_+ for positive, $f_\times$ for neutral and f_- for negative sentiments) with respect to the total number of sentences in the book. The values shown are the median (inside the box) and the lower and upper quartile. The whiskers extend from the box to show the range of the data, while the flier points are those past the end of the whiskers and are considered as outliers.

In order to investigate further the bias towards positive sentiment in language, for each book, we obtain the normalized histograms for the compound sentiment series. Figure 6 shows the overlay of the histograms. As can be seen, there is a peak for the sentiments around the neutral values of sentiment. Moreover, we compute the area under the positive (denoted by A_+) and the negative (A_-) sides, which offer the probability of finding positive or negative sentences in the text, respectively. The scatter plot of A_+ vs A_- in the inset of Figure 6 shows that for most of the cases, the probability of finding positive sentences is larger than the one for the negative ones. Moreover, we compute the empirical cumulative distribution function for the series of compound series and compare the positive and negative tails (see Figure 7). As can be seen, the probability of finding sentences with a compound value lower than a certain value c_0 decreases faster for the negative tail.

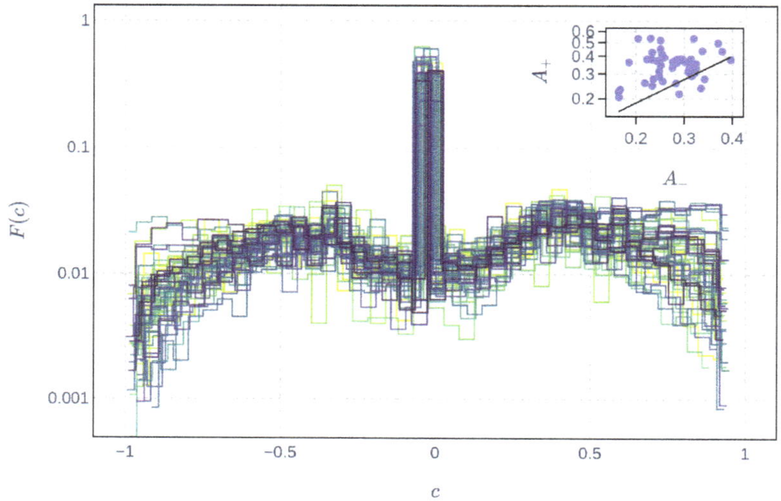

Figure 6. Normalized histogram ($F(c)$) for the compound sentiment c, where each trace with different color corresponds to a book. The inset is a scatter plot of the areas under the histograms for the positive and negative sides, which shows that the probability of finding sentences with positive sentiment is higher than with negative sentiment (the identity line is provided as a visual guide).

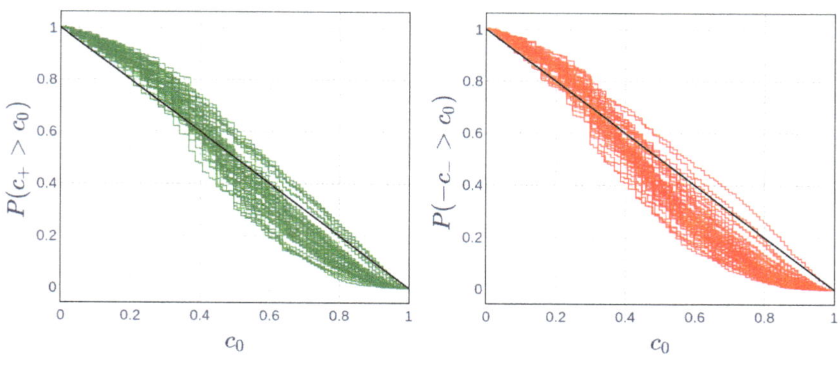

Figure 7. Cumulative distribution function for the compound values for the positive sentiment (**left**) and the negative one (**right**). Each trace corresponds to a book, green color for positive values and red for negative ones. The straight line is provided as a visual guide.

5.2. Observations from the Transition Coefficients

As mentioned in the Methods section, we discretize the compound sentiment series by applying a classification approach. After counting the number of sentiment states transition, we come up with a state transition matrix for each book. Figure 8 shows box plots for the coefficients of each possible transition, for both populations: original text and shuffled text. As can be seen, the most likely transition is from a neutral sentence to another neutral one, followed by the transitions from a positive (negative) sentences to a positive (negative) one.

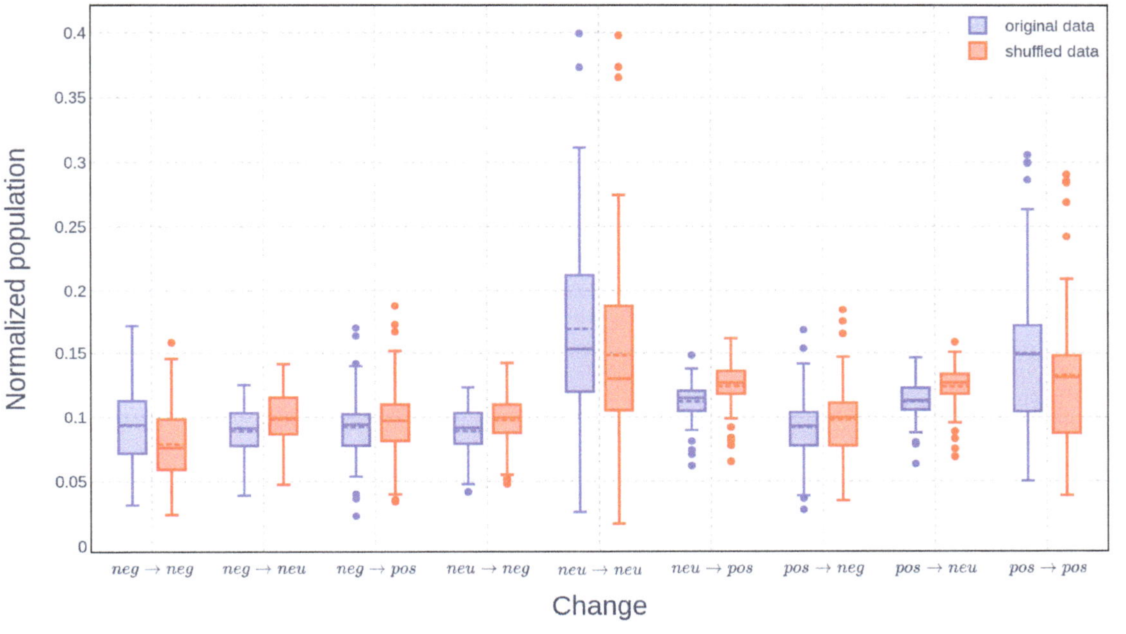

Figure 8. Box plots for the normalized populations of each state transition coefficient. The values for the original text and its shuffled version are given side by side (box plots in red color represent the shuffled text). The median values are marked within each box plot with a dotted line, while the mean values are marked with a solid line. The whiskers extend from the box to show the range of the data, while the flier points are those past the end of the whiskers and are considered as outliers.

We see that for the three states, the transition to a neutral sentence is the one with higher probability, which suggests that the neutral sentence is an inflection point for the sentiment when changing emotion (positive to negative or vice versa) or that these sentences are providing general and contextual information in the narrative. Starting from a positive sentence, it is more likely to move to a positive sentence, and from a negative sentence to a negative one, except that the latter transition is less differentiated with respect to the transitions to neutral or positive sentences, while moving from a neutral to a neutral sentence is markedly more likely compared to the other two transitions. Moreover, the medians of the transition coefficients show that the transition matrices are not symmetric, since there is a certain bias for transitions to positive and to neutral sentences. In summary, Table 1 shows the list of state transitions in descending order on the probabilities of transitioning to a certain state given a start on a particular one.

Table 1. List of state transitions in descending order of transition probabilities.

Initial State	First Most Likely Transition	Second	Third
positive	positive	neutral	negative
neutral	neutral	positive	negative
negative	negative	positive	neutral

On the other hand, Figure 8 also shows the state transition coefficients for the shuffled sentences. As can be seen, the transition matrix between states of the same type (*pos–pos*, *neg–neg* and *neu–neu*) exhibit mean values that are smaller than the values corresponding to the original data, while for the other transitions, the differences between the mean values is less noticeable. We see that for the shuffled sentences, the transition coefficient to a certain state is the same independently of on which state we started with, while there is a bias towards neutral sentences followed by positive ones. Again, the transition to negative sentences has the lower probability. Therefore, even in this case of shuffled sentences, there is a bias towards positive sentiment in human language, as previously reported in other studies [56]. One interesting thing to note here is that the median values of the transition coefficients for the shuffled texts follow the same proportion that the fraction of text that it is in a certain sentiment state (see Figure 5).

The long-term correlations in the sentiment data series that are revealed by the DFA analysis are somehow expected since, by construction, the writing process has memory given that the narrative is about concatenating sentences that are related. Our results on the presence of long-term correlations with values in fractal exponents, which reveal slight persistence, are in agreement with previous results reported for sentiment value sequences and those based on word-length [35,37,38], sentence-length [57], and sentiment arcs [58]. In addition, this approach could eventually be used to evaluate certain individual characteristics of the texts, which would provide an alternative way of identifying them through their organization across different scales. On the other hand, by introducing a Markov chain approach, we find that the sentiment state of a sentence depends on the immediately preceding one. This approach allows us to reveal the biases on the transitions to neutral and positive sentences in the evolution of the sentiment along the text. The narrative has sentiment scores that are correlated, but the story being told can vary in emotion and intensity from one sentence to the next; therefore, the sentiment evolution along the text could be mapped to a Markov chain. In other words, the long-term correlation approach allows to make a global assessment of the book sentiment, while the state transition matrix approach provides local information on the evolution of sentiment along the text. These local and global properties have been recognized as features present in systems that exhibit, at the same time, the presence of event "clustering" and long-term correlations [59–61]. The main limitation of this study lies in the sentiment values returned by VADER, where the compound sentiment construction may exhibit biases when analyzing content with sarcasm or other representations where the tool is not robust. Although these evaluations can be made more robust by considering other sentiment analysis tools, it remains a complex task. Further studies are needed to explore the feasibility of obtaining specific features of sentiment evolution in literary texts, and whether the levels of correlations are representative of the type of text being analyzed to determine properties such as literary genres, authors, etc.

6. Conclusions

We perform a sentence-level sentiment analysis of several literary works in English. This study has two approaches: (i) a global one through the assessment of the correlations in the sentiment along the text and (ii) a local one through the analysis of the transitions of sentiment from a sentence to the next. The global assessment, performed by applying the Higuchi Fractal Dimension and the Detrended Fluctuation Analysis methods, shows that the data series of sentiment scores is monofractal with long-term correlations, which can be explained by the fact that the writing process has memory by construction with a sentiment evolution that is self-similar. The local assessment, performed by counting the sentiment state transitions, shows that there are biases that make more likely the transitions to neutral and positive sentences, implying a bias towards positive sentiment in the texts. Previous studies based on word-level sentiment analysis have found a similar bias to positive sentiment [56]. These two approaches supplement each other because the long-term correlation approach allows a global assessment of the sentiment of the book, while the state transition matrix approach provides local information about the sentiment evolution along the text.

Author Contributions: Conceptualization, R.H.-P. and L.G.-V.; methodology, R.H.-P., P.L.-M., B.O.-Q. and L.S.L.; software, R.H.-P. and P.L.-M.; validation, R.H.-P., P.L.-M., B.O.-Q. and L.S.L.; formal analysis, R.H.-P., B.O.-Q., L.S.L. and L.G.-V.; investigation, R.H.-P., P.L.-M., B.O.-Q., L.S.L. and L.G.-V.; resources, B.O.-Q. and L.G.-V.; data curation, R.H.-P. and P.L.-M.; writing—original draft preparation, R.H.-P.; writing—review and editing, R.H.-P., P.L.-M., B.O.-Q., L.S.L. and L.G.-V.; visualization, R.H.-P. and P.L.-M.; supervision, R.H.-P. and L.G.-V.; project administration, R.H.-P. and L.G.-V.; funding acquisition, B.O.-Q. and L.G.-V. All authors have read and agreed to the published version of the manuscript.

Funding: This research received no external funding.

Institutional Review Board Statement: Not applicable.

Informed Consent Statement: Not applicable.

Data Availability Statement: All corpora used in this study are available from the repository at https://figshare.com/articles/dataset/A_sentence-level_sentiment_analysis_of_some_literary_texts_inEnglish_language/27092008, last accessed day: 30 September 2024.

Acknowledgments: The plots in this paper were produced with `matplotlib (3.9.2)` [62]. This work was partially supported by COFAA-IPN, EDI-IPN, UNAM-PAPIIT (IN111822) and CONAHCYT (México).

Conflicts of Interest: The authors declare no conflicts of interest.

References

1. Dodds, P.S.; Danforth, C.M. Measuring the Happiness of Large-Scale Written Expression: Songs, Blogs, and Presidents. *J. Happiness Stud.* **2010**, *11*, 441–456. [CrossRef]
2. Dodds, P.S.; Harris, K.D.; Kloumann, I.M.; Bliss, C.A.; Danforth, C.M. Temporal Patterns of Happiness and Information in a Global Social Network: Hedonometrics and Twitter. *PLoS ONE* **2011**, *6*, e26752. [CrossRef] [PubMed]
3. Chmiel, A.; Sobkowicz, P.; Sienkiewicz, J.; Paltoglou, G.; Buckley, K.; Thelwall, M.; Hołyst, J.A. Negative emotions boost user activity at BBC forum. *Physica A Stat. Mech. Its Appl.* **2011**, *390*, 2936–2944. [CrossRef]
4. Chmiel, A.; Sienkiewicz, J.; Thelwall, M.; Paltoglou, G.; Buckley, K.; Kappas, A.; Hołyst, J.A. Collective Emotions Online and Their Influence on Community Life. *PLoS ONE* **2011**, *6*, e22207. [CrossRef] [PubMed]
5. Wankhade, M.; Rao, A.C.S.; Kulkarni, C. A survey on sentiment analysis methods, applications, and challenges. *Artif. Intell. Rev.* **2022**, *55*, 5731–5780. [CrossRef]
6. Calvo, R.A.; Mac Kim, S. Emotions in text: Dimensional and categorical models. *Comput. Intell.* **2013**, *29*, 527–543. [CrossRef]
7. Jain, M.; Jindal, R.; Jain, A. Building Domain-Specific Sentiment Lexicon Using Random Walk-Based Model on Common-Sense Semantic Network. In *International Conference on Innovative Computing and Communication*; Springer: Singapore, 2023; pp. 193–204.
8. Cambria, E.; Poria, S.; Hazarika, D.; Kwok, K. SenticNet 5: Discovering conceptual primitives for sentiment analysis by means of context embeddings. In Proceedings of the AAAI Conference on Artificial Intelligence, New Orleans, LA, USA, 2–7 February 2018; Volume 32.
9. Akhtar, M.S.; Ekbal, A.; Cambria, E. How intense are you? Predicting intensities of emotions and sentiments using stacked ensemble [application notes]. *IEEE Comput. Intell. Mag.* **2020**, *15*, 64–75. [CrossRef]
10. Nandwani, P.; Verma, R. A review on sentiment analysis and emotion detection from text. *Soc. Netw. Anal. Min.* **2021**, *11*, 81. [CrossRef]
11. Xie, H.; Lin, W.; Lin, S.; Wang, J.; Yu, L.C. A multi-dimensional relation model for dimensional sentiment analysis. *Inf. Sci.* **2021**, *579*, 832–844. [CrossRef]
12. Roy, B.; Das, S. Perceptible sentiment analysis of students' WhatsApp group chats in valence, arousal, and dominance space. *Soc. Netw. Anal. Min.* **2022**, *13*, 9. [CrossRef]
13. Rizhinashvili, D.; Sham, A.H.; Anbarjafari, G. Enhanced speech emotion recognition using averaged valence arousal dominance mapping and deep neural networks. *Signal Image Video Process.* **2024**, *18*, 7445–7454. [CrossRef]

14. Sharma, S.S.; Dutta, G. SentiDraw: Using star ratings of reviews to develop domain specific sentiment lexicon for polarity determination. *Inf. Process. Manag.* **2021**, *58*, 102412. [CrossRef]
15. Baldwin, J.; Brunsdon, T.; Gaudoin, J.; Hirsch, L. Comparative Analysis of Lexicon-Based Sentiment Analysis Methods. 2023. Available online: https://ssrn.com/abstract=4531226 (accessed on 27 May 2024).
16. Oh, N. sentibank: A Unified Resource of Sentiment Lexicons and Dictionaries. *Proc. Int. AAAI Conf. Web Soc. Media* **2024**, *18*, 2003–2013. [CrossRef]
17. Ophir, Y.; Walter, D. Computational Sentiment Analysis. In *Emotions in the Digital World: Exploring Affective Experience and Expression in Online Interactions*; Oxford University Press: Oxford, UK, 2023; p. 114.
18. Taboada, M.; Brooke, J.; Tofiloski, M.; Voll, K.; Stede, M. Lexicon-based methods for sentiment analysis. *Comput. Linguist.* **2011**, *37*, 267–307. [CrossRef]
19. Deng, S.; Sinha, A.P.; Zhao, H. Adapting sentiment lexicons to domain-specific social media texts. *Decis. Support Syst.* **2017**, *94*, 65–76. [CrossRef]
20. Itani, M.; Roast, C.; Al-Khayatt, S. Developing resources for sentiment analysis of informal Arabic text in social media. *Procedia Comput. Sci.* **2017**, *117*, 129–136. [CrossRef]
21. Thelwall, M. The Heart and Soul of the Web? Sentiment Strength Detection in the Social Web with SentiStrength. In *Cyberemotions. Understanding Complex Systems*; Springer: Cham, Switzerland, 2017. [CrossRef]
22. Sebastiani, F.; Esuli, A. Sentiwordnet: A publicly available lexical resource for opinion mining. In Proceedings of the 5th International Conference on Language Resources and Evaluation, Genoa, Italy, 22–28 May 2006; European Language Resources Association (ELRA): Genoa, Italy, 2006; pp. 417–422.
23. Khan, F.H.; Qamar, U.; Bashir, S. SentiMI: Introducing point-wise mutual information with SentiWordNet to improve sentiment polarity detection. *Appl. Soft Comput.* **2016**, *39*, 140–153. [CrossRef]
24. Warriner, A.B.; Kuperman, V.; Brysbaert, M. Norms of valence, arousal, and dominance for 13,915 English lemmas. *Behav. Res. Methods* **2013**, *45*, 1191–1207. [CrossRef]
25. Lee, L.H.; Li, J.H.; Yu, L.C. Chinese EmoBank: Building Valence-Arousal Resources for Dimensional Sentiment Analysis. *ACM Trans. Asian Low-Resour. Lang. Inf. Process.* **2022**, *21*, 65. [CrossRef]
26. Bradley, M.; Lang, P.J. *Affective Norms for English Words (ANEW): Instruction Manual and Affective Ratings*; Technical Report C-1; The Center for Research in Psychophysiology, University of Florida: Gainesville, FL, USA, 1999. Available online: https://pdodds.w3.uvm.edu/teaching/courses/2009-08UVM-300/docs/others/everything/bradley1999a.pdf (accessed on 21 October 2024).
27. Nielsen, F.Å. A new ANEW: Evaluation of a word list for sentiment analysis in microblogs. *arXiv* **2011**, arXiv:1103.2903.
28. Ribeiro, F.N.; Araújo, M.; Gonçalves, P.; Gonçalves, M.A.; Benevenuto, F. SentiBench—A benchmark comparison of state-of-the-practice sentiment analysis methods. *EPJ Data Sci.* **2016**, *5*, 23. [CrossRef]
29. Hutto, C.J.; Gilbert, E.E. VADER: A Parsimonious Rule-Based Model for Sentiment Analysis of Social Media Text. *Proc. Int. AAAI Conf. Web Soc. Media* **2014**, *8*, 216–225. [CrossRef]
30. Garcia, D.; Garas, A.; Schweitzer, F. Positive words carry less information than negative words. *EPJ Data Sci.* **2012**, *1*, 3. [CrossRef]
31. Kloumann, I.M.; Danforth, C.M.; Harris, K.D.; Bliss, C.A.; Dodds, P.S. Positivity of the English Language. *PLoS ONE* **2012**, *7*, e29484. [CrossRef]
32. Yuri, B.; Pascale, F. Sentiment Analysis for Literary Texts: Hemingway as a Case-study. *J. Data Min. Digit. Humanit.* **2024**, *NLP4DH*. [CrossRef]
33. Yeruva, V.K.; Chandrashekar, M.; Lee, Y.; Rydberg-Cox, J.; Blanton, V.; Oyler, N.A. Interpretation of sentiment analysis in aeschylus's Greek tragedy. In Proceedings of the 4th Joint SIGHUM Workshop on Computational Linguistics for Cultural Heritage, Social Sciences, Humanities and Literature, Barcelona, Spain, 12 December 2020; pp. 138–146.
34. Vinodini, S. Analyzing Sentiments in Paulo Coelho's Literary Works Using VADER Sentiment Analysis. In Proceedings of the 2023 International Conference on Innovative Computing, Intelligent Communication and Smart Electrical Systems (ICSES), Chennai, India, 14–15 December 2023; pp. 1–6.
35. Ausloos, M. Generalized Hurst exponent and multifractal function of original and translated texts mapped into frequency and length time series. *Phys. Rev. E* **2012**, *86*, 031108. [CrossRef]
36. Rodriguez, E.; Aguilar-Cornejo, M.; Femat, R.; Alvarez-Ramirez, J. Scale and time dependence of serial correlations in word-length time series of written texts. *Physica A Stat. Mech. Its Appl.* **2014**, *414*, 378–386. [CrossRef]
37. Guzmán-Vargas, L.; Obregón-Quintana, B.; Aguilar-Velázquez, D.; Hernández-Pérez, R.; Liebovitch, L.S. Word-Length Correlations and Memory in Large Texts: A Visibility Network Analysis. *Entropy* **2015**, *17*, 7798–7810. [CrossRef]
38. Drożdż, S.; Oświęcimka, P.; Kulig, A.; Kwapień, J.; Bazarnik, K.; Grabska-Gradzińska, I.; Rybicki, J.; Stanuszek, M. Quantifying origin and character of long-range correlations in narrative texts. *Inf. Sci.* **2016**, *331*, 32–44. [CrossRef]
39. Gromov, V.A.; Dang, Q.N. Semantic and sentiment trajectories of literary masterpieces. *Chaos Solitons Fractals* **2023**, *175*, 113934. [CrossRef]
40. Ausloos, M. Measuring complexity with multifractals in texts. Translation effects. *Chaos Solitons Fractals* **2012**, *45*, 1349–1357. [CrossRef]
41. Carrizales-Velazquez, C.; Donner, R.V.; Guzmán-Vargas, L. Generalization of Higuchi's fractal dimension for multifractal analysis of time series with limited length. *Nonlinear Dyn.* **2022**, *108*, 417–431. [CrossRef]

42. Higuchi, T. Approach to an irregular time series on the basis of the fractal theory. *Physica D Nonlinear Phenom.* **1988**, *31*, 277–283. [CrossRef]
43. Peng, C.K.; Buldyrev, S.V.; Havlin, S.; Simons, M.; Stanley, H.E.; Goldberger, A.L. Mosaic organization of DNA nucleotides. *Phys. Rev. E* **1994**, *49*, 1685–1689. [CrossRef]
44. Shannon, C.E. A mathematical theory of communication. *Bell Syst. Tech. J.* **1948**, *27*, 623–656. [CrossRef]
45. Griffths, T.L. Rethinking language: How probabilities shape the words we use. *Proc. Natl. Acad. Sci. USA* **2011**, *108*, 3825–3826. [CrossRef]
46. Markov, A.A. An Example of Statistical Investigation of the Text Eugene Onegin Concerning the Connection of Samples in Chains. *Sci. Context* **2006**, *19*, 591–600. [CrossRef]
47. Malamud, B.D.; Turcotte, D.L. Self-affine time series: Measures of weak and strong persistence. *J. Stat. Plan. Inference* **1999**, *80*, 173–196. [CrossRef]
48. Peng, C.K.; Havlin, S.; Stanley, H.E.; Goldberger, A.L. Long-range anti-correlations and non- Gaussian Behavior of the heartbeat. *Phys. Rev. Lett.* **1995**, *70*, 1343–1346. [CrossRef] [PubMed]
49. Rangarajan, G.; Ding, M. Integrated approach to the assessment of long range correlation in time series data. *Phys. Rev. E* **2000**, *61*, 4991–5001. [CrossRef] [PubMed]
50. Higuchi, T. Relationship between the fractal dimension and the power law index for a time series: A numerical investigation. *Physica D Nonlinear Phenom.* **1990**, *46*, 254–264. [CrossRef]
51. Guzmán-Vargas, L.; Angulo-Brown, F. Simple model of the aging effect in heart interbeat time series. *Phys. Rev. E* **2003**, *67*, 052901. [CrossRef] [PubMed]
52. Peng, C.K.; Mietus, J.; Hausdorff, J.; Havlin, S.; Stanley, H.E.; Goldberger, A.L. Quantification of Scaling Exponents and Crossover Phenomena in Nonstationary Heartbeat Time Series. *Chaos* **1995**, *5*, 82–87. [CrossRef]
53. Telesca, L.; Lapenna, V.; Macchiato, M. Multifractal fluctuations in seismic interspike series. *Physica A Stat. Mech. Its Appl.* **2005**, *354*, 629–640. [CrossRef]
54. Bashan, A.; Bartsch, R.; Kantelhardt, J.W.; Havlin, S. Comparison of detrending methods for fluctuation analysis. *Physica A Stat. Mech. Its Appl.* **2008**, *387*, 5080–5090. [CrossRef]
55. Feder, J. *Fractals*; Springer: New York, USA, 1988.
56. Dodds, P.S.; Clark, E.M.; Desu, S.; Frank, M.R.; Reagan, A.J.; Williams, J.R.; Mitchell, L.; Harris, K.D.; Kloumann, I.M.; Bagrow, J.P.; et al. Human language reveals a universal positivity bias. *Proc. Natl. Acad. Sci. USA* **2015**, *112*, 2389–2394. [CrossRef]
57. Yang, T.; Gu, C.; Yang, H. Long-range correlations in sentence series from a story of the stone. *PLoS ONE* **2016**, *11*, e0162423. [CrossRef]
58. Bizzoni, Y.; Moreira, P.; Thomsen, M.R.; Nielbo, K.L. The fractality of sentiment arcs for literary quality assessment: The case of Nobel laureates. In Proceedings of the 2nd International Workshop on Natural Language Processing for Digital Humanities, Taipei, Taiwan, 20 November 2022; pp. 31–41.
59. Yamasaki, K.; Muchnik, L.; Havlin, S.; Bunde, A.; Stanley, H.E. Scaling and memory in volatility return intervals in financial markets. *Proc. Natl. Acad. Sci. USA* **2005**, *102*, 9424–9428. [CrossRef]
60. Hernández-Pérez, R.; Guzmán-Vargas, L.; Reyes-Ramirez, I.; Angulo-Brown, F. Evolution in time and scales of the stability of heart interbeat rate. *Europhys. Lett.* **2011**, *92*, 68006. [CrossRef]
61. Reyes-Ramírez, I.; Guzmán-Vargas, L. Scaling properties of excursions in heartbeat dynamics. *Europhys. Lett.* **2010**, *89*, 38008. [CrossRef]
62. Hunter, J.D. Matplotlib: A 2D graphics environment. *Comput. Sci. Eng.* **2007**, *9*, 90–95. [CrossRef]

information

Article

Quickly Finding the Semantically Optimal Presentation Order for a Set of Text Artifacts

Daniel S. Soper

Department of Information Systems & Decision Sciences, California State University, Fullerton, CA 92831, USA; dsoper@fullerton.edu

Abstract: This study considers how to quickly find the order in which to present a set of text artifacts on mobile apps or websites such that those artifacts are maximally semantically separated. Semantic separation is desirable because it ensures that users experience as much novelty as possible from one item to the next, thereby improving user attention and engagement. Since an exhaustive search of all possible sequences of text items becomes increasingly infeasible as the length of the sequence grows, a new algorithm is proposed to quickly find the semantically optimal presentation order for a set of text artifacts. The performance of the proposed algorithm is evaluated using an extensive set of experiments involving three different types of text artifacts, seven different sequence lengths, and more than 600 experimental trials. The results demonstrate that the proposed algorithm can select statistically optimal sequences of text artifacts extremely quickly, regardless of the type of text artifacts being used as input or the length of the sequence. App and website developers who are seeking to hold users' attention and improve user engagement may therefore find the proposed algorithm very attractive in comparison to an exhaustive search.

Keywords: text mining; semantic separation; content presentation order; web design; app design; pagination; infinite scroll; user engagement

1. Introduction

It is very common for modern apps and websites to present content in the form of a sequence of items through which users can browse. Video-sharing apps, for example, present users with a sequence of video previews, while news websites present users with a sequence of news article headlines. Streaming television and music apps present users with sequences of available shows and recordings, while social media platforms present users with sequences of photos, messages, and other posts. Similarly, search engines present information to users in the form of a sequence of items, as do online retailers. These sequences of content items are typically displayed to users either through the interface design pattern known as "pagination" or through the pattern known as "infinite scroll" [1,2]. Both of these interface design patterns allow users to browse through a subset of available content items, and if none of the currently displayed items is of interest, to fetch another sequence of content items, either by loading the next page of results in the case of pagination [3], or by scrolling downward in the case of infinite scroll [4].

Regardless of whether an app or website implements pagination or infinite scroll, each sequence of content items is finite in length. No universal agreement exists regarding the optimal number of items that should be included in each sequence, but sequences of length 10 have been observed to be common for search results [5]. For any set of content items of length $k > 1$, app and website developers must determine the order in which the items will

https://doi.org/10.3390/info16010059

be presented to users, thus transforming the unordered set into a sequence. Search engines, for example, commonly order content items according to their relevance to the user's query, while news articles are typically presented in reverse chronological order. Alphabetical order, numerical order, ordering by popularity, and ordering by user ratings are just a few of the many other ways in which the presentation order for content items is often determined.

For apps and websites that rely on an advertising-based revenue model, a common design goal is to keep users engaged on the app or website as long as possible, thus allowing more advertisements to be displayed and more revenue to be generated [6]. It follows, of course, that in order to keep a user engaged, the app or website must hold the user's attention. Past research has demonstrated that novelty plays a significant role in human attention processes, with novel stimuli leading to increased attention [7,8]. Physiologically, novel stimuli trigger the release of the neurotransmitter dopamine, which heightens attention through cognitive pleasure and reward mechanisms that make the novel stimuli more enticing [9,10]. Ensuring that users experience novelty while browsing from one content item to the next can therefore be expected to heighten their attention and bolster their engagement with an app or website. This theoretical connection between novelty and user engagement is supported by a variety of empirical studies, including research that found positive impacts of novelty on user engagement on streaming media platforms [11], research connecting novelty to user engagement with online news articles [12], and research showing how novelty improves user engagement with blog posts [13]. By contrast, a lack of novelty, as manifested through excessive redundancy or similarity from one content item to the next, can be expected to lead to waning attention and lower user engagement.

Many of the content items that appear on apps and websites take the form of text artifacts, including, for example, search results, product descriptions, reviews, news headlines, social media messages, blog posts, frequently asked questions (FAQs), and tutorials and how-to articles, among many others. In light of the discussion above, developers of apps and websites on which text artifacts appear as sequences of content items should consider the extent to which those items exhibit novelty from one item to the next. Given a set of text artifacts, maximal novelty can be achieved by ensuring that the semantic distance between the artifacts in the sequence is as large as possible, with semantic distance referring to the extent to which the meaning of two text artifacts differs [14]. For a finite set of text artifacts, however, many different sequences are possible. To maximize the novelty experienced by the user, the app or website must therefore find the specific sequence of those artifacts that exhibits the largest total semantic distance, as determined by the sum of the semantic distances between each adjacent pair of text artifacts. To date, however, no systematic study has been undertaken that considers how to identify the semantically optimal presentation order for a set of text artifacts in an efficient manner. The current paper seeks to fill this gap in the extant literature.

To better clarify the nature of this semantic similarity problem, consider a set of three text artifacts $\{A, B, C\}$, the possible sequences of which are shown in Table 1.

Table 1. Possible sequences for a set of three text artifacts $\{A, B, C\}$.

Sequence	
$A \rightarrow B \rightarrow C$	$C \rightarrow B \rightarrow A$
$A \rightarrow C \rightarrow B$	$B \rightarrow C \rightarrow A$
$B \rightarrow A \rightarrow C$	$C \rightarrow A \rightarrow B$

As a general rule, there are $k!$ possible sequences (i.e., permutations) of length k for a set containing k elements. In the context of semantic similarity, however, it is important to recognize that the semantic distance between any two text artifacts is symmetric, such that the semantic distance between artifact *A* and artifact *B* is identical to the semantic distance between artifact *B* and artifact *A*. By extension, a sequence of text artifacts is bidirectional insofar as the sum of the semantic distances for a sequence $A \to B \to C$ is identical to the sum of the semantic distances for its symmetric counterpart $C \to B \to A$. Since sequences of text artifacts are semantically bidirectional, the symmetric version of each sequence can be excluded from consideration when using the sequence as a whole as the unit of analysis. The three sequences in the rightmost column of Table 1, for example, can be ignored because they are all symmetric versions of the three sequences that appear in the leftmost column of the table. Excluding symmetric versions, the number of possible sequences of length k for a set of k text artifacts is thus equal to $k!/2$.

Although a sequence in which all pairs of adjacent text artifacts are equidistantly spaced may be theoretically appealing, in the absence of any duplicate artifacts, such an outcome would be highly improbable in the real world because the semantic content of each artifact in the sequence would differ in some way from the semantic content of every other artifact in the sequence. Given a finite set of distinct text artifacts as input and the objective of maximizing the semantic novelty from one artifact to the next, the best we can do is therefore to identify the sequence for which the sum of semantic distances between each pair of adjacent artifacts is as large as possible. This notion is illustrated for two different sets of text artifacts in Figure 1 below, with the optimal sequences highlighted in green.

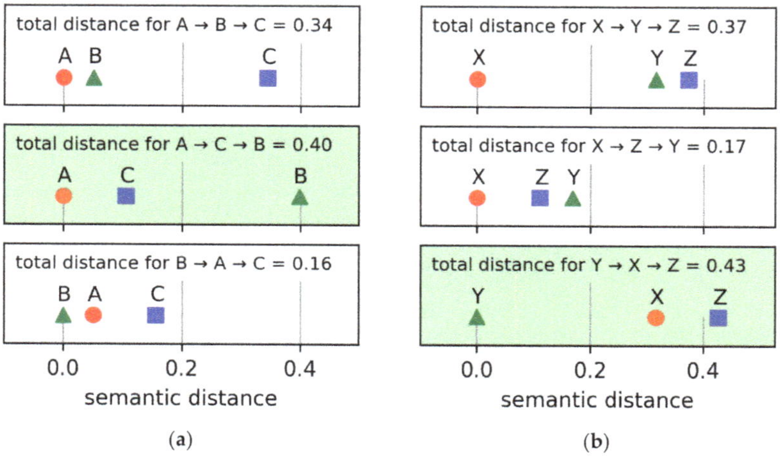

Figure 1. Semantic distances for all possible bidirectional sequences of two sets of text artifacts. The optimal presentation order is the sequence for which the sum of the semantic distances between each adjacent pair of items in the set is as large as possible. (**a**) The optimal sequence for the set of text artifacts $\{A, B, C\}$ is $A \to C \to B$ (or its symmetric equivalent, $B \to C \to A$). (**b**) The optimal sequence for the set of text artifacts $\{X, Y, Z\}$ is $Y \to X \to Z$ (or its symmetric equivalent, $Z \to X \to Y$).

As shown in Figure 1, the sum of semantic distances for a sequence of text artifacts depends on the order in which those artifacts appear in the sequence. In panel (a) of Figure 1, for example, the total semantic distance for the sequence $B \to A \to C$ is 0.16, while the total semantic distance for the same text artifacts when arranged into the sequence $A \to C \to B$ is 0.40. Since the semantic distance between each pair of adjacent artifacts reflects the degree to which their topical content differs, the transition from artifact *C* to artifact *B* would be experienced by a user as a more substantial or novel shift in content than the transition from, say, artifact *B* to artifact *A*, whose small semantic distance suggests a much greater degree of topical redundancy or overlap. For a finite set of text artifacts, the greatest possible amount of novelty that the user can experience is obtained from the sequence with the largest total semantic distance, and for that purpose, the sequence with the greatest length can be considered optimal.

While finding the best possible sequence should be of great interest to developers of apps and websites, it is also critical to be able to find the best sequence quickly in order to ensure a high-quality user experience. As noted previously, the total number of possible bidirectional sequences of length k for a finite set of text artifacts containing k elements is equal to $k!/2$. Finding the semantically optimal presentation order for a set of text artifacts can therefore be easily and quickly accomplished using an exhaustive search when the number of artifacts in the set is small. For a larger set of text artifacts, however, providing a high-quality user experience would be infeasible using an exhaustive search due to exponential growth in both the number of possible sequences and the wall-clock time that would be required to examine those sequences. A set of five text artifacts, for example, could only be arranged into $5!/2 = 60$ different bidirectional sequences, while a total of $10!/2 = 1{,}814{,}400$ bidirectional sequences would be possible for a set of 10 artifacts. For a set of 15 text artifacts, however, a total of $15!/2 = 653{,}837{,}184{,}000$ bidirectional sequences would be possible, making an exhaustive search computationally infeasible in any reasonable amount of wall-clock time.

In light of the discussion immediately above, the goal of the current paper is to develop and evaluate the performance of an algorithm that can quickly find the semantically optimal presentation order for a set of text artifacts, even when the number of artifacts in the set is comparatively large. If proven tenable, the resulting algorithm could be used by developers of a wide variety of apps and websites to present content items to users in a sequence that is intentionally designed to hold the users' attention, thus increasing both user engagement and its attendant revenues.

The balance of this paper is organized as follows: the next section presents the proposed algorithm for quickly finding the semantically optimal presentation order for a set of text artifacts, as well as descriptions of the data, experiments, and methods of evaluation that were used to assess the algorithm's performance. Section 3 presents the results obtained from the experiments, and those results are subsequently discussed in Section 4. This paper concludes in Section 5 with a summary, a discussion of this study's limitations, and opportunities for future research.

2. Materials and Methods

2.1. Encoding and Measuring the Semantic Distance Between Text Artifacts

While there are many methods of capturing the semantic content of text artifacts, the current study adopted the common and well-established approach in which the semantic content of each artifact is encoded into a vector in a shared n-dimensional space [15]. A simple two-dimensional example of this vector-space model is illustrated in Figure 2 below.

Representing text artifacts as vectors of length n in a shared n-dimensional space is convenient because it allows the degree of semantic similarity (or dissimilarity) among the text artifacts to be measured as a function of the distance between their corresponding vectors. For the current study, the cosine distance metric was used to quantify the semantic distance between text artifacts because its values are naturally constrained to the closed interval [0.0, 1.0], with a value of 0.0 indicating that two text artifacts are semantically identical and a value of 1.0 indicating that two artifacts are semantically orthogonal [16]. All text artifacts used in the current study were encoded into vectors using the pretrained "all-MiniLM-L6-v2" model, which is freely available as part of the Sentence Transformers library in Python [17]. This particular model maps each text artifact to a vector space consisting of 384 dimensions.

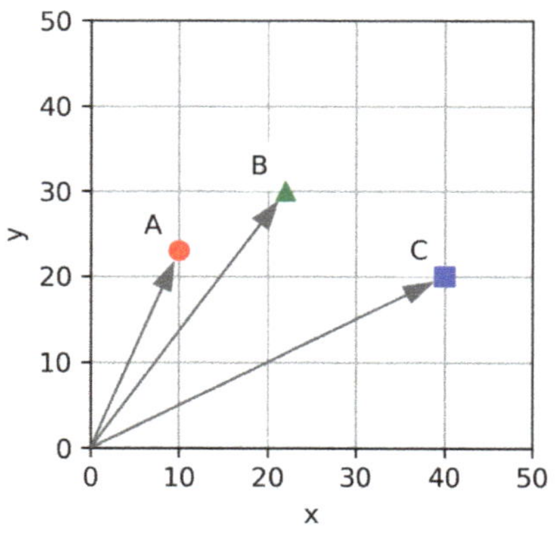

Figure 2. A set of three text artifacts {*A*, *B*, *C*} represented as vectors in a two-dimensional space.

2.2. The Proposed Algorithm

Having described the methods that were used in the current study to encode text artifacts into vectors and measure the semantic distance between them, we are now equipped to proceed with a complete description of the proposed algorithm for quickly finding the optimal presentation order for a set of text artifacts. As noted previously and as illustrated in Figure 1, the optimal presentation order is defined as the bidirectional sequence for which the sum of the semantic distances between all adjacent pairs of text artifacts in the sequence is as large as possible. The steps in the algorithm (Algorithm 1) below are described textually rather than symbolically in order to ensure clarity.

Algorithm 1: Quickly finding the semantically optimal presentation order for a set of text artifacts

1. Encode all text artifacts that will appear in the sequence into vectors in a shared high-dimensional space.
2. Compute the cosine distances between all possible pairs of text artifact vectors.
3. Initialize storage locations to hold the best observed sequence of text artifacts and the total semantic distance of that sequence.
4. For each text artifact in the set, complete the following:
    a. Initialize storage locations to hold a new candidate sequence and the total semantic distance of the candidate sequence.
    b. Use the current text artifact as the first item in the new sequence.
    c. While text artifacts remain to be added to this candidate sequence, complete the following:
        i. Among the remaining (unused) text artifacts, find the artifact whose cosine distance from the most recent item in the sequence is largest, and add that artifact to the sequence.
        ii. Update the total semantic distance of the candidate sequence to include the cosine distance between the two most recent items.
    d. If the current candidate sequence has the largest total semantic distance thus far observed, complete the following:
        i. Update the value of the largest total semantic distance thus far observed.
        ii. Store the current candidate sequence as the best sequence thus far observed.
5. Return the best sequence (i.e., the sequence with the largest total semantic distance that was observed during the search).

A simplified graphical representation of the proposed algorithm is provided in Figure 3 below.

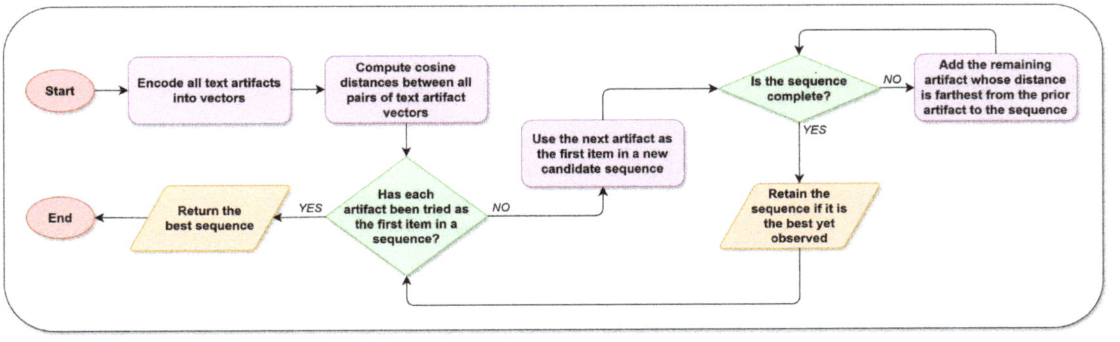

Figure 3. A simplified graphical representation of the proposed algorithm.

Notably, for a set of *k* text artifacts, the proposed algorithm constructs and considers just *k* candidate sequences, with each text artifact being used exactly once as the first item in a sequence. After placing the first text artifact in a candidate sequence, the proposed algorithm greedily uses whichever of the remaining artifacts has the largest cosine distance from the most recent item as the next item in the sequence. This process continues until the candidate sequence is complete. The newly completed candidate sequence is then retained if it has the largest total semantic distance thus far observed or is discarded otherwise. After constructing and considering each of the *k* candidate sequences, the proposed algorithm returns the best-observed sequence and then terminates. Since the number of candidate sequences considered by the proposed algorithm corresponds directly to the number of text artifacts in the input set, it follows that the wall-clock time required by the algorithm scales linearly with the size of the set (or equivalently, with the length of the sequence). Given that the proposed algorithm has an O(n) complexity, while an exhaustive search has an $O(2^n)$ complexity, it is reasonable to expect that the total execution time of the proposed algorithm will be very fast in comparison to an exhaustive search.

2.3. Data

If found to be viable, the proposed algorithm could be usefully applied to determine the semantically optimal sequence of a set of text artifacts in a very wide variety of scenarios. As a means of evaluating and demonstrating this broad applicability, the data set that was used to evaluate the performance of the algorithm was intentionally designed to contain text artifacts from three distinct domains, including (1) synopses of movie plots, (2) news articles about many different topics, and (3) lyrics for popular songs. In total, 30 of each of these different types of text artifacts were included in the data set, yielding a total of 90 unique text artifacts for use in the experiments.

The movie synopses were obtained from the Internet Movie Database (IMDb), which describes itself as "the world's most popular and authoritative source for information on movies, TV shows, and celebrities" [18]. Specifically, the IMDb synopses for the 30 highest-grossing movies of all time were used in the experiments, according to the worldwide gross box office revenue figures published by Box Office Mojo as of October 2024 [19]. The 30 news articles used in the experiments were derived from the freely available Reuters Corpus that is included as part of the Natural Language Toolkit (NLTK) suite of Python libraries [20]. The 30 specific news articles that were included in the data set were chosen at random from among the 10,788 articles contained in the NLTK Reuters Corpus. Finally, the song lyrics included in the data set were for the 30 greatest songs of all time as of October 2024, according to the songs' performances in the United States on the Billboard Hot 100 Singles Chart [21], with the song lyrics themselves being obtained from LyricFind's Lyrics Database [22]. Interested readers may download all of the raw data used in the experiments by following the instructions in the Data Availability Statement that appears near the end of this paper.

2.4. Experiments

Three sets of experiments were conducted in order to evaluate the performance of the proposed algorithm, with each set of experiments using one of the text sources described immediately above (i.e., movie synopses, news articles, or song lyrics). Each set of experiments examined sequences of text artifacts of length $k = \{5, 6, \ldots, 11\}$. A total of 30 trials were carried out for each combination of text source and sequence length (i.e., for each experimental condition) in order to ensure that the distributions of the resulting performance metrics would be approximately Gaussian, per the central limit theorem [23]. The k specific text artifacts used in each trial were chosen at random from among the set of 30 artifacts for the trial's corresponding source of text. The experiment design thus involved three sources of text and seven different sequence lengths, yielding 21 unique experimental conditions. Since each experimental condition was tested 30 times, a total of $21 \times 30 = 630$ experimental trials were conducted in the current study. All of the experimental trials were carried out sequentially using identical hardware on the Google Colaboratory platform [24].

The proposed algorithm itself was assessed in two different ways, both of which involved comparing the algorithm's performance in each experimental trial against that of a corresponding exhaustive search that used the same text artifacts and sequence length. First, the wall-clock time required by the algorithm was compared against that of an exhaustive search, and second, the quality of the sequence chosen by the proposed algorithm in each trial was compared against the globally optimal sequence for that trial, as determined by the exhaustive search. This involved both a comparison of the total semantic distance of the sequence chosen by the proposed algorithm against the total semantic distance of the globally optimal sequence, as well as calculating the percentile of the algorithm's chosen sequence in comparison to all possible sequences for the current experimental trial. Specific details about the methods that were used for evaluating the proposed algorithm are provided in the following subsection. Interested readers may also download all of the Python source code that was used to conduct the experiments by following the instructions in the Data Availability Statement that appears near the end of this paper.

2.5. Methods for Evaluating the Proposed Algorithm

As noted above, the performance of the proposed algorithm was evaluated both in terms of its wall-clock execution time relative to an exhaustive search and in terms of the quality of the algorithm's chosen sequence of text artifacts. With respect to wall-clock time, the total execution time of the proposed algorithm and its corresponding exhaustive search were recorded for each of the 30 trials that were carried out in each of the 21 different experimental conditions. Welch's t-tests were then used to compare the wall-clock times from the proposed algorithm and its matching exhaustive searches for each experimental condition. Welch's t-tests were used for this purpose because they allow for unequal variances, and there was no reason to expect that the variances of the distributions of the wall-clock times for the proposed algorithm and the exhaustive searches would be equal [25].

Comparing the wall-clock times of the proposed algorithm and an exhaustive search was necessary but insufficient for fully assessing the algorithm's viability since being faster than an exhaustive search would be of little value if the quality of the sequences chosen by the proposed algorithm were poor. For this reason, the total semantic distances of the sequences of text artifacts chosen by the proposed algorithm were statistically compared against those of the globally optimal sequences for each experimental condition, as determined by a matching set of exhaustive searches. Again, Welch's t-tests were used for this purpose because there was no reason to expect that the variances in the distributions of semantic distances for the sequences chosen by the algorithm and those identified as optimal via an exhaustive search would be equal [25]. For each experimental condition, if the proposed algorithm was found to require significantly less wall-clock time than an exhaustive search while simultaneously choosing sequences of text artifacts that were statistically indistinguishable from their corresponding optimal sequences, then it could be reasonably concluded that the proposed algorithm is superior to an exhaustive search.

Finally, the quality of the sequence of text artifacts chosen by the proposed algorithm in each experimental trial was also quantified by computing the percentile of the chosen sequence relative to all possible sequences for that trial. Specifically, the percentile of a chosen sequence was calculated as *1 − (number of superior sequences/total sequences)*, with superior sequences being defined as those whose total semantic distance was greater than that of the sequence chosen by the proposed algorithm. For example, a set of six text artifacts would have a total of *6!/2* = 360 possible bidirectional sequences. If two of those sequences had a larger total semantic distance than the sequence chosen by the algorithm, then the quality of the sequence chosen by the algorithm would be quantified as *1 − (2/360)* ≈ 0.994, yielding a percentile for the algorithm's chosen sequence of 99.4%. The wall-clock times, total semantic distances, and percentiles of the proposed algorithm's chosen sequences are presented in the following section.

3. Results

The results of the experiments that were described in the previous section are presented in Tables 2–4 below, with the tables respectively showing the comparative performance of the proposed algorithm relative to an exhaustive search for the movie synopses, news articles, and song lyrics text artifacts.

Table 2. Proposed algorithm performance on movie synopses relative to an exhaustive search.

Sequence Length	Mean Wall-Clock Time (Seconds)		Mean Cosine Distance of Best Sequence		Average Quality of Algorithmic Sequence
	Proposed Algorithm	Exhaustive Search	Proposed Algorithm	Exhaustive Search	
5	0.00028 ***	0.00316	3.52583	3.53478 ns	0.99278
6	0.00031 ***	0.00797	4.44218	4.45140 ns	0.99722
7	0.00029 ***	0.02623	5.29985	5.32438 ns	0.99827
8	0.00041 ***	0.23103	6.27516	6.31719 ns	0.99788
9	0.00050 ***	2.16796	7.14110	7.19904 ns	0.99986
10	0.00057 ***	22.07154	8.12200	8.16449 ns	0.99998
11	0.00072 ***	256.39432	9.08820	9.19619 ns	0.99996

*** $p < 0.001$, ns p = not significant.

Beginning with wall-clock time, it is immediately evident in Tables 2–4 that the average time required by the proposed algorithm to choose a sequence of text artifacts is much less than the average wall-clock time required by an exhaustive search. Moreover, this difference was highly significant at $p < 0.001$ for all 21 combinations of text sources and sequence lengths considered in the experiments. As expected, the average wall-clock time required by the proposed algorithm was observed to grow linearly with the length of the sequence (or, equivalently, with the number of text artifacts in the input set), while the average wall-clock time required by an exhaustive search was observed to grow exponentially. These characteristics are illustrated in Figure 4 below.

Table 3. Proposed algorithm performance on news articles relative to an exhaustive search.

Sequence Length	Mean Wall-Clock Time (Seconds)		Mean Cosine Distance of Best Sequence		Average Quality of Algorithmic Sequence
	Proposed Algorithm	Exhaustive Search	Proposed Algorithm	Exhaustive Search	
5	0.00036 ***	0.00074	3.59040	3.59219 ns	0.99500
6	0.00026 ***	0.00363	4.50808	4.51811 ns	0.99833
7	0.00034 ***	0.02710	5.39192	5.41109 ns	0.99923
8	0.00044 ***	0.23080	6.37339	6.44631 ns	0.99881
9	0.00053 ***	2.05910	7.27462	7.33826 ns	0.99959
10	0.00063 ***	22.24218	8.30702	8.39426 ns	0.99992
11	0.00070 ***	256.20882	9.17250	9.29327 ns	0.99997

*** $p < 0.001$, ns p = not significant.

Table 4. Proposed algorithm performance on song lyrics relative to an exhaustive search.

Sequence Length	Mean Wall-Clock Time (Seconds)		Mean Cosine Distance of Best Sequence		Average Quality of Algorithmic Sequence
	Proposed Algorithm	Exhaustive Search	Proposed Algorithm	Exhaustive Search	
5	0.00021 ***	0.00061	2.48525	2.49249 ns	0.99278
6	0.00045 ***	0.00373	3.06495	3.09022 ns	0.99324
7	0.00037 ***	0.02884	3.70566	3.74845 ns	0.99595
8	0.00041 ***	0.23391	4.39472	4.46422 ns	0.99781
9	0.00051 ***	2.12178	4.98578	5.08293 ns	0.99752
10	0.00064 ***	22.08317	5.77806	5.92306 ns	0.99865
11	0.00068 ***	255.74082	6.30305	6.49257 ns	0.99877

*** $p < 0.001$, ns p = not significant.

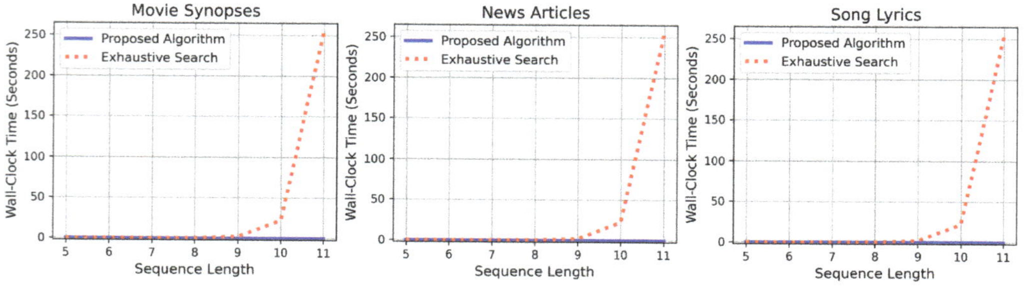

Figure 4. Average wall-clock time required by the proposed algorithm in comparison to an exhaustive search.

Moving next to a consideration of sequence quality, it is evident in Tables 2–4 that, on average, the total semantic distance of the sequence of text artifacts chosen by the proposed algorithm is slightly less than the total semantic distance of the optimal sequence identified via an exhaustive search. Importantly, however, this difference was not observed to be statistically significant for any of the 21 different combinations of text sources and sequence lengths evaluated in the experiments. Thus, although the total semantic distances of the sequences of text artifacts identified by the proposed algorithm are nominally smaller than those identified via an exhaustive search, they are, in fact, statistically identical in all cases to the optimal sequences. It can therefore be concluded that, on average, the proposed algorithm selects sequences of text artifacts that are statistically optimal.

Finally, Tables 2–4 reveal that the average quality of the sequences chosen by the proposed algorithm—as measured by their percentiles relative to all possible sequences—not only consistently exceeds 99% but also tends to approach 100% as the length of the sequence grows. Put differently, the average performance of the proposed algorithm in terms of the quality of the sequences of text artifacts that it selects tends to improve as the sequence grows longer. The observed improvement in the relative quality of the sequences selected by the algorithm is attributable to the exponential growth in the total number of sequences that are possible as the length of the sequence grows. If, for example, the algorithm chose the second-best option out of 100 possible sequences, then the quality of the chosen sequence would be 99.0%. If the algorithm chose the second-best option out of 1000 possible sequences, however, the quality of the chosen sequence would be 99.9%. This behavior is illustrated in Figure 5 below, which shows how the average quality of the proposed algorithm's chosen sequences approaches 100% according to a logarithmic function.

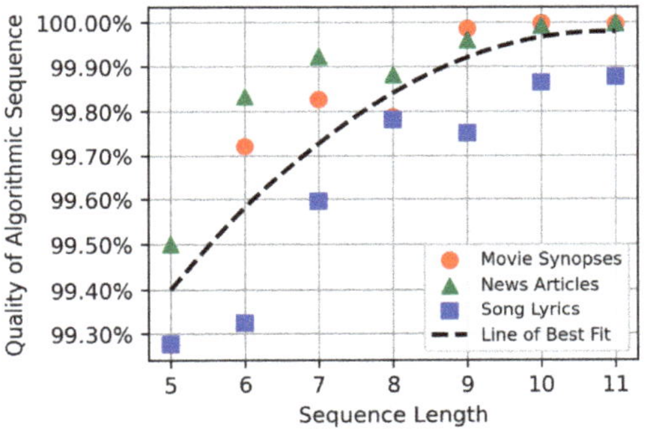

Figure 5. Average quality of sequences identified by the proposed algorithm relative to all possible sequences of the same length.

The results obtained from the experiments and their implications for practitioners are discussed in greater detail in the following section.

4. Discussion

Collectively, the results of the experiments reported in the previous section suggest that the proposed algorithm runs very quickly and yields sequences of text artifacts whose total semantic distances are statistically optimal. The fact that the proposed algorithm is consistently able to deliver statistically optimal sequences of text artifacts in a very short amount of time has important implications for developers of apps and websites that present sequences of textual content to users. Namely, unless the set of input text artifacts is very small, finding the semantically optimal sequence of artifacts using an exhaustive search simply requires too much wall-clock time to provide a high-quality experience to users. In the experiments, for example, the proposed algorithm was consistently observed to find a statistically optimal sequence in an average of less than 0.001 s, regardless of the number of text items in the sequence. By contrast, an exhaustive search running on identical hardware typically required more than 20 s to find the optimal sequence for a set of 10 text artifacts and required more than 250 s to perform the same task for a set of 11 text artifacts. It would be very difficult indeed to argue that a mobile app or data-driven website provides a high-quality user experience if it requires its users to wait for more than 20 s while new content is being loaded, let alone waiting for more than 250 s!

Its dramatic superiority in wall-clock time notwithstanding, the proposed algorithm was also observed to identify sequences of text artifacts whose total semantic distances were statistically indistinguishable from the globally optimal sequences. Put differently, there were no statistically significant differences between the quality of the sequences chosen by the proposed algorithm and the optimal sequences identified via an exhaustive search. Moreover, the quality percentiles of the sequences of text artifacts selected by the proposed algorithm were observed to improve according to a logarithmic function as the length of the sequences grew, increasing from an overall average of 99.35% for sequences of length $k = 5$ to an overall average of 99.96% for sequences of length $k = 11$. Given that the quality of the sequences selected by the proposed algorithm improves as the length of the sequence grows, and given that the amount of wall-clock time required for an exhaustive search increases exponentially under the same conditions, the proposed algorithm should be very attractive to app and website developers, particularly when working with larger sets of text artifacts.

In addition to the above general observations, the proposed algorithm was also observed to work equally well for all of the different types of textual content that were included in the experiments, and there is no theoretical reason to expect that the proposed algorithm would perform in any notably different manner for any other type of textual content. Moreover, the vector-space model upon which the proposed algorithm relies ensures that the algorithm will perform well regardless of how much semantic variation exists among the text artifacts in the input set. We might, for example, expect the total amount of semantic variation in a set of news articles about the FIFA World Cup to be less than the total amount of semantic variation in a set of news articles about a wider variety of topics such as politics, technology, business, and entertainment. The degree of semantic variation among the set of input articles will, of course, naturally constrain the total amount of semantic separation that can be achieved, but as long as that degree of variation is greater than zero, the proposed algorithm can be relied upon to find a high-quality solution.

The proposed algorithm has the virtues of being simple, being very fast in comparison to an exhaustive search, and being able to select statistically optimal sequences of text artifacts. Developers seeking to implement the algorithm in real-world scenarios will, however, need to consider a few important points related to the vector-space model upon which the proposed algorithm relies. First, the dimensions of the vector-space model directly influence how much of the semantic content of the underlying text artifacts is captured by each vector. The current study obtained good results with a freely available 384-dimension model, but models with more or fewer dimensions may be appropriate based on the developer's specific use case. Second, developers must decide whether to compute vector representations for and cosine distances between text artifacts in real time or in advance. For text artifacts whose content is static, computing and storing vector representations and cosine distances just once may prove advantageous, but for text artifacts whose content is subject to change, more frequent or real-time calculations may be more appropriate.

Finally, it should be noted that the proposed algorithm can also be applied to content items that are not inherently textual in nature. Modern artificial intelligence tools, for example, can readily generate textual descriptions of images using computer vision techniques [26,27] and can easily extract spoken words from video or audio recordings using speech-to-text models [28]. Generative AI tools are also capable of writing accurate textual summaries of a wide variety of multimedia artifacts [29]. Using such tools to preprocess non-textual content items can thus transform almost any form of media into a textual proxy that is suitable for input into the proposed algorithm with very little effort. Indeed, as long as a set of non-textual content items—such as images, videos, songs, or other audio recordings—can be reduced to textual descriptions, the proposed algorithm can be used to quickly find the sequence in which those items should be presented to users in order to maximize the overall novelty from one item to the next. In this way, the proposed algorithm can be applied to find the statistically optimal sequence for a wide and mixed variety of content items, thus dramatically enhancing its potential usefulness for developers of apps and websites.

5. Conclusions

The primary goal of this paper was to address the problem of how to quickly find the optimal order in which to present a set of text artifacts to users such that the artifacts exhibit the widest possible degree of semantic separation, thereby bolstering user engagement by maximizing novelty from one artifact to the next. Although an exhaustive search could be used for this purpose, the wall-clock time required to conduct an exhaustive search increases exponentially as the number of text artifacts in the sequence grows. Since past research has established that users are unwilling to wait for more than a few seconds before being presented with new content [30–32], a solution that relies on an exhaustive search is infeasible if app and website developers hope to provide a high-quality experience to their users. The current paper therefore proposed an algorithm for quickly finding the semantically optimal presentation order for a set of text artifacts. An extensive set of experiments involving 21 different experimental conditions and more than 600 experimental trials was carried out in order to evaluate the performance of the algorithm, the results of which revealed that the proposed algorithm consistently selects sequences of text artifacts that are statistically optimal while simultaneously being extremely fast.

Although careful and methodical efforts were taken to evaluate the performance of the proposed algorithm, this study nevertheless has several limitations that merit acknowledgment. First, the proposed algorithm was evaluated using text artifacts from just three different domains—movie synopses, news articles, and song lyrics. The results of the experiments indicate that the proposed algorithm performed equally well across all of these domains, but confidence in the proposed algorithm could be improved by testing it using text artifacts from other domains. Next, the performance of the proposed algorithm was evaluated only for sequences of text artifacts of length $k = \{5, 6, \ldots, 11\}$. Longer sequences were not examined in the current study due to the excessive amount of wall-clock time that would be required to conduct exhaustive searches for such sequences. Evidence obtained from the experiments suggests that the quality of the sequences selected by the proposed algorithm tends to improve as the length of the sequence grows, but whether this pattern holds for sequences of length $k > 11$ cannot be known in the absence of additional exhaustive searches. In addition to testing the algorithm in other textual domains, evaluating the algorithm's performance on longer sequences of text artifacts also represents an opportunity for future research. Moreover, it is reasonable to assume that other non-exhaustive algorithmic approaches could be developed to address the problem of maximizing inter-item novelty in a sequence of text artifacts, making the development and comparison of such algorithms another specific avenue for future work in this area.

The limitations above notwithstanding, the algorithm proposed in this paper appears to be very promising. Holding users' attention is critical for apps and websites that rely on advertising-based revenue models, and since past research suggests that novelty is strongly associated with increased attention, taking steps to ensure that the content items presented to users are as novel as possible from one item to the next has obvious advantages. It is hoped that the algorithm proposed in this paper will prove useful in that regard.

Funding: This research was generously supported by a senior intramural grant from the Office of Research and Sponsored Projects at California State University, Fullerton.

Institutional Review Board Statement: Not applicable.

Informed Consent Statement: Not applicable.

Data Availability Statement: The raw data, analytical results, and Python source code for the algorithm and experiments described in this paper can be downloaded from the following URL: https://drive.google.com/file/d/1JjLpUxZINcttmr7c8TFkZU9xJhmrOJGG/view?usp=sharing, accessed on 15 October 2024.

Acknowledgments: This work benefited greatly from informal conversations with the author's colleagues in the Department of Information Systems & Decision Sciences at California State University, Fullerton. Their thoughts and insights are very much appreciated.

Conflicts of Interest: The author declares no conflicts of interest.

References

1. Kim, J.; Thomas, P.; Sankaranarayana, R.; Gedeon, T.; Yoon, H.-J. Pagination Versus Scrolling in Mobile Web Search. In Proceedings of the 25th ACM International on Conference on Information and Knowledge Management, New York, NY, USA, 24–28 October 2016.
2. MacDonald, D. *Practical UI Patterns for Design Systems: Fast-Track Interaction Design for a Seamless User Experience*; Apress: New York, NY, USA, 2019.
3. Tidwell, J. *Designing Interfaces: Patterns for Effective Interaction Design*; O'Reilly Media: Sebastopol, CA, USA, 2010.
4. Bernstein, G. *Unwired: Gaining Control over Addictive Technologies*; Cambridge University Press: Cambridge, UK, 2023.
5. Kelly, D.; Azzopardi, L. How Many Results Per Page? A Study of SERP Size, Search Behavior and User Experience. In Proceedings of the 38th International ACM SIGIR Conference on Research and Development in Information Retrieval, Santiago, Chile, 9–13 August 2015.
6. Claussen, J.; Kretschmer, T.; Mayrhofer, P. The Effects of Rewarding User Engagement: The Case of Facebook Apps. *Inf. Syst. Res.* **2013**, *24*, 186–200. [CrossRef]
7. Wu, F.; Huberman, B.A. Novelty and Collective Attention. *Proc. Natl. Acad. Sci. USA* **2007**, *104*, 17599–17601. [CrossRef] [PubMed]
8. Ernst, D.; Becker, S.; Horstmann, G. Novelty Competes with Saliency for Attention. *Vis. Res.* **2020**, *168*, 42–52. [CrossRef] [PubMed]
9. Costa, V.D.; Tran, V.L.; Turchi, J.; Averbeck, B.B. Dopamine Modulates Novelty Seeking Behavior During Decision Making. *Behav. Neurosci.* **2014**, *128*, 556–566. [CrossRef] [PubMed]
10. Duszkiewicz, A.J.; McNamara, C.G.; Takeuchi, T.; Genzel, L. Novelty and Dopaminergic Modulation of Memory Persistence: A Tale of Two Systems. *Trends Neurosci.* **2019**, *42*, 102–114. [CrossRef] [PubMed]
11. Ping, Y.; Li, Y.; Zhu, J. Beyond Accuracy Measures: The Effect of Diversity, Novelty and Serendipity in Recommender Systems on User Engagement. *Electron. Commer. Res.* **2024**, 1–28. [CrossRef]
12. O'Brien, H.L. Exploring User Engagement in Online News Interactions. *Proc. Am. Soc. Inf. Sci. Technol.* **2011**, *48*, 1–10. [CrossRef]
13. Carmel, D.; Roitman, H.; Yom-Tov, E. On the Relationship Between Novelty and Popularity of User-Generated Content. *ACM Trans. Intell. Syst. Technol. (TIST)* **2012**, *3*, 1–19. [CrossRef]
14. Rips, L.J.; Shoben, E.J.; Smith, E.E. Semantic Distance and the Verification of Semantic Relations. *J. Verbal Learn. Verbal Behav.* **1973**, *12*, 1–20. [CrossRef]
15. Lee, D.L.; Chuang, H.; Seamons, K. Document Ranking and the Vector-Space Model. *IEEE Softw.* **1997**, *14*, 67–75. [CrossRef]
16. Deerwester, S.; Dumais, S.T.; Furnas, G.W.; Landauer, T.K.; Harshman, R. Indexing by Latent Semantic Analysis. *J. Am. Soc. Inf. Sci.* **1990**, *41*, 391–407. [CrossRef]
17. Reimers, N.; Gurevych, I. Sentence-BERT: Sentence Embeddings Using Siamese BERT-Networks. In Proceedings of the 2019 Conference on Empirical Methods in Natural Language Processing, Hong Kong, China, 3–7 November 2019; pp. 3982–3992.
18. IMDb. *Internet Movie Database*; Amazon: Seattle, WA, USA, 2024; Available online: https://www.imdb.com (accessed on 15 October 2024).
19. Box Office Mojo. *Worldwide Lifetime Gross Box Office Revenues*; IMDb Pro: Seattle, WA, USA, 2024; Available online: https://www.boxofficemojo.com (accessed on 15 October 2024).
20. Bird, S.; Loper, E.; Klein, E. *Natural Language Toolkit*; NLTK Project: Philadelphia, PA, USA, 2024; Available online: https://www.nltk.org (accessed on 15 October 2024).
21. Billboard Magazine. *Billboard Hot 100 Singles Chart*; Penske Media Corporation: Los Angeles, CA, USA, 2024.
22. LyricFind. *Song Lyrics Database*; LyricFind, Inc.: Toronto, ON, USA, 2024; Available online: https://www.lyricfind.com (accessed on 15 October 2024).

23. Wasserman, L. *All of Statistics: A Concise Course in Statistical Inference*; Springer: New York, NY, USA, 2013.
24. Google LLC. *Google Colaboratory*; Alphabet Inc.: Mountain View, CA, USA, 2024.
25. Welch, B.L. The Generalization of "Student's" Problem When Several Different Population Varlances Are Involved. *Biometrika* **1947**, *34*, 28–35. [CrossRef] [PubMed]
26. He, X.; Deng, L. Deep Learning for Image-to-Text Generation: A Technical Overview. *IEEE Signal Process.* **2017**, *34*, 109–116. [CrossRef]
27. Apostolidis, E.; Adamantidou, E.; Metsai, A.I.; Mezaris, V.; Patras, I. Video Summarization Using Deep Neural Networks: A Survey. *Proc. IEEE* **2021**, *109*, 1838–1863. [CrossRef]
28. Trivedi, A.; Pant, N.; Shah, P.; Sonik, S.; Agrawal, S. Speech to Text and Text to Speech Recognition Systems—A Review. *IOSR J. Comput. Eng.* **2018**, *20*, 36–43.
29. Epstein, Z.; Hertzmann, A.; Creativity, I.O.H.; Akten, M.; Farid, H.; Fjeld, J.; Frank, M.R.; Groh, M.; Herman, L.; Leach, N. Art and the Science of Generative AI. *Science* **2023**, *380*, 1110–1111. [CrossRef] [PubMed]
30. Nah, F.F.-H. A Study on Tolerable Waiting Time: How Long Are Web Users Willing to Wait? *Behav. Inf. Technol.* **2004**, *23*, 153–163. [CrossRef]
31. Lee, Y.; Chen, A.N.; Ilie, V. Can Online Wait Be Managed? The Effect of Filler Interfaces and Presentation Modes on Perceived Waiting Time Online. *MIS Q.* **2012**, *36*, 365–394. [CrossRef]
32. Hong, W.; Hess, T.J.; Hardin, A. When Filling the Wait Makes it Feel Longer: A Paradigm Shift Perspective for Managing Online Delay. *MIS Q.* **2013**, *37*, 383–406. [CrossRef]

information

MDPI

Article

Temporal Dynamics in Short Text Classification: Enhancing Semantic Understanding Through Time-Aware Model

Khaled Abdalgader [1,*], Atheer A. Matroud [2] and Ghaleb Al-Doboni [1]

1 School of Engineering and Computing, American University of Ras Al Khaimah, Ras Al Khaimah P.O. Box 10021, United Arab Emirates; ghaleb.aldoboni@aurak.ac.ae

2 Cyber Security Program, De Montfort University-Dubai, Dubai P.O. Box 294345, United Arab Emirates; atheer.al-mousa@dmu.ac.uk

* Correspondence: khaled.balawafi@aurak.ac.ae

Abstract: Traditional text classification models predominantly rely on static text representations, failing to capture temporal variations in language usage and evolving semantic meanings. This limitation reduces their ability to accurately classify time-sensitive texts, where understanding context, detecting trends, and addressing semantic shifts over time are critical. This paper introduces a novel time-aware short text classification model incorporating temporal information, enabling tracking of and adaptation to evolving language semantics. The proposed model enhances contextual understanding by leveraging timestamps and significantly improves classification accuracy, particularly for time-sensitive applications such as News topic classification. The model employs a hybrid architecture combining Convolutional Neural Networks (CNNs) and Bidirectional Long Short-Term Memory (BiLSTM) networks, enriched with attention mechanisms to capture both local and global dependencies. To further refine semantic representation and mitigate the effects of semantic drift, the model fine-tunes GloVe embeddings and employs synonym-based data augmentation. The proposed approach is evaluated on three benchmark dynamic datasets, achieving superior performance with classification accuracy reaching 92% for the first two datasets and 85% for the third dataset. Furthermore, the model is applied to a different-fields categorization and trend analysis task, demonstrating its capability to capture temporal patterns and perform detailed trend analysis of domain-agnostic textual content. These results underscore the potential of the proposed framework to provide deeper insights into the evolving nature of language and its impact on short-text classification. This work advances natural language processing by offering a comprehensive time-aware classification framework, addressing the challenges of temporal dynamics in language semantics.

Keywords: sentence classification; hybrid architecture; attention mechanism; synonym augmentation; GloVe embeddings; temporal sensitivity; ensemble learning

1. Introduction

Short text classification is a critical task in natural language processing (NLP), with applications ranging from sentiment analysis [1–3] and news categorization [4–6] to decision support systems [7,8]. Traditional short-text classification models, however, rely on static text representations, which ignore the temporal aspect of language evolution [9–14]. Over time, words and phrases change in meaning or importance due to cultural, social, and technological shifts. For example, the word "cloud" once predominantly referred to a meteorological phenomenon, but in recent years, it has become more closely associated with cloud computing technology. Ignoring these shifts can lead to inaccurate classifications in time-sensitive applications, such as trend analysis [15,16], public opinion tracking [17], and historical text classification [18]. Time-aware text classification, however, addresses this limitation by incorporating temporal information into the classification process [19–23], enabling models to account for the evolving nature of language [21,24–27].

Traditional models, such as Naive Bayes [28,29], Support Vector Machines (SVMs) [30–32], Convolutional Neural Networks (CNNs) [33–36], and Recurrent Neural Networks (RNNs) [37,38], have achieved significant success in text classification tasks by focusing on static content [39]. These models typically use static word embeddings like Word2Vec [39] or GloVe [40], which represent words as fixed vectors, regardless of the context or time period in which they appear. While adequate for many NLP tasks, these static embeddings do not capture semantic drift—changes in word meaning over time—or the evolving contexts in which words are used [41–43]. This limitation becomes especially apparent in domains where terminology shifts rapidly, such as technology, politics, and economics [44].

To address these limitations, we propose a time-aware sentence (i.e., short-text) classification model that integrates temporal data to evolve with language. By leveraging timestamps and time-aware word embeddings, our model captures the temporal dynamics of language, ensuring more accurate and contextually relevant classifications. This approach significantly enhances the model's adaptability and performance in tasks where language evolution plays a key role, such as analyzing news trends or shifts in public sentiment.

One of the core challenges addressed by our model is *semantic drift*, the gradual change in word meanings over time, which was addressed in [41–44]. For instance, the word "viral" once referred exclusively to biological infections, but today, it is commonly associated with the rapid spread of media on the internet (e.g., "viral videos"). Static models trained on older datasets may misclassify contemporary texts by failing to account for such shifts in meaning. Our model integrates temporal information, allowing it to track these changes and adjust its predictions accordingly. This is particularly useful in time-sensitive tasks like news classification or social media analysis, where word meanings can evolve rapidly.

Contextual relevance is another critical factor in temporal-aware sentence classification. The meaning of a text can vary depending on the period in which it was written. For example, terms like "housing market crash" may carry different implications during an economic recession than during a period of economic stability. Without temporal awareness, models may fail to recognize these contextual shifts, leading to misclassification. By incorporating timestamps into our model, we ensure that it distinguishes between historical and contemporary contexts, offering more accurate classifications based on the time period of the text.

Moreover, traditional models quickly become outdated as language evolves [45–47]. This is particularly problematic in fast-changing fields like technology, where new terms emerge frequently. For example, words like "blockchain" and "artificial intelligence" have gained prominence in recent years, whereas they were virtually unknown a decade ago. Our model addresses this issue by dynamically updating its understanding of word meanings through the fine-tuning of pre-trained embeddings and synonym-based data augmentation. This *dynamic learning* process ensures the model remains relevant and accurate, even as language evolves.

Recent advances in NLP, such as BERT [45] and XLNet [47], have revolutionized the field by introducing contextualized embeddings, allowing for a better understanding of word meaning in context. However, these models do not account for temporal shifts in language, limiting their effectiveness in time-sensitive tasks. While they excel at providing context-sensitive word representations, they fail to incorporate the temporal dimension, leaving a gap in their ability to adapt to evolving language. Our model addresses this gap by explicitly integrating temporal data, allowing for a more accurate and adaptable understanding of language over time.

This paper introduces several key contributions to advanced time-aware sentence classification, with its primary contribution being a hybrid approach that incorporates temporal-aware embeddings. The proposed model seamlessly integrates temporal dynamics into a hybrid Bidirectional Long Short-Term Memory (BiLSTM) [48,49] and Convolutional Neural Networks (CNN) [34,35] architecture. The novelty of this approach lies in its combination of Temporal-Aware Word Embeddings, which enable the model to capture semantic changes over time, and attention mechanisms that enhance focus on the most relevant portions of the text. The detailed contributions of this study are as follows: First, we introduce the *Temporal-Aware word embeddings model*, which integrates temporal information directly into the word embedding process. Unlike previous approaches that treated temporal information as supplementary, we directly embed temporal data into the word embedding process. Second, our model employs a *hybrid CNN-BiLSTM architecture* with an attention mechanism, combining the strengths of CNNs for local feature extraction and BiLSTMs for capturing long-range dependencies. This hybrid architecture enhances the model's flexibility, while the attention mechanism allows the model to focus on the most relevant parts of each sentence, improving both interpretability and classification accuracy. Third, our model operates within a *dynamic learning process*, which fine-tunes pre-trained GloVe embeddings and employs synonym-based data augmentation to adapt to evolving language contexts. This ensures the model remains relevant even in rapidly changing environments, offering improved performance in long-term applications. We also employ a *comprehensive evaluation framework*, including metrics such as accuracy, F1 score [50], Cohen's Kappa [51], Matthews Correlation Coefficient (MCC) [52], Mean Squared Error (MSE), and Mean Absolute Error (MAE) [53]. These metrics, combined with time-specific evaluations, provide a thorough analysis of the model's ability to handle semantic drift and adapt to temporal changes in language, validating its effectiveness in time-sensitive classification tasks. Finally, we report results obtained by applying the proposed classification model (i.e., in vivo evaluation) to a domain-agnostic (i.e., different-fields) categorization and trend analysis task. The implementation results demonstrated that incorporating temporal information within the embedding process leads to favorable performance among time-sensitive text classification.

The remainder of the paper is organized in the following manner. Section 2 describes relevant work in text classification methods and relevant language models. Section 3 presents preliminaries to the sentence classification task, and Section 4 describes the proposed time-aware model. Empirical results are presented in Section 5, and Section 6 concludes the paper.

2. Related Work

2.1. Traditional Approaches to Sentence Classification

Sentence classification is a fundamental task in natural language processing, underpinning various applications, including sentiment analysis [1–3], topic categorization [54–56], and spam detection [57,58]. Early approaches to text classification primarily relied on statistical methods like Naive Bayes [28,29] and Support Vector Machines (SVMs) [30–32], utilizing bag-of-words and n-gram representations to classify sentences based on word frequency and occurrence patterns [39]. These models, while effective in capturing basic patterns in text, suffered from a key limitation: they treated sentences as unordered sets of words, thus failing to capture contextual relationships between words. Consequently, they were not well-suited to tasks that required an understanding of word order or syntactic structure.

The development of word embeddings, such as Word2Vec [39] and GloVe [40], transformed the field by mapping words into continuous vector spaces, capturing semantic relationships, and allowing models to represent words with more meaningful features [59]. These embeddings significantly improved the performance of text classification models. However, they remained context-free—each word had a single, fixed representation, irrespective of the sentence or time period it appeared [60]. As a result, they struggled with tasks requiring a nuanced understanding of word meaning in context, such as sarcasm detection or sentiment analysis.

The advent of deep learning, however, marked a turning point in sentence classification. Convolutional Neural Networks (CNNs) [33–36], originally developed for image processing, were adapted to text by treating sequences of words as visual patterns. Kim (2014) [61] demonstrated that CNNs could effectively capture local dependencies in text, such as n-grams, making them highly effective for classification tasks. CNNs' ability to detect local features in textual data enabled them to outperform traditional statistical models in a range of sentence classification tasks [55].

Meanwhile, Recurrent Neural Networks (RNNs) [37,38] and their variants, such as Long Short-Term Memory (LSTM) [62] networks, were designed to handle sequential data. These models were adept at capturing long-term dependencies in text by retaining information over time. Bidirectional LSTMs (BiLSTMs) [48,49] enhanced LSTMs by processing input text in both forward and backward directions, offering a deeper contextual understanding of words. Graves et al. (2013) [63] showed that BiLSTMs outperformed CNNs on tasks requiring understanding sentence structure and sequence order, such as language modeling and named entity recognition.

Despite the advancements made by CNNs and BiLSTMs, these techniques encounter challenges in capturing long-range dependencies and handling text that requires deeper context. The introduction of the attention mechanism by Bahdanau et al. (2014) [64] addressed this limitation. Attention mechanisms allowed models to selectively focus on the most relevant parts of the input when making predictions, improving performance in tasks like machine translation [65], text summarization [66], and sentence classification [67].

Although these models were effective in capturing short-term and local dependencies, they fell short in accounting for language evolution over time. By treating language as static, they overlooked the temporal dynamics that can influence word meaning and usage in various contexts.

2.2. Contextualized Embeddings: BERT, GPT, and XLNet

The development of contextualized embeddings, epitomized by models like BERT (Bidirectional Encoder Representations from Transformers) [45] and GPT (Generative Pre-trained Transformer) [46], marked a significant leap forward in NLP. Unlike static embeddings, these models generated context-sensitive embeddings that varied depending on the surrounding words. BERT's bidirectional architecture enabled it to simultaneously capture both left and right contexts, leading to improved performance in various tasks, including question answering, text classification, and natural language inference.

However, despite their contextual sensitivity, models like BERT, RoBERTa [68], and XLNet [47] did not incorporate an explicit approach to modeling the temporal dynamics of language. They treated text as temporally static, failing to account for word meanings and connotations changing over time. This limitation becomes especially significant in applications where understanding language evolution is essential, such as analyzing decades of news articles or monitoring shifts in public sentiment on social media platforms.

For example, while BERT can provide a highly contextualized representation of the word "Apple" based on its immediate context (technology vs. fruit), it cannot account for the temporal evolution of the term. Whether the text was written in the 1980s, when Apple was an emerging technology company, or in the 2020s, when it became a dominant player in the global market, BERT would use the same underlying pre-trained embedding. This limitation in capturing temporal context led to the exploration of time-aware models that integrate temporal information into word representations.

2.3. Time-Aware Models: Capturing Language Evolution

Recent research has increasingly recognized the need to incorporate temporal information into NLP models to capture the evolving nature of language. Language is not static—words shift in meaning, usage, and significance over time, reflecting broader cultural, societal, and technological changes. To address these dynamics, several approaches have been developed to incorporate temporal aspects directly into the training and representation of language models [21,24–27,41–44,69].

Yao et al. (2018) [70] introduced Dynamic Word Embeddings; a model designed to capture shifts in word meaning across different time periods. By embedding temporal metadata into the training process, the model was able to produce word representations that evolve with time. For instance, the word "cloud" could be represented differently in datasets from the 1990s compared to more recent contexts where "cloud" refers to cloud computing. This capability allowed the model to distinguish between different meanings of the same word depending on the historical context.

Similarly, Bamler and Mandt (2017) [71] proposed Dynamic Embeddings that explicitly modeled semantic drift by adjusting word representations over time. This approach addressed one of the critical limitations of static embeddings like Word2Vec or GloVe: their inability to reflect how word meanings change. The dynamic embeddings model accounted for the evolving context in which words are used, making it particularly effective for tasks like historical text analysis or trend detection. For example, the term "virus" primarily referred to biological infections many years ago, but recently, its meaning expanded to include references to viral social media content and digital computer viruses.

More recently, several studies have focused on integrating temporal dynamics into more complex architectures like CNNs, LSTMs, and transformers [72,73], addressing a key gap in earlier models [21,24–27]. Gururangan et al. (2020) [74] introduced domain-adaptive pre-training (DAPT) and task-adaptive pre-training (TAPT) approaches, which adapt models like BERT to specific domains or tasks, including temporally sensitive contexts. Although these methods do not explicitly track temporal changes, they provide a pathway for better domain-specific language modeling. However, they still lack the ability to capture fine-grained temporal shifts in language.

Building on these efforts, Wang et al. (2023) [75] presented BiTimeBERT, a model designed to capture temporal changes in language by modifying BERT's architecture to include temporal embeddings. This approach incorporates time as an explicit input to BERT, allowing it to generate temporally contextualized word embeddings. BiTimeBERT demonstrated significant improvements in tasks such as sentiment analysis, where the meaning of words like "stock" or "inflation" shifts depending on the time period. The model's integration of temporal information allows it to adapt to changing word meanings, leading to more accurate classifications.

Similarly, Gong et al. (2020) [76] introduced a framework for enriching word embeddings with temporal and spatial information. This approach explicitly models semantic drift by conditioning word representations on time and location, enabling a better understanding of evolving word usage. The embeddings preserve the geometric consistency of semantically stable words while also capturing different degrees of meaning change across conditions. For example, the model could distinguish the usage of the word "cloud" as a meteorological term in older texts and its association with cloud computing in modern contexts. This method highlights the importance of incorporating temporal and spatial metadata into word representations to reflect linguistic and sociocultural dynamics over time.

Another recent contribution was by Tang et al. (2023) [77], who proposed a template-based temporal adaptation method for pre-trained masked language models (MLMs) to generate dynamic contextualized word embeddings (DCWEs). By fine-tuning pre-trained MLMs using time-sensitive templates, the model adapts to changing word meanings across two time periods. The approach reduces perplexity and outperforms state-of-the-art models such as TemporalBERT, showcasing its efficacy in capturing temporal variations in word semantics. For instance, terms like "mask" shifted their associations from "hide" (2010) to "vaccine" (2020), demonstrating the ability to adapt to emerging contexts.

Despite these advances, most time-aware models are still limited by treating temporal information as a supplementary feature rather than a core component of the model architecture. While models like BiTimeBERT and dynamic embeddings have made strides in capturing temporal shifts in word usage, they often rely on static embeddings augmented with external temporal metadata rather than integrating temporal awareness directly into the learning process. These systems fail to adapt to evolving linguistic contexts and struggle to address long-term semantic drift, particularly in complex architectures like CNNs, LSTMs, and transformers.

Our proposed approach addresses these limitations by fully embedding temporal information into the model architecture at its core. Unlike existing methods, our model integrates temporal-aware word embeddings directly into the training process, ensuring that temporal metadata is inherently learned alongside word representations. Specifically, our hybrid CNN-BiLSTM architecture dynamically uses pre-trained GloVe embeddings to reflect temporal variations in language use. This integration allows the model to adapt in real time to semantic shifts, capturing both content and context while preserving temporal dynamics.

Additionally, our proposed model employs attention mechanisms to selectively focus on the most relevant portions of text, further enhancing its ability to align temporal information with semantic meaning. By incorporating a dynamic learning process with synonym-based data augmentation, the model ensures robust generalization and continual adaptation to emerging trends and evolving language. This integrated approach not only mitigates the limitations of treating temporal data as a supplementary feature but also ensures that the model dynamically adjusts to linguistic shifts, delivering more accurate and contextually relevant predictions.

As a result, our model demonstrates significant improvements in time-sensitive tasks such as trend analysis, news categorization, and historical text classification. By embedding temporal metadata as a core learning component, this approach addresses gaps in existing models, enabling deeper insights into the interplay between language evolution and text semantics. This novel approach ensures that the model remains relevant and effective as the language evolves.

3. Preliminaries and Technical Details

This section introduces the foundational concepts, key terminologies, and formal notations used throughout our proposed time-aware sentence classification model. By establishing a clear mathematical framework, we provide the necessary background to understand the temporal dynamics incorporated into the model. We first describe the static sentence classification process, followed by the temporal extensions that form the basis of our approach.

3.1. Static Sentence Classification

In traditional sentence classification, the task is to predict the label $y \in Y$ for a given input sentence $s \in S$, where Y is the set of possible labels (e.g., news categories) and S is the set of sentences in a given dataset D. Each sentence s consists of a sequence of words $s = [w_1, w_2, \ldots, w_n]$, where $w_i \in V$ represents the i-th word from a vocabulary V.

The classification function (i.e., classifier) $f : S \to Y$ typically relies on a feature representation $\mathbf{h}(s)$, which is obtained by transforming the sentence into a continuous vector space through word embeddings such as Word2Vec or GloVe. The task is to learn a function f, often represented by a neural network such as a CNN or RNN, that maps the feature representation of the sentence $\mathbf{h}(s)$ to the corresponding class y.

Formally, the classifier can be expressed as follows:

$$\hat{y} = \underset{y \in Y}{\operatorname{argmax}} P(y|\boldsymbol{h}(s)) \tag{1}$$

where $P(y|\boldsymbol{h}(s))$ is the conditional probability of the label y given the sentence embedding $\mathbf{h}(s)$. The goal is to minimize the classification error by learning an optimal mapping from sentences to labels.

However, traditional methods assume that word meanings remain constant, leading to limitations when applied to text spanning multiple time periods, where word meanings may shift. This static approach does not account for *semantic drift*, which is crucial for handling time-sensitive classification tasks.

3.2. Problem Formalism: Time-Aware Sentence Classification

The core challenge in time-aware sentence classification is to extend the static model by incorporating *temporal information* to capture the evolution of word meanings over time. In this regard, we introduce temporal dependencies into the classification process, allowing the model to dynamically adjust its predictions based on the time context in which a sentence was written.

Let $t \in T$ denote a timestamp, where T represents the set of all possible time periods. The input sentence is now represented as $s_t = (s, t)$, where s is the sequence of words, and t is the timestamp associated with the sentence. The task is to predict the label $y \in Y = \{y_1, y_2, \ldots, y_T\}$ based not only on the content of the sentence but also on the time period t.

Formally, the time-aware classification problem can be expressed as finding a function $f : S \times T \to Y$, which maps the sentence and its timestamp to a label:

$$\hat{y} = \underset{y \in Y}{\operatorname{argmax}} P(y|\boldsymbol{h}(s_t)), \tag{2}$$

where $\mathbf{h}(s_t)$ is the time-aware sentence embedding that incorporates both the semantic content of the sentence and its temporal context.

In contrast to static embeddings, we aim to compute a time-dependent representation $\mathbf{h}(s_t)$, where the embedding of each word $w_i \in S$ evolves over time. This allows us to capture the semantic drift that occurs when word meanings change across different time periods.

3.3. Temporal-Aware Word Embeddings

Traditional word embeddings, such as Word2Vec and GloVe, treat word representations as static. However, words can change their meaning over time. To address this, we introduce *Temporal-Aware Word Embeddings*, which incorporate the timestamp $t \in T$, where T is the set of possible time periods. Let w_i be a word at time t, the corresponding embedding is represented as follows:

$$e(w_i,\ t) = f_{embed}(w_i, t), \tag{3}$$

where $f_{embed}\ : V \times T\ \rightarrow R^d$ maps the word and its timestamp into a d-dimensional embedding space. These embeddings evolve with time, capturing the semantic drift of words. The sentence embedding at time t, denoted as $\mathbf{h}(s_t)$, is then computed by aggregating the dynamic word embeddings as more details are provided in Section 4.3.

3.4. Time-Aware Sentence Classification with Hybrid Architecture

In our model, we integrate both *Convolutional Neural Networks (CNNs)* and *Bidirectional LSTMs (BiLSTMs)* with attention mechanisms to process the time-aware sentence embeddings. This hybrid architecture leverages CNNs to capture local dependencies within sentences and BiLSTMs to capture long-range dependencies across time-aware embeddings. Additionally, the attention mechanism focuses on the most relevant parts of the sentence, further enhancing the model's ability to adapt to temporal changes.

The classification model is formalized as follows:

$$\mathbf{h}(s_t) = \text{Attention (BiLSTM (CNN } (\mathbf{e}(w_1, t), \ldots, \mathbf{e}\ (w_n, t)))), \tag{4}$$

where the *attention mechanism* is used to selectively weight important time-dependent word embeddings $\mathbf{e}(w_i, t)$ for the final sentence representation. The classification function is then computed by a fully connected layer and a *softmax* operation to predict the probability distribution over the possible labels:

$$P\ (y|h(s_t)) = softmax\ (Wh\ (s_t) + b), \tag{5}$$

where W and b are learned parameters of the model.

3.5. Loss Function

The model is trained by minimizing the cross-entropy loss, which is defined as follows:

$$L = -\sum_{j=1}^{N} \sum_{y \in Y} y_j \log P\left(y \middle| \boldsymbol{h}\left(s_{t_j}\right)\right), \tag{6}$$

where N is the number of training examples, y_j is the true label for the j-th sentence, and $P\left(y \middle| \boldsymbol{h}\left(s_{t_j}\right)\right)$ is the predicted probability of label y given the sentence s_{t_j}.

This temporal-aware loss ensures that the model optimizes both the content and the temporal context, adapting to the dynamic evolution of language.

4. Proposed Approach

This section presents the technical details and the underlying rationale for the time-aware sentence classification model, including data preprocessing and augmentation strategies, dynamic embedding, the proposed hybrid architecture, attention mechanisms, ensemble learning, and computational complexity analysis. Figure 1 shows the general architecture of the proposed time-aware sentence classification model.

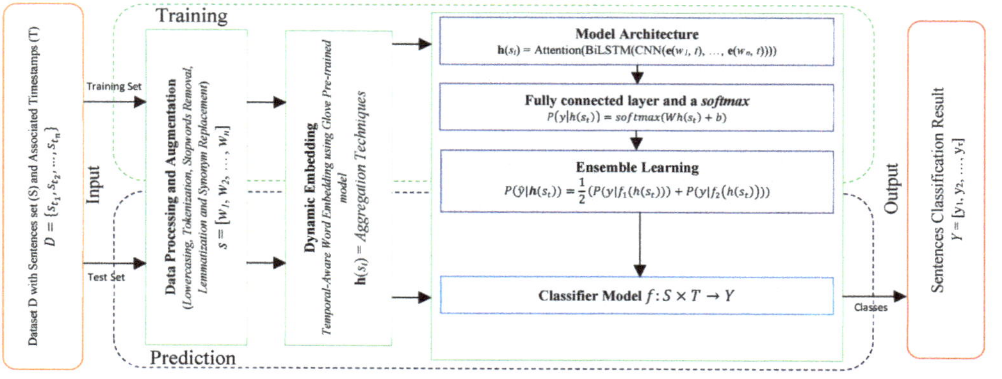

Figure 1. Time-aware sentence classification model.

4.1. Data Processing and Augmentation

Before feeding sentences into the model, text preprocessing ensures that raw text is converted into a clean, usable format. Each sentence s undergoes the following steps:

- **Lowercasing**: All words are converted to lowercase.
- **Tokenization**: Sentences are split into tokens $w_i \in V$, where V is the vocabulary.
- **Stopwords Removal**: Words from a predefined stopword list are removed.
- **Lemmatization**: Words are reduced to their base forms using a lemmatizer, ensuring that inflected forms are handled correctly.

Let $s = [w_1, w_2, \ldots, w_n]$ represent a sentence with n words. After processing, each word w_i is ready to be mapped to its corresponding embedding $\mathbf{e}(w_i, t)$, which includes the temporal context. To improve the model's robustness, we employ *synonym-based data augmentation*. For each sentence s, we replace a random selection of words w_i with their synonyms with a probability $p_{augment}$. This process can be formalized as follows:

$$\tilde{w}_i = \begin{cases} synonym(w_i) & with\ probability\ P_{augment} \\ w_i & Otherwise. \end{cases} \tag{7}$$

This ensures variability in the training data, helping the model generalize better. The augmented sentences $\tilde{s}$ are concatenated with the original data to create a more diverse dataset.

4.2. Dynamic Embedding

A central component of our model is the integration of *Temporal-Aware Word Embeddings*, which is designed to address the limitations of traditional static embeddings by incorporating temporal dependencies. Given a word $w_i \in V$, the embedding $\mathbf{e}(w_i, t)$ is dynamic, based on the corresponding timestamp t. This allows the model to reflect the temporal nuances of word meanings. Figure 2 shows the general process of temporal-aware word embedding.

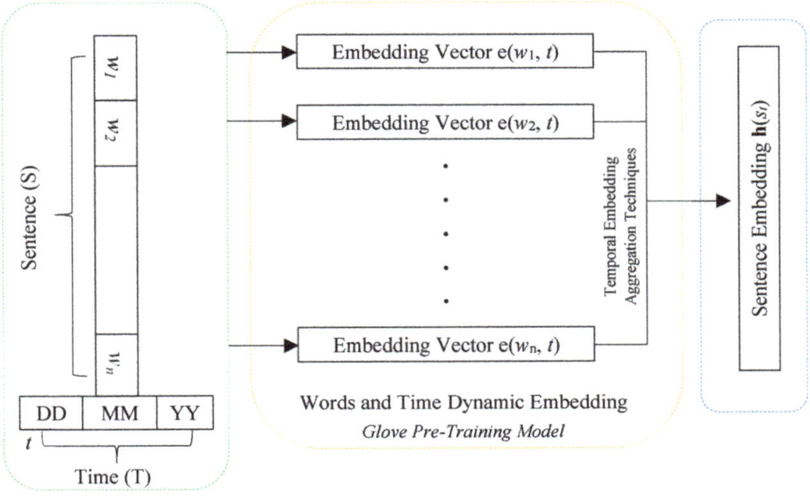

Figure 2. Temporal-Aware Word Embeddings.

Mathematically, the embedding $\mathbf{e}(w_i, t)$ is a time-varying function:

$$e(w_i,\ t) = f_{embed}(w_i,\ t), \tag{8}$$

where $f_{embed} : V \times T \rightarrow R^d$ maps each word and its corresponding timestamp to a d-dimensional vector space. This mapping function adjusts the embedding of each word based on the specific time period, effectively capturing semantic drift. To construct the sentence embedding $\mathbf{h}(s_t)$ at the corresponding time t, however, we explore three different temporal embedding aggregation techniques:

Aggregate-based Embedding Fusion (ABEF): The aggregate function computes a single embedding vector for each word by averaging its temporal embeddings across all available timestamps. Given a word w_i, the aggregate embedding $\mathrm{e}(w_i)_{agg}$ is calculated by averaging its embeddings over all timestamps:

$$e(w_i)_{agg} = \frac{1}{T}\sum_{t=1}^{T} e(w_i,\ t) \tag{9}$$

The sentence embedding $\mathbf{h}(s_t)$ is then constructed by aggregating these time-independent word embeddings:

$$\mathbf{h}(s_t) = \text{Aggregate}(\mathbf{e}(w_1, t), \mathbf{e}(w_2, t), \ldots, \mathbf{e}(w_n, t)), \tag{10}$$

where the aggregation function captures forward and backward dependencies within the sentence.

Time-weighted Embedding Fusion (TAEF): In this technique, recent meanings are prioritized by weighting embeddings according to a temporal decay parameter λ. The time-weighted embedding for a word w_i is computed as follows:

$$e(w_i,\ t)_{tw} = \sum_{t=1}^{T} \alpha_t e(w_i,\ t) \ where\ \alpha_t = e^{-\lambda(\mathrm{T}-\mathrm{t})}. \tag{11}$$

Here, α_t decays exponentially, emphasizing recent embeddings. The sentence embedding $\mathbf{h}(s_t)$ is derived by aggregating the weighted word embeddings:

$$\mathbf{h}(s_t) = \text{Aggregate}(\mathbf{e}(w_1, t), \mathbf{e}(w_2, t), \ldots, \mathbf{e}(w_n, t)), \tag{12}$$

Self-Attention with Temporal Positional Encoding (SATPE): This method enhances temporal awareness by incorporating positional encoding into the embeddings. For each word embedding $\mathrm{e}(w_i, t)$ at a corresponding timestamp t, a temporal positional encoding P_t is added:

$$\mathrm{e}(w_i, t)_{\text{temp}} = \mathrm{e}(w_i, t) + P_t \tag{13}$$

The temporal sentence embedding is obtained by applying multi-head self-attention on these temporally enriched embeddings. For each attention head, the weighted embeddings is computed as follows:

$$A\left(e(w_i,\ t)_{temp}\right) = softmax\left(\frac{QK^T}{\sqrt{d_k}}\right)V \tag{14}$$

where Q, K, and V represent the query, key, value matrices, and d represents the dimensionality of the key and query vectors within the self-attention mechanism. The sentence embedding $\mathbf{h}(s_t)$ is then constructed by aggregating these time-independent word embeddings:

$$\mathbf{h}(s_t) = \text{Aggregate}\ (A\ (\mathbf{e}(w_1, t)_{\text{temp}}), A\ (\mathbf{e}(w_2, t)_{\text{temp}}), \ldots, A\ (\mathbf{e}(w_n, t)_{\text{temp}})) \tag{15}$$

In this way, $\mathbf{h}(s_t)$ encodes the entire sentence's content, adjusted by the temporal position of each word, allowing the model to capture both semantic relationships and time-based word evolution within the sentence.

4.3. Model Architecture

The architecture of our model combines the strengths of CNNs and BiLSTMs. CNNs capture local dependencies, while BiLSTMs capture long-term dependencies in the sentence sequence.

Convolutional Neural Networks (CNNs): The convolutional layers extract local features from the input sentence embeddings. Given the sentence embedding matrix $h(s_t) \in R^{n\times d}$, where each row corresponds to a word embedding, the CNN applies filters to capture local n-grams. The output of the convolutional layer is:

$$\mathbf{C}(\mathrm{s_t}) = \mathrm{CNN}(\mathbf{h}(s_t)) \tag{16}$$

where $C(s_t)$ represents the extracted local features. These features are then passed through a max-pooling layer to retain the most salient information.

Bidirectional Long Short-Term Memory Networks (BiLSTMs): The BiLSTM layer processes the sentence embeddings to capture both forward and backward dependencies. For a sequence $\mathbf{h}(\mathrm{s_t})$, the BiLSTM computes:

$$\boldsymbol{h}_{BiLSTM} = BiLSTM(\boldsymbol{C}(s_t)), \tag{17}$$

where $\boldsymbol{h}_{BiLSTM}$ is the output representation that captures both the past and future context for each word in the sentence.

4.4. Attention Mechanism

To further improve the model's ability to focus on relevant information, we incorporate an *attention mechanism*. The attention mechanism allows the model to assign different weights to different words based on their relevance to the classification task. The attention score for each word is computed as follows:

$$\alpha_i = \frac{\exp\left(\boldsymbol{v}^T \tanh(\boldsymbol{W}_h \boldsymbol{h}_i)\right)}{\sum_j \exp\left(\boldsymbol{v}^T\ tant(\boldsymbol{W}_h \boldsymbol{h}_j)\right)}, \tag{18}$$

where $\boldsymbol{h}_i$ is the hidden state for the i-th word, and $\boldsymbol{v}$ and $\boldsymbol{W}_h$ are learnable parameters. The final sentence representation is then computed as a weighted sum of the hidden states:

$$\boldsymbol{h}_{attn} = \sum_i \alpha_i \boldsymbol{h}_i \tag{19}$$

This mechanism ensures that the model attends to the most important parts of the sentence when making predictions.

4.5. Ensemble Learning

To enhance robustness and accuracy, we incorporate *ensemble learning* by training two models: a CNN-based model and a BiLSTM-based model. The predictions from each model are combined using an averaging strategy. Given two models f_1 and f_2, the final prediction $\hat{y}$ is computed as follows:

$$P(\hat{y}|\boldsymbol{h}(s_t)) = \frac{1}{2}(P(y|f_1(h(s_t))) + P(y|f_2(h(s_t)))) \tag{20}$$

This approach leverages the complementary strengths of the two models to improve overall performance and stability.

4.6. Computation Complexity Analysis

The computational complexity of our model is driven by the following factors:

Convolutional Layers: The complexity of the CNN layer is O($n \cdot k \cdot d \cdot f$), where n is the sentence length, k is the kernel size, d is the embedding dimension, and f is the number of filters.

BiLSTM Layers: The BiLSTM layer has a complexity of O($n \cdot h^2$), where n is the sentence length, and h is the number of hidden units.

Attention Mechanism: The attention mechanism adds a complexity of O($n \cdot d$) for computing the attention scores and the weighted sum of the hidden states.

In total, the model's complexity scales with O(n $\cdot$ ($h^2 + k \cdot d \cdot f$)), making it efficient for large-scale datasets while maintaining flexibility to capture local and global features.

5. Experiments and Results

In this section, we evaluate the effectiveness of the proposed method on three freely available benchmark datasets: Ireland-news-headlines (https://www.kaggle.com/therohk/ireland-historical-news, accessed on 10 February 2025), Sentiment140 [78] and 20 News Groups (https://www.kaggle.com/crawford/20-newsgroups, accessed on 10 February 2025) datasets. We first describe the benchmark datasets, experiment setup, and evaluation criteria. Then, we discuss the obtained results and compare the performance of the proposed model with that of other existing approaches. In addition, as an end-to-end evaluation, we apply the proposed sentence classification model to a news categorization and trend analysis task across different fields.

5.1. Benchmark Datasets

To evaluate our proposed Time-Aware Sentence Classification Model, we tested our method on three distinct datasets: the Ireland-news-headlines dataset, the Sentiment140 dataset and 20 News Groups dataset. These datasets offer diverse temporal and contextual information, allowing us to assess the robustness and adaptability of our model across different language dynamics and classification tasks. Figure 3 shows the distribution of categories (labels) in the selected benchmark datasets.

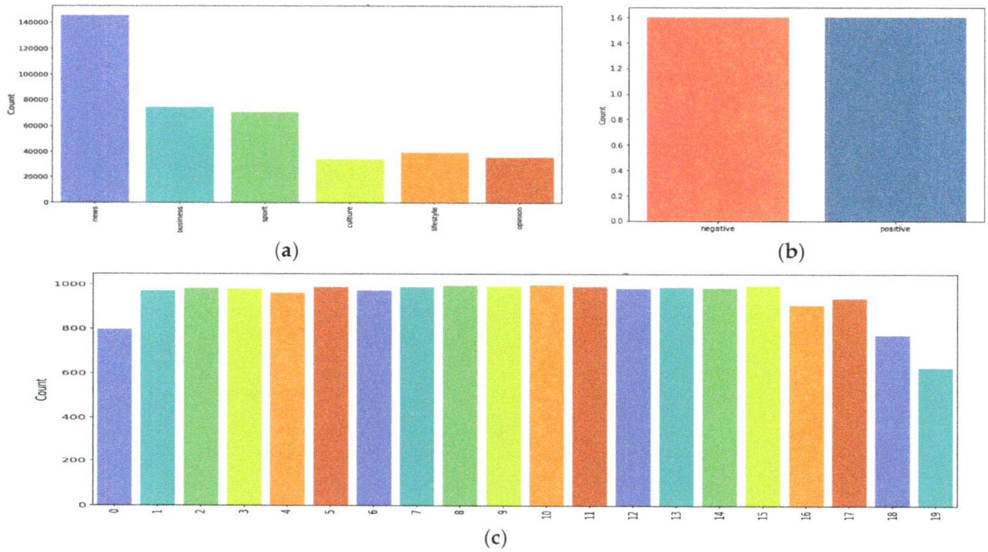

Figure 3. Benchmark Datasets Distribution: (**a**) Ireland-news-headlines, (**b**) Sentiment140, (**c**) 20 News Groups.

Ireland-news-headlines Dataset: This dataset consists of over 1.6 million headlines from the Irish Times, spanning multiple decades. Each headline is labeled with a category, such as *news*, *culture*, *opinion*, *business*, *sport*, and *lifestyle*, and is associated with a timestamp in DD, MM, YY format. The category distribution is imbalanced, with the majority of headlines falling under *news*, followed by *sport* and *business*, while categories such as *culture*, *opinion*, and *lifestyle* are less frequent as can be seen from Figure 3a. This dataset provides a unique opportunity to capture temporal shifts in language usage and track semantic evolution over time.

Sentiment140 Dataset: This dataset contains also 1.6 million tweets, each labeled as *positive* or *negative* (associated with a timestamp) based on sentiment. The distribution is approximately balanced, with similar proportions of positive and negative sentiments as can be seen in Figure 3b. The Sentiment140 dataset was created by gathering tweets containing emoticons, which were then used as noisy labels. This dataset provides a shorter text format with temporal data, enabling us to test the model's effectiveness in sentiment analysis over time.

20 News Groups Dataset: This dataset comprises 18,000+ news articles (1995–2000) across 20 domain-agnostic topics (see Figure 3c), including *politics*, *sports*, *business*, *technology* and etc. It serves as a benchmark for multi-class text classification and evaluates the model's ability to generalize across varied textual domains while incorporating temporal context.

The Ireland-news-headlines dataset captures the temporal dynamics of news articles, making it suitable for tasks that require understanding the evolution of language in long-form content. In contrast, the Sentiment140 dataset allows for the analysis of short, sentiment-driven texts, enabling the model to handle both sentiment analysis and time-sensitive classification tasks across different domains. Additionally, the 20 News Groups dataset provides a diverse range of topics across multiple categories, making it ideal for evaluating the model's ability to classify multi-topic documents (i.e., domain-agnostic) over time while handling semantic variations in different domains. Table 1 shows the summarized key statistics for the three datasets, including the number of instances, time span, average text length, and category distribution.

Table 1. Statistical Information for Benchmark Datasets.

Dataset	Sentences	Time Span	Avg. Sentence Length (Tokens/Words)	Labels
Ireland-news-headlines	1,610,000	1996–2021	15	news, culture, opinion, business, sport, lifestyle
Sentiment140	1,600,000	2009–2020	13	Positive, Negative
20 News Groups	18,846	1995–2000	150	20 domain-agnostic topic categories

5.2. Experiment Setup

In the experiment setup, we explored three different embedding techniques to evaluate the impact of temporal information on classification performance:

Aggregated Temporal Embeddings: This method computes the word embeddings for each word in a sentence and aggregates them through averaging to form a sentence representation, taking into account the timestamp of each word.

Time-Weighted Embedding Fusion: In this approach, embeddings are adjusted by applying time-based weights to enhance the influence of recent or temporally relevant information.

Self-Attention with Temporal Positional Encoding: In this approach, self-attention mechanisms incorporate temporal positional encodings, allowing the model to assign different levels of importance to words based on their position and time context.

We conducted our experiment usingthe following hyperparameters:

- Embedding dimension: 100.
- Maximum sequence length: 100 tokens.
- BiLSTM units: 128.
- Attention dropout: 0.3.
- Conv1D filters: 128 with kernel size 5.
- Dense layers: Two layers with 256 and 128 units, respectively, followed by dropout layers.
- Learning rate: 0.00005 with early stopping and learning rate reduction strategies.

Each model variant was trained using categorical cross-entropy as the loss function and the Adam optimizer [79], with early stopping and learning rate scheduling to prevent overfitting and optimize training convergence.

5.3. Evaluation Criteria

To rigorously evaluate the model performance, we employed a comprehensive set of metrics, each providing unique insights into different aspects of classification:

Accuracy [50]: Measures the overall proportion of correctly classified samples:

$$Accuracy = \frac{Number\ of\ correct\ predictions}{Total\ number\ of\ predictions} \quad (21)$$

Cohen's Kappa Score (CK) [51]: Assesses the agreement between predicted and true labels, accounting for chance:

$$\kappa = \frac{p_o - p_e}{1 - p_e} \quad (22)$$

where p_o is the observed agreement and p_e is the expected agreement by chance.

F1 Score (Macro and Micro) [50]: The F1 score provides a balanced evaluation of precision and recall, offering a comprehensive measure of classification performance: Macro F1 calculates the mean F1 score across all classes, treating each class equally and Micro F1 aggregates contributions of all classes to compute an average score. The F1 score for each class c is defined as follows:

$$(F1)_c = 2 \times \frac{Precision_c \times Recall_c}{Precision_c + Recall_c} \quad (23)$$

Matthews Correlation Coefficient (MCC) [52]: Provides a balanced measure even when classes are imbalanced:

$$MCC = \frac{TP \times TN - FP \times FN}{\sqrt{(TP + FP)(TP + FN)(TN + FP)(TN + FN)}} \quad (24)$$

where TP, TN, FP, and FN are true positives, true negatives, false positives, and false negatives, respectively.

Mean Squared Error (MSE) and **Mean Absolute Error (MAE)** [53]: Used for error-based evaluation, capturing the magnitude of classification errors:

$$MSE = \frac{1}{n}\sum_{i=1}^{n}(\hat{y}_i - y_i)^2,\ MSE = \frac{1}{n}\sum_{i=1}^{n}|\hat{y}_i - y_i| \quad (25)$$

Precision-Recall and ROC Curves [50]: These curves, along with their AUC values, help in understanding the model's performance in distinguishing between classes.

5.4. Results on Benchmark Datasets

The proposed time-aware short text classification model was evaluated using three benchmark datasets: the Ireland-news-headlines dataset, Sentiment140 dataset and 20 News Groups dataset. Three dynamic embedding techniques—*Aggregate-based Embedding Fusion*, *Time-weighted Embedding Fusion*, and *Self-Attention with Temporal Positional Encoding*—were employed to assess the model's robustness in tracking semantic drift and handling time-sensitive tasks. The results, as shown in Table 2, demonstrate that the proposed approach achieves consistently high performance across all datasets, with accuracy reaching up to 92% for Ireland-news-headlines and Sentiment140 datasets, and 85% for 20 News Groups dataset in the best-performing configurations respectively.

For the Ireland-news-headlines dataset, the model achieves its highest performance with Self-Attention with Temporal Positional Encoding and Aggregate-based Embedding Fusion, achieving an accuracy of 92%. This result underscores the effectiveness of integrating temporal information with attention mechanisms and demonstrates the model's ability to capture both local and global dependencies. The corresponding F1 Macro and Micro scores, at 90% and 92% respectively, further validate the model's reliability in handling class imbalances while ensuring consistent performance. Metrics such as Cohen's Kappa and Matthews Correlation Coefficient (MCC), both at 0.89, confirm the robustness of the model's predictions. On the other hand, the Time-weighted Embedding Fusion technique performs slightly lower, achieving 91% accuracy, which suggests that its effectiveness may depend on the specific characteristics of the dataset.

Table 2. Performance results (%) of the proposed time-aware classification model on the used datasets.

Dynamic Embedding Techniques	Acc	CK	F1 Macro	F1 Micro	MCC	MSE	MAE
Ireland-news-headlines dataset							
Aggregate-based Embedding Fusion	**0.92**	0.89	0.90	0.92	0.89	0.75	0.23
Time-weighted Embedding Fusion	0.91	0.88	0.89	0.91	0.88	0.83	0.25
Self-Attention with Temporal Positional Encoding	**0.92**	0.89	0.90	0.92	0.89	0.75	0.23
Sentiment140 dataset							
Aggregate-based Embedding Fusion	0.87	0.74	0.87	0.87	0.74	0.13	0.13
Time-weighted Embedding Fusion	**0.92**	0.81	0.91	0.92	0.80	0.09	0.09
Self-Attention with Temporal Positional Encoding	0.89	0.78	0.87	0.89	0.78	0.11	0.11
20 News Group dataset							
Aggregate-based Embedding Fusion	0.73	0.71	0.71	0.73	0.72	11.5	1.30
Time-weighted Embedding Fusion	**0.85**	0.85	0.85	0.85	0.85	3.2	0.80
Self-Attention with Temporal Positional Encoding	0.82	0.81	0.82	0.82	0.82	6.3	0.97

On the Sentiment140 dataset, the Time-weighted Embedding Fusion technique outperforms the other approaches, achieving an accuracy of 92%, alongside F1 Macro and Micro scores of 91% and 92%, respectively. This result highlights the importance of time-weighted embeddings in sentiment analysis tasks, where language usage and tone evolve rapidly. While Self-Attention with Temporal Positional Encoding demonstrates slightly lower accuracy (89%), its consistent performance underscores its adaptability to noisy, real-world datasets. In comparison, the Aggregate-based Embedding Fusion approach achieves an accuracy of 87%, showing its effectiveness in more straightforward time-aware tasks but its limitations in more dynamic language contexts.

For the 20 News Groups dataset, the model exhibits a wider performance gap across different techniques. The Time-weighted Embedding Fusion method achieves the highest accuracy of 85%, highlighting its ability to capture temporal dependencies in multi-class text classification. Self-Attention with Temporal Positional Encoding follows closely with 82% accuracy, demonstrating its robustness in handling longer text structures and diverse topics. However, the Aggregate-based Embedding Fusion approach performs significantly lower (73% accuracy), indicating its limitations in adapting to the highly varied textual content present in this dataset. The observed trends suggest that time-aware representations are crucial for effectively classifying diverse topics while maintaining temporal consistency.

The learning curves presented in Figure 4 further illustrate the stability and efficiency of the proposed model during training. For the Ireland-news-headlines dataset, the accuracy curve shows a steady increase over epochs, converging at approximately 92% (Figure 4a), while the loss decreases consistently (Figure 4b). The alignment between training and validation losses demonstrates that the model effectively learns without overfitting. Similarly, for the Sentiment140 dataset, the accuracy curve exhibits a smooth upward trend, reaching around 92% (Figure 4c). In contrast, the loss curve (Figure 4d) decreases despite minor fluctuations, which can be attributed to the noisy nature of the sentiment-based text. For the 20 News Groups dataset, however, the learning curves exhibit a different pattern due to the greater textual diversity across multiple topics. The accuracy curve steadily improves, converging at 85% (Figure 4e) with Time-weighted Embedding Fusion, while the loss curve (Figure 4f) follows a consistent downward trajectory. However, compared to the other datasets, training progresses more gradually, indicating that the model requires more epochs to effectively generalize across the dataset's longer and more varied textual content. The stability of the validation loss further supports the model's ability to capture temporal dependencies while handling diverse topics.

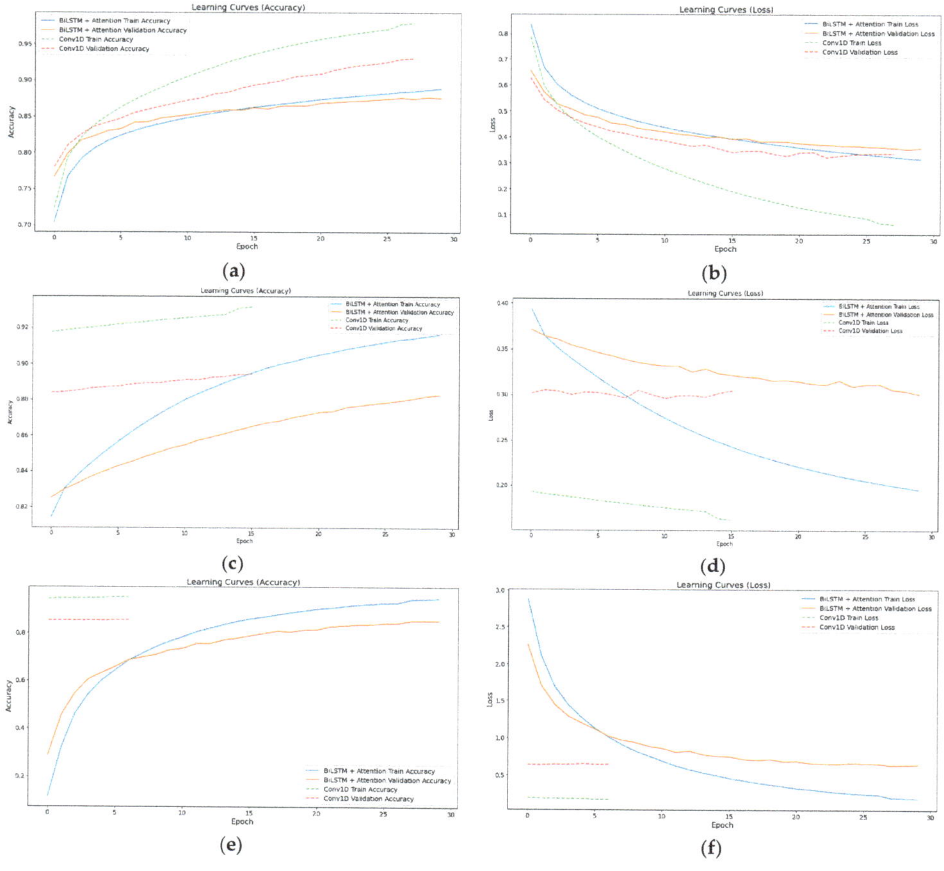

Figure 4. Performance (Learning Curves) of the proposed model on three datasets: (**a**) accuracy for Ireland-news-headlines, (**b**) loss for Ireland-news-headlines, (**c**) accuracy for Sentiment140, (**d**) loss for Sentiment140, and (**e**) accuracy for 20 News Groups and (**f**) loss for 20 News Groups.

Figure 5 presents the ROC curves and precision-recall curves, providing deeper insights into the model's classification performance. For the Ireland-news-headlines dataset, the ROC curve indicates near-perfect classification with an AUC approaching 1.0, validating the model's ability to distinguish between classes effectively. The precision-recall curve reinforces this result, showing a strong balance between precision and recall, particularly in handling time-sensitive categories. For the Sentiment140 dataset, while the ROC curve remains strong, the AUC is slightly lower due to the inherent complexity and variability of sentiment data. Nevertheless, the precision-recall curve demonstrates that the model maintains reliable predictions despite the noisy nature of the sentiment-labeled text. For the 20 News Groups dataset, the ROC and precision-recall curves reveal the model's ability to generalize across diverse topics. The ROC curve shows an AUC close to 1.0 for most categories, indicating high separability. However, certain topics exhibit slight variations, suggesting that some categories have overlapping textual patterns. The precision-recall curve displays variability across different topics, with some classes maintaining high precision, while others show a gradual decline in recall, reflecting the challenges posed by long-form, multi-domain text classification. These results highlight the effectiveness of the proposed model in handling diverse textual structures and evolving semantic patterns over time.

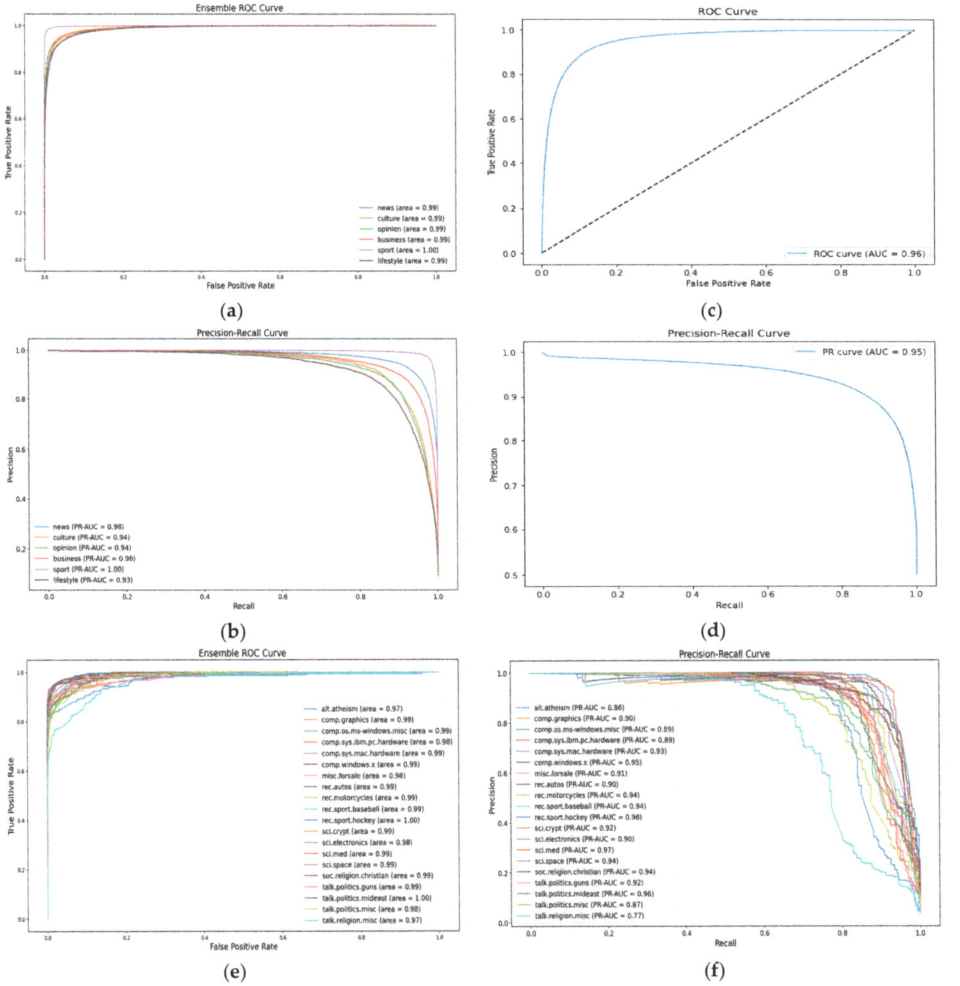

Figure 5. Performance (ROC Curves) of the proposed model on two datasets: (**a**) ROC for Ireland-news-headlines, (**b**) precision-recall for Ireland-news-headlines, (**c**) ROC for Sentiment140, (**d**) precision-recall for Sentiment140, (**e**) ROC for 20 News Groups and (**f**) precision-recall for 20 News Groups.

The correlation matrices in Figure 6 highlight the alignment between predicted and true classes. For the Ireland-news-headlines dataset (Figure 6a), the matrix shows clear diagonal dominance, indicating that the model consistently predicts the correct class with high confidence. Misclassifications are minimal, reflecting the model's precision in handling evolving semantic meanings. For the Sentiment140 dataset (Figure 6b), the correlation matrix also exhibits strong diagonal dominance, with only minor misclassifications observed.

These errors occur primarily between semantically similar classes, which is expected in sentiment classification tasks due to subtle variations in word tone and usage. For the 20 News Groups dataset (Figure 6c), the matrix illustrates the model's effectiveness in multi-class classification across diverse topics. While most categories exhibit strong diagonal patterns, indicating high classification accuracy, some categories, particularly those related to technology, religion, and politics, show slight misclassifications. This suggests some semantic overlap among these topics, where textual similarities may lead to ambiguities in classification. Despite this, the model demonstrates robust generalization across multiple domains, reinforcing its ability to adapt to heterogeneous text categories with temporal variations.

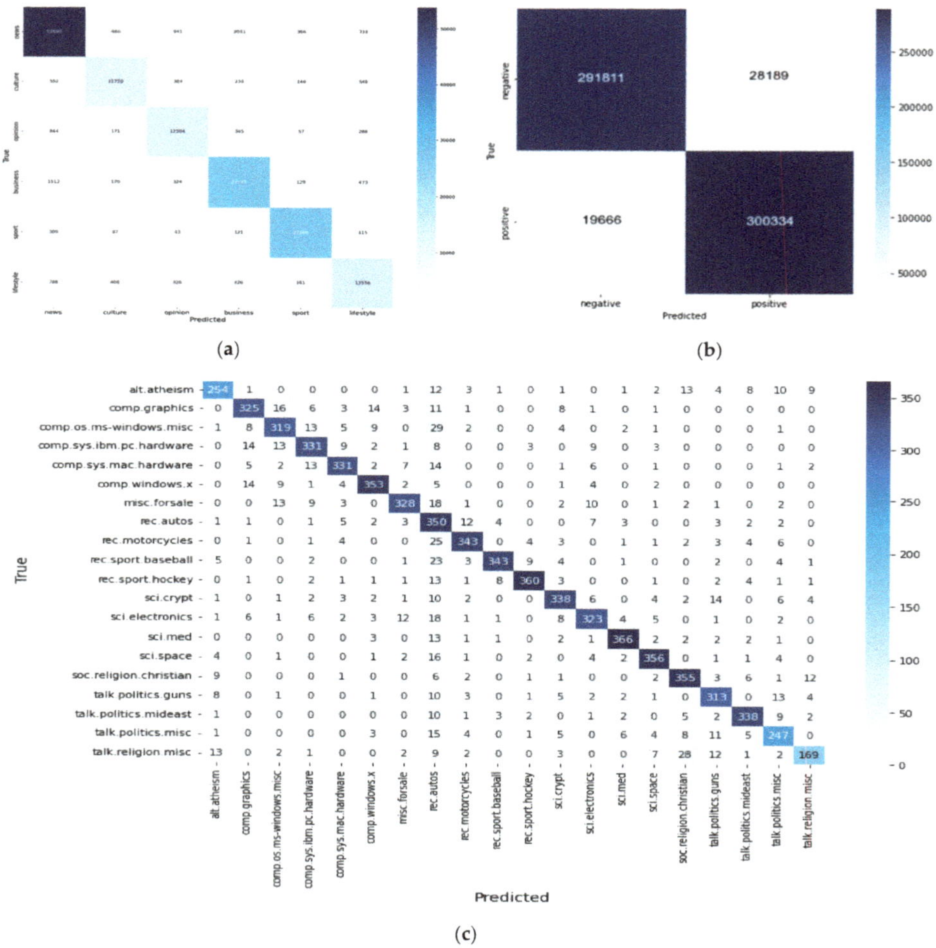

Figure 6. Performance (Correlation matrices) of the proposed model on three datasets: (**a**) Ireland-news-headlines, (**b**), Sentiment140 and (c) 20 News Groups.

The true versus predicted class distribution in Figure 7 further validates the model's ability to preserve class balance while maintaining high classification accuracy. For the Ireland-news-headlines dataset (Figure 7a), the predicted class distributions closely align with the true labels, demonstrating the model's robustness in tracking evolving language semantics and ensuring accurate classification across diverse news categories. For the Sentiment140 dataset (Figure 7b), the distribution remains highly consistent, with minimal deviation between true and predicted classes. While minor discrepancies exist, particularly in sentiment polarity shifts, these are expected due to the dataset's complex and evolving sentiment expressions. For the 20 News Groups dataset (Figure 7c), the model effectively captures multi-topic classification, as indicated by the similarity between true and predicted class distributions. However, slight variations occur in certain categories such as *rec.autos* and *soc.religion.christian*, suggesting that some topics exhibit semantic overlap that challenges precise categorization. Despite these differences, the overall distribution confirms the model's generalization capability across diverse textual domains while maintaining high classification reliability.

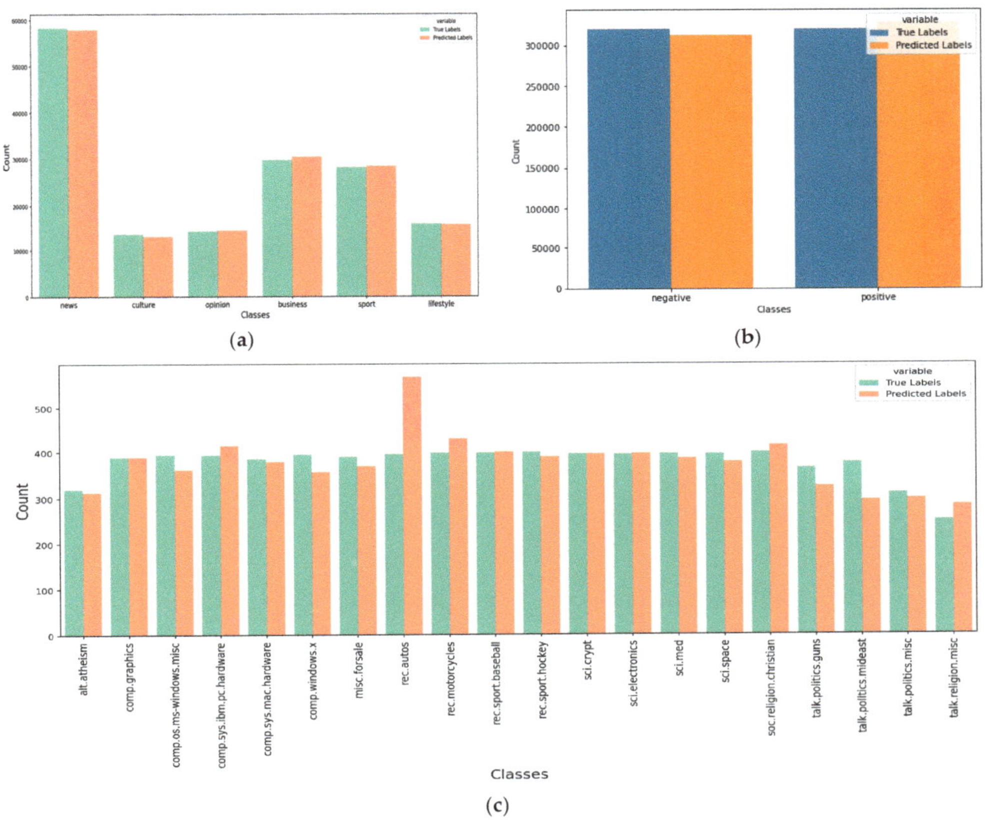

Figure 7. Performance (True vs Predicted) of the proposed model on three datasets: (**a**) Ireland-news-headlines, (**b**), Sentiment140 and (c) 20 News Groups.

The above results confirm the effectiveness and robustness of the proposed time-aware short-text classification model across all used benchmark datasets in capturing semantic drift and evolving language usage. The integration of Self-Attention with Temporal Positional Encoding and Time-weighted Embedding Fusion proves particularly effective, achieving high accuracy across news categorization, sentiment analysis, and multi-topic classification. The model's strong performance across accuracy, F1 scores, Cohen's Kappa, MCC, and AUC highlights its reliability and adaptability to time-sensitive classification tasks, outperforming static approaches.

5.5. Results on Lager Temporal Gap

To evaluate the model's ability to handle long-term semantic drift, we conducted an experiment on the Ireland-news-headlines dataset, using 1996–2008 as the training period and 2009–2012 as the test period. This setup introduced a significant temporal gap, allowing us to assess the model's generalization performance across evolving language patterns.

Among the dynamic embedding techniques, Time-weighted Embedding Fusion achieved the best performance, with an accuracy of 91%, F1 Macro of 89%, and Cohen's Kappa of 0.87, as shown in Table 3. These results confirm that the model effectively generalizes across different time periods despite evolving linguistic trends. The MCC score of 0.87 further reinforces its consistency and reliability in maintaining robust classification decisions even in the presence of significant language shifts.

Table 3. Performance results (%) of the proposed time-aware classification model with larger temporal gap on the Ireland-news-headlines datasets.

Dynamic Embedding Techniques	Acc	CK	F1 Macro	F1 Micro	MCC	MSE	MAE
			Ireland-news-headlines dataset				
Time-weighted Embedding Fusion	0.91	0.87	0.89	0.91	0.87	0.92	0.27

The Mean Squared Error (MSE) of 0.92 and Mean Absolute Error (MAE) of 0.27 indicate that while the classification model remains highly effective, there is a slight increase in error metrics compared to shorter temporal gaps, which is expected due to the natural evolution of language. The learning curves (Figure 8a,b) demonstrate a stable convergence pattern, with the model gradually improving its accuracy while reducing loss over epochs. Furthermore, the ROC curves (Figure 8c) indicate strong classification performance across all categories, with an AUC exceeding 0.96 for each class, demonstrating a well-calibrated predictive capability.

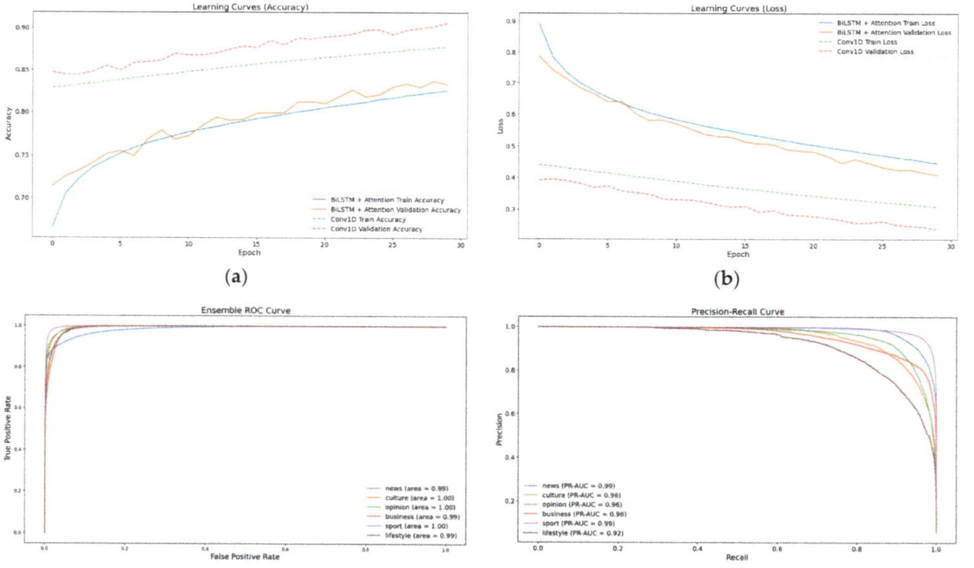

Figure 8. Performance (Learning Curves (**a**,**b**) & ROC Curves (**c**,**d**)) of the proposed model on the Ireland-news-headlines dataset with larger temporal gap.

The precision-recall curves (Figure 8d) further support the effectiveness of the model in distinguishing between different categories, with high AUC values ensuring that the model maintains strong precision-recall trade-offs. The ability to retain high classification accuracy, even when encountering extended time intervals, highlights the effectiveness of the time-weighted embedding approach in mitigating the effects of semantic drift. By dynamically adjusting word importance over time and incorporating both recent and historical language patterns, this method enhances the model's adaptability to evolving textual distributions.

5.6. Comparison with Well-Known Temporal Models

The comparison between our Time-Aware Sentence Classification Model and various time-aware and traditional classification models [25,80], as presented in Table 4, highlights the effectiveness of our approach in handling temporal text classification. The results demonstrate that our model, particularly when utilizing dynamic word embeddings, achieves state-of-the-art accuracy across multiple datasets, outperforming several established temporal models.

Table 4. Performance results (% accuracy) of proposed time-aware classification model and baselines.

Approaches	System	Accuracy (%)	Datasets
Time-Aware Classification	RoBERTa with date as text [25]	87.84	Ireland-news-headlines
		91.13	Sentiment140
	RoBERTa with added embeddings [25]	86.82	Ireland-news-headlines
		91.04	Sentiment140
	RoBERTa with stacked embeddings [25]	87.65	Ireland-news-headlines
		91.1	Sentiment140
	Text GloVe with Triples [80]	86.9	20 News Group
	Text BERT with Triples [80]	77.7	20 News Group
Traditional/Static Classification	RoBERTa without date [25]	82.35	Ireland-news-headlines
		89.27	Sentiment140
	Most frequent class baseline [25]	51.10	Ireland-news-headlines
		49.88	Sentiment140
	Naive Bayes Classifier [25]	85.00	Sentiment140
	Hybrid Stacked Ensemble Model [25]	99.00	Sentiment140
Proposed Classification Model	Time-Aware Sentence Classification Model with *traditional/static word embeddings*	85.6	Ireland-news-headlines
		82.1	Sentiment140
		77.00	20 News Group
	Time-Aware Sentence Classification Model with *dynamic word embeddings*	**92.00**	Ireland-news-headlines
		92.00	Sentiment140
		85.00	20 News Group

Among the time-aware classification models, RoBERTa with date as text achieved 87.84% on Ireland-news-headlines and 91.13% on Sentiment140, leveraging date metadata as textual input to enhance its temporal awareness. Other RoBERTa-based approaches, such as RoBERTa with added embeddings and RoBERTa with stacked embeddings, also showed competitive performance, demonstrating that incorporating time-related embeddings contributes to classification accuracy [25]. Similarly, Text GloVe with Triples (86.9%) and Text BERT with Triples (77.7%) on 20 News Group further emphasizes the importance of encoding temporal aspects in text representations [80].

In contrast, traditional/static classification models exhibited inferior performance due to their lack of temporal modeling. RoBERTa without date saw a notable drop in accuracy

(82.35% on Ireland-news-headlines, 89.27% on Sentiment140), reinforcing the necessity of temporal integration. The Naïve Bayes classifier (85.00%) and Most Frequent Class Baseline (51.10%) underperformed, confirming that static models struggle with evolving semantics. While the Hybrid Stacked Ensemble Model achieved 99.00% on Sentiment140, its performance on other datasets was not reported, limiting its comparative insight [25].

Our proposed Time-Aware Sentence Classification Model consistently outperformed these baselines, achieving 92.00% accuracy on both Ireland-news-headlines and Sentiment140 and 85.00% on 20 News Group when using dynamic word embeddings. This confirms the superiority of time-aware embeddings in learning evolving semantics over time. In contrast, when using traditional/static embeddings, our model's accuracy was 85.6% on Ireland-news-headlines, 82.1% on Sentiment140, and 77.0% on 20 News Group, further validating that temporal dynamics play a crucial role in classification accuracy. The following are the key important points of our proposed model compared with the well-known approaches:

- **Temporal Awareness Significantly Improves Classification**: The substantial gap between RoBERTa without date and time-aware models emphasizes the necessity of incorporating temporal information into text classification.
- **Dynamic Word Embeddings Enhance Performance**: Our model's superior accuracy with dynamic embeddings confirms that capturing semantic drift over time is essential for effective classification.
- **Generalizability Across Datasets**: Unlike certain models, such as Hybrid Stacked Ensemble, which perform well on Sentiment140 but lack evaluations on multiple datasets, our approach maintains high accuracy across diverse text domains.
- **Comparison with Well-Known Work**: Our model consistently outperforms existing temporal classification approaches, demonstrating the effectiveness of direct time-aware embedding integration rather than treating time as an external input feature.

5.7. Application to News Categorization and Trend Analysis

To demonstrate the effectiveness of the proposed time-aware sentence classification model for time-sensitive tasks, we applied it to a compiled news dataset specifically designed for categorization and trend analysis, as presented in Table 5. The dataset consists of 25 samples distributed evenly across five categories: *News*, *Opinion*, *Sport*, *Business*, and *Culture*. Each sample includes a timestamp and a corresponding headline, reflecting real-world events and trends between January 2020 and May 2020. The headlines span diverse themes, such as economic stimulus measures, climate policies, ethical debates surrounding AI, remote work trends, championship victories, stock market developments, and the digital transformation of cultural events during the pandemic.

The model (with Time-weighted Embedding Fusion) successfully classified the dataset into its respective categories, achieving exceptional performance across all evaluation metrics. As shown in Figure 9a, the per-class precision, recall, and F1-scores consistently reached near-perfect values of 1.0, indicating the model's ability to effectively differentiate between categories. This strong performance demonstrates the model's capacity to capture both content and temporal nuances, enabling accurate classifications even in time-sensitive contexts. The alignment between true and predicted labels, illustrated in Figure 9b, further highlights the reliability of the model, with no significant misclassifications observed.

Table 5. A compiled dataset for news categorization and trend analysis task.

Timestamp	News Headlines	Category
1 January 2020	Government announces economic stimulus package.	News
8 January 2020	World leaders meet to discuss global climate goals.	News
15 January 2020	New policies aim to stabilize economic growth.	News
22 January 2020	Climate crisis takes center stage at global summit.	News
29 January 2020	Global literacy programs gain global traction.	News
1 June 2020	Remote work should remain post-pandemic.	Opinion
10 June 2020	Is technology making us more disconnected from reality?	Opinion
17 June 2020	The future of work: Balancing remote and in-office setups.	Opinion
24 June 2020	Ethical concerns in AI dominate opinion columns.	Opinion
1 July 2020	Healthcare debates spark discussions on innovation.	Opinion
5 February 2020	Football team wins championship after dramatic final.	Sport
12 February 2020	Olympics postponed amid global uncertainty.	Sport
19 February 2020	Local soccer team secures thrilling playoff victory.	Sport
26 February 2020	World championships highlight resilience amid challenges.	Sport
4 March 2020	Global sports events thrive with new safety measures.	Sport
11 March 2020	Tech industry sees surge in remote collaboration tools.	Business
18 March 2020	Stock market rallies as companies report strong earnings.	Business
25 March 2020	E-commerce giants report record profits in Q2 earnings.	Business
1 April 2020	Tech startups lead innovation in green energy solutions.	Business
8 April 2020	Small businesses adopt AI for competitive edge.	Business
22 April 2020	Art exhibition explores human connection in isolation.	Culture
29 April 2020	Digital concerts gain popularity among younger audiences.	Culture
6 May 2020	Local artists adapt to virtual mediums during pandemic.	Culture
13 May 2020	Virtual reality performances redefine cultural experiences.	Culture
20 May 2020	Museum curates digital exhibitions for global audiences.	Culture

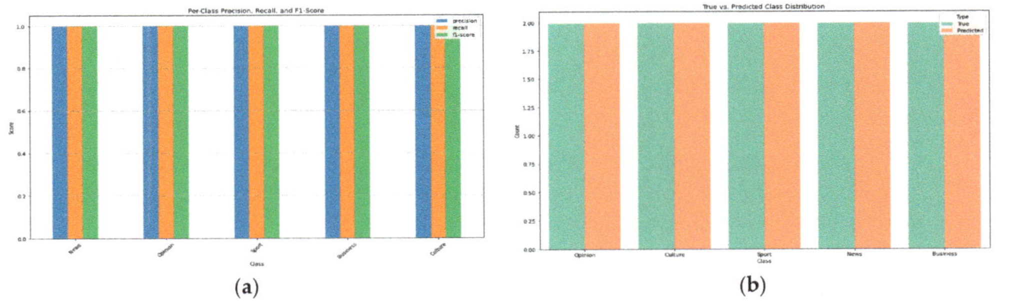

(a) (b)

Figure 9. Performance of the proposed model on the compiled news categorization dataset: (**a**) per-class precision, recall, and F-score, and (**b**) True vs Predicted results.

The confusion matrix presented in Figure 10a confirms these findings, as all predictions align perfectly with the true labels, underscoring the model's robustness in distinguishing semantically similar categories such as *News* and *Business* or *Opinion* and *Culture*. Additionally, Figure 10b showcases the prediction probability distribution, revealing high confidence scores for correct predictions and minimal uncertainty across all classes. This result emphasizes the model's ability to generalize effectively, even with a relatively small dataset.

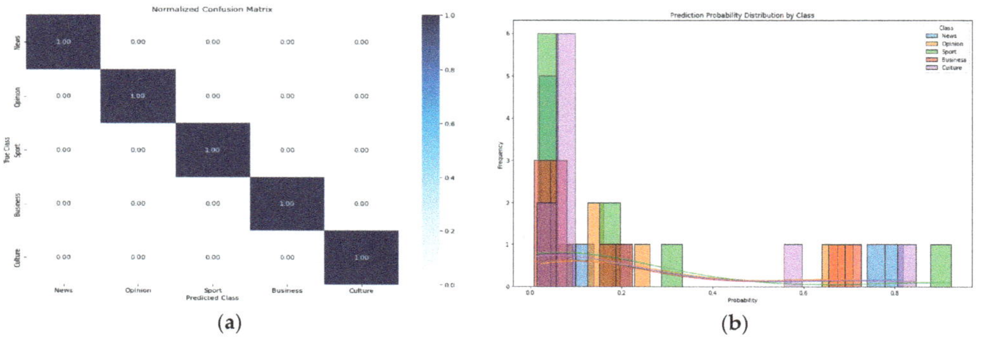

Figure 10. Performance of the proposed model on the compiled news categorization dataset: (**a**) confusion matrix, and (**b**) prediction probability distribution by class.

The learning curve in Figure 11a illustrates a steady and consistent improvement in both training and validation accuracy over the epochs, converging at near-optimal levels without signs of overfitting. Simultaneously, the loss curve in Figure 11b shows a smooth and continuous decline in training and validation loss, further validating the model's stability and capacity to generalize well to unseen data.

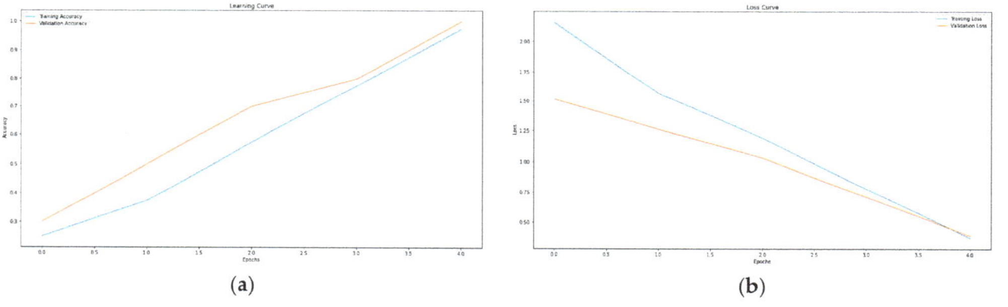

Figure 11. Performance of the proposed model on the compiled news categorization dataset: (**a**) learning curve, and (**b**) loss curve.

The results also highlight the model's ability to adapt to evolving semantics and capture temporal dynamics. For instance, terms like "remote work" and "AI adoption" reflect societal shifts during the pandemic, enabling the model to distinguish these trends accurately within relevant categories such as *Opinion* or *Business*. This capability makes the model particularly suitable for downstream applications, including tracking trends in public sentiment, identifying business developments, and analyzing cultural adaptations over time.

In summary, the application of the proposed time-aware sentence classification model to this dataset demonstrates its effectiveness in handling time-sensitive text classification tasks. The model achieves near-perfect accuracy and exhibits robust generalization, successfully integrating temporal dynamics into its predictions. These results validate the model's utility for real-world applications such as news categorization, trend analysis, and historical text classification, where understanding the temporal evolution of language is essential for capturing meaningful insights.

6. Conclusions

This paper introduced a novel time-aware sentence classification model that incorporates temporal dynamics to address the limitations of traditional static models in natural language processing. By explicitly integrating temporal information into the word embedding process, the proposed model effectively tracks and adapts to evolving language semantics over time. Leveraging a hybrid architecture that combines Convolutional Neural Networks (CNNs) and Bidirectional Long Short-Term Memory (BiLSTM) networks, enriched with attention mechanisms, the model captures both local and global dependencies while maintaining focus on the most relevant parts of the text.

The proposed approach was validated through rigorous experimentation on benchmark datasets and applied to real-world tasks such as news categorization and trend analysis. The results demonstrated superior performance compared to well-known temporal and static models, achieving high accuracy, precision, and F1 scores. Specifically, the model achieved a classification accuracy of 92% in benchmark experiments, significantly outperforming traditional baselines and comparable time-aware approaches. The model's ability to capture temporal semantics was further highlighted in its application to news categorization, where it accurately classified headlines across multiple time-sensitive categories and provided meaningful insights into evolving trends.

The key contributions of this study include the introduction of Temporal-Aware Word Embeddings, the design of a hybrid CNN-BiLSTM architecture, and a dynamic learning process that integrates fine-tuned pre-trained embeddings and synonym-based data augmentation. These innovations ensure that the model adapts to semantic drift and maintains relevance as language evolves, making it suitable for various time-sensitive NLP tasks.

By addressing the challenges of temporal dynamics and semantic evolution, this work advances the field of NLP and provides a comprehensive framework for time-aware sentence classification. The proposed model opens new avenues for applications in trend analysis, historical text classification, and sentiment tracking, where understanding the temporal evolution of language is critical. Future work will focus on expanding the model to larger datasets, incorporating domain-specific temporal features, and exploring its applicability to multilingual and cross-lingual contexts. In conclusion, the proposed time-aware sentence classification model effectively bridges the gap between static text representations and evolving language semantics. It offers a robust and adaptable solution for time-sensitive NLP tasks, paving the way for deeper insights into the dynamic nature of language and its impact on modern text classification challenges.

Author Contributions: K.A.: Conceptualization; K.A. and G.A.-D.: Data curation; K.A.: Formal analysis; Funding acquisition; Investigation; Methodology; K.A. and A.A.M.: Project administration; Resources; Software; K.A., A.A.M. and G.A.-D.: Supervision; Validation; Visualization; Roles/Writing—original draft; Writing—review & editing. All authors have read and agreed to the published version of the manuscript.

Funding: The research leading to these results has received funding from the Mohammed Bin Rashid Smart Learning Program, UAE, under the Funding Agreement No: MBRSLP/02/23.

Data Availability Statement: The data that has been used is publicly available.

Acknowledgments: We are grateful to the American University of Ras Al Khaimah (AURAK) for its valuable support.

Conflicts of Interest: The authors declare that they have no known competing financial interests or personal relationships that could have appeared to influence the work reported in this paper.

References

1. Liu, B. *Sentiment Analysis and Opinion Mining*; Springer Nature: Berlin/Heidelberg, Germany, 2022.
2. Mayur, W.; Annavarapu, C.S.R.; Chaitanya, K. A survey on sentiment analysis methods, applications, and challenges. *Artif. Intell. Rev.* **2022**, *55*, 5731–5780.
3. Khaled, A.; Aysha, A.S. Experimental results on customer reviews using lexicon-based word polarity identification method. *IEEE Access* **2020**, *8*, 179955–179969.
4. Bogery, R.; Nora, A.B.; Nida, A.; Nada, A.; Yara, A.H.; Irfan, U.K. Automatic Semantic Categorization of News Headlines using Ensemble Machine Learning: A Comparative Study. *Int. J. Adv. Comput. Sci. Appl.* **2019**, *10*, 689–696. [CrossRef]
5. Agarwal, J.; Sharon, C.; Aditya, P.; Anand, K.M.; Guru, P. Machine Learning Application for News Text Classification. In Proceedings of the 13th International Conference on Cloud Computing, Data Science & Engineering (Confluence), Noida, India, 19–20 January 2023; pp. 463–466.
6. Sukhramani, K.; Harshika, K.; Akhtar, R.; Abhishek, J. Binary Classification of News Articles using Deep Learning. In Proceedings of the IEEE International Students' Conference on Electrical, Electronics and Computer Science (SCEECS), Bhopal, India, 24–25 February 2024; pp. 1–9.
7. Hiremath, B.N.; Malini, M.P. Enhancing Optimized Personalized Therapy in Clinical Decision Support System using Natural Language Processing. *J. King Saud Univ.-Comput. Inf. Sci.* **2022**, *34*, 2840–2848. [CrossRef]
8. Eguia, H.; Carlos, L.S.-B.; Franco, V.; Fernando, A.-L.; Francesc, S.-R. Clinical Decision Support and Natural Language Processing in Medicine: Systematic Literature Review. *J. Med. Internet Res.* **2024**, *26*, 39348889. [CrossRef]
9. Palanivinayagam, A.; Claude, Z.E.-B.; Robertas, D. Twenty Years of Machine-Learning-Based Text Classification: A Systematic Review. *Algorithms* **2023**, *16*, 236. [CrossRef]
10. Sun, X.; Xiaoya, L.; Jiwei, L.; Fei, W.; Shangwei, G.; Tianwei, Z.; Guoyin, W. Text classification via large language models. *arXiv* **2023**, arXiv:2305.08377.
11. Duarte, J.M.; Berton, L. A review of semi-supervised learning for text classification. *Artif. Intell. Rev.* **2023**, *56*, 9401–9469. [CrossRef]
12. Zhao, H.; Haihua, C.; Thomas, A.R.; Yunhe, F.; Debjani, S.; Hong-Jun, Y. Improving Text Classification with Large Language Model-Based Data Augmentation. *Electronics* **2024**, *13*, 2535. [CrossRef]
13. Kamal, T.; Paul, D.Y.; Chan, Y.; Dirar, H.; Aya, T. A comprehensive survey of text classification techniques and their research applications: Observational and experimental insights. *Comput. Sci. Rev.* **2024**, *54*, 100664.
14. Wu, Y.; Jun, W. A survey of text classification based on pre-trained language model. *Neurocomputing* **2025**, *616*, 128921. [CrossRef]
15. Hyojung, K.; Minjung, P. Discovering fashion industry trends in the online news by applying text mining and time series regression analysis. *Heliyon* **2023**, *9*, 2405–8440.
16. Hardin, G. Disinformation; Misinformation, and Fake News: The Latest Trends and Issues in Research. In *Encyclopedia of Libraries, Librarianship, and Information Science*, 1st ed.; Academic Press: Cambridge, MA, USA, 2025; pp. 519–530.
17. Hu, T.; Siqin, W.; Wei, L.; Mengxi, Z.; Xiao, H.; Yingwei, Y.; Regina, L. Revealing public opinion towards COVID-19 vaccines with Twitter data in the United States: Spatiotemporal perspective. *J. Med. Internet Res.* **2021**, *23*, e30854. [CrossRef] [PubMed]
18. Sun, G.; Cheng, Y.; Dong, F.; Wang, L.; Zhao, D.; Zhang, Z.; Tong, X. Multi-Label Text Classification model integrating Label Attention and Historical Attention. *Knowl.-Based Syst.* **2024**, *296*, 111878. [CrossRef]
19. Ren, H.; Wang, H.; Zhao, Y.; Ren, Y. Time-Aware Language Modeling for Historical Text Dating. In Proceedings of the 2023 Conference on Empirical Methods in Natural Language Processing (EMNLP-2023), Singapore, 6–10 December 2023.
20. Khan, S.U.R.; Muhammd, A.I.; Muhammad, A.; Muhammad, A.I. Temporal specificity-based text classification for information retrieval. *Turk. J. Electr. Eng. Comput. Sci.* **2018**, *26*, 2916–2927. [CrossRef]
21. He, Y.; Li, J.; Song, Y.; He, M.; Peng, H. Time-evolving Text Classification with Deep Neural Networks. In Proceedings of the Twenty-Seventh International Joint Conference on Artificial Intelligence (IJCAI-18), Stockholm, Sweden, 13–19 July 2018.
22. Rabab, A.; Elena, K.; Arkaitz, Z. Building for tomorrow: Assessing the temporal persistence of text classifiers. *Inf. Process. Manag.* **2023**, *60*, 103200.
23. Salles, T.; Leonardo, R.; Gisele, L.P.; Fernando, M.; Wagner, M.J.; Marcos, G. Temporally-aware algorithms for document classification. In Proceedings of the 33rd International ACM SIGIR Conference on Research and Development in Information Retrieval, Geneva, Switzerland, 19–23 July 2010.
24. Raneen, Y.; Abdul, H.; Zahra, A. MTS2Graph: Interpretable multivariate time series classification with temporal evolving graphs. *Pattern Recognit.* **2025**, *152*, 110486.
25. Pokrywka, J.; Filip, G. Temporal language modeling for short text document classification with transformers. In Proceedings of the 2022 17th Conference on Computer Science and Intelligence Systems (FedCSIS), Sofia, Bulgaria, 4–7 September 2022; pp. 121–128.
26. Santosh, T.; Vuong, T.; Grabmair, M. Time-aware Incremental Training for Temporal Generalization of Legal Classification Tasks. *arXiv* **2024**, arXiv:2405.14211.

27. Chen, X.; Qiu, P.; Zhu, W.; Li, H.; Wang, H.; Sotiras, A.; Wang, Y.; Razi, A. TimeMIL: Advancing Multivariate Time Series Classification via a Time-aware Multiple Instance Learning. *arXiv* **2024**, arXiv:2405.03140.
28. Frank, E.; Bouckaert, R. Naive Bayes for Text Classification with Unbalanced Classes. In Proceedings of the 10th European conference on Principle and Practice of Knowledge Discovery in Databases, Berlin, Germany, 18–22 September 2006; Volume 4213.
29. Jiang, L.; Li, C.; Wang, S.; Zhang, L. Deep feature weighting for naive Bayes and its application to text classification. *Eng. Appl. Artif. Intell.* **2016**, *52*, 26–39. [CrossRef]
30. Cortes, C.; Vapnik, V. Support-vector networks. *Mach. Learn.* **1995**, *20*, 273–297. [CrossRef]
31. Ramesh, B.; Sathiaseelan, J.G.R. An Advanced Multi Class Instance Selection based Support Vector Machine for Text Classification. *Procedia Comput. Sci.* **2015**, *57*, 1124–1130. [CrossRef]
32. Parashjyoti, B.; Deepak, G.; Barenya, B.H. ConCave-Convex procedure for support vector machines with Huber loss for text classification. *Comput. Electr. Eng.* **2025**, *122*, 109925.
33. Wu, J. *Introduction to Convolutional Neural Networks*; National Key Lab for Novel Software Technology, Nanjing University: Nanjing, China, 2017; Volume 5, p. 495.
34. Albawi, S.; Mohammed, T.A.; Al-Zawi, S. Understanding of a convolutional neural network. In Proceedings of the 2017 International Conference on Engineering and Technology (ICET), Antalya, Turkey, 21–23 August 2017.
35. Zhao, Z.; Wu, Y. Attention-Based Convolutional Neural Networks for Sentence Classification. In Proceedings of the Interspeech, San Francisco, CA, USA, 8–12 September 2016; Volume 8, pp. 705–709.
36. Vieira, J.; Paulo, A.; Raimundo, S.M. An analysis of convolutional neural networks for sentence classification. In Proceedings of the 2017 XLIII Latin American Computer Conference (CLEI), Córdoba, Argentina, 4–8 September 2017.
37. Lai, S.; Xu, L.; Liu, K.; Zhao, J. Recurrent convolutional neural networks for text classification. In Proceedings of the AAAI Conference on Artificial Intelligence, Austin, TX, USA, 25–30 January 2015; Volume 29.
38. Tarwani, K.M.; Swathi, E. Survey on recurrent neural network in natural language processing. *Int. J. Eng. Trends Technol.* **2016**, *48*, 301–304. [CrossRef]
39. Tomas, M.; Kai, C.; Greg, C.; Jeffrey, D. Efficient estimation of word representations in vector space. *arXiv* **2013**, arXiv:1301.3781.
40. Pennington, J.; Richard, S.; Christopher, D.M. Glove: Global vectors for word representation. In Proceedings of the 2014 Conference on Empirical Methods in Natural Language Processing (EMNLP), Doha, Qatar, 25–29 October 2014; pp. 1532–1543.
41. Giulianelli, M.; Marco, D.T.; Raquel, F. Analysing lexical semantic change with contextualised word representations. *arXiv* **2020**, arXiv:2004.14118.
42. Bhuwan, D.; Jeremy, R.C.; Julian, M. Time-Aware Language Models as Temporal Knowledge Bases. *Trans. Assoc. Comput. Linguist.* **2022**, *10*, 257–273.
43. Rosin, G.D.; Ido, G.; Kira, R. Time masking for temporal language models. In Proceedings of the Fifteenth ACM International Conference on Web Search and Data Mining, Tempe, AZ, USA, 21–25 February 2022; pp. 833–841.
44. Rosin, G.D.; Kira, R. Temporal attention for language models. *arXiv* **2022**, arXiv:2202.02093.
45. Devlin, J.; Chang, M.W.; Lee, K.; Toutanova, K. BERT: Pre-training of Deep Bidirectional Transformers for Language Understanding. In Proceedings of the NAACL 2019, Minneapolis, MN, USA, 2–7 June 2019; pp. 4171–4186.
46. Radford, A.; Narasimhan, K.; Salimans, T.; Sutskever, I. Improving Language Understanding by Generative Pre-Training. 2018. Available online: https://openai.com/research/language-unsupervised (accessed on 10 February 2025).
47. Yang, Z.; Dai, Z.; Yang, Y.; Carbonell, J.; Salakhutdinov, R.R.; Le, Q.V. XLNet: Generalized Autoregressive Pretraining for Language Understanding. In Proceedings of the Advances in Neural Information Processing Systems (NeurIPS), Vancouver, BC, Canada, 8–14 December 2019; Volume 32, pp. 5754–5764.
48. Schuster, M.; Kuldip, K.P. Bidirectional Recurrent Neural Networks. *IEEE Trans. Signal Process.* **1997**, *45*, 2673–2681. [CrossRef]
49. Grisoni, F.; Michael, M.; Robin, L.; Gisbert, S. Bidirectional molecule generation with recurrent neural networks. *J. Chem. Inf. Model.* **2020**, *60*, 1175–1183. [CrossRef]
50. Powers, D.M. Evaluation: From precision, recall and F-measure to ROC, informedness, markedness and correlation. *arXiv* **2020**, arXiv:2010.16061.
51. Cohen, J. A coefficient of agreement for nominal scales. *Educ. Psychol. Meas.* **1960**, *20*, 37–46. [CrossRef]
52. Matthews, B.W. Comparison of the predicted and observed secondary structure of T4 phage lysozyme. *Biochim. Biophys. Acta (BBA)-Protein Struct.* **1975**, *405*, 442–451. [CrossRef]
53. Willmott, C.J.; Kenji, M. Advantages of the Mean Absolute Error (MAE) Over the Root Mean Square Error (RMSE) in Assessing Average Model Performance. *Clim. Res.* **2005**, *30*, 79–82. [CrossRef]
54. Sheng, L.; Lizhen, X. Topic Classification Based on Improved Word Embedding. In Proceedings of the 14th Web Information Systems and Applications Conference (WISA), Liuzhou, China, 11–12 November 2017; pp. 117–121.
55. Luo, W. Research and Implementation of Text Topic Classification Based on Text CNN. In Proceedings of the 2022 3rd International Conference on Computer Vision, Image and Deep Learning & International Conference on Computer Engineering and Applications (CVIDL & ICCEA), Changchun, China, 20–22 May 2022; pp. 1152–1155.

56. Ding, H.; Yang, J.; Deng, Y.; Zhang, H.; Roth, D. Towards Open-Domain Topic Classification. In Proceedings of the 2022 Conference of the North American Chapter of the Association for Computational Linguistics: Human Language Technologies: System Demonstrations, Seattle, WA, USA, 10–15 July 2022; pp. 90–98.
57. Ghazala, N.; Muhammad, M.K.; Muhammad, Y.; Bushra, Z.; Muhammad, K.H. Email spam detection by deep learning models using novel feature selection technique and BERT. *Egypt. Inform. J.* **2024**, *26*, 100473.
58. Maged, N.; Faisal, S.; Aminu, D.; Abdulaziz, A.; Mohammed, A.-S. Topic-aware neural attention network for malicious social media spam detection. *Alex. Eng. J.* **2025**, *111*, 540–554.
59. Mariano, M.; Fernando, D.; Fernando, T.; Ana, M.; Evangelos, M. Detecting ongoing events using contextual word and sentence embeddings. *Expert Syst. Appl.* **2022**, *209*, 118257.
60. Elena, M.; Eva, W. Temporal construal in sentence comprehension depends on linguistically encoded event structure. *Cognition* **2025**, *254*, 105975.
61. Kim, Y. Convolutional Neural Networks for Sentence Classification. In Proceedings of the EMNLP, Doha, Qatar, 25–29 October 2014; pp. 1746–1751.
62. Nguyen, A.; Srijeet, C.; Sven, W.; Leo, S.; Martin, M.; Bjoern, E. Time matters: Time-aware lstms for predictive business process monitoring. In Proceedings of the Process Mining Workshops: ICPM 2020 International Workshops, Padua, Italy, 5–8 October 2020; pp. 112–123.
63. Graves, A.; Navdeep, J.; Abdel-rahman, M. Hybrid speech recognition with deep bidirectional LSTM. In Proceedings of the 2013 IEEE Workshop on Automatic Speech Recognition and Understanding, Olomouc, Czech Republic, 8–12 December 2013; pp. 273–278.
64. Bahdanau, D. Neural machine translation by jointly learning to align and translate. *arXiv* **2014**, arXiv:1409.0473.
65. Raffel, C.; Noam, S.; Adam, R.; Katherine, L.; Sharan, N.; Michael, M.; Yanqi, Z.; Wei, L.; Peter, J.L. Exploring the limits of transfer learning with a unified text-to-text transformer. *J. Mach. Learn. Res.* **2020**, *21*, 1–67.
66. Luo, M.; Xue, B.; Niu, B. A comprehensive survey for automatic text summarization: Techniques, approaches and perspectives. *Neurocomputing* **2024**, *603*, 128280. [CrossRef]
67. Huang, Y.; Bai, X.; Liu, Q.; Peng, H.; Yang, Q.; Wang, J. Sentence-level sentiment classification based on multi-attention bidirectional gated spiking neural P systems. *Appl. Soft Comput.* **2024**, *152*, 111231. [CrossRef]
68. Liu, Y. Roberta: A robustly optimized bert pretraining approach. *arXiv* **2019**, arXiv:1907.11692 364.
69. Röttger, P.; Janet, B.P. Temporal adaptation of BERT and performance on downstream document classification: Insights from social media. *arXiv* **2021**, arXiv:2104.08116.
70. Yao, Z.; Yifan, S.; Weicong, D.; Nikhil, R.; Hui, X. Dynamic word embeddings for evolving semantic discovery. In Proceedings of the Eleventh ACM International Conference on Web Search and Data Mining, Los Angeles, CA, USA, 5–9 February 2018; pp. 673–681.
71. Bamler, R.; Stephan, M. Dynamic word embeddings. In Proceedings of the International Conference on Machine Learning, Sydney, Australia, 6–11 August 2017; pp. 380–389.
72. Turner, R.E. An introduction to transformers. *arXiv* **2023**, arXiv:2304.10557.
73. Reimers, N. Sentence-BERT: Sentence Embeddings using Siamese BERT-Networks. *arXiv* **2019**, arXiv:1908.10084.
74. Gururangan, S.; Ana, M.; Swabha, S.; Kyle, L.; Iz, B.; Doug, D.; Noah, A.S. Don't stop pretraining: Adapt language models to domains and tasks. *arXiv* **2020**, arXiv:2004.10964.
75. Wang, J.; Jatowt, A.; Yoshikawa, M.; Cai, Y. BiTimeBERT: Extending Pre-Trained Language Representations with Bi-Temporal Information. In Proceedings of the 46th International ACM SIGIR Conference on Research and Development in Information Retrieval (SIGIR '23), Taipei, Taiwan, 23–27 July 2023.
76. Gong, H.; Suma, B.; Pramod, V. Enriching word embeddings with temporal and spatial information. *arXiv* **2020**, arXiv:2010.00761.
77. Tang, X.; Yi, Z.; Danushka, B. Learning dynamic contextualised word embeddings via template-based temporal adaptation. *arXiv* **2023**, arXiv:2208.10734.
78. Go, A.; Richa, B.; Lei, H. *Twitter Sentiment Classification Using Distant Supervision*; S224N Project Report; Stanford University: Stanford, CA, USA, 2009; Volume 1.
79. Diederik, P.K.; Jimmy, B. Adam: A Method for Stochastic Optimization. *arXiv* **2014**, arXiv:1412.6980.
80. Nagumothu, D.; Peter, W.E.; Bahadorreza, O.; Reda, B.M. Linked Data Triples Enhance Document Relevance Classification. *Appl. Sci.* **2021**, *11*, 6636. [CrossRef]

information

MDPI

Article

Perspective-Based Microblog Summarization †

Chih-Yuan Li [1,*], **Soon Ae Chun** [2,*] **and James Geller** [3]

[1] Computer Science Program, Department of Management and Information Technology, St. Francis College, Brooklyn, NY 11201, USA
[2] Information Systems and Informatics Program, College of Staten Island, City University of New York, New York, NY 10314, USA
[3] Department of Data Science, New Jersey Institute of Technology, Newark, NJ 07102, USA; james.geller@njit.edu
* Correspondence: cli@sfc.edu (C.-Y.L.); soon.chun@csi.cuny.edu (S.A.C.)
† This article is a revised and expanded version of a paper entitled Multiple View Summarization Framework for Social Media, which was presented at FLAIRS-36: 36th International Florida Artificial Intelligence Research Society Conference, Clearwater Beach, Fl, USA, 14–17 May 2023.

Abstract: Social media allows people to express and share a variety of experiences, opinions, beliefs, interpretations, or viewpoints on a single topic. Summarizing a collection of social media posts (microblogs) on one topic may be challenging and can result in an incoherent summary due to multiple perspectives from different users. We introduce a novel approach to microblog summarization, the Multiple-View Summarization Framework (MVSF), designed to efficiently generate multiple summaries from the same social media dataset depending on chosen perspectives and deliver personalized and fine-grained summaries. The MVSF leverages component-of-perspective computing, which can recognize the perspectives expressed in microblogs, such as sentiments, political orientations, or unreliable opinions (fake news). The perspective computing can filter social media data to summarize them according to specific user-selected perspectives. For the summarization methods, our framework implements three extractive summarization methods: Entity-based, Social Signal-based, and Triple-based. We conduct comparative evaluations of MVSF summarizations against state-of-the-art summarization models, including BertSum, SBert, T5, and Bart-Large-CNN, by using a gold-standard BBC news dataset and Rouge scores. Furthermore, we utilize a dataset of 18,047 tweets about COVID-19 vaccines to demonstrate the applications of MVSF. Our contributions include the innovative approach of using user perspectives in summarization methods as a unified framework, capable of generating multiple summaries that reflect different perspectives, in contrast to prior approaches of generating one-size-fits-all summaries for one dataset. The practical implication of MVSF is that it offers users diverse perspectives from social media data. Our prototype web application is also implemented using ChatGPT to show the feasibility of our approach.

Keywords: Multiple-View Summarization; COVID-19 vaccine tweet summarization; microblog summarization; social feature-focused summarization; entity-based summarization; distance-centered summarization

1. Introduction

In 2023, Twitter (now "X") had around 450 million monthly active users, and 6000 tweets were posted on average every second [1,2]. When extrapolating the counts, there are 360,000 tweets posted every minute, 518 million tweets a day, and 189 billion tweets a year. Due to the large volume, it is infeasible for humans to review all relevant tweets if they want to investigate a certain topic or event. A number of machine learning and deep learning algorithms for social media summarization have been proposed, e.g., [3–10] using reinforcement learning along with attention layers and a deep learning-based model, based on using a recurrent neural network (RNN) and a Bi-LSTM (bidirectional long short-term memory) network. Others have used K-means clustering, and a Twitter Online Word Graph Summarizer for a set of related tweets.

However, social media posts can talk about the same topic or content but reflect different user perspectives, such as negative or positive sentiments, emotions, biases, political views, distorted opinions (so-called fake vs. real news), etc. Thus, providing a single summary of social posts may be misleading or not represent different perspectives of users, such as their emotions, opinions, and attitudes toward content.

In addition, despite the potential that social media platforms have to democratize access to diverse social and political perspectives [11], the meteoric rise of these platforms has further fueled the creation and ossification of "echo chambers" [12–14]. Echo chambers are environments where the opinions, political leanings, or beliefs of users about a topic are reinforced due to repetitive interactions with peers with similar tendencies and attitudes [15]. The echo chamber effect usually arises concerning controversial topics, e.g., gun control, vaccinations, abortion, school prayer, etc. [15]. Spending time in communities of like-minded individuals not only raises individuals' exposure to pro-attitudinal messages but also decreases their exposure to counter-attitudinal information. This leads to the issue of echo chambers, where citizens do not see or hear different topics or ideas. This issue limits their capacity to reach common ground on political issues [16].

A number of methods have been researched to overcome echo chamber effects, for example, increasing the diversity of information sources [17]. Receiving information from different sources will help users better understand a topic from different perspectives, develop more in-depth opinions, and make better decisions [18,19]. However, users often restrict their personal exposure to only like-minded individuals or platforms [20]. According to [21], the primary cause of polarization and extremism is the loss of truly public platforms/forums. Therefore, recreating a new environment where people are more likely to encounter opposing perspectives and opinions could counteract this tendency, as having trust in "the media" is likely to increase confidence in seeking and receiving information from diverse sources [22]. It is plausible that the greater a person's media trust, the more likely they are to explore different views from these sources, thereby becoming less susceptible to echo chambers [20].

In this paper, we propose the *perspective-based summarization approach* to address the challenges posed by the overwhelming volume and echo chamber issues in social media. This approach is designed to summarize and compare the subtle nuances between different viewpoints, e.g., the dissemination and reception of fake and real news. By employing this comparative analysis, our framework aims to highlight the discrepancies between authentic and manipulated content, which are important in our big data world. The proposed summarization framework, the Multiple-*View Summarization Framework (MVSF)*, generates different perspective-based summaries from the same set of social media posts based on user-centered views, opinions, or emotions by flexibly combining those to match different desired perspectives expressed in social media posts. Providing summaries with different perspectives of the same social media content may help individuals understand the contrary opinions and diverse perspectives on the same topic.

In our MVSF, a "perspective" refers to a distinct viewpoint or angle interpreted or analyzed. This encompasses a range of elements such as sentiments (both positive and negative), political views, and the authenticity of information (distinguishing between fake and real news). The framework identifies these perspectives through a combination of natural language-processing techniques, including sentiment analysis, and fact-checking models. Each perspective is integrated into the summarization process by filtering content that aligns with the user-defined perspectives. This approach allows for personalized summaries that reflect user interests. Therefore, the approach enhances the relevance and engagement of the summary.

With the MVSF, users can obtain summaries reflecting specific interests and viewpoints expressed on social media. For example, a positive summary on Pfizer vaccines in COVID-19 related posts, or a summary with only negative sentiment regarding the same vaccines. These can help policymakers realize how the vaccines are perceived by different groups. The summaries can also allow further content analyses, to gain an understanding of positivity vs. negativity or who the influential figures are in these different perspective summaries.

To address the issue of echo chambers, our MVSF is designed to expose users to a broad range of viewpoints. By aggregating and summarizing diverse perspectives, the MVSF ensures that summaries include viewpoints from across the ideological spectrum. Thus, the MVSF provides users with a balanced view of the topic. This is achieved through algorithms including identifying and quantifying sentiment biases and diversifying other perspectives included in the summaries. Such an approach enriches the user's understanding as well as fosters more informed discussions. The integration of diverse perspectives is important in combating the polarization and misleading information prevalent on social media.

Our MVSF has two components, summarization and perspective computing components. The summarization component summarizes the social media data using one of three summarization methods: entity-based (EbS), triple-based (TbS), and social signal-based (SbS). The perspectives computing component is intended to detect specific user perspectives expressed in social media posts, such as negative sentiments. The combination of two components enables a wide range of fine-grained summaries, such as a summary of only negative sentiment views whose focus is the topical entity. As another example, it can combine a triple-based summary with positive sentiments.

The summarization methods use the semantic analysis of each social media post in the form of *<subject, predicate, object>* triples [23]. We show that the semantic analysis-based summarization outperforms state-of-the-art extractive and abstractive summarization models from the literature, as indicated by better Rouge F-1 scores [24] of around 14%.

The perspectives can be combined to convey summaries with multiple perspectives. For example, when a journalist writes a story on social media posts on a politician's policy, they can focus on one perspective, such as a summary of negative opinions about the policy, or a summary of user posts that are negative *and* fake opinions about the policy. In this way they can convey summaries that contain one or multiple perspectives. By employing MVSF's various methods and perspectives, users can navigate widespread social media content, gaining deeper insights and enhancing information extraction. The framework's adaptability underpins its significance in providing comprehensive and user-centric summarization solutions. The work in this paper contributes in the following ways:

1. We have developed three summarization methods for social media posts: entity-based, triple-based and social feature-focused summarization.
2. We have developed the Multiple-View Summarization Framework (MVSF), which is capable of generating summaries based on multiple *perspectives*, such as political orientations, sentiments, or fake opinions, combining them with any of the three summarization methods. The framework provides greater flexibility of choosing summarization methods as well as combining different perspectives, generating fine-grained and personalized summaries tailored to the end-user's preferences.
3. Theoretical implications are the integration of multiple perspectives and extractive methods within a unified framework, in contrast to one-size-fits-all summarization.

This enables comprehensive information extraction from social media content and constitutes an extended paradigm for summarization research. On the practical side, we have developed summarization algorithms for the MVSF to allow users to tailor summaries to their needs.

4. Through extensive performance experiments, we compared the summaries generated by our entity-based and triple-based methods, both independently and in conjunction. When benchmarking the results against prominent summarization models from the literature, such as Bart-large-CNN 5, Text-To-Text-Transfer-Transformer (T5) [25], BertSum [26], and SBert [27], our summaries achieved a performance improvement of 14% in terms of Rouge scores.
5. Our framework was effectively applied to an X/Twitter dataset of 18,047 COVID-19 vaccine-related tweets, demonstrating the flexibility of presenting different summaries of this topic.
6. We leverage our MVSF to present a comparative analysis of fake and real news, to enhance its utility in discerning truth and misleading information distributed across social media platforms, which is increasingly important in today's world.
7. We have developed a user-friendly web prototype (http://ai4sg.njit.edu/ai4sg/Summarize, accessed on 1 September 2023) leveraging the power of OpenAI ChatGPT (text-davinci-003) [28] for text summarization. This application works within the MVSF, while not suffering from the hardware-intensive resource use of our algorithms. The application allows users to input text and customize summarization preferences based on the MVSF's methods and perspectives, serving as an accessible perspective-based summarization tool.

These contributions collectively underscore the significance and practical applicability of the MVSF in addressing the challenges of efficiently summarizing extensive social media content, while catering to diverse user needs. Our summarization approach is novel as opposed to a one-size-fits-all summarization algorithm.

This paper is organized as follows. In Section 2, we provide a synopsis of related work. We present our summarization framework in Section 3. In Sections 4–6, we detail each component of the MVSF, including knowledge triple extraction and processing, perspective analysis and detection models, and our summarization methods, respectively. The evaluation of our summarization method is presented in Section 7. We present the application of our summarization framework to a large dataset, the results, and our findings in Section 8. We compare and present the findings of summaries of fake news and real news in Section 9. In Section 10, we present our web prototype application, which leverages the power of OpenAI ChatGPT [28] to perform text summarization within our MVSF. Section 11 contain the Discussion, Conclusions, and Future Work.

2. Related Work

In this section, we introduce general social media summarization approaches along with different applications, as well as echo chamber effects on social media.

2.1. General Summarization Approaches

Researchers distinguish between abstractive and extractive summarization methods [29]. Abstractive summarization generates a summary by capturing the prominent ideas of the source text. The summaries contain new sentences that do not exist in the original text. The abstractive summarization methods in the literature include Bart-large-CNN [30], Text-To-Text Transfer Transformer (T5) [25], FactSumm [31], FAIRSEQ [32], PEGASUS [33], XNLG [34], ChatGPT [28], GPT-2 [35], etc. On the other hand, extractive summarization selects a subset of the sentences that are able to best represent the original document. The extractive summarization models in the literature include BertSum [26], SBert [27], RankSum [36], HAHSum [37], NeRoBERTa [38], DebateSum [39], MemSum [40], Gensim [41], etc. While abstractive summarization is beneficial in situations where high rates of compression are required [42], microblogs are the antithesis to long documents. Abstractive systems usually perform best in limited domains, since they require outside knowledge sources. The abstractive approaches might not work so well with microblog posts, as they are unstructured and diverse in their subject matter. Furthermore, the summaries generated by abstractive models usually face factual inconsistency problems [43]. There is also a huge inference speed gap between the abstractive and extractive summarization methods [44]. Extractive techniques are known to scale better in highly diverse domains [45]. It is also beneficial to work with tweet fragments rather than entire tweets [46]. Therefore, in this paper, we work on extractive summarization along with this tweet post fragment approach.

To specifically summarize large content, the LOCOST model [47] is introduced as a recent advancement in handling extensive texts. LOCOST is designed to manage documents exceeding 600,000 tokens. This capability makes it suitable for summarizing entire books or comprehensive documents longer than the typical input length limitations of models.

Joshi et al. [36] proposed a method based on LDA (Latent Dirichlet Allocation) [48] topic modeling and word embedding [49] for the extractive summarization of single documents. Their work, based on CNN Daily Mail datasets [50], achieved a state-of-the-art performance at the time. LDA and word embedding are effective when sentences are coherent; however, when sentences are not coherent, which often happens in social media, extra contextual information is needed [51]. One of our summary methods identifies contextual information and bridges this gap.

Our MVSF integrates user perspectives such as sentiments, political biases, and authenticity, which these traditional models often overlook. This personalized approach allows the MVSF to produce summaries that reflect the nuanced views of social media users, enhancing the relevance and comprehensiveness of summaries.

2.2. Microblogging Summarization Approaches

Many algorithms for social media summarization have been proposed, e.g., [3–10]. Yadav et al. [3] used reinforcement learning along with attention layers and a deep learning-based model, by using a recurrent neural network (RNN) and a Bi-LSTM (bidirectional long short-term memory) network for summarization tasks. Their work achieved a state-of-the-art performance when evaluated with BLEU and ROUGE scores. Modhe et al. [4] made use of TF-IDF encoding to obtain both single-post and multi-post summaries of Twitter activity, based on the rankings of words and a user-defined threshold. Geng et al. [5] proposed a microblogging cluster stream (Microblog Cluster Vectors) and a ranking method, by using K-means clustering [52] and query-lexical-rank to generate a query-focused extractive summaries of Twitter data. Dutta et al. [7] performed the first systematic analysis of approaches towards summarizing Twitter posts during disasters. They found that different algorithms applied to the same input yielded summaries with significant differences, which is superficially similar to our results. However, we achieve different summaries *intentionally* and as part of a unified framework. Olariu et al. [8] introduced a Twitter Online Word Graph Summarizer, which was the first online abstractive summarization algorithm for tweets. In their experiments, for a set of related tweets, they generated a high-quality summary. However, when applied to unrelated tweets, the initially generated summary lacked meaning. This happened because event-related signals (in their case, bigrams) stand out when analyzing similar tweets. As a better solution, they built a word graph from trigrams to solve the issue.

Sharifi et al. [9] chose an extractive approach, since it is more appropriate for the structure and diversity of microblogs. They first applied Phrase Reinforcement [53], which generates summaries by looking for the most commonly occurring phrases. Then, they processed the results of the Phrase Reinforcement approach with their proposed Hybrid TF-IDF algorithm, where the TF (term frequency) component is computed from the entire collection of posts, whereas the IDF (inverse document frequency) component is computed from a single post. Inouye [10] proposed a clustering-based algorithm and a threshold-based Hybrid TF-IDF algorithm. The first step performs clustering by combining the K-Means++ algorithm [54] with the bisecting K-means algorithm [52] to cluster posts into subtopics, and then each cluster [55] is summarized individually. The second step uses the modified Hybrid TF-IDF summarization algorithm [9], so that it can produce multiple post summaries. Originally [9], the algorithm only selected the best summarizing topic sentence, but later, Inouye [10] modified the method to select the top four highest weighted posts.

2.3. Other Summarization Approaches

Gunaratna et al. [56] selected related features among entities while maintaining the diversity and saliency of features within entity sets. By selecting (i) inter-entity facts that are similar and (ii) intra-entity facts that are important and diverse, the approach summarizes facts about a collection of entities. Entity summarization has been categorized into extractive and non-extractive methods. Among extractive methods, the summarization is further divided into single-entity and multi-entity categories. For single-entity categories, Gunaratna et al. [57] proposed FACES to incorporate diversity in summarization. For multi-entity categories, FACES-E [58] uses focus term detection and aligns these focus terms with ontology classes and entities present in knowledge graphs [59]. FACES-E showed the usefulness of type-computed literals in creating comprehensive entity summaries. For the non-extractive categories, REMES was introduced [56] to maximize the relatedness of facts between entity summaries and importance and diversity of facts within each entity summary. One of our methods performs entity-based summarization.

Amplayo et al. [60] presented an abstractive opinion summarization model that generates input aspect-based summaries for a set of product or hotel reviews. Their aspect-based summaries use transformer models, and for the generation of summaries, users need to input a specific aspect code or keywords. Li and Chaturvedi [61] presented the Rationale-based Opinion Summarization system (RATION), which generates summaries of user reviews by extracting the representative opinions as well as one or more corresponding rationales as supporting details for opinions. They use transformer-based opinion extraction and Gibbs sampling to sample a user-specified number of sentences as rationales by approximating this joint probability distribution.

Unlike most of the approaches in the literature, which focus on a single aspect, our framework focuses on separate or combined perspectives expressed in social media posts, and it ranks the extracted information based on respective criteria to obtain fine-grained extractive summaries.

3. Multiple-View Summarization Framework

The MVSF is designed to address the complex nature of social media data, allowing for customized summaries based on multiple perspectives. In the MVSF, the terms "views" and "perspectives" are used synonymously to describe the different angles of content analyzed and summarized. Figure 1 illustrates the general architecture of our framework, which consists of the following components:

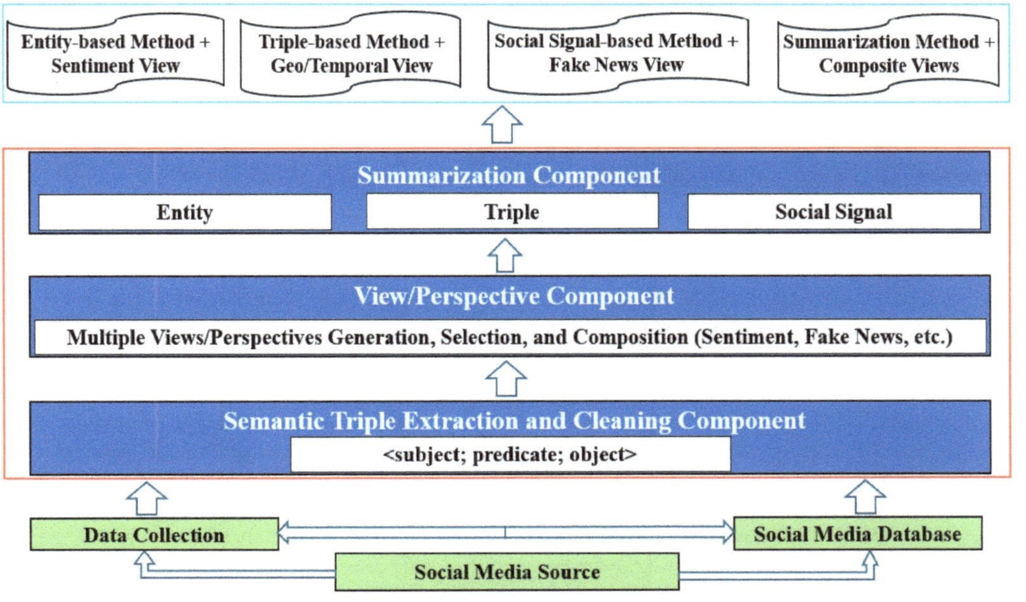

Figure 1. Multiple-View Summarization Framework (MVSF).

Data Cleaning and Semantic Triple Extraction Component: The collected data undergo standard preprocessing, which includes the removal of non-ASCII characters, redundant spaces, and URLs. To capture the essence of social media posts, such as described events or activities [62], we implement semantic triple extraction. This process extracts <subject (S), predicate (P), object (O)> triples from each post. This structures the content by identifying key entities, actions, and relationships. These triples serve as the foundational data, and they are used to generate perspective-based summaries.

View/Perspective Component: This component analyzes the extracted text to identify multiple perspectives, such as sentiments or potential misinformation. Using advanced NLP techniques, it performs sentiment analysis to gauge public emotions and perceptions [63] and applies fake news detection algorithms to identify and flag potentially misleading information. The outcomes of this component are tagged with metadata, which categorize each post according to detected sentiments, biases, or factual accuracies.

Summarization Component: After perspectives are identified, the summarization component processes the enriched data to generate summaries. It employs three distinct methods: *Entity-based (EbS) summarization* focuses on key individuals, organizations, or locations mentioned in the content. *Triple-based (TbS) summarization* groups posts related to specific events or statements. *Social signal-based (SbS) summarization* leverages social media interaction metrics such as follower counts and retweets to highlight content with popularity. This component integrates the perspectives from the previous component that match the user-defined criteria for summarization and reflect the desired perspectives.

Output Component: The final summaries are generated based on the users' selection of summarization methods and perspectives. Users have the flexibility to select from simple sentiment-driven summaries to complex composites that merge various perspectives, such as combining sentiment analysis results with fake news detection. For instance, a user might request a summary focusing solely on negative sentiments about a policy, or a combined summary addressing both negative sentiments and misleading information.

Users can utilize the MVSF to generate multiple summaries from the same social media posts, reflecting different perspectives or a combination of perspectives. This offers multiple views of the discourse surrounding a topic. This capability also highlights the framework's adaptability and the potential to enhance decision-making processes in various analytical scenarios.

4. Semantic Triple Extraction and Cleaning

The *Semantic Triple Extraction and Cleaning Component* (in Figure 1) is a fundamental and important component in the MVSF. Semantic triple extraction transforms unstructured social media text data into structured knowledge triple representations. Social media content usually contains irregular sentence structures, hashtags, URLs, and abbreviations [64]. Thus, it is challenging to perform analysis directly on social media content. To address this issue, we extract meaningful insights by capturing relationships between key entities in the form of *<subject; predicate; object> (SPO) triples*. The triples capture events and actions expressed in the text, and they serve as the foundation for generating diverse summaries in our framework. For instance, a post like *"The CDC announced new vaccine guidelines"* would yield a triple *<CDC; announced; new vaccine guidelines>*, which showcases the key information in the sentence.

We used the Stanford Open Information Extraction (Open IE) model [65] to extract the triples. The model first breaks down sentences into shorter logical clauses. The model then identifies the <subject; predicate; object> for each clause, and it predicts whether an edge in the dependency graph should form a new independent clause [66]. For example, the sentence "The CDC and WHO announced that vaccines will be distributed by March" can be broken into two triples: <CDC; announced; vaccines distribution> and <WHO; announced; vaccines distribution>. Each extracted triple is then converted to lowercase to achieve a unified text representation, ensuring consistency across the dataset.

5. Perspective Analytics for Summarization

The Perspective Detection Component in our framework is used to identify different perspectives expressed in each social media post. Perspective detection can use different methods. For instance, a negative perspective can be identified by sentiment analysis, and a fake content view can be detected by a machine learning model to classify a post as fake or not. These perspectives are essential to provide unique insights, such as a summary with a particular sentiment, or a summary of a particular political bias. In this section, we provide the perspective analysis approaches we used. With the proliferation of AI models available with APIs, our framework assumes that the appropriate perspective detection model is available to be utilized for the summarization.

5.1. Sentiment Perspective Analysis

To distinguish between different emotions expressed from the text, we performed sentiment analysis using the Stanford Sentiment Analyzer [67]. The choice of that analyzer was based on human evaluation [63] among the Stanford Sentiment Analyzer, VADER [68], and TextBlob [69]. In addition, based on the literature, the Stanford Sentiment Analyzer has the best accuracy among the three, at 80.7% [67], while VADER has an accuracy of 76.8% and TextBlob has an 68.8% accuracy [70]. Thus, we chose the Stanford Sentiment Analyzer.

The Stanford Sentiment Analyzer labels each input phrase either as *"(Very) Negative"*, *"Neutral"*, or *"(Very) Positive"*. With sentiment labels, we can choose to focus only on the *<S, P, O>* triples with a specific sentiment, e.g., triples expressing negative sentiments towards mandatory COVID-19 policies.

5.2. Fake News or Real News Perspectives

Social media platforms have been flooded with misinformation, so-called fake news, which confuses citizens, causes conflicts, and drowns out authentic information [71]. Therefore, summarizing large fake news item sets can produce a readable summary. This will enable concerned users to counteract the spread of misleading information. That can be achieved by training a machine learning model to classify social media posts and collecting those labeled as fake news.

5.3. Political Bias Perspectives

To systematically discern the political biases in a posted text, we can employ a machine learning model trained on data labeled either as 'left' or 'right' political viewpoints or biases. This binary classification approach, inspired by the approaches in [72], allows the detection of political orientations within content. By integrating this method into our framework, we enhance the granularity of our summarization, ensuring a comprehensive representation of the political landscape within the data.

In addition to these, one can consider contextual perspectives such as temporal or location-specific perspectives for summaries of the public reactions to restrictive government COVID-19 policies, e.g., right after their introduction and again after six months. This could allow us to evaluate the acceptance or rejection of a policy, which would allow government agencies to fine-tune the policy. This view can be derived from the time stamps of social media posts. A summary based on specific locations, or at different administrative levels, such as country, state/province, etc., can capture location-specific perspectives [73], which can be compared with summaries from different locations to determine differences.

5.4. Composition of Multiple Perspectives

Our MVSF allows users to select and combine multiple perspectives to generate customized summaries. This showcases its adaptability to the complex nature of social media data.

User-Driven Composition: In the MVSF, the composition of perspectives is entirely user-driven, allowing for a customized summarization. Users can choose and combine different perspectives to generate a summary, i.e., a *fake news-only view with negative sentiments*. The *composite perspectives* are achieved through aggregation:

$$c_v = compose\ (v_1, v_2, \ldots, v_n)$$

where n is the number of perspectives and v_i is a single view or perspective. This process emphasizes the framework's flexibility, as it accommodates a combination of perspectives without internal weighting or prioritization.

Handling of Perspective Outputs: Each perspective operates independently and analyzes social media content to produce insights from its specific viewpoint. When combined, the outputs are presented collectively, without automated conflict resolution. This allows users to view and interpret composite summaries that incorporate diverse analytical angles, therefore enabling informed decision-making.

Independence from Summarization Methods: While perspectives are combinable, the summarization methods within the MVSF operate independently. For example, the entity-based method focuses on key entities, the triple-based method organizes data around specific events, and the social signal-based method highlights content with significant social engagement. These methods are designed to address different aspects of the data, and they are used individually or combined with selected perspectives.

6. Microblogging Summarization Methods

6.1. Entity-Based Summarization (EbS)

In this method (EbS), the entities define the primary subjects and objects for obtaining summaries. Unlike in other research where the user provides the entities of interest (e.g., "Joe Biden"), we discover the most prominent entities mentioned in the social media posts by first finding the triple verbs that contain the same semantic events, and by identifying the salient entities in triple subjects and objects.

1. **Identify the same events in triples using WordNet:** Important entities can appear in semantically similar events that are expressed by different predicates/actions. Thus, we need to identify predicates expressing similar or identical meanings with different verbs, such as "offer", "pass", and "transfer", or different forms of the same verb, e.g., "provide", and "provided", all of which express a similar meaning of "giving something to someone". Groups of semantically similar verbs can be subsumed by one *root verb*, using the appropriate synset from WordNet [74]. A synset is a set of one or more synonyms. WordNet organizes synset into generalization hierarchies. A verb in a hierarchy that is the most general is referred to as a root verb. For triples using verbs expressing similar/identical meanings with different words or tense forms, we replaced the verbs as follows. To disambiguate the meaning of a predicate and find the closest synsets, we compared two methods and used a human evaluator to determine the better one. The first method is the Lesk algorithm [75]. Given a verb and the triple where it occurs, Lesk returns a synset that represents its context meaning. However, Lesk often failed at finding the correct synset. Among a set of 80 randomly picked triples, only 37 verb synsets were correctly identified, according to the human evaluator. The second method was that we selected "v.01" (primary meaning returned by WordNet) as the verb synset. Although this is a simple approach, it produced a better result (78/80) according to the human review. Therefore, we used the "v.01" meaning for each verb to find the root synset. For each synset vx.v.01 of the verb vx, we followed its hypernym (superclass) chain upward until reaching its root synset. We identified the frequent events by selecting triples whose root verbs occur more often than a threshold θ. Given a triple set TS = $\{ts_1, ts_2, \ldots\}$ where $ts_i = <s, p, o>$, find $ts_j = <s, root(p), o>$. We select triples that have frequent root verbs root(p), i.e., frequency(root(p)) > θ. We present the program to identify the synset hierarchy in Table 1, and an example synset hierarchy in Figure 2, where all verbs are summarized by "give."
2. **Identifying Salient Entities:** The second task in this method is to identify important entities to focus on. Each triple includes two entities, a subject and an object. As noted, this method is based on the entities (subject/object) that occur most often in the triple sets. To identify the frequencies of *meaningful* words, for each entity, we removed numbers, stop words, and words with fewer than three characters and performed lemmatization. If a preprocessed entity became an empty string, we removed its triple from the triple set. If a preprocessed subject consisted of more than two words, we removed all words except for the last two (which are likely to contain "most of the meaning").

Each subject is labeled with its frequency in the triple set. If there is more than one word in a subject, we obtain the subject score based on the word with the higher frequency. For example, if there are 77 mentions of "COVID" and 100 of "vaccine," the subject score of "COVID" is 77, of "vaccine" is 100, and of "COVID vaccine" is also 100. The same method is applied to objects for computing object scores. The preprocessing and score calculation of triple entities is shown in Table 2.

Table 1. Pseudo code to identify the root verb synset by using WordNet.

```
highestSuperclass = []

for v in tripleVerb:
    currentV = v + '.v.01' # we apply v.01 (most natural) synset to all triple verbs

    while (len(wordNet.synset(currentV).hypernyms()) == 1):
        currentV = wordNet.synset(currentV).hypernyms()[0] # replace current synset
with its direct superclass synset

    highestSuperclass.append(currentV)
```

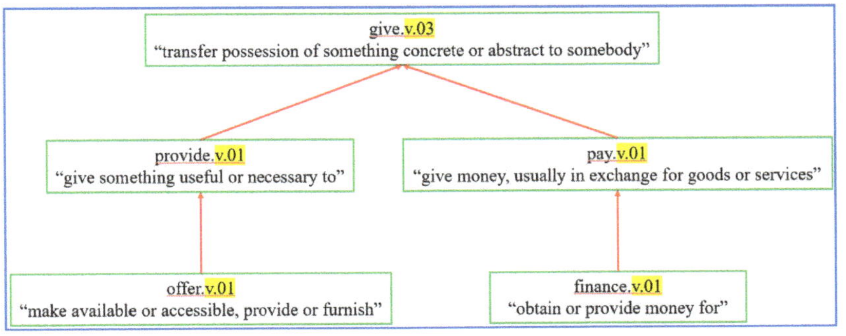

Figure 2. Example of synset for all verbs related to the root "give".

Table 2. Pseudo code for identifying top entities.

```
def preprocess (entity):
    entity = remove stop words and numbers from entity
    if (length of entity) < three characters:
        entity = empty string
    entity = lemmatization (entity)
    return entity

subjectWord = [ ] // a list that collects all words in triple subjects
objectWord = [ ] // a list that collects all words in triple objects

for each subject s, object o, triple t in triple set ST: // (s, o) is the (subject, object) of triple t in ST,
    s = preprocess (s)
    o = preprocess (o)
    if s == empty string or o == empty string:
        remove t from ST

      s = s.split(" ")[:-2] // if s have more than two words, remove all except for the last two words

    subjectWord.extend (s.split(" "))
    objectWord.extend (o.split(" "))

for each word x in subjectWord:
    label x with an integer score of its frequency in subjectWord

for each word y in objectWord:
    label y with an integer score of its frequency in objectWord

for each subject s, object o, triple t in triple set ST: // (s, o) is the (subject, object) of triple t in ST
    Subject Score of s = highest score of the word in s
    Object Score of o = highest score of the word in o
```

To identify the summary with the best accuracy, we experimented with assigning different weights (α) to the subjects and $(1 - \alpha)$ to the objects. We select the top-scoring $\mathbf{m_E}$ triples and the corresponding original sentences. The parameter $\mathbf{m_E}$ controls the length of the summary.

$$\boldsymbol{TripleScore} = \alpha \times (Subject\ Score) + (1 - \alpha) \times (Object\ Score) \tag{1}$$

where $\alpha \in [0.0, 1.0]$.

6.2. Triple-Based Summarization (TbS)

In this method, we capture the important contextual meaning (the whole statement instead of entities) by using triple sentence representations. To create sentence representations, we use BERT [76] sentence embeddings. BERT reads the entire input sequence at one time, which allows BERT to learn the contextual information of each word based on its neighboring (left and right) words. We used an autoencoder [77] to learn a 32-dimensional vector representation to ensure that we achieved a lower-dimensional representation [51]. Instead of focusing on specific entities, we produced a summary based on important statement information in triples. We used the distance measures to the centroid of the triple vectors to select the salient triples for summarization.

For each triple t, its vector representation v is

$$v_t = [v_{t1}, v_{t2}, v_{t3}, \ldots, v_{t32}] \tag{2}$$

The centroid vector v_c of all triple vectors is calculated:

$$v_c = \frac{1}{n}\left(\sum\nolimits_{t=1}^{n} v_t\right) = [v_{c1}, v_{c2}, v_{c3}, \ldots, v_{c32}] \tag{3}$$

where n is the triple count.

The Euclidean distance d from a triple t to the centroid c is

$$d_{tc} = sqrt\left(\sum\nolimits_{i=1}^{32} (v_{ti} - v_{ci})^2\right) \tag{4}$$

We selected triples with the shortest distances to the centroid c as top summarization triples. The original sentences corresponding to the selected triples were recovered to form the summary.

6.3. Social Signal-Based Summarization (SbS)

In this method (SbS), we exploit the social signals (i.e., a tweet's retweet count, and its poster's follower count) to identify the salience of tweets. A tweet is more important if it is (1) posted by a user with many followers, and (2) retweeted many times, according to [62], where the salience score of a tweet is the multiplication of the retweet count, user follower count, and readability. Our goal is to identify summaries with social prominence on social media. Thus, we modified the formula and defined the salience score of a tweet:

$$\boldsymbol{SalienceScore} = \begin{cases} follower + retweet \times 707, & follower > 0 \\ 0, & follower = 0 \end{cases} \tag{5}$$

where 707 is the average number of followers of a Twitter user [9]. When a post is retweeted, there will be on average 707 people who will see it. We rank triples based on the scores of their original tweets and select the $\mathbf{m_{SF}}$ top-scoring triples. The corresponding original sentences of the triples are selected to form the summary.

We also acknowledge the limitations of using social signals such as followers and retweets to represent the importance of content. A study "The Million Tweets Fallacy" [78] indicates that engagement metrics such as retweets and followers may not always correlate with the content relevance or quality. These metrics often reflect visibility more than value, leading to potential biases in assessment [79].

7. Evaluation of Microblogging Summarization Methods

To evaluate our summarization approaches, we compared them with extractive and abstractive summarization models from the literature. The extractive models are BertSum [26] and SBert [27], variants of BERT used in our method (TbS). Abstractive summarization models are Bart-large-CNN [30] and T5 [25], which according to [63], generate better summaries than TextRank [41] and GPT-2 [35].

In our pursuit of evaluation, we encountered a challenge: we could not locate a social media dataset with a gold-standard summary. Nonetheless, we could perform an evaluation by leveraging an alternative dataset—the BBC news items set [80]. Originally designed as a benchmark for machine learning research, we repurposed this dataset to evaluate the performance of summaries in our specific task. The dataset comprises 2225 documents, each sourced from the BBC news website, spanning five diverse topical areas, namely business, entertainment, sport, politics, and technology. This dataset serves as a trustworthy foundation for our assessment of summary generation by providing human extractive summaries for each document.

We selected 20 news documents from the business category. We summarized them using our entity-based (EbS) and triple-based summarization (TbS) approaches, with and without a sentiment perspective (S). Because this dataset lacks social signals, we excluded the SbS method from our evaluation process. Each of our generated summaries adheres to a consistent length of approximately 300 words, aligning with both our chosen methods and the published results.

We employed Rouge scores [24] to quantify performance, which measure the overlap between the generated summaries and human-crafted reference summaries. The evaluation focused on 1-g (unigram overlap), 2-g (bigram overlap), and LCS (Longest Common Subsequence). Our summaries based on an entity and triple with or without a perspective outperformed those by the benchmarking models (Table 3). The triple-based summaries with a sentiment view, i.e., TbS + S performed best with the highest score for 1-g and LCS, while the method TbS performed best for 2-g. This result shows that our summaries are more consistent with the gold-standard summaries than existing models. The inclusion of *negative* sentiment analysis in our TbS model helps with focusing on emotionally charged and impactful phrases, which are often important in news reporting. This focus aligns the summaries more closely with the nuances and tones of the source documents.

Table 3. Rouge scores of summarization models.

Rouge Score	1-g	2-g	LCS
Method (EbS), $\alpha = 0.7$	0.465	0.310	0.444
Method (TbS)	0.557	**0.427**	0.551
TbS with View (S)	**0.58**	0.416	**0.572**
EbS with View(S), $\alpha = 0.7$	0.459	0.299	0.433
BertSum	0.406	0.174	0.394
SBert	0.444	0.152	0.428
bart-large-cnn	0.402	0.150	0.394
T5	0.304	0.104	0.304

8. Application of MVSF to COVID-19 Vaccine Tweets

This section demonstrates the application of the MVSF to a dataset of COVID-19 vaccine-related tweets. Our objective is to illustrate how the MVSF captures diverse perspectives, providing insights on critical health issues like vaccinations.

8.1. Data

We used 18,047 tweets [81] about widely used COVID-19 vaccines worldwide, Pfizer/BioNTech, Sinopharm, Sinovac, Moderna, AstraZeneca (AZ), Covaxin, and Sputnik V. The tweets were posted between December 2020 and November 2021 *(this dataset may not fully represent all tweets concerning COVID-19 vaccines)*. The dataset's columns include tweet ID, tweet content text, timestamp, user ID, retweets, likes, hashtags, and user locations.

8.2. Preprocessing

We removed non-ASCII codes, URLs, and redundant spaces. We assigned each post an integer *post index*. We then performed sentence tokenization [82] to split posts into sentences, because a tweet may contain multiple sentences. It is beneficial to work with post fragments (sentences) rather than entire posts [46]. We assigned to each sentence an integer *sentence index*, as this sentence tokenization is used for tracing back to the corresponding original sentences from the selected knowledge triples. Table 4 shows an example of a post with two sentences. We obtained 28,242 sentences from 18,047 posts.

Table 4. A post with two sentences in the dataset.

Post Index	Post Text	Sentence Index	Sentence Text
484	A shipment of Sputnik V vaccine arrived in Vietnam. The handover ceremony took place at Noi Bai airport.	0	A shipment of Sputnik V vaccine arrived in Vietnam.
		1	The handover ceremony took place at Noi Bai airport.

8.3. Triple Extraction and Cleaning Process

Using triple extraction methods (OpenIE) [65] from the Stanford CoreNLP package [83], we extracted 101,432 triples and linked them to their sentences and their original posts.

We further filtered out triples with auxiliary verbs that carry little meaning, e.g., "be" or "have". This reduced the triples from 101,432 to 67,049. In a number of cases, there were overlapping triples from the same sentence, but of different lengths. For triples from the same post and sentence, and using the same verb, we eliminated all but the one triple, retaining the most information (words). The final 16,270 triples were used as the input for each summarization method.

8.4. Experimental Results

This subsection presents the application of the MVSF to COVID-19 vaccine-related tweets, demonstrating how the framework generates summaries from social media data. The following subsections illustrate the summarization results both with and without integrating specific perspectives, showcasing the flexibility of the MVSF in capturing different viewpoints.

8.4.1. Summaries Without Perspectives

We use all the 16,270 triples (from Section 8.3) to generate a summary for each method (EbS, TbS, SbS), respectively.

Figure 3 shows a knowledge graph [59] of the summary triples using entity-based summarization (EbS). We used Gephi, Version 0.10.1 [84] as our visualization tool. The size of each node is proportional to its degree, with a size range (10, 20) implemented in Gephi. The edge color expresses the sentiment expressed by the triple, with red (=1) for "Negative", yellow (=2) for "Neutral", and green (=3) for "Positive." The edge thickness represents the triple's rank. The thicker an edge, the higher its rank in the summary set (i.e., higher (triple/salience) score, or shorter distance to the centroid). For the summary generation, we selected the top-scoring $\mathbf{m_e}$ triples from the triple set, with their corresponding original sentences, such that the total number of words in the summary was approximately 300. The details of the summary triples are in Table 5. The corresponding original sentences of the selected summary triples are in Table 6 in temporal order of the original tweets.

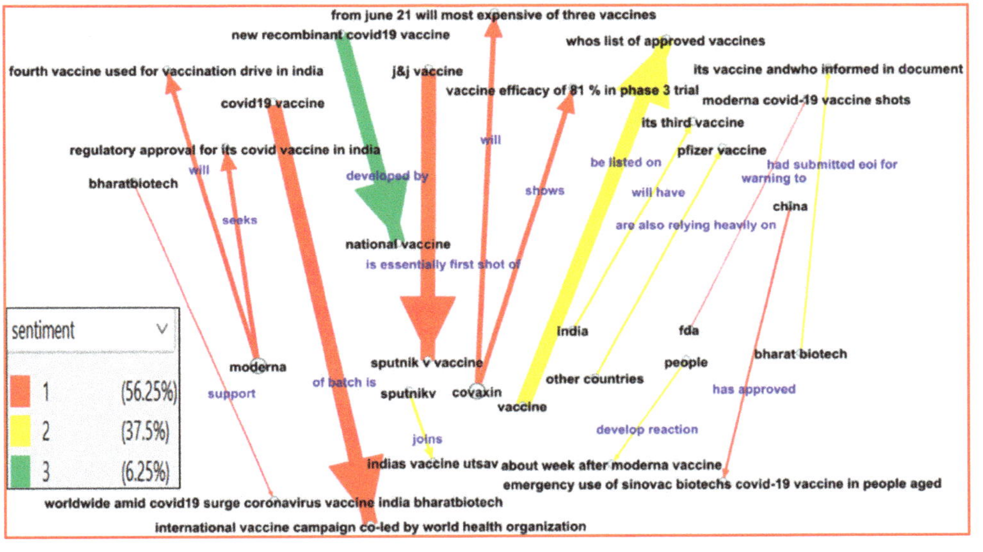

Figure 3. Knowledge graph visualization of summary triples of view (EbS).

Table 5. Summary triples of method (EbS), their triple scores, sentiments, and vaccines, in rank order.

Triples	Sentiment	Triple Score	Vaccine
j&j vaccine is essentially first shot of sputnik v vaccine	1	1646	sputnik
new recombinant COVID-19 vaccine developed by national vaccine	3	1646	sinopharm
COVID-19 vaccine of batch is international vaccine campaign co-led by world health organization	1	1646	sinopharm
vaccine be listed on whos list of approved vaccines	2	1646	covaxin
covaxin shows vaccine efficacy of 81% in phase 3 trial	1	1153.2	covaxin
covaxin will from june 21 will most expensive of three vaccines	1	1153.2	covaxin
moderna seeks regulatory approval for its COVID vaccine in india	1	1129.4	moderna
moderna will fourth vaccine used for vaccination drive in india	1	1129.4	moderna
sputnikv joins indias vaccine utsav	2	1028.6	sputnik
india will have its third vaccine	2	1002.7	sputnik

Table 5. *Cont.*

Triples	Sentiment	Triple Score	Vaccine
china has approved emergency use of sinovac biotech's COVID-19 vaccine in people aged	1	999.2	sinovac
other countries are also relying heavily on pfizer vaccine	2	994.3	pfizer
bharat biotech had submitted eoi for its vaccine andwho informed in document	2	978.2	covaxin
people develop reaction about week after moderna vaccine	2	974	moderna
bharatbiotech support worldwide amid COVID-19 surge coronavirus vaccine india bharatbiotech	1	962.8	covaxin
fda warning to moderna COVID-19 vaccine shots	1	939.7	moderna pfizer

Table 6. Entity-based summary (in temporal order).

Other countries in the Middle East, including Saudi Arabia, Qatar, Kuwait, and Oman, are also relying heavily on the Pfizer vaccine, developed by the US company PfizerVaccine. This is also another validation of Sputnik V pioneering technology as J&J vaccine is essentially a first shot of Sputnik V vaccine (Ad 26—human adenoviral vector 26). Covaxin shows vaccine efficacy of 81% in phase 3 trial. About a week after the Moderna vaccine, some people develop a reaction. The new recombinant COVID-19 vaccine, developed by the National Vaccine &Serum Institute, a R&D center of Sinopharms bioscience subsidiary the China National Biotec Group, got approval from the National Medical Products Administration on April 9. SputnikV joins Indias vaccine utsav. Once DCGI approves SputnikV, India will have its third vaccine after Covishield and Covaxin. Bharat Biotech announces COVAXIN capacity expansion to support vaccination campaigns in India & worldwide amid COVID-19 surge Coronavirus Vaccine India BharatBiotech. The first batch of COVID-19 vaccine supplied by Chinas Sinopharm to COVAX, the international vaccine campaign co-led by the World Health Organization, was officially rolled off the production line on Tuesday. China has approved emergency use of Sinovac Biotechs COVID-19 vaccine in people aged between 3 and 17. From June 21 Covaxin will be the most expensive of the three vaccines which will be available in private hospitals. The vaccine is yet to be listed on the WHOs list of approved vaccines. FDA adds warning to Pfizer, Moderna COVID-19 vaccine shots to indicate the rare risk of heart inflammation after its use Pfizer Moderna COVID-19 Vaccine US FDA. Moderna seeks regulatory approval for its COVID vaccine in India. Moderna will be the fourth vaccine to be used for the vaccination drive in India. Bharat Biotech had submitted EOI (Expression of Interest) on April 19 for its vaccine and WHO informed in a document that the assessment status for Covaxin is ongoing

Similarly, for methods (TbS) and (SbS), the goal was again to retain the $\mathbf{m_t}$ and $\mathbf{m_S}$ top-ranking triples that could be used to generate readable summaries of a length of approximately 300 words, respectively. Visualizations of method (TbS), method (SbS), and the selected triples are omitted, but we show the summary results in Tables 7 and 8, respectively.

As shown in the summary results, three different methods yielded completely different triple sets, and therefore produced different summaries. Each corresponding original sentence in our summaries is unique, meaning there is no common sentence among our methods. As desired, this shows that the three methods generate different results, focusing either on entities, triple statements, or social features.

Table 7. Triple-based summarization (in temporal order).

The Food and Drug Administration on Wednesday gave its approval for Sinovac use on the elderly after considering the recommendation of the experts and the current situation of high COVID-19 transmission and limited available vaccines. The Moderna COVID-19 jab is now available at 11 of 38 vaccination centres in Singapore, while the rest are offering the PfizerBioNTech product. The CoronaVac vaccine developed by the Chinese biopharmaceutical company Sinovac Biotech has effectively reduced the risk of COVID-19 symptoms in medical workers by 94%, showed a study by the Indonesian Health Ministry. On the picture Deepak Sapra, Global Head of Custom Pharma Services at drreddys Laboratories is getting a shot of Sputnik V in Hyderabad. unless you had J&J) Moderna Pfizer As of today154,199,664 Americans are fully vaccinated, according to the CDC! The first validation samples taken from the produced batch will be shipped to the Gamaleya Center for quality control. The WorldHealthOrganizations pandemic programme plans to ship 100 million doses of the Sinovac and Sinopharm COVID-19 shots by the end of next month, mostly to Africa and Asia, in its first delivery of Chinese vaccines, a WHO document shows. Your queries answered Deadline for booster dose for Sinopharm announced, if you received vaccine over six months PfizerBiontech COVID-19. USA doesnt recognise Indian vaccine COVAXIN PM Modi has gone to US and possibly he took doses of COVAXIN Whether all Indians are allowed to visit US with COVAXIN doses? days after PM Modis vaccine diplomatic push, Covaxin gets WHO nod; propaganda by anti-govt voices falls flat. Sinopharm approved for travel to UK From Nov. 22, the Sinopharm vaccine will be added to the UKs list of approved vaccines for inbound travel, benefiting more fully vaccinated people travelling from to Sinopharm is the leading vaccine administered in SriLanka.

Table 8. Social signal-based summary (in temporal order).

India gets third coronavirus vaccine as Russias SputnikV is cleared for emergency use COVIDVaccine. Dr Reddys administers first dose of the SputnikV vaccine in Hyderabad. The second consignment of SputnikV arrives in Hyderabad, Telangana. There are plans to introduce single-dose vaccine soon in India-Sputnik Lite. JustIn. A PIL has been moved in Delhi High Court challenging Centres notification which has accorded permission to conduct the Phase II/III clinical trial of Covaxin in the age group 2 to 18 years to its manufacturer Bharat Biotech. Bharat Biotech Amid Travel Fears NDTVs Shonakshi Chakravarty reports Read more. Malta firm wants to supply 60 million doses of SputnikV to Haryana, state government writes to Centre. Assam Covaxin Shortage Grows Into Crisis, Some Miss Second Dose Deadline. Made in India Covaxin is the third costliest vaccine globally. The appointment slots can be booked via CoWIN portal, according to the hospital administration. Delhis Madhukar Rainbow Childrens Hospital will start administering Russias COVID-19 vaccine SputnikV, tentatively by June 20. children are undergoing trials for the vaccine across the country. After Covaxin, Zydus Cadilla is the second indigenously produced vaccine for children currently under trial in India. This will also benefit people travelling abroad for education, jobs or business. I request for your kind intervention so that an early approval is received for Covaxin from WHO. Moderna approved for emergency use, 4th vaccine okayed by India COVID-19 Vaccine. Accept Covishield, Covaxin Or Face Mandatory Quarantine, India Tells EU. COVAXIN effective against DeltaPlus variant of COVID-19, says Indian Council of Medical Research study. DCGI gives nod to study mixing of Covishield and Covaxin. Subject Expert Committee recommends Covaxin for kids aged between 2 and 18 NDTVs Meher Pandey reports. Covaxin Cleared By UK, Relief For Indian Students And Tourists.

8.4.2. Summarization with Sentiment Perspectives

In this subsection, we generate summaries based on negative and positive sentiments (view S) as follows. The different view compositions show the power of our framework, which provides summaries with different perspectives from a single post set. We performed sentiment analysis on each of the data items using the Stanford Sentiment Analyzer [67]. This analyzer uses a fine-grained analysis based on both words and labeled phrasal parse trees to train a Recursive Neural Tensor Network (RNTN) model. The RNTN model computed the sentiments based on (1) the sentiment values of each word, and (2) the sentiment of the parse-tree structure composed of the sentiment values of words and sub-phrases. Each post will be labeled either as negative, very negative, neutral, positive, or very positive.

We present the (1) S view + social signal-based method (S + SbS) (Table 9), (2) S view + triple-based method (S + TbS) (Table 10), and (3) S view + entity-based method (S + EbS) (Table 11). We compare summaries with negative sentiments and positive sentiments. Among the 16,270 triples from Section 8.3, there are 926 positive or very positive triples and

5423 negative or very negative triples, which we combined into just two classes, positive and negative.

In the (S + SbS) summary (Table 9), the positive-sentiment summary focuses on encouraging vaccine developments, such as approval and distribution progress, and highlights Sinovac and Sinopharm in countries like China and regions supportive of these vaccines. The negative-sentiment summary addresses topics about vaccine discussions, primarily focusing on Sputnik V and Covaxin. The negative-sentiment summary expresses concern about vaccine supply issues, regulatory actions, and logistical challenges. For example, the summary discusses high-profile reports and decisions around emergency authorizations, delays, and shortages, reflecting a current public concern. This difference between sentiment-based summaries reveals that negative views emphasize obstacles and critical opinions, while positive views celebrate advancements and achievements in vaccine deployment.

Table 9. Composite view summaries of positive (left) and negative (right) views with SbS.

The 80-year-old three-time World Cup champion called it an unforgettable day and urged discipline to preserve lives. The COVID-19 vaccine developed by Chinas Sinopharm has been approved for emergency use in the Maldives, the Maldives Food and Drug Administration announced at a press conference Monday afternoon. Azerbaijan on Thursday received a batch of Sinovacs COVID-19 vaccines that it directly purchased from China. Serbian President Aleksandar Vucic avucic received a dose of Chinese Sinopharm COVID-19 vaccine on Tuesday, encouraging more people to join the immunization, according to local media. Delhi high court refuses to stay Covaxin trial among children (RichaBanka reports) I request for your kind intervention so that an early approval is received for Covaxin from WHO The U.S. drug regulator on Friday added a warning to the literature that accompanies Moderna and Pfizer-BioNTech COVID-19 vaccine shots, indicating the rare risk of heart inflammation after its use. Accept Covishield, Covaxin Or Face Mandatory Quarantine, India Tells EU The Union health ministry cited a large-scale, real-life study conducted by the ICMR and said that two doses of COVIDvaccines, irrespective of Covishield and Covaxin, were successful to extend 95% protection from death. Covaxin receives certificate of Good Manufacturing Practice from Hungarian authorities. ICMR study Watch for details We want to ensure equitable access of the vaccine to every Indian citizen, and the expansion of Covaxin production facilities by Bharat Biotech will take us closer to this goal. Dr Sumit Ray, Holy Family Hospital, on delay in Covaxin approval by the World Health Organisation. Bharat Biotechs Covaxin, the vaccine against COVID-19, has received the recommendation of a SEC for use in children between the ages 2 to 18 PM NarendraModi jis visionary decision to back our scientists & researchers is now a perfect Diwali Gift from to the World. This video fits the last almost 2 years into 2 min.	Covaxin 81% Effective, Works Against UK Variant, Claims Bharat Biotech Read more: India to get its third COVID-19 vaccine; Subject Expert Committee recommends Russias SputnikV vaccine for Emergency Use Authorisation NDTVs Sukirti Dwivedi with the latest updates India gets third coronavirus vaccine as Russias SputnikV is cleared for emergency use COVIDVaccine Dr Reddys administers first dose of the SputnikV vaccine in Hyderabad There are plans to introduce single-dose vaccine soon in India-Sputnik Lite. JustIn. A PIL has been moved in Delhi High Court challenging Centres notification which has accorded permission to conduct the Phase II/III clinical trial of Covaxin in the age group 2 to 18 years to its manufacturer Bharat Biotech Malta firm wants to supply 60 million doses of SputnikV to Haryana, state government writes to Centre. After Malta Firm Offers 6 Crore Sputnik Jabs, Haryana Seeks Centres Help NDTVs Mohammad Ghazali reports SputnikV Assam Covaxin Shortage Grows Into Crisis, Some Miss Second Dose Deadline VaccinationDrive COVIDVaccine Assam Covaxin Shortage Grows Into Crisis, Some Miss Second Dose Deadline Made in India Covaxin is the third costliest vaccine globally Delhis Madhukar Rainbow Childrens Hospital will start administering Russias COVID-19 vaccine SputnikV, tentatively by June 20. The appointment slots can be booked via CoWIN portal, according to the hospital administration. After Covaxin, Zydus Cadilla is the second indigenously produced vaccine for children currently under trial in India. Moderna approved for emergency use, 4th vaccine okayed by India COVID-19Vaccine COVAXIN effective against DeltaPlus variant of COVID-19, says Indian Council of Medical Research study Union Minister of Health and Family Welfare, Mansukh Mandaviya launches the first commercial batch of Bharat Biotechs Covaxin manufactured in Gujarats Ankleshwar. Subject Expert Committee recommends Covaxin for kids aged between 2 and 18 NDTVs Meher Pandey reports The Lancet peer-review confirms the efficacy analysis of Bharat Biotechs Covaxin. As per phase-three clinical trials data, Covaxin demonstrates 77.8% efficacy against symptomatic COVID-19.

Table 10. Composite view summaries of positive (left) and negative (right) views with TbS.

Only the PfizerBioNtech vaccine has received EUL approval, so far. Sinovac vaccine works on UK, South African variants—Brazil institute SLnews SriLanka Sinovac US President JoeBiden announces that US will share US-authorized vaccines doses of Pfizer, Moderna and Johnson & Johnson, as they become available, with the rest of the world. India cant afford to fail because India will lead the fightback by mass production of vaccines for the developing world. Haryana government has received an expression of interest from an international pharmaceutical company headquartered in Malta to provide up to 60 million doses of SputnikV vaccine. NSTworld Israel will receive in return the doses that Pfizer is to send to the PalestinianAuthority. The state has reportedly received a fresh consignment of 693,210 doses of Covaxin and Covishield vaccines from the central govt. Top sources tell CNNnews18 Authorisation of Covaxin internationally will happen by end of Aug WHO rep Meeting Health Minister today COVID-19 Vaccination Drive to Resume In Mumbai From Tomorrow As BMC Receives Fresh Stock of Vaccines COVID-19 COVID-19 A new study by the Centers for Disease Control and Prevention revealed that Modernas COVID-19 vaccine is somewhat more effective than those offered by Pfizer and Johnson & Johnsons vaccines Following the arrival of more Sinopharm vaccines to SriLanka, doses will be released to the North to begin administering on the 20–29 age group. Subject Expert Committee has given a recommendation to Official sources to ANI NSTnation Individuals who have been vaccinated with Sinovac are allowed to perform the umrah in SaudiArabia on the condition that they get a third dose of the vaccine. The last-minute addition comes less than one week before the US launches its new travel system, granting entry to travellers who have received a vaccine that has been approved by the FDA or WHO US Covaxin Travel	But with the general pool eligible for the vaccine expanding 2.5 times to 345 million from April 1, Covaxin will need to step up to service demand MintPlainFacts rashmi kundu As you can see, the UK could conceivably restrict AstraZeneca vaccine to older people and lean on Moderna, Novavax and $JNJ jabs for the younger crowd. My COVID vaccine volunteering experience Vaccinated GetVaccinated COVID Moderna Pfizer Maryland Central Govt recently gave BharatBiotech permission to test Covaxin on 2–18 yrs age group, marking it an important milestone in vaccine development. Indonesia aims to be regional vaccine making hub. According to researchers data, both Pfizer and Moderna vaccines remain highly effective at preventing severe illness and death, even amid surging DeltaVariant cases and a booster is not required. The U.S. Food and Drug Administration on Thursday authorized a booster dose of COVID-19 vaccines from Pfizer Inc and Moderna Inc for people with compromised immune systems US FDA COVID-19 COVID-19Vaccine CDCgov now recommends COVID-19 BoosterShots for all eligible Americans. Egypt to roll out a vaccination campaign with local produced additional 5 million doses Chinese Sinovac vaccines in Sept, Consultant to Minister of Health and Population for Research Noha Assem stated in a TV interview. Your queries answered Deadline for booster dose for Sinopharm announced, if you received vaccine over six months PfizerBiontech COVID-19 BharatBiotech releases a statement after the Subject Expert Committee on COVID-19 recommends the emergency use of Covaxin for children 2–18 years of age If the US FDA signs off on Modernas booster, the U.S. Centers for Disease Control and Prevention will make specific recommendations on who should get the shots. Indias COVID-19 vaccine Covaxin will be added to the UK governments approved list of vaccines for international travellers from 22 November. BharatBiotechs Covaxin now recognized by HongKong COVID-19

For S + TbS (Table 10), the summaries illustrate how different sentiments shape the narrative around vaccine distribution and public policy. The negative-sentiment summary focuses on policies and actions by governments and institutions about vaccine regulations, meanwhile highlighting delays, supply chain issues, and public dissatisfaction.

On the other hand, the positive-sentiment summary emphasizes successful implementation and the progress of vaccine campaigns. This difference captures the essence of sentiment-specific discussions by focusing on the relational dynamics between policies and outcomes.

In the (S + EbS) summaries (Table 11), the negative-sentiment summary focuses on discussions about the supply, import, and regulatory approval of vaccines, particularly during the early stages of vaccine availability in Asian countries like China, India, and Thailand. The summary reflects a sensitivity to logistical and regulatory challenges, which aligns with prevalent concerns at that time.

Table 11. Composite view summaries of positive (left) and negative (right) views with EbS.

Peru launched the first stage of its national vaccination campaign against the novel coronavirus disease on Feb. 9, using vaccines developed by Chinese company Sinopharm to immunize healthcare workers. Argentina on Sunday approved the COVID-19 vaccine developed by Chinese company Sinopharm for emergency use. PM narendramodi was administered a shot of Covaxin, the vaccine fully Researched & Developed as well as Made in India by BharatBiotech to mark phase 2 of COVID-19 inoculation campaign. CDSCO expert panel recommends moving Covaxin out of clinical trial mode Covaxin The COVID-19 vaccine developed by Chinas Sinopharm has been approved for emergency use in the Maldives, the Maldives Food and Drug Administration announced at a press conference Monday afternoon. Mauritius arms itself with COVAXIN, Indias indigenously developed vaccine, in its fight against COVID-19 India stands strong with Mauritius in these tough times Consignment to arrive tomorrow A time-tested and enduring partnership IndiaMauritius The new recombinant COVID-19 vaccine, developed by the National Vaccine &Serum Institute, a R&D center of Sinopharms bioscience subsidiary the China National Biotec Group, got approval from the National Medical Products Administration on Apr. 9. Covaxin, developed completely in India, can effectively neutralise multiple variants of SARS-CoV-2. Covaxin BharatBiotech developed Covaxin effective on B.1.617 and B.1.1.7, emerging variants first identified in India and UK respectively—Study by Journal Clinical Infectious Diseases PIBKochi COVIDNewsByMIB PIB India KirenRijiju BSF India CISFHQrs CRPF sector GMSRailway A study published in NEJM found that a 3rd dose of the Moderna or Pfizer vaccine significantly improved its effectiveness in organ transplant recipients who take immunosuppressant drugs. Moderna created the COVID-19 vaccine using the sequence data released on the Internet. New study shows which vaccine offers the best protection against COVID-19. As of now, Covaxin seems to be the most effective & long lasting vaccine against the Delta variant!	Cambodian Prime Minister Hun Sen emphasized that Chinas vaccines are very safe and effective, and China will become the safest and most stable supplier of COVID-19 vaccines. Sinopharms COVID-19 vaccines have just arrived in this first EU country approving the Chinese vaccine. Bharat Biotech confirms deal with Brazil to supply 20 million doses of COVAXIN vaccine CoronavirusVaccine BharatBiotech Covaxin Brazil India on Friday began using SputnikV in its battle against COVID-19 with the first dose of the vaccine from Russia administered in Hyderabad. BharatBiotech announces the quick ramp-up of additional manufacturing capacities for COVAXIN at Chiron Behring Vaccines, Ankleshwar, Gujarat, a wholly-owned subsidiary of Bharat Biotech. The Kings sister had just approved on Thursday the Sinopharm COVID-19 vaccine be imported into Thailand as alternative vaccines to help the nation cope with the pandemic. Centre recently gave BharatBiotech permission to test Covaxin on 2–18 yrs age group, marking it an important milestone in vaccine development. The first batch of COVID-19 vaccine supplied by Chinas Sinopharm to COVAX, the international vaccine campaign co-led by the World Health Organization, was officially rolled off the production line on Tuesday. From June 21 Covaxin will be the most expensive of the three vaccines which will be available in private hospitals. The Drugs Controller General of India allowed Indian pharmaceutical Cipla to import the Moderna mRNA COVID-19 vaccine on Tuesday making it the fourth vaccine that will be available to Indians. Moderna approved for emergency use, 4th vaccine okayed by India COVID-19Vaccine Global coronavirus death toll surpasses 468 million COVID-19 vaccines Moderna COVIDVictoria An expert committee recommended a booster dose of Modernas anti-COVID vaccine in the United States for certain at-risk groups, a month after making a similar decision for the Pfizer shot. He further added that 96 countries have recognized both Covishield and Covaxin vaccines.

In contrast, the positive-sentiment summary brings attention to the successful development and effectiveness of vaccines, highlighting endorsements by various entities and governments. The positive perspective often includes mentions of vaccine approvals and endorsements, which underscore trust in vaccine efficiency and safety.

The divergent sentiments in the summaries show how different viewpoints can provide diverse insights into public opinions on vaccines. In a polarized environment, some users might prefer summaries that reflect positive perspectives, like those from the governing party, while others may focus on the critical opinions that are prevalent in opposition narratives.

The generated summaries provide insights into public sentiments surrounding COVID-19 vaccines, as well as illustrate both the challenges and achievements in vaccine deployment. They underscore the utility of MVSF in public health communication by offering a quick, precise, and concise synthesis of diverse public opinions.

This case study serves as a practical demonstration of the MVSF's applicability, and it is illustrative rather than evaluative. It highlights the framework's utility in real-world events, offering a quick, perspective-driven summarization. This allows for informed decision-making in public health.

9. Summary with Perspective of Fake and Real News

In this section, the perspective analysis utilizes fake news detection models to distinguish between fake and real news. This section presents a comparative summary derived from a dataset consisting of 4080 fake news items and 4480 real news items, collected by Patwa et al. [85].

This dataset, which discerns between fake and real news related to COVID-19, was compiled through automated and manual verification methods. For real news, the collection process involved using the Twitter API to gather tweets from verified accounts, including those of the WHO, CDC, and other governmental and medical organizations. Each item underwent a review process by human annotators to ensure its factual accuracy and relevance to COVID-19. The data items focus on updates about vaccine progress, governmental responses, and pandemic statistics. For fake news, verification involved scrutinizing social media posts, news articles, and public declarations previously identified as misleading. Fact-checking platforms such as Politifact, Snopes, and Boomlive were utilized to validate the falsehoods. This involved comparing content from various platforms, including Facebook and Twitter, against original documents or reliable sources to ascertain their falsity.

Additionally, researchers evaluated the dataset using several machine learning models, including Decision Trees, Logistic Regression, Support Vector Machines (SVMs), and Gradient Boosting Trees. The SVM model exhibited a superior performance, achieving an accuracy of 93.46%, precision of 93.48%, recall of 93.46%, and F1-score of 93.46% on the validation data. The dataset comprises two columns, text and label, illustrated in Table 12.

Table 12. Examples of fake news and real news.

Text	Label
Politically Correct Woman (Almost) Uses Pandemic as Excuse Not to Reuse Plastic Bag #coronavirus #nashville	Fake
COVID Act Now found "on average each person in Illinois with COVID-19 is infecting 1.11 other people. Data shows that the infection growth rate has declined over time this factors in the stay-at-home order and other restrictions put in place".	Real

We leverage our MVSF to explore how different summarization perspectives capture the nuances to differentiate deceptive content from factual reporting. This section aims to enhance the MVSF's support for informed decision-making. We present the experimental result of summaries generated by method (EbS) and method (TbS), and we perform a comparative analysis of fake news and real news.

9.1. Entity-Based (EbS) Summarization of Fake News and Real News

In this subsection, we generate entity-based summaries of fake news and real news (Table 13). The real news summaries focus on systemic and governmental responses to public health situations. The prominent entities *(state, case, death)*, supported by the consistent triple score of 311.5 (Table 14), show a high level of organization and relevance to public policy and safety. All except for one sentiment are neutral, which reflects the factual and informative nature of the content.

Table 13. Summary sentences of real news (left) and fake news (right) using method (EbS).

Indias Total Recoveries continue to rise cross 32.5 lakh today 5 States contribute 60% of total cases 62% of active cases and 70% of total fatality reported in India. Sometimes when a state reports a large number of deaths it is because they caught up on a reporting backlog of deaths that occurred long in the past. Few states reported race and ethnicity data at the beginning of April. State decides testing rates of COVID-19 for pvt labs. Several states are seeing outbreaks of in meat and poultry processing facilities. To protect the lives of healthcare workers every state needs stay-at-home orders NOW. Together with the States of Uttar Pradesh and Tamil Nadu these 5 states contribute nearly 60% of the total active cases. Some states also provide data about the date of death. These States are seeing a sudden surge in the number of cases and some of them are also reporting high mortality. States contribute 60% of total cases 62% of cases and 70% of total repo. Seven states saw the number of people hospitalized rise by 100 or more today. States reported relatively low numbers of tests (713 k) and cases (60 k). Six states saw a rise of over 100 (FL CA TX AZ GA TN) in their number of currently hospitalized COVID-19 patients. But looking at other metrics today the state reported record hospitalizations and its 2nd-highest number of deaths. Reporting gaps in 20+ states leave the public in dark about the true scope of the pandemic.	A photo shows people infected with coronavirus lying on the sidewalk in China. Video shows coronavirus patients and doctors. Video of a doctor fainted on the floor after getting infected with coronavirus. A long message attributed to Bill Gates, the Microsoft billionaire, encouraging people to reflect positively on their lives during the coronavirus outbreak has been shared in multiple countries. Chinese government is burning down people infected with Coronavirus. People shouting Allahu Akbar in Europe after the coronavirus outbreak. A video shows a man spitting inside food packets during the coronavirus crisis. Video shows Canadian PMs wife talking about the effects of Coronavirus. People in Ukraine will be forcibly vaccinated against the new coronavirus. Video shows people behaving abnormally in China due to coronavirus. A video shows a new hospital for coronavirus patients in China. People in Ahmedabad tested positive, 11 in Kanpur and 8 in Lucknow after being exposed to vegetable infected with coronavirus. Video shows Bodies of dead novel coronavirus patients in Russia. Video showing dead bodies of coronavirus patients in Osmania Hospitals mortuary. Video shows coronavirus infected notes scattered on Indore streets being sanitized. People who have never died before are now dying from coronavirus. A video showing a police officer briefing about cases being registered against the WhatsApp group admins is shared in the context of coronavirus lockdown. People died in Hyderabad due to the 2019 coronavirus. People infected with coronavirus die in the street while doctors travel through the infection zone.

Table 14. Summary triples of real news using method (EbS).

Triple	Sentiment	Triple Score
5 states contribute 60% of total cases	2	311.5
state reports large number of deaths	2	311.5
few states reported race data at beginning of april	2	311.5
state decides testing rates of COVID-19 for pvt labs	2	311.5
several states are seeing outbreaks of in meat	2	311.5
state protect lives of healthcare workers	2	311.5
5 states together contribute nearly 60% of total active cases	1	311.5
states also provide data about date of death	2	311.5
states are seeing sudden surge in number of cases	2	311.5
states contribute 60% of total cases	2	311.5
seven states saw number of people	2	311.5
states reported relatively low numbers of tests	2	311.5
six states saw rise of over 100 in their number of currently hospitalized COVID-19 patients	2	311.5
state reported its 2nd-highest number of deaths	2	311.5
states leave public in dark about true scope of pandemic	2	311.5

On the other hand, fake news summaries are characterized based on the depiction of vivid scenarios such as people infected, or dramatic events related to health crises. The prominent entities (*people, video, coronavirus*) include individual actions and localized events, with triple scores ranging slightly and generally lower than real news. The sentiments expressed are slightly more negative than for real news, which suggests a focus on shocking the audience and emotional content (Table 15). These summaries appear to capture attention through specific and impactful imagery and scenarios.

Table 15. Summary triples of fake news using method (EbS).

Triple	Sentiment	Triple Score
people infected with coronavirus	2	175.3
video shows coronavirus patients	2	177.4
video fainted getting with coronavirus	2	177.4
people reflect positively on their lives during coronavirus outbreak	2	175.3
people infected with coronavirus	2	175.3
people shouting allahu akbar after coronavirus outbreak	1	175.3
video shows man spitting inside food packets during coronavirus crisis	1	177.4
video shows canadian pms wife talking about effects of coronavirus	2	177.4
people will forcibly vaccinated against new coronavirus	2	175.3
people behaving abnormally due to coronavirus	2	175.3
video shows new hospital for coronavirus patients in china	2	177.4
people tested exposed to vegetable infected with coronavirus	2	175.3
video shows bodies of dead novel coronavirus patients in russia	1	177.4
video showing dead bodies of coronavirus patients in osmania hospitals mortuary	2	177.4
video shows coronavirus infected notes scattered on indore streets	1	177.4
people are now dying from coronavirus	2	175.3
video is shared in context of coronavirus lockdown	2	177.4
people died due to 2019 coronavirus	2	175.3
people infected with coronavirus	2	175.3

The emphasized entities are apparently different between real news and fake news. Real news summaries focus on systemic and governmental responses, such as *state actions*, *case updates*, and *death tolls*. This shows a consistent approach in how these entities are scored, which is supported by the consistent triple score, 311.5. This consistency indicates a standardized method of evaluating the importance of each entity, reinforcing the objective and factual nature of real news reporting.

On the other hand, fake news summaries frequently spotlight individual, localized, or even imaginary events, including *specific people*, *dramatic videos*, or *aspects related to the coronavirus*. The triple scores in fake news vary between 175.3 and 177.4, reflecting a broader and less consistent approach to how information is valued. This variability suggests that the evaluation of entities in fake news does not adhere to a consistent standard. This inconsistency is likely due to the more sensational and diverse topics covered, aiming to engage the audience on an emotional level.

Understanding these differences in entity focus and scoring consistency is important. It helps to discern the reliability and intent of news content. This also helps emphasize the need for critical evaluation when consuming news, especially in distinguishing between credible and misleading information. Our analytical results underscore the importance of recognizing the veracity in news summaries.

9.2. Triple-Based (TbS) Summarization of Fake News and Real News

Table 16 shows triple-based summaries of fake news and real news. The real news summary illustrates a focus on responses to current public health challenges. The summary discusses *strategies, initiatives*, and *evaluations surrounding public health crises.* The results reflect a systematic approach to managing and communicating about public health events. By choosing triples with shortest distances from the centroid, we ensure that the topics discussed are central to the ongoing discourse and aligned with the core issues. Therefore, the experimental result suggests a focused and relevant dissemination of information.

Table 16. Summary sentences of real news (left) and fake news (right) using method (TbS).

Principal Secretary to Prime Minister directed all concerned for an evidence based preparedness of all aspects of with active participation of Districts and States for effectiveness. Testing a drug will determine if an emergency use authorization comes by late fall. Our estimates suggest that once an effective vaccine has been distributed and international travel and trade is fully restored the economic gains will far outweigh the $38 billion investment required for the ACT Accelerator-Dr Tedros. India records more than 82,000 Recoveries for two days in a row Total Recoveries cross 40 lakhs Recovered Cases exceed Active Cases by more than 30 lakhs. CDCMMWR finds steps that help slow the spread of may also reduce if widely practiced. We continue to call on all countries to use every tool at their disposal to suppress transmission & save lives until & after we have a vaccine- Dr Tedros. The recovered cases (4,674,987) exceed active cases (966,382) by more than 37 lakh. In Cross River our Rapid Response Team (R) is supporting the state to enhance sample collection and ramp-up testing for The also worked with the Cross River State Response Team to assess a 100-bed isolation facility in Adiabo Tinapa. County health depts (Maricopa AZ and St. Louis, MO) provide both states most reliable source of LTC data. High level teams will assist State/UT in strengthening public health measures for surveillance drharshvardhan Prakash Javdekar PIB India. Across 50 states and DC we've tracked 16,502 total 1953 positive 13,419 negative and 1130 pending.	During Lock down period such a fantastic natural scenery on sea beach near Chandrabhaga, Puri to Konark marine drive road. BBC replaces Nichola Sturgeons pandemic briefings with Jamie Oliver making curried haggis. Spain corrected their number of deaths by COVID-19 from more than 26,000 to 2000. Nigel Farage to teach kids climate change denial for balance in BBC Lockdown Learning Scheme. Canadas COVID alert app warns that the virus is calling from inside the house. Well, I think climate change still counts as the worst federal response to a national emergency in our nations history. Are you struggling to work out the difference between real and fake news during the crisis? We fact checked Night 3 of Trumps actions to prevent COVID-19 Biden on school choice and defunding the police. Military COVID infected 118,984. A majority of COVID-19 deaths in the United States happen in a medical facility but people die at home too. Mr. Mandetta singles out the presidents COVID-19 denialism as the biggest problem in tackling the pandemic. Takes us back to our childhood when the first line of defence against a common cold sore throat was an iodine tincture, or Betadine gargle. Trump ensures Americas stimulus checks will bounce by writing his name on them. There are sterilization agents in the COVID vax which can cause sterility not only in the patient but also in the sexual partners of people who have taken the shot. Rock Legend Beats Bug. Hindu gods quarantined due to COVID-19.

On the other hand, the fake news summary is characterized by the distortion of facts, including the misleading presentation and incorrect information under the guise of news. These narratives often include sensational or controversial topics to attract attention or provoke emotional responses. The content involves outrageous claims or conspiracy theories that diverge from genuine news reporting.

The difference in method (TbS) between real and fake news lies in the alignment and integrity of the presented information. Real news aligns with current public discourse, reflecting ongoing societal or governmental responses. The real news summary aims to provide data and updates to promote knowledge and safety. In contrast, fake news deviates from such discussions, instead introducing irrelevant topics to distort perceptions or manipulate readers' emotions. Fake news lacks integrity and focuses on generating engagement through controversial or sensational content at the expense of relevance and truthfulness.

10. Prototype Application

In this section, we present our web prototype (Figure 4). This app allows users to easily summarize social media discussions and other input text. Users can input a segment of text such as a social media thread or article and customize summarization preferences based on key elements of the MVSF including the method (entity-based or triple-based), sentiment perspective (negative or positive), or political perspective (left or right).

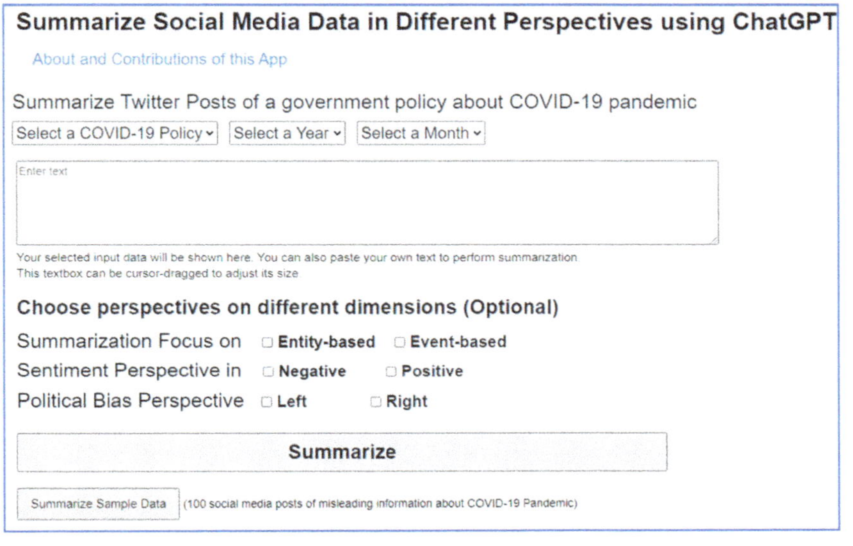

Figure 4. Screenshot of web prototype of the webpage.

We also offer an ongoing dataset that captures COVID-19 government health policies [63], organized on a policy and monthly basis. Additionally, the website contains a built-in sample set of 100 social media posts of fake news [71] about the COVID-19 pandemic. Users can utilize these datasets to create summaries according to their preferred summarization techniques and viewpoints. With an input token limit of 4096 for each month's policy tweet compilation, the application employs a random selection mechanism to ensure it stays within this token boundary.

Figure 5 shows the summary of tweets about the Business Closing policy in Dec. 2021 (Table 17), using the entity-based method, combined with the perspectives of negative sentiment and left political bias, while Figure 6 shows the summary of the same tweet set using the triple-based method, combined with the perspectives of positive sentiment and right political bias.

In our experiments we were not able to coax ChatGPT into using extractive summarization. Thus, our algorithms differ from the web application built with ChatGPT.

The two summaries differ in emphasis and tone based on the requested perspectives. The first (Figure 5), leaning left, emphasizes entities and negative sentiments: it accentuates Ted Cruz's controversial vote, underscores pandemic-induced hardships, and critiques some pandemic responses. The second summary (Figure 6), in contrast, is leaning right, and highlights positive events: it applauds the Senate's actions and emphasizes business resilience during the pandemic. Through selective extraction and strategic phrasing, the same input is transformed to resonate with different biases and foci.

Table 17. Summary of Business Closing policy tweets in 2021-12.

I managed a restaurant in BH during COVID, not only did we never close, but business was booming due to delivery services being the main option of that soft shutdown. It never felt safe the entire time
Senate passes stopgap funding bill, avoiding shutdown, despite TED CRUZ VOTING TO SHUT DOWN GOVERNMENT. @SenTedCruz
Its crazy how in the beginning of the pandemic we were closing down and disinfecting everything because of the chance of COVID now when everyone basically has it its business as usual.
we need to shutdown the nation and pay people and business owners to stay home and let COVID-19 run it's course. It's absolutely clear you can't make Americans take the jab. Capitalism only benefit the few. #COVID-19
This is pretty important information. We are closing in on looking at COVID in a very different way, and the messaging should support that. Get vaccinated. Get boostered. Time to trust science and live your lives.
So we learned nothing from last year or the social justice work that was done? Business as usual @BroadwayLeague not considering industry shutdown amid COVID cancellations l
The restaurant i work at just got shutdown bc we dont get enough business due to COVID and ion really know how im gonna pay for the hotel i live in this week, or even this month. really not tryna live n my car again but ill do what i got to. soon as im almost up they push me down

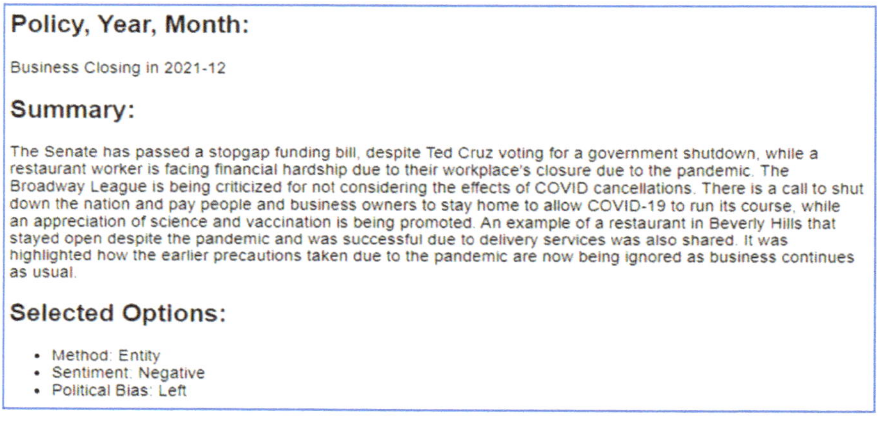

Policy, Year, Month:

Business Closing in 2021-12

Summary:

The Senate has passed a stopgap funding bill, despite Ted Cruz voting for a government shutdown, while a restaurant worker is facing financial hardship due to their workplace's closure due to the pandemic. The Broadway League is being criticized for not considering the effects of COVID cancellations. There is a call to shut down the nation and pay people and business owners to stay home to allow COVID-19 to run its course, while an appreciation of science and vaccination is being promoted. An example of a restaurant in Beverly Hills that stayed open despite the pandemic and was successful due to delivery services was also shared. It was highlighted how the earlier precautions taken due to the pandemic are now being ignored as business continues as usual.

Selected Options:

- Method: Entity
- Sentiment: Negative
- Political Bias: Left

Figure 5. Summary text of tweets about COVID-19 Business Closing policy in December 2021, using entity method, negative sentiment, and left political bias perspectives.

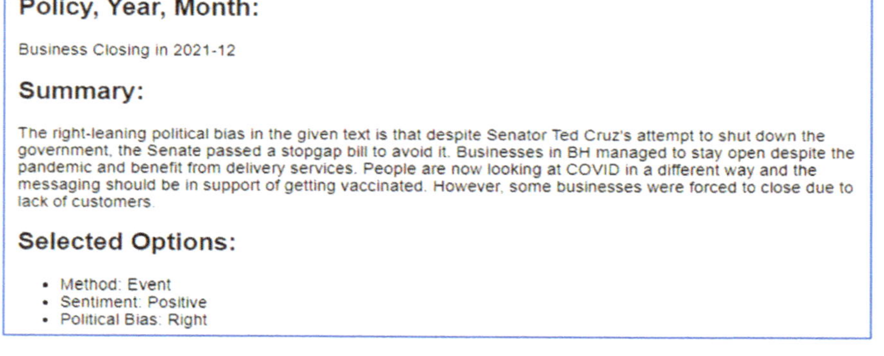

Policy, Year, Month:

Business Closing in 2021-12

Summary:

The right-leaning political bias in the given text is that despite Senator Ted Cruz's attempt to shut down the government, the Senate passed a stopgap bill to avoid it. Businesses in BH managed to stay open despite the pandemic and benefit from delivery services. People are now looking at COVID in a different way and the messaging should be in support of getting vaccinated. However, some businesses were forced to close due to lack of customers.

Selected Options:

- Method: Event
- Sentiment: Positive
- Political Bias: Right

Figure 6. Summary text of tweets about COVID-19 Business Closing policy in December 2021, using event method, positive sentiment, and right political bias perspectives.

Leveraging the power of ChatGPT [28], the application can rapidly produce a customized summary highlighting the most relevant information tailored to the user's preferences. This provides an accessible and user-friendly tool for text summarization that can supplement the computationally demanding algorithms within our framework. The integration of ChatGPT enables high-quality summarization capabilities within the overall MVSF architecture, while opening up these techniques to a broader general audience.

11. Discussion and Conclusions

We presented the Multiple-View Summarization Framework (MVSF), which enables users to generate summaries of diverse perspectives with diverse methods from the same dataset. Entity-based (EbS) summarization focuses on frequent entities, triple-based (TbS) summarization emphasizes the events by ranking prominent triples, while social signal-based (SbS) summarization captures social prominence of tweets. Additionally, combining methods and views enables users to narrow down summaries to specific topics or sentiments. For instance, a user may focus on a summary of entities that are related to negative sentiments or possibly derived with a fake news analysis [71]. A notable challenge for our evaluation was the lack of a dataset of social media posts with gold-standard summaries. Despite this, the MVSF's competitive performance against state-of-the-art models on a news dataset showcases its efficacy.

Our MVSF offers several key theoretical implications for the field of summarization. By combining multiple extractive summarization perspectives within a unified framework, the MVSF enables targeted information extraction from social media content. This provides a more nuanced understanding of the underlying data. Additionally, the MVSF's ability to cater to specific user interests and viewpoints introduces a novel approach to personalized summarization. It contributes to the advancement of research in extractive summarization by demonstrating the effectiveness of a multi-perspective approach.

The practical implications of the MVSF are to offer content curation and decision-making support in the era of vast social media datasets. By offering personalized and fine-grained summaries, the MVSF empowers users to efficiently extract vital information aligned with their specific interests and requirements. This capability might be particularly valuable for professionals, journalists, politicians, and social media analysts, who deal with large volumes of daily information.

The MVSF sets itself apart from existing work in several key ways. While traditional transformer-based models [86] such as BertSum, SBert, T5, and Bart-Large-CNN are limited in handling long input sequences due to the performance of their attention mechanism [87], the MVSF is more flexible when accepting input text of greater length. The comparative evaluations of state-of-the-art models demonstrate the MVSF's better performance, with an average gain of 14% in Rouge scores.

However, it is important to recognize the limitations of Rouge, which measures lexical overlap and may not fully capture semantic accuracy. This suggests a potential undervaluation if summaries are paraphrased or semantically similar but lexically different from source texts. To enhance evaluation robustness, integrating metrics like BERTScore [88] or MoverScore [89] could provide deeper semantic insights. We also acknowledge the limitation of not including a comparison against human-generated summaries. Human evaluation is considered a gold standard as it can capture nuances in coherence, informativeness, and readability that automated metrics might miss. Human evaluation through crowdsourcing could validate coherence and readability from a human perspective. Such approaches would help overcome the limitations of Rouge and offer a more comprehensive assessment. Future research could incorporate a human evaluation, where human evaluators rate the summaries based on various criteria such as relevance, accuracy, and overall quality. This can potentially provide a more comprehensive understanding of approach performance.

Another challenge we encountered is the ongoing instability of Twitter (now X), our primary source of social media posts. With policies changing frequently and new restrictions being imposed, such as limitations on the number of tweets users can access, Twitter's dynamics have become unpredictable. Additionally, Twitter is now charging fees. Despite these challenges, we have tailored our methods to effectively handle Twitter's unique characteristics, including its short, disconnected, and often ungrammatical posts. Moreover, we believe that the MVSF holds potential for applications beyond Twitter, including other social networks such as Reddit. As digital landscapes evolve, we anticipate adapting our framework to suit varying contexts. Looking ahead, the MVSF's adaptability and user-centric approach render it a valuable tool for comprehending the diverse perspectives of online discussions. For example, our MVSF study has incorporated a comparative analysis of fake and real news. This offers a unique method for discerning and contrasting the reliability of information on social media. It facilitates the development of a deeper understanding of misleading information dynamics and enhances media literacy among users. By addressing user preferences and offering comprehensive insights into social media content, our framework paves the way for a more informed and insightful exploration of social media data by lay audiences and decision-makers alike.

In conclusion, the MVSF represents an advance in the field of extractive summarization, with its combination of multiple perspectives and extractive methods within a unified framework. The practical implications of the MVSF are that it offers insights for decision-making support and analysis, while its theoretical implications contribute to the understanding of multiple information extraction perspectives and methods within a unified framework.

We are currently integrating the disparate elements of our summarization methodology into a unified real-time summarization web application. The design of this web application will enable users who are not affiliated with this research group to *choose a set of keywords*, a time range, a geographical range, and a collection period for tweets from X. Common-sense limitations will be imposed, and password registration will be required. Users can then return after the end of the collection period and select the exact combinations of methods and views that can help them comprehend "what Twitter/X users say about their topic of interest". This web application will be based on our own algorithms, as opposed to ChatGPT.

Our MVSF primarily employs extractive summarization techniques, which select significant pieces from the source text, maintaining the original phrasing and factual accuracy. However, this approach potentially misses subtler nuances that abstractive methods can capture. Abstractive summarization, by contrast, involves generating entirely new sentences, sometimes leading to a more coherent and concise representation. This method can offer fresh perspectives and synthesize broader themes that extractive techniques may overlook. Future work could explore hybrid models that integrate the reliability of extractive methods with the fluidity of abstractive techniques to improve both the accuracy and readability of generated summaries.

To address the limitations that social signals may not always correlate with the content quality, as stated in Section 6.3, future research could explore integrating additional metrics that provide a better content quality. Metrics such as stance detection [90] could offer more nuanced evaluations of tweet importance. Stance detection assesses the sentiment and position expressed in the content regarding a specific topic. These enhancements would contribute to a more comprehensive understanding of content value, reducing the reliance on simple engagement metrics.

The introduction of ChatGPT has allowed us to build a rapid web frontend within our MVSF that is not inhibited by the hardware limitations of the system on which we are running our own summarization algorithms. It remains to be determined, in a comparative study between ChatGPT and our implementation, whether our purpose-built algorithms perform better than ChatGPT. While tailored methods often have an edge over generalized implementations, the question is still open as to whether this is the case for MVSF text summarization. Furthermore, we plan to experiment with having ChatGPT generate triples from social media posts and then use our methods to summarize them. This exploration will further allow us to compare the effectiveness of our customized algorithms with ChatGPT's handling of similar tasks.

Lastly, we are carefully monitoring the rapid advancement of ChatGPT, Google Bard, and their kin. These generative AI tools have enabled many new approaches to all AI tasks, while reducing long-established AI methods to technological anachronisms. We intend to make full use of the power of these new tools in our research.

Author Contributions: Conceptualization, S.A.C. and J.G.; Methodology, C.-Y.L., S.A.C. and J.G.; Software, C.-Y.L.; Resources, J.G.; Data curation, C.-Y.L.; Writing—original draft, C.-Y.L.; Writing—review & editing, S.A.C. and J.G.; Supervision, S.A.C. and J.G. All authors have read and agreed to the published version of the manuscript.

Funding: Research reported in this publication was partially supported by the Professional Staff Congress—City University of New York (PSC-CUNY) Research Award Program under PSC Cycle 54 Award 66510-00 54, and in part supported by the National Center for Advancing Translational Sciences (NCATS), a component of the National Institute of Health (NIH) under award number UL1TR003017.

Institutional Review Board Statement: Not Applicable.

Informed Consent Statement: Not Applicable.

Data Availability Statement: The raw data supporting the conclusions of this article will be made available by the authors on request.

Acknowledgments: Michael Renda has substantially contributed to the implementation of the MVSF and the web application.

Conflicts of Interest: The authors declare no conflict of interest.

References

1. Li, C.; Chun, S.A.; Geller, J. Multiple View Summarization Framework for Social Media. In Proceedings of the International Florida Artificial Intelligence Research Society Conference, FLAIRS-36, Clearwater, FL, USA, 14–17 May 2023. [CrossRef]
2. Petrov, C. 50+ Stunning Twitter Statistics You Need to Know in 2023. 2023. Available online: https://techjury.net/blog/twitter-statistics/ (accessed on 1 March 2023).
3. Yadav, A.K.; Singh, A.; Dhiman, M. Extractive text summarization using deep learning approach. *Int. J. Inf. Technol.* **2022**, *14*, 2407–2415. [CrossRef]
4. Modhe, S.V.; Panse, N.S.; Rathi, M.U.; Chavan, S. Extractive Based Approach For Microblogs Summarization. *Int. Res. J. Mod. Eng. Technol. Sci.* **2021**, *3*.
5. Geng, F.; Liu, Q.; Zhang, P. A time-aware query-focused summarization of an evolving microblogging stream via sentence extraction. *Digit. Commun. Netw.* **2020**, *6*, 389–397. [CrossRef]
6. Saini, N.; Saha, S.; Bhattacharyya, P. Multiobjective-based approach for microblog summarization. *IEEE Trans. Comput. Soc. Syst.* **2019**, *6*, 1219–1231. [CrossRef]
7. Dutta, S.; Chandra, V.; Mehra, K.; Ghatak, S.; Das, A.K.; Ghosh, S. Summarizing Microblogs During Emergency Events: A Comparison of Extractive Summarization Algorithms. In *Emerging Technologies in Data Mining and Information Security*; Abraham, A., Dutta, P., Mandal, J., Bhattacharya, A., Dutta, S., Eds.; Advances in Intelligent Systems and Computing; Springer: Singapore, 2019; Volume 813. [CrossRef]

8. Olariu, A. Efficient Online Summarization of Microblogging Streams. In Proceedings of the 14th Conference of the European Chapter of the Association for Computational Linguistics, Volume 2: Short Papers, Association for Computational Linguistics, Gothenburg, Sweden, 26–30 April 2014; pp. 236–240. [CrossRef]
9. Sharifi, B.; Hutton, M.A.; Kalita, J.K. Experiments in Microblog Summarization. In Proceedings of the 2010 IEEE Second International Conference on Social Computing, Minneapolis, MN, USA, 20–22 August 2010; pp. 49–56. [CrossRef]
10. Inouye, D. Multiple post microblog summarization. *REU Res. Final. Rep.* **2010**, *1*, 34–40.
11. Shirky, C. The Political Power of Social Media: Technology, the Public Sphere, and Political Change. *Foreign Aff.* **2011**, *90*, 28–41.
12. Saveski, M.; Gillani, N.; Yuan, A.; Vijayaraghavan, P.; Roy, D. Perspective-Taking to Reduce Affective Polarization on Social Media. *Proc. Int. AAAI Conf. Web Soc. Media* **2022**, *16*, 885–895. [CrossRef]
13. Bakshy, E.; Messing, S.; Adamic, L. Exposure to Ideologically Diverse News and Opinion on Facebook. *Science* **2015**, *348*, 1130–1132. [CrossRef]
14. Sunstein, C.R. *#Republic: Divided Democracy in the Age of Social Media*; Princeton University Press: Princeton, NJ, USA, 2017. [CrossRef]
15. Cinelli, M.; Morales GD, F.; Galeazzi, A.; Quattrociocchi, W.; Michele, S. The echo chamber effect on social media. *Proc. Natl. Acad. Sci. USA* **2021**, *118*, e2023301118. [CrossRef]
16. Barberá, P. Social Media, Echo Chambers, and Political Polarization. In *Social Media and Democracy: The State of the Field, Prospects for Reform (SSRC Anxieties of Democracy, pp. 34–55)*; Persily, N., Tucker, J., Eds.; Cambridge University Press: Cambridge, UK, 2020.
17. Kitchens, B.; Johnson, S.L.; Gray, P. Understanding Echo Chambers and Filter Bubbles: The Impact of Social Media on Diversification and Partisan Shifts in News Consumption. *MIS Q.* **2020**, *44*, 1619–1649. [CrossRef]
18. Jehn, K.A.; Northcraft, G.B.; Neale, M.A. Why Differences Make a Difference: A Field Study of Diversity, Conflict, and Performance in Workgroups. *Adm. Sci. Q.* **1999**, *44*, 741–763. [CrossRef]
19. Mutz, D.C.; Martin, P.S. Facilitating Communication across Lines of Political Difference: The Role of Mass Media. *Am. Political Sci. Rev.* **2001**, *95*, 97–114. [CrossRef]
20. Chan, C.K.; Zhao, M.M.; Lee, P.S. Determinants of escape from echo chambers: The predictive power of political orientation, social media use, and demographics. *Glob. Media China* **2023**, *8*, 155–173. [CrossRef]
21. Rule, J.B. Going to Extremes: How Like Minds Unite and Divide. *Soc. Serv. Rev.* **2010**, *84*, 309–312. [CrossRef]
22. Mourão, R.; Thorson, E.; Chen, W.; Tham, S. Media repertoires and news trust during the early Trump administration. *Journal. Stud.* **2018**, *19*, 1945–1956. [CrossRef]
23. Sintek, M.; Decker, S. TRIPLE—A Query, Inference, and Transformation Language for the Semantic Web. In *The Semantic Web—ISWC 2002. Lecture Notes in Computer Science*; Springer: Berlin/Heidelberg, Germany, 2002; Volume 2342. [CrossRef]
24. Lin, C.-Y. ROUGE: A Package for Automatic Evaluation of Summaries. In *Text Summarization Branches Out*; Association for Computational Linguistics: Barcelona, Spain, 2004; pp. 74–81. Available online: https://aclanthology.org/W04-1013 (accessed on 1 January 2023).
25. Raffel, C.; Shazeer, N.; Roberts, A.; Lee, K.; Narang, S.; Matena, M.; Zhou, Y.; Li, W.; Liu, P.J. Exploring the Limits of Transfer Learning with a Unified Text-to-Text Transformer. *arXiv* **2019**. [CrossRef]
26. Liu, Y. Fine-tune BERT for Extractive Summarization. *arXiv* **2019**. [CrossRef]
27. Reimers, N.; Gurevych, I. Sentence-BERT: Sentence Embeddings using Siamese BERT-Networks. *arXiv* **2019**. [CrossRef]
28. Lund, B.D.; Wang, T.; Mannuru, N.R.; Nie, B.; Shimray, S.; Wang, Z. ChatGPT and a new academic reality: Artificial Intelligence-written research papers and the ethics of the large language models in scholarly publishing. *J. Assoc. Inf. Sci. Technol.* **2023**, *74*, 570–581. [CrossRef]
29. Widyassari, A.P.; Rustad, S.; Shidik, G.F.; Noersasongko, E.; Syukur, A.; Affandy, A.; Setiadi, D.R.I.M. Review of automatic text summarization techniques & methods. *J. King Saud Univ.-Comput. Inf. Sci.* **2022**, *34*, 1029–1046. [CrossRef]
30. Lewis, M.; Liu, Y.; Goyal, N.; Ghazvininejad, M.; Mohamed, A.; Levy, O.; Stoyanov, V.; Zettlemoyer, L. BART: Denoising Sequence-to-Sequence Pre-training for Natural Language Generation, Translation, and Comprehension. In Proceedings of the 58th Annual Meeting of the Association for Computational Linguistics, Online, 5–10 July 2020; pp. 7871–7880. [CrossRef]
31. Zhang, S.; Niu, J.; Wei, C. Fine-grained Factual Consistency Assessment for Abstractive Summarization Models. In Proceedings of the 2021 Conference on Empirical Methods in Natural Language Processing, Punta Cana, Dominican Republic, 7–11 November 2021; pp. 107–116. [CrossRef]
32. Ott, M.; Edunov, S.; Baevski, A.; Fan, A.; Gross, S.; Ng, N.; Grangier, D.; Auli, M. fairseq: A Fast, Extensible Toolkit for Sequence Modeling. In Proceedings of the 2019 Conference of the North American Chapter of the Association for Computational Linguistics (Demonstrations), Minneapolis, MN, USA, 2–7 June 2019; pp. 48–53. [CrossRef]
33. Zhang, J.; Zhao, Y.; Saleh, M.; Liu, P.J. PEGASUS: Pre-training with Extracted Gap-sentences for Abstractive Summarization. *arXiv* **2019**. [CrossRef]
34. Chi, Z.; Dong, L.; Wei, F.; Wang, W.; Mao, X.L.; Huang, H. Cross-Lingual Natural Language Generation via Pre-Training. *arXiv* **2019**. [CrossRef]

35. Radford, A.; Wu, J.; Child, R.; Luan, D.; Amodei, D.; Sutskever, I. Language Models Are Unsupervised Multitask Learners. 2019. Available online: https://api.semanticscholar.org/CorpusID:160025533 (accessed on 2 January 2023).
36. Joshi, A.; Fidalgo, E.; Alegre, E.; Alaiz-Rodriguez, R. RankSum—An unsupervised extractive text summarization based on rank fusion. *Expert Syst. Appl.* **2022**, *200*, 116846. [CrossRef]
37. Jia, R.; Cao, Y.; Tang, H.; Fang, F.; Cao, C.; Wang, S. Neural Extractive Summarization with Hierarchical Attentive Heterogeneous Graph Network. In Proceedings of the 2020 Conference on Empirical Methods in Natural Language Processing (EMNLP), Association for Computational Linguistics, Online, 16–20 November 2020; pp. 3622–3631. [CrossRef]
38. Kwon, J.; Kobayashi, N.; Kamigaito, H.; Okumura, M. Considering Nested Tree Structure in Sentence Extractive Summarization with Pre-trained Transformer. In Proceedings of the 2021 Conference on Empirical Methods in Natural Language Processing, Association for Computational Linguistics, Online, 7–11 November 2021; pp. 4039–4044. [CrossRef]
39. Roush, A.; Balaji, A. DebateSum: A large-scale argument mining and summarization dataset. *arXiv* **2020**. [CrossRef]
40. Gu, N.; Ash, E.; Hahnloser, R.H.R. MemSum: Extractive Summarization of Long Documents Using Multi-Step Episodic Markov Decision Processes. *arXiv* **2021**. [CrossRef]
41. Barrios, F.; López, F.; Argerich, L.; Wachenchauzer, R. Variations of the Similarity Function of TextRank for Automated Summarization. *arXiv* **2016**. [CrossRef]
42. Vodolazova, T.; Lloret, E. Towards Adaptive Text Summarization: How Does Compression Rate Affect Summary Readability of L2 Texts? In Proceedings of the International Conference on Recent Advances in Natural Language Processing (RANLP 2019), Varna, Bulgaria, 2–4 September 2019; pp. 1265–1274. [CrossRef]
43. Goyal, T.; Durrett, G. *Annotating and Modeling Fine-Grained Factuality in Summarization*; North American Chapter of the Association for Computational Linguistics: Seattle, WA, USA, 2021. [CrossRef]
44. Li, S.; Xu, J. MRC-Sum: An MRC framework for extractive summarization of academic articles in natural sciences and medicine. *Inf. Process. Manag.* **2023**, *60*, 103467. [CrossRef]
45. Hahn, U.; Mani, I. The challenges of automatic summarization. *Computer* **2000**, *33*, 29–36. [CrossRef]
46. Rudra, K.; Ghosh, D.; Ganguly, N.; Goyal, P.; Ghosh, S. Extracting Situational Information from Microblogs during Disaster Events: A Classification-Summarization Approach. In Proceedings of the 24th ACM International on Conference on Information and Knowledge Management, Melbourne, VIC, Australia, 19–23 October 2015; pp. 583–592. [CrossRef]
47. Le Bronnec, F.; Duong, S.; Ravaut, M.; Allauzen, A.; Chen, N.; Guigue, V.; Lumbreras, A.; Soulier, L.; Gallinari, P. LOCOST: State-Space Models for Long Document Abstractive Summarization. In Proceedings of the 18th Conference of the European Chapter of the Association for Computational Linguistics, St. Julian's, Malta, 17–22 March 2024; Graham, Y., Purver, M., Eds.; Association for Computational Linguistics: Stroudsburg, PA, USA, 2024. Volume 1: Long Papers. pp. 1144–1159. Available online: https://aclanthology.org/2024.eacl-long.69/ (accessed on 10 March 2025).
48. Blei, D.M.; Ng, A.Y.; Jordan, M.I. Latent dirichlet allocation. *J. Mach. Learn. Res.* **2003**, *3*, 993–1022. [CrossRef]
49. Pennington, J.; Socher, R.; Manning, C. GloVe: Global Vectors for Word Representation. In Proceedings of the 2014 Conference on Empirical Methods in Natural Language Processing (EMNLP), Doha, Qatar, 25–29 October 2014; pp. 1532–1543. [CrossRef]
50. Hermann, K.M.; Kočiský, T.; Grefenstette, E.; Espeholt, L.; Kay, W.; Suleyman, M.; Blunsom, P. Teaching machines to read and comprehend. In Proceedings of the 28th International Conference on Neural Information Processing Systems—Volume 1 (NIPS'15), Montreal, QC, Canada, 7–12 December 2015; MIT Press: Cambridge, MA, USA, 2015; pp. 1693–1701.
51. Khatri, C.; Goel, E.; Hedayatnia, B.; Metanillou, A.; Venkatesh, A.; Gabriel, R.; Mandal, A. Contextual Topic Modeling For Dialog Systems. In Proceedings of the 2018 IEEE Spoken Language Technology Workshop (SLT), Athens, Greece, 18–21 December 2018; pp. 892–899. [CrossRef]
52. Jin, X.; Han, J. K-Means Clustering. In *Encyclopedia of Machine Learning*; Sammut, C., Webb, G.I., Eds.; Springer: Boston, MA, USA, 2011. [CrossRef]
53. Sharifi, B.; Hutton, M.A.; Kalita, J. Automatic Summarization of Twitter Topics. National Workshop on Design and Analysis of Algorithm, Tezpur, India. 2010. Available online: https://api.semanticscholar.org/CorpusID:17725346 (accessed on 1 January 2023).
54. Arthur, D.; Vassilvitskii, S. K-means++: The advantages of careful seeding. In Proceedings of the eighteenth annual ACM-SIAM symposium on Discrete algorithms (SODA '07); Society for Industrial and Applied Mathematics: Philadelphia, PA, USA, 2007; pp. 1027–1035.
55. Zhao, Y.; Karypis, G. Criterion Functions for Document Clustering: Experiments and Analysis. Retrieved from the University of Minnesota Digital Conservancy. 2001. Available online: https://hdl.handle.net/11299/215490 (accessed on 1 January 2023).
56. Gunaratna, K.; Yazdavar, A.H.; Thirunarayan, K.; Sheth, A.; Cheng, G. Relatedness-based multi-entity summarization. In Proceedings of the Twenty-Sixth International Joint Conference on Artificial Intelligence Main Track, Melbourne, VIC, Australia, 19–25 August 2017; pp. 1060–1066. [CrossRef]
57. Gunaratna, K.; Thirunarayan, K.; Sheth, A. FACES: Diversity-Aware Entity Summarization Using Incremental Hierarchical Conceptual Clustering. *Proc. AAAI Conf. Artif. Intell.* **2015**, *29*, 1. [CrossRef]

58. Gunaratna, K.; Thirunarayan, K.; Sheth, A.; Cheng, G. Gleaning Types for Literals in RDF Triples with Application to Entity Summarization. In *The Semantic Web. Latest Advances and New Domains*; ESWC, 2016, Sack, H., Blomqvist, E., d'Aquin, M., Ghidini, C., Ponzetto, S., Lange, C., Eds.; Springer: Cham, Switzerland, 2016; Volume 9678. [CrossRef]
59. Li, C.; Chun, S.A.; Geller, J. Knowledge graph analysis of Russian trolls. In Proceedings of the 10th International Conference on Data Science, Technology and Applications, DATA 2021, Virtual, 6–8 July 2021; Quix, C., Hammoudi, S., van der Aalst, W., Eds.; SciTePress: Setúbal, Portugal, 2021; pp. 335–342. [CrossRef]
60. Amplayo, R.K.; Angelidis, S.; Lapata, M. Aspect-controllable opinion summarization. *arXiv* **2021**, arXiv:2109.03171.
61. Li, H.; Chaturvedi, S. Rationale-based Opinion Summarization. *arXiv* **2024**, arXiv:2404.00217.
62. Liu, X.; Li, Y.; Wei, F.; Zhou, M. Graph-Based Multi-Tweet Summarization using Social Signals. In Proceedings of the COLING 2012, Mumbai, India, 8–15 December 2012; pp. 1699–1714. Available online: https://aclanthology.org/C12-1104 (accessed on 1 January 2023).
63. Li, C.; Renda, M.; Yusuf, F.; Geller, J.; Chun, S.A. Public Health Policy Monitoring through Public Perceptions: A Case of COVID-19 Tweet Analysis. *Information* **2022**, *13*, 543. [CrossRef]
64. Chowdhary, M.; Chahal, P. A Systematic Review of Challenges in Information Retrieval from Online Social Networking Platforms. In Proceedings of the International Conference on Artificial-Business Analytics, Quantum and Machine Learning, Faridabad, India, 14–15 July 2023; Springer Nature: Singapore, 2023; pp. 719–734. [CrossRef]
65. Angeli, G.; Premkumar, M.J.J.; Manning, C.D. Leveraging Linguistic Structure For Open Domain Information Extraction. In Proceedings of the 53rd Annual Meeting of the Association for Computational Linguistics and the 7th International Joint Conference on Natural Language Processing (Volume 1: Long Papers), Beijing, Chian, 27–31 July 2015; pp. 344–354. [CrossRef]
66. Niklaus, C.; Cetto, M.; Freitas, A.; Handschuh, S. A Survey on Open Information Extraction. In Proceedings of the 27th International Conference on Computational Linguistics, Santa Fe, NM, USA, 20–26 August 2018; pp. 3866–3878. Available online: https://aclanthology.org/C18-1326 (accessed on 1 November 2022).
67. Socher, R.; Perelygin, A.; Wu, J.; Chuang, J.; Manning, C.D.; Ng, A.; Potts, C. Recursive Deep Models for Semantic Compositionality Over a Sentiment Treebank. In Proceedings of the 2013 Conference on Empirical Methods in Natural Language Processing, Seattle, WA, USA, 18–21 October 2013. Available online: https://aclanthology.org/D13-1170 (accessed on 1 January 2023).
68. Hutto, C.J.; Gilbert, E. VADER: A Parsimonious Rule-Based Model for Sentiment Analysis of Social Media Text. In Proceedings of the International AAAI Conference on Web and Social Media, Ann Arbor, MI, USA, 1–4 June 2014; Volume 8, pp. 216–225. Available online: https://ojs.aaai.org/index.php/ICWSM/article/view/14550 (accessed on 1 January 2023).
69. Loria, S. TextBlob Documentation. Release 0.16.0. 2020. Available online: https://buildmedia.readthedocs.org/media/pdf/TextBlob/latest/TextBlob.pdf (accessed on 1 January 2023).
70. Sentiment Analysis Without Modeling: TextBlob vs. VADER vs. Flair. Available online: https://pub.towardsai.net/sentiment-analysis-without-modeling-textblob-vs-vader-vs-flair-657b7af855f4 (accessed on 15 January 2023).
71. Li, C.Y.; Chun, S.A.; Geller, J. Stemming the Tide of Fake News about the COVID-19 Pandemic. *Int. Flairs Conf. Proc.* **2022**, *35*. [CrossRef]
72. Chun, S.; Holowczak, R.; Dharan, K.; Wang, R.; Basu, S.; Geller, J. Detecting Political Bias Trolls in Twitter Data. In Proceedings of the 15th International Conference on Web Information Systems and Technologies (WEBIST 2019), Vienna, Austria, 18–20 September 2019; SCITEPRESS—Science and Technology Publications, Lda: Setubal, Portugal, 2019; pp. 334–342. [CrossRef]
73. GeoPy's Documentation. 2023. Available online: https://geopy.readthedocs.io/en/stable/ (accessed on 13 March 2023).
74. Fellbaum, C. WordNet and wordnets. In *Encyclopedia of Language and Linguistics*, 2nd ed.; Brown, K., Ed.; Elsevier: Oxford, UK, 2005; pp. 665–670.
75. Lesk, M. Automatic Sense Disambiguation Using Machine Readable Dictionaries: How to Tell a Pine Cone from an Ice Cream Cone. In Proceedings of the 5th Annual International Conference on Systems Documentation, Toronto, Canada; 1986; pp. 24–26. [CrossRef]
76. Devlin, J.; Chang, M.-W.; Lee, K.; Toutanova, K. BERT: Pre-training of Deep Bidirectional Transformers for Language Understanding. In Proceedings of the 2019 Conference of the North American Chapter of the Association for Computational Linguistics: Human Language Technologies, NAACL-HLT 2019, Minneapolis, MN, USA, 2–7 June 2019; Burstein, J., Doran, C., Solorio, T., Eds.; Association for Computational Linguistics: Stroudsburg, PA, USA, 2019; Volume 1, (Long and Short Papers). pp. 4171–4186. [CrossRef]
77. Bank, D.; Koenigstein, N.; Giryes, R. Autoencoders. *arXiv* **2020**. [CrossRef]
78. Vilenchik, D. The Million Tweets Fallacy: Activity and Feedback Are Uncorrelated. In Proceedings of the Twelfth International AAAI Conference on Web and Social Media. 2018; Volume 12. Available online: https://cdn.aaai.org/ojs/15062/15062-28-18581-1-2-20201228.pdf (accessed on 10 March 2025).
79. Davies, S.W.; Putnam, H.M.; Ainsworth, T.; Baum, J.K.; Bove, C.B.; Crosby, S.C. Promoting inclusive metrics of success and impact to dismantle a discriminatory reward system in science. *PLoS Biol.* **2021**, *19*, e3001282. [CrossRef]

80. Greene, D.; Cunningham, P. Practical Solutions to the Problem of Diagonal Dominance in Kernel Document Clustering. In Proceedings of the 23rd International Conference on Machine Learning, Pittsburgh, PA, USA, 25–29 June 2006; pp. 377–384. [CrossRef]
81. Preda, G. COVID-19 All Vaccines Tweets. Kaggle. 2021. Available online: https://www.kaggle.com/datasets/gpreda/all-covid19-vaccines-tweets (accessed on 1 October 2022).
82. Qi, P.; Zhang, Y.; Zhang, Y.; Bolton, J.; Manning, C.D. Stanza: A Python Natural Language Processing Toolkit for Many Human Languages. In Proceedings of the 58th Annual Meeting of the Association for Computational Linguistics: System Demonstrations, Seattle, WA, USA, 6–8 July 2020; pp. 101–108. [CrossRef]
83. Manning, C.D.; Surdeanu, M.; Bauer, J.; Finkel, J.; Bethard, S.J.; McClosky, D. The Stanford CoreNLP Natural Language Processing Toolkit. In Proceedings of the 52nd Annual Meeting of the Association for Computational Linguistics: System Demonstrations, Baltimore, MD, USAA, 23–24 June 2014; pp. 55–60. [CrossRef]
84. Bastian, M.; Heymann, S.; Jacomy, M. Gephi: An Open Source Software for Exploring and Manipulating Networks. 2009. Available online: http://www.aaai.org/ocs/index.php/ICWSM/09/paper/view/154 (accessed on 3 January 2023).
85. Patwa, P.; Sharma, S.; Pykl, S.; Guptha, V.; Kumari, G.; Akhtar, M.S.; Ekbal, A.; Das, A.; Chakraborty, T. Fighting an Infodemic: COVID-19 Fake News Dataset. In *Combating Online Hostile Posts in Regional Languages during Emergency Situation*; Springer International Publishing: Berlin/Heidelberg, Germany, 2021; pp. 21–29. [CrossRef]
86. Vaswani, A.; Shazeer, N.; Parmar, N.; Uszkoreit, J.; Jones, L.; Gomez, A.N.; Kaiser, L.; Polosukhin, I. Attention Is All You Need. *arXiv* **2017**. [CrossRef]
87. Rohde, T.; Wu, X.; Liu, Y. Hierarchical Learning for Generation with Long Source Sequences. *arXiv* **2021**. [CrossRef]
88. Zhang, T.; Kishore, V.; Wu, F.; Weinberger, K.Q.; Artzi, Y. BERTScore: Evaluating text generation with BERT. In Proceedings of the International Conference on Learning Representations (ICLR), Virtual, 26 April–1 May 2020. Available online: https://arxiv.org/abs/1904.09675 (accessed on 11 March 2025).
89. Zhao, W.; Peyrard, M.; Liu, F.; Gao, Y.; Meyer, C.M.; Eger, S. MoverScore: Text Generation Evaluating with Contextualized Embeddings and Earth Mover Distance. In Proceedings of the Conference on Empirical Methods in Natural Language Processing, Hong Kong, 3–7 November 2019. Available online: https://aclanthology.org/D19-1053.pdf (accessed on 11 March 2025).
90. Burnham, M. Stance detection: A practical guide to classifying political beliefs in text. *Political Sci. Res. Methods* **2024**, 1–18. [CrossRef]

information

MDPI

Article

CHTopo: A Multi-Source Large-Scale Chinese Toponym Annotation Corpus

Peng Ye [1,2], Yujin Jiang [3,4] and Yadi Wang [5,*]

1 Urban Planning and Development Institute, Yangzhou University, Yangzhou 225127, China; 007839@yzu.edu.cn
2 College of Civil Engineering and Transportation, Yangzhou University, Yangzhou 225127, China
3 Zhejiang Academy of Culture and Tourism Development, Hangzhou 311231, China; jiangyujin@tourzj.edu.cn
4 School of Applied Digital Technology, Tourism College of Zhejiang, Hangzhou 311231, China
5 School of Management, Henan University of Urban Construction, Pingdingshan 467041, China
* Correspondence: 20221051@huuc.edu.cn

Abstract: Toponyms are fundamental geographical resources characterized by their spatial attributes, distinct from general nouns. While natural language provides rich toponymic data beyond traditional surveying methods, its qualitative ambiguity and inherent uncertainty challenge systematic extraction. Traditional toponym recognition methods based on part-of-speech tagging only focus on the surface-level features of words, failing to effectively handle complex scenarios such as alias nesting, metonymy ambiguity, and mixed punctuation. This leads to the loss of toponym semantic integrity and deviations in geographic entity recognition. This study proposes a set of Chinese toponym annotation specifications that integrate spatial semantics. By leveraging the XML markup language, it deeply combines the spatial location characteristics of toponyms with linguistic features, and designs fine-grained annotation rules to address the limitations of traditional methods in semantic integrity and geographic entity recognition. On this basis, by integrating multi-source corpora from the *Encyclopedia of China: Chinese Geography* and *People's Daily*, a large-scale Chinese toponym annotation corpus (CHTopo) covering five major categories of toponyms has been constructed. The performance of this annotated corpus was evaluated through toponym recognition, exploring the construction methods of a large-scale, diversified, and high-coverage Chinese toponym annotated corpus from the perspectives of applicability and practicality. CHTopo is conducive to providing foundational support for geographic information extraction, spatial knowledge graphs, and geoparsing research, bridging linguistic and geospatial intelligence.

Keywords: Chinese text; toponym; annotated corpus; toponym recognition

1. Introduction

Toponyms refer to the specific names assigned to geographical entities in particular locations or areas. As some of the most commonly used pieces of public information, toponyms are closely related to people's daily lives and are indispensable foundational geographic information resources for national administration, economic development, and domestic and international exchanges [1–3]. The primary sources of toponym data include surveying, mapping, and natural language [4]. Toponyms are a crucial aspect of informatized surveying, encompassing names, coordinates, and types of geographical features [5]. However, although toponym information obtained through surveying is current,

https://doi.org/10.3390/info16070610

(2) A multi-source heterogeneous large-scale Chinese toponym annotation corpus (CHTopo) was constructed. By integrating encyclopedic authoritative texts with dynamic news corpora, this resource comprehensively covers five major categories of geographic names including administrative regions, natural landscapes, and transportation facilities. The hybrid training strategy effectively enhanced the model's generalization capability across cross-domain texts. The corpus provides high-quality foundational data support for geographic information extraction and spatial knowledge graph construction.

The main chapters of this paper are as follows: Section 2 introduces the methods of annotation specification of Chinese toponyms, Section 3 explains the annotation of the Chinese toponym corpus, Section 4 presents the experimental evaluation and discussion of the methods, and Section 5 presents the conclusions and future work.

2. Description Characteristics and Annotation Specification of Chinese Toponyms

2.1. Description Characteristics

Spatial location is one of the key features distinguishing toponyms from general nouns. To determine whether a noun in a text is a toponym, it is not only necessary to consider linguistic aspects such as part of speech and word integrity but, more importantly, whether the "toponym" explicitly conveys its inherent spatial location semantics. For instance, in descriptions like "Nanjing leaders went to Shanghai for research" and "Nanjing salted duck is very famous," the actual spatial location of "Nanjing" is not the focus and does not need to be understood as a toponym. Toponym descriptions in Chinese texts also have the following characteristics:

(1) Characteristic Words: Toponyms often end with characteristic words that indicate administrative regions and divisions (e.g., province, city) or types of toponyms (e.g., road, mountain, river, island). These characteristic words help in recognizing toponyms, especially in determining the right boundary of the toponym.
(2) Variable Length: Toponyms do not have a strict length limit and can include multi-character words or named entities. Examples include "京" ("Jing" in Chinese), "双江拉祜族佤族布朗族傣族自治县" ("Shuangjiang Lahuzu Wa Autonomous County" in Chinese), and "中山路" ("Zhongshan Road" in Chinese).
(3) Homonyms: Different types and ranges of geographical features often share the same name in Chinese texts, such as mountains and cities (e.g., "黄山", Huangshan in Chinese, refers to Huangshan Mountain or Huangshan City), lakes and cities (e.g., "巢湖", Chaohu in Chinese, refers to Chaohu Lake or Chaohu City), and cities and counties (e.g., "芜湖", Wuhu in Chinese, refers to Wuhu City or Wuhu County).
(4) Historical and Audience Variability: The spatial location of a toponym with the same name can vary across different historical periods and for different audiences. For instance, Beijing during the Jin Dynasty was located near present-day Baling Left Banner in Inner Mongolia, while the jurisdiction of Beijing in the year 1949 differed from its current extent.

2.2. Markup Language

Using XML as the markup language, and considering the characteristics of Chinese toponym descriptions, this study references the "Rules for the Classification and Codes of Geographical Names" (GB/T 18521-2001) [24] to categorize Chinese toponyms into five major classes: Area, Water, Sea, Landscape, and Transport. Based on this categorization, we have designed a standard for annotating Chinese toponyms. In this annotation standard, toponyms are tagged using the <Place> tag, and each <Place> tag includes three attributes:

it is relatively limited in quantity and often lacks alternate names, historical names, and low-level toponyms.

Toponyms are also an essential component of maps, which are venues for the mass, systematic appearance of toponyms. However, due to the scarcity of map data, difficulties in updating maps, and issues like multiple names for the same location and duplicate names, toponym data are challenging to acquire and share effectively [6,7]. Natural language serves as another important medium for conveying toponym information, supplementing the aforementioned data acquisition methods [8–10]. This includes traditional paper documents, electronic files, statistical tables, and web pages. Despite the richness and diversity of toponyms in natural language, they are characterized by qualitative, ambiguous, and uncertain properties [11]. The lack of standardized and structured methods for acquiring and organizing these toponyms hampers large-scale collection and retrieval [12].

Deep learning is the primary technology currently used to extract toponyms from natural language, mainly through training toponym recognition models on annotated corpora [13,14]. A toponym annotated corpus is a specially collected, structured, and sizeable collection of representative texts in which toponyms are marked according to a specific format [15]. The annotation standards for toponyms differ significantly across languages. For English texts, notable standards include the Generalized Upper Model (GUM), Toponym Resolution Markup Language (TRML), GeoTagger, and SpatialML [16–19]. Representative Chinese toponym annotated corpora include the *People's Daily* corpus and the Microsoft corpus.

Related research has gained attention in the field of geo-information science. For instance, using 432 samples from *Aesop's Fables*, entities such as toponyms, people, and objects, along with their spatial relationships, were annotated [20]. Methods for annotating spatial entities, spatial relationships, and spatial processes based on semantic roles have been proposed [21]. Additionally, annotation guidelines for geographical entities and spatial relationships in Chinese texts have been developed, leading to the construction of an annotated corpus based on the *Encyclopedia of China: Chinese Geography* [22,23]. Overall, existing toponym annotation methods are primarily divided into two categories: One category is based on linguistic part-of-speech tagging, which only identifies toponyms in texts through "toponym" part-of-speech tags without considering the core essence of toponyms—"spatial location semantics." The other category relies on fundamental entity recognition techniques, which can recognize "toponym" entities but do not design annotation specifications tailored to the particularities of the geographic domain. Consequently, they cannot distinguish between geographic element types of toponyms and exhibit insufficient coverage in annotating professional geographic terms.

This study proposes a methodology for constructing a Chinese toponym annotation corpus, with its innovation lying in the deep integration of spatial semantics and linguistic features. This approach not only preserves the capability of traditional methods to capture surface-level linguistic features but also resolves annotation ambiguity in complex scenarios through spatial semantic constraints. The main contributions of this study include the following two aspects:

(1) We propose a spatial-semantic integrated annotation framework for Chinese toponyms. To address prevalent challenges including nested aliases, metonymic expressions, and mixed punctuation in Chinese geographic nomenclature, we developed fine-grained XML annotation rules that integrate spatial attributes with linguistic features. This approach overcomes the limitations of traditional part-of-speech tagging methods in preserving semantic integrity and identifying geographic entities, which provides a novel technical framework for standardized processing of Chinese toponyms.

(1) ID: The serial number of the annotation unit.
(2) Type: The type of geographical feature described by the toponym.
(3) StartNode and EndNode: The start and end positions of the toponym in the original text.

The core advantage of adopting XML markup language lies in the modular design of its structured tags. First, the tag hierarchy is extensible. The base tag <Place> supports nested sub-tags; when new annotation dimensions are added, only new attributes or sub-tags need to be appended under the <Place> tag without modifying existing annotation rules. Second, namespace isolation is implemented. By using custom namespaces, conflicts with tags from other XML standards are avoided, enabling parallel expansion of multi-dimensional annotations. Finally, XSD (XML Schema Definition) constraints are applied. XML Schema is employed to clarify tag types, mandatory requirements for attributes, and other specifications, ensuring the standardization of newly added annotations. To support rapid adaptation to mainstream natural language processing frameworks such as HuggingFace and spaCy, XML markup language can be integrated through format conversion. For named entity recognition tasks in HuggingFace and spaCy, XML is converted to JSON formats supported by these frameworks via XSLT (Extensible Stylesheet Language Transformation). The converted JSON can be directly input into HuggingFace and spaCy to generate the data formats required for training, thereby supporting downstream natural language processing tasks such as named entity recognition.

2.3. Annotation Specification

Considering the complexity of toponym descriptions and expressions in Chinese texts, this paper defines several special annotation patterns, which include the following aspects. In particular, square brackets [ ] denote the span of a toponym in the original text. Parentheses ( ) within examples provide supplementary explanations (e.g., abbreviations) and are not part of the annotation.

(1) Toponym alias phenomenon: Toponyms often have aliases, abbreviations, and acronyms, which typically need to be annotated. However, words indicated by terms such as "meaning" in the description are not annotated (Table 1).

Table 1. Example 1 of annotated result.

	Example 1
Original text (in Chinese)	[扎什伦布寺]最早称 "[康建曲批]"，意为 "雪城兴佛"。
Translation text (in English)	The [Tashilhunpo Monastery] was originally called "[Kangjianqupi]", meaning "Xue Cheng Xing Fo". [1]
Annotated text	<Place Id = "1" Type = "Area" StartNode = "1" EndNode = "5">扎什伦布寺 ("Tashilhunpo Monastery" in Chinese)</Place> <Place Id = "2" Type = "Area" StartNode = "10" EndNode = "13">康建曲批 ("Kangjianqupi" in Chinese)</Place>

[1] The English translations in parentheses are not part of the annotations.

(2) Derived toponym phenomenon: In Chinese texts, the combination of "toponym + geographical concept" is often used to describe features associated with the toponym, such as "九华山主峰" (the main peak of Jiuhuashan Mountain in Chinese). This phenomenon is referred to as derived toponyms. Derived toponyms are annotated differently due to their expression of features distinct from the recognized geographical entity. When toponyms are followed by terms indicating topography, geographical scope, or organizations, generally only the main toponym is annotated (Table 2).

Table 2. Examples 2 and 3 of annotated result.

	Example 2
Original text (in Chinese)	枯水期时[鄱阳湖]湖面急剧萎缩。
Translation text (in English)	During the dry season, the lake surface of [Poyang Lake] shrinks dramatically. [1]
Annotated text	<Place Id = "3" Type = "Water" StartNode = "5" EndNode = "7">鄱阳湖 ("Poyang Lake" in Chinese)</Place>
	Example 3
Original text (in Chinese)	[华西县]县府搬迁。
Translation text (in English)	The county government of [Huaxi County] has been relocated.[1]
Annotated text	<Place Id = "4" Type = "Area" StartNode = "1" EndNode = "3">华西县 ("Huaxi County" in Chinese)</Place>

[1] The English translations in parentheses are not part of the annotations.

Some combinations require contextual judgment to determine whether they represent toponyms. When a term only indicates a type of landform and does not refer to a specific location, it should not be annotated as a toponym. For instance, in the phrase "江南丘陵低丘盆地作物可一年三熟或两熟" ("In the Jiangnan hilly low hill basin, crops can be grown three times or twice a year" in Chinese), "江南丘陵低丘盆地" (Jiangnan hilly low hill basin in Chinese) only describes a type of basin. In geography, specific combinations are sometimes used to describe a natural landscape unit as a whole, such as "河西走廊" (Hexi Corridor in Chinese). Since such a term refers to a determinable location, it should be annotated as a toponym (Table 3).

Table 3. Example 4 of annotated result.

	Example 4
Original text (in Chinese)	[昆仑山脉][塔什库尔干谷地]的海拔3100–3900米。
Translation text (in English)	The elevation of the [Kunlun Mountains] and the [Tashkurgan Valley] ranges from 3100 to 3900 m. [1]
Annotated text	<Place Id = "5" Type = "Landscape" StartNode = "1" EndNode = "4">昆仑山脉 ("Kunlun Mountains" in Chinese)</Place> <Place Id = "6" Type = "Landscape" StartNode = "5" EndNode = "11">塔什库尔干谷地 ("Tashkurgan Valley" in Chinese)</Place>

[1] The English translations in parentheses are not part of the annotations.

In addition, commonly recognized general derived toponyms such as "黄河下游" (Lower Yellow River in Chinese) and "长江中下游平原" (Yangtze Plain, Middle and Lower in Chinese) can be annotated as whole toponyms.

(3) Metonymy in toponyms: The phenomenon of metonymy in toponyms is both common and complex, and generally, such instances do not require annotation as toponyms. For instance, when a toponym is used as an adjectival phrase to modify another object, implying a certain association but not expressing geographical meaning or spatial location, it should not be annotated as a toponym. An instance of this is "南京盐水鸭" (Nanjing salted duck in Chinese), where "Nanjing" is used to describe a type of duck rather than a geographic location. Additionally, when toponyms in texts imply institutions, units, or organizations, and the focus is not on their geographic location, such terms do not possess geographic semantics and are not annotated as toponyms. For instance, terms like "江苏省规定…" ("Jiangsu Province regulations …" in Chinese) or "日本方面认为…" ("The Japanese side believes …" in Chinese) are used to refer to entities or perspectives without geographic significance and should not be annotated as toponyms.

(4) Spatial relations in toponym expressions: Toponyms often accompany spatial relationship terms. Some commonly used toponyms that imply omitted reference objects,

such as "华北" (North China in Chinese) and "东南亚" (Southeast Asia in Chinese), should be annotated as a whole, provided there is no public recognition discrepancy. The most frequent occurrence involves expressions of geographical ranges in the form "toponym + spatial relationship," indicating a specific relationship with reference objects. To ensure the completeness and consistency of the primary toponym, only the primary toponym should be annotated (Table 4).

Table 4. Example 5 of annotated result.

Example 5	
Original text (in Chinese)	[蒲圻市]南部为低山丘陵。
Translation text (in English)	The southern part of [Puqi City] consists of low mountain hills. [1]
Annotated text	<Place Id = "7" Type = "Area" StartNode = "1" EndNode = "3">蒲圻市("Puqi City" in Chinese)</Place>

[1] The English translations in parentheses are not part of the annotations.

(5) Challenges with mixed punctuation in toponyms: Mixed punctuation in toponyms can make it difficult to determine the start and end positions for annotation. When annotating such names, the independence and completeness of linguistic elements should be considered. Firstly, for composite toponyms with shared elements. When two or more toponyms share common linguistic elements and are connected by punctuation, they are presented as a composite toponym (Table 5).

Table 5. Example 6 of annotated result.

Example 6	
Original text (in Chinese)	[兴安岭]由[大、[小兴安岭]]组成。
Translation text (in English)	The [Xing'an Mountains] are composed of [Daxing'an Mountains] and [Xiaoxing'an Mountains]. [1]
Annotated text	<Place Id = "8" Type = "Landscape" StartNode = "1" EndNode = "3"> 兴安岭 ("Xing'an Mountains" in Chinese)</Place> <Place Id = "9" Type = "Landscape" StartNode = "7" EndNode = "10">小兴安岭 ("Xiaoxing'an Mountains" in Chinese)</Place> <Place Id = "10" Type = "Landscape" StartNode = "5" EndNode = "10" >大、小兴安岭 ("Daxing'an and Xiaoxing'an Mountains" in Chinese)</Place>

[1] The English translations in parentheses are not part of the annotations.

Secondly, the combination of multiple simple toponym elements needs to be considered, when multiple simple toponym elements are combined to express a higher-level geographical concept (Table 6).

Table 6. Example 7 of annotated result.

Example 7	
Original text (in Chinese)	[[黑河]–[腾冲]线]是我国地理上非常重要的一条分界线。
Translation text (in English)	The [[Heihe]–[Tengchong] Line] is a very important geographical boundary in China. [1]
Annotated text	<Place Id = "11" Type = "Area" StartNode = "1" EndNode = "2">黑河 ("Heihe" in Chinese)</Place> <Place Id = "12" Type = "Area" StartNode = "5" EndNode = "6">腾冲 ("Tengchong" in Chinese)</Place> <Place Id = "13" Type = "Landscape" StartNode = "1" EndNode = "6">黑河–腾冲线 ("Heihe–Tengchong Line" in Chinese)</Place>

[1] The English translations in parentheses are not part of the annotations.

Thirdly, the expansion of abbreviated toponyms, which provides a complete form of abbreviated toponyms to offer detailed explanations (Table 7). The parentheses indicate expanded forms, but only the full compound term (Baotou–Lanzhou Railway) is annotated as a single toponym.

Table 7. Example 8 of annotated result.

	Example 8
Original text (in Chinese)	[包（头）兰（州）铁路]全长990公里。
Translation text (in English)	The [Baotou–Lanzhou Railway] has a total length of 990 km. [1]
Annotated text	<Place Id = "14" Type = "Transport" StartNode = "1" EndNode = "10" >包（头）兰（州）铁路 ("Baotou–Lanzhou Railway" in Chinese)</Place>

[1] The English translations in parentheses are not part of the annotations.

3. Annotation of Chinese Toponym Corpus

3.1. Corpus Data Source

In general, the selection of data sources for corpora should adhere to the following principles: (1) Authenticity: the data should originate from real language usage and reflect actual applications of toponyms. (2) Diverse genres: incorporate texts from various genres to ensure a balanced representation of toponym types and coverage. For instance, travel writings focus on city and geographical landscape names, whereas city-level news reports often include numerous street and community names. (3) Scale and representativeness: the data source should be of sufficient scale and representativeness. (4) Public availability: preferably, the data sources should be publicly available to ensure accessibility and shareability.

This study selects two different types of corpus data sources: (1) the *Encyclopedia of China: Chinese Geography* (referred to as C1). This is a specialized popular science work that introduces various geographical elements. The descriptions of toponyms in this source are highly standardized, with a large number of toponyms and diverse types. (2) *People's Daily* (April to June 1998) (referred to as C2). This source covers a wide range of fields including society, economy, sports, and education. The toponym descriptions in this source are flexible and diverse, with a relatively scattered distribution, predominantly featuring administrative regions and territorial divisions. To ensure the balance of toponym annotation results, this study employs a stratified sampling method to select the corpus. For the *Encyclopedia of China: Chinese Geography*, classification is conducted based on China's provincial administrative divisions, where the proportion of the sample size for each province aligns with its proportion in the total entries of the entire book. For *People's Daily*, themes are categorized into "current political news," "economic development," "cultural tourism," and "ecological protection," with proportional sampling implemented within each theme. Additionally, each text entry in the *Encyclopedia of China: Chinese Geography* contains approximately 800 characters, with a relatively long length and dense toponym distribution, whereas most texts in *People's Daily* have around 300 characters, with a relatively short length and sparse toponym distribution. Thus, fewer texts are sampled from the *Encyclopedia of China: Chinese Geography*, while a relatively larger number of texts are sampled from *People's Daily*.

3.2. Corpus Annotation and Consistency Control

The annotation team comprised 3 graduate students majoring in geographic information science and 1 linguistics expert. To ensure the accuracy and consistency of annotation results, this study established a full-process quality control system following the workflow of "training–pre-annotation–calibration–verification–revision." All team members completed two phases of training: first, rule training, involving systematic study of the Chinese Toponym Annotation Specifications and unified understanding of "spatial location semantics" through simulated annotation of 100 typical texts and expert explanations; and second, tool training, focusing on mastering the operation of XML annotation tools to ensure technical implementation aligned with the rules.

Prior to formal annotation, inter-annotator consistency was calibrated through pre-annotation tests. Four annotators independently annotated a common batch of 200 texts (100 from the *Encyclopedia of China: Chinese Geography* and 100 from *People's Daily*). Cohen's kappa statistic was used to evaluate consistency, with a focus on alignment in annotation boundaries, type labeling, and handling of special patterns. The initial average kappa value from pre-annotation was 0.72. Discrepant cases were discussed by experts, and rules were revised. After two rounds of calibration, the final kappa value increased to 0.85, meeting the requirement for annotation consistency.

During formal annotation, a three-level verification mechanism of "cross-validation + expert review + automated checking" was adopted. For every 500 annotated texts, 10% were randomly selected for re-annotation by members not involved in the original process. Discrepancies such as boundary errors and type misclassifications were recorded, with the correction rate controlled within 3%. An audit group composed of linguistics experts and geographic information experts conducted full-volume reviews of batches with an error rate $\geq$ 2%, focusing on complex cases (e.g., metonymy scenarios and mixed punctuation). The final correction rate was reduced to 1.2%. Under this full-process quality control system, the annotation results for these two data sources are presented in Table 8.

Table 8. Statistics of annotation results for the two toponym data sources.

Data Source	Number of Parts	Area	Water	Sea	Landscape	Transport	Total
Encyclopedia of China: Chinese Geography	1382	38,543	10,258	10,949	2658	2638	65,053
People's Daily	8199	32,223	796	1067	530	852	35,480

The Chinese dataset "zh_msra.tar.gz" created by Microsoft Research Asia (MSRA) and the New Era People's Daily Segmented Corpus (NEPD) are both highly significant annotated corpora for modern Chinese. When comparing the CHTopo corpus with these two existing corpora, the following observations can be made: First, NEPD only provides word segmentation annotation and cannot directly determine whether a segment corresponds to a toponym based on segmentation results; thus, it is not applicable for toponym recognition tasks. The zh_msra corpus, derived from real news texts, employs the BIO tagging scheme to annotate Chinese named entities, including 36,517 toponym entities in total. Notably, the zh_msra corpus is designed for general name entity recognition tasks and does not specifically focus on Chinese toponym annotation. In contrast, the CHTopo corpus demonstrates advantages in both the richness of corpus sources and the granularity of toponym annotation.

4. Testing and Analysis of Chinese Toponym Annotation Corpus

The quality evaluation of toponym annotation corpora is a complex task, with different evaluation methods suited to different applications. Toponym recognition is one of the most important applications of toponym annotation corpora. Therefore, this study aims to assess the quality of the annotated corpora through performance evaluation of toponym recognition, including closed testing and open testing. The toponym recognition model employs Conditional Random Fields (CRFs) [25]. As a classical sequence labeling model, its advantages lie in its strong interpretability, well-defined feature functions, low computational cost, and suitability for small-sample scenarios. The CRF method utilized manually designed feature templates based on the experimental corpus [26], and these templates were created according to the requirements of the CRF tool's corpus format. The template design is illustrated in Table 9. The feature template design of a CRF is closely integrated with the word-formation rules of Chinese toponyms and the requirements of sequence labeling tasks. First, from a linguistic motivation perspective, it needs to cover the core patterns of toponyms. Chinese toponyms are typically composed of "specific name + generic name," and their key patterns can be captured by unigrams and bigrams. Second, from the perspective of task adaptability, it must match the needs of sequence labeling. The design of the CRF's feature functions requires direct association with the character information at the current position (i) and contextual positions (i − 1, i + 1) to predict toponym boundaries. Unigram features (i − 1, i, i + 1) and bigram features (i − 1, i; i, i + 1) exactly cover the core contextual windows for sequence labeling, avoiding the explosion of feature dimensions caused by excessively large feature windows.

Table 9. The feature templates of CRF.

No.	Feature Templates of CRF
1	# Unigram U00:%x[−2,0] U01:%x[−1,0] U02:%x[0,0] U03:%x[1,0] U04:%x[2,0] U05:%x[−2,0]/%x[−1,0] U06:%x[−1,0]/%x[0,0] U07:%x[0,0]/%x[1,0] U08:%x[1,0]/%x[2,0] U09:%x[−1,0]/%x[0,0]/%x[1,0]
2	# Bigram B

The CRF model was trained using a feature set including character-level n-grams ($n = 1$), part-of-speech tags, and contextual position indicators. The regularization parameter was set to 0.1 via grid search.

This experiment utilized three evaluation metrics from the field of natural language processing to assess the results of Chinese toponym recognition: Precision (P), Recall (R), and $F1$ Score.

$$P = \frac{TP}{TP + FP} \times 100\% \quad (1)$$

$$R = \frac{TP}{TP + FN} \times 100\% \quad (2)$$

$$F1 = \frac{P \times R \times 2}{P + R} \quad (3)$$

In the formula, TP is the number of positive samples correctly identified as positive; FP is the number of negative samples incorrectly identified as positive; FN is the number of positive samples incorrectly identified as negative; and TN is the number of negative samples correctly identified as negative. These metrics allow for a comprehensive evaluation of the toponym recognition model's performance, providing insights into its accuracy, completeness, and overall effectiveness in processing toponym annotations.

4.1. Closed Testing

Closed testing involves developing a recognition model using a subset of the annotated corpus and then evaluating the model on the remaining portions of the corpus. This testing approach is categorized into two types based on the source of the training corpus: single-corpus testing and mixed-corpus testing.

4.1.1. Single-Corpus Testing

Firstly, 300 texts were randomly selected from C1 to create training datasets, with three iterations denoted as C11, C12, and C13. Similarly, 1000 texts were randomly chosen from C2 for training, resulting in datasets C21, C22, and C23. These six training datasets were used to develop corresponding toponym recognition models. Subsequently, C1 and C2 were used as test corpora for toponym recognition. The test results are presented in Table 2, where C1 + C2 represents the combined corpus of C1 and C2.

From Figure 1, it is evident that C11, C12, and C13 achieved similar precision and recall rates for C1, indicating a high degree of similarity within the C1 corpus. Randomly selecting different subsets of this corpus yields comparable results. In contrast, C21 and C22 produced similar recognition results for C2, while C23 showed significant deviations, suggesting variability in the *People's Daily* corpus and indicating that the testing outcomes are influenced by the selected texts.

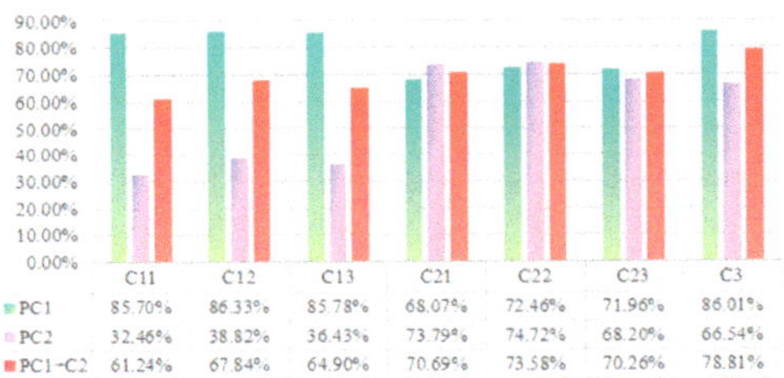

(a)

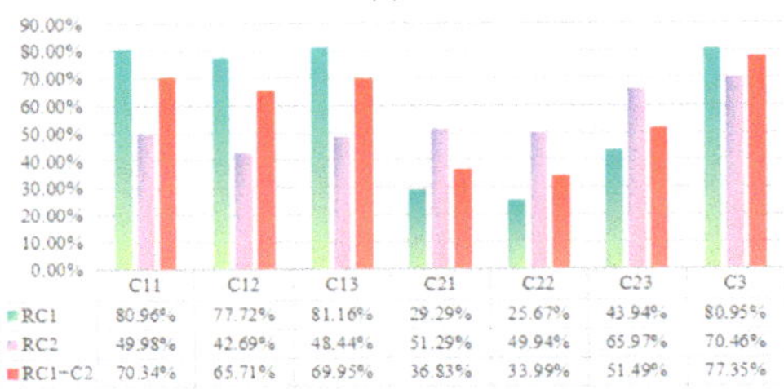

(b)

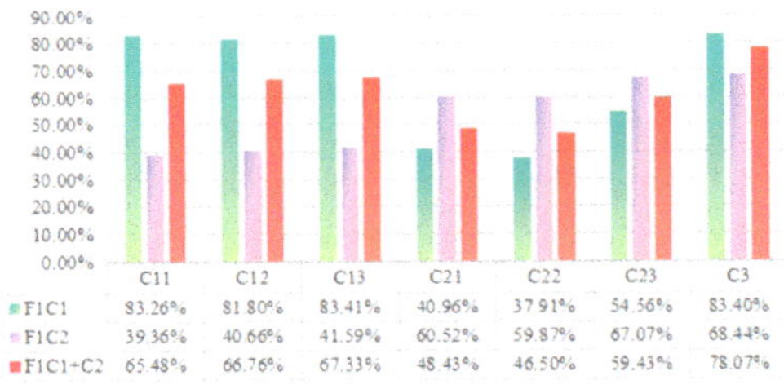

(c)

Figure 1. The results of closed tests. (**a**) The precision of closed tests. (**b**) The recall of closed tests. (**c**) The F1 value of closed test.

The recognition performance of C11, C12, and C13 on C2 was relatively poor, while C21, C22, and C23 performed inadequately on C1. This suggests that the toponym description features in the *Encyclopedia of China: Chinese Geography* and *People's Daily* corpora differ substantially, making cross-corpus recognition challenging. Notably, the model trained with C13 showed slightly better performance for recognizing C1, whereas the recall rate for C2 using the C23 model was significantly higher than other models, indicating that, overall, C23 achieved the best performance.

Comparing the test results of C11, C12, and C13 with those of C21, C22, and C23, it is observed that there are more significant differences in test performance among different CRF models trained on C21, C22, and C23. This is primarily attributed to the corpus sources of C21, C22, and C23 being *People's Daily*, where reports on different topics exhibit substantial variations in toponym types, character lengths of toponyms, and contextual features. For instance, regional administrative toponyms appear more frequently in reports on current political news and economic development. These toponyms have clear boundaries and iconic generic names, contributing to more stable boundary recognition. However, regional administrative toponyms involved in current political news and economic development reports also differ: current political news reports often feature administrative divisions (e.g., "Beijing Municipality," "Jiangsu Province") with relatively short character lengths, whereas economic development reports involve economic development zones (e.g., "Suzhou Industrial Park") with longer character lengths, which may affect the accuracy of boundary recognition. Additionally, cultural and tourism-themed reports involve a large number of scenic spot toponyms (e.g., "Zhouzhuang Ancient Town," "National Forest Park"). These toponyms typically adopt a composite structure of "specific name + multi-level generic name," imposing higher requirements on the model's ability to capture contextual information. It can be concluded that the inherent differences in corpus features of randomly sampled test data exert an impact on the toponym recognition performance of CRF models.

4.1.2. Mixed-Corpus Testing

The models trained on single corpora exhibited varying performance for C1 and C2, each showing strengths and weaknesses. To enhance the recognition accuracy and recall rates for both datasets, a mixed training approach was adopted. In this approach, portions of both C1 and C2 corpora were combined to create new training datasets for recognition and testing. Given that C13 and C23 showed the best recognition results in single-corpus testing, they were selected as representative corpora for C1 and C2, respectively, and were mixed to form a new training dataset, C3.

The testing results indicate that C3 leverages the advantages of C13 and C23, providing robust recognition performance for both C1 and C2. This improvement leads to enhanced precision and recall rates overall, and broadens the model's recognition capabilities. Closed testing results show that models trained on single corpora reflect the toponym and description characteristics of their respective types of text, but may not be directly applicable to corpora with significant differences. The mixed-corpus approach addresses the limitations of single-corpus models, offering a more comprehensive reflection of the overall toponym description features within the corpus. This approach better aligns with the design goals of achieving universality and broad applicability in Chinese toponym annotation corpora.

4.2. Open Testing

Open testing refers to the evaluation of recognition models using texts outside of the annotated corpora. For this purpose, 282 specialized texts were collected from sources such as the internet and news outlets, covering topics like natural disasters, influenza, and the South China Sea issues. These texts were manually annotated, resulting in 2914 toponyms. To comprehensively assess the performance differences in toponym recognition using various corpora, models trained on C13, C23, and C3 were tested on this specialized dataset. The experimental results indicate that the model trained with the mixed corpus C3 achieved approximately a 10% increase in F1 score compared to models trained on C13 and C23. This improvement underscores the broader recognition capability of the mixed corpus (Figure 2).

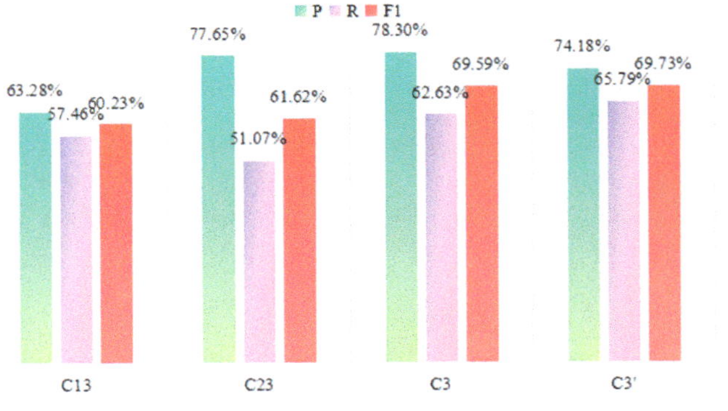

Figure 2. The results of open tests.

Both the *Encyclopedia of China: Chinese Geography* and *People's Daily* corpora primarily focus on domestic toponyms and cover a limited range of locations, notably lacking many global toponyms and administrative divisions of counties and towns, which are relatively common in the specialized texts used for open testing. To address this gap, we selected simple texts from online geographical encyclopedias that include these missing toponyms to construct a new web-based corpus data source (C4). The supplementary corpus C4 was constructed by scraping 500 web pages from Baidu Encyclopedia containing county-level toponyms not covered in C1/C2.

The experiments demonstrated that by combining C4 with C13 and C23 to form a new training dataset, C3′, targeted supplementation of toponyms was achieved, thereby enhancing toponym recognition capabilities. Through this open testing, we further realized that constructing an effective toponym recognition model requires not only ensuring the diversity of the training corpus but also ensuring comprehensive coverage of toponyms.

4.3. Extended Experiments with Deep Learning

Pre-trained models exemplified by BERT (Bidirectional Encoder Representations from Transformers) demonstrate exceptional capabilities in text representation and comprehension. The prevailing paradigm for named entity recognition (NER) tasks predominantly employs BERT or BERT-BiLSTM as foundational text feature encoders. Long Short-Term Memory (LSTM) networks effectively learn sentence-level contextual features, while the Bidirectional LSTM (BiLSTM) [27] architecture integrates forward and backward LSTMs through concatenated outputs. This bidirectional mechanism ensures that predictions are jointly determined by preceding and subsequent inputs, thereby enhancing output accuracy. Overall, combining the contextual semantic representation capability of pre-trained language models (BERT) with the sequence modeling advantages of BiLSTM demonstrates excellent performance in Chinese name entity recognition tasks, serving as one of the mainstream choices to balance performance and complexity.

In the BERT-BiLSTM-CRF framework, input text sequences first undergo contextual feature extraction through BERT's character embedding layer, generating low-dimensional character vectors. These vectors subsequently pass through a BiLSTM-based bidirectional encoding layer for higher-dimensional feature extraction. The processed features then enter a CRF decoding layer incorporating MFM (Multi-Feature Mapping) or TLP (Tag Label Projection) mechanisms, which enforces strict compliance with entity category formats during sequence output. This hierarchical architecture ultimately accomplishes the entity prediction task through coordinated multi-layer feature transformation.

This study further implements the BERT-BiLSTM-CRF model for Chinese toponym recognition, with detailed training parameters specified in the accompanying table. To address the catastrophic forgetting phenomenon where BERT may overwrite pre-trained knowledge during fine-tuning, we empirically set the pre-training layer's learning rate to 0.0001 based on existing research [28] and experimental validation. A dropout rate of 0.2 was applied to randomly deactivate specific neuron units during training, effectively mitigating overfitting risks. The C3 corpus underwent random partitioning into training, validation, and test sets following a 7:2:1 ratio. Additionally, XML-formatted annotated data was systematically converted into the BIOES tagging format for model compatibility. (See Table 10).

Table 10. Training parameter settings for the BiLSTM networks.

Parameter	Value
Learning rate	0.0001
Dropout	0.2
Maximum gradient	5
Model iterations	100
Label categories	5 types (BIEOS)

To benchmark against state-of-the-art methods, we fine-tuned a BERT-BiLSTM-CRF model on the CHTopo corpus. The model achieved an F1 score of 92.30% on C1 (vs. 83.40% for CRF) and 78.10% on C2 (vs. 68.44% for CRF), demonstrating superior performance in handling ambiguous and long-tail toponyms. Moreover, we simulated low-resource scenarios by training on 10% of C3. CRF achieved 72.1% F1 (vs. 68.5% for BERT-BiLSTM-CRF), indicating traditional models may still benefit from handcrafted features in limited data.

Comparing the recognition results of the BERT-BiLSTM-CRF model with those of the CRF model, it is observed that generally lower recognition rates are evident for the following three categories of toponyms (Table 11). It can be seen that both the CRF and BERT-BiLSTM-CRF models still exhibit recognition shortcomings in scenarios involving derived toponyms, mixed punctuation toponyms, and metonymic toponyms. To address these issues, it is necessary to integrate the annotation rules and coverage limitations of the CHTopo corpus, and continue to optimize and improve along directions such as corpus supplementation, feature template refinement, and the integration of multi-recognition models.

Table 11. Analysis of toponym recognition results based on CRF and BERT-BiLSTM-CRF models.

Error Type	Original Text	Recognition Result	Annotated Result	Error Analysis
Boundary omission of derived toponyms	枯水期时鄱阳湖湖面急剧萎缩。(in Chinese)	鄱阳湖湖面 (in Chinese)	鄱阳湖 (in Chinese)	The feature template of CRF only covers the current character and adjacent characters, failing to capture that "lake surface" is a non-toponymic derived description.
	During the dry season, the lake surface of Poyang Lake shrinks sharply. (in English)	Poyang Lake surface (in English)	Poyang Lake	
Structural misjudgment of mixed punctuation toponyms	秦岭一淮河线是中国地理区分北方地区和南方地区的地理分界线。(in Chinese)	秦岭; 淮河 (in Chinese)	秦岭一淮河线; 秦岭; 淮河 (in Chinese)	Not optimized for mixed punctuation, splitting "Qinling–Huaihe Line" into independent toponyms.
	The Qinling–Huaihe Line is a geographical dividing line in China that distinguishes northern and southern regions. (in English)	Qinling; Huaihe (in English)	Qinling–Huaihe Line; Qinling; Huaihe (in English)	
Over-annotation of metonymic toponyms	南京盐水鸭是江苏特产。(in Chinese)	南京 (in Chinese)	——	Due to the high-frequency feature of the generic name "Jing" ("capital"), the model fails to combine context (where "salted duck" indicates a specialty) to identify "Nanjing" as a metonym.
	Nanjing salted duck is a specialty of Jiangsu. (in English)	Nanjing (in English)	——	

4.4. Extended Experiments with Practical Applications

In the current big data environment, social media has gradually been applied to the prevention, preparation, response, and recovery work of disaster management. Identifying toponyms from social media texts has become a fundamental task in the promotion and application of disaster big data. Based on the CHTopo corpus and the CRF model trained therefrom, experiments were conducted using social media data from typical disasters. Super Typhoon Lekima (international number: 1909), the strongest typhoon to make landfall in China in 2019, and Sina Weibo (one of the most widely used social media platforms in China) were selected for this study [29]. This research collected Weibo posts containing the keywords "typhoon" and "Lekima" from 9–12 August 2019, and processed/analyzed posts from the major affected regions (Zhejiang Province, Jiangsu Province, Shanghai Municipality, and Shandong Province). A total of 34,825 eligible Weibo posts were obtained [30].

Applying the CRF model trained on the C3 corpus to toponym recognition in Sina Weibo texts yields results with P = 81.98%, R = 76.34%, and F1 = 79.06%, with partial toponym recognition results shown in Table 12. It can be observed that in social media texts related to natural disaster monitoring and emergency response, the toponyms involved are primarily administrative divisions. As this type of toponym has been extensively annotated in the CHTopo corpus, the trained CRF model also excels at recognizing administrative division-based toponyms. However, since Weibo users share various disaster-related information at any time and place, the texts may contain descriptions of toponyms at lower administrative levels, which poses challenges to toponym recognition. For instance, "Dongyuan Sicun" (a residential community name) in Table 12 was not identified by the CRF model. Overall, applying the CRF model to social media texts can achieve relatively accurate recognition results in most scenarios. Based on the toponym recognition results from social media texts, more extensive research can be further conducted, such as toponym-based disaster information aggregation, disaster status identification, and disaster process analysis.

Table 12. Analysis of toponym recognition results for Sina Weibo.

Original Weibo Text	Recognition Result	Correct Result
台风终于放过广东 广州。(in Chinese) The typhoon has finally spared Guangdong and Guangzhou. (in English)	广东; 广州 (in Chinese) Guangdong; Guangzhou (in English)	广东; 广州 (in Chinese) Guangdong; Guangzhou (in English)
安吉县综合执法局执法人员巡查到孝源街道皈山场村时, … 土房就倒塌了… (in Chinese)	安吉县; 孝源街道皈山场村 (in Chinese)	安吉县; 孝源街道; 皈山场村 (in Chinese)
When law enforcement officers from the Anji County Comprehensive Law Enforcement Bureau patrolled to Guishanchang Village, Xiaoyuan Subdistrict, … the adobe house collapsed … (in English)	Anji County; Xiaoyuan Subdistrict Guishanchang Village (in English)	Anji County; Xiaoyuan Subdistrict; Guishanchang Village (in English)
台风天都不用出门了啦啦啦。上海·东园四村 (in Chinese)	上海 (in Chinese)	上海东园四村 (in Chinese)
No need to go out on this typhoon day, la la la. Shanghai·Dongyuan Sicun (in English)	Shanghai (in English)	Shanghai Dongyuan Sicun (in English)
…中心位于浙江省金华市磐安县内，… (in Chinese)	浙江省金华市磐安县 (in Chinese)	浙江省金华市磐安县 (in Chinese)
…the center is located within Pan'an County, Jinhua City, Zhejiang Province, … (in English)	Pan'an County, Jinhua City, Zhejiang Province (in English)	Pan'an County, Jinhua City, Zhejiang Province (in English)

4.5. Discussion

The CHTopo corpus constructed in this study provides high-quality foundational resources for Chinese toponym annotation. However, limited by data sources, annotation rules, and technical implementation, it still has the following limitations in aspects such as the absence of temporal dimension annotation, insufficient coverage of dialectal toponyms, limited quantity of global toponyms, and lack of a dynamic update mechanism. Future extensions may focus on the following directions:

(1) Expanding temporal dimension annotation to support historical context analysis

A "Time" attribute will be added to the existing XML annotation scheme to record the existence time range or change time points of toponyms. By supplementing temporal attributes, the corpus can support tasks such as "spatial location comparison of the same toponym across different historical periods" and "statistical analysis of toponym change frequency," thereby providing data support for historical geography research.

(2) Supplementing dialectal corpora to improve the cultural dimension of toponyms

Expand data sources to include dialectal texts (e.g., local county annals, dialectal literary works, and dialectal versions of local news), and add a "Dialect" attribute to XML tags (recording dialectal pronunciation or regional cultural backgrounds). The supplementation of dialectal annotations will enhance the application value of the corpus in scenarios such as dialectal toponym recognition and regional cultural dissemination.

(3) Adding new global toponym data sources to enhance coverage breadth

Building on the existing data sources of the *Encyclopedia of China: Chinese Geography* and *People's Daily*, three new categories of corpus data sources for international toponyms will be added. First, the authoritative geographical literature, including the *Encyclopedia of World Geography* and *United Nations Geospatial Information Management Documents on Toponymic Standardization*, containing multilingual official toponyms. Second, international news corpora, including the *China Daily International Edition*, BBC Chinese Website, and *Xinhua News Agency International News*, covering multiple fields such as politics, economy, and culture. Finally, social media and travelogues, including Ctrip International Travelogues and the Zhihu "Global Travel" Topic, which is beneficial for supplementing niche toponyms.

(4) Constructing a dynamic update system to support real-time toponym annotation

Develop an automated annotation tool based on natural language processing that integrates real-time data sources such as news and government announcements, enabling dynamic extraction and automatic annotation of toponyms. For example, upon detecting an establishment announcement of "Changbai Korean Autonomous County," the tool can automatically extract the toponym information and supplement it to the corpus while generating a <Place> tag. The dynamic update system will upgrade the corpus from a "static resource" to "living data," better supporting real-time application scenarios.

5. Conclusions

The construction of toponym annotation corpora requires careful consideration of the balance, representativeness, and scale of the data. It is essential to use a comprehensive annotation system to ensure the completeness of spatial semantic information. In practical annotation processes, the determination of whether toponyms reflect spatial semantics may involve a degree of subjectivity, which can impact subsequent training and recognition.

Moreover, comparative analysis of annotation results with those from tokenization software reveals that while common and simple toponyms are relatively consistent, there is a significant discrepancy for complex toponyms. Models trained on multi-source corpora not only effectively capture the descriptive features and patterns within the toponym annotation corpus but also enhance the recognition of a wider array of toponyms.

In practical applications, the toponym recognition model can be expanded based on specific needs. For instance, in the open testing conducted in this study, incorporating web-based corpus data effectively addressed issues with out-of-vocabulary terms and broadened the scope of toponym recognition. This study demonstrates that expanding the corpus through web-sourced texts, particularly targeting administrative divisions such as countries, cities, and towns, offers a more efficient and expedient alternative to traditional methods. This approach is particularly valuable for the challenging task of collecting toponym data for other regions.

Author Contributions: Conceptualization, P.Y.; data curation, Y.J.; formal analysis, Y.J.; investigation, P.Y. and Y.J.; methodology, P.Y.; project administration, P.Y.; validation, Y.J.; visualization, Y.W.; writing—original draft, P.Y.; writing—review and editing, Y.W. All authors have read and agreed to the published version of the manuscript.

Funding: This research was funded by the National Natural Science Foundation of China (grant no. 42301522), and the Humanities and Social Sciences Foundation of Yangzhou University (grant no. xjj2021-08).

Institutional Review Board Statement: Not applicable.

Informed Consent Statement: Not applicable.

Data Availability Statement: The raw data supporting the conclusions of this article will be made available by the authors on request.

Conflicts of Interest: The authors declare no conflicts of interest.

References

1. DeLozier, G.; Baldridge, J.; London, L. Gazetteer-independent toponym resolution using geographic word profiles. In Proceedings of the Twenty-Ninth AAAI Conference on Artificial Intelligence (AAAI'15), Austin, TX, USA, 25–30 January 2015; AAAI Press: New York, NY, USA, 2015; pp. 2382–2388.
2. Kumar, A.; Singh, J.P. Location reference identification from tweets during emergencies: A deep learning approach. *Int. J. Disaster Risk Reduct.* **2019**, *33*, 365–375. [CrossRef]

3. Speriosu, M.; Baldridge, J. Text-driven toponym resolution using indirect supervision. In Proceedings of the 51st Annual Meeting of the Association for Computational Linguistics (Volume 1: Long Papers), Sofia, Bulgaria, 4–9 August 2013; Association for Computational Linguistics: Sofia, Bulgaria, 2013; pp. 1466–1476.
4. Karimzadeh, M.; Pezanowski, S.; MacEachren, A.M.; Wallgrun, J.O. GeoTxt: A scalable geoparsing system for unstructured text geolocation. *Trans. GIS* **2019**, *23*, 118–136. [CrossRef]
5. Buscaldi, D. Approaches to disambiguating toponyms. *SIGSPATIAL Spec.* **2011**, *3*, 16–19. [CrossRef]
6. Hu, Y.; Mao, H.; McKenzie, G. A natural language processing and geospatial clustering framework for harvesting local place names from geotagged housing advertisements. *Int. J. Geogr. Inf. Sci.* **2018**, *33*, 714–738. [CrossRef]
7. Gritta, M.; Pilehvar, M.T.; Collier, N. A pragmatic guide to geoparsing evaluation: Toponyms, named entity recognition and pragmatics. *Lang. Resour. Eval.* **2020**, *54*, 683–712. [CrossRef] [PubMed]
8. Mehta, S.; Jain, G.; Mala, S. Natural Language Processing Approach and Geospatial Clustering to Explore the Unexplored Geotags Using Media. In Proceedings of the 2023 13th International Conference on Cloud Computing, Data Science & Engineering (Confluence), Noida, India, 19–20 January 2023; pp. 672–675.
9. Kuai, X.; Guo, R.; Zhang, Z.; He, B.; Zhao, Z.; Guo, H. Spatial context-based local toponym extraction and Chinese textual address segmentation from urban POI data. *ISPRS Int. J. Geo-Inf.* **2020**, *9*, 147. [CrossRef]
10. Berragan, C.; Singleton, A.; Calafiore, A.; Morley, J. Transformer-based named entity recognition for place name extraction from unstructured text. *Int. J. Geogr. Inf. Sci.* **2023**, *37*, 747–766. [CrossRef]
11. Halterman, A. Mordecai: Full text geoparsing and event geocoding. *J. Open Source Softw.* **2017**, *2*, 91. [CrossRef]
12. Weissenbacher, D.; Magge, A.; O'Connor, K.; Scotch, M.; Gonzalez-Hernandez, G. SemEval-2019 task 12: Toponym resolution in scientific papers. In Proceedings of the 13th International Workshop on Semantic Evaluation, Minneapolis, MN, USA, 6–7 June 2019; Association for Computational Linguistics: Minneapolis, MN, USA, 2019; pp. 907–916.
13. Wang, S.; Zhang, X.; Ye, P.; Du, M. Deep belief networks based toponym recognition for Chinese text. *ISPRS Int. J. Geo-Inf.* **2018**, *7*, 217. [CrossRef]
14. Wallgrun, J.O.; Karimzadeh, M.; MacEachren, A.M.; Pezanowski, S. GeoCorpora: Building a corpus to test and train microblog geoparsers. *Int. J. Geogr. Inf. Sci.* **2018**, *32*, 1–29. [CrossRef]
15. Karimzadeh, M.; MacEachren, A.M. GeoAnnotator: A collaborative semi-automatic platform for constructing geo-annotated text corpora. *ISPRS Int. J. Geo-Inf.* **2019**, *8*, 161. [CrossRef]
16. Mani, I.; Hitzeman, J.; Richer, J.; Harris, D.; Quimby, R.; Wellner, B. SpatialML: Annotation scheme, corpora, and tools. In Proceedings of the 6th International Conference on Language Resources and Evaluation, Marrakech, Morocco, 28–30 May 2008; LPEC: Marrakech, Morocco, 2008.
17. Talmy, L. The fundamental system of spatial schemes in language. In *From Perception to Meaning: Image Schemes in Cognitive Linguistics*; Hampe, B., Ed.; De Gruyter: Berlin, Germany, 2005; pp. 199–263.
18. Leidner, J.L. Toponym Resolution in Text. Ph.D. Thesis, University of Edinburgh, Edinburgh, UK, 2007.
19. Mani, I.; Doran, C.; Harris, D.; Hitzeman, J.; Quimby, R.; Richer, J.; Wellner, B.; Mardis, S.; Clancy, S. SpatialML: Annotation scheme, resources, and evaluation. *Lang. Resour. Eval.* **2010**, *44*, 263–280. [CrossRef]
20. Li, H. Research on Spatial Conceptual Model Based on Natural Language Processing. Ph.D. Thesis, Harbin Institute of Technology, Harbin, China, 2007.
21. Le, X.; Yang, C.; Yu, W. Spatial concept extraction based on spatial semantic role in natural language. *Geomat. Inf. Sci. Wuhan Univ.* **2005**, *30*, 1100–1103.
22. Zhang, X.; Zhu, S.; Zhang, C. Annotation for geographical named entities in Chinese text. *Acta Geod. Cartogr. Sin.* **2012**, *41*, 115–120.
23. Zhang, X.; Zhang, C.; Zhu, S. Annotation for geographical spatial relations in Chinese text. *Acta Geod. Cartogr. Sin.* **2012**, *41*, 468–474.
24. *GB/T 18521-2001*; Rules for Classification of Geographical Names and Code Representation. National Standard: Beijing, China, 2001.
25. Sutton, C.; McCallum, A. An introduction to conditional random fields. *Found. Trends Mach. Learn.* **2010**, *4*, 267–373. [CrossRef]
26. Song, S.; Nan, Z.; Huang, H. Named entity recognition based on conditional random fields. *Cluster Comput.* **2017**, *1*, 5195–5206. [CrossRef]
27. Qiu, Q.; Xie, Z.; Wu, L.; Tao, L.; Li, W. BiLSTM-CRF for geological named entity recognition from the geoscience literature. *Earth Sci. Inform.* **2019**, *12*, 565–579. [CrossRef]
28. Sun, C.; Qiu, X.; Xu, Y.; Huang, X. How to Fine-Tune BERT for Text Classification? In Proceedings of the Chinese Computational Linguistics: 18th China National Conference on Computational Linguistics, Kunming, China, 18–20 October 2019; Springer: Cham, Switzerland, 2019; pp. 194–206.

29. Ye, P.; Zhang, C.; Chen, M.; Li, S. Typhoon disaster state information extraction for Chinese texts. *Sci. Rep.* **2024**, *14*, 7925. [CrossRef] [PubMed]
30. Ye, P.; Zhang, X.; Huai, A.; Tang, W. Information Detection for the Process of Typhoon Events in Microblog Text: A Spatio-Temporal Perspective. *ISPRS Int. J. Geo-Inf.* **2021**, *10*, 174. [CrossRef]

01010
01010
01010 *information*

MDPI

Article

Automated Classification of Public Transport Complaints via Text Mining Using LLMs and Embeddings

Daniyar Rakhimzhanov [1,*], Saule Belginova [2,*] and Didar Yedilkhan [1,*]

1 Big Data and Blockchain Technologies Research Innovation Center, Astana IT University, 020000 Astana, Kazakhstan
2 Department of Information Technology, University Turan, 050013 Almaty, Kazakhstan
* Correspondence: d.rahimzhanov@astanait.edu.kz (D.R.); s.belginova@turan-edu.kz (S.B.); d.yedilkhan@astanait.edu.kz (D.Y.)

Abstract: The proliferation of digital public service platforms and the expansion of e-government initiatives have significantly increased the volume and diversity of citizen-generated feedback. This trend emphasizes the need for classification systems that are not only tailored to specific administrative domains but also robust to the linguistic, contextual, and structural variability inherent in user-submitted content. This study investigates the comparative effectiveness of large language models (LLMs) alongside instruction-tuned embedding models in the task of categorizing public transportation complaints. LLMs were tested using a few-shot inference, where classification is guided by a small set of in-context examples. Embedding models were assessed under three paradigms: label-only zero-shot classification, instruction-based classification, and supervised fine-tuning. Results indicate that fine-tuned embeddings can achieve or exceed the accuracy of LLMs, reaching up to 90 percent, while offering significant reductions in inference latency and computational overhead. E5 embeddings showed consistent generalization across unseen categories and input shifts, whereas BGE-M3 demonstrated measurable gains when adapted to task-specific distributions. Instruction-based classification produced lower accuracy for both models, highlighting the limitations of prompt conditioning in isolation. These findings position multilingual embedding models as a viable alternative to LLMs for classification at scale in data-intensive public sector environments.

Keywords: multilingual complaint classification; large language models; embedding models; instruction-based classification; zero-shot learning; few-shot inference; public transportation; resource-efficient NLP; supervised fine-tuning; public sector NLP

1. Introduction

Public transportation complaints represent a strategically important but underutilized source of operational data for urban mobility systems. With the expansion of digital communication channels, transit authorities are exposed to increasingly large volumes of free-text feedback generated by passengers [1–3]. Historically, most text classification systems in civic contexts have relied on sentiment analysis or topic modeling approaches, which reduce feedback to binary polarity or general thematic clusters [4–6]. Recent works on multilingual cyber threat detection underscore the significance of architectures capable of addressing contextual volatility in high-stakes environments, such as social media and civic communication channels [7].

Earlier comparative studies in grammar acceptability classification have shown that transformer-based models substantially outperform POS-tagging and BoW-based methods in linguistic tasks of similar structural complexity [8]. While sufficient for broad trend monitoring, such techniques lack the semantic resolution needed for fine-grained categorization and actionable understanding. In high-throughput, multilingual data environments such as municipal transportation systems, the ability to separate overlapping intents and accurately localize service-specific issues is critical. Novel developments in LLMs and multilingual embedding models have enabled more context-aware and resource-efficient approaches to multilingual classification [9–11]. These paradigms are especially relevant in infrastructure-heavy domains, where low-latency inference and scalable deployment are critical constraints [12–15], as shown in prior applications involving automated review analysis and clinical information extraction [16,17].

Despite the progress in using LLMs and embeddings, there remains a notable gap in the literature: no prior work has thoroughly compared these two paradigms side-by-side on public service complaint classification nor fully explored the trade-offs between accuracy and resource efficiency in this context. Existing studies tend to focus on one class of models in isolation. For example, [11] applied a reasoning-augmented LLM to consumer complaint texts, demonstrating improved detection of complaint categories with chain-of-thought prompts. In a separate approach [14], the authors combined multiple LLM-based classifiers (an ensemble of large models) to boost complaint classification accuracy. These works underscore the growing interest in LLMs for complex classifications. However, they primarily emphasize accuracy gains and do not address the practical drawbacks of relying solely on LLMs, namely the high computational cost and latency, as well as dependence on proprietary APIs or large infrastructure.

On the other hand, research on embedding models in multilingual contexts shows they can be highly effective (e.g., achieving cross-lingual semantic alignment) [18], but their use in fine-grained complaint categorization is under-explored. There is little insight into whether a properly tuned embedding model can match an LLM's performance on this task or how an instruction-based embedding classifier compares to a zero-shot LLM prompt. This represents a critical gap, given that public agencies need solutions that are both accurate and efficient. Therefore, a strong rationale exists to investigate which approach (LLM vs. embeddings) is more suitable for public transport complaint classification under real-world conditions. The current study is motivated by this gap and aims to provide clarity on the comparative effectiveness of LLMs and embedding models when balancing performance with operational constraints.

Closely relevant to our study, works [19,20] proved that fine-tuning embeddings outperformed prompting. However, unlike these studies, which typically evaluate one or two model types in isolation, our work systematically compares a broad spectrum of architectures across both embedding-based and LLM-based paradigms. The evaluation covers multiple multilingual architectures and explores differences in classification accuracy, latency, and deployment feasibility under varied inference conditions.

In this study, we investigate the comparative effectiveness of LLMs and embedding-based architecture across several classification setups. We hypothesize that embedding models, when properly configured, can deliver performance comparable to LLMs while exhibiting superior inference efficiency. Our results enhance a comprehensive insight into model selection under resource constraints and provide evidence for the viability of embedding-based systems in public-sector language processing pipelines. Emphasis is placed on performance trade-offs across paradigms and the operational feasibility of integrating such models into multilingual, high-volume environments.

2. Materials and Methods

2.1. Dataset

The dataset used in this study is derived from public transport complaints submitted by residents of Astana, Kazakhstan, throughout 2023. These complaints were collected through official municipal platforms, where users described various transit-related issues in free-text format. From a corpus of over 58,000 transport-related entries, a representative subset of 2400 complaints was selected for manual annotation and used in the present study. Each complaint contains a natural-language narrative, varying in length from 47 to over 2000 characters. These texts exhibit significant linguistic diversity, including unstructured phrasing, grammatical inconsistencies, and frequent code-switching between Russian and Kazakh. These characteristics reflect real-world data distributions and provide a rigorous testbed for classification under variability [5].

Each complaint was independently labeled by two native-speaking annotators with domain expertise in urban mobility and transportation systems. Annotation was performed according to a predefined taxonomy consisting of seven functionally distinct categories, the descriptions and examples of which are presented in Table 1. Inter-annotator reliability was assessed using Cohen's kappa coefficient, which yielded $\kappa = 0.7065$, indicating substantial agreement. In cases of disagreement, the final label was determined by a senior annotator, whose judgments served as the reference due to their deeper involvement in the development of the annotation protocol.

Table 1. Complaint categories with descriptions and representative examples (translated to English).

Code	Category	Description	Example
0	Transport problems	Complaints related to transport delays, overcrowded buses, vehicle breakdowns, and insufficient service on routes.	"It's 06:45, but route N has still not arrived. . ."
1	Personnel problems	Complaints concerning driver misconduct, missed stops, or inappropriate behavior of ticket inspectors.	"The inspector walked through the bus without checking tickets. . ."
2	Bus stop infrastructure	Complaints about the condition and equipment of bus stops, including absence or malfunction of heated shelters, damaged structures, and broken information displays.	"We request the installation of an information display at N bus stop. . ."
3	Equipment faults	Complaints regarding broken equipment inside buses, such as validators, air conditioning units, or heating systems.	"The onboard announcer is not working on this route. . ."
4	Praise	Expressions of gratitude or positive feedback related to the performance of the transport system or personnel.	"Thank you. . . for your professionalism. . ."
5	Organizational and technical problems	Complaints involving transport card top-ups, public information dissemination, route maps, and schedule updates.	"Please extend route No. N to Koktal Park. . ."
6	Other complaints	Complaints that either span multiple categories or do not fit into any of the predefined ones.	"The manhole cover is open across from the checkpoint. . ."

While Table 1 provides concise examples, other complaints are linguistically more complex, featuring code-codeswitching as shown in Table 2.

Table 2. Code-switched complaints.

Category	Original Complaint	Kazakh Segment	Russian Segment	English Translation
Transport problems	XX таңғы 7-де келмеді, хотя расписание указано	XX таңғы 7-де келмеді,	хотя расписание указано	Bus XX did not arrive at 7 a.m., even though it is shown in the timetable.
Personnel problems	Маршрут № XX гос. номер XXX Умбетей жырау аялдамасында, ж/м Караоткель-2 аялдамысна қарай бағытта, автобус тоқтаған жоқ, өтіп кетті.	Умбетей жырау аялдамасында, ж/м Караоткель-2 аялдамысна қарай бағытта, автобус тоқтаған жоқ, өтіп кетті.	Маршрут № XX гос. номер XXX	Bus route No. XX, state number XXX, did not stop at the Umbetey Zhyrau stop in the direction of Karaotkel-2.
Bus stop infrastructure	На остановке Нажимиденова в направления Нұрлы жол не работает информационное табло	Нұрлы жол	На остановке Нажимиденова в направления … не работает информационное табло	The information board at the Nazhimidenov stop in the direction of Nurly Zhol is not working
Organizational and technical problems	100 тг каспи. Перезалив жасау керек, чек бар Каспида.	100 тг каспи. … жасау керек, чек бар Каспида.	Перезалив	100 tenge Kaspi. Need to top up, there is a check in Kaspi.

The dataset was randomly sampled to preserve the natural distribution of complaint types across categories, including underrepresented and context-dependent cases (see Table 3). The annotated entries were divided into 75% training and 25% testing partitions, applied consistently across all modeling paradigms, including supervised fine-tuning, few-shot prompting, and embedding-based zero-shot classification. All the few-shot prompts were drawn exclusively from the training set to prevent data leakage.

Table 3. Distribution of annotated complaints by category with a consistent 75/25 train–test split.

No	Name of Category	Number of Annotated Complaints		
		Total	Training Dataset	Test Dataset
1	Transport Problems	1214	910	304
2	Personnel problems	605	454	151
3	Bus stop infrastructure	104	78	26
4	Equipment faults	117	88	29
5	Praise	28	21	7
6	Organizational and technical problems	175	131	44
7	Other complaints	157	118	39
	TOTAL	2400	1800	600

Several categories in the dataset have low support in the test split due to their natural rarity. For example, expressions of gratitude occur far less frequently than complaints about service disruptions. These categories were retained to preserve the authenticity of user input and to support targeted qualitative analysis. Evaluation reports both class-specific and macro-averaged metrics to account for class imbalance.

2.2. Models and Experimental Configurations

To compare the performance of LLMs and embedding models, we evaluate five models representing these two major classes as shown in Figure 1. For LLMs, classification is performed using few-shot prompting, where the model is given a small number of labeled examples within the prompt to guide prediction. For embedding-based models, we consider three approaches: (1) zero-shot classification using label descriptions, where the model assigns a class based solely on semantic similarity to label names or definitions; (2) instruction-based classification, which uses task prompts to guide inference without retraining; and (3) supervised fine-tuning, where model weights are adjusted using labeled training data.

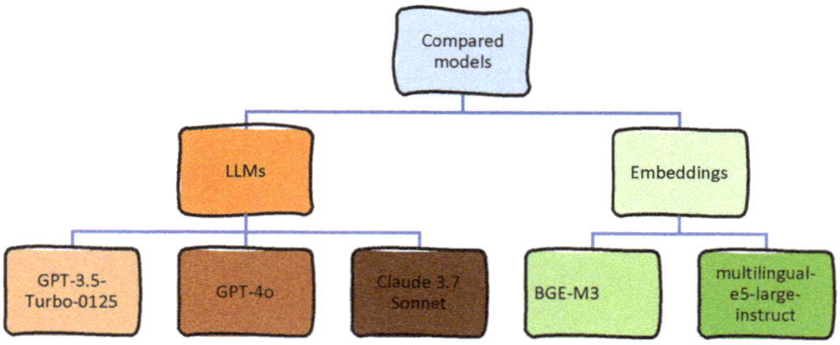

Figure 1. Models under evaluation.

2.2.1. Few-Shot Prompting Configuration for LLMs

Few-shot prompting configuration avoids any model fine-tuning or parameter adjustment and relies exclusively on in-context learning capacity [11]. Each LLM receives a structured prompt with three labeled examples per class, covering all seven target categories (21 examples total). Samples are drawn from the training set and kept constant across all experiments to ensure consistency. The prompt lists classification categories and instructs the model to return one label per complaint. Messages follow a role-tagged format, compatible with both OpenAI and Claude APIs to ensure consistency across models. Listing 1 shows the input format while Figure 2 illustrates the overall workflow. Without task-specific tuning, this setup enables a fair evaluation of generalization in multilingual, low-supervision settings.

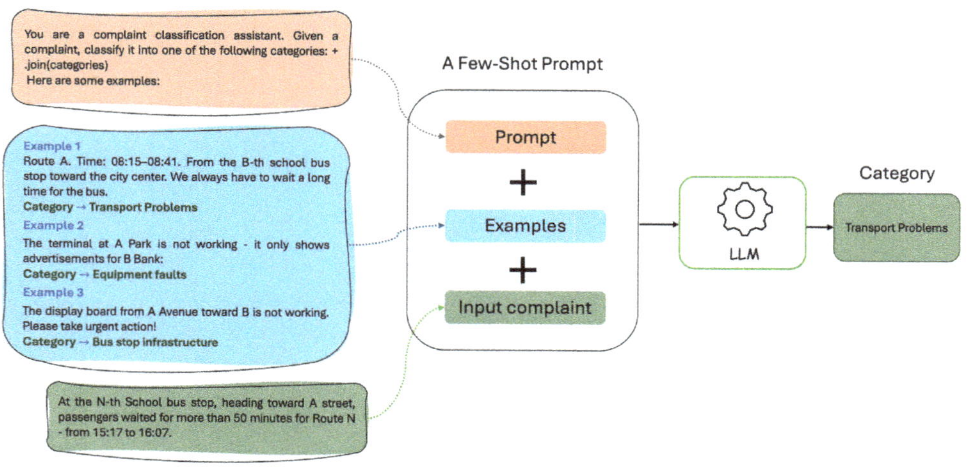

Figure 2. The workflow for few-shot classification using LLMs and prompt-based inputs.

Listing 1. Prompt template used in few-shot classification with LLMs.

```
messages = [
{
"role": "system",
"content":
"You are a complaint classification assistant."
"Given a complaint, classify it into one of the following
categories: "+", "join (categories)"
"Here are some examples:\n\n"
},
{
"role": "user",
"content":
"Now, classify the following complaint:\nComplaint:
{complaint_text}\nCategory:"
}
]
```

This few-shot prompting setup enables direct comparison between LLMs and embedding-based classifiers under comparable data and task conditions [14,18]. It follows evidence that contextual examples improve LLM generalization in complex classification tasks [19,20], including prompt-based extraction in domains like clinical reports [16]. Henríquez-Jara et al. [21] also demonstrated ChatGPT's (GPT-3.5-turbo) effectiveness for classifying affective content in multilingual public transport feedback.

2.2.2. Zero-Shot Configuration for Embeddings

As a baseline for classification without supervision, we implemented a label-only zero-shot approach using multilingual embedding models. This method excludes the use of labeled examples, natural language instructions, or any form of fine-tuning. Instead, both the complaint texts and the category labels are independently encoded into dense vector representations. Classification is performed by computing the cosine similarity between the embedded complaint and each label embedding, with the highest similarity score determining the predicted class (see Figure 3).

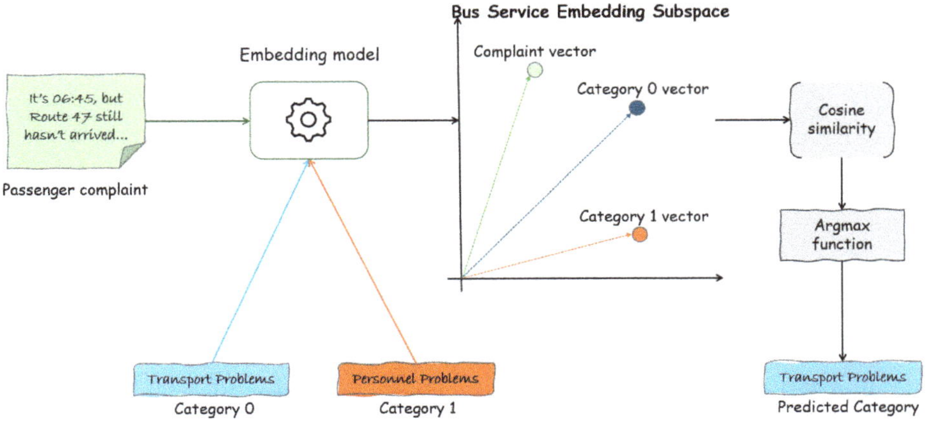

Figure 3. The workflow for embedding-based zero-shot classification with cosine similarity.

2.2.3. Instruction-Based Configuration for Embeddings

While the label-only method provides a simple and fully unsupervised baseline by matching complaints to category names via embedding similarity, it does not supply the model with any explicit information about the task or the semantic distinctions between classes. To address this limitation, we extended the zero-shot paradigm with an instruction-based classification approach, which incorporates task descriptions directly into the input through natural language prompts. This setup allows embedding models to perform zero-shot classification by leveraging prompt semantics, without requiring any task-specific fine-tuning or labeled data [9,22].

Each input was created by concatenating a classification instruction with the complaint text, forming a single natural-language input (see Listing 2). Likewise, each category was represented by pairing the same instruction with a brief, class-specific description drawn from a manually curated desc_map. This setup generated two types of embedding inputs: (1) the instruction plus complaint text and (2) the instruction plus a label description. The cosine similarity between these two types of embeddings was used to determine the most semantically aligned category for each complaint. To address the multilingual nature of the dataset, all prompts were constructed in both Russian and English. Each instruction listed all seven target categories, with a concise and distinctive description for each class to improve inter-class differentiation and reduce ambiguity during inference. We do not include the workflow figure, as it closely resembles Figure 3.

Listing 2. Instruction-based prompt template for multilingual embedding models.

```
    categories = [
"Transport Problems",
"Personnel Problems",
"Bus Stop Infrastructure",
"Equipment Faults",
"Praise",
"Organizational and Technical Problems",
"Other Complaints"
]

desc_map = {
"Transport Problems": "bus delays, route cancellations, irregular schedules",
"Personnel Problems": "driver rudeness, negligence, impolite staff behavior",
"Bus Stop Infrastructure": "missing shelters, poor signage, broken stop markings",
"Equipment Faults": "broken terminals, air conditioning issues, malfunctioning doors",
"Praise": "positive feedback, gratitude for service quality",
"Organizational and Technical Problems": "schedule errors, mobile app failures",
"Other Complaints": "issues not covered by the main categories"
}

instruction = "Classify the complaint into one of the following categories:\n"
for cat, desc in desc_map.items():
instruction += f "- {cat}: {desc}\n"
instruction += "\nComplaint:"
```

2.2.4. Supervised Fine-Tuning Configuration for Embeddings

Fine-tuning was conducted to evaluate model performance under explicit supervision. A contrastive learning objective was used to adjust the embedding space by pulling together representations of complaints from the same category and pushing apart those from different categories, as illustrated in Figure 4. This approach improves the model's ability to distinguish between semantically similar classes. The training data consisted of labeled complaint pairs from the annotated dataset. No additional preprocessing was applied, and raw user-generated inputs were preserved, including punctuation, inconsistent casing, and multilingual fragments. This ensured that training reflected real-world input conditions and maintained natural linguistic variation.

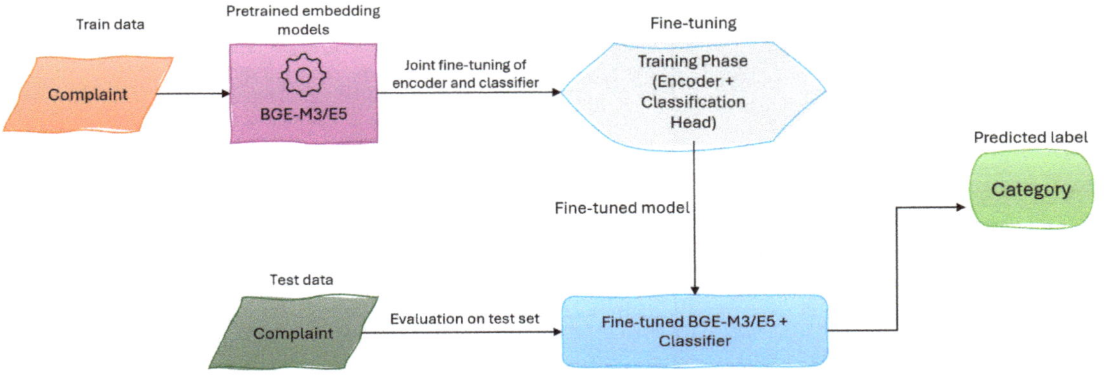

Figure 4. Workflow of fine-tuning pretrained embedding models (BGE-M3/E5) for multi-class complaint classification.

Fine-tuning affected only the upper layers of the model architecture, including the projection layer and selected encoder components, while pretrained weights remained frozen to retain multilingual generalizability. Optimization was conducted for three epochs using a batch size of 64 and a learning rate of 2×10^{-5}. Following training, complaint texts from the test set were embedded into fixed-size vectors and compared to class-level prototype representations. These prototypes were computed as mean embeddings of training examples belonging to each category. Final predictions were derived via cosine similarity between the complaint embedding and the centroids, selecting the nearest semantic match.

This fine-tuning strategy enables embedding models to learn domain-aligned representations that capture the structural and lexical variation specific to transportation complaint data. It offers a resource-efficient method for adapting pretrained models to real-world deployment environments characterized by linguistic variability, high-volume input, and the need for low-latency inference.

2.3. Evaluation Strategy

To ensure fair comparison across modeling paradigms, we applied a unified evaluation protocol using a shared test split. Performance was primarily measured by exact match accuracy, reflecting the proportion of cases where the predicted category matched the ground truth. To address class imbalance, we also computed weighted precision, recall, and F1-score. All results were derived via a consistent post-processing pipeline and recorded in tabular format to facilitate reproducibility and category-level diagnostics.

2.3.1. Confusion Matrix Analysis

To complement aggregate metrics, we analyzed confusion matrices to visualize inter-class misclassifications. Heatmaps highlighted correct predictions along the diagonal and confusion patterns off-diagonal, enabling interpretation of common errors. These visualizations revealed frequent misclassifications between lexically overlapping categories, class-specific prediction biases, and imbalances in precision-recall dynamics.

2.3.2. Bootstrap-Based Confidence Estimation

To quantify the statistical reliability of classification accuracy and assess the significance of observed differences between models, we employed a non-parametric bootstrap resampling procedure [23]. This approach enables the estimation of confidence intervals without assuming any underlying distribution of prediction errors, making it especially suitable for evaluation under limited test set sizes or class imbalance.

Let $D = \{(x_i, y_i)\}_{i=1}^{n}$ denote the test set of n samples, where x_i is the complaint text and y_i is the ground-truth category. For each model M, predictions $\hat{y}_i$ are obtained, and classification accuracy is computed as follows:

$$\text{Accuracy} = \frac{1}{n}\sum_{i=1}^{n} II(\hat{y}_i = y_i) \quad (1)$$

To construct a bootstrap distribution of accuracy, we repeatedly sample with replacement from the test set to generate $B = 1000$ bootstrap replicates $D^{(b)}, b \in \{1, \ldots, B\}$, each of size n. For each replicate, accuracy $Acc^{(b)}$ is computed. To ensure reproducibility, all bootstrap procedures were conducted using a fixed random seed of 42. The resulting distribution allows for the construction of a 95% confidence interval by extracting the 2.5th and 97.5th percentiles, as follows:

$$CI_{95\%} = \left[Precentile_{2.5}\left(Acc^{(1:B)}\right), Precentile_{97.5}\left(Acc^{(1:B)}\right)\right] \quad (2)$$

To assess the robustness of the performance estimates, bootstrap resampling was applied to all tested models. The resulting confidence intervals were subsequently used to determine whether the observed differences in classification accuracy could be considered statistically significant.

3. Results

The following subsections provide a stratified breakdown of model performance by classification paradigm, emphasizing trade-offs in representational generalization, instruction sensitivity, and inference efficiency under high-volume multilingual input conditions.

3.1. *Model-Level Accuracy Comparison*

3.1.1. Language-Specific Instruction Adaptation

To assess the influence of instruction language, we evaluated both models using prompts formulated in Russian and English. As shown in Table 4, E5 achieved higher accuracy with English instructions (85.83%) compared to Russian (82.00%), while BGE-M3 showed a slight preference for Russian (81.83% vs. 80.67%).

Table 4. Instruction-based classification accuracy across models and instruction languages.

Model	Russian Instruction (%)	English Instruction (%)
BGE-M3	81.83	81.67
E5	82.00	85.83

These results suggest that E5 is more attuned to English, likely due to its instruction-tuning process, whereas BGE-M3 may benefit from closer alignment between prompt and input language. Confidence intervals from 1000 bootstrap iterations confirmed this trend: for E5, 83.8–87.8% in English vs. 80.1–83.9% in Russian, indicating modest statistical significance. Full category-level metrics are reported in Appendix A, Tables A1 and A2.

This highlights the importance of prompt-language alignment in multilingual settings, particularly when leveraging instruction-conditioned embeddings.

3.1.2. Zero-Shot Performance Across Embedding Models

We evaluated the zero-shot classification performance of two multilingual embedding models (E5 and BGE-M3) using cosine similarity between complaint texts and static label embeddings, without fine-tuning or prompt-based conditioning. Results are presented in Table 5, with class-level metrics in Appendix B, Table A3.

Table 5. Zero-shot classification accuracy for E5 and BGE-M3 models.

Model	Accuracy (%)
BGE-M3	80.67
E5	89.67

E5 outperformed BGE-M3 by nearly 9 percentage points, indicating stronger generalization in zero-shot settings. This difference likely stems from E5's instruction-tuned pretraining, which yields more semantically aligned embeddings. In contrast, BGE-M3 exhibited greater variability across classes, particularly in abstract or sparsely represented categories (e.g., "Other Complaints"), suggesting reduced robustness to semantic ambiguity.

Bootstrap-based confidence intervals confirm the significance of the gap, as follows:

- E5 (zero shot): Mean Precision = 89.69%, 95% CI = 87.17–92.00%
- BGE-M3 (zero shot): Mean Precision = 80.71%, 95% CI = 77.50–83.83%

The non-overlapping intervals highlight E5's superior performance in zero-shot classification without adaptation.

3.1.3. Fine-Tuned Performance Across Embedding Models

We fine-tuned both embedding models on 75% of the annotated data and evaluated them on the held-out 25%. As shown in Table 6, BGE-M3 achieved 93.00% accuracy, slightly outperforming E5 (92.68%). Full class-wise metrics are available in Appendix C, Table A4.

Table 6. Accuracy scores following supervised fine-tuning (75% training, 25% testing).

Model	Accuracy (%)
BGE-M3	93.00
E5	92.68

Bootstrap resampling with 1000 iterations produced overlapping confidence intervals as follows:

- E5 (fine-tuned): Mean Accuracy = 92.83%, 95% CI = 90.83–94.83%
- BGE-M3 (fine-tuned): Mean Accuracy = 93.00%, 95% CI = 91.00–95.00%

The marginal difference (0.17 percentage point) is not statistically significant, indicating comparable performance under supervised conditions.

However, error distribution analysis suggests divergent model behavior. BGE-M3 showed greater stability in structurally simple categories (e.g., "Gratitude" or "Personnel Issues"), while E5 was more accurate on complaints with nested structures or ambiguous phrasing (e.g., "Organizational and Technical Issues"). Additionally, BGE-M3 benefited more from fine-tuning relative to its zero-shot baseline, whereas E5 remained consistent across both modes. This suggests complementary strengths: BGE-M3 adapts well to labeled data, while E5 demonstrates stronger baseline generalization.

3.1.4. Few-Shot Classification with LLMs

Few-shot classification was conducted using in-context prompts that included three labeled examples per category. We applied this setup uniformly across three instruction-tuned LLMs: Claude 3.7 Sonnet, GPT-4o, and GPT-3.5-turbo-0125. Table 7 summarizes the resulting accuracies and cost estimates. Full category-wise results are provided in Appendix D, Tables A5–A7.

Table 7. Accuracy and estimated inference cost for LLMs using few-shot prompting.

Model	Accuracy (%)	Cost (USD)
Claude 3.7 Sonnet	90.00	4.41
GPT-4o	89.00	3.19
GPT-3.5-turbo-0125	67.00	0.81

Claude slightly outperformed GPT-4o, while GPT-3.5 lagged. Bootstrap estimates confirmed the differences:

- Claude: Mean Accuracy = 89.68%, 95% CI = 87.17–92.00%
- GPT-4o: Mean Accuracy = 89.00%, 95% CI = 86.33–91.50%
- GPT-3.5: Mean Accuracy = 66.92%, 95% CI = 63.00–70.50%

All inference calls were executed in batches of 100 complaints. This batch size was chosen to reflect realistic deployment scenarios in production pipelines. The per-batch cost reported in Table 7 was recorded directly from API logs and includes all associated token and request overhead. Accordingly, the cost per one complaint is approximately USD 0.0441 for Claude 3.7 Sonnet, USD 0.0319 for GPT-4o, and USD 0.0081 for GPT-3.5-turbo-0125. These values ensure reproducibility and clarity in practical deployment scenarios.

While these per-complaint costs are manageable at test scale, they increase significantly in high-volume public sector deployments. For instance, classifying 10,000 complaints daily would incur approximately USD 441/day with Claude 3.7 Sonnet, USD 319/day with GPT-4o, and USD 81/day with GPT-3.5-turbo, translating to monthly expenditures ranging from USD 2430 to over USD 13,000 depending on the model. This cost burden becomes particularly critical in resource-constrained municipal contexts, where budget allocations for digital services are limited.

In addition to financial cost, LLM-based inference introduces non-negligible environmental impact. LLMs are energy-intensive during inference, contributing to increased carbon emissions per query. According to recent benchmarks, models like GPT-4 and Claude 3.7 can consume an order of magnitude more energy per inference than distilled or embedding-based counterparts. These environmental and financial considerations highlight the necessity of balancing predictive accuracy with sustainability and scalability when selecting models for real-world public service applications.

3.2. Error Patterns and Category-Level Insights

To move beyond aggregate metrics, we examined model behavior at the category level using confusion matrices. This allowed us to assess not only classification accuracy, but also error distribution across semantically adjacent and infrequent classes, which were deliberately preserved in the dataset to reflect real-world complaint frequencies. Misclassification patterns revealed tendencies such as systematic overlap in ambiguous categories and uneven treatment of low-resource labels. This approach supports a more nuanced understanding of model performance, particularly under conditions of multilingual input and class imbalance.

3.2.1. Instruction-Based Models: Language-Specific Confusion Pattern

Figures 5 and 6 visualize the confusion matrices for BGE-M3 and E5 under instruction prompts in Russian and English. BGE-M3 produces consistent predictions in high-frequency categories (e.g., transport problems, personnel problems) but shows instability in sparse or semantically diffuse classes such as praise and other complaints. Russian prompts yield a more concentrated diagonal, whereas English prompts improve precision in structured categories like bus stop infrastructure while increasing confusion among adjacent labels, indicating high sensitivity to prompt language and reliance on explicit linguistic alignment. In contrast, E5 maintains coherent class separation across both languages, with strong diagonal focus and limited off-axis dispersion. English prompts further enhance separability in low-frequency categories, suggesting that E5 generalizes more effectively across linguistic contexts, likely due to training exposure skewed toward English.

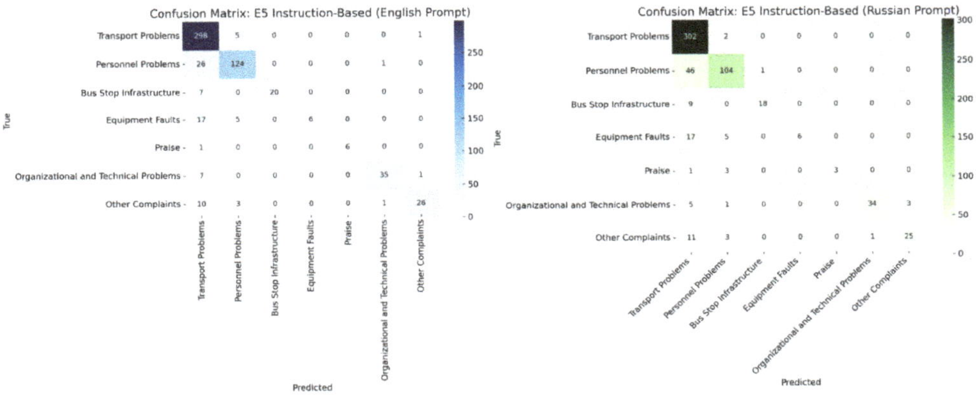

(a) (b)

Figure 5. Confusion matrices for the instruction-based E5 model: (**a**) English-language instructions; (**b**) Russian-language instructions.

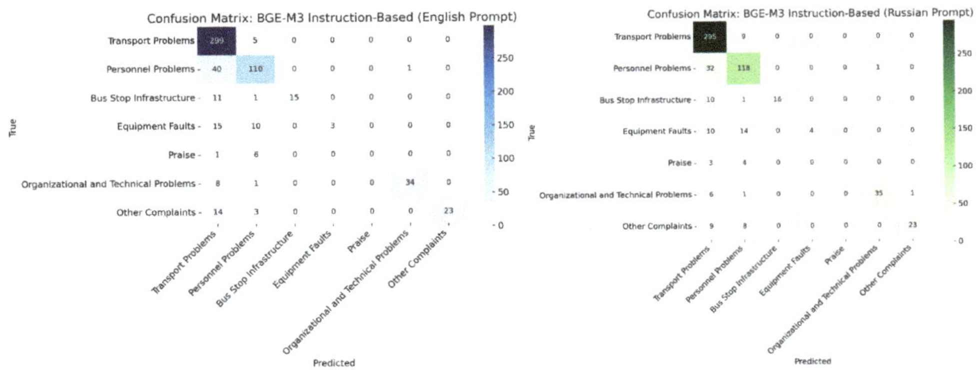

(a) (b)

Figure 6. Confusion matrices for the instruction-based BGE-M3 model: (**a**) English-language instructions; (**b**) Russian-language instructions.

Overall, Figures 5 and 6 illustrate that instruction-based classification remains language-sensitive, with BGE-M3 benefitting from prompt–input alignment, while E5 demonstrates greater cross-lingual stability.

3.2.2. Label-Only Zero-Shot Classification

In the label-only setup, models classified complaints based solely on cosine similarity between text and static label embeddings, without fine-tuning or prompts. As shown in Figure 7, E5 produced clearer category boundaries, with strong diagonal focus across both frequent and infrequent classes. This suggests a well-structured embedding space, likely shaped by instruction-tuned multilingual pretraining. BGE-M3, while accurate on high-volume categories like transport problems, exhibited more off-diagonal confusion in overlapping classes such as organizational and technical problems, indicating reduced semantic separation.

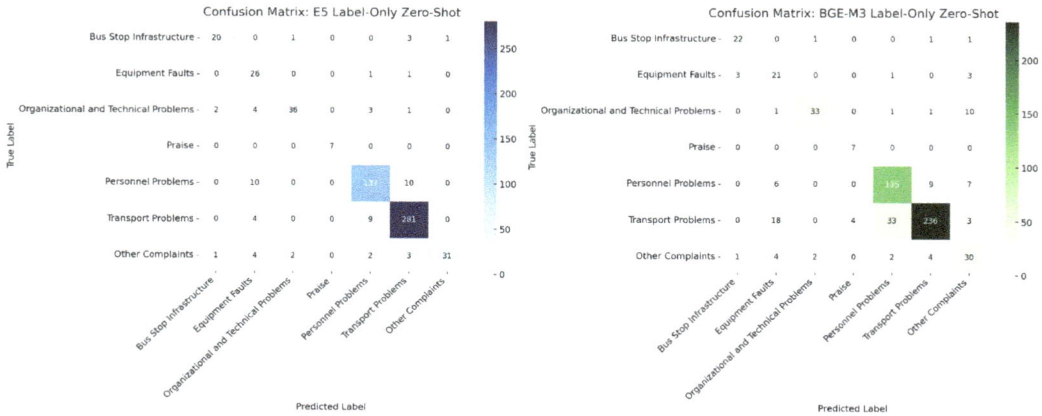

(a) (b)

Figure 7. Confusion matrices for label-only zero-shot classification: (**a**) E5 model; (**b**) BGE-M3 model.

These results confirm that E5 better generalizes under zero-shot constraints, particularly in multilingual, imbalanced data. When deployed at scale, label-only classification with robust embeddings offers a lightweight yet effective strategy for public service feedback analysis.

3.2.3. Fine-Tuned Embedding Models

Figure 8 shows the confusion matrices for fine-tuned E5 and BGE-M3 models. Both exhibit high accuracy, with most predictions concentrated along the diagonal. E5 shows minimal confusion, with errors mainly in semantically close categories like organizational and technical problems and other complaints. BGE-M3 displays slightly more off-diagonal activity in low-resource classes, possibly due to greater sensitivity to intra-class variation.

These patterns suggest that both models, once fine-tuned, handle multilingual, imbalanced data effectively. Their performance confirms their applicability for large-scale feedback classification, though E5 may offer marginally stronger category separation in ambiguous cases.

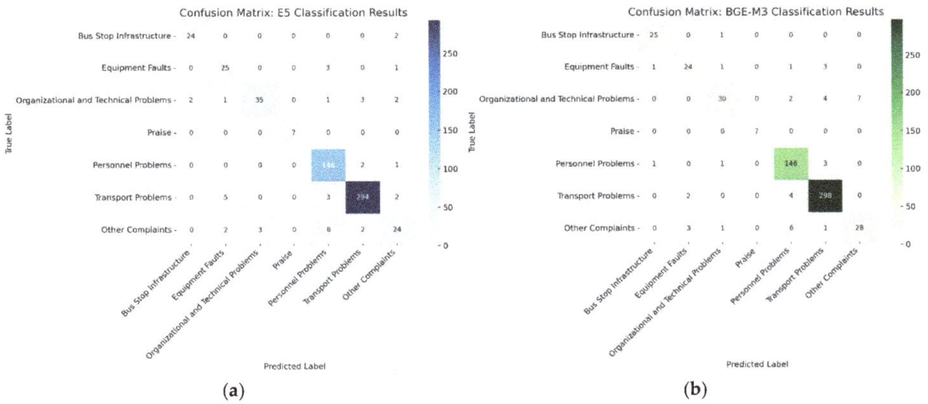

Figure 8. Confusion matrices for complaint classification models: (**a**) confusion matrix of the fine-tuned E5 model; (**b**) confusion matrix of the fine-tuned BGE-M3 model.

3.2.4. LLM-Based Few-Shot Classification Performance

Figure 9 presents confusion matrices for GPT-3.5-turbo-0125, GPT-4o, and Claude 3.7 Sonnet under few-shot prompting with three examples per class. Across all models, categories like transport problems and personnel problems were classified with high consistency, reflecting lexical regularity and class dominance. Claude achieved the most distinct class separation, particularly in low-frequency categories, while GPT-4o showed strong performance in structurally defined labels such as organizational and technical problems. GPT-3.5-turbo-0125 exhibited greater confusion, especially in semantically diffuse or underrepresented classes.

LLM performance in few-shot classification reveals distinct behavioral patterns. Claude minimizes confusion in low-resource and adjacent categories, making it a strong candidate for imbalanced multilingual tasks. GPT-4o provides competitive accuracy with lower inference cost, while GPT-3.5 exhibits reduced precision, particularly on semantically diffuse inputs, indicating limited contextual abstraction.

A deeper qualitative error analysis was conducted to examine divergence between LLMs and embedding-based models. Specifically, we categorized all classification outcomes into four types: (1) both models correct, (2) only the LLM correct, (3) only the embedding model correct, and (4) both incorrect. Table 8 summarizes the distribution of these outcomes. Among 216 test complaints, both models provided correct predictions in 192 cases. The LLM correctly classified four instances that the embedding model misclassified, while the embedding model outperformed the LLM on thirteen complaints. In seven instances, both models failed to identify the correct category. These results indicate a high level of agreement between the two models while highlighting complementary capabilities in handling ambiguous or underspecified complaints.

A close examination of misclassified examples revealed consistent patterns in model behavior. Errors made by LLMs typically stemmed from ambiguity in complaints involving overlapping categories, such as infrastructural issues framed as organizational failures. In contrast, the embedding model often misinterpreted nuanced or implicit references, particularly in messages with code-switching or indirect phrasing. For instance, the LLM correctly classified complaints about inoperative validation terminals as equipment failures, whereas the embedding model defaulted to broader categories such as transport issues. These discrepancies suggest that while LLMs excel at inferring latent intent from free-form text, embedding models may rely more heavily on lexical cues and learned associations. This distinction underlines the LLMs' strength in pragmatic reasoning and contextual flexibility and the embedding models' precision in domain-specific regularities, especially when fine-tuned on well-structured datasets.

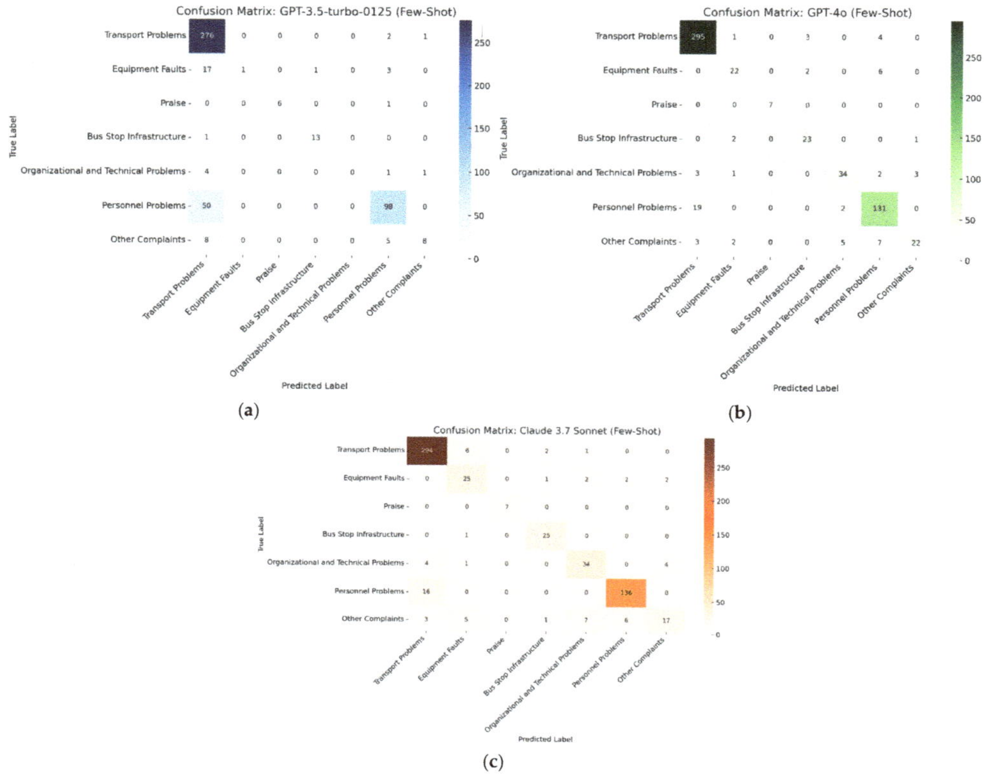

Figure 9. Confusion matrices for LLM-based few-shot classification models: (**a**) GPT-3.5-turbo-0125; (**b**) GPT-4o; (**c**) Claude 3.7 Sonnet.

Table 8. Qualitative comparison of classification correctness for LLMs and embeddings.

Outcome Type	Count	Complaint Excerpt	True Category	LLM Prediction	Embedding Prediction
Both correct	192	"Why does route N stop and go unpredictably?"	Transport Problems	Transport Problems	Transport Problems
Only LLM correct	4	"Route N, vehicle number NUMBER, failed to operate at 19:08"	Equipment faults	Equipment faults	Transport Problems
Only embedding correct	13	"I can't register my child's transport card..."	Other complaints	Organizational and technical problems	Other complaints
Both incorrect	7	"Bus N didn't stop at bus stop..."	Personnel problems	Transport Problems	Transport Problems

4. Discussion

4.1. Misclassification Trends and Error Distribution

Across all models, misclassification trends were concentrated in semantically adjacent or underrepresented categories such as organizational and technical problems, praise, and other complaints. These classes often lacked clear operational boundaries, contributing to consistent confusion in both LLMs and embedding-based models. A common issue was the misattribution of behavior-driven complaints, such as driver conduct, to infrastructural or vehicle-related classes, especially when cues were ambiguous or indirect.

For example, the complaint "Bus N, stop at BUS_STOP. The driver did not open the doors" ("Автобус N, остановка BUS_STOP. Водитель не открыл двери") was misclassified as a transport problem by all LLMs, despite reflecting a personnel problem. This illustrates a broader pattern in which models rely on lexical anchors (e.g., "bus," "stop") rather than contextual cues that indicate agency or responsibility.

Fine-tuned embeddings exhibited improved precision overall but similarly struggled with intent-driven edge cases. One such example is "Bus N, two identical buses arrived at BUS_STOP. One of them did not stop" ("Автобус N, BUS_STOP аялдамасына екі бірдей автобус келді. Біреуі тоқтамады"), which was also misclassified as transport problems despite describing a behavioral issue consistent with Personnel problems.

Errors in distinguishing between infrastructure and operational categories were also observed. The complaint "The stop on BUS_STOP Street for routes N is not equipped with a shelter" ("Улица BUS_STOP, остановка маршрутов N не оборудована павильоном") was frequently labeled as a transport problem, although it clearly falls under bus stop infrastructure. Zero-shot models were particularly sensitive to such surface-level features and often failed to infer pragmatic roles in the absence of fine-tuning.

These observations point to structural limitations in handling subtle or overlapping category definitions, especially when complaints encode implicit behavioral or operational context.

Figure 10 illustrates that misclassification rates for code-switched complaints consistently exceed those of monolingual inputs, particularly among embedding-based models. This performance gap highlights persistent challenges in processing mixed-language content, where syntactic and semantic cues are split across linguistic systems. Notably, LLMs display greater robustness, likely due to their multilingual pretraining and subword tokenization. Although the difference in error rates is not statistically significant ($p = 0.1146$), the observed trend suggests that LLMs may better generalize over multilingual variability. These findings emphasize that code-switching introduces latent structural ambiguity, which is insufficiently addressed by current embedding-based approaches.

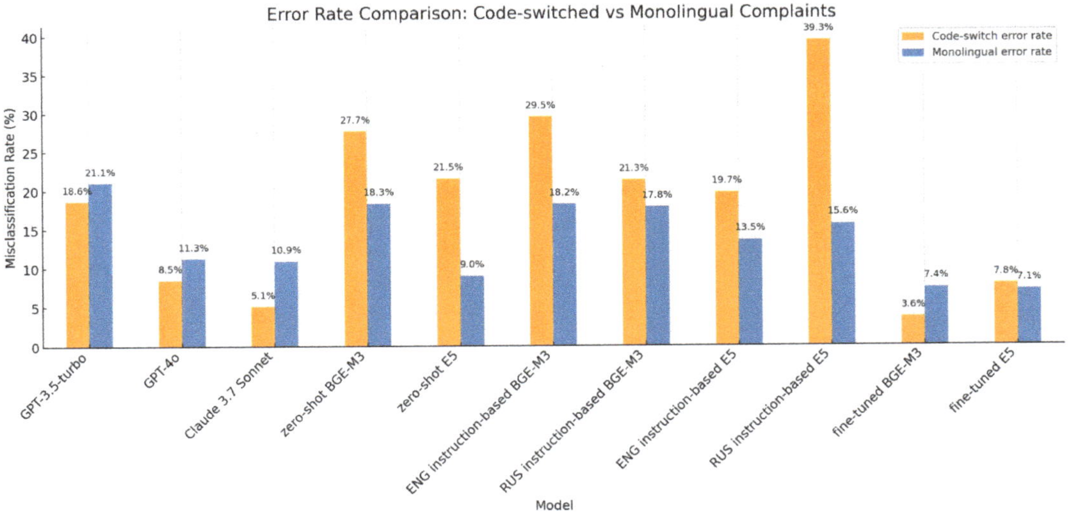

Figure 10. Classification error breakdown by model: monolingual vs. code-switching inputs.

Code-Switching and Contextual Ambiguity

Multilingual complaints combining Russian and Kazakh posed a distinct challenge, particularly in differentiating between driver behavior (personnel problems) and service-level issues (transport problems). In such cases, surface-level tokens like route numbers and stop names obscured the intended meaning, especially when action or agency was conveyed through Kazakh verbs.

Representative examples include the following:

- "Route N, vehicle number NUMBER, at stop BUS_STOP, departed toward the school direction" ("Маршрут N, гос. номер NUMBER, аялдама BUS_STOP, мектеп бағытына кетті")
- True category: Personnel problems predicted as transport problems due to focus on route and stop markers.
- "Route N did not stop at the final stop BUS_STOP" ("Маршрут N не остановился на конечной аялдаме BUS_STOP")
- True category: Personnel problems classified as transport problems based on location emphasis.
- "The bus on route N at stop BUS_STOP did not open the door" ("Автобус по маршруту N, остановка BUS_STOP, не открыл дверь")
- True category: Transport problems interpreted as personnel problems, likely due to verb-driven phrasing.

These trends are further illustrated through visual analysis. As shown in Figure 11, a confusion heatmap of code-switched misclassifications reveals dominant error clusters between personnel problems and transport problems, as well as between equipment faults and transport problems.

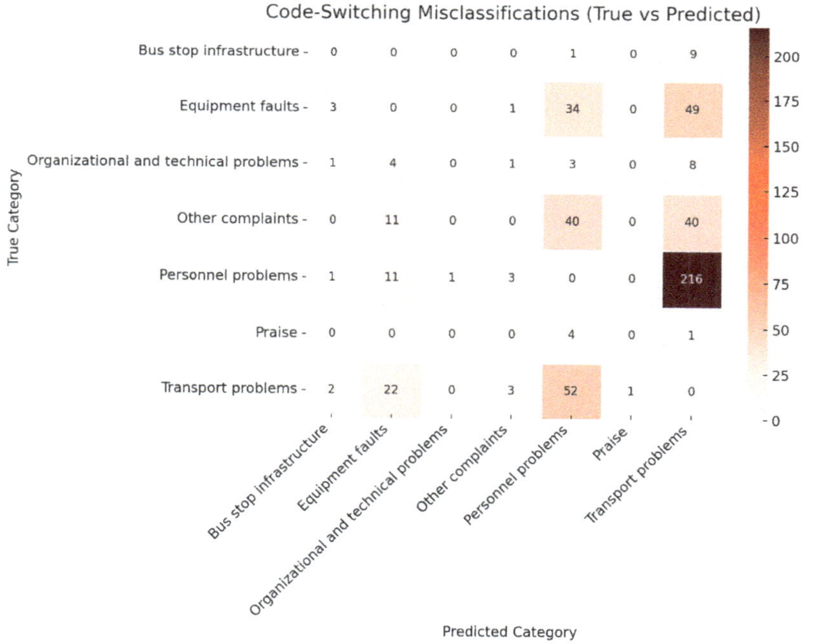

Figure 11. Confusion heatmap of misclassified code-switched complaints.

In parallel, Figure 12 presents a Sankey diagram that exposes the model-wise contribution to these systematic errors. Notably, models such as GPT-3.5 and E5 zero-shot show a higher concentration of misclassifications in these ambiguous categories.

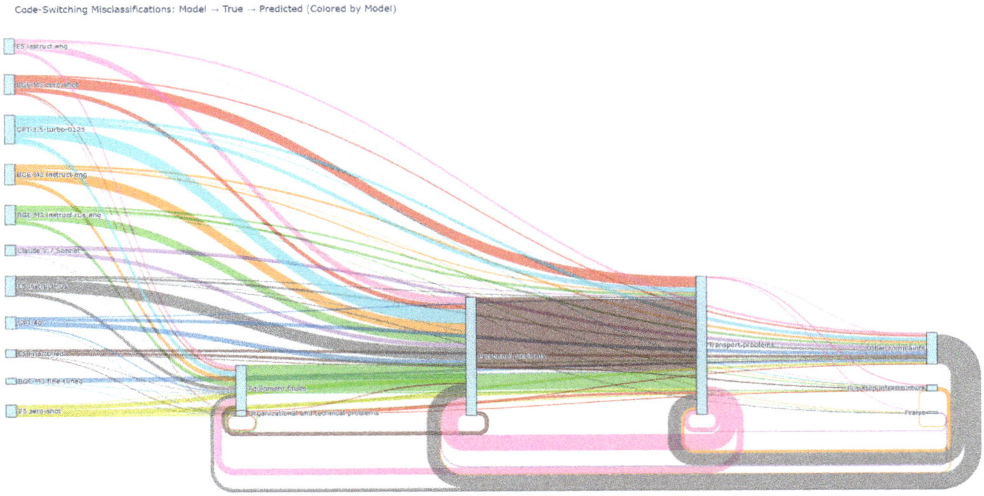

Figure 12. Sankey diagram of model-wise contributions to code-switching misclassifications.

Many of these errors appear to be triggered by Kazakh verb forms (e.g., "кетті", "тоқтамады") that encode intent or agentive action but are underrepresented or unanchored in model pretraining data, leading to semantic drift in multilingual inference.

To further examine the nature of these failures, Figure 13 compares the distribution of misclassification causes across model types. It reveals that embedding-based models were disproportionately prone to errors arising from code-switching and syntactic ellipsis, while LLMs more frequently exhibited surface lexical confusion. These findings suggest that embedding models struggle to resolve multilingual structural ambiguity, whereas LLMs are more vulnerable to misinterpreting semantically overloaded terms in the absence of explicit grounding.

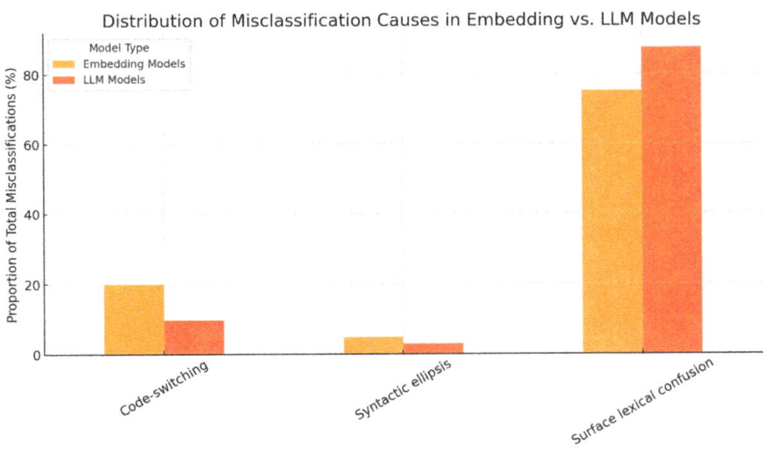

Figure 13. Distribution of misclassification causes in embedding-based versus LLMs.

In sum, code-switching amplifies semantic ambiguity and highlights limitations in models' ability to assign roles across languages. Embedding-based methods were particularly sensitive to surface-level cues, while LLMs generalized broadly but frequently overlooked behavioral intent without explicit contextual grounding.

To mitigate these issues, future improvements should include the following:

- Task-specific fine-tuning with annotated code-switched data,
- Multilingual pretraining with better coverage of functional Kazakh expressions,
- Architectures sensitive to discourse roles (actor, action, object), beyond flat semantic categorization.

4.2. Comparative Performance of Modeling Approaches

Figure 14 summarizes the overall accuracy of all tested models across classification paradigms. It highlights key performance differences between fine-tuned, few-shot, instruction-based, and zero-shot setups.

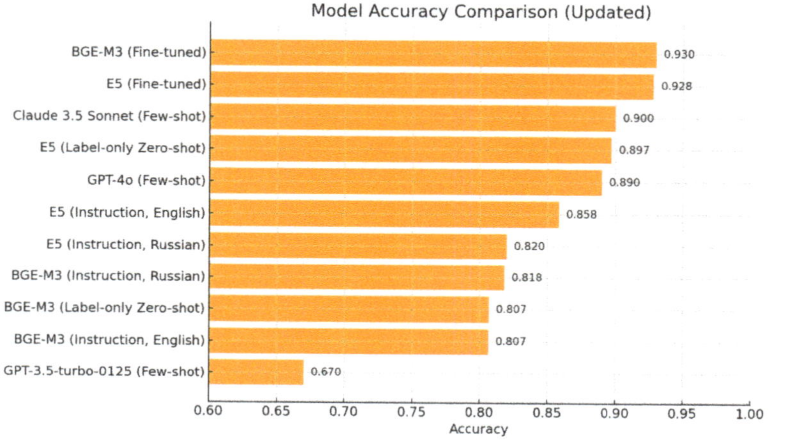

Figure 14. Comparative accuracy scores for fine-tuned, zero-shot, instruction-based, and few-shot classification models.

4.3. Discovery of Latent Categories Through Embedding-Space Clustering

One promising avenue for future research involves the discovery of latent complaint categories through unsupervised clustering of embedding representations. Given the semantic granularity of instruction-aligned embeddings, techniques such as HDBSCAN and UMAP-based projection have proven effective in identifying fine-grained groupings within complex datasets [24,25]. Applied to multilingual civic feedback, these methods may reveal emerging complaint types or context-dependent subcategories not captured by existing taxonomies. As prior work has shown, clustering dense semantic spaces can support adaptive classification in evolving public discourse environments [26]. Integrating such techniques with current zero-shot frameworks could reduce reliance on manual annotation and enable more flexible, data-driven taxonomy expansion.

5. Application Case Study: Web-Based Complaint Classification System

To demonstrate practical applicability, we deployed a lightweight web-based system for real-time classification of transportation complaints. The service leverages a fine-tuned multilingual-E5 model and operates entirely on local infrastructure without reliance on external APIs or GPU resources. It accepts free-text input in Russian and Kazakh and outputs both the predicted category and associated similarity scores for all seven classes.

Classification is performed by embedding each input and computing cosine similarity to pre-defined category prototypes. A visual overview of the pipeline is shown in Figure 15. The system's transparent output and minimal latency make it suitable for integration into municipal feedback channels.

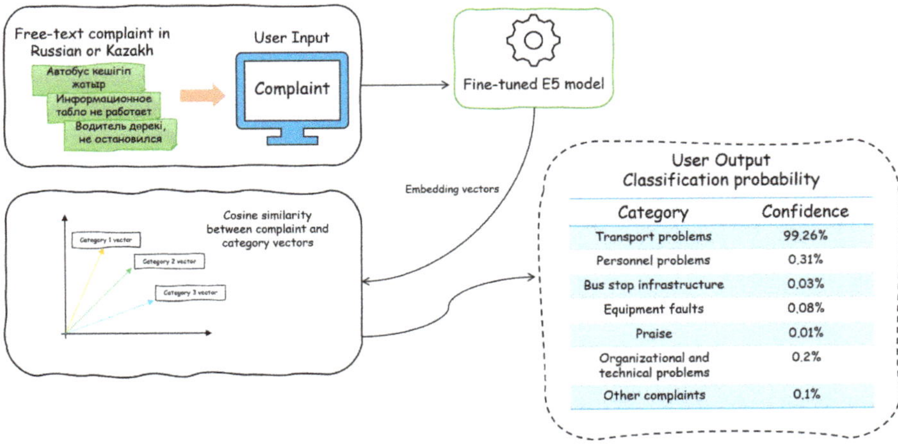

Figure 15. A flowchart summarizing the classification process in the web-based complaint categorization service using the fine-tuned E5 model.

In real-world usage, the model showed robust performance even on noisy or emotionally charged inputs. As illustrated in Figure 16, the classifier confidently identified a Kazakh-language complaint about wait times as "Transport Problems" and correctly labeled a sanitation-related message as "Equipment Faults," despite informal phrasing.

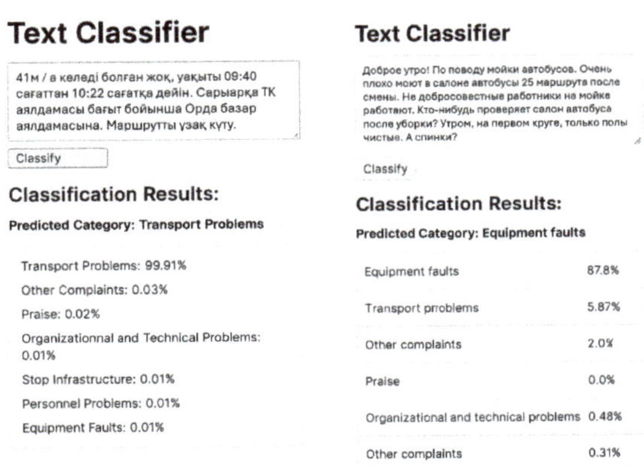

(**a**) (**b**)

Figure 16. Sample output screens from the web interface of the deployed classification system: (**a**) complaint in Kazakh classified as "Transport Problems" with 99.91% confidence (English translation: "Bus 41 did not arrive between 09:40 and 10:22. From Saryarka TC stop in the direction of Orda Bazar stop. Long waiting time for the route."); (**b**) sanitation complaint classified as "Equipment Faults" with 87.8% confidence (English translation: "Good morning! Regarding bus cleaning. The buses on route 25 are poorly cleaned inside after shifts. The car wash staff are not doing their job properly. Does anyone check the bus interior after cleaning? In the morning, on the first run, only the floors are clean. What about the seat backs?").

This deployment demonstrates the feasibility of using fine-tuned multilingual embedding models in civic feedback systems under real-world constraints. Operating in a fully non-parametric inference regime, the model does not require retraining, parameter updates, or prompt engineering at deployment time. Its modular architecture further facilitates integration into e-government platforms and analytics dashboards for transport authorities. As such, it enables scalable and interpretable real-time classification of public feedback with minimal computational overhead.

6. Conclusions

This study examined the practical viability of embedding-based and instruction-tuned architectures for multilingual complaint classification in civic infrastructure.

Rather than reiterating accuracy benchmarks, the conclusions emphasize system-level implications: embedding models offer a non-parametric alternative that facilitates real-time classification without dependence on prompt engineering or frequent retraining. Moreover, the observed language sensitivity in instruction-based setups highlights the need for context-aware adaptation strategies when dealing with multilingual input streams.

Beyond current deployments, this research opens new directions for semantically grounded civic analytics. Future work may focus on extending embedding-based pipelines to support unsupervised category discovery, multilingual taxonomy refinement, and multimodal feedback integration. Collectively, these approaches point toward a scalable framework for responsive digital governance.

Author Contributions: Conceptualization, D.R. and S.B.; methodology, D.R. and S.B.; software, D.R.; validation, D.R. and S.B.; formal analysis, D.R.; investigation, D.R.; resources, D.Y.; data curation, D.Y.; writing—original draft preparation, D.R.; writing—review and editing, D.R. and S.B.; visualization, D.R.; supervision, S.B.; project administration, D.Y. All authors have read and agreed to the published version of the manuscript.

Funding: This research has been funded by the Ministry of Science and Higher Education of the Republic of Kazakhstan, grant number BR24992852 «Intelligent models and methods of Smart City digital ecosystem for sustainable development and the citizens' quality of life improvement».

Institutional Review Board Statement: Not applicable.

Informed Consent Statement: Not applicable.

Data Availability Statement: The data presented in this study are available on request from the corresponding author.

Conflicts of Interest: The authors declare no conflicts of interest.

Abbreviations

The following abbreviations are used in this manuscript:

NLP	Natural Language Processing
LLM	Large Language Model
E5	intfloat/multilingual-e5-large-instruct
BGE-M3	BAAI/bge-m3
AI	Artificial Intelligence
UMAP	Uniform Manifold Approximation and Projection
HDBSCAN	Hierarchical Density-Based Spatial Clustering of Applications with Noise
F1-score	Harmonic Mean of Precision and Recall
CI	Confidence Interval

Appendix A. Instruction-Based Classification Reports for Public Transportation Complaints

Table A1. Classification report—BGE-M3 with Russian/English instructions.

Category	Precision		Recall		F1-Score		Support
	Russian	English	Russian	English	Russian	English	
Transport Problems	0.81	0.77	0.97	0.98	0.88	0.86	304
Personnel problems	0.76	0.81	0.78	0.73	0.77	0.77	151
Bus stop infrastructure	1.00	1.00	0.59	0.56	0.74	0.71	27
Equipment faults	1.00	1.00	0.14	0.11	0.25	0.19	28
Praise	0.00	0.00	0.00	0.00	0.00	0.00	7
Organizational and technical problems	0.97	0.97	0.81	0.79	0.89	0.87	43
Other complaints	0.96	1.00	0.57	0.57	0.72	0.73	40
Accuracy	-	-	-	-	0.82	0.81	600
Macro avg	0.79	0.79	0.55	0.53	0.61	0.59	600
Weighted avg	0.83	0.82	0.82	0.81	0.80	0.78	600

Table A2. Classification report—E5 with Russian/English instructions.

Category	Precision		Recall		F1-Score		Support
	Russian	English	Russian	English	Russian	English	
Transport Problems	0.77	0.81	0.99	0.98	0.87	0.89	304
Personnel problems	0.88	0.91	0.69	0.82	0.77	0.86	151
Bus stop infrastructure	0.95	1.00	0.67	0.74	0.78	0.85	27
Equipment faults	1.00	1.00	0.21	0.21	0.35	0.35	28
Praise	1.00	1.00	0.43	0.86	0.60	0.92	7
Organizational and technical problems	0.97	0.95	0.79	0.81	0.87	0.88	43
Other complaints	0.89	0.93	0.62	0.65	0.74	0.76	40
Accuracy	-	-	-	-	0.82	0.86	600
Macro avg	0.92	0.94	0.63	0.73	0.71	0.79	600
Weighted avg	0.84	0.87	0.82	0.86	0.81	0.85	600

Appendix B. Zero-Shot Classification Reports for Public Transportation Complaints

Table A3. Zero-shot classification performance across categories using BGE-M3 and E5 models.

Category	BGE-M3			E5			
	Precision	Recall	F1-Score	Precision	Recall	F1-Score	Support
Transport Problems	0.94	0.80	0.87	0.94	0.96	0.95	294
Personnel problems	0.78	0.86	0.82	0.90	0.87	0.89	157
Bus stop infrastructure	0.85	0.88	0.86	0.87	0.80	0.83	25
Equipment faults	0.42	0.75	0.54	0.54	0.93	0.68	28
Praise	0.64	1.00	0.78	1.00	1.00	1.00	7
Organizational and technical problems	0.92	0.72	0.80	0.92	0.78	0.85	46
Other complaints	0.56	0.70	0.62	0.97	0.72	0.83	43
Accuracy	-	-	0.81	-	-	0.90	600
Macro avg	0.73	0.82	0.76	0.88	0.87	0.86	600
Weighted avg	0.84	0.81	0.82	0.91	0.90	0.90	600

Appendix C. Fine-Tuned Classification Reports for Public Transportation Complaints

Table A4. Fine-tuned classification performance across categories using BGE-M3 and E5 models.

Category	BGE-M3			E5			
	Precision	**Recall**	**F1-Score**	**Precision**	**Recall**	**F1-Score**	**Support**
Transport Problems	0.96	0.98	0.97	0.98	0.97	0.97	304
Personnel problems	0.92	0.97	0.94	0.91	0.98	0.94	151
Bus stop infrastructure	0.93	0.96	0.94	0.92	0.92	0.94	26
Equipment faults	0.83	0.80	0.81	0.83	0.80	0.81	30
Praise	1.00	1.00	1.00	1.00	1.00	1.00	7
Organizational and technical problems	0.88	0.70	0.78	0.92	0.80	0.78	43
Other complaints	0.80	0.72	0.76	0.75	0.62	0.76	39
Accuracy	-	-	0.93	-	-	0.93	600
Macro avg	0.90	0.87	0.89	0.89	0.88	0.89	600
Weighted avg	0.93	0.93	0.93	0.93	0.93	0.93	600

Appendix D. Few-Shot Classification Reports for Public Transportation Complaints

Table A5. Few-shot classification performance across categories using Claude 3.7 Sonnet models.

Category	Precision	Recall	F1-Score	Support
Transport Problems	0.92	0.97	0.95	303
Personnel problems	0.87	0.86	0.87	152
Bus stop infrastructure	0.82	0.88	0.85	26
Equipment faults	0.79	0.73	0.76	30
Praise	1.00	1.00	1.00	7
Organizational and technical problems	0.83	0.79	0.81	43
Other complaints	0.85	0.56	0.68	39
Accuracy	-	-	0.90	600
Macro avg	0.87	0.83	0.84	600
Weighted avg	0.89	0.89	0.89	600

Table A6. Few-shot classification performance across categories using GPT-4o models.

Category	Precision	Recall	F1-Score	Support
Transport Problems	0.92	0.97	0.95	303
Personnel problems	0.87	0.86	0.87	152
Bus stop infrastructure	0.82	0.88	0.85	26
Equipment faults	0.79	0.73	0.76	30
Praise	1.00	1.00	1.00	7
Organizational and technical problems	0.83	0.79	0.81	43
Other complaints	0.85	0.56	0.68	39
Accuracy	-	-	0.89	600
Macro avg	0.87	0.83	0.84	600
Weighted avg	0.89	0.89	0.89	600

Table A7. Few-shot classification performance across categories using GPT-3.5-turbo-0125 models.

Category	Precision	Recall	F1-Score	Support
Transport Problems	0.78	0.91	0.84	303
Personnel problems	0.89	0.64	0.75	152
Bus stop infrastructure	0.93	0.50	0.65	26
Equipment faults	1.00	0.03	0.06	30
Praise	1.00	0.86	0.92	7
Organizational and technical problems	0.00	0.00	0.00	43
Other complaints	0.80	0.21	0.33	39
Accuracy	-	-	0.67	600
Macro avg	0.77	0.45	0.51	600
Weighted avg	0.77	0.67	0.68	600

References

1. Yona, M.; Birfir, G.; Kaplan, S. Data science and GIS-based system analysis of transit passenger complaints to improve operations and planning. *Transp. Policy* **2021**, *101*, 133–144. [CrossRef]
2. Çapalı, B.; Küçüksille, E.; Alagöz, N.K. A natural language processing framework for analyzing public transportation user satisfaction: A case study. *J. Innov. Transp.* **2023**, *4*, 17–24. [CrossRef]
3. Liu, W.K.; Yen, C.C. Optimizing bus passenger complaint service through big data analysis: Systematized analysis for improved public sector management. *Sustainability* **2016**, *8*, 1319. [CrossRef]
4. Shaikh, S.; Yayilgan, S.Y.; Abomhara, M.; Ghaleb, Y.; Garcia-Font, V.; Nordgård, D. Multilingual User Perceptions Analysis from Twitter Using Zero-Shot Learning for Border Control Technologies. *Soc. Netw. Anal. Min.* **2025**, *15*, 19. [CrossRef]
5. Cai, H.; Dong, T.; Zhou, P.; Li, D.; Li, H. Leveraging Text Mining Techniques for Civil Aviation Service Improvement: Research on Key Topics and Association Rules of Passenger Complaints. *Systems* **2025**, *13*, 325. [CrossRef]
6. Fu, X.; Brinkley, C.; Sanchez, T.W.; Li, C. Text Mining Public Feedback on Urban Densification Plan Change in Hamilton, New Zealand. *Environ. Plan. B Urban Anal. City Sci.* **2025**, *52*, 646–666. [CrossRef]
7. Murad, S.A.; Dahal, A.; Rahimi, N. Multi-Lingual Cyber Threat Detection in Tweets/X Using ML, DL, and LLM: A Comparative Analysis. *arXiv* **2025**, arXiv:2502.04346.
8. Benlahbib, A.; Boumhidi, A.; Fahfouh, A.; Alami, H. Comparative Analysis of Traditional and Modern NLP Techniques on the CoLA Dataset: From POS Tagging to Large Language Models. *IEEE Open J. Comput. Soc.* **2025**, *6*, 248–260. [CrossRef]
9. Wang, Y.; Zheng, X.; Zhang, J.; Ma, X.; Li, M.; Zhou, Y. Instruction Tuning for Large Language Models: A Survey. *arXiv* **2023**, arXiv:2312.03857.
10. Zeng, H.; Zhang, J.; He, Z. M3-Embedding: Multi-Linguality, Multi-Functionality, Multi-Granularity. *arXiv* **2024**, arXiv:2402.03216.
11. Roumeliotis, K.I.; Tselikas, N.D.; Nasiopoulos, D.K. Think Before You Classify: The Rise of Reasoning Large Language Models for Consumer Complaint Detection and Classification. *Electronics* **2025**, *14*, 1070. [CrossRef]
12. Edwards, A.; Camacho-Collados, J. Language Models for Text Classification: Is In-Context Learning Enough? *arXiv* **2024**, arXiv:2403.17661.
13. Liu, F.; Li, Z.; Yin, Q.; Liu, F.; Huang, J.; Luo, J.; Thakur, A.; Branson, K.; Schwab, P.; Wu, X.; et al. A multimodal multidomain multilingual medical foundation model for zero shot clinical diagnosis. *NPJ Digit. Med.* **2025**, *8*, 86. [CrossRef]
14. Airani, P.; Pipada, N.; Shah, P. Classification of Complaints Text Data by Ensembling Large Language Models. In Proceedings of the 17th International Conference on Agents and Artificial Intelligence (ICAART 2025), Rome, Italy, 24–26 February 2025; SciTePress: Setúbal, Portugal, 2025; Volume 3, pp. 679–689, ISBN 978-989-758-737-5.
15. Mei, P.; Zhang, F. Network Public Opinion Environment Shaping for Sustainable Cities by Large Language Model. *SSRN Electron. J.* **2024**, 1–19. Available online: https://ssrn.com/abstract=5117779 (accessed on 22 July 2025).
16. Pendyala, V.S.; Kamdar, K.; Mulchandani, K. Automated Research Review Support Using Machine Learning, Large Language Models, and Natural Language Processing. *Electronics* **2025**, *14*, 256. [CrossRef]
17. Mondal, C.; Pham, D.-S.; Gupta, A.; Tan, T.; Gedeon, T. Leveraging Prompt Engineering with Lightweight Large Language Models to Label and Extract Clinical Information from Radiology Reports. In Proceedings of the ACM on Web Conference 2025 (WWW '25), Sydney, NSW, Australia, 28 April–2 May 2025; Association for Computing Machinery: New York, NY, USA, 2025; pp. 1616–1625.
18. Oro, E.; Granata, F.M.; Ruffolo, M. A Comprehensive Evaluation of Embedding Models and LLMs for IR and QA Across English and Italian. *Big Data Cogn. Comput.* **2025**, *9*, 141. [CrossRef]
19. Kokkodis, M.; Demsyn-Jones, R.; Raghavan, V. Beyond the Hype: Embeddings vs. Prompting for Multiclass Classification Tasks. *arXiv* **2025**, arXiv:2504.04277.

20. Al Faraby, S.; Romadhony, A. Analysis of llms for educational question classification and generation. *Comput. Educ. Artif. Intell.* **2024**, *7*, 100298. [CrossRef]
21. Henríquez-Jara, B.; Arriagada, J.; Tirachini, A. Evidence of the Impact of Real-Time Information on Passenger Satisfaction across Varying Public Transport Quality in 13 Chilean Cities. *SSRN Electron. J.* **2024**. [CrossRef]
22. Wang, L.; Yang, N.; Huang, X.; Yang, L.; Majumder, R.; Wei, F. Multilingual E5 Text Embeddings: A Technical Report. *arXiv* **2024**, arXiv:2402.05672.
23. Efron, B.; Tibshirani, R.J. *An Introduction to the Bootstrap*; Chapman and Hall/CRC: New York, NY, USA, 1993.
24. Islam, K.M.S.; Karri, R.T.; Vegesna, S.; Wu, J.; Madiraju, P. Contextual Embedding-Based Clustering to Identify Topics for Healthcare Service Improvement. *arXiv* **2025**, arXiv:2504.14068.
25. Petukhova, A.; Matos-Carvalho, J.P.; Fachada, N. Text Clustering with Large Language Model Embeddings. *Int. J. Cogn. Comput. Eng.* **2025**, *6*, 100–108. [CrossRef]
26. Vrabie, C. Improving Municipal Responsiveness through AI-Powered Image Analysis in E-Government. CEE e | Dem e | Gov Days 2024. pp. 1–27. Available online: https://www.ceeol.com/search/article-detail?id=1330925 (accessed on 22 July 2025).

information

MDPI

Article

Internet Governance in the Context of Global Digital Contracts: Integrating SAR Data Processing and AI Techniques for Standards, Rules, and Practical Paths

Xiaoying Fu [1], Wenyi Zhang [2] and Zhi Li [3,*]

[1] Xiangshan Film and Television Academy, Ningbo University of Finance & Economics, Ningbo 315175, China; fuxiaoying@nbufe.edu.cn
[2] School of Information Management, Nanjing University, Nanjing 210023, China; 602024140037@smail.nju.edu.cn
[3] School of Media and Law, NingboTech University, Ningbo 315000, China
* Correspondence: lizhi@nbt.edu.cn

Abstract: With the increasing frequency of digital economic activities on a global scale, internet governance has become a pressing issue. Traditional multilateral approaches to formulating internet governance rules have struggled to address critical challenges such as privacy leakage and low global internet defense capabilities. To tackle these issues, this study integrates SAR data processing and interpretation using AI techniques with the development of governance rules through international agreements and multi-stakeholder mechanisms. This approach aims to strengthen privacy protection and enhance the overall effectiveness of internet governance. This study incorporates differential privacy protection laws and cert-free cryptography algorithms, combined with SAR data analysis powered by AI techniques, to address privacy protection and security challenges in internet governance. SAR data provides a unique layer of spatial and environmental context, which, when analyzed using advanced AI models, offers valuable insights into network patterns and potential vulnerabilities. By applying these techniques, internet governance can more effectively monitor and secure global data flows, ensuring a more robust defense against cyber threats. Experimental results demonstrate that the proposed approach significantly outperforms traditional methods. When processing 20 GB of data, the encryption time was reduced by approximately 1.2 times compared to other methods. Furthermore, satisfaction with the newly developed internet governance rules increased by 13.3%. By integrating SAR data processing and AI, the model enhances the precision and scalability of governance mechanisms, enabling real-time responses to privacy and security concerns. In the context of the Global Digital Compact, this research effectively improves the standards, rules, and practical pathways for internet governance. It not only enhances the security and privacy of global data networks but also promotes economic development, social progress, and national security. The integration of SAR data analysis and AI techniques provides a powerful toolset for addressing the complexities of internet governance in a digitally connected world.

Keywords: global digital contract; internet governance standards; internet governance rules; SAR data processing; AI techniques

1. Introduction

With the increasing frequency of digital economic activities around the world, internet governance has become a pressing issue. Traditional multilateral rulemaking methods

https://doi.org/10.3390/info16080697

are unable to cope with key challenges such as privacy breaches and weak global network defense capabilities [1]. This study aims to solve the privacy protection and security problems in internet governance by integrating SAR data processing and AI technology, combining international agreements and multi-stakeholder mechanism governance rule-making in the context of global digital contracts, building a more accurate and scalable governance mechanism, and optimizing the standards, rules, and practice paths of internet governance [2].

Recent advancements in digital technology are catalyzing the emergence of new business models within virtual environments, particularly within the context of metaverses. This shift is giving rise to a new economy where traditional, physical-world business models are adapted, new virtual-world models are developed, and hybrid approaches that blend both are explored. The integration of these evolving business models with internet governance is crucial. It ensures that as businesses expand into virtual spaces, they do so within a framework that promotes transparency, security, and accountability, aligning with broader regulatory standards and contributing to the sustainable growth of digital ecosystems [3].

Digital twins are sophisticated digital models of assets that play a crucial role across the Industry 4.0 value chain. As industrial processes become increasingly digitized, the use of digital twins is expected to become more prevalent. Integrating digital twins with internet governance will enhance the oversight and efficiency of these technological advancements, ensuring they align with broader regulatory and operational frameworks. This integration will likely lead to more robust, transparent, and accountable digital ecosystems in various industrial sectors [4,5].

With the continuous development of the economy, the status of the internet has become increasingly important, but it has also triggered various network security risks. Therefore, how to improve the level of internet governance and establish reasonable governance standards and rules has become the focus of many scholars' research, and some research results have been achieved. Wang (2018) explored the role of the public in the debate on internet governance and linked public theory and technological research to internet governance, believing that they are of great help to stakeholders in internet governance [6]. White (2019) believed that the internet, as a facilitator of the peace-building process, had great potential and might become a tool for oppression or a channel for the dissemination of false information [7]. Therefore, studying internet governance is of great significance for international peace and stability. Tjahja et al. (2022) examined how individual participants identify themselves within the framework of the Internet Governance Forum and how they understand the internet governance ecosystem, based on the list of participants in the Public Internet Governance Forum, opening up a new path for further research on the legitimacy of multiple stakeholders [8]. Flonk (2020) analyzed the conflicts between norms and institutions in internet governance, helping to address the low level of institutionalization in dispute resolution in this emerging field [9]. For the development of internet governance rules, Malcic (2018) established a digital identity management system by utilizing a digital address allocation agency [10]. The system itself was the infrastructure of the global identity industry and used infrastructure configuration to connect global internet governance with the digital identity terminology data base. Guan (2019), considering the characteristics of the internet, conducted an experiment on the internet governance model with multiple stakeholders as the core, using internet startups as carriers [11]. He also posed challenges to the subject qualifications, operational rules, and other aspects of traditional sovereignty models. In summary, many scholars have conducted various studies on the rules and standards of internet governance using different methods. However, these studies have shortcomings in areas such as privacy breaches and security. As a new type of contractual tool, global digital contracts have significant advantages in privacy protection and security, which can solve the problems existing in the aforementioned research.

As a new type of contract, digital contracts store and transmit contract content in electronic form, providing convenient, efficient, and secure signing and execution methods for all parties. Therefore, it has significant advantages in privacy protection and security and is also a current research hotspot. Zhang (2018) utilized the technical characteristics of digital financial assets to study the illegal behavior of digital currency and used digital contracts to study legislation in this area, improving the rationality of utilization and also improving the security of currency [12]. Jiang (2023) believed that global digital economy regulation has been continuously improved in practice [13]. Therefore, he used digital contracts to set basic rules to reflect national or regional characteristics, so as to strengthen industry compliance and fairness, improve data governance, and jointly formulate international rules. Wylde (2023) aimed to advance the United Nations' goal of "an open, free, and secure digital future for all" by reviewing the requirements of the Global Digital Compact in order to better address potential risks of the future internet [14], such as national isolation, sovereignty, and internet fragmentation, and enhance privacy protection efforts. Saravistha et al. (2022) discussed the issue of optimizing consumer protection in the context of new forms of contracts [15], where standard digital contracts and new cross-border market mechanisms coexisted in the business world to better protect consumer privacy. Ong (2021) conducted a comparative analysis and interpretation of the enforceability of digital contracts in contract law between New Zealand and Indonesia, using normative legal research to ensure the enforceability of digital contracts and improve legal security [16]. In summary, digital contracts have absolute advantages in terms of privacy protection and network security. Applying them to internet governance can effectively solve the current problem of low security in internet governance.

This study studies the standards, rules, and practice paths of internet governance, with the aim of exploring and analyzing how to effectively conduct internet governance under the framework of the global digital contract, including the formulation of appropriate standards, rules, and practice paths. Its goal is to create a transparent, fair, and stable network environment to support global social progress and the development of the digital economy. The main ways to achieve this goal include formulating laws, regulations, and standards for internet governance and using these laws and regulations to protect the security and privacy of users. Through international cooperation and multilateral consultation, differentiated privacy protection measures are adopted to maintain the privacy of members. It aims to promote the construction of a stable, fair, and transparent internet ecosystem and provide practical guidance and support for global internet governance.

To this end, this paper proposes the following hypotheses:

H1. *The governance model that integrates SAR data processing and AI technology will have significantly better encryption efficiency when processing data than traditional governance methods and can effectively improve the technical feasibility of internet governance.*

H2. *The user satisfaction of Internet governance rules formulated based on the multi-stakeholder mechanism (MSM) will be higher than that of rules formulated based on traditional methods such as multilateralism and international agreements and can better balance the interests of all parties.*

H3. *The internet governance standards constructed using the OSI model are superior to other governance standards in terms of rationality and applicability and can better meet the requirements for the uniformity and security of network protocols in the context of global digital contracts.*

2. Formulation of Standards and Rules for Internet Governance

2.1. Formulation of Internet Governance Standards

Internet governance is a standard for managing and using the internet formulated by multiple parties based on actual situations, aimed at regulating and promoting the development of the internet and forming consensus, legal regulations, technical norms, etc. [17,18]. The purpose of internet governance is to enable the development of the internet to benefit various countries and fields and to benefit the world. With the help of Abood Amany et al. (2021) and Wang et al. (2018), the hierarchy of Transmission Control Protocol/Internet Protocol (TCP/IP) for internet transmission is studied, and internet governance standards are created based on different functions at different levels [19,20]. The summary is shown in Table 1.

Table 1. Functional tasks and behaviors of internet governance.

Functional Area	Task	Main Behavior Subject
Key internet resources	Central supervision of domain names and addresses	Number internet name and word address allocation agency, the internet number administration
	Technology and design of IP addresses	Internet engineering task force
	Domain name allocation	Internet registration authority
	Automatic digital distribution system	Internet numbering authority and regional internet registration
	IP address allocation	Regional internet registration, local internet registration, internet numbering authority
Setting up internet standards	Protocol number distribution	Internet numbering authority
	Core internet standard design	Internet engineering task force
	Core web page standard design	Internet alliance
Access and connection coordination	Multi-layer network interconnection	Internet exchange center and network operator
	Network management	Private network operator
	Access management	National government
Network security governance	Network infrastructure security	Operator
	Encryption standard design	Standard-setting agency
	Network security management	National governments and multilateral protocols
	Software security vulnerability repair	Software company
	Software patch management	End user
	Routing and address security	Operator and registrar
	Website security certification	Certification body
Information transmission	Commercial trading institutions	E-commerce agency
	Content review	Search engines and social media
	Private policy	Social networks and service providers
	Manage privacy and speech	Law and constitution

As shown in Table 1, the functions and tasks of network governance are divided into five aspects, mainly including key internet resources, internet standard setting, access and connection coordination, network security governance, and information transmission. These five aspects are subdivided, and then the behavioral objects of these subdivided subjects are introduced.

Internet governance requires the development of a series of technical standards to ensure the security, stability, and interoperability of the internet in order to ensure the relevance and interoperability of digital contracts. The global digital contract proposes requirements to support network security to prevent network attacks and data leakage. Internet governance standards should include the best practices and technical standards for cybersecurity to help protect the cybersecurity of online users and various international organizations. Among them, network protocol is a special communication standard designed by humans to improve communication, helping global digital contracts better manage the internet. Due to special needs, based on the research on network protocol standards [21–23], the details of internet protocols were identified and extracted. Network protocols often use specific formats, and identifying these fixed features can help analysts identify formats and protocol types, analyze protocol types and formats, and differentiate content. The schematic diagram of the internet protocol architecture is shown in Figure 1.

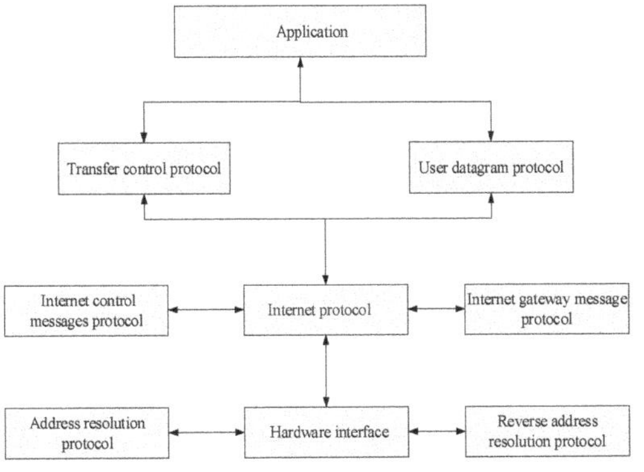

Figure 1. Schematic diagram of internet protocol architecture.

As shown in Figure 1, the composition of protocols on the internet is often tree-shaped. Any high-level application layer protocol relies on the existence of lower-layer protocols, and in front of each application layer message, there are several lower-layer protocol frame headers. Therefore, the prerequisite for parsing high-level protocols is to first parse low-level protocols. Different data frames of the same protocol often have similar structures. Therefore, they can be compared and processed by searching for similarities between them.

In order to facilitate better communication between different parts of the network on the internet, an open communication model is studied using the standards proposed by ISO, which is known as the OSI model (Open System Interconnection model). It is used to study the most important standard in internet governance standards, namely, network protocols. The OSI model can divide the communication process of the internet architecture into seven layers from bottom to top, with interfaces used to communicate between each layer, maximizing the utilization of internet network protocols and helping to better govern the internet in the future. Figure 2 shows the ISO/OSI of the network protocols corresponding to each layer in the OSI model.

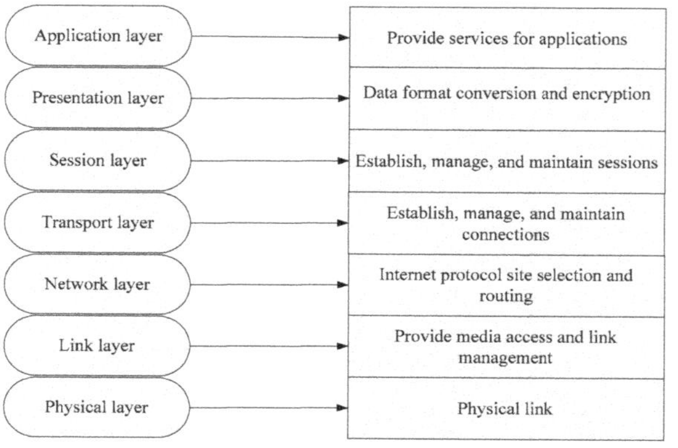

Figure 2. ISO/OSI of network protocols corresponding to each layer in the OSI model.

As shown in Figure 2, the main steps for designing and creating network protocol models based on different levels are as follows. Firstly, with the emergence of demand for internet governance business and the growth of data processing volume, the complexity of management and operation is also increasing exponentially. Adopting a layered system makes it easier for operation and maintenance personnel to maintain and develop the internet in the future. Next, operations are standardized to enable different products to communicate according to the same communication standard. Unknown processes built in unknown environments can also follow the same hierarchical process, but the process structure of each layer may differ from the hierarchical standards of governance on the internet. Data frames are the foundation of communication between link layers, and all content above the link layer in a network is ultimately encapsulated in frames layer by layer.

SAR data has unique spatial and environmental contextual characteristics. By capturing geospatial information, network infrastructure distribution, and environmental interference factors, it can provide a correlation perspective between the physical layer and the network layer for internet governance. SAR data can reflect the geographical distribution density of global network nodes, the environmental risks of submarine cable routes, or the correspondence between the physical location of cross-border data centers and the scope of sovereign jurisdiction. After being processed by AI technology, this information can be converted into an assessment basis for the vulnerability of network topology, the physical path risks of cross-border data flow, and the security of infrastructure, thereby providing data support for the formulation of targeted governance rules. This connection extends internet governance from a purely digital level to a "physical–digital" fusion dimension, enhancing the spatial accuracy and risk predictability of governance.

2.2. *Transformer Architecture in SAR Data-Driven Applications*

The Transformer architecture can effectively process the spatial characteristics and temporal dynamic changes in the network infrastructure in SAR images by virtue of its self-attention mechanism's ability to capture long-distance dependencies, providing technical support for network security governance. In the SAR image feature extraction and infrastructure identification process, an improved Vision Transformer (ViT) model is used to segment SAR images into fixed-size image patches based on the scattering characteristics of facilities such as base stations and data centers. The spatial location information is retained through linear embedding and position encoding, and the multi-head self-attention mechanism is used to calculate the association between patches and extract key features such as the geometric shape and scattering intensity of the facilities. The feature extraction process can be expressed as

$$Embedding_i - Linear(Patch_i) + Positional\ Encoding(i) \quad (1)$$

$$Feature_i = MultiHeadAttention(Embedding_i, Embedding_j) \quad (2)$$

Among them, $Positional\ Encoding(i)$ ensures that the model captures the spatial position relationship of image blocks, and $MultiHeadAttention$ strengthens the focus on features such as facility edges and signal coverage, thereby achieving accurate positioning and classification of network infrastructure.

In terms of time series analysis and load pressure prediction, we combined historical SAR data and network traffic data to build a time series Transformer model. This model captures the dependencies in the time dimension through the self-attention mechanism, and the prediction formula is

$$Load_t = Transformer(Feature_{t-1}, Feature_{t-2}, \ldots, Feature_{t-n}) \quad (3)$$

Among them, $Feature_{t-k}$ is the fusion vector of SAR features and network traffic features at the $t-k$th moment. By setting the load threshold θ, when $Load_t > \theta$, the load overload warning is triggered, providing a basis for resource scheduling and improving the foresight of network governance.

2.3. Formulation of Internet Governance Rules

Internet governance should establish a comprehensive and inclusive set of rules to manage all aspects of the internet. The content involved in global internet governance is very rich. For these contents, some have already existed before the emergence of the internet, and others have occurred after the emergence of the internet. Therefore, it is necessary to conduct research on internet governance rules in the context of global digital contracts based on this characteristic. Firstly, it is necessary to divide the problems, and then collect, combine, and derive governance rule elements based on the impact of existing problems. The main rules of global internet governance include six aspects, as shown in Figure 3. Among them, key resource management, network, and security are special rights of the internet. Intellectual property protection is an extension of existing internet rights. With the development of the internet, specialized internet rules are gradually being established, and the extension of existing rules to the internet is constantly deepening.

As shown in Figure 3, the management of critical resources includes root server management, IP address allocation, and domain name resource allocation and management. At the same time, the participants in the formulation of key resource management policies include a wide range of sectors, such as the private sector, the public sector, governments, and international organizations. Economic trade and market competition: Due to the growth of internet e-commerce and communication networks, business, marketing, and market competition are becoming more complex, and these complexities are reflected on the internet. The purpose of all parties has expanded from professional standards and key resource management to cross-border internet business, e-commerce, and other businesses.

At present, most of the rules in Figure 3 are extensions of the relevant rules formulated by the World Trade Organization on the internet, as well as protocols reached in bilateral and multilateral negotiations. In order to better study the rules of internet governance, utilizing the MSM to institutionalize rules in the context of global digital contracts is a way or approach to solve problems [24,25]. The MSM typically requires the participation of government agencies, private organizations, civil society groups, and international organizations to negotiate and formulate internet rules. Therefore, in the context of the global digital contract, the MSM is used to formulate internet governance rules, which can take into account the interests and requirements of all parties, follow the jointly formulated governance rules and norms, and adopt the same solution measures for problems in the same field through activities. The multiple-stakeholder mechanism is shown in Figure 4.

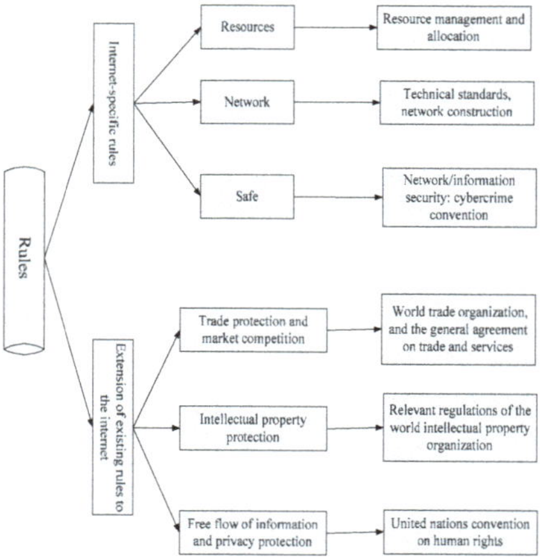

Figure 3. Attribute classification of international internet governance rules.

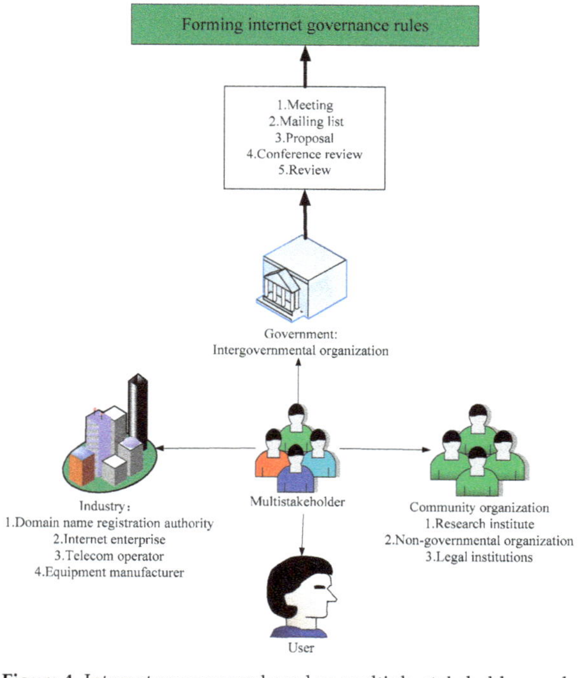

Figure 4. Internet governance based on multiple-stakeholder mechanisms.

The formation of the core rules of the internet is determined by the participation of multiple stakeholders and follows established processes. As shown in Figure 4, the openness of non-governmental platforms is generally very high, and all governments, organizations, enterprises, and individuals worldwide can participate in activities on non-governmental platforms. On this platform, all parties participate in the formulation of rules and regulations in a certain way and procedure. The processes and procedures they follow include multiple ways and means.

The use of multilateral mechanisms has always been a common practice among governments around the world in international trade events. Although there have always been voices in the internet community opposing the use of multilateral mechanisms to formulate internet governance rules, governments of various countries are representatives of the public interest, and their mission is to provide public services and safety for their own people, safeguard their legitimate rights and interests, and ensure that the public can use the internet safely and reliably. Therefore, in some areas of internet governance rulemaking, multiple approaches still need to be taken. However, for different levels of problems, different decisions should be appropriately chosen. For example, the government should play an important role in policymaking in areas such as managing critical internet resources, maintaining cybersecurity, preventing cybercrime, and protecting citizens. According to the above analysis, the "multilateral mechanism" and the "multi-stakeholder" mechanism are not mutually exclusive. As long as they are properly operated, both can play a role and effectively address the complex issues of the global internet.

In global internet governance, the importance of specific internet rules is higher than the extension of existing internet rules. Among the special rules of the internet, the rules of internet resources are more important as they are the foundation for the development of the internet. Therefore, the special rules of the internet are the main rules of the global internet, and the key resource rules of the internet are the core rules of international internet governance. The quadrant diagram of global internet governance rules and methods is shown in Figure 5.

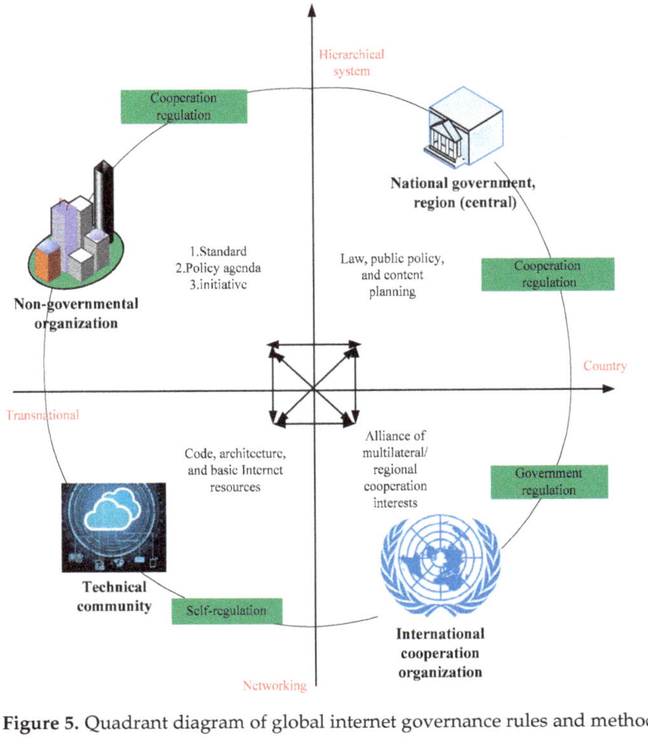

Figure 5. Quadrant diagram of global internet governance rules and methods.

As shown in Figure 5, by setting up management platforms and governance rule categories horizontally and vertically, a four-quadrant analysis matrix can be obtained to analyze the main controls and their corresponding regulations mentioned above. It can be seen that in the formulation of governance rules in some special areas of the internet, the number of government cooperations is limited, while the scale of non-intergovernmental platforms is still very large. Many non-governmental platforms have specific rights on the internet, responsible for developing internet resources and formulating network technology standards and rules. Unlike the organizational approach and rules of intergovernmental platform processes, the cooperation approach of non-governmental platforms involves all stakeholders, and their organizational approach and rulemaking are often based on the principle of multiple stakeholders.

2.4. Legal and Policy Development

Creating and developing a legal and policy framework that adapts to the global digital contract can protect user privacy and data security, enable internet governance legislation to have relatively high liquidity, and enable legislation to involve data protection laws, cybersecurity laws, digital identity verification systems, and more. Legal reform is a way of social change, but as a relationship with the implementation of national coercive force, it has stability and lag. In contrast, the internet seeks more innovation, and the governance ideas and methods of internet platforms are adjusted according to the new models and functions that have emerged on the internet. Therefore, legal regulations are very limited in the field of the internet, and it is necessary to find ways to ensure that they can help internet governance play its due role and make up for the failure of platform governance. Among them, the most important task is to address the legal issues related to internet governance, as shown in Table 2.

Table 2. Legal issues in internet governance.

Number	Legal Dilemma	Category	Explain
1	The dilemma in legislation	Lawmaking lags behind the development of internet governance	The legal system of network governance is still being improved.
		Imbalance of rights of the internet governance platform	1. There is a lack of statutory rules to divide the power of different attributes. 2. The scientific structure of the authority and responsibility of the network platform is lacking.
2	The dilemma of regulatory enforcement	There is a problem with the supervision system of administrative outsourcing	1. The division of authority within the government is not clear. 2. Regulatory and law enforcement agencies are not scientific enough in setting up.
		Imperfect regulatory mechanism	The prevention mechanism is not sound.
		Complex regulatory and law enforcement environment	1. Sufficient culture of the rule of law in cyberspace has not been established. 2. The pattern of collaborative governance of network information content needs to be strengthened.
3	Insufficient privacy protection	Data collection infringes on citizens' privacy rights	Internet platforms pose a threat to users' privacy rights during data collection.
		Governance platform infringes on privacy	With the continuous development of the internet, violations of rights that have brought physical and mental trauma to different groups of people are more common, infringing on the privacy rights of consumers.
		Problems in the data security protection phase	The instability of the internet has led internet companies to infringe on consumer privacy.

As shown in Table 2, there are many problems in the process of internet governance, which are not conducive to the formulation of laws and regulations related to internet governance. In order to address the above issues, it is necessary to leverage the global digital contract to help laws better safeguard the privacy of users in various countries and protect personal and national information through new forms of contracts. At the same time, it also helps global networks to share and develop, allowing multiple parties to participate in the formulation of internet governance laws and regulations and formulate more reasonably and in line with the development of the internet. The specific measures are as follows.

2.4.1. Privacy Protection

In the process of internet governance, public privacy protection is very important [26]. In the process of collecting network data, it is necessary to improve data protection work and expand the scope of protection laws based on the primary protection of user data rights. In the process of protecting users' right to know, more effective ways should be created to clarify data content, while rejecting the use of personal data as an additional condition for customers' right to refuse. It is also necessary to enhance the ability to handle erroneous information and enhance the ability to collect information by modifying or deleting learning materials. In addition, the public's willingness to seek security in online information governance can affect competition in the internet market, thereby encouraging the internet industry to meet higher security standards, enhance privacy protection, and meet customer needs [27].

2.4.2. Personal Information Protection

Personal information security is the most important security requirement for users on internet platforms and also the most concerning issue for internet users [22]. Internet platforms are indeed unable to fulfill their responsibility to protect users' personal data. When the number of internet platform users is large, various internet platforms may face public security issues in terms of personal information protection. Therefore, in the context of the global digital contract, it is necessary to better govern the internet through various means and legislative methods to protect personal information, taking China as an example. In order to successfully govern the internet and combat crime, China saves information about its citizens in internal public security institutions. Public information is held by government departments, and citizens are very confident about it. However, with the development of the internet, the information about users on the internet is also more complex and ever-changing. Therefore, relying solely on internet platforms for user data protection cannot guarantee user data security. In this case, legal regulations are needed to address issues related to user information security.

3. Practical Path of Internet Governance

3.1. International Cooperation and Multilateral Consultation

International cooperation is crucial for global internet governance in the context of the global digital contract. Countries should strengthen international cooperation, formulate rules and standards through mutual consultation and cooperation, and solve cross-border internet problems. International organizations such as the United Nations and the World Trade Organization play an important role in internet governance. Under the influence of the global digital contract, international cooperation has been utilized to study the implementation of internet governance practices, mainly in the following three steps. Firstly, the private sector, the internet technology community, and individual citizens are united to negotiate multiple interests. Secondly, developing countries should use multilateral consultations and combine with international organizations such as the United Nations to govern the internet. Thirdly, developed countries collaborate with their own governments and citizens to carry out internet governance through a multi-agent governance approach.

Utilizing multilateralism is a way to address various common human challenges, resolve international conflicts, and provide good guarantees for global internet governance [28]. As the most representative and authoritative international government in the world today, the United Nations should be the best place for the international community to practice many things. After years of competitive gaming in internet governance, technological standards and key internet resources are still held by a few developed countries, while developing countries are still in an unequal position in technological standards and related governance. Therefore, international governance of the internet should pay more attention to fairness and justice, involve more participants, and establish accountability mechanisms and legal frameworks. By utilizing multilateralism, it is easier to help the global internet formulate governance practice rules and paths. At the same time, due to the multilateral system of the United Nations, the universal support of all member states has been received, and the internet governance rules designed for international standards have unique authority.

3.2. Data Privacy Protection

Standards and rules related to privacy protection have been established to ensure the proper storage of personal information and data involved in digital contracts. Differential privacy (DP) is a method of protecting privacy in cryptography, with the goal of creating a method that improves the accuracy of requested information while collecting as much information as possible and reduces the likelihood of recording errors when searching for data [29,30]. In other words, while ensuring commonality, personal characteristics are removed to maintain the privacy of internet users. DP's privacy protection mainly relies on accurate data provided by information providers when attackers impersonate users. Based on this, the user's original privacy data is inferred. Based on the inferred results, a pattern of adding different types of noise interference to the original privacy data has been derived to achieve data modification, thereby preventing internet attackers from obtaining effective data and protecting the privacy of internet users. Using DP can predict the future development trend of internet privacy management. It can also protect various types of privacy of internet users, predict the probability of attackers attacking, and further propose methods to prevent such predictive inference attacks, thereby better governing the internet.

The core terms used in this study are defined as follows: "Privacy budget" refers to a total threshold for measuring privacy leakage risks in differential privacy protection, which controls the degree of data perturbation; a smaller value indicates a higher level of privacy protection. "Global sensitivity value" represents the maximum difference in the output results of the same query function between adjacent datasets, serving as a key parameter to determine the amount of noise required for privacy protection. "Global Digital Compact" is a UN-led international cooperation framework aimed at establishing open, secure, and inclusive digital governance rules through multilateral negotiations to address global issues such as the digital divide and data security. "Certificateless Cryptography (CC) algorithm" is an encryption technology that enables key management without certificates, ensuring secure data transmission through the collaborative generation of users' public keys and partial private keys.

By adding noise to the output results of the original data, it is ensured that even if the data in the original data is deleted or changed, the results are still generated, and the results are the same as the actual results. The specific expression is

$$Pr[N(X_1) \in Q] \leq exp(\mu) * Pr[N(X_2) \in Q] \tag{4}$$

Among them, Q represents a possible set of outputs, and μ represents privacy budget parameters. From the formula, it can be seen that the smaller the privacy budget μ, the higher the degree of privacy protection.

Differential privacy mainly protects the personal information of users in the data by adding some noise, which is very important for noise control. It is necessary to protect user privacy while avoiding too much noise affecting the effectiveness of data usage. The expression for calculating the global sensitivity of noise is as follows:

$$SF_k = \max_{X_1,X_2} ||k(X_1) - k(X_2)||_1 \tag{5}$$

When the global sensitivity value is high, a large number of voices need to be added to the function query results to confirm the user's identity, resulting in poor data availability.

The amount of noise is very important. The amount of noise in the dataset can cause too much interference, resulting in the unavailability of the data. The noise density is

$$q(j) = \frac{1}{2\gamma} exp\left(-\frac{|j|}{\gamma}\right) \tag{6}$$

Among them, γ = Δk/μ. The amount of noise is directly proportional to the value of function sensitivity Δk and inversely proportional to privacy budget μ. γ represents the noise density parameter, which is determined by the function sensitivity Δk and the privacy budget μ. j represents the discrete index value in the noise sequence, which is an integer, used to quantify the distribution state of the noise; i represents the number of iterations or sample index, which is a positive integer and represents the budget share of the i-th iteration in the privacy budget allocation.

When calculating the privacy budget under a fixed number of iterations scenario, the implementation method is to evenly allocate the privacy budget in each iteration, that is, h value, 0 < h < 1. When the initial budget allocation is determined, the entire budget sequence is fixed and adjustable and meets the requirements of differential privacy protection. The privacy budget allocation formula is shown in Formula (4), and the evaluation function is shown in Formula (5).

$$\mu_i = \frac{h\mu}{(i-1)^!} (ln\frac{1}{h})^{i-1}, i \in N^+ \tag{7}$$

$$F(n) = \sum\nolimits_{j=1}^{n} (\frac{1}{\mu_i})^2 = \frac{1}{h^2\mu^2} * \sum\nolimits_{j=1}^{n} (\frac{[(i-1)^!]^2}{(ln\frac{1}{h})^{2(i-1)}})^2 \tag{8}$$

Among them, μ_i is the privacy budget for each score search, and μ is the total budget.

With the continuous development of the internet, personal and national information is easier to publish on the internet. In the context of global digital contracts, understanding privacy protection in internet governance is crucial. In order to ensure data security during data transmission, the use of cryptographic technology has been strengthened in practice. A secure and effective certificate without a signature can be established based on the Certificateless Cryptography (CC) system [31]. When generating partial private keys, this scheme uses a secure hash function to bind the user's public key with the generation of partial private keys, making it impossible for attackers to delete the results of the hash function by changing the user's public key. By analyzing the effectiveness of this strategy, compared with other strategies, it is found that this strategy reduces the number of bilinear and exponential operations, improves computational efficiency and accuracy, and reduces communication overhead, ensuring that data can only be accessed and used by authorized individuals.

This method continuously optimizes the virtual gradient value to approach the real gradient value, which can make the virtual data approach the user's real data. The formula is as follows:

$$(a^*, b^*) = \underset{a',b'}{argmin}||\nabla M' - \nabla M||^2 = \underset{a',b'}{argmin}||\frac{\delta\vartheta(H(a', M), b')}{\delta M} - \nabla M||^2 \quad (9)$$

When virtual gradient ∇M′ continuously approaches real gradient ∇M, the false information created by malicious attackers approaches the user's true information, leading to indirect leakage of user privacy to the attacker.

Each participant negotiates keys with other participants to generate a joint mask, and then the local gradient parameters are converted. The specific expression is as follows:

$$\hat{m}_i = m_i + \sum\nolimits_{j \in V: i<j} PRG(f_{i,j}) - \sum\nolimits_{j \in V: i>j} PRG(f_{i,j}) \quad (10)$$

The server receives gradient parameters from various participants but cannot obtain the correct gradient parameters from the user. Therefore, attackers are unable to recover the user's data, thereby ensuring the privacy and security of the user's data.

Differential privacy controls the risk of privacy leakage by adding noise, and the CC algorithm improves encryption efficiency by optimizing key management. These technologies provide practical tools for the ongoing research on "Data Security Governance under the Global Digital Contract Framework".

3.3. Transparency and Accountability

On a global scale, the number of international internet governance platforms is constantly increasing, and these governance platforms are all different. Choosing the correct partitioning method is a necessary foundation for using governance platforms to govern the internet. When a user conflicts with a platform company, the government and industry need to supervise the governance policies formulated by the platform company to protect the legitimate rights of users. In order to urge users to consciously comply with market behavior, the government and public organizations should clarify the boundaries of governance, jointly improve policies, and create a healthy online environment. The governance mechanism diagram of the internet supervision platform is shown in Figure 6.

To ensure more openness and transparency in internet governance, an internet governance supervision platform is established to monitor the behavior and information of internet service providers. Platform enterprises need to create business information networks, connect key personnel, and carry out a series of value activities. At the same time, in order to better govern the behavior of various groups, enterprises can develop a comprehensive policy system as operators and supervise as platform supervisors to ensure the effectiveness of policy implementation and timely revise and supplement the governance policy system. Due to the virtual nature of the internet, governance is mainly achieved through the unilateral formulation of governance rules by enterprise platforms in order to avoid attacks from other platforms and solve the problem of threats to user information caused by significant changes in the macro environment. By analyzing Figure 6, it can be seen that creating a cohesive business and a strong business ecosystem requires the platform to maintain a high degree of neutrality in overseeing governance policies during formulation and implementation.

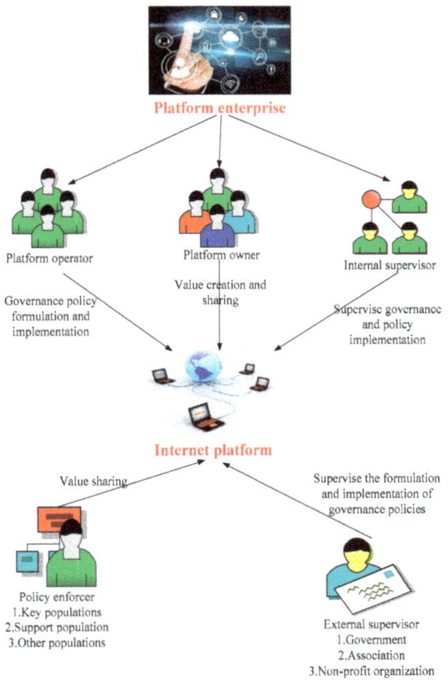

Figure 6. Governance mechanism of internet supervision platform.

4. Experiments Related to Internet Governance

The term "Software updates over the Air", or "SOTA", describes the updating of apps via communication without establishing a connection with the programmer. For the following reasons, nevertheless, it is not appropriate for internet administration within the framework of the Global Digital Compact: (1) there are several domains and tiers involved in internet governance under the framework of the global digital agreement. The SOTA baseline approach finds it challenging to completely address all facets of internet governance because it primarily concentrates on the most recent advancements and industry best practices in a certain subject or technology. (2) The process of internet governance is dynamic in nature, with new practices, laws, and technologies always emerging. It is challenging to modify the SOTA baseline method to accommodate the quickly evolving governance environment since it frequently concentrates on summarizing and evaluating currently used technology and processes. (3) The game of internet governance requires the cooperation and coordination of several parties. Effective solutions are hard to come by when using the SOTA baseline approach, which typically solely concentrates on technical and practical problems while neglecting the demands and conflicts of interest of stakeholders. (4) A wide range of considerations, including social impact, economic cost, and technical viability, must be thoroughly taken into account when governing the internet. The SOTA baseline approach frequently ignores the impact of other elements in favor of concentrating solely on the development and efficacy of technology, making it challenging to offer thorough direction and assistance for internet governance.

The OSI model, multilateralism, international agreements, and traditional methods, as core elements of internet governance, have three significant commonalities: First, they all have "regulating network behavior and ensuring interconnection" as their core goal, aiming to solve the problem of disorder in cyberspace through a standardized framework or rule system. Second, they rely on a multi-subject participation mechanism. Whether it is the layered collaboration of the OSI model, the intergovernmental coordination of multilateralism, or the cross-border cooperation of international agreements, they all emphasize the division of rights and responsibilities among multiple parties. Third, they have certain timeliness limitations. With the iteration of the digital economy and technology, their adaptability to new issues such as privacy protection and cross-border data flow has gradually decreased, and it is necessary to improve governance effectiveness through innovation and optimization.

A questionnaire survey was conducted among all users, primarily collecting user ratings through scoring. The user rating scale uses a 1–10 scale, with 1 representing the lowest rating and 10 representing the highest. Scores are determined based on users' actual experience, understanding, and needs regarding internet governance standards/rules. Specifically, the scores cover three core dimensions: satisfaction, reflecting users' recognition of the standards/rules' effectiveness in protecting privacy and balancing the interests of all parties; practicality, measuring the operability of the standards/rules in actual internet governance scenarios; and applicability, assessing their alignment with the Global Digital Compact framework, including whether they are adapted to the economic development levels of different regions and meet the differentiated needs of multiple stakeholders. During the scoring process, users independently rated the governance standards/rules under different models based on their own experience in internet usage, governance practices, or research. The average value was then calculated to present an overall evaluation.

The experimental data for this article comes from a randomly selected user sample from an international online research platform. This sample covers regions with varying levels of economic development worldwide, taking into account the proportion of users in both developed and developing countries. The sample is categorized by identity, including individual users, internet company technicians, government network regulators, and academic researchers. All participants signed informed consent forms to clarify their understanding of internet governance rules. Data selection strictly adhered to the principles of coverage and randomness, excluding samples with regional or identity biases. During data processing, statistical analysis was performed on user ratings, and averages were calculated to reflect user evaluations of different governance models. For algorithm performance testing, the performance of different algorithms was compared on metrics such as encryption time and feature extraction accuracy, by controlling for variables such as data volume, to ensure that the data effectively supports the rationality of the experimental conclusions.

This article used digital contracts and the OSI model to study global internet governance standards. For this purpose, 15 internet users were randomly selected, and the governance standards studied in this article were rated with a score of 1–10. The higher the score, the higher the level of evaluation and satisfaction. In order to better demonstrate the superiority of the OSI model, the experimental results were compared and analyzed with internet governance standards based on multilateralism, international protocols, and traditional methods (that is, before using the OSI model). The specific results are shown in Table 3.

As shown in Table 3, different models were utilized to study internet governance standards. Through the comparison of experimental results, it can be found that in the context of global digital contracts, the OSI model was used to formulate internet governance standards. The user rating was much higher than the internet governance standards developed based on other methods. Among them, the user rating of the internet governance standard based on the OSI model was above 8.99 points, and the average score of 15 users was 9.2 points. The internet governance standards based on multilateralism, international protocols, and traditional methods had user ratings below 8.91, 8.96, and 8.71, respectively, and the average scores were 0.6, 0.54, and 0.72 points lower than the internet governance standards studied in this article. The average user rating of internet governance standards developed using the OSI model in this article was the highest compared to traditional methods. This once again indicates that in the context of global digital contracts, using the OSI model to study internet governance standards can effectively improve the rationality of governance standards. The opinions of multiple parties are integrated to develop more scientific governance standards, so that the global internet can be shared more securely.

Table 3. User ratings of internet governance standards under different models.

Number	OSI	Multilateralism	International Protocol	Traditional Method
1	9.2	8.4	8.5	8.2
2	9.3	8.5	8.6	8.6
3	9.4	8.5	8.8	8.4
4	9.3	8.7	8.5	8.6
5	9.2	8.9	8.5	8.6
6	9.1	8.8	8.85	8.5
7	9.1	8.8	8.95	8.4
8	9.1	8.4	8.8	8.3
9	9.3	8.6	8.6	8.6
10	9	8.7	8.75	8.4
11	9.1	8.7	8.85	8.5
12	9.2	8.6	8.4	8.5
13	9.2	8.5	8.65	8.6
14	9.3	8.5	8.45	8.7
15	9.2	8.4	8.7	8.3
Average value	9.2	8.6	8.66	8.48

In the context of the global digital contract, the rules of internet governance were studied. By utilizing digital contracts and combining multiple-stakeholder mechanisms (MSMs), global internet governance rules were studied. For this purpose, 20 internet users were randomly selected, and the governance standard rules studied in this article were rated with a score of 1–100. The higher the score, the higher the level of evaluation and satisfaction. In order to better demonstrate the superiority of the MSM model, the experimental results were compared and analyzed with internet governance rules based on multilateralism, international protocols, and traditional methods (that is, before using the MSM model). The specific results are shown in Figure 7.

In Figure 7, the x-axis represents different governance rule models, and the y-axis represents the scores scored by users. The dotted elements in the figure represent the specific scoring of the 20 internet users selected, and the horizontal line in the middle represents the average scoring of these 20 users. As shown in Figure 7, it can be clearly observed that in the context of global digital contracts, user ratings for internet governance rules formulated using the MSM model were much higher than those based on other models. Among them, the rule users based on the MSM model scored above 91.49 points, and the average score of 20 users was 93.3 points. However, users scored governance rules based on multilateralism, international protocols, and traditional methods below 91.01 points, 89.01 points, and 86.51 points, respectively. The average score of 20 users was 6.3 points, 6.55 points, and 10.7 points lower than the average score of users based on the MSM model.

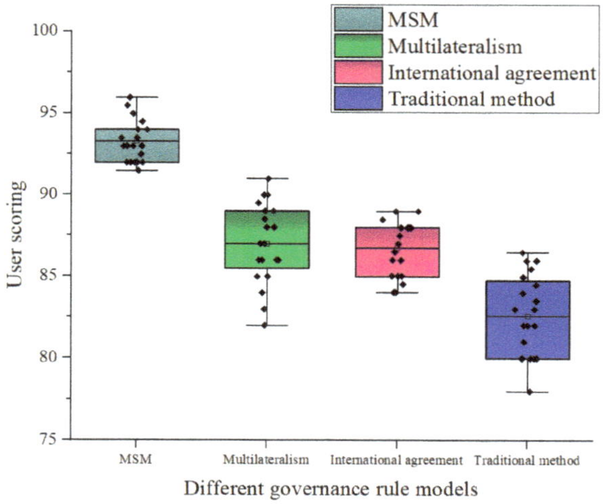

Figure 7. User ratings of internet governance rules formulated under different methods.

In the practical path of internet governance, special attention should be paid to the privacy protection of internet data. In the context of the global digital contract, the Certificateless Cryptography (CC) algorithm was utilized to encrypt data generated during the practice of internet governance. This has not only enhanced privacy protection and the security of internet governance but also increased the speed of encryption and saved encryption time. In order to further demonstrate the superiority of internet data encryption based on the CC algorithm, the experimental results obtained were compared with the Data Encryption Algorithm (DEA), Homomorphic Encryption (HE), and Secure Hash Algorithm (SHA). The comparison results are shown in Figure 8.

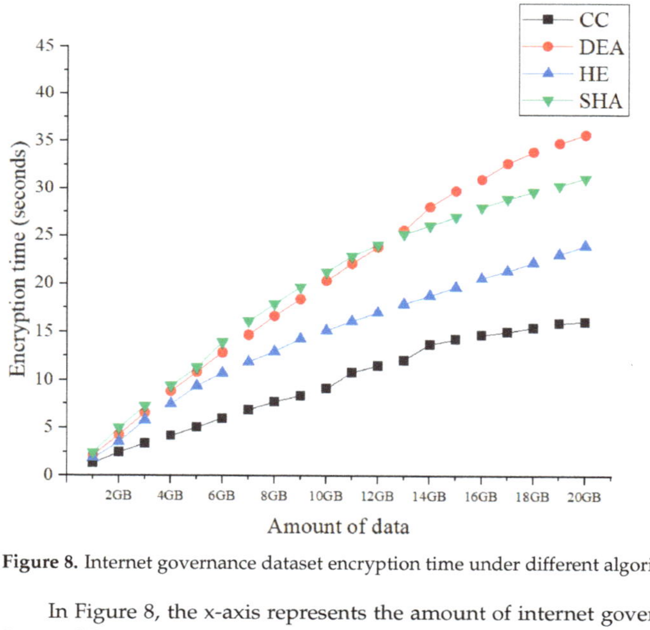

Figure 8. Internet governance dataset encryption time under different algorithms.

In Figure 8, the x-axis represents the amount of internet governance data, ranging from 1 GB to 20 GB, and the y-axis represents the time required to encrypt the data. As shown in Figure 8, it is clear that using the CC algorithm to encrypt internet governance data required much less time than other algorithms, and the encryption speed was faster. Among them, encrypting data based on the HE algorithm required more time than the CC algorithm, but less time than encrypting data based on the DEA and SHA. When the amount of data was below 12 GB, the time required for data encryption based on the DEA was lower than that required for encryption based on the SHA, but higher than the time required for encryption using the other two algorithms. However, when the amount of data exceeded 13 GB, the time required for data encryption based on the DEA was much higher than the other three algorithms. When the data quantity was 1 GB, the encryption time based on the CC algorithm was 1.31 s, which was 0.83 s, 0.57 s, and 1.16 s lower than the encryption time based on the DEA, HE, and SHAs. When the data quantity was 20 GB, the time required for encryption based on the CC algorithm was 16.14 s, which was 19.64 s, 7.94 s, and 15.05 s lower than the time required for encryption based on the DEA, HE, and SHAs.

To verify the technical advantages of the Transformer and SAR data fusion method proposed in this paper in network infrastructure governance, CNN, BiLSTM, SVM, and random forest algorithms commonly used in the current internet governance field were selected for comparison. Experiments were conducted from multiple dimensions, such as feature extraction accuracy, load prediction error, and abnormal warning response time. The datasets used and the performance comparison results of each algorithm are shown in Table 4.

Table 4. Performance comparison of different algorithms.

Evaluation Metrics	Transformer + SAR	CNN	BiLSTM	SVM	RF
Feature Extraction Accuracy (%)	96.2	90.5	88.7	82.4	89.1
Load Forecast Error (MAE)	3	4.9	3.6	6.8	5.7
Anomaly Warning Response Time (ms)	16.8	28.3	23.5	40.2	34.7
Encryption Compatibility (%)	91.5	78.6	75.3	62.5	73.8
Spatial Feature Long-Distance Correlation Capture Rate (%)	93.8	72.6	76.4	56.8	70.3
Multi-Source Data Fusion Efficiency (GB/s)	2.6	1.7	2.1	1	1.4

Judging from the results in Table 4, in internet governance under the background of the global digital contract, the Transformer + SAR fusion method shows significant advantages in all evaluation indicators. Its feature extraction accuracy reaches 96.2%, far exceeding SVM's 82.4%, and higher than CNN's 90.5%, BiLSTM's 88.7%, and random forest's 89.1%. This is due to the Transformer's multi-head attention mechanism's accurate capture of the spatial characteristics of SAR data and the network runtime characteristics; the load prediction error is only 3.0, lower than other algorithms, reflecting the ability to accurately predict dynamic network loads; the anomaly warning response time is 16.8 ms, which can quickly respond to network anomalies and ensure the timeliness of governance; the encryption compatibility is 91.5%, which has strong synergy with certificateless encryption algorithms and meets the needs of privacy protection; the spatial feature long-distance correlation capture rate of 93.8% and the multi-source data fusion efficiency of 2.6 GB/s also highlight its advantages in integrating multi-dimensional and cross-regional network data, fully verifying the effectiveness of this method in improving the accuracy, security, and efficiency of internet governance.

5. Discussion

Theoretically, this article offers a thorough understanding and methodology for an examination of internet governance within the framework of the Global Digital Compact. Even though internet governance is discussed in the literature that is now available, it is performed within the larger framework of the Global Digital Compact, which highlights recent advancements and trends in the field. This offers an alternative viewpoint for comprehending the guidelines, policies, and procedures of internet governance. In actuality, it offers legislators, internet firms, and pertinent stakeholders a useful resource. The swift advancement of digital technology has presented previously unheard-of difficulties for internet administration. Not only have the governance models and procedures already been examined in use, but also, specific, doable routes have been suggested to offer direction for real-world operations.

Despite the fact that internet governance is the subject of a lot of current work, the majority of studies tend to begin from a single national or regional viewpoint. In order to analyze the issues of internet governance more thoroughly and take into account the differences and similarities between various countries and regions, this article highlights the history of the Global Digital Compact. This makes it more thorough and in-depth than research that only stays at the theoretical level or concentrates on a single practice. This article's primary output is a thorough examination and debate of internet governance's guidelines, policies, and best practices within the framework of the Global Digital Compact. This offers direction for the realm of practice as well as fresh theoretical insights for academics. Additionally, it can offer academics fresh viewpoints and research techniques that can advance the field of internet governance research and growth. Policymakers, internet corporations, and other pertinent stakeholders can find great inspiration and reference value in the research findings. In order to make better decisions and more informed choices, it can assist these entities in better understanding their duties and obligations within the framework of the Global Digital Compact.

So, the primary focus of this paper is a thorough analysis and discussion of internet governance within the framework of the Global Digital Compact, which has both theoretical and practical significance. This article is deeper and more comprehensive in perspective and content than previous works. The findings have guiding implications for the realm of practice in addition to having a significant impact on academia.

6. Conclusions

In the context of the global digital contract, this paper constructs the standards, rules, and practice paths of internet governance by integrating SAR data processing and the Transformer model, combining differential privacy protection and certificateless cryptographic algorithms. This study shows that the governance standards based on the OSI model, the rules of the multi-stakeholder mechanism, and the data encryption of the CC algorithm are superior to traditional methods in terms of efficiency and satisfaction and effectively improve privacy protection and network security. However, there are shortcomings in this study: the core relationship between SAR and internet governance is not explained enough, and the innovative expansion of the existing framework is limited. Future research can deepen the integration mechanism of SAR data and network governance, optimize sample design to enhance repeatability, and explore new governance frameworks to break through the limitations of the existing model and further improve the internet governance system under the global digital contract.

Author Contributions: X.F., W.Z. and Z.L.; Writing, Editing, and Software, Z.L.; Data Analysis, X.F. Resources, Z.L. and W.Z.; Data Analysis and Software. All authors have read and agreed to the published version of the manuscript.

Funding: This study was supported by the National Social Science Fund of China 'The Practical Dilemmas and Chinese solutions of Global Governance of Cross-border Data Flows (Grant: 24BXW043)'.

Data Availability Statement: The data presented in this study are available on request from the corresponding author.

Conflicts of Interest: The authors declare no conflicts of interest.

References

1. Liu, J.; Liu, L.Y.; Tu, Y.; Li, S.X.; Li, Z.M. Multi-stage Internet public opinion risk grading analysis of public health emergencies: An empirical study on Microblog in COVID-19. *Inf. Process. Manag.* **2022**, *59*, 2–21. [CrossRef]
2. Li, Z.; Zhang, W.Y.; Zhang, H.T.; Gao, R.; Fang, X.D. Global Digital Compact: A Mechanism for the Governance of Online Discriminatory and Misleading Content Generation. *Int. J. Hum.-Comput. Interact.* **2024**, *3*, 1381–1396. [CrossRef]
3. Mancuso, I.; Petruzzelli, A.M.; Panniello, U. Digital business model innovation in metaverse: How to approach virtual economy opportunities. *Inf. Process. Manag.* **2023**, *60*, 103457. [CrossRef]
4. Putz, B.; Dietz, M.; Empl, P.; Pernul, G. Ether Twin: Blockchain-based Secure Digital Twin Information Management. *Inf. Process. Manag.* **2021**, *58*, 102425. [CrossRef]
5. Khan, S.D.; Basalamah, S. Multi-Branch Deep Learning Framework for Land Scene Classification in Satellite Imagery. *Remote Sens.* **2023**, *15*, 3408. [CrossRef]
6. Wang, J.S.; Yang, G.H. Data-driven methods for stealthy attacks on TCP/IP-based networked control systems equipped with attack detectors. *IEEE Trans. Cybern.* **2018**, *49*, 3020–3031. [CrossRef]
7. White, P.A. Cyberpeace: Why Internet Governance Matters for Global Peace and Stability. *Peace Change* **2019**, *44*, 441–467. [CrossRef]
8. Tjahja, N.; Trisha, M.; Jamal, S. Who do you think you are? Individual stakeholder identification and mobility at the Internet Governance Forum. *Telecommun. Policy* **2022**, *46*, 102410–102411. [CrossRef]
9. Flonk, D.; Markus, J.; Anke, S.O. Authority conflicts in internet governance: Liberals vs. sovereigntists? *Glob. Const.* **2020**, *9*, 364–386. [CrossRef]
10. Malcic, S. Proteus online: Digital identity and the Internet governance industry. *Convergence* **2016**, *24*, 205–225. [CrossRef]
11. Guan, S.; Xie, Y.; Zhai, Y.M. The Model Selection and Optimization of Global Internet Governance—Based on Reflection on the Multi stakeholder Model. *Gov. Res.* **2018**, *35*, 112–113.
12. Zhang, J.W. How to Regulate Digital Financial Assets: Cryptocurrency and Smart Contracts—Review of the Draft Law on Digital Financial Assets of the Russian Federation. *J. Shanghai Univ. Political Sci. Law Rule Law Ser.* **2018**, *33*, 14–23.
13. Jiang, L. New Trends and Policy Implications for Global Digital Economy Regulation. *J. Beijing Norm. Univ. Soc. Sci. Ed.* **2023**, *3*, 58–65.
14. Wylde, A. The UN Global Digital Compact (GDC), Achieving a trusted, free, open, and Secure Internet: Trust-building. *Eur. Conf. Cyber Warf. Secur.* **2023**, *22*, 544–551. [CrossRef]
15. Saravistha, D.B.; Sukadana, I.K.; Suryana, K.D. Urgency of Contract Model Settings in the Global Digital Market Related to Tourism Business: A Study on Consumer Protection and Electronic Information and Transactions. *Bp. Int. Res. Crit. Inst.-J. BIRCI-J.* **2022**, *5*, 4549–4556.
16. Ong, J.P. The Enforceability of Digital Contract: A Comparative Analysis on Indonesia and New Zealand Law. *Lawpreneurship J.* **2021**, *1*, 30–42. [CrossRef]
17. Tjahja, N.; Meyer, T.; Shahin, J. What is civil society and who represents civil society at the IGF? An analysis of civil society typologies in internet governance. *Telecommun. Policy* **2021**, *45*, 102141. [CrossRef]
18. Cheung, M.; Chen, Z.T. Power, Freedom, and Privacy on a Discipline-and-Control Facebook, and the Implications for Internet Governance. *IEEE Trans. Prof. Commun.* **2022**, *65*, 467–484. [CrossRef]
19. Abood, A.M.; Hussein, M.S.; Faisal, Z.G.; Tawfiq, Z.H. Design and simulation of video monitoring structure over TCP/IP system using MATLAB. *Indones. J. Electr. Eng. Comput. Sci.* **2021**, *24*, 1840–1845. [CrossRef]
20. Wang, L.M. Harmony but Difference: The Rule Boundary and Application of Privacy and Personal Information. *Leg. Rev.* **2021**, *39*, 15–24.
21. Feng, W.B.; Hong, Z.; Wu, L.F.; Fu, M.L. Overview of Network Protocol Recognition Technology. *Comput. Appl.* **2019**, *39*, 3604–3605.

22. Zharova, A. Ensuring the information security of information communication technology users in Russia. *Int. J. Cyber Criminol.* **2019**, *13*, 255–269.
23. Joseph, I.; Ituabhor, O.; Zhimwang, J.T.; Ikechi, R. Achievable Throughput over Mobile Broadband Network Protocol Layers: Practical Measurements and Performance Analysis. *Int. J. Adv. Netw. Appl.* **2022**, *13*, 5037–5044. [CrossRef]
24. Raha, A.; Hajdini, I. Franchisees with multiple stakeholder roles: Perceptions and conflict in franchise networks. *J. Strateg. Mark.* **2022**, *30*, 160–179. [CrossRef]
25. Daigo, E.; Kevin, F. Exploring the value sponsors co-create at a charity sport event: A multiple stakeholder perspective of sport value. *Sport Manag. Rev.* **2022**, *25*, 656–678. [CrossRef]
26. Dai, L. On the Protection of Personal Privacy Rights in the Context of Digital Trade. *Contemp. Law* **2020**, *34*, 148–160.
27. Isaak, J.; Hanna, M.J. User data privacy: Facebook, Cambridge Analytica, and privacy protection. *Computer* **2018**, *51*, 56–59. [CrossRef]
28. Cheng, S. Multilateralism: A New Phenomenon in International Politics. *J. Soc. Sci. Jilin Univ.* **2020**, *60*, 127–133.
29. Hassan, M.U.; Rehmani, M.H.; Chen, J. Differential privacy techniques for cyber physical systems: A survey. *IEEE Commun. Surv. Tutor.* **2019**, *22*, 746–789. [CrossRef]
30. Feng, D.; Zhang, M.; Ye, Y. Research on location trajectory publishing technology based on differential Privacy Model. *J. Electron. Inf. Technol.* **2020**, *42*, 74–88.
31. Qiao, Z.; Yang, Q.; Zhou, Y.; Zhang, M. Improved secure transaction scheme with certificateless cryptographic primitives for IoT-based mobile payments. *IEEE Syst. J.* **2021**, *16*, 1842–1850. [CrossRef]

MDPI AG
Grosspeteranlage 5
4052 Basel
Switzerland
Tel.: +41 61 683 77 34

Information Editorial Office
E-mail: information@mdpi.com
www.mdpi.com/journal/information